RSAC

DEC 1995

PLEASE RETURN THIS ITEM
BY THE DUE DATE TO A
TULSA CITY-COUNTY LI

FINES ARE 5¢ PER DAY; A
MAXIMUM OF $1.00 PER ITEM.

D0084766

DATE DUE

SEP 23 1996			
JUN 27 1997			
			Printed in USA

HIGHSMITH #45230

THE RISE AND FALL OF MERRY ENGLAND

THE RISE

AND FALL OF

MERRY

ENGLAND

The Ritual Year 1400–1700

RONALD HUTTON

Oxford   New York

OXFORD UNIVERSITY PRESS

Oxford University Press, Walton Street, Oxford OX2 6DP
Oxford New York
Athens Auckland Bangkok Bombay
Calcutta Cape Town Dar es Salaam Delhi
Florence Hong Kong Istanbul Karachi
Kuala Lumpur Madras Madrid Melbourne
Mexico City Nairobi Paris Singapore
Taipei Tokyo Toronto
and associated companies in
Berlin Ibadan

Oxford is a trade mark of Oxford University Press

Published in the United States by
Oxford University Press Inc., New York

© Ronald Hutton 1994

First published 1994

All rights reserved. No part of this publication may be reproduced,
stored in a retrieval system, or transmitted, in any form or by any means,
without the prior permission in writing of Oxford University Press.
Within the UK, exceptions are allowed in respect of any fair dealing for the
purpose of research or private study, or criticism or review, as permitted
under the Copyright, Designs and Patents Act, 1988, or in the case of
reprographic reproduction in accordance with the terms of the licences
issued by the Copyright Licensing Agency. Enquiries concerning
reproduction outside these terms and in other countries should be
sent to the Rights Department, Oxford University Press,
at the address above

British Library Cataloguing in Publication Data
Data available

Library of Congress Cataloging in Publication Data
Hutton, Ronald.
The rise and fall of merry England: the ritual year, 1400-1700 / Ronald Hutton.
p. cm.
Includes bibliographical references.
1. England—Social life and customs—16th century. 2. England—Social life
and customs—17th century. 3. England—Social life and customs—1066-1485.
4. Rites and ceremonies—England—History. 5. Popular culture—England—
History. 6. Calendar—England—History. 7. Folklore—England—History.
8. Ritual. I. Title.
DA320.H87 1994 942—dc20 93-43092
ISBN 0-19-820363-2

3 5 7 9 10 8 6 4 2

Printed in Great Britain
on acid-free paper by
Biddles Ltd.
Guildford and King's Lynn

942 H979r 1994
Hutton, Ronald.
The rise and fall of merry E

For three Cambridge ladies:

Penelope Gwendolyn Ashbrook

Antonia Galloway

and

Prudence Jones

TULSA CITY-COUNTY LIBRARY

PREFACE

THIS book is one product of a long-cherished design to write a history of the ritual year in the British Isles. My collection of information upon the subject predated my undergraduate career, but only in 1981 did I resolve to undertake the book. I drafted a plan of research that year and commenced steady work upon it in 1983, alongside the very different enterprise of a life of Charles II. My intention was to pursue each in alternate months for about ten years, publishing essays upon both as my research advanced. This system operated until 1985, when I decided to concentrate upon the royal biography. This was partly because the competition in that field was increasing, and threatened to render pointless many of my original intentions if I attended to them at so slow a pace. It was also because my material on the ritual year now seemed likely to give birth to at least three books instead of one. I completed *Charles II* in 1988, and by 1989 I had added a short textbook on the Interregnum to close a gap in my writing on the mid-seventeenth century. The way was now clear for me to resume my other work, first by producing a survey of what was known of the pagan religions of the ancient British Isles, intended to prove how little of certainty could be said about them. This was finished in 1990, and I commenced the second instalment of publication, covering the years 1400 to 1700 and represented by the present book. The general history of calendar customs which I planned in 1981, *The Stations of the Sun*, can now follow upon a foundation made much stronger by the first two works.

Inevitably, scholarly interest in aspects of the subject of this book has increased considerably during the past ten years, resulting in a string of publications which have stimulated my own ideas and added to my knowledge, but also, inevitably, rendered some of my earlier research redundant. The late 1980s saw the publication of important books by David Underdown and David Cressy which accomplished all those results, and after most of this one was written the rapid appearance of more by Julian Davies, Kevin Sharpe, and Eamon Duffy resulted in the deletion of several passages which covered matters now well represented by them. I can only hope that more will not be overtaken during the time in which this work is passing through the press. The problem is the natural consequence of treating a subject which sprawls across such a long span of time and into so many other issues; it certainly reflects well on the condition of early modern English studies.

RONALD HUTTON

27 January 1993

ACKNOWLEDGEMENTS

―――――

THREE different kinds of debt have been incurred in the writing of this book. The first is to the British Academy, for having made a grant towards the archival research, and to the Bristol University Staff Travel Fund, for assisting some additional journeys when the main body of work was done. The second is to the members of staff of those archives who responded to a bombardment of requests from me with magnificent patience and efficiency. The vast majority of library and record office personnel fall into this category, so it is very high praise indeed to single out for special mention those of the Doncaster City Archives, Essex Record Office, Cheshire Record Office, Clwyd (Hawarden) Record Office, and Dorset Record Office. My third sort of gratitude is owed to Tony Morris of Oxford University Press, for being the sort of publisher who adds considerably to the pleasures of being an author.

CONTENTS

INTRODUCTION

THIS book considers certain themes in the history of the ritual year in England during the late Middle Ages and the Tudor and Stuart periods. A small amount of Welsh material is included, but so little of relevance survives from Wales until the late seventeenth century that the title 'Merry England' suffices for most of the work. Its concern is essentially with those annual festivals which were celebrated, regionally or nationally, with public rituals or customary pastimes. It includes those which were part of religion, those which were secular entertainments, and those which spanned the two spheres. It treats of élite customs, those of the populace, and those which were common to both or moved from one to another. It begins by attempting to identify those activities, and to determine how widespread they were across the nation and among different kinds of community, in the period immediately preceding the English Reformation. It then looks backward to consider the approximate antiquity of each activity by that time, asking whether the religious rituals of early Tudor England were those of the Anglo-Saxons, and whether the folk customs were derived from an ancient, ultimately pre-Christian, past. It subsequently moves forward to examine how this calendar of activities altered under the impact of the successive religious, political, and social changes of the sixteenth and seventeenth centuries, intervening in a set of historiographical controversies. Ultimately, its main contribution is to a much bigger issue: the question of whether economic and social factors had more impact upon cultural change in early modern England than those of religion or politics, or even an autonomous cultural determinism.

In the process, several aspects of the subject are excluded. There is no attempt to consider private customs associated with numinous dates (such as divinatory magic), or rites unique to individual communities, however colourful these may be. Public holy days not noted for communal customs are usually passed over, and there is little treatment of activities, such as sports, which very commonly took place at festivals but were not particular to them. Nor does this book attempt to join the debates over the meaning of the words 'ritual', 'ceremony', or 'custom', preferring to use those terms in a crude fashion sufficient (I hope) to carry the arguments and convey the information at stake. Those unfamiliar with the discussions concerned need only consult David Sills's *International Encyclopedia of the Social Sciences* (1968) and G. Duncan Mitchell's *Dictionary of Sociology* (1968), or more recent publications such as Peter Borsay's essay in Peter Clark (ed.), *The Transformation of English Provincial Towns 1600–1800* (1984), to see how sociologists and anthropologists have completely failed to arrive at a single, generally agreed working definition of any one of those terms after a hundred years of disputation. I am not suggesting that their arguments are not fascinating and important in themselves, only that I did not feel it necessary to join them. Likewise, I have not attempted any discussion of the social function of the different categories of ritual, being satisfied with the broad categories already provided in a book such as Peter Burke's *Popular Culture in Early Modern Europe* (1978).

If the work has been selective in its subject-matter, so has it been in its source material. It makes very heavy use of churchwardens' accounts, each set of which could furnish information of value. Indeed, having begun with the intention of concentrating upon those from a sample of counties, I gradually came to attempt the task of reading every one available to the public which dated from before 1690; the full list is printed as an appendix. I also set out to consult every set of household accounts surviving from before 1530, in which quest I was greatly helped by the work of Christopher Dyer. My third and final attempt at a comprehensive survey was of the works listed in the *Short Title Catalogue* of books published before 1640. I had less luck with manuscript records of church courts, quarter sessions, and corporations, which did indeed include items of importance to my interests but so rarely that the time and cost of reading systematically through any of these classes of document became prohibitive. I searched the archives of the diocesan courts of Salisbury, Bath and Wells, and Oxford, of the archdeaconry of Essex, of the Staffordshire and Wiltshire Quarter Sessions, and the unpublished sections of those of the municipalities of Plymouth and Nottingham. They were selected for their quality and their convenience of access, but the lay and ecclesiastical court papers of Wiltshire and Somerset turned out to have been well used for my purpose by David Underdown and Martin Ingram, and the others provided only a handful of relevant entries after a lot of work. These kinds of source in other areas probably contain some items which would have been of considerable use to me, but I can only leave them to emerge in future research by historians concerned with the bulk of the issues reflected in them. Otherwise, I read all of these categories of evidence which I could find in publication, along with a variety of other printed and manuscript items. As in the case of my remarks upon the preoccupations of this book, these comments upon its sources are not intended to extenuate any weaknesses or shortcomings but to indicate the large quantity of even elementary research which remains to be done within its field.

I

The Ritual Year in England
*c.*1490–*c.*1540

NOBODY has hitherto attempted to provide a systematic portrait of English seasonal rituals and pastimes in the half-century before the Reformation. There have been excellent studies of aspects of the subject and of its place in particular communities,[1] but until now there has been no overall view. The evidence for such a project is supplied chiefly by sets of accounts, left by churchwardens, urban corporations, colleges, monasteries, monarchs, and nobles, which detail the expenditure upon ceremonies, decorations, and entertainments. These can be elucidated at times by a small number of works of literature, belonging to the period in question and to those immediately before and after. From such materials it is possible to build up a fragmentary picture, which raises as many problems as it solves and may be seriously misleading unless it is interpreted with care. None the less it is also colourful, exciting, and in some respects very consistent.

It was Charles Phythian-Adams, one of the pioneers in the field, who identified the existence of a 'ritual year', or rather half-year, in early Tudor England.[2] He argued, convincingly, that it commenced with Christmas and ended around Midsummer. This being so, for most people the first sign of the opening of the season of ceremony would have been the decorating of buildings with holly and ivy on or just before Christmas Eve. The urban churchwardens' accounts for the period virtually all show payments for these evergreens,[3] and their absence from the accounts of country churches is almost certainly due to the fact that they were freely available in the parish. Occasionally there are glimpses of the kind of decorations which resulted, such as the frame which was made at St Mary on the Hill, Chester, covered in holly, stuck with candles, and suspended from a line. At Rye the prickly plant was wound up with broom and also had candles placed in it.[4] The same sorts of adornment were found in private homes, for John Stow, nostalgically remembering the London of the young Henry VIII, stated that 'every man's house' was decked with holly and ivy at this season.[5] A fifteenth-century poem proclaimed

> Nay, ivy, nay, it shall not be, I wys,
> Let holly have the master as the manner is,
> Holly stood in the hall, fair to behold,
> Ivy stood without the door, she is full sore a-cold.[6]

This may accurately reflect a tradition whereby the holly was fastened in the interior and the ivy in the porch, or it may have embodied a strictly local or personal taste. Certainly there appears to have been no sense that either of these plants was chosen for arcane properties. It was the custom to fill buildings with greenery for feasts, and holly and ivy were simply, in Stow's words, 'whatsoever the season of the year afforded to be green'. Broom, as said, also featured at Rye, and Stow mentions bays in addition. But whatever its significance in ancient times, nobody in England at this period seems to have paid attention to mistletoe at Christmas.

Another item of expenditure which is found in virtually all the surviving churchwardens' accounts is for candles, made or bought in bulk for Christmas morning. The book of ceremonies most widely used in England, that originally written for Salisbury Cathedral, specified that three masses should be held on the feast of the Nativity. At that season proceedings would have to commence well before dawn, and a lovely effect could be achieved by making the church blaze with light to salute the great festival. Some accounts made special mention of illumination of the rood loft, the carved wooden balcony fixed above the screen which divided nave from chancel and laity from clergy. Its principal feature was the rood, the large effigy of the crucified Christ flanked by the Virgin and St John. It may well have seemed appropriate to light up the form of the Christian saviour upon his birth-feast, but there was also a practical reason for the expenditure. The Salisbury rite directed that during the opening service somebody should stand in the loft and read the genealogy of Christ from St Matthew's Gospel, and it was necessary both that they should be visible and that they could see their text. By process of association, a collection often followed to pay for the candle or lamp which lit up the rood at services throughout the year.[7]

When the people left church they could enjoy, if they wished, their first really ample meal for over four weeks. From Advent Sunday, the fourth before the Nativity, they had been enjoined to restrict their diet. For the wealthy, this apparently meant having soups, stews, and fish instead of roasts or pies. The poorer, however, could find the reduction quite burdensome. In the fifteenth century James Ryman complained of eating 'no puddings nor sauce, but stinking fish not worth a louse'.[8] Christmas Eve was kept as a strict fast, meat, cheese, and eggs all forbidden. The feasting upon the Day was thus something of an emotional release, and also an occasion for generosity. The ideal was expressed by Thomas Tusser:

> At Christmas we banquet, the rich with the poor,
> Who then (but the miser) but openeth his door?[9]

The wealthy, of course, were expected to open theirs with particular munificence, although in reality they entertained their social equals and immediate inferiors. In the 1510s the earl of Northumberland and duke of Buckingham received a string of clerical dignitaries and local gentlefolk. The earl's dinner always included four swans, the duke's several barrels of malmsey wine. In the 1520s Sir Henry Willoughby, a midland landowner, entertained all his tenants. But Henry Rogers, mayor of Coventry in 1517, seems genuinely to have kept 'open house' for all.[10] This meal ushered in the twelve days of merriment which were to last until the feast of the Epiphany, and included a wide range of amusements. In the Twelve Days of 1520–1, the duke of Buckingham watched a troupe of French players, as well as three jesters, the municipal musicians of Bristol, and an acrobat. During a later Christmas season the earl of Rutland paid for players from Lincoln and Wighen, minstrels from Derbyshire, and a performance by 'the children of Newark'. These aristocrats were exceptional in their appetite for entertainment. Most watched only one or two plays and concerts, and Henry VIII himself marked his first Christmas season as monarch with just three dramatic productions and one sequence of music.[11] Religious houses and municipal corporations frequently, but not invariably, invited in the same sorts of entertainers as the nobles,[12] and parishioners sometimes pooled their resources to hire players or to mount their own productions in the village church. The latter were occasionally turned into fund-raising events, with food and drink sold by the churchwardens.[13] In addition there was a large amount of card-playing and board-gaming, and there were very many private parties.[14]

We can only guess at the nature of the great majority of the plays which were performed. From the evidence of the next century, when theatrical records become more detailed, we can surmise that many would simply have been the current repertoire of the groups which staged them, without relevance to the season. Some would have been upon the theme of the Nativity, like one acted annually before the fifth earl of Northumberland.[15] Until very recently it could have been stated confidently that others would have consisted of what was presumed to be the most archaic and persistent form of English folk drama, the Mummers' play. This survives in some villages up to the present day, and during the early twentieth century it was regarded by scholars as an authentic relic of prehistoric ritual. Its simple plot, hinging upon a combat, death, and resurrection, its performance in midwinter, and its fairly wide geographical distribution within Britain, all seemed to bear out this idea. The latter only began to be challenged at the end of the 1970s, when further research indicated that this type of play was at its most popular between 1780 and 1900, and that it was spread in part by printed chapbooks. No trace of it has yet been discovered before 1738, despite copious evidence of other popular customs.

Those who have continued to argue for an earlier period of origin have therefore to do so from silence. Some point out similarities of character and structure in medieval and early modern literature, without disposing of the possibility that the literature itself might have influenced the Mummers' play, rather than the other way round. Another has found still more remarkable parallels in folk plays of northern Greece and Trebizond. If he can manage to prove that the similarities are too many to be coincidental, he has, however, yet to establish when it was that Greek and English folk drama came into such a close relationship. It is certainly true that even if the English plays are an eighteenth-century tradition, they still preserve within them echoes of much earlier periods. Several of the stock personalities are recognizably Tudor and Stuart favourites, while another, the quack doctor, performs much the same function and in the same way in a piece of early sixteenth-century religious drama. Most remarkable is the regular appearance of one usually named Beelzebub and characterized by the carrying of a club and frying-pan. He can hardly be anything other than a pagan god-figure known in Ireland as the Daghda and in Gaul as Sucellus, and how he leaped one and a half millennia to turn up in an English folk play is a fascinating, and apparently baffling, question.[16] What does seem to be clear is that despite these touches the play concerned has at present to be left out of a discussion of pre-Reformation festivities.

On the other hand there were certainly plenty of mummers around in fifteenth- and sixteenth-century England, in the broad contemporary usage of the term. It signified people disguised in festive costumes, and these, also known as 'maskers' and 'guisers', were a feature of the Twelve Days. They appeared in the dramatic performances at the royal court and in great households, and passed through the streets of towns on their way to private fancy-dress parties. In the larger urban centres they clearly posed an unintentional problem to law and order, because the combination of dark evenings and the presence of many people in disguises afforded marvellous opportunities for street criminals to escape unrecognized. As a result, between 1400 and 1560 London, Bristol, Chester, and probably other towns whose records have not survived for this period, forbade anybody to walk about masked during the Christmas season.[17]

But an element of legitimized disorder was built into the Twelve Days. One expression of it was in the figure of the Lord of Misrule, also known as Abbot of Misrule, Christmas Lord, and by local names. One was appointed at the royal court, and given a full panoply of kingship, including throne, canopy, armoury, jester, and a gibbet for mock executions of those who offended him. John Stow declared them to have existed 'in the house of every nobleman, of honour or good worship, be he spiritual or temporal'. Despite this opinion, rewards to them are absent from most of the surviving household accounts, but the fifth earl of Northumberland and Lady Margaret Beaufort certainly did maintain them. They were also employed by the Lord Mayor and sheriffs of London, the mayor of Coventry, the corporation of New Romney (in Kent), and probably by some other municipalities. They featured at university colleges and in the London law schools known as Inns of Court. At the latter the multiplicity of them could become quite elaborate. Thus at Lincoln's Inn during 1519–20 there was a 'King over Christmas Day' and also a 'King over New Year's Day'. They could be the same person, normally a high-ranking officer of the Inn, and were attended by a Sewer and Cupbearer, chosen from colleagues who were fined if they refused to serve. But there was also a 'King of Cockneys' on the feast of Holy Innocents, 28 December, who had his own Marshal, Butler, and Constable and was apparently chosen or elected from the students. The figure that the governing body of the Inn would not tolerate was 'Jack Straw', named after a leader of the Peasants' Revolt of 1381 and clearly an instigator of pranks and wild behaviour among the young men. At Christmas 1516–17 a 'Jack Straw' and his followers had broken down doors and invaded rooms at the Inn, resulting in a fine, a dismissal, and the formal prohibition of his reappearance. In addition to all these mock monarchs among the intellectual and social élite, some parishes in East Anglia also supplied them.

Despite all this information, it is difficult to provide a detailed portrait of what Lords of Misrule actually did in pre-Reformation England. Stow states that they made 'the rarest pastimes to delight the beholders', but if they were simply there to devise entertainments then it is hard to see why the king and Northumberland both also paid a Master of Revels, who certainly had this function. Polydor Vergil, writing in the 1500s, emphasized instead that they were mock-rulers, to whom the usual leaders of households or of official institutions became subservient during the Christmas merry-making. Where their status can be identified, they were drawn from the junior officers of the lord or corporation by whom they were appointed. At Harwich one was elected by the youth of the town gathered in its church, from among their own number, 'to solace the parish'. It seems, then, that the essence of the office lay in role-reversal, in the elevation of a servant to a position of apparent authority. This alteration of the 'natural' order seems to have been the 'misrule' involved, and a suitable symbol for a season of revelry and of release from work. But no information survives upon precisely how any of the 'Lords' and 'Abbots' in great households or towns carried out their duties. The latter were presumably a mixture of those of the Master of the Revels and the Fool, both of whom were apparently disqualified from the Christmas office because it too closely resembled their permanent position. The Harwich 'Lord' went about the town with musicians, to draw other young people into the streets for public merry-making. Seven sets of early sixteenth-century churchwardens' accounts from Norfolk, Suffolk, and Essex record sums handed in by such figures, who had gathered money in the course of their activities. But the nature of the latter, again, can only be presumed. They may have simply consisted of processions with costumes and music, or may have included games and performances. Some of the household or college Lords of Misrule held office for a long period, the one at the royal court 'reigning' from late October until early January, but they were clearly only active for parts of this span. Northumberland's 'Abbot' only officiated during the Twelve Days, while the Harwich 'Lord' was elected on 26 December. The activities and terms of appointment of these characters were probably as disparate as they are mysterious.[18]

Their parallel in the ecclesiastical world was the Boy Bishop, also known as the Bairn Bishop or St Nicholas Bishop. This was a child clad in episcopal vestments, who officiated to some degree in religious activities during December. His presence is best attested in the cathedrals themselves, being recorded in all those from which late medieval documents have survived: Wells, Salisbury, York, St Paul's, Exeter, Lincoln, Lichfield, Durham, and Hereford. His activities are most clearly described at Salisbury, where he was elected by the choirboys from amongst their number. He first appeared in public after vespers (evensong) upon 27 December, the day before the feast of the Holy Innocents, the infants killed at Bethlehem by King Herod in an attempt to destroy the new-born Christ. The little 'bishop' led the choristers in procession to the high altar, dressed in full episcopal robes with his companions clad in silk copes (mantles) like higher clergy, carrying candles and singing. Then he censed the altar and its images, while the genuine bishop and chapter followed the procession bearing books and candles as the boys normally did. They then gave up their stalls to the choristers and the boy leader presided over all services from then until the end of the feast of Holy Innocents, except mass itself. The same pattern seems to have obtained in other cathedrals, with variations. At St Paul's the Boy Bishop was chosen by the senior clergy, and was expected to preach a sermon. Three of these have survived, all clearly written by adults but with a great deal of dry humour at the expense of authority. At York the 'Bairn Bishop' went upon visitation, accompanied by stewards, a preacher, and singers, collecting money from noble households and monasteries. Until the early fifteenth century, prelates occasionally expressed disquiet about the degree of irreverence and disorder associated with the custom, but after then it seems to have been both generally accepted and well disciplined.[19]

Around 1500 it was also observed in some major abbeys which included schools, including Westminster, Bury St Edmunds, and Winchester. From the last of these the boys were also taken to St Mary's Convent dressed as girls, to sing and dance before the nuns. Such 'bishops' also appeared at important schools such as Eton and Winchester, and wealthy collegiate churches such as St Peter's, Canterbury, and Ottery St Mary in Devon. They are recorded at the university colleges of Magdalen and All Souls, Oxford, and King's, Cambridge. However, at King's and (for most of the period) at Magdalen, they presided not at Holy Innocents but on 6 December, the feast of St Nicholas, a special patron of children. The accounts at King's also provide us with our only detailed description of a Boy Bishop's costume, specially made to fit his size and including a white wool coat, a scarlet gown with its hood furred with white ermine, fine knitted gloves, gold rings, a crozier, and a mitre of white damask with a rose, a star, and a cross embroidered upon it in pearls and green and red gems. At King's he presided not only at services but over theatrical performances upon St Nicholas's Day. On that feast also the king himself presented money to his own 'St Nicholas Bishop', apparently chosen from the choristers of the Chapel Royal. Most nobles do not seem to have gone to the trouble of copying this royal example, but the festivity-loving fifth earl of Northumberland did reward a 'Bairn Bishop' upon Holy Innocents' Day, and as the child's robes and ornaments were listed in the earl's inventory of goods he was presumably selected from the household.[20]

Most of this is fairly well known to historians. What is perhaps less appreciated is the part which these little characters played in parish affairs. At Bristol it was appropriately enough the church of St Nicholas which set forth a Boy Bishop upon its patron's feast, with a procession bearing eight banners. The corporation came to receive his blessing and then entertained him and his retinue of boys to a banquet. But at least seven London parishes which had no association with the saint paraded robed and mitred children upon his feast. The same was true of others in Norwich, Cambridge, Nottingham, Coventry, Leicester, Lincolnshire, Yorkshire, Derbyshire, Staffordshire, Shropshire, Worcestershire, Somerset, Dorset, Sussex, Kent, Surrey and Suffolk. Records of more have doubtless perished. The surviving entries make plain that while going on procession the boys collected money from spectators which was handed over to the churchwardens. Not all of them stayed within their parish boundaries. The 'Bishop' from New Romney in Kent visited nearby Lydd, while Lydd's Lord of Misrule paid a reciprocal call upon New Romney. The 'Bishop' from Lambeth toured the surrounding countryside with his entourage. What exactly they did is recorded in no contemporary source, but there seems little reason to doubt the assertion of a writer in 1655, that they had sung and blessed the people whom they encountered. The communities in whose records they appear span not only a great part of England but also a considerable range of size and economic function. Yet they represent a small minority of the parishes in each locality for which records survive. No evidence is available to explain why they, and not their neighbours, should have adopted the custom. Nor does the surviving material support the notion that parishes which produced Boy Bishops were geographically spaced so that each had a 'catchment area' of contributions and that most districts had access to such a 'bishop' if they wished to see one.[21] On the other hand, towns and university colleges which provided them do seem to have been different from those which had Lords of Misrule, with the exception of London. Yet, as said, the royal court and Northumberland's household included both, so that their presence was by no means mutually exclusive.

The contributions made by each to parish funds were paralleled by those gathered by a more mysterious group of people, known variously as Hognells, Hogglers, Hogans, Hogners, or Hoggells, or by variant spellings of these names. In the fifteenth and sixteenth centuries, they are recorded at a total of twenty-one rural parishes, in Gloucestershire, Somerset, and

Devon, Surrey, Sussex, and Kent, and the Lincolnshire fens. In the south-western counties and in Sussex and Surrey, they appear in the majority of (but not all) country parishes for which Tudor accounts survive. In some, especially in Devon and Somerset, they provided the largest single contribution to parochial finances. In the two neighbouring Lincolnshire villages where they are known to have existed, they maintained their own light burning in the churches. At Pilton and Tintinhull in Somerset and Ashburton and Chagford in Devon, they were formally organized into a guild, Tintinhull's having a steward and Chagford's possessing wardens. At times they included some of the wealthiest people in the village. At Ashburton they handed in their contribution at Easter, but most of the accounts imply what those of Surrey and some in Sussex make explicit, that their period of activity was during the Christmas holiday. At Bolney in Sussex 'the hognel time' lasted longer, until 2 February. What we are never told is what exactly happened in that time. The derivation of the name or names is unknown. The Old English 'hogenhune' meant a protected guest, while the Norman 'hoguinane' signified a New Year present, but neither provides a real indication of the activities of these Tudor villagers. The Scots 'hogmanay', first meaning a gift made to the poor or to children at the New Year, is itself obscure in its origins and not recorded before the seventeenth century. And with these the dictionary runs out of clues. We do not know whether the Hogglers, or Hogners, performed any service or gave any performance in return for their collections. We cannot account for their curious geographical distribution. We can only say that, according to a late Elizabethan Somerset source, their fundamental activity was to go about the parish gathering money for it, and that every piece of evidence testifies to their efficiency in doing so.[22]

A different sort of group activity at this season concerned the wassail cup or bowl. A fourteenth-century text by Peter de Langtoft describes in detail the custom involving this vessel, to which the Tudor sources only refer in passing; the leader of a gathering took it, and cried 'Wassail', Old English for 'your health'. He was answered 'Drinkhail', and then passed it to another person with a kiss, so that these actions could be repeated by each. At the early Tudor court it was accompanied into the king's presence by the chief officers of the household, bearing staves. In great families it was made of precious metal—Edmund, earl of March, leaving a silver one upon his death in 1382. By about 1600 it had become a custom for commoners to take a wassail bowl about the streets and probably from house to house, offering drink from it and sometimes expecting money in return. A song, first recorded in 1550, runs

> Wassail, wassail, out of the milk pail,
> Wassail, wassail, as white as my nail,
> Wassail, wassail, in snow, frost and hail,
> Wassail, wassail, that much doth avail,
> Wassail, wassail, that never will fail.

The song may have been intended to accompany the bowl on its rounds of a village, and so the inception of that custom may lie in the early Tudor period or considerably before. But the song may equally well have been part of the passage of the wassail within a household.[23] A similar problem of projection concerns the related custom of 'wassailing' orchards in the Christmas season, by wishing the trees health and abundant crops in the coming year. It is apparently first recorded at Fordwich, Kent, in 1585, and reappears in Devon in the 1630s, according to the poem by Robert Herrick:

> Wassail the Trees, that they may bear
> You many a plum, and many a pear . . .

It appears to feature again in the diary of a Sussex parson in 1670, and is quite frequently recorded thereafter. The fact that traces of it are found in so many fruit-growing areas of England under Elizabeth and the Stuarts argues for an origin at the latest in the early Tudor or medieval periods.[24] Modern guides to English folk-customs have frequently described it as a relic of pre-Christian ritual, and so indeed it may be. It may, nevertheless, also be an extension of the custom of the household wassail, made after the end of the Middle Ages.

The song quoted above was one of a very large number associated with the season. 'At Christmas of Christ many carols we sing' wrote Tusser in 1555, and scores have survived from the fifteenth and early sixteenth centuries. Most are religious in nature, while a few celebrate feasting or deal with ways of predicting the weather. In 1521 Wynken de Worde issued the first printed handbook of them. Some of those which have not survived were apparently bawdy or satirical, for in 1497 a biographer of St Thomas à Becket could regard them as a bad influence upon the young. No record survives of the setting for their performance. Some were by their nature suited to the home, but many could have been sung door to door as they have been in modern times. There is no evidence, however, that it was usual to perform them in church during the pre-Reformation period.[25]

Many of the customs and diversions mentioned above were common to all or most of the Christmas season. But certain days among the Twelve were more important than others. The first such, after Christmas itself, was 1 January, known as New Year's Day even though the date of the year did not officially change until 25 March, and had not done since the early Middle Ages. Nevertheless, the older Roman tradition, of the turn of the year at the opening of January, still universally persisted in late medieval Europe. As the king put on his shoes that morning, trumpets sounded and a present arrived from the queen, followed by servants of the leading courtiers each bearing gifts from them. In her own chamber, the queen received hers. The royal couple had arranged for reciprocal presents, usu-ally in cash, to be sent out to the officers of the household and to the chief lay and clerical dignitaries of the realm. If the latter were at their own seats, the gifts were carried thither by Yeomen of the Guard. Upon the same morning the fifth earl of Northumberland was awoken by minstrels playing before his door, followed by his own fanfare of trumpets. He then received his gifts, making them in turn to his sovereigns and his own household. Similar scenes were enacted in the residences of other magnates, while gentry exchanged presents with their servants, not usually receiving any from royalty but often dispatching them to local aristocrats. Some great nobles, like the earl of Rutland, sent gifts to servants of the king and of other peers, from whom they expected or had received favours. Religious houses gave to their own staff and to each other. These New Year's gifts, forerunners of modern Christmas presents, appear in every full set of household accounts surviving from the period 1450–1550, underpinning the social and political order. What is not clear is whether they were exchanged between commoners. Polydor Vergil, at the opening of the six-teenth century, stated that they were sent only by those who served lords; but Tusser, in the middle of the same century, commented that Christmas was a time when people in general 'gave many gifts', so the matter must remain in doubt.[26]

At the end of the morning the monarch, Northumberland, and probably all the other nobles and gentry who were keeping Christmas at home, presided over a banquet. The king went in procession to it with the sword of state carried before him, while Northumberland's herald cried his hon-ours as the feasting commenced. The evening was a notable one for enter-tainments, from royal to parish level.[27] The same was even more true of Twelfth Night, which ended the Christmas holiday. Just as Christmas Day itself had done, Twelfth Day, 6 January, began with a dramatic religious service. This time it was the feast of the Epiphany, the recognition of Christ by the Three Kings. A feature of this was a Star of Bethlehem, sometimes gilded and sometimes made of brass, suspended from the rood loft or in 'the body of the church'. It seems to have been used almost wholly in urban parishes, Holbeach in Lincolnshire being the only rural one where it is recorded before the Reformation.[28] Once again, it was apparently only favoured by some churches even within towns, and it is striking that none of the several surviving sets of London parish accounts ever mention it. It may have played a part in a dramatic performance featuring the Three Kings, but of this there is no evidence from this period. Whatever exactly did happen during this service, it was followed by feasting just like that on Christmas morn. The king presided over his feast, wearing the crown and royal robes. For him and for Northumberland, Buckingham, Rutland, and many others of all social ranks, the festivities that night were the most sumptuous of the whole year. In the 1510s Northumberland regularly had a play followed by a masked dance interspersed with pageants. In 1486 Henry VII held a banquet and then went in procession to Westminster Hall to watch a play, and then a pageant of St George and the dragon, and then a 'disguising' by various courtiers. For Henry VIII in 1512 the Master of the Revels prepared the pageant of 'The Dangerous Fortress', a castle complete with towers, bulwarks, iron chains, cannon, and a banner, inhabited by six ladies and seven gentlemen in yellow and russet, six lords in gold and russet, and twelve great nobles in yellow and blue.[29]

Upon the 7th the merry-making was over for everybody, and in arable districts preparations commenced for the ploughing. It was an activity with its own rites and religious associations. In the East Midlands there were 'plough lights' kept burning in many churches, in some cases definitely maintained by special guilds. Each probably had a plough placed in front, for at Holbeach in Lincolnshire and at Great Yarmouth there were certainly ploughs mounted in churches upon special stands. Lincolnshire was especially fond of the 'lights', which are recorded in the majority of its surviving early Tudor churchwardens' accounts. They are also mentioned in four Northamptonshire parishes, and one in Cambridgeshire, with a single possible reference in Norfolk. Yet even in Lincolnshire the custom was not universal, for records of churches in the same districts as those which maintained 'plough lights' show no trace of them.[30] It seems likely that the ploughs kept in churches, and perhaps some that were not, were blessed upon Plough Sunday, the first after Epiphany. John Bale, a Protestant writing under Edward VI, condemned 'conjuring of ploughs' among various other rites which had until his time been enacted in English churches. It may have been accompanied by private ceremonies to ensure the same effect, outside the Church and so less approved by it. Over a hundred years before Bale an anonymous cleric had inveighed against 'leading of the plough abouten the fire as for good beginning of the year'.[31]

The formal opening of the ploughing season was upon the next day, Plough Monday. It often took place with a great deal of jollity. Tusser recorded a custom whereby the ploughmen tried to put an object beside the fire before the young women could put a kettle of water onto it: the maidens succeeded or failed in gaining a prize according to the result.[32] In villages and towns scattered across Essex, Suffolk, Norfolk, Cambridgeshire, Lincolnshire, and Northamptonshire, a plough (perhaps that from the church) was dragged around the streets and money collected behind it for the parish funds. In East Anglia this collection is mentioned in virtually all (but again not all) of the accounts for arable parishes. Boxford in Suffolk and Great Dunmow in Essex held feasts, and Leverington in Lincolnshire had a scheme whereby upon that day arrangements were made to loan out money and a plough to poor farmers. At Saxilby in Lincolnshire and Brundish in Suffolk it was specifically the young men of the village who made the gathering, and so it may have been everywhere. Sometimes the proceeds went directly to the upkeep of the 'plough light'.[33] What is never recorded is whether those who dragged the plough upon these occasions performed a special song, dance, or play as they did so. By the late eighteenth century the lads of many east midland villages certainly had a Plough Monday play. Generally it was a version of that of the Mummers, based around a combat, death, and revival, but tacked onto a tale of how a Fool courts and marries.[34] But it is not recorded before the 1760s, and although great efforts have been made by some modern scholars to find traces of it before then,[35] none are convincing, and so, like the drama of the Mummers, it must be left out of this portrait.

After Plough Monday there were no more national or regional ceremonies for at least two weeks. Then came February, and upon the second day of that month fell the Christian feast of the Purification of the Virgin Mary and the recognition of Christ as the Messiah by Simeon. The latter's words 'a light to lighten the Gentiles' provided a cue for the activity associated with that festival, the kindling and blessing of candles in churches. Furthermore, the spectacle of light growing against the shadows was also an appropriate one with which to open the month which drove the darkness from the afternoon and (usually) restored the first flowers and buds to England. The words of the Salisbury rite, which was (as said before) the one most commonly used, played upon the notion of the retreating of the dark. The popular name for the feast was Candlemas. Good Christians were expected to eat only bread and to drink only water upon the previous day, to enhance the sense of celebration as the feast began. Then churches, in the words of a Shropshire monk, 'made great melody', and worshippers offered their candles and tapers for benediction. They were placed before the altar, sprinkled with holy water, and perfumed with incense. That of the king was carried at his right-hand side by the Lord Chamberlain as he processed into the Chapel Royal. The fifth earl of Northumberland presented them on behalf of himself and his family, while in the Midlands Sir Henry Willoughby offered them for his servants as well.[36] Some parish churches bought them in bulk for the feast, either to present them to parishioners or to light up the building still further. Some made a trendle, a circular frame which either operated as a chandelier in the conventional sense or rotated each candle in turn beneath the priest's hands for benediction.[37] The service was followed by municipal banquets at Grimsby, Coventry, and Cambridge (where the town musicians toured the streets), and probably in other places as well. At Beverley in the East Riding of Yorkshire, the Guild of the Blessed Virgin assembled in the morning to process to church. One of its female members was attired as the Virgin, carrying a doll to represent Christ. She was followed by two men costumed as Joseph and Simeon, two people dressed as angels bearing a structure which held twenty-four candles, and then the remaining sisters and brothers, bearing their own, with musicians. At the church the Virgin offered the doll to Simeon at the high altar and the others presented their candles to be blessed.[38]

Candlemas marked the formal end of winter, and after about two weeks more the first courtship flights of birds (especially members of the crow family) would usually be visible. Humans provided a self-conscious parallel to this upon 14 February, the feast of the patron saint of birds, Valentine, by sending each other tokens of affection. What seems to have distinguished these from the modern cards is that none were anonymous and that the recipients were chosen by chance, from within a group of friends. Intriguingly, although mentioned by the fifteenth-century poet John Lydgate, who wrote principally for members of the royal court, the custom does not feature among royalty and the aristocracy of this time so much as among the gentry. The letters of the Paston family of Norfolk mention it three times in the 1470s, while the generous Sir Henry Willoughby paid 2s. 3d. for his Valentine in 1523, a large sum for a token.[39] Unhappily, we shall never know what his gift was, and no other late medieval or early Tudor Valentine has survived or been described. Nor can we tell whether the custom was prevalent among commoners.

Either before or after this flirtation, the English were involved in a much larger celebration, that of Shrovetide, which lasted from the seventh Sunday before Easter until the end of the following Tuesday. It was the occasion for eating up the remaining stocks of meat, eggs, cheese, and other commodities which could not be consumed during the long season of fasting now at hand. The second day was called 'Collop Monday', after the roasting of collops, or slices, of meat.[40] The third was known as 'Fasting's Even' or, more commonly, as Shrove Tuesday, a name taken from the 'shriving' or confession of sins, and absolution from them, which the devout were expected to undertake before the fast began. It was far more celebrated, however, for eating and merry-making, with the prospect of austerity to come lending a peculiar fervour to both. A Protestant preacher in 1570 remembered it as having been 'a day of great gluttony, surfeiting and drunkenness',[41] and it was also a time for street sports. The two most notorious had been identified together at London in 1409, when the collection of money for them had been forbidden: football and 'cockthreshing'.[42] Shrovetide football was banned altogether by the corporation of Chester in 1540, because of 'great inconvenience' caused by 'evil disposed persons'. Formerly the Shoemakers' Company had provided the ball, but henceforth they were to sponsor a foot race instead. The 'inconvenience' at Chester can only be imagined, but it must have been very great indeed, as Tudor football normally possessed neither teams nor rules. The gracious Sir Thomas Elyot described it in 1531 as 'nothing but beastly fury and extreme violence, whereof procedeth hurt'. 'Cockthreshing' referred to the entertainment of tethering a cockerel by a leg and attempting to knock it over, or to kill it, with missiles. It combined at Shrovetide with the more regular cock-fighting, and both were popular at all levels of society. John Stow recalled Shrovetide cockfights in the streets of early Tudor London, while Henry VII paid for cocks to be delivered to his palace for Shrovetide 1493. The fourth Lord Berkeley, who died in 1417, was a notable 'thresher', and although no aristocrats were similarly reputed in the years around 1500, it seems fairly certain that they indulged in the same pleasure as their king.[43]

Upon the morning after Shrovetide the English, some of them bruised or badly hung over, were expected to make their way to church and to kneel before a priest. He would bless ashes, sprinkle them with holy water, and place the mixture upon the heads of the people, with the Latin words for the phrase 'Remember O Man that thou art dust and to dust thou shalt return.'[44] It was Ash Wednesday and Lent had begun. For six and a half weeks there was to be a restricted diet and no festivity, while individuals considered to be especially sinful by priest and community were excluded from the church. Those admitted had to endure the sight of the rood, and images of saints, veiled to hide their comforting faces and to bring home the immediacy of sin. None the less the cloths used as veils were clearly sometimes objects of beauty in their own right. From inventories drawn up in the reigns of Henry VIII and Edward VI, it is clear that they were made of linen or silk and either white, black, or blue, usually with red crosses in the centre of the white examples and sometimes with white crosses upon the others. The rood's veil was drawn by a line, attached to a pulley, and could be painted or embroidered with pictures from Scripture. White cloths covered the altars and the lectern, while a large veil hid the chancel from the nave, let down like the rood cloth by a line worked by pulley. For most of Lent it was raised only when the gospel was read at mass. Once again, it was usually white but could bear crosses or be of a variety of single or mixed colours. The clergy also wore robes which were wholly or mostly white.[45]

Nothing relieved the sobriety of most of the Lenten season, although the steady growth of daylight, flowers and new leaves, and the number of nesting birds must have added some pleasure to it. The custom of turning the fourth Sunday in Lent into Mother's Day is not known before the seventeenth century.[46] The Cambridgeshire village of Bassingbourn rather bravely held an annual feast upon that day, to mark the middle of Lent, but the rules of the fast could not have allowed them an extensive diet or much revelry.[47] Only in the last two weeks, called Passiontide, did excitement begin to mount. Upon Passion Sunday, the fifth in Lent, the clergy were supposed to alter their white robes to red.[48] A week later came Palm Sunday, and one of the longest passages of ceremony of the whole ecclesiastical year. Where the Salisbury rite was fully observed, it took the following form. First the priest blessed water and the story of Christ's entry into Jerusalem from St John's Gospel was read to the congregation. Then the priest blessed branches, apparently gathered and presented by the people, of what was supposed to be palm in memory of the palms said to have been strewn before Jesus in that entry. In England fronds of willow or sallow in fresh leaf, or of box, yew, or other evergreens, were usually employed instead. The consecrated host was put in a shrine or monstrance and carried out by the clergy into the churchyard. The laity followed in their own procession, bearing the branches behind a priest with a plain cross, and the two groups halted to hear the story of the entry read from St Matthew's Gospel. Now the two processions met, and one or more people read or sang the prophetic lesson, being rewarded later with bread and ale or a potation of wine. The processions merged and moved to a scaffold at the south door of the church, from which seven boys sang 'Gloria, Laus et Honor', and flowers and cakes were thrown to the congregation.

The procession then entered the church through the west door and watched as the rood cloth was drawn aside to reveal the image of Christ, while an anthem was sung. It remained drawn as mass was sung, incorporating the Passion from the gospel of Matthew sung, if possible, by a tenor voice providing the narrative, trebles for the parts of Jews or disciples, and a bass representing Christ. During this either the priest or the congregation made small wooden crosses, perhaps from the branches, and the former may have blessed them in turn; certainly the laity believed that they possessed protective powers. At the end of the service the rood was veiled again and the proceedings concluded.[49]

What now needs to be emphasized is that this full Palm Sunday rite was enacted in relatively few places. The blessing of branches seems to have been very widespread and perhaps universal, to judge both from literary comment and the number of local names for the day which relate to the custom. Apart from 'Palm Sunday' itself, 'Branch', 'Sallow', 'Willow', and 'Yew' Sunday are all recorded.[50] But the singing of the Passion by a choir appears almost wholly in urban parishes and in cathedrals. The only village church where it is recorded is Denton in Norfolk. The presence of a 'prophet' to read the lesson seems to have been confined entirely to towns. Even there not all churches appear to have adopted the practice: some in London, for example, did not make any payment for it. Others, by contrast, went to great lengths to achieve as dramatic an effect as possible. Thus, St Peter Cheap hired a wig or false beard to make its own 'prophet' look more patriarchal. In the overwhelming majority of rural parishes, Palm Sunday was almost wholly a festival for the blessing of foliage, a Christian rite of spring.[51] It opened Holy Week, which culminated in a series of increasingly crowded ceremonies. First, upon Wednesday, the passage concerning the rending of the veil in the Temple at Jerusalem was read, and at that moment the cloth hung before the high altar was torn or dropped away, and remained so. After dark that evening the first of the Tenebrae, the Services of Shadows, could occur. A triangular or cruciform candleframe was placed on the south side of the altar and lit with twenty-four candles representing the apostles and the prophets. When the office was sung, one was sometimes extinguished at the opening of each response, until only a single taper, representing Christ, was left burning. In other places they were snuffed in groups, or simultaneously, but the taper always remained. The custom was part of the Salisbury rite, but recorded almost wholly in cathedrals and important urban churches.[52]

The next day was Maundy Thursday, the feast of the Last Supper, at which Christ gave his final instructions to his disciples. As a gesture of fellowship and humility he also (according to Scripture) washed their feet, an action imitated by many royal and ecclesiastical dignitaries in Europe around the year 1500. The English kings traditionally performed the act for as many poor men as they themselves had years of life (not reign). The individuals thus honoured were chosen by the royal almoner for their unusual virtue, and each was rewarded with gifts of money, food, drink, and clothing. That connoisseur of ceremony, the fifth earl of Northumberland, imitated this one down to the last detail, but no other noble is recorded as having done so in this period. Archbishops, bishops, abbots, and priors did observe it (excluding the point about years of age), although there is no way of telling how many of them did so. Only at Durham is there a full description of the rite, the prior of the cathedral church (which was also an abbey) performing the action at 9 a.m. in the cloisters, for eighteen old men seated upon a long bench. The usual donations were then made to them. The term 'maundy' may derive from the Old English 'maund', a basket, denoting the container for the gifts, or from the Latin 'mandatum', a directive, in memory of Christ's instructions.[53] To many English people, however, it was 'Sheer', 'Char', 'Shrift', or 'Sharp' Thursday, all names which the fourteenth-century writer John Mirk held to derive from the cutting of hair or beards in preparation for Easter. This was apparently part of a personal process of renewal, and the same spirit extended to the rites of the church for that day. Altars were unveiled, washed, and scrubbed with birch besoms. Those excluded from the churches during Lent were now readmitted upon confession, and many others went through the same act. Bishops blessed holy oil, to be used in the unction of the sick and the consecration of priests during the next year.[54]

That evening the Tenebrae were sung again in those parishes where they were observed, and the following morning began Good Friday, the commemoration of the crucifixion and entombment of Christ. In some places the altar slabs were sprinkled or rubbed with herbs. Those individuals whose sense of sin had not been assuaged by confession sometimes asked a priest to beat their hands with 'disciplining rods'.[55] The king demonstrated again the semi-divine nature of his office, by blessing 'cramp rings' which were given to epileptics in the belief that their fits would be moderated by the royal magic.[56] But most references to Good Friday in the early sixteenth century take note of its two most celebrated ecclesiastical rites, 'Creeping to the Cross' and the Easter sepulchre. The first was the popular name for the veneration of the figure of the crucified Christ. The Salisbury service book laid down that a crucifix was to be held up veiled behind the high altar by two priests while the responses were sung, and then uncovered and laid upon the third step in front of the altar. The clergy present would then crawl shoeless to it upon hands and knees and kiss it, while hymns were sung. It was then carried down to the laity, who could kiss it in turn, genuflecting, before it was taken back to the high altar. At Durham the ceremony was very similar, the crucifix being of gold and laid upon a velvet cushion embroidered with the arms of St Cuthbert in gold thread. It was held on the lowest steps of the choir by the two oldest monks of the abbey. Royalty, like clergy, seem to have made the full ritual crawl: the young Henry VIII and his first queen, Catherine of Aragon, were provided with a rich carpet for the purpose. But monarchs also led the laity in making offerings to the Church after the action. They, and nobles such as the earl of Northumberland, gave money. Poorer people presented in kind, eggs and apples being favourite items. Once again, it is hard to tell how widespread the ritual was. It is recorded at the cathedrals of York, Lincoln, Hereford, and Wells in addition to Salisbury and Durham, in several Benedictine and Augustinian monasteries, and in some urban churches, and literary comment suggests that it was very widely known. But Cistercian and Carthusian monks did not use it and it does not feature in the records of any rural parishes.[57]

The Easter sepulchre was a miniature tomb within which a representation of Christ was laid. In the Salisbury rite, the crucifix which had been laid on the high altar after adoration was taken down after vespers (the evening service), washed with wine and water, and placed in the sepulchre. With it was lodged a consecrated wafer enclosed in a casket. Much the same ceremony existed in the cathedrals at Durham, Lincoln, and York: at Durham, crucifix and casket were combined as the host was placed in a crystal container set into the breast of an image of Christ. The nature of the sepulchre itself varied considerably by the early sixteenth century. Some were simple recesses in the wall of the choir or chancel, others richly carved stone structures with decorated arches and human figures, others small masonry chests in the chancel's corner, and yet others chambers built into the tombs of wealthy and pious individuals who had provided for this in their wills. But most often they were wood, canvas, and paper constructions, remade in most years and fastened together by pins, nails, or wires. Sometimes, as at Leverton in Lincolnshire, they were gilded. When the host was within one, a cloth was draped over it or hung before it: at Durham this was of red velvet embroidered with gold, while even in rural parishes it could be richly painted. Sometimes the sepulchre was surrounded by candles, and in the early 1480s a Duchess of Norfolk made regular payments to ensure this. Sometimes it was illuminated by a smaller number of large tapers, three being specified at the London church of St Andrew Hubbard in 1510–12. But more commonly it had its own 'light', a big candle or lamp paid for in many places by a particular collection and cared for by its own guild. At Heybridge in Suffolk the unmarried youth of the village maintained it. St Lawrence, Reading, built a special loft for it in 1516. In many parishes, especially in towns, volunteers watched the sepulchre from the moment that it was closed until the Easter morning, in memory of the soldiers who guarded Christ's tomb. The churchwardens provided bread and ale for them, and sometimes coals to keep them warm at night. At St Mary at Hill, London, the number of watchers was recorded, as three. The Easter sepulchre is mentioned in the majority of parishes for which early Tudor accounts survive, and its popularity is demonstrated by the number of bequests made to support it or its light. A survey of Northamptonshire wills for the period 1490–1546 reveals an average of just over one bequest per parish, far exceeding that for sums left to any other seasonal rite.[58] On the other hand, there remains a total of twenty-three parishes which have left good early Tudor churchwardens' accounts entirely lacking a reference to the custom.[59] This number represents about a seventh of all those surviving from the period. They span the country and most types of farming practice, and all that they have in common is that they are rural. It seems that there were many districts of countryside in which the sepulchres never appeared.

That night the Tenebrae were sung for the last time in those churches which observed them, and in came the Saturday, Easter Eve. Excitement would have mounted until after nightfall, when those who gathered in churches would witness the extinguishing of every light and the striking of fire anew from flints by the priest. Urban churchwardens' accounts usually record the purchase of coals or wood to be kindled by this means,[60] while country people would almost certainly have used their own local supplies of fuel. The new flames were blessed and censed, and from them was lit the largest candle to burn in any church, the paschal. It normally weighed about 20 pounds, but specimens as small as 3 pounds in weight and as gigantic as 300 (in cathedrals) have been mentioned. It was sometimes wreathed with ribbons, or painted, or made of coloured wax. It could be set upon a wooden stick, painted to look like a continuation of the candle and nicknamed a 'Judas'. With or without this, the great candle was sometimes put in a metal candlestick proportionately bigger than the norm. The one at Durham cathedral stood upon the steps before the high altar and was so tall that the paschal candle itself had to be lighted from the roof. The metal was wrought with flowers, dragons, soldiers, and other forms. In some parish churches the candle was stuck upon a wooden post or hung in a basin. The circumstances of its lighting varied—that at Durham, for example, being kindled upon Maundy Thursday—but it is found in every surviving set of fifteenth- and early sixteenth-century churchwardens' accounts and was probably universal: usually a special collection was made to pay for it. Once it was burning, another taper could be lit to illuminate a procession to the font, to bless the water there anew for baptisms. After that the sepulchre light and all the others of the church could be renewed.[61]

In most churches the first ceremony of Easter Day was the opening of the sepulchre. At Durham this took place before 4 a.m., and it was probably held before dawn in other places as well. The Durham monks placed the crucifix bearing the host upon a velvet cushion and carried it to the middle of the high altar. The anthem 'Christ is Risen' was sung, and then the crucifix and host were carried about the cathedral under a canopy of purple velvet fringed with gold and hung with red silk tassels. Elsewhere the rite of opening seems to have been similar, if rarely so gorgeous and never so well described. A few urban parish churches placed carved angels beside the empty sepulchre, in memory of those said to have appeared beside the tomb of Christ.[62] The ceremony of the opening may have been part of the 'play of the Resurrection' recorded in some parishes and in the earl of Northumberland's chapel, though the payments for this piece of drama indicate that it must have been something more than merely the sepulchre rite. It was probably an acting out of the events set around Christ's tomb in the gospels. At Dartmouth in Devon the parishioners themselves painted the costumes.[63] At the mass on Easter Day, the Salisbury service book prescribed the blessing of herbs sprinkled upon the altar, which must have added fragrance to the joyous atmosphere in the churches which followed the custom. It is perhaps a little disappointing that only a few, in London and Bristol, can be demonstrated to have done so.[64] Everywhere the figures of saints, veiled since Ash Wednesday, now stood benign and accessible once more, and the rood was revealed upon its loft.

Even the most irreligious of the early Tudor English must have enjoyed Easter Day, for Lent was over and all except regular clergy could now eat as freely as they could afford. It was traditionally also a time for cleaning houses and sprinkling the floor with fresh rushes and flowers,[65] an opportunity both to reaffirm the Christian faith and to celebrate the presence of spring. A symbol of this was the consumption, and the blessing in church, of eggs. But if Easter eggs are a genuine link between late medieval and modern practice, that other celebrated Holy Week foodstuff, the hot cross bun, is not. Its first appearance is in the early eighteenth century, and no such treats relieved the dietary gloom of the pre-Reformation Lent.[66] The succeeding few days were a time for sport and feasting second only to Christmastide. Among the more notable local events were the archery contest held by the sheriffs of Chester and the parish festival at Melton Mowbray in Leicestershire which had an 'Easter Lord', like those in other places at Christmas.[67]

Just as Christmastide culminated in the merry-making of Twelfth Night, so the celebrations which began on Easter Day could find a climax in Hocktide, the second Monday and Tuesday following. The derivation of the name is obscure, but the custom associated is well documented. Upon one of the days the men of a settlement could capture and tie up any woman upon the streets and release her for a fee which was paid into the parish funds. Upon the other the women did the binding. For them the action was a symbolic reversal of their usual position of social subservience, and they seem accordingly not only to have carried it out with gusto but to have found more willing victims. At any rate they invariably raised considerably more money. Indeed, by contemporary standards their sums were handsome, occasionally (for example at Lambeth) furnishing more than any other parish collection of the year. In most places it was specifically the married women who were responsible, but at Badsey in Worcestershire the maidens went out with the ropes. In a few of the parishes where the custom is recorded, the men never did the binding at all, while at St Mary at Hill, London, they gave up the competition in 1526. On the whole it was an urban custom, but some rural parishes, scattered across southern England, practised it enthusiastically. Yet there were still some remarkable restrictions in its distribution, for it is not recorded at Bristol, in the four south-western counties, north of Cambridge and Coventry, or in most London parishes.[68] Over much of the country, Hocktide was an opportunity to hold manorial court leets to settle business, and not one for this slightly *risqué*, if highly effective, way of raising funds.

As Easter Day was always fixed upon the first Sunday after the full moon following the spring equinox, it could fall anywhere in late March or early to mid-April. As a result, Hocktide could be followed by a fortnight of lull in merry-making or might itself follow the first calendar feast to be widely celebrated since St Valentine's. This was St George's Day on 23 April. Already the national saint, his cult seems to have expanded considerably at all levels of English society during the fifteenth and early sixteenth centuries. Large numbers of guilds were founded in his name and many churchwardens' accounts record payment for the setting-up of his image and that of the dragon which he was said to have slain. Some of these figures were probably paraded on the day of his feast, but for the purposes of this book it is possible to cite only that evidence which clearly indicates public festivities upon that date.

The most spectacular of all were at Norwich, where the whole corporation heard mass at the cathedral upon St George's Eve and then held a banquet. The next day, the guild dedicated to the saint provided a procession with a model dragon and people dressed up as George himself, St Margaret, and their retinue. The George wore a gilt helmet and coat armour of white damask with a red cross, the Margaret a gown of tawny velvet. He rode a horse harnessed in black velvet with copper ornaments, while her steed was caparisoned in crimson velvet with gold flowers. Their followers were dressed variously in more crimson velvet, green satin, red buckram, and red and white wool or satin. Upon the same day the corporation of Newcastle-upon-Tyne paraded its own dragon, of canvas nailed onto a wooden frame. The St George's Guild of Leicester held its own costumed parade, while the town council followed behind it and contributed towards the expenses. Another George and dragon went forth on behalf of the guild at Stratford-upon-Avon. All the guilds of Chester processed through its streets, while at York St Christopher and a 'royal family' appeared along with a George. The king mustered the Order of the Garter for its annual service at Windsor Castle, while the fifth earl of Northumberland, ever anxious to show that noblemen were almost the peers of royalty, had a banquet of his own with a generous distribution of gifts. Bristol and Coventry parish churches held processions with the carrying of a cross at the head, Croscombe in Somerset provided a parish feast, and more dragons were carried or towed around Little Walsingham in Norfolk and Lostwithiel in Cornwall.[69] Again, there were many communities in which the feast was not apparently celebrated. No festivities are recorded in London and other towns for which good early Tudor records survive, nor in the vast majority of the period's churchwardens' accounts. Yet St George's Day can still be described as one of the national festivals of early sixteenth-century England.

A more important celebration fell only a week later upon May Day, the formal beginning of summer. From the fourteenth to the nineteenth centuries there is abundant literary evidence that a common custom on May Morning was to go into the nearest countryside before sunrise and to return with flowers and greenery to deck streets and houses. For the period under study here, the authorities are Edward Hall, Polydor Vergil, and John Stow. Hall (copied by Stow) tells a now celebrated story of May

Morn in 1515, when Henry VIII and his queen, Catherine of Aragon, rode from Greenwich Palace to Shooter's Hill with their court, and ate and drank in the woodland. Stow adds that 'on May Day in the morning, every man, except impediment, would walk into the sweet meadows and green woods, there to rejoice their spirits with the beauty and savour of sweet flowers, and with the harmony of birds.' He goes on to say that the London parishes, singly or in groups, 'did fetch in may-poles, with diverse warlike shows . . . and other pastimes all the day long and towards the evening they had stage plays and bonfires in the streets'. Vergil, much earlier and more briefly, had commented upon the fetching home of garlands.[70] But then May Day ushered in a season, lasting into July, during which the festivities described by these writers could occur upon any date which a community chose. Although it is very likely that many people did go out upon May Morning itself, most of the recorded merry-makings of this sort occurred within the next two months.

They were known variously as May ales or May games (even if held in June or July), church ales, summer games, or summer plays. All were a celebration of summer and of communal life, and many made another contribution to parish funds. In many communities, especially in the countryside, they were the largest single source of parochial revenue. They are recorded in a total of 104 parishes in the century 1450–1550, representing the overwhelming majority for which accounts or other information survive. Norwich, Coventry, Lincolnshire, Lancashire, and the four northernmost counties apparently did not have them, although all are either relatively or severely lacking in evidence. In London and Bristol they seem to have been very occasional. The wardens of All Saints, Derby, seem to have resorted to them only in the year 1532–3, when they desperately needed cash to finish rebuilding the tower. They did not provide any in the town itself, but made a tour of three nearby villages, holding an ale in each and returning with the profits. But across most of the rest of the country they were found regularly, whether in small villages, in the northern capital of York, or in towns such as Oxford, Reading, Salisbury, Worcester, and Plymouth. They were not a universal custom even where they were common. Nettlecombe in Somerset, St Aldate's in Oxford, and Dartmouth in Devon are all examples of parishes set in districts notable for such events, which none the less do not seem to have adopted them. Furthermore, where they did occur they varied considerably in frequency, date, and venue. Most communities which held ales or games did not do so every year: for many, indeed, they were occasional events intended to generate a large quantity of money for a particular purpose. But they were annual at Wimborne

Minster in Dorset, Stogursey in Somerset, and Thame in Oxfordshire, while Brundish in Suffolk and Denton in Norfolk had an average of three per year. In some districts a rota may have operated, whereby villages held them in turn. Thus the churchwardens of Yatton, in Somerset, were regular guests at the feasts of four other parishes and made donations of money to them. Tintinhull, also in Somerset, had a reciprocal arrangement of gifts with the ales of three other villages. Individuals could go on 'ale-crawls' each year, so that the sociable or conscientious Sir Henry Willoughby patronized three in as many Warwickshire villages during May 1526. In 1537 the inhabitants of Wing, Crofton, Ascot, and Burcot, in Buckinghamshire, attended each other's celebrations. Sometimes private persons would hold such feasts for their own needs, hiring church property for the purpose. Of five ales held at Cratfield, Suffolk, in 1490, two were of this sort.[71] Most of the parish celebrations were held at Whitsun, and most of the remainder at some other time during May. But they could be found from Easter until the end of the summer, and occasionally at other times of the year. Their physical location is rarely specified, but at Saffron Walden in Essex, Elham in Kent, and St Lawrence, Reading, they were definitely held in the church, and at St Edmund, Salisbury, and at Yatton, in Somerset, in a special hall owned by the parish. In Yorkshire the proceeds were also used to maintain a special 'summer game light' in some churches, but the custom is not known elsewhere.[72]

From time to time a menu survives from one of these events. Ale itself was, of course, always brewed and sometimes, as at Snettisham in Norfolk, only bread added to it. But the Hampshire village of Bramley also required veal, mutton, chicken, butter, and cheese for its Whitsun feast in 1530. At Huntingfield, Suffolk, in 1534, eight parishes pooled their resources and came up with beer, milk, bread, cream, eggs, honey, spices, veal, and mutton.[73] Specific entertainments featured at some of these occasions. Music seems to have been fairly common, often played by an individual piper, drummer, or harper hired for the day.[74] There was also at times the mysterious 'May'. In 1422–4 the corporation of New Romney, Kent, 'paid to the men of Lydd, when they came with their May'. In the 1430s Launceston, in Cornwall, had expenses 'about le May'. In 1492 Henry VII gave ten shillings 'to the maidens of Lambeth for a May'. Seven years later the Wiltshire parish of St Mary, Devizes, paid for 'the making of the May'. And the mayor and young men of Nottingham went out to 'bring in May' in 1541.[75] There are similar references in other records. Some of them may refer to entertainments, being short for 'May game', but the Nottingham entry appears to record the fetching of flowers and foliage described by

Stow and Vergil. It is possible that some or all of the other examples were actually prompted by the making of a garland or floral decoration of the sort well known in nineteenth-century village Maytime celebrations.

It is interesting that maypoles, of the kind described by Stow, are rarely mentioned in the parish or municipal accounts. This could be because they were cut without cost, but such a consideration can hardly apply to the urban churches which had to pay for items such as holly and ivy. Snettisham in Norfolk did buy such a pole in May 1501 and again in 1536,[76] but on the whole it seems that either they were not often provided from parish funds or they did not feature very often in *parish* revels at this time. Nevertheless, some of them were clearly around. Stow, reflecting upon the early Tudor period, not only made the general comments quoted above but cited the specific example of the Cornhill maypole in London. Until 1517 it was set up annually in the middle of that street, outside St Andrew's church. So tall was it that it stood higher than the steeple. Its erection only ended in 1517 because the riots in the city upon that May Day produced such feelings of shock amongst government and citizens that the festival was henceforth celebrated more soberly in London. The great pole was left stored in an alley.[77]

A feature of these summer revels was the crowning of individuals as mock-kings and (more rarely) mock-queens, to preside over them. Such figures are mentioned at seventeen out of the 104 parishes in which such ales or games are recorded for the period 1450–1550. They are scattered all over England. The crowning at Wistow in Yorkshire in the 1460s was held by the youth of the parish, who elected two of their number to be king and queen. They gathered in a 'summerhouse', apparently a barn, on the Sunday before Midsummer Eve. The royal couple processed in, attended by a seneschal, a guard, and two soldiers, and presided all afternoon over theatrical and musical entertainments which their elders considered 'appropriate and respectable'. The whole gathering numbered over a hundred people, and presumably consisted of almost the entire village community. In the parish of St Edmund, Salisbury, a queen and king were also chosen, and were fined 8*d.* each if they refused to serve. The records do not tell us about their duties, but in 1461 their various 'plays' raised over £23, a colossal sum by the standards of parochial collections. At St Lawrence, Reading, and Henley in Buckinghamshire, the early sixteenth-century 'king plays' were specifically 'of the young men', and they may everywhere have been the special concern of local youth. At St Lawrence a bough or sapling was dragged into the market-place for the event, and presumably decorated. At Sherborne in Dorset, in 1525, 'posts' were set up for the revel in the churchyard, perhaps as the framework for an arbour or bower. At Winterslow, Wiltshire, and at St Edmund, Salisbury, the church owned a special hall for the proceedings. The Leicestershire market town of Melton Mowbray issued arrows to its Whitsun 'lord' in the 1540s, either as part of his costume or for a display of archery. The 'King game' of Kingston upon Thames was sent on visits to Croydon, another Surrey market town. Clearly some of these temporary monarchs had activities more exciting than those of the decorous young couple who presided at Wistow.[78]

At twenty-four known places in the period 1450–1550, the character of the 'King' as centre of the revels was replaced or accompanied by the dashing outlaw hero of contemporary ballads, Robin Hood. All these communities were in the South and the Midlands, from Cornwall to Kent and from Leicestershire to Worcestershire, with particular concentrations in the Thames and Severn valleys and the three westernmost counties. They tended also to be lowland market towns, apparently because these contained or attracted a large enough number of people to make the provision of a Robin Hood 'play', and associated collection of money, financially worthwhile. But villages would sometimes mount them, and occasionally would send the players to perform and to ask for donations at nearby settlements, aristocratic seats, and monasteries. By contrast the biggest urban centres, London, Bristol, and Coventry, all appear to have lacked them, and they were also missing from East Anglia and from the very counties north of the Trent in which the hero's deeds were set. In some places Robin Hood was a regular feature of the May games and summer ales. At Little Croscombe in Somerset, certain villagers kept the part for a number of successive years, chosen for their popularity or theatrical ability. The entertainment appeared there almost annually from 1475 to 1526. But at Tintinhull in the same county there was a Robin Hood ale 'only this once' in 1513. He appeared in Henley, Buckinghamshire, at regular intervals between 1499 and 1520, while the Surrey market town of Kingston upon Thames expended great efforts to set him forth from 1509 to 1537. At the other places in which he is recorded he seems to have appeared more rarely, and sometimes the resources of a number of different villages were required to provide a Robin Hood play or game. Thus in 1498 three in Staffordshire joined forces to send a Robin out to a local fair to raise money for their churches.

The main reason for the apparent trouble and expense of such an entertainment was that it required a full cast of costumed characters in addition to Robin himself. Its most celebrated performance in this period was upon May Day 1515, when Henry VIII and Catherine of Aragon, making their well-recorded excursion to Shooter's Hill, were met by 200 of the royal guard, dressed in green as the outlaw's band. They fired a volley of arrows and led their sovereigns to an arbour constructed in the woods, decorated with flowers and aromatic herbs, to feast upon venison. The payments for this extravaganza show that Robin Hood's company included Lady May and her retinue, Little John, Friar Tuck, and Maid Marian. It was not the first appearance that the famous outlaw had made before the young king, for Robin and Marian had both featured in a court entertainment in 1510. These two occasions do, however, seem to have been the only times at which he played a part in royal revelry. The description of the May Day outing of 1515 nevertheless furnishes details of several features recorded more sparsely in the churchwardens' accounts. Robin Hood often, and perhaps always, had a 'company', in costume. Kingston had all the characters who performed before Henry VIII, except Lady May. Robin and Little John had special coats, the friar a habit, and Maid Marian a hooded cloak and gloves. In 1520 Robin and John wore satin jackets lined with canvas, while their fourteen followers were in dark green coats. Over the years there was a great deal of wear and tear of costumes, and loss of hats and feathers, although the receipts more than justified the expense. The players seem to have handed coloured paper strips, or pins, to those who gave them money: in most years between 3,000 and 4,000 of these had to be provided, so that the crowds who watched, even divided between five days of performances, must have been large. Marian was played by a woman until 1516, when a male actor took over, perhaps (as David Wiles has suggested) because in that year the players began to dance and it was considered improper for a female to cavort in a male troupe. Nowhere else are parish festivities as well recorded as at Kingston, but we know that Little John joined Robin at Ombersley in Worcestershire and sometimes at Croscombe in Somerset, while one of the players at Leicester in 1534 was lent a sword and buckler (which he almost lost).[79]

It seems very likely that Robin Hood 'ales', 'plays', or 'games' took very different forms. The costumed characters who greeted Henry VIII apparently did nothing but conduct him to his feast in the woods. It is distinctly possible that some of the village Robins did little other than to preside over celebrations in the manner of some of the mock kings and queens. Even when attended by full companies in costume, they may have merely paraded. But it is fairly certain that pieces of drama were sometimes performed. A fragment of a script for a Robin Hood play survives upon the back of a sheet of financial reports, to and from persons unknown, for the year 1475–6.[80] It recounts a tale similar to those found in contemporary ballads, in which the outlaw foils the forces of authority by cunning and skill with weapons. It would have made an exciting entertainment.

As David Wiles, the leading authority upon the genre, has pointed out,[81] the figure of Robin served a number of different symbolic functions in the summer revels. His green clothing and association with the woodlands made him an appropriate addition to the seasonal celebrations. But as an outlaw chief, he was also an ideal Lord of Misrule. Certainly his plays and games could be the occasion for serious misbehaviour. One at Willenhall Fair, Staffordshire, in 1498, ended in a riot which cost lives. In the same year, the corporation of Wells, Somerset, was wondering what had happened to all the money which the players had raised, and which had vanished with them instead of being added to municipal funds according to the prior arrangement. In 1509 the city fathers of Exeter banned Robin Hood plays altogether because of the disorders committed by young men associated with them (the order was ineffectual). The Lord Warden of the Cinque Ports of Kent and Sussex did the same in 1528.[82] During the same season genuine Lords of Misrule, of the Christmas variety, appeared in a few places. The Essex village of Great Dunmow chose one to preside over its May ales. The corporation of Shrewsbury appointed an 'Abbot' for its revels, complete with robes and ornaments. Another such mock cleric, leading his own company, joined forces with Robin Hood's band for the ill-fated fair at Willenhall in 1498.[83]

The only dance specified at the summer festivities was the morris. It was performed at the royal court and in noble households as well as in villages, although in the former situations it did not have any special association with the warm green months. Henry VII watched it several times, at all seasons, while Henry VIII saw it mainly at Christmastide and Shrovetide, and it was a regular feature of the Twelfth Night revels of the fifth earl of Northumberland. But in municipal and parochial celebrations it was clearly a feature of the summer. It appeared occasionally in London guild pageants and was prominent in the May games at Kingston upon Thames, at first taking its place alongside Robin Hood and then replacing him. A troupe from Winchelsea in Kent visited nearby Lydd in 1518, while the corporation of Nottingham paid for a morris dance upon May Day 1530. The dance also became part of the 'King play' at St Lawrence, Reading.[84] But during the early Tudor period it was apparently restricted to the wealthiest households and to towns, not being mentioned in the villages.

Nor is there any clear picture of what the dance looked like at this time.[85] The earlier performances before royalty may have been by people with faces darkened to resemble the 'Moors' or Arabs after whom the morris is possibly named. At Shrovetide 1509 Henry VIII had torchbearers 'apparelled in crimson satin and green like Moriskoes, their faces black'. But by Christmas 1515 the 'moresk' dancers at court certainly appeared something like the modern morris sides: six people wearing white and green jackets with hanging sleeves, tiny dangling pieces of copper, and a large number (348 between them) of small bells. They were accompanied by a fool in a yellow silk coat and two ladies in satin representing Beauty and Venus. A gold cup owned by the king was decorated with five morrismen and a lady, while the Christmas revels of the princess Mary, in 1522, included nine dancers in coats and bells. At Kingston the coats and bells had already appeared in 1507. By 1520 the former were specified as being of spangled twilled cotton and the latter were apparently strung on garters as they were later in the century, and have been ever since. There were always six in the troupe.[86] So the costume of the morris, if not the number of performers, was becoming standardized. But we have no record of the steps.

A feature of later Tudor May games which is met with occasionally at this earlier period is the hobby-horse, with which a person would dance for the entertainment of onlookers. It appeared in revels at the royal court and in London guild processions. It is also referred to in the Cornish play *Beunans Meriasek*, finished in 1504, and formed an important part of the celebrations of a few midland parishes. At St Mary, Stafford, its cavortings represented one of the main means of fund-raising. At Culworth, Northamptonshire, a troupe which included one obtained most of the money for the church candles upon the annual 'hobby-horse night'. The Nottinghamshire parish of Holme Pierrepoint also depended heavily before the Reformation upon gatherings 'with hobby horse and lights'.[87] But again, the nature of these pieces of equipment, whether sticks with carved heads upon the end or canvas frames worn by the dancer, is a matter for conjecture at this period.

Meanwhile the calendar of festivals anchored to the moveable feast of Easter proceeded alongside that related to the fixed days of the year. The sixth Thursday after Easter Day was chosen to commemorate the ascension of Christ into heaven. Upon the preceding Monday, Tuesday, and Wednesday, many or most parishes held a procession around their streets or fields and up to or along their boundaries. It was led by the priest and involved open-air services in which the land and boundary-markers were blessed. A cross and banners were carried, the church bells were rung, and a communal meal was frequently provided for those who went on the walk.

Whereas the ales and games represented a celebration of summer, these processions were also a solemn ritual to ask the protection of the Christian deity for the whole parish at the time when crops were growing. They took place upon what were variously known as the Rogation, Cross, or Gang Days, the first term being taken from the Latin 'rogare', meaning 'to ask', and the last signifying 'going', in the sense of 'going around'. The process is unusually well described at St Edmund, Salisbury, where seventeen banners were carried during the early sixteenth century, depicting saints and scenes from the life of Christ. The people taking part were described as being boys and men, and they were rewarded in some years with bread and ale and in others with cash. At Durham the monks of the cathedral made a procession to one of the town's parish churches upon each of the three days, and one of their number delivered a sermon.[88]

It is very difficult to demonstrate how widely the rite was observed. Payments for the meal or to those who carried cross and banners appear almost wholly in urban churchwardens' accounts, such as those of London, Bristol, Reading, Chester, Oxford, Dover, and Salisbury. Otherwise they are confined to the small market town of Tavistock and a few villages in Norfolk, Cambridgeshire, Lincolnshire, Essex, and Worcestershire.[89] Yet a fourteenth-century commentary upon holy days held that to avoid going on the Rogation processions was as sinful as failing to attend church. Medieval English ecclesiastical law made these rites compulsory, and a very quick glance at diocesan records reveals very few cases of alleged neglect of them. In the biggest diocese of all, that of Lincoln, only three priests were reported for failing to lead the processions during the years 1517–20. Between 1499 and 1530 a single case respecting these events appeared in the Norwich consistory court, and that was the denunciation of some building work which had blocked the processional route of one parish.[90] This may, of course, argue not for widespread acceptance and enactment so much as for widespread indifference, with reluctance to report those who neglected the custom. The evidence of wills is inconclusive, for in contrast with the hundreds of bequests to the Easter sepulchre in early Tudor Northamptonshire, there survive only seven in that county (from five parishes) for the entertainment of Rogation processioners.[91] Yet the custom is so well and so widely documented in rural parishes after the Reformation (albeit in a truncated form), that it was indeed probably common before that event. The relative lack of reference to it in rural churchwardens' accounts may be due to the fact that in these smaller communities, with crops to be blessed, people were willing to contribute without any payment.

The Rogation Days were supposed to be times of fasting as well as per-ambulating, and the compensation for this came upon the Thursday, the feast of the Ascension. Then the church bells were rung again and the paschal candle, which had burned through the services of Easter Week and upon all festivals since then, was lighted for the last time and then removed.[92] London parishes had the tradition of decking their churches with garlands, not recorded elsewhere.[93] At Durham the cathedral clergy processed around the town carrying gold and silver crosses and the relics of saints. They wore copes (mantles), that of the Prior being golden.[94] Other processions are recorded in parishes at Oxford, Salisbury and the small Suffolk town of Bungay.[95]

At the end of the following week more people were parading, to cele-brate Whitsun or Pentecost, the feast which commemorated the inspiration of Christ's apostles by the Holy Ghost. Sometimes the Holy Ghost itself appeared in parish churches, in the form of a white dove let through a hole in the ceiling. The records do not make clear whether it was a model bird or a real one, although common sense favours the former idea. It seems to have been a rare custom but widely scattered, being recorded at tiny Walberswick, in Suffolk, in 1500, at the Lincolnshire town of Louth in 1500 and 1518, and in the London church of St Mary at Hill during 1540–2.[96] That afternoon, and the day following, were the most common times for the holding of church ales.

Whit Monday was also, as indicated above, a notable date for proces-sions. In most communities those of the Rogation Days, just past, and of Corpus Christi, soon to come, were observed instead. But in four county towns Whitsun was the occasion for some of the most splendid of all. At Leicester in the early sixteenth century the parishioners of St Mary le Castro and of St Martin made their way to the third church of St Mary Magdalen. The former carried the image of the Virgin, richly robed and crowned, beneath a canopy supported by four of them. She was preceded by minstrels and followed by statues of the twelve Apostles, or perhaps by people dressed to represent them, their names fixed to their bonnets. Then came the unmarried young women, and fourteen men carrying banners. The parishioners of St Martin carried their own patron, and another set of images of the Apostles. Both processions made offerings at the altar of St Mary Magdalen, and then were paid or feasted by their respective church-wardens. At Exeter in the fifteenth century a 'May' (presumably in the sense of a huge garland, as six men were needed to lift it) was carried through the streets, along with a huge elephant. How far this tradition sur-vived into the Tudor period is concealed by the failure of the sequence of accounts. The craft guilds of Chester provided a cycle of biblical pageants, which appear with the beginning of the relevant records in 1519. By that time the cycle had grown so much that it consisted of twenty-four different subjects and took up not only the Monday but two more days. It may have been more glamorous than the parallel series of pageants at Norwich, which required only the Monday and Tuesday and had only eleven subjects in 1528. But these were still apparently very impressive, ranging from 'The Creation' to 'The Holy Ghost' and including an Ark and a view of Hell. In 1534 the Grocers supplied 'Paradise', mounted upon a cart hung with cloths and drawn by four horses. At both Chester and Norwich the pageants made a wide circuit of the city and seem to have included some spoken drama. At Norwich it is certainly recorded that people flocked in from the countryside for the spectacle, and upon the Tuesday the corporation appointed a Lord of Misrule to preside over the festivities.[97]

After this it might be only a matter of about a week before the year rose to its zenith of foliage, flowers, and daylight at midsummer. In the Christian world this was formally recognized as falling upon 24 June, the feast of St John the Baptist. In one of his most famous passages, the London antiquary John Stow described the customs kept up in the city before 1540 upon the eve of that feast:

there were usually made bonfires in the streets, every man bestowing wood or labour towards them: the wealthier sort also before their doors near to the said bonfires, would set out tables . . . furnished with sweet bread and good drink . . . whereunto they would invite their neighbours . . . every man's door being shadowed with green birch, long fennel, St John's Wort, Orpin, white lilies and such like, garnished upon with garlands of beautiful flowers, had also lamps of glass with oil burning in them all the night.

He went on to recall how the corporation and livery companies, 4,000 strong, paraded through the streets carrying torches or weapons. They were accompanied by morris dancers, model giants, and pageants.[98]

At first sight, Stow's description seems like a classic piece of nostalgic romanticism, over-estimating the merriment and generosity of a former age. But something very similar to it, and contemporary to the scenes described, is preserved in the sober pages of the Journal of the Corporation of London, for 1526. In March that year Henry VIII ordered a celebration to be held in the city, to accompany one of his state visits, modelled upon those of Midsummer Eve. The jurats, issuing the necessary order, portrayed bonfires in the streets, with children sitting around them wearing garlands of flowers. Beside them minstrels would play and neighbours drink together joyously, while the parish constables patrolled in their best clothes and arms. And all the customs itemized by Stow can be found in other sources, both for the capital and for provincial communities. A monk of Winchcombe Abbey, Gloucestershire, had preached in the mid-fifteenth century against the 'vain, stupid, profane games' carried on at midsummer, with much drinking and lighting of fires. He spoke of the burning of piles of bones, which gave off dark, reeking smoke, the carrying of torches around fields, and the rolling of flaming wheels down hillsides. From the prosperous cloth-making town of Long Melford, in Suffolk, comes an affectionate description of how one of its wealthiest inhabitants had a fire made in front of his house each Midsummer Eve in the early sixteenth century. He gave bread and a tub of ale to the local poor and had a table set for himself near the blaze, to which he called 'some of the friends and more civil poor neighbours' to feast with him.

Stow commented that the particular purpose of the fires was to 'purge the infection of the air'. A Protestant minister preaching in Dorset in 1570 mocked the belief of the pre-Reformation English that the midsummer flames had special beneficial properties. The same notion was recalled more sympathetically by an author in 1616, recalling the torches in the London parade described by Stow:

A thousand sparks dispersed throughout the sky
Which like to wandering stars about did fly,
Whose wholesome heat, purging the air, consumes
The earth's unwholesome vapours, fogs and fumes.

A fourteenth-century Shropshire monk distinguished between three kinds of St John's Eve blaze, the 'bonfire', made of bones and intended to drive away evil with its stench, the 'wakefire', built of wood and intended to be a focal point of merry-making, and the 'St John's fire', composed of wood and bones and fulfilling both functions.[99] It seems clear that there was a widespread belief in late medieval and Tudor England that the midsummer fires gave protection against the particular dangers of late summer and early autumn: the threat to crops from wet weather and blight, and the threat to humans from plague and other infections especially common at that season. Many such ailments of humans and vegetation had origins quite inscrutable to the science of the time, and appeared to many to emanate from the atmosphere.

What is much less clear is whether the making of the bonfires was a universal custom. The comments reproduced above obviously indicate that it was widespread, and there are other specific local references to it in the century before the Reformation. The king had his own fire in most years for which royal payments survive, made in the palace hall by its pages and grooms on a variety of dates in the last week of June. None of the aristocratic account books record them, but Sir Henry Willoughby supplied bread and ale for one at Maxstoke, Warwickshire, on Midsummer Eve 1521. In 1448 the Leet Book of Coventry mentioned them as being made annually in the streets upon that night. At the other end of our present span of interest, in the 1540s and 1550s, the chapter of the newly established cathedral of Chester provided one at midsummer in some years. They would presumably not have done so had the practice not been both well established and popular in the city. And the corporation of Sandwich, Kent, paid for them in the early sixteenth century.[100] But that appears to be all that has survived. The fact that the fires did not play any part in parochial fund-raising means that they do not appear in our principal set of sources for seasonal customs in the period. As in the case of maypoles, it seems wise to assume that they were common without being able to substantiate the assumption fully.

The decorating of buildings with greenery is another practice mentioned by Stow which is recorded elsewhere. At Coventry in 1448 the fronts of houses were being festooned with it in just the manner described for early Tudor London. Payments for birch, the foliage which heads Stow's list, are found in the churchwardens' accounts for most London parishes at midsummer in the early sixteenth century. At St Martin Outwich broom was added, and at St Andrew Hubbard the birch boughs, mixed with flowers and fennel, were specifically fixed in the church porch, in the manner portrayed by Stow upon secular buildings.[101] None of the accounts surviving for parishes in other towns show similar payments, and the custom of decorating churches in this way may have been a metropolitan one. But at Tavistock in Devon, rushes were regularly strewn on the church floor upon Midsummer Day, and extra candles were lighted upon the same feast at Pilton in Somerset and Saffron Walden in Essex.[102]

The London Midsummer Watch, as described by Stow, is also well attested in other sources. The records of the city's craft guilds, in particular, preserve vivid evidence for the entertainments provided with it. In 1521 the Lord Mayor was a Draper, and his guild made a particularly lavish contribution. It included five pageants; 'the Castle of War', 'the Story of Jesse', 'St John the Evangelist', 'St George', and 'Pluto', the last of these being accompanied by a serpent which spat fireballs. All were carried on platforms. The same craft also set forth a model giant called 'Lord Marlinspikes', morris dancers, naked boys dyed black to represent devils, armoured halberdiers, and a King of the Moors clad in black satin robes, with silver paper shoes and a turban crowned with white plumes. The latter character walked or was carried under his own canopy, and 'wild fire' went with him. In 1541 the same guild agreed to make another great effort, sending out 'the Assumption of the Virgin Mary', 'Christ disputing with the Doctors', 'the Rock of Roche' and 'St Margaret'. Sixteen porters were needed to drag these tableaux. Margaret was to be accompanied by four children dressed as angels, all in yellow wigs and two with wings of peacock feathers. Christ had a black wig, and the Doctors long hair and beards. The Drapers also hired another wooden giant, a morris side 'well trimmed after the gorgeous fashion', twelve 'mummers with visors and hats', eight 'players with two-handed swords', banner-bearers, and a dragon with 'aqua vitae' burning in its mouth. The writer who recalled the Marching Watch nostalgically in 1616 commented upon the glow sent up against the sky by all the torches, visible far out into the countryside.[103]

Midsummer 'marching watches' are also recorded in the early sixteenth century at Coventry, Chester, Totnes (in Devon), Nottingham, Exeter, Bristol, Liverpool and Barnstaple. At Gloucester, Carlisle, Salisbury, and Kendal, they appear as soon as the municipal records begin in the late Tudor period, and almost certainly began before then.[104] Thus they were a feature of several important towns, although not of all, as York, Leicester, Norwich, Newcastle-upon-Tyne, and others have left good records for the time without any trace of the custom. York had instead minstrels strolling the streets upon the Eve and a play upon the Day. At Newcastle members of the Shipmen's Guild occasionally danced before the mayor upon the Eve.[105] But the marching watches were nevertheless the most distinctive municipal celebration of midsummer. All seem to have included torches, armed men, and music. At Coventry the craft guilds also carried staves with pails over a foot long dangling from the end, filled with blazing resin-soaked rope. At Chester in 1564 the traditional 'ornaments' of the procession were four giants, a unicorn, two camels, an ass, a lynx, a dragon, six hobby-horses, and sixteen 'naked boys'.[106]

Midsummer Day was also the last possible date upon which might fall the feast of Corpus Christi, the culmination of the Easter cycle of fast and celebration. This took up the second Thursday after Whitsun, and its principal feature was the bearing through streets of a consecrated host, enclosed within a shrine and protected from weather and birds by a canopy. The procession was often organized by the Corpus Christi guild of a community, dedicated to the revering of the Christian eucharist. In corporate towns the councillors and craft guilds marched behind the clergy who carried the shrine, while the populace in general were expected to kneel bareheaded as it passed. Banners, torches, and crosses featured in the procession, and hymns were sung by those who took part in it. At Leicester the mayor and other leading officers always carried the canopy. At York the shrine was of silver and crystal, and the house-fronts along the processional route were hung with tapestries and the doorways strewn with rushes and flowers. The banners carried at Coventry were of damask and velvet worked with gold. At Durham the shrine was gilded, and kept at the parish church of St Nicholas, from which it was paraded up to the cathedral for a service and then back again. The cathedral's own clergy went before it and behind it came the guilds, carrying torches on the east side of their line and banners upon the west.

At London the main procession was supplied by the Skinners' Company, and contained 200 clergy and 100 candles. But the individual parishes of the metropolis provided their own celebrations as well, decorating their churches with roses which were sometimes mixed with sweet white woodruff. Garlands were also carried upon the processions of these London parishes, so that in 1521 the wardens of St Mary at Hill paid for thirty-six portable bunches of roses and lavender and another twenty-four of greenery. At Bristol, St John's church paid for candles to be carried by children behind the shrine, while the sexton rang the bells throughout and a quart of muscatel wine was prepared for all who participated. The rite is recorded in every English town for which early Tudor parochial, municipal, or guild documents survive.[107] In the countryside, however, it is much more difficult to trace, and it may be that the village communities, lacking large populations with a complex social hierarchy, and competing parishes and guilds, did not usually feel the need for it. It is represented only in the churchwardens' accounts of places which, although not chartered, were still local centres and markets, such as East Dereham and Swaffham in Norfolk, Saffron Walden and Great Dunmow in Essex, and Ashburton in Devon.[108] Yet it did still occur in quite tiny places such as Streatham in the Isle of Ely, being carried on there not by the parish but by the village guild dedicated to Corpus Christi. The destruction of the records of most of these rural fraternities has left little possibility of knowing how many of them held the annual processions.[109]

Almost half a millennium later, the feast of Corpus Christi remains famous among scholars, not so much for its religious significance as for the place which it occupies in the development of English drama. By the early sixteenth century the theatrical productions of the day occurred at various levels. Upon the lowest, in some market towns, they consisted of a single play, performed after the procession. This was the case at Ashburton, where the participants performed in tunics, with crests on heads and staves in hands, against a background of painted cloths. Productions of this sort also featured regularly at Great Dunmow and at Sherborne in Dorset, and were occasional at St Lawrence, Reading, and in the east midland and East Anglian towns of Louth, Sleaford, Stamford, Peterborough, Yarmouth, Eye, Ipswich, King's Lynn, Bungay, and Bury St Edmunds. In 1500 the library at the church of St Dunstan, Canterbury, contained a set of texts described as suitable for staging at Corpus Christi. All were biblical.[110]

These fixed performances need to be distinguished from the pictures of saints and scriptural stories, and model beasts, which were often carried in the processions. Thus East Dereham in Norfolk paraded a 'monster' on Corpus Christi Day 1493, while nearby Swaffham more demurely set forth an angel in 1515 or 1516.[111] But the difference is not always made clear in the records, and often vanishes in the case of those towns in which pageants were drawn upon carts. Such places seem to have been relatively numerous. At present they are known to include Beverley, Bungay, Bury St Edmunds, Doncaster, Hereford, Ipswich, Kendal, Louth, Newcastle-upon-Tyne, Preston, Shrewsbury, and Worcester. In every case the tableaux were the responsibility of the craft guilds, sometimes individually and sometimes grouped together; hence in 1536 the Goldsmiths, Glaziers, Plumbers, Pewterers, and Painters of Newcastle united to provide 'The Three Kings of Cologne'. The result was a total number of spectacles varying widely between places, so that there were fourteen at Ipswich in the 1520s, twenty-seven at Hereford in 1503, and thirty-five at Beverley in about 1520. The order in which the guild pageants moved was carefully prescribed by municipal ordinance, and was quite frequently the subject of bitter dispute. A fund was often levied upon the freemen of the towns or on the producers of cheaper pageants in order to maintain the most elaborate productions. In many places, also, a very light rate was laid upon the whole community to help defray expenses.[112]

In a class of their own were the cycles of plays presented at a few important towns. Those at Coventry were the most famous in their time and the most visited by royalty. They were also the first to be subjected to something like a scholarly study (by Thomas Sharp in 1825). The city's crafts spent lavishly on costumes and musicians, and the waggons which carried the performers must have been unusually large if all were like the Cappers', which had to be moved by twelve men. The performances were true plays, probably no more than ten in number and both lengthy and elaborate, so that only the richest guilds could stage them single-handed. All were biblical, and two have survived. York by contrast had fifty-two, each much briefer and covering between them the whole of Christian cosmic history from Creation to Doomsday. They also were performed upon wheeled vehicles, apparently with a screened lower chamber for a changing-room, and although short they required trained players. The texts for most of them have come down to the present, and along with the two from Coventry and two cycles which have no clearly identified place of origin, they represent our total collection of Corpus Christi cyclical drama and the most celebrated products of the medieval English stage. They were arguably the most truly popular theatrical achievements of all time, staging the largest action ever attempted by any drama in the western world. The prevailing mood in most of the plays was one of celebration, a triumphant review of Christian belief provided at the end of the 'ritual half' of the year and at what was normally its warmest and most comfortable time.[113]

There remain two very large problems concerning these plays. One is that, as Alan Nelson first pointed out, we do not know exactly how they were in fact produced. Sharp had suggested that the waggons were hauled between 'stations' at which performances took place. But the enormous length of the York cycle, and the wildly variant length of its individual components, would make it impossible for sequence and order to be maintained in such a progression. And it would have required at least twenty-one hours and over 300 actors (unless some doubled in other roles). This conundrum has provoked the suggestions that only some of the cycle was presented each year, and that the whole thing took place in an open space at the end of the procession. Either or neither may be correct.[114] The second important puzzle is one already encountered (without solution) in the case of many other customs noted in this chapter. Although a large number of towns provided Corpus Christi pageants and plays, others which have left good records clearly did not. They include London itself, Bristol, Nottingham, Leicester, Salisbury, and Exeter. For once this difficulty has already been squarely faced by a historian, Mervyn James.[115] His solution is that the cycles developed in urban centres which contained a tension and free play of political and social forces and required a continual affirmation of unity, order, and degree. Those towns always dominated by a self-co-opting élite, he argues, never experienced the need for them. The argument is ingenious, and may be correct, but is not susceptible of proof in the existing condition of the evidence. As Professor James himself noted, conflicts over precedence in the procession could be an occasion for division in themselves. And we simply do not know enough about the political arrangements of most late medieval English towns, whether those which produced pageants or those which did not, to tell whether the distinction holds up. At London and Exeter the point was not that the craft guilds failed to parade with pageants, but that they chose to do so in the Midsummer Watch instead of at Corpus Christi. At issue was not a difference in social mechanisms but in favoured festivals, based apparently upon local whims or accidents which have not been recorded.

After Midsummer itself, and the last possible date for Corpus Christi, only four days elapsed before St Peter's Eve, 28 June, and a chance to re-enact all the midsummer festivities. Once again torch-bearing armed processions made their way through Coventry, Bristol, Liverpool, Carlisle, Exeter, and Gloucester. At Newcastle-upon-Tyne the guilds sometimes paid for minstrels or provided a play or parade. Once again bonfires were made and porches decked and lit at London, Coventry, Sandwich, and elsewhere. Sir Henry Willoughby provided ale for a St Peter's Eve fire in Warwickshire in 1521, and gave a penny to a maiden who presented him with a garland beside it.[116] And upon this night the 'ritual half' of the English year came to an end. Local summer games would continue, here and there, until that season itself formally ended upon 31 July. In July also Canterbury and Lincoln held their own processions of pageants of the sort provided by other towns at Whitsun and Corpus Christi. The former was upon the 6th, the eve of the feast of the greatest local saint, Thomas à Becket, and the latter twenty-one days later upon the festival of St Anne. The Canterbury parade included the militia, torchbearers, the aldermen in scarlet gowns, model giants, gunners, and musicians. There were also floats from each ward, of which one was always 'The Martyrdom of St Thomas', with children playing the murderous knights and a liberal splashing of pig's blood. At Lincoln the churches and priory lent religious ornaments for use in the pageants, and each alderman contributed a silk gown to dress the actors representing kings.[117]

On 1 August came Lammas, the 'Loaf Mass', formal opening of the harvest season and of autumn. It also ushered in the main period for the holding of fairs, which provided a set of entertainments as varied and exciting as many of the more ritualized celebrations in the first half of the year. Harvest suppers, held to mark the end of the gathering of the most important crop on a farm or manor or in a village, were notable opportunities for festivity and the reaffirmation of neighbourly feeling.[118] There is very little trace of harvest customs surviving from the century 1450–1550, but some recorded in that immediately following almost certainly obtained earlier. They include the crowning of girls as harvest queens by sets of reapers, the bringing home of the last load of corn covered in garlands, with loud acclamations, and the weaving of images from grain stalks.[119]

The season of fairs ended with October, from which it was only eleven days to Martinmas, centre-point of the annual slaughter of surplus livestock and the salting down of their meat for winter, with much attendant feasting. After that only about three more weeks elapsed to the beginning of Advent, the time of fasting before Christmastide. But in all the half-year between the eves of St Peter and of Christmas, there were only two customs which occurred across much of the nation at the same time. One was the appearance of Boy Bishops upon St Nicholas's Day, 6 December, as described above. The other took place upon the feast of All Saints, the first day of November. It marked the formal opening of winter, falling at the time of the first frosts when most of the leaves and flowers had withered and the darkness had trickled back into the afternoon. At this time of death, it was the human dead who were remembered. Upon All Saints' Day the king dressed in purple velvet and his courtiers in black, the colours of mourning.[120] For that evening many churches laid in extra supplies of candles and torches, to be carried in procession and to illuminate the building. Some of them (and more which apparently did not invest in extra lighting) made payments for the most famous custom of the night, the ringing of church bells to comfort those departed souls which were enduring the torments of Purgatory. In the chapel of the fifth earl of Northumberland, the peals rang out from the moment that the evening service ended until midnight, and so it probably was in the parish churches. Likewise the prayers of the service itself were devoted to the dead, especially those (presumed to be the majority) who were undergoing purgation. In a few places the rites were repeated, or took place upon, the following evening, known as the feast of All Souls.[121] In this way the opening of the season of darkness and cold was made into an opportunity to confront the greatest fear known to humans, that of death, and the greatest known to Christians, that of damnation. In the heart of that dreaded season, the feast of Christmas would provide an opportunity for defiant merry-making, and would open the 'ritual half' of the year which would carry the English up to midsummer again.

So that is the picture which was described earlier as colourful and exciting, consistent in some respects and seriously misleading in others. The moment has come to confront that last characteristic directly. The account provided has not been as fallacious as was easily possible, because it has taken care to demonstrate that many of the customs recorded were confined to particular regions, while the full extent of others remains a mystery. It has also tried to avoid another obvious error, by trying to distinguish between practices which are recorded annually in communities and those which were intermittent or infrequent. But it is still flawed in three major respects. One is that it takes no account of rituals and festivals important to individual communities or to small districts. At Stafford in the 1520s, especially important festivities marked by bell-ringing and music were held upon Holy Rood Eve (13 September) and upon the evening of St Nicholas's Day (without a Boy Bishop). This is a pattern not known anywhere else.[122] The corporation of Grimsby chose to feast upon St Mary Magdalen's Day, in July. There and in Hull, facing it across the Humber, a model ship was dragged through the streets on Plough Monday instead of the usual plough.[123] Many or most parishes held a wake, a communal feast on the dedication day of their church and in honour of its patron; in theory this should have been upon the actual date of the dedication, but at a later period, and perhaps always, they were in practice concentrated in the summer and early autumn. Eamon Duffy has questioned the whole concept of a 'ritual half' to the year originally identified by Charles Phythian-Adams, on the grounds that the period from July to November contained the feasts of important saints, including apostles and some who were the focus of intense local affection, as well as guild festivities.[124] He is certainly correct in making the point that the latter part of the annual cycle was by no means 'secular', although he misses the one at which Dr Phythian-Adams was aiming, that it contained strikingly few nationwide rituals. In pastoral districts the celebrations at the end of haymaking or sheep-shearing would have been among the major yearly festivities. None of these activities deserve a place in an account confined to those which were shared by a large number of communities at the same time; but to the people who combined in them they would have been at least as important as some of those which have been included.

The second shortcoming of this chapter is that it is almost wholly dependent upon records surviving from the period under consideration. It cannot therefore take account of customs which did not enter into parochial, municipal, royal, or aristocratic finance, or did not attract the attention of poets, clerics, or nostalgic conservatives. In particular, it cannot include some popular rituals which have been identified by nineteenth- and twentieth-century folklorists as relics of pre-Christian religious custom, not because of any objective evidence but because of their intrinsic nature. They include the Mummers' play and the Plough Monday play, which have already been considered. To this list should now be added the widespread custom of carrying carved animals' heads or skulls around streets at Christmastide, usually requesting money and singing. The animal concerned could be a horse (in South Wales, Kent, Derbyshire, and Yorkshire), a ram (in Derbyshire and Yorkshire), or a bull (in Wiltshire and Gloucestershire). In all these areas it was amply recorded in the nineteenth century, but in all, also, it was first mentioned between 1800 and 1840. Yet the writings of early medieval churchmen contain several complaints, spanning western Europe, about the donning of antlers or horns by human beings as part of the New Year festivities. In England this is condemned in texts ascribed to Aldhelm and Theodore of Tarsus, both dating from the end of the seventh century. The obvious question arising is whether the two groups of references are to the same tradition, which may have survived for more than a millennium without official or literary notice being taken of it. E. C. Cawte, who has made the definitive study of the nineteenth-century effigies, was prepared to argue cautiously that it could have done so, for the heads were taken around only by commoners, for their private profit.[125] The suggestion is a good one, but a powerful case can be built against it. Other activities which fell into the same category, such as apple-wassailing, are mentioned almost 200 years earlier. Maypoles and midsummer fires played little part in parochial fund-raising but are still well attested in medieval and Tudor literature. Charivaris or 'rough music', the ritual humiliation of unpopular villagers by their neighbours, found their way into art and written records in the early Stuart period. In this context the complete lack of references to the animals' heads, as to Mummers' plays, is remarkable. It does not rule out the possibility that such folk practices did go unrecorded. But it does mean that no assumption of existence can be made in default of evidence. There is a possibility that the heads discussed here were all modern developments of the early modern hobby-horse dance.

There is in fact a case of the ritualized carrying of animal heads which is described in an early modern source, and which moreover has survived until the present and corresponds better than any of the other recent examples to the practices condemned in the early middle ages. It is the famous Horn Dance held at Abbots Bromley in Staffordshire, performed by six men bearing a set of antlers each. The sheer size and weight of the latter mean that they are carried upon stands, projecting around heads and shoulders, instead of being worn on the head. None the less, the dancers make an image corresponding quite well to those conjured up by the invectives of the early churchmen, who mentioned stags (rather than horses, rams, or bulls) as the animals which were imitated in particular. And the dance was certainly in existence by the first half of the seventeenth century, and held at the Christmas season like the ancient disguisings.[126] But even the Horn Dance cannot necessarily be regarded as a direct link with the pagan past. It is too similar to another sort of celebration known in early modern England, the triumphal bearing of antlers to mark the end of a successful hunt. At the present day the best-known example of this is found in Shakespeare's *As You Like It*. The one closest to Abbots Bromley was a dozen miles away at Tutbury Priory, to which the woodmaster and keepers of Needwood Chase (in which Abbots Bromley lies) presented a buck every year. They carried its head in procession to the church and were thanked with a feast (after which, for general entertainment, a bull was turned loose among the musicians).[127]

So it is impossible to know how far the picture of the 'ritual year' provided in this chapter has been guilty of the second major charge which can be lodged against it. But there is no doubt of its deficiency in the third respect, that it is far too static. Not only does it give little indication of whether customs developed or altered within the span of time considered, but it provides no sense of their relative antiquity. These problems must be the whole matter of the next chapter.

2

The Making of Merry England

Just as there has hitherto been no systematic account of the most common seasonal rituals of early Tudor England, so nobody has made any sustained attempt to determine the age of the various customs involved. Were the ecclesiastical ceremonies those of the Anglo-Saxons? Were the secular customs equally old, or indeed yet more ancient so that they represented relics of pagan religion? Were both part of an unchanging, immemorial culture? Excellent case-studies have been made of the origins of specific rites, and folklorists have collected materials for an investigation of more, but this information needs to be rationalized and extended before an overall view can be obtained. The sources concerned are much the same in nature as those employed for the preceding chapter. Literary and legal records furnish some important data, and are the only evidence available until the later Middle Ages. Then accounts appear, of the sort which have featured so prominently in the discussion of the sixteenth-century year. In theory, they should provide a fairly precise guide to the inception of particular customs.

Two objections, again theoretical, can be lodged against this idea. The first is that an activity may have been in existence before it became paid for by households, parishes, or other bodies. Against this there is no straightforward defence, as it is an argument from silence. It can only be countered by placing upon the critic the burden of showing why it is likely that a ceremony or celebration should have existed before a certain time either without incurring expense or without having that expense entered in accounts. The second objection is that the evidence may not have survived in sufficient quantity to provide a meaningful sample. For this study I have located churchwardens' accounts from 196 parishes for the years 1500–49, from seventy-five for the years 1450–99, from thirty-three for the years

1400–49, and from nine for the fourteenth century.[1] They are overwhelmingly concentrated in the southern two-thirds of the country, the four northernmost counties and Lancashire supplying two sets between them for the early sixteenth century and none for the fifteenth. None survive from rural Yorkshire in the whole period up to 1549. South of the Trent the situation is much better, with towns and villages being well represented in most regions, although material from the counties which border Wales is still scanty. Before the fifteenth century the sample is so tiny that it might be deemed worthless were it not for the fact that it comes from small towns scattered from Devon to Yorkshire. The range of geography involved does allow some basis for comparison. Similar considerations apply to the use of household accounts. I have located twenty-three sets from the establishments of secular landowners, seated all over southern England and the Midlands and representing a social range from great nobles to fairly minor gentry.[2] To these are added another five left by bishops[3] and eight from religious houses and university colleges.[4] Between them they are spaced quite evenly across the period 1269–1478. The expenditure of the royal household, recorded so well around 1500 in the King's Books of Payments, is itemized during the early thirteenth century in the Liberate Rolls and later in the Wardrobe Accounts. The best examples of both categories of document have been published.[5] And relevant records from several towns extend back into the fourteenth century.

Thus there does appear to be enough evidence to make such an enquiry worthwhile. It can in itself possess pitfalls. Some of the churchwardens' accounts now exist only as published extracts made by antiquaries, although the latter were generally interested in precisely this sort of material. Virtually all expenses before the mid-fifteenth century were entered in Latin, often abbreviated and closely written, and it is possible to miss items among them with only a little inattention. Furthermore, if a custom is recorded at the beginning of every set of accounts in which it appears, and does not feature in any other type of source, its time of origin is quite mysterious. There are, fortunately, only two which fall into this category, the gatherings of the 'hogglers' or 'hognels' and upon Plough Monday. They feature in the first year of every book of expenses in which they occur, but none of those books are older than the 1450s in the case of the 'hogglers' and 1413 in the case of Plough Monday. The antiquity of these traditions is therefore an open question. Some conclusions, however tentative, can be drawn for all the others and they can now be considered in order of apparent antiquity.

There are in fact only two customs, among all of those described in the last chapter, which can be documented in pre-Christian times. One is the giving of New Year gifts. They were exchanged in first-century Rome, and subsequently found across much of Europe in the Middle Ages. In England the thirteenth-century monarch Henry III was criticized for extorting them from his subjects.[6] The other seasonal activity which can be firmly assigned to the ancient world is the decking of holy places with greenery and flowers for festivals. In a much-quoted letter from Pope Gregory the Great to Abbot Mellitus, sent in the year 601, specific reference is made to this custom among the heathen Anglo-Saxons. It included the construction of bowers of summer foliage of the sort which were to feature in the late medieval and Tudor revels.[7] Classical Greek and Roman texts also constantly mention the garlanding of temples and religious processions. In addition there is a third custom which can safely be assumed to have come down from pagan times, the kindling of bonfires and rolling of blazing wheels on Midsummer Eve. It is recorded in England only as far back as the mid-thirteenth century, when the villagers of East Monckton, Wiltshire, carried torches around their lord's cornfield upon that night. In France the fires were described as being very common in the 1140s, but there are no previous references to them anywhere in Europe.[8] By the nineteenth century folklorists found them all across northern Europe from Ireland to Russia, and assumed them to be an equally extensive prehistoric seasonal rite. Although it seems impossible positively to prove this, we can document ancient parallels for it. The pagan Romans and Irish believed with equal conviction in the power of bonfires to purify the air and to protect crops and livestock, although they kindled them in April and May respectively.[9] In Aquitaine at the beginning of the fourth century a blazing wheel was customarily rolled down a hillside, although we are not told at which date. It was expected to end its run by falling into water; almost one and a half millennia later the people of Buckfastleigh, Devon, were still carrying out exactly the same rite. All over the north-western provinces of the Roman Empire, including Britain, the wheel was the most common symbol of the sun. The same sign, almost certainly with the same solar significance, is found in Scandinavian rock art of the second millennium BC and Irish metalwork from the end of the third millennium.[10] It therefore has a record in the British Isles which spans about 4,000 years.

We can turn now to Christian customs. The principal festivals, of Easter, Christmas, Candlemas, Pentecost, and Rogationtide, were all present in Anglo-Saxon times. Easter must have arrived with Christianity itself under the Roman Empire, although not until the eighth century were the English, Welsh, and Cornish churches all celebrating it on the same date. Christmas seems to have been established all over the western Roman provinces by the year 400, as was Pentecost, which acquired its English name Whitsun by the mid-eleventh century. The feast of the Purification, which became Candlemas, appears among those listed around the year 730 by the famous monastic writer Bede. The hallowing of candles upon it was ordered by Pope Sergius in 684, and is first mentioned in England in directions issued by St Dunstan during the late tenth century. The English Rogation Days were established in 747 by the Council of Cloveshoo, although they almost certainly drew upon ancient traditions of blessing fields during early summer such as the pagan Roman Ambarvalia. The hallowing of fronds on Palm Sunday is first enjoined in a mid-eighth-century pontifical of Archbishop Egbert of York, while 'Creeping to the Cross' on Good Friday appears in 957, as part of the Canons of Elfric. But the latter rite, as indicated before, was never observed in some religious houses. Although a few thirteenth-century prelates enjoined it upon all clergy in their dioceses, and it formed part of the most popular late medieval service book, it may still not have been present in some parishes by the Tudor period.[11] Furthermore, while some of these very old rituals were continuing to spread at the end of the Middle Ages, others were being further elaborated then. The prophet appears on Palm Sunday for the first time in the churchwardens' accounts of the 1490s, and becomes more common in those of the next thirty years, while the scattering of cakes and flowers as part of the same feast seems to have been adopted only in the early sixteenth century.[12]

Other venerable ecclesiastical customs were adopted or developed at a yet slower pace. The feast of All Saints was fixed upon 1 November in the year 837, but it is not clear when the English began to associate it with the dead, as they clearly did by the fourteenth century. There are no payments for bell-ringing until the middle of the fifteenth, and they do not become common until the end of that century. The paschal candle was certainly known in western Christendom in the sixth century, but during the twelfth it was still consecrated in different places in England at different times, and thirteenth-century prelates showed concern that it should be more generally adopted. This was eventually what occurred, because the taper is recorded in all the surviving churchwardens' accounts, from their first appearance in the fourteenth century.[13] The Easter sepulchre was known in southern England by the mid-tenth century, being used especially at Winchester Cathedral.[14] But how far it had trickled into the parishes after 500 years is suggested by an inventory of church goods taken in the Archdeaconry of Norwich (hardly a remote corner of the realm) in about 1360. Out of a total of 358 town and village churches, five had the cloth which traditionally covered the sepulchre when the host was lying inside it.[15] The surviving accounts show that it was employed in some urban parishes during the late fourteenth century and in most of them by the middle of the fifteenth. In the early sixteenth century it was present in all of them and becoming popular in the countryside but (as said in the previous chapter) on the eve of the Reformation about a seventh of the rural parishes in our sample had apparently still not taken it up.[16] It had at that time been present in the realm for at least 600 years. The veiling of images and of the chancel during Lent may well have been Saxon in origin, and certainly had made greater progress than Easter sepulchres by the fourteenth century. That marvellous 'snapshot' of the situation in the archdeaconry of Norwich reveals that 261 out of the 358 churches owned cloths for the purpose. On the other hand, only two of them had the larger veils needed to cover the rood, the big figure of Christ on the cross above the entrance to the chancel.[17] This may well have been because most parish churches did not at the date possess either roods or the wooden lofts upon which they, and the statues of Mary and John, were mounted. Certainly the fifteenth-century churchwardens' accounts often contain payments for the construction of such lofts. Although it cannot be proved that they were being built instead of rebuilt at these times, the entries never give any suggestion of mere refurbishing. Under Mary Tudor, when several lofts were replaced after destruction in the previous reign, the same sources frequently specify that a restoration, not a first building, was involved.

Other religious customs were of considerably more recent origin, although that did not necessarily mean a less general popularity by the early Tudor period. One was the Boy Bishop. The practice of giving honours to children on particular feasts was already known in the fourth- and fifth-century Roman Empire, where it was defended by the writers Rufinus, Athanasius, and Socrates. In tenth-century Germany it became accepted that the inferior clergy as well as the choirboys should be given periods of licence in the three days after Christmas, and this custom was taken up in France in the twelfth century as the 'feast of fools'. That period also saw the blossoming of the cult of St Nicholas in western Christendom, and the two seem to have come together by about 1200 to produce the institution of the little bishop.[18] It was known in France and Germany, but was especially popular in England where it is first recorded at York, in a statute which dates from 1220 at the latest. After then it is attested at every cathedral which has left a medieval archive.[19] During the course of the thirteenth and fourteenth centuries several prelates made rules to stop irreverent and disorderly behaviour which had become associated with it and to ban the 'feast of fools' altogether. The latter gave more offence for the simple reason that adults were capable of greater excess. By 1450 the process was complete, and the children alone were permitted a moment of role-reversal at Christmastide. Furthermore they seem henceforth to have behaved perfectly.[20] The tradition seems to have taken longer to get into religious houses, being absent from the accounts of Beaulieu and Westminster Abbeys in the late thirteenth century, and appearing in those of Durham in 1355 although they commence in 1303. It is first recorded in an abbey at Hyde, Hampshire, in 1327.[21] But its importance in parish religion does seem to have begun quite early, to judge by the fact that Edward II gave money to a Boy Bishop from St Mary's church, Nottingham, in 1317, and that two, from rival parishes, were going the rounds of Cambridge in 1386.[22] Despite this, the churchwardens' accounts suggest that Boy Bishops, like Easter sepulchres, were a recent innovation in some local churches in the early sixteenth century, and never became as common as the other custom.[23]

The feast of Corpus Christi was wholly a product of the fourteenth century. As is well known, it was proclaimed in 1317 by Pope John XXII, as a means of drawing greater attention to the sanctity of the eucharist and to the Real Presence of Christ in the consecrated host. The papal bull did not specify a procession, only a liturgy. Within one year the latter had been taken up across Catholic Europe, being recorded in England at St Peter's Abbey, Gloucester, and at Wells Cathedral. In 1322 the archbishop of York ordered it to be kept all over his province, and in 1325 a Corpus Christi guild was founded at Ipswich with responsibility for a procession. Another appeared at Louth in 1326, a further one at Leicester in 1343, the Coventry guild dated from 1348, and that at Cambridge was processing by 1349. Nevertheless, the adoption of the custom was only rapid in certain places. Most of the surviving English service missals composed before the mid-fourteenth century do not contain the liturgy for the feast, and most of those kept in the archdeaconry of Norwich around 1360 still omitted it. Still, the years 1350–70 saw a surge in the foundation of the guilds, and in 1388 a royal enquiry identified forty-two in existence, making Corpus Christi the third most popular dedication for such fraternities after the Virgin and the Trinity.[24] By the early fifteenth century every urban corporation and parish which has left records was observing the processions, and throughout the century these were being embellished, notably by the addition of torches and banners.[25] As mentioned in the previous chapter, they never seem to have penetrated very far into rural parish life, although guilds may have provided them in a number of villages.

Religious guilds were also very important to the 'ridings' of St George upon that saint's feast day, which (as shown) were mostly supported by the fraternities dedicated to him. Thus the processions must have developed with these bodies, which were almost all founded in the late fourteenth and fifteenth centuries and were still appearing in the early sixteenth. They reflected a growth in the standing of George as the national saint from the 1340s onward, propelled by royal patronage and observable at all levels of society.[26] The most famous 'riding' of all, at Norwich, is first recorded in 1420, and the guild responsible was founded in 1385.[27] All the earliest references to the St George processions in other towns fall after this date.[28] The establishment of new shrines of the saint after 1490 is recorded in the churchwardens' accounts of parishes in Somerset, Yorkshire, Salisbury, Reading, and Westminster.[29] These entries testify to a continued burgeoning of his cult up to the Reformation.

We come now to secular or semi-secular customs which can first be detected in the high Middle Ages. Of these, the most universal was the feasting and merry-making at Christmastide. This almost certainly represented a continuation of pre-Christian midwinter celebrations in Britain of which we have no details at all. Every single one of the sample of medieval household accounts employed for this chapter contains payments for banquets on Christmas Day itself and some of the following days until Twelfth Night. Often the food consumed is carefully itemized: thus we know, for example, that in 1289 the bishop of Hereford ensured a boar's head as a stylish touch for his table.[30] What alters over time is that whereas the earlier expenses are almost all for foodstuffs, with the very occasional entertainment, by the beginning of the fifteenth century it was becoming common for landowners of most incomes to be visited regularly by theatrical troupes and musicians. Thus Dame Alice de Bryene paid for a harper to perform repeatedly from Christmas to New Year 1412, as she fed a succession of different guests. At the other end of the scale of aristocracy, the earl of Warwick's family spent the feast at Berkeley Castle in 1420 hearing a minstrel retained by the duke of Clarence, six players from Slimbridge, and four from Wotton under Edge.[31] The best literary portraits we possess of an earlier Christmas season are in the famous poem *Sir Gawaine and the Green Knight*, composed at some time in the fourteenth century.[32] They bear out what the accounts up to and including that period suggest: that even quite wealthy households tended to find amusements within themselves, rather than receiving the entertainers who feature so prominently in the fifteenth-century records.

It is likewise a safe assumption that English villagers were holding summer games and revels long before Christianity. None the less, the first specific references to them to survive are from the thirteenth century, when they attracted the unfavourable attention of two unusually severe and energetic churchmen. In 1240 Walter de Cantelupe, bishop of Worcester, condemned clerics who attended 'games to be made of a king and a queen', who sound exactly like the mock-monarchs of later May games. At about the same time his colleague Robert Grosseteste, bishop of Lincoln, complained about priests who encouraged 'games which they call the bringing-in of summer and autumn'. The former seem very much like the fetching in of the May, although whether the latter were a harvest-home celebration or something else is anybody's guess.[33] In the late four-teenth century references to the summer revels appear with more detail. Chaucer wrote joyously about the bringing home of blooms and greenery upon May morning, his heroine Emelie going out at sunrise for a garland, singing. Her knight Arcite rides forth with a squire to gather woodbine or hawthorn, and the people of their court pluck flowers.[34] At about the same time an anonymous Life of St Anne portrayed a procession of children 'each a green branch in his hand, even like a summer play'.[35] In the following century the literary references proliferate and court records and churchwar-dens' accounts add their evidence. This is a case in which there are absolutely no grounds to argue that a greater quantity of material indicates a greater prevalence of the custom concerned. The kind of sources which supply the late medieval data, vernacular literature and parish records, are simply not available earlier.

Yet, as in the case of Christmastide, it is possible to suggest that very old seasonal celebrations came to include novel activities in the course of the Middle Ages. Some of those associated with the summer games will be discussed below, but here it is appropriate to consider the question of may-poles. The first unequivocal references to them are fourteenth century. One occurs in an English poem dating from the last two decades, *Chaunce of the Dice*, which speaks of the pole maintained permanently at Cornhill, London. The other consists of a piece of Welsh poetry, by Gryffydd ap Adda ap Dafydd, describing one set up at Llanidloes in the middle of the century.[36] A charter of King John's reign, about 150 years before, refers to a 'mepul' as a permanent feature used to mark a boundary. Unhappily, his-torians have long pointed out that the vagaries of medieval spelling could here equally well conceal a 'mew pool' (the mew being a waterfowl), or a maple tree.[37] Nor are there any earlier notices on the Continent, although in the last few centuries maypoles have been found across the north of Europe almost as widely as midsummer bonfires. Thus the question of their antiquity would be completely open, were it not for one tiny piece of evidence which might indicate that in the British Isles at least they have not descended from prehistory. This consists of the references in the earliest Irish literature to pagan rituals. Although the works concerned are all written by Christians, and their portraits of pre-Christian ways are increasingly regarded as the merest shadow of the reality, there seems to be general agreement that the descriptions of the May Day rite record a genuine custom. It consisted of the rekindling and blessing of fire, as on the Christian Easter Eve. These flames were still lit in Ireland, Highland Scotland, and Wales (the principal 'Celtic' areas of the archipelago) until the present century, but have never been recorded across most of England.[38] It is possible that they preceded maypoles there as the focal point of the day's celebrations before the poles were introduced by the Anglo-Saxons or even during the Middle Ages. Certainly, the poles were only known in Ireland in districts where the English had settled during the latter period.[39] But this is mere speculation.

Other traditions first mentioned in high medieval records include the playing of ball games and staging of cock-fights upon Shrove Tuesday, which feature in a description of London life contained within a late twelfth-century biography of St Thomas Becket by William Fitzstephen.[40] Every one of the sample of medieval household accounts which cover the Shrovetide season record feasting at that time. The washing of poor peoples' feet by royalty on Maundy Thursday, and the giving of presents to them, certainly began at the opening of the thirteenth century. Churchmen had performed this ceremony long before then, and according to Bede it was already established prior to 700 in the Northumberland monastery of Lindisfarne. On the Continent clerics had used the custom for almost 200 years before that, and French kings had taken it up by the beginning of the eleventh century. But the first English monarch to practise it was John, almost certainly as part of an attempt to demonstrate his piety in the wake of his excommunication by the Pope. The earliest surviving payment for the robes and money given to the paupers concerned occurs in the year 1210. Thirteen men received them, being a very common number selected for medieval almsgiving (perhaps being that of Christ and the Apostles). It remained standard for the 'royal maundy' until 1361, when Edward III showed a yet greater generosity by introducing the tradition of benefiting as many individuals as the monarch had years of life (he being then 50).[41] Not until the early sixteenth century, however, does the practice seem to have been followed by secular English magnates.

Secular midwinter songs were probably composed before the dawn of history, and the earliest extant examples in England are twelfth century. But the Christian Christmas carol was devised by Italian Franciscans in the thirteenth, and the genre does not seem to have reached the English until the fourteenth.[42] Likewise the wassail cup or bowl must have drawn upon very old ideas but seems to be a high medieval invention. From the eighth-century poem *Beowulf* to fourteenth-century literature such as the conduct book of Robert of Brunne, the word 'wassail' appears as a toast. It is simply the Old English for 'be of good health'. The bowl is first mentioned by Matthew Paris in the thirteenth century, as one in which cakes and fine white bread were communally dipped. Near the end of the same century Robert of Gloucester retold the legend of the marriage of the British king Vortigern with the Saxon princess Rowena, making the latter drink to the former with the words 'waes heal'. When Peter de Langtoft repeated the story in the 1320s, he portrayed people drinking alternately from the same cup with the exchange 'wassaille' and 'drinkhaille', exactly as in Tudor England.[43] The sequence raises the possibility that the exchange became customary around 1300, but this, again, cannot be proved.

Other Tudor seasonal customs had apparently evolved yet more recently. When Chaucer mentioned St Valentine's Day, near the end of the fourteenth century, he described the belief that the birds chose their mates then. But he completely failed to refer to what would later be the more obvious human activity, of sending love tokens. This is first mentioned by the early fifteenth-century poet John Lydgate, writing in praise of Queen Katherine, wife of Henry V. After Lydgate's time the evidence multiplies rapidly, in literature and accounts, suggesting that the presentation of tokens was a fifteenth-century innovation.[44] As Lydgate was a courtier poet, one might argue that it was conceived within the royal entourage and then spread out among the aristocracy, but this is to erect one unproven probability upon another. Far more certain, and better documented, is the evolution of Corpus Christi pageants and plays. The first records of the carrying of images or tableaux in the day's processions are at York in 1376 and Beverley in 1377. At King's Lynn, Norfolk, plays began to be performed in 1384 and 'tabernacles' carried in 1388. The archive at Lynn is so full that there seems little doubt that these were indeed the first appearances of such activities in the town upon the feast. That at York is sufficiently good to rule out the possibility that the pageants were carried more than a few years before the first reference to them.[45] At Coventry the earliest such records are in 1392, at Exeter in 1413, at Chester in 1422, and at Newcastle-upon-Tyne in 1427, all referring to a custom already established, although in the Exeter case it was a very recent one.[46] The first appearances in other municipalities are later, and there a much worse survival rate of documents prevents us from determining whether their tableaux or performances also originated at the end of the fourteenth century or afterward. But some towns were definitely still taking up the practice in the early sixteenth century, such as Louth in Lincolnshire, where an annual Corpus Christi play was instituted in the 1510s and pageants in 1520.[47] The famous cycles of religious drama at Coventry and York developed a generation after the processional tableaux. The records for the former town are ample enough to show the plays taking form rapidly in the 1440s, while at York the process occurred between 1433 and 1460. The Chester cycle expanded much later, from a single play in 1474 which was subsequently moved to Whitsun, into the full three-day sequence which evolved between 1521 and 1532.[48]

The development of the urban midsummer watches was precisely synchronized with that of the Corpus Christi pageants. The most famous of all, at London, is also the earliest for which a record survives. It is mentioned in 1378, in an order which may well have marked the inception of the event. That at Exeter was apparently first set forth in 1415, while the Coventry parade may have resulted from a suggestion made by the Prior in 1421, although the first clear reference to it is in 1445. The only other such procession for which we have something like a date of origin is at Chester, where the midsummer watch was later said to have been organized in 'about 1499'.[49] Thus, like the pageants, the watches seem to have been a product of the late fourteenth century which greatly increased their range in the fifteenth.

Church ales also seem to have become more popular in the latter century. Communal drinkings, for the profit of individuals or for a public cause, were common in England during the high Middle Ages. From 1220 to 1364, and especially in the mid-thirteenth century, bishops repeatedly forbade the attendance of clergy at such gatherings, and the holding of them in churches.[50] Yet there does seem to have been a tendency during the mid- to late fifteenth century for ales to become a regular means of raising parish funds, and it was in this period that they achieved the prominence which they were to occupy in early Tudor parochial finance. In several villages they replaced levies or gatherings as a more enjoyable way of raising money, often being held in a newly constructed church house or hall.[51] Another great parish moneyspinner, Hocktide, seems to have been wholly a fifteenth-century invention. Folklorists have linked it to a payment in the Wardrobe Accounts of Edward I, 'to seven ladies of the

Queen's Bedchamber who took the king in bed on the morrow of Easter and made him fine himself'.[52] This refers instead to a medieval courtly game whereby ladies who caught gentlemen still abed could exact a forfeit from them: it features prominently in the next century in the poem *Sir Gawaine and the Green Knight*.[53] It is just possible that it helped to inspire the custom of holding the other sex hostage in the street, but this is first mentioned at London in 1406, when the corporation identified it quite specifically, apparently as a novelty, and banned it as a source of disorder. The prohibition was repeated in 1409, and echoed furiously by a bishop of Worcester in 1450, who thought it a 'disgraceful sport'.[54] Within two decades of this, for reasons which remain quite mysterious, it had become respectable enough to take its part in parish fund-raising. The first appearance of it in this capacity is at Cambridge in 1469–70,[55] and it became widespread during the next three decades,[56] reaching its full recorded range during the early sixteenth century.[57]

The story of the Robin Hood plays is very similar. The first record of one is at Exeter in 1427, performed before the mayor, but after that none are known until they reappear as parish entertainments in Oxfordshire in 1469 and then in Somerset in 1474. During the 1490s references to them are found across most of their subsequent range, and multiply in the early sixteenth century. Almost certainly it was the printing of the ballads about the hero and his band which ensured the popularity of the plays based upon them.[58] Robin's opposite number in the Christmastide revels, the Lord of Misrule, is not heard of until the 1480s, when he appears at the royal court. In all probability he represented a self-conscious Renaissance classicism, for such mock-rulers are mentioned in Tacitus and Lucian as presiding over the midwinter festivities of ancient Rome. But he had some important English forerunners. In the reigns of Edward II and Edward III the monarchs took up a French fashion of choosing a 'king' for Twelfth Night revels by dropping a bean into a cake mix and awarding the title to the man who found it in his slice. But then royalty abandoned it, and it reappears only in the later fifteenth century at Merton College, Oxford. The immediate predecessors of the Lords of Misrule seem to have been figures chosen to preside over festivities at Oxford in the early fifteenth century. A 'Prester John' was operating at Canterbury College (later dissolved) in 1414–30, while 'King Balthasar' held court at a nameless one in December 1432. The example of the classical texts mentioned, and perhaps of the Boy Bishop, may have lain behind these academic 'sovereigns', who in turn may have helped to inspire the royal Lords fifty years later. Certainly, as noted in the previous chapter, they persisted at the universities, and became a feature of aristocratic households by 1500, thereafter getting into the parishes and corporations.[59]

The first definite reference to the English morris dance is in 1458, when Alice de Wetehalle, a widow with property in London and Suffolk, left to her heirs a silver cup 'sculpted with moreys dauns'. At about the same time the English translation of a Norman French romance, *The Knight of the Swan*, included 'morishes'. They appeared at court in 1492, when Henry VII paid for the first of what became a favourite royal entertainment. Market towns were taking the morris up from the 1500s. During the late fifteenth century its cast of characters, the Lady, the Fool, and the set of dancers, became a common motif for artists all over western and central Europe. The plot of their action was the wooing of the lady by all the others, and the winning of her hand by the Fool. The dance which they performed was distinguished by its exceptional vigour, with much capering and rapid arm movements. But although it was clearly a very widespread phenomenon, none of the European appearances seem to be earlier than Alice de Wetehalle's bequest. Several are, on the other hand, roughly contemporary or only a little later. Thus we do not seem at present able to tell if the dance was an English invention or an importation. Nor is there any certain explanation for its name, as it had usually no obvious association with Moors, the Spanish Arabs.[60] It has been suggested that it developed out of earlier English leaping dances, called routs and reyes, because those terms vanish as the morris appears,[61] but they may have been different altogether, and have given way to the new fashion. The hobby-horse, which was to be included in some morris troupes, appeared a little earlier but its progress is more difficult to chart. The first surviving reference to it is in a late fourteenth-century Welsh poem by Gryffydd Gryg, who implied that it was a new development. It features as part of parochial finance at St Andrew Hubbard, London, in 1460, when a child raised money for the churchwardens by dancing with it. By 1500 it was part of the entertainments at the royal court and familiar in Cornwall, where the author of the play *Beunans Meriasek* seems to describe it as travelling with a troupe. Thereafter it is encountered in the midland churchwardens' accounts mentioned in the previous chapter, but none are earlier than 1528, and they supply no evidence for when their communities took it up.[62]

By now the point ought to have been substantiated that although some of the rituals and customs carried on in early Tudor communities were very old, many had been either introduced or embellished only a few generations before or even within living memory. The churchwardens' accounts from the years around 1400 show few of them compared with those from the period around 1500, and the fourteenth-century household accounts likewise refer to them much less than those of the early sixteenth century. Literary evidence and the edicts of churchmen suggest that some earlier customs had died away by the later middle ages, to be replaced by others. The 'feast of fools' once permitted to the lesser clergy is a classic example. The importance of the New Year festival, the Kalendae, seems to have declined relatively during the medieval period, while that of Christmas and Twelfth Night increased. From the fifth to the tenth centuries clerical writers denounced the excesses of the Kalendae all over western Christendom, concentrating especially upon the associated custom of dressing up in animal skins, antlers, and horns.[63] In the famous Welsh epic poem *Y Gododdin*, composed at any time between the sixth and tenth centuries, it is the New Year Feast which ranks as the greatest. Later, however, no more complaints are heard of it from the Church and the animal disguises cease to attract attention (and perhaps vanish). It may well be that other seasonal activities waxed and waned during the same span of time, concealed from us by the lack of documentation. But the evidence for accumulation of communal customs and for the elaboration of the ritual year in England between about 1350 and about 1520 is still very strong.

It fits into a pattern of progressive physical embellishment of the churches with which many of these activities were associated. There is abundant architectural and documentary evidence for large-scale rebuilding of their basic fabric during the fifteenth and early sixteenth centuries: the so-called 'wool churches' and 'perpendicular towers' are still notable monuments of the English landscape. The parish accounts and wills of the period record the purchase and bequest of increasing numbers of images, altars, permanent lights, and other decorations, a process maintained until the very eve of the Reformation. A comparable growth is well attested for chantries, parish guilds, obits, and other local religious institutions.[64] The payments made by urban corporations to travelling groups of players and musicians, whether or not associated with particular festivals, show the same sort of increase. By the early sixteenth century they were more frequent and more ample than ever before.[65]

So why did all this happen? At first sight there seem to be three different sorts of possible explanation. One is to argue that fashions have their own impetus, largely independent of practical considerations, and that this period just had an increasing taste for physical and ceremonial display. In many ways it appears to evade the issue and to answer a puzzle with a mystery. But, however unsatisfying it may be, if the other two theories prove unsound it may be all that we can fall back upon. The second of these theories is one of economic determinism. The late middle ages was a time in which all social groups have been credited with prosperity by one or another writer. Thorold Rogers, in a very famous phrase, described the fifteenth century as the 'golden age of the English labourer'. Sir Michael Postan extended the same phrase to the peasantry of the period. F. W. Maitland called the fourteenth century 'the golden age of the boroughs', and Joel Rosenthal labelled the whole 200 years 'a golden age for the nobility'.[66] With all this gold around it would not be surprising if some of it had spilled over into the institutions and activities described above. The latter would therefore have been largely a matter of surplus wealth seeking investment. The third theory is one of what might be called spiritual determinism. It is based upon the undoubted fact that many of the favourite religious institutions of the age, obits, chantries, and guilds, were directly related to the belief that the suffering of the dead in purgatory could be reduced by prayer. Other prominent aspects of the religion of the time, such as the cult of the saints as intercessors, could be directed towards the same end. In the past this aspect of late medieval piety, all over Europe, has sometimes been linked to the recurrence of plague epidemics after the 1340s, presenting the spectacle of rapid and agonizing mass mortality. Thus, runs the argument, people were more than usually concerned with what Joel Rosenthal has termed 'the purchase of paradise', investing heavily in religious decoration and ceremonial to ensure a happier afterlife. The logic could be extended, far more weakly, to suggest that the comparable elaboration of secular pastimes stemmed from a need to forget the fear of death.

These explanations are not, of course, mutually exclusive, and substantiating any one of them, let alone quantifying the importance of each, is extremely difficult. The economic argument ought in principle to be the easiest to check against objective evidence, but the data concerned is incomplete, complex, and at times controversial.[67] The following assertions appear to be more or less generally accepted. During the fifteenth century virtually the whole of the six northern counties were either certainly or probably in a state of economic depression. Only pastoral farming seems to have remained buoyant there, as most ports declined and the old cloth-making centres collapsed. In western Yorkshire a new textile industry created wealth for a few small towns. The Midlands also experienced prolonged recession in many places, especially in the north and west. On the other hand, southern England, and particularly the three south-western counties, underwent discernible economic growth in the second half of the century. This produced a notable improvement in the fortunes of some market towns. The fate of the larger urban centres was often less happy. The period 1380–1440 was a good one at York, Norwich, King's Lynn, Colchester, Coventry, Salisbury, Reading, Southampton, Bristol, and Chester, although Lincoln and Winchester were in decline and scores of petty boroughs and local markets decayed. The rest of the century was a bad time for major towns and ports in general, and those of the east coast in particular. The exceptions were connected to expanding rural industry, such as London, Newcastle-upon-Tyne, Ipswich, Exeter, Chester, Worcester, Reading, Newbury, Leicester, Nottingham, and Derby. The same pattern seems to have held into the sixteenth century, when London, Exeter, Leicester, and Worcester all joined the list of those experiencing losses in trade.

The following observations have been made concerning social changes. The landed aristocracy lost income steadily between 1350 and 1450 because of a fall in the price of most agricultural produce, an increase in the cost of labour, and a shortage of tenants. The total fall in their receipts was probably about a quarter, making retrenchment necessary for those not lucky enough to acquire more land or the profits of state service and war. Many noble and gentry families reduced the number of their servants, residences, and luxury goods. Religious houses recruited fewer members. Merchants in general suffered from the decline of so many towns after about 1430, although there were of course some who rose with the few urban centres still prospering. Tenants gained from lower rents and lost because of the lower value of farm products. Wage-earners gained absolutely if they lived in a flourishing community. Mobility of labour increased after 1450, especially into market towns and the south-eastern and south-western counties. In economically buoyant areas the proportion of servants in the population increased, and everywhere the percentage of smallholders and wage-earners grew. So did the involvement of local laity in the affairs of their parish churches, expressed in gifts, bequests, and the foundation of religious guilds.

Much of all this can be related to the apparent growth in ritual and seasonal celebration. A lot of the evidence for the latter derives from those parts of southern England where economic growth has been noted, and especially from the flourishing market towns. The appearance of Corpus Christi pageants, midsummer watches, and St George 'ridings' in the larger urban centres seems to fit quite nicely within the period from 1370 to 1440 in which so many were prospering. Those in which late adoption or continuing elaboration of pageantry has been detected, such as Chester and Nottingham, were also generally those which continued to gain trade during the succeeding hundred years. The greater investment by ordinary people in their local church's ornaments and activities may be attributed to the greater opportunities for smallholders and wage-earners. There remain, however, serious objections to this model. The greater elaboration of calendar customs in the South of England may be in large part a reflection of the much greater survival of evidence from there. The multiplication of entertainments in the households of landowners runs contrary to all the logic of economic reality. Lincoln is an example of a local capital in a consistent state of depression after 1350 which none the less produced pageants and spent more upon visiting groups of players, just like the expanding towns. The same expenditure is visible in the Cinque Ports of Kent, which were likewise in prolonged decline. At Canterbury the procession of St Thomas was actually made more colourful and elaborate in order to attract back trade to a community which was losing it.[68] Pressures of prestige and competition could make economic boom and economic slump produce identical results in different places. The same forces of fashion and emulation ensured that local laity invested more in their parish churches and parochial institutions even in the less prosperous regions. The strengthening of the belief in purgatory and in salvation by good works must be held accountable for much of this activity, although whether this was in turn galvanized by plague epidemics is impossible to say. It must be concluded, very lamely, that there is no clear and obvious reason for the apparent greater investment in English seasonal ceremony during the later Middle Ages. Both economic stimulants and religious needs seem to have played a part in it, but specific aspects of it (such as the household diversions of landowners) cannot be explained other than in such intangible terms as developments of taste.

Certainly it proceeded despite marked fluctuations in social tension, which can be charted by prosecutions for offences such as fornication, the bearing of illegitimate children, gambling, and the keeping of alehouses. In the 1970s it was demonstrated, notably by Keith Wrightson, that the late sixteenth century in England witnessed a dramatic increase in such charges which peaked in the first part of the seventeenth. This was ascribed to a combination of moral fervour associated with evangelical Protestantism and practical responses to population growth. The latter, pressing upon an insufficiently elastic economy, created a novel scale of poverty, vagrancy, unemployment, hunger, and potential disorder which caused local élites to fear, supervise, and discipline their social inferiors more than before. In 1985 this model was questioned in part by Margaret Spufford,[69] who compared the decades around 1600 with those around 1300, also a time of severe population pressure with consequent social difficulties. She found that both periods produced unusually high levels of presentation of poor people for sexual incontinence and the bearing of bastards. From this she argued that the Protestantism of Elizabethan parish leaders was irrelevant to their behaviour towards 'moral' offences, and that economic factors were all-important. This sequence of work is relevant to the concerns of the present chapter. For if the period from 1350 to 1500 was one in which the English population did not press hard upon its resources, and therefore when poverty was relatively slight and real wages relatively high, might not this have manifested itself in a greater propensity to, and freedom for, popular celebration? Certainly Drs Wrightson and Spufford and their colleagues have between them characterized the late fourteenth and the early sixteenth centuries as periods in which the leaders of local communities made relatively little attempt to regulate the behaviour of their poorer neighbours.

In 1986, however, there appeared Marjorie McIntosh's study of the late fifteenth century,[70] which demonstrated that it was also a time marked by such concern. She found a sharp rise in prosecutions for gambling, sexual misdeeds, and alehouse-keeping, most obvious in south-eastern market towns but spread far across the country. Furthermore, her research endorsed what had earlier been believed about the relative absence of such activity in the years 1350–1450 and again 1500–50. Clearly, the upsurge between these epochs could not be explained in terms of a growing population, and she ascribed it instead to a reaction to greatly increased mobility of population as the distribution of labour adjusted to a changing pattern of geographical opportunity. Between them, her study and those cited above suggest that the evolution of seasonal celebrations continued across periods with very different levels of social concern and regulation. It may just be possible to argue that rituals which reaffirmed communal solidarity were encouraged by a situation in which mobility was the chief stress. But this notion is not supported by the evidence that the rituals continued to develop even when the perceived threat to communities was waning.

It is necessary at this point to address the fact that the process of accumulation carried on alongside one of rejection. Some communities took up customs only to drop them after a few years. The most capricious of all was of course the most sophisticated, the royal court. It took up Robin Hood plays only after 1510, when the publication of the most famous collection of tales about the hero, the *Geste*, created an enhanced interest in him. By 1520 Henry VIII and his companions had wearied of the subject, and never returned to it.[71] After 1525 they also got bored with the morris dance.[72] Commoners could also lose their taste for pastimes. The most vulnerable were, again, those involving Robin Hood. As mentioned, at Tintinhull in Somerset an ale including the theme was held 'only this once' in 1513. At other places the popularity of the outlaw lasted for a generation, but still came to an end. In another Somerset village, Croscombe, he appeared from 1475 to 1525, in the Reading parish of St Lawrence between 1498 and 1507, at Thame in Oxfordshire from 1474 to 1501, and at Henley in Buckinghamshire from 1499 to 1520. By the mid-1520s, in fact, the popularity of the Robin Hood theme was waning all over the West Midlands and the Thames basin.[73] It was easy, however, for people to get bored with a character, even featured in a series of different plots. The other seasonal pastimes endured far better, and ecclesiastical rituals, even when not actually enjoined by the Church, were difficult to shed in a society which regarded religious ceremony as a means to divine pleasure.

Nevertheless, given the increasing economic problems of many towns it would be surprising if the quantity of civic pageantry which they were supporting by 1500 did not produce some strains. There are certainly signs of these. At Coventry, which suffered a catastrophic fall in population between 1440 and 1530, there were complaints of the cost of the plays and marching watches in the 1530s. During the previous decade the corporations of Leicester and Salisbury decided to fine the masters of the towns' St George guilds if the annual 'ridings' of the saint did not take place. Norwich craft guilds had to restrict their annual feasts in 1495, 1531, and 1543 because their junior officers were leaving the town rather than pay the necessary expenses. After 1527 that dedicated to St Luke could no longer carry out its traditional responsibility for providing the Whitsun pageants. The bill had henceforth to be shared out among all the crafts. At Bristol in 1518 one of the sheriffs, William Dale, brought a legal action to recover some of his outlay upon ceremonies and entertainments, which took up fully 30 per cent of the total expenditure of his office and could not be covered by its profits. Nor was he allowed to evade any of them.[74] But complaints by guilds of the burdens of providing pageants or other contributions to urban festivity began almost as soon as the activities themselves, and it does not seem that they increased over time in the great majority of towns which have left relevant records.[75] Nor did any municipality before the Reformation deal with economic pressures by abolishing a single ceremony.

Thus, there may have been stresses in the observance of the ritual year in particular places by the 1520s, and one custom was apparently waning over a large part of its range. But these developments were more than balanced by the continued adoption of other rites and pastimes in many communities. Up till 1530 the English calendar of celebrations, like the religion to which so many of them were attached, was still flourishing and expanding rapidly along traditional lines. There was no sign of the changes which were soon to transform both almost out of recognition. Within ten years that process had begun, and its inception will be the subject of the next chapter.

3

Reformation of Religion

URING the 1970s and 1980s the English Reformation was one of the most exciting fields of historiography, both in the quantity of new research and in the controversies which this helped to generate. Much of the former consisted of local studies, each concerned with a particular city, county, or region.[1] For the purposes of this present book, however, the utility of each was limited by geographical scope, the period covered, or the balance of interests. Few gave much space to the fate of ecclesiastical rituals or any to that of secular calendar customs. The same was even more true of general surveys, of which only one was substantially devoted to these matters.[2] That survey, which represents the preliminary research for this chapter, was based upon an incomplete set of sources, ignored municipal ceremonies, and had additional preoccupations which are less relevant to this book. It was also possibly a little rash in some of its conclusions.

The main source for the impact of the Reformation at parish level consists of churchwardens' accounts, supported by information from visitation returns, corporation records, sermons, official correspondence, and literary sources. Most of the sets of accounts are incomplete, various years being unrepresented or damaged beyond legibility, or else furnishing mere annual totals of income and expenditure. In large part these faults are the work of time, personal inclination, or local tradition, but they also reflect the tensions prevailing in the period. Detailed sets often, infuriatingly, break off or become summary as the religious changes commence, and some items were erased as regimes and policies altered. Thus, of the books and rolls of accounts from the period 1535–62 which have been used for this study, representing 205 parishes,[3] only eighteen cover all those years in detail.[4] Furthermore the sample is geographically limited. The third of England north of the Trent is reflected in only a thirteenth of the accounts, while the four northernmost counties and the whole of Wales have yielded just two sets between them. The total represents only about 2 per cent of the parishes of the age. Nevertheless it is still of considerable value, for it provides our principal evidence for the rituals and celebrations carried on by the local communities of Tudor England. The sample derives from settlements of all sizes, terrains and economies, scattered widely across the southern two-thirds of England with a few examples from other regions. Most of the customs recorded in different sources upon the eve of the Reformation were the responsibility of guilds and municipalities, which have, again, left some good collections of documents.

As indicated at times in the previous chapters, the attitude of the pre-Reformation religious and secular authorities towards merry-making was not one of unqualified tolerance. Churchmen were chiefly concerned with sanctity and lay magistrates with order, and some customs offended either or both. Ecclesiastical leaders were intent above all upon ensuring that festivity did not involve the abuse of holy buildings, the temptation of clergy into indecorous behaviour, or the subtraction of audiences from religious services. This was probably true from the beginning of English Christianity: in the late tenth century a letter directed to the bishop of Sherborne forbade priests to drink at funeral wakes, while an almost exactly contemporary capitula prohibited all activities in churches except 'prayer and the love of God'.[5] From Anglo-Saxon times also date the first decrees to discourage excessive or unruly merriment upon Sundays, a theme continued all through the Middle Ages.[6] Likewise, a succession of medieval statutes, canons, sermons, and works of piety kept up a condemnation of feasting, dances, and games in either church or churchyard, especially during service time.[7] Reforming bishops of the thirteenth century tried to ensure that their clergy did not attend ales or 'summer games'.[8] How effective all these measures were is very difficult to determine. It seems, as said above, that many church ales were held in a parish house, specially built to provide a secular venue for such assemblies. A tiny number of breaches of the regulations is recorded, which may reflect a general tendency to observe them or a general tolerance of disobedience. The trivial character of the offences prosecuted suggests the former. At Ottery St Mary in east Devon, tennis matches in the churchyard were stopped by a bishop of Exeter in 1451, after the balls had caused damage. At the Hertfordshire market town of Bishops Stortford the parish 'drinking' in 1490 was definitely held in the church, but apparently not thereafter. So was the ale at Elham, near the coast of Kent, in 1511, but it was decisively 'put down'. In 1535 the curate at the Essex port of Harwich, a notable defender of the traditional religion, caught the town's youth choosing a Lord of Misrule in the nave, beat their minstrel over the head with his own pipe, and ordered them out.[9]

Occasionally the concern of the Church for its own property and personnel, and to maintain its congregations, merged into a more general distaste for festivities. The latter was propelled by two enduring themes within Christian teaching: that disorder must be as abhorrent to the divine magistrate as to the human one, and that merry-making and sins of the flesh are wont to be found in partnership. The case has already been cited of the bishop of Worcester who banned the 'Hokedays' in that city in 1450. So has that of the Winchcombe monk who complained about the midsummer fires. The angry curate at Harwich, having expelled the adolescents from his church, preached the next Sunday against dancing and piping as sinful activities in themselves. Over 200 years before, in 1303, another preacher had inveighed against 'summer games', holding that they encouraged much evil, especially lechery and pride.[10] Such attacks emerged naturally enough from a late medieval Christianity which was prone to stress the vanity of worldly joys, but seem to have been rare in the specific nature of their targets. More common were the municipal orders against mummers and Robin Hood plays, mentioned above, which were wholly motivated by a fear of crime and riot. They do not, however, seem to have become more common during the early Tudor period, any more than the complaints of churchmen about popular celebrations. As will be seen below, there was certainly a growing feeling, expressed in the Reformation Parliament, that holy days were too abundant and thus gave too many opportunities for misbehaviour. But no rites or customs observed upon them were regarded as scandalous. The poet Alexander Barclay, writing under the young Henry VIII, could speak of these days as times when 'the beastly sort' could banquet, jest, and dance. But his tone was light and he did not suggest that a reform programme was needed.[11] It seems sensible to draw from all this evidence the conclusion which Peter Burke has suggested for the whole of Europe: that popular customs and celebrations were attacked by particular authorities at specific times and places, but that there was no general campaign against them.[12] Certainly what was to follow was out of all proportion to this earlier criticism.

One charge which never seems to have featured in late medieval English denunciations of popular festivities was that they were survivals of older, pagan, religions. The latter suggestion has however aroused considerable interest among modern folklorists. This is partly because of the influence of the late nineteenth-century Cambridge School of anthropology, and in particular of Sir James Frazer, but as will be seen the preoccupation has a much longer history. It is more or less completely irrelevant to a consideration of fifteenth- and sixteenth-century calendar customs. As David Cressy has already pointed out, there is absolutely no evidence that the people who kept these customs were anything but Christian or had any notion that by carrying on these activities they were commemorating older deities.[13] Furthermore, as has been indicated above, only a few folk rituals can be traced back beyond the Christian era with any certainty. Many of those confidently labelled pagan survivals in the early twentieth century, such as mummers' plays, apple-wassailing, carrying of animal heads, maypoles, and the morris dance, may actually be nothing of the kind.[14] The description of the ritual year in about 1500, given earlier, ought to demonstrate how well the cycle of English Christian feasts had accommodated the exposition of the faith to the rhythm of the seasons. The readings given in the churches upon each holy day were intended to elucidate and to inculcate the Scriptures.[15] Those purely secular celebrations which marked some of the days were of a sort which could take their place alongside almost any religion. Medieval churchmen *did* condemn some popular practices as relics of heathenism, but all these consisted of activities belonging to the realm of magic, superstition, and divination.[16] None of the communal rites and pastimes described above were perceived as falling into this category. The question of pagan origins is not one which need enter into any discussion of attitudes to the ritual year upon the eve of the English Reformation.

Nor does it seem helpful in this context to draw distinctions between popular and élite culture or religion. These have proved valuable when considering other periods and questions, although a considerable debate has developed over the definitions and applications of the terms.[17] But they seem hardly relevant to a treatment of calendar customs in early Tudor England. Some of these, like midsummer bonfires and going a-Maying, were common alike to kings and labourers, to town and country. Some, like Robin Hood plays, seem to have begun at parish level and travelled upwards in society to the royal court. The morris dance, and perhaps the wassail cup, seem to have moved from a courtly to a popular level. The village summer lord was a much older figure than the aristocratic Lord of Misrule, but the latter may have had an independent, literary, origin. Corpus Christi processions and midsummer watches embodied within them a complete local social order. So, in its way, did the interchange between Sir Henry Willoughby and the maiden beside the St Peter's Eve bonfire, when the one gave a garland and the other a present of cash. The many ecclesiastical rituals were performed or observed by the whole of society. Only a few customs, such as Hocktide and 'hoggling', were not found above the parish level, and there they seem to have involved the miniature hierarchy of that administrative unit. The sneers of such as Barclay were directed at the behaviour of common people upon festive occasions, not at the occasions themselves.

So it is time now to consider the nature of the changes which commenced with Henry VIII's decision to become the head of the Church of England. Christopher Haigh, perhaps the most important of the recent historians of these changes, has characterized possible interpretations of them as falling into four categories: rapid reformation from above, rapid reformation from below, slow reformation from above, and slow reformation from below.[18] He himself favoured a mixture of the last two, and there will be much in this present study to support his view. But in one very significant respect, the churchwardens' accounts testify to a rapid reformation from above. They reveal that parish representatives had repeatedly to entertain or attend upon agents of the Crown, bishops, or archdeacons, who instructed and cross-examined them. Thus, the churchwardens of Yatton, in the coastal marshes of northern Somerset, had to attend visitations at Chew Magna in 1547–8, Bedminster and Wells in 1548–9, and Axbridge and Wells in 1549–50. In the single financial year 1550–1, the wardens of Stoke Charity, on the chalk downs of Hampshire, had to report twice to royal commissioners and once to the archdeacon. The villagers of Great Packington, in Warwickshire's Forest of Arden, succeeded in preserving their rood loft intact for a year after Queen Elizabeth had ordered that such structures be cut down; but then they were faced by a furious representative of the local archdeacon, and it was removed immediately.[19] Such examples are typical, and will be multiplied below. The Tudor religious reforms and counter-reforms were not measures taken by a weak and remote central government, taking many years to filter through to the provinces. They were enforced rapidly and energetically at parish level. Whether they were imposed upon willing parishioners is, however, a very different question.

The first acts of the Henrician Reformation, from 1529 to 1537, made a tremendous impact upon the English Church and helped to provoke the largest rebellion of the Tudor period, the Pilgrimage of Grace. But these measures, the establishment of the royal supremacy, the dissolution of the religious houses, the rejection of some traditional theology, and the abrogation of the cults of some saints, had little effect upon the ritual year. The main consequence was to restrict the number of holy days. In 1532, as part of their complaints about the state of the Church, the House of Commons stated that such feasts had grown too numerous, encouraging vice and idleness and diluting piety. The bishops replied that a stricter enforcement of devotion upon the days, rather than a reduction in their number, would improve the quality of religion.[20] In this as in other respects, Henry VIII took the part of the Commons, and his first injunctions as Supreme Head, in 1536, repeated their accusation. The injunction concerned went on to abolish a large number of feasts of minor patrons of parishes. It directed that all celebrations of the foundation of churches be held nationally on the same day, the first Sunday in October. It forbade any public religious services and any rest from labour between 1 July and 29 September, the time of harvest, except upon Sundays and dates dedicated to apostles and to the Virgin Mary (four in all). The royal instructions did nothing to abrogate a single seasonal rite, although they did to some extent undermine the sanctity of Candlemas candles, Ash Wednesday ashes, Palm Sunday 'palms', 'Creeping to the Cross', and the water hallowed upon Easter Eve, by insisting that these things were mere symbols and could not confer grace by themselves.[21]

As Eamon Duffy has pointed out, the abrogation of so many minor holy days was one of the biggest changes made by this stage of the Henrician Reformation, and aroused considerable popular resentment. The package also had some effect upon local seasonal customs. The abolition of the cult of St Thomas Becket (for whom, as an opponent of royal authority, Henry reserved particular venom) meant the removal of the centrepiece of Canterbury's annual marching watch. In place of the pageant of his martyrdom, the corporation hurriedly substituted some giants.[22] At the big Suffolk port of Ipswich, the Corpus Christi play was 'laid for ever aside by order' in 1531, although we shall never know why. The town's procession of pageants continued to follow the sacrament upon that feast.[23] In balance to these small losses, the reforms benefited the ritual impedimenta of some parish churches by allowing them to acquire items from a nearby religious house as the latter was dissolved. The record scoop was at Halesowen in northern Worcestershire, where the rood, organ, images, and pictures were obtained from the abbey.[24]

But then this last process overlapped with the effects of the next set of royal injunctions, which were issued in 1538 and which introduced the first major alteration in local worship. They instructed every parish to purchase a Bible; to extinguish all lights in the church except those on the altar, in the rood loft, and before the Easter sepulchre (saving illumination for a practical and not a religious purpose); to remove any images which had been 'abused with pilgrimages or offerings'; to regard the surviving representations of saints simply as memorials and to be prepared for the removal of more later; and to reject the veneration of holy relics.[25] The last direction affected only those few parishes which had relics to venerate. At Halesowen and at All Saints, Bristol, they were promptly delivered to the local bishop for destruction.[26] Four villages beside the dunes and cliffs of north Cornwall lost the major part of their Rogation week rites, which had consisted of exhibiting the bones and crosses of their patron saints upon four raised stones in the chapel yard at St Newlyn East.[27] The decree against 'abused' images halted the St George's Day procession at Canterbury, because the statue of the saint carried in it was deemed to have fallen within the prohibition. It was promptly removed from public view by the warden and curates of its church, but this was not enough for Archbishop Cranmer, whose commissary sought it out a few years later and had it broken into pieces.[28] The other St George's Day 'ridings' seem to have been maintained, but no more were instituted.

The greatest consequence of the 1538 injunctions for parish churches was the snuffing-out of the candles and lamps which had burned before saints. With them went the 'plough lights' maintained by the Plough Monday collections in East Anglia and the East Midlands, promptly extinguished like all the many others prohibited by the command. At two villages in western Norfolk and three in eastern Suffolk[29] the collections are recorded as continuing, the proceeds being added to the general church fund, but elsewhere they ceased to relate to religious matters. Such an obedience to the royal will is apparent in all the surviving sets of accounts, and is all the more impressive in that these injunctions were not enforced by the teams of visitors and commissioners which were to follow up later instructions. The obvious question is whether such acquiescence proceeded from a widespread early Protestantism or from a disinclination to resist the royal will, reinforced by the many executions following the Pilgrimage of Grace. Against the former conclusion can be pitted the conspicuous fact that the single positive injunction was also the most widely ignored. This was the purchasing of the Bible, to which the reformers appealed to justify their beliefs. Most of the accounts in the sample do not record this by the end of 1540, and most of those which do derive from London and other large towns.[30] The reason for the neglect was simple: that the order was not supported by any effective penalty. On the other hand the royal directions did have some impact upon faith as well as outward conformity, for the cult of the saints, flourishing until the 1530s, never recovered from the restrictions now placed upon it. Heavy blows were being inflicted upon traditional religion without a new one yet being substituted for it in many places.[31]

The Crown simultaneously brought another important custom to an end, by forbidding the London midsummer watch, the most famous of its kind, in 1539. Its motives for doing so seem to have been upon grounds of security, for by 1533 the royal Council was already sufficiently worried about the marching watches of Midsummer Night and St Peter's Night to consider doing away with at least some of them; a tradition which had appeared merely colourful in settled times had begun to appear menacing now that rebellion had become a real danger with the royal decision to reform the Church. To admit this would of course have been a display of weakness, and the possibility of offending local pride by prohibiting the watches was an additional deterrent to action. Thus the government hesitated until 1539 before moving against the biggest, and then pleaded a financial excuse, that the City had already been put to considerable expense for defensive measures consequent upon a threat of invasion by Catholic powers. The royal direction stated that the parade, being largely ceremonial, was an expensive waste of time when genuine military preparations were needed. It only arrived on 21 June, by which time various pageants and torches had already been prepared, and this compounded a widespread irritation at the ban among the citizens. Their feelings were, however, quite ineffectual, and from the next year their appetite for pageantry was fed instead by floats depicting Bible stories pulled through the streets before the inauguration of the year's Lord Mayor in November. Although not at first repeated annually, such displays at this purely civic occasion became during the 1540s the successors to the midsummer watches as the principal public shows of the London year.[32] In 1540 Henry made his last payment for a midsummer bonfire in his hall,[33] and with these two moves it seems that the celebrations of the metropolis upon Midsummer Eve, formerly so famous, began to wane generally. A few other corporations apparently took advantage of the developments in London to attempt a pruning of their own seasonal rituals. In 1539 that of Coventry, a town severely beset by economic and demographic decline, divided over whether or not to abolish the Corpus Christi plays and the Midsummer and St Peter's Eve watches. The mayor wrote to the royal minister most closely associated with reform, Thomas Cromwell, asking him to resolve the dispute by obtaining a royal order for the abolition. But apparently none came.[34] Likewise at Lincoln, another local capital in decline, the council considered seizing the plate of the two religious guilds which it controlled. The annual

St Anne's Day procession depended upon one of them. In the end it drew back from this step and, as at Coventry, the pageants continued.[35] At Chester the trouble was not economic but social, as the traditional Shrove Tuesday football match had run into 'great inconveniences' created by 'evil disposed persons', who presumably had exceeded even the customary levels of violence associated with the sport. It was therefore banned in 1540, and a foot-race and horse-race were substituted, with prizes awarded by the couple of trade guilds which had sponsored the match.[36]

Thus far none of the Henrician changes had extended either to removing or to instituting any category of seasonal custom. At some time in the years 1538–40 one of the government's propagandists and reformist intellectuals, Sir Richard Morison, did indeed propose to do just that. He suggested that the king forbid Robin Hood plays because they celebrated disobedience to royal officials, and issue texts of others directed against the Pope, to be performed instead at summer games. In the same period another member of this group, and client of Cromwell's, Richard Taverner, produced a book of homilies for non-preaching clergy containing the opinion that the Rogation ceremonies had been so abused by 'those uplandish processions and gangings about which be spent in rioting and in belchery' that they deserved to be abolished altogether.[37] The advice of both was, however, ignored. Instead, upon 26 February 1539, Henry proclaimed his support for a set of important ceremonies of the old Church—Candlemas candles, Ash Wednesday ashes, Palm Sunday 'palms', and 'Creeping to the Cross'—against Protestant criticism. All were justified as a means of honouring Christ or illustrating Scripture, without investing any of the objects concerned with sanctity as the traditional religion had claimed to do. In 1540 he followed this up by ordering that the Rogation processions should be held with special care because the season was one of drought and pestilence.[38] These actions were part of a series which disassociated the regime from both the former faith and from Protestantism. Others included the reaffirmation of certain points of traditional doctrine and the execution of some leading reformers. Yet what ensued in the 1540s could hardly be described as a period of reaction. In 1541 the king at last ordered all churchwardens to obtain a Bible or to pay fines. Under this pressure virtually all parishes which have left accounts did buy one within three years, although a few took longer.[39] In 1541 also he at last abrogated a ritual, although a rather marginal one, by forbidding the appearance of Boy Bishops on the grounds that they affronted the dignity of the Church.[40] In the Chapel Royal itself, the choirboys continued to receive a cash present upon St Nicholas's Day, but no little bishop appeared there again.[41] In the tiny number of parishes which observed it and which have left accounts for the years 1541–3, the custom was also terminated immediately.[42]

For the rest of Henry's lifetime, England had not so much a reformed Catholic Church as a mutilated one in decay, being picked away piecemeal. No more royal orders were issued for the removal of images, but the threat of such a step had been made in 1538. Largely because of it, but also probably because of a loss of faith in divine intercessors, only one new statue of a saint is recorded as being erected after that date,[43] in comparison with the dozens purchased in the 1520s. The same combination of factors probably accounts for the rapid decline in the number and importance of parish guilds. This was certainly warranted, for in his last year Henry took the first measures for a survey of the wealth of these bodies, intending to confiscate at least some of it.[44] In 1544 his churchmen began the process of translating the liturgy from Latin into the vernacular, by issuing a processional in English. Within the next three years the majority of churches which have left accounts recorded the purchase of it. Yet when the London and Westminster churches in that number are excluded, the majority almost vanishes, and it is probably misleading. Some country churches, scattered across England, did obtain the processional, and some in London did not, but most of the parishes which failed to buy it were either rural or in remote provincial capitals such as Worcester. The smaller number of accounts surviving from such communities produces an imbalance in the picture, and when this is appreciated the pattern indicates once more the limited interest in the positive aspects of reformation.[45]

Overall, the surviving evidence indicates that most of the traditional rituals, like the traditional ornaments, remained in English churches during Henry VIII's last years. Images were washed, utensils, banners, veils, and vestments mended or replaced, and sacred and secular ceremonies carried on much as before. But they existed upon a fragile royal sufferance. An official guide to religious belief and conduct was published in 1543 under the title *A Necessary Doctrine and Erudition of any Christian Man*, popularly known as 'The King's Book'. It placed a heavy new stress upon the traditional notion that Sunday should be devoted to worship and pious works. Indeed, it added that bodily labour was less sinful upon that day than 'vain or idle pastime' such as dancing. This threatened an end to any revels which were held on the Sabbath, either because it coincided with a calendar feast or because it happened to be the only day of the week usually free for leisure pursuits.[46] In January 1546 Archbishop Cranmer drafted a letter for Henry's signature to abolish three major rituals: ringing for the dead upon All Saints' Night, veiling images during Lent, and 'Creeping to the Cross'. He was also rumoured to have persuaded the king to order the pulling-down of roods. But all these reforms were aborted, apparently because a more conservative adviser, Stephen Gardiner, convinced Henry that his hoped-for *rapprochement* with the Catholic powers of France and the Holy Roman Empire would be endangered by them.[47] It is hardly surprising that, against such an official background, local rites were occasionally subject to neglect or abuse. At Great Witchingham in Norfolk the collections to keep the rood light burning ceased in 1543. In 1546 the traditional St John's lamp which was burned on Midsummer Eve in the hall of Lincoln's Inn, the London law school, was replaced by a horse's head. The prank was the work of three students, none of whom seem to have been Protestants and all of whom had already been in trouble for whoring, brawling, and damage to property. But their choice of target was still significant, for such ornaments had not been attacked before by the pupils of the Inns of Court, notorious as they were for endemic violence and boisterous high spirits.[48]

The four months after Henry's death, from January to May 1547, saw the last replay of the traditional spring and early summer ceremonies of Church and populace, using the accumulated props of the past few hundred years. There were a few omens of dramatic change in London. The church-wardens of St Martin Ironmonger Lane removed all its images, including the rood, and painted scriptural texts upon the walls. But they were hauled before the bishop and Lord Mayor, made excuses that they had intended to replace these objects, and were bound over to do so. The wardens of St Botolph Aldgate bought six books of psalms in English, although the curate refused to use them. Images were broken at Portsmouth.[49] These episodes are signs of the strength of Protestant feeling in certain parishes of the metropolis and in the seaport concerned. But they are completely overshadowed by the number of cases of provincial churches, extending across the country, in which new investment was made in the old order during these same months. New altar cloths and vestments were bought, roods, crosses, and rood lofts repaired, processional banners painted, and the cords which drew up rood cloths and lenten veils replaced.[50] All this argues powerfully for the conclusion that the overwhelming majority of the English certainly did not expect, and probably did not want, the reformation which was about to occur.

It began on 31 July, when the government of Lord Protector Somerset, acting for the young Edward VI, issued its first injunctions for the Church. They ordered the destruction of all shrines and pictures of saints, and of all images to which offerings had been made or before which candles had burned. They limited the number of lights in the church to two upon the high altar, doing away with those before the rood and the sepulchre. They forbade processions in or around the church when mass was celebrated, striking at one of the principal Palm Sunday ceremonies. They banned another, the making and blessing of wooden crosses, outright. And they ordered wardens to buy the *Paraphrases* of Erasmus, a favourite text of reformers. To enforce these injunctions the realm was divided into six circuits, Archbishop Cranmer and the Privy Council naming from four to six visitors for each. All the men chosen were either known Protestants or reliable servants of the regime; a carefully selected handful of activists. Their presence is recorded in all the surviving churchwardens' accounts during the rest of that year and in the next, including those for Lancashire and Cumberland. It was frequently felt heavily. Some Salisbury wardens had to produce two bills for the visitors, one certifying the condition of the church before their coming and the other detailing the changes that had been made since. At Sheriff Hutton in the farmland north of York and Banwell beside Somerset's Mendip Hills, the parish officials had to return a fresh bill after their first had been rejected. At Worfield, in the Severn valley near the southern border of Shropshire, they had to send in eight bills. At the major Yorkshire port of Hull, the visitors broke the statues in the church in person. At St Paul's Cathedral, they destroyed most of the images in September and pulled down the remainder (including the rood) two months later, at night to avoid opposition. In the West Country, and probably elsewhere, they exceeded their public instructions by forbidding ringing for the dead upon All Saints' Night. Every team made wardens present evidence on oath, and sometimes summoned other parishioners in addition to obtain alternative information.[51]

Even while the visitation was proceeding, government policy toughened. In September 1547, in response to uncertainty upon the part of the corporation of London, the privy council directed that images which had not been cult objects could also be removed if the parish priest, the churchwardens, *or* the visitors objected to them.[52] On 6 February a royal proclamation forbade four of the major ceremonies of the religious year: the blessing of candles at Candlemas, ashes upon Ash Wednesday and foliage upon Palm Sunday, and 'Creeping to the Cross'.[53] Two weeks later, the council ordered the removal of *all* remaining images, upon the grounds that their continued presence was creating dissension and disorder.[54] In the autumn of 1547, two acts of Parliament had carried the Reformation further, one instructing that the laity be allowed to drink the communion wine along with the priest and the other decreeing the seizure by the state of the endowments of chantries, religious guilds, and perpetual obits. All were institutions dedicated to prayers for the dead, and the act declared that the falsity of the doctrine of Purgatory made such supplication unnecessary. For this task the privy council employed county commissions, numbering between five and thirteen and mixing royal financial officials with local gentry. The latter were not, however, a cross-section of shire leaders but individuals handpicked for loyalty and zeal. They began their surveys in February 1548, and the expropriations after Easter.[55] Also in early 1548, Cranmer issued further articles to prohibit three Easter ceremonies: the sepulchre, the paschal candle, and the hallowing of the fire.[56]

The impact of these measures upon the parishes was profound, but slightly blurred for the historian by the fact that few accounts dated individual items, so that the precise chronology of change is usually irrecoverable. Two parishes alone show unmistakable evidence of Protestant zeal: the Sussex port of Rye, where the images were removed before September 1547 and called 'idols', and St Botolph Aldgate in London, where the congregation got rid of their curate in October after a fierce tussle with the Lord Mayor, and adopted an English service. All observers agree that images were cleared from the churches of London by the end of that year, and the surviving accounts bear this out. In the provinces the process was virtually complete by the end of 1548, in most cases as a consequence of the royal visitation, and in the autumn of 1547 the Privy Council punished two cases of resistance. Both were at market towns, St Neots in Huntingdonshire and High Wycombe in Buckinghamshire. The surviving Lancashire account does not mention the removal of images by name, but after the visitation the wardens sold much brass, pewter, and iron, which probably marks the same process. The remaining account from York records that the statues were taken away in 1547, and the curate of a living near Doncaster, in south Yorkshire, stated firmly that all in the county were plucked down by mid-1548. The only full Cornish account from these years includes the removal of the 'rood and pageants' in 1548. The last recorded clearances of images took place at St Dunstan, Canterbury, in 1549, and at Worfield in Shropshire and Ashburton in Devon during 1549–50. Thus it looks as if the campaign against representations of saints had triumphed all over England within three years, and across most of it within one. In seventeen parishes out of the 114 which have left accounts used for this study, the rood lofts themselves were demolished. No provision for this had been made in the official instructions, but as we have seen the visitors freely interpreted these. In some of the urban parishes it may have been caused by reforming enthusiasm on the part of inhabitants, but in others it may well be that the visitors found the lofts to be so heavily carved with saints as to seem worthy of complete destruction.[57]

Having no statues to veil in Lent, the churches began to part with the cloths which had served this purpose, many of them textiles of considerable beauty and value. The sale of them was recorded in some London parishes in 1547–8[58] and in some in the provinces in 1547–50,[59] and by the early 1550s, as will be described below, most had met this fate. Among the images taken down were those of St George, bringing to an end the 'ridings' upon his feast. The special significance of his cult is indicated by the fact that churchwardens tended to specify the removal of his statues (and of the horse and dragon which often accompanied one),[60] while failing to name almost any of the other saints whose representations were being stripped away. The process should in theory have left those processions, like the most famous one at Norwich, in which the part of George was played by a human actor. But they perished with the guilds which had staged them. At Norwich itself the corporation did preserve the institution, but only by removing its religious function and using its funds to clean the river. The three men appointed to arrange the annual dinner upon St George's Day 1548 flatly refused to do so unless the old situation were restored, and suffered the punishment of being disenfranchised. The dinner became a municipal feast instead, and in April 1550 the council sold all the costumes of the 'riding'. The corporation of York at first could not believe that the government intended to dissolve the city's St George guild, and sent a clerk to discover the truth and to argue for a reprieve if necessary. But none could be obtained. At Leicester the trappings of the shrine and horse were sold in 1547, and no longer was a townsman paid to act the part of the saint.[61] The government of the Protector thus made an absolute end of the custom. For a time the Crown retained its own procession and service upon St George's Day, of the Knights of the Garter, rather than abolish the principal means of display for the realm's highest chivalric order. In 1548 its rites were reformed to make them more acceptable to Protestants. But many of the latter were still offended by them, and they included the boy king himself. At one ceremony he demanded, 'What saint is Saint George that we do here honour him?' The marquis of Winchester replied gamely, 'St George mounted his charger, out with his sword and ran the dragon through with his spear.' 'And pray you my lords,' riposted Edward, convulsed with laughter, 'and what did he with his sword the while?' In 1552 the feast was struck out of the English religious calendar.[62]

The dissolution of the guilds also stopped the processions at Corpus Christi, which had depended so heavily upon these bodies. The ritual had in any case incurred the bitter hostility of Protestants, who regarded it as idolatry.[63] In parishes where it was not coupled with any guild, it ought in theory to have been able to continue, but in practice the government discouraged it so strongly in London in 1548 that no clergy dared to perform it there. As a compensation the Protector and his colleagues revived the midsummer watch that year, for once only. In 1549 neither the watch nor the processions were allowed, although many citizens kept Corpus Christi as a holiday and some priests held services.[64] News of official disapproval apparently reached provincial towns, because there likewise the processions, held as expensively as ever in 1547, did not appear the next year.[65] The celebrated cycles of plays which accompanied the feast at Coventry and York did continue, with the excision of passages which offended Protestant sensibilities. The same was true of the Chester cycle at Whitsun. But the Lincoln pageants vanished with the guild of St Anne which had sponsored them, and those at Norwich also went into abeyance after 1547.[66] Nor do the surviving records from lesser towns mention any after that year, for the rest of the reign. No churchwardens' accounts of that period contain a reference to the village plays at Corpus Christi which had been a feature of the early Tudor age. The greatest drama of the feast survived, but all the luxuriant undergrowth of pageantry and plays had vanished, withering with the processions under the eye of a hostile regime.

All the other ecclesiastical ceremonies proscribed by the government were as swiftly abandoned. After the proclamation of 6 February 1548 there is no more sign in either accounts or contemporary comment of Candlemas candles, Ash Wednesday ashes, Palm Sunday 'palm', and 'Creeping to the Cross'. The curate serving in south Yorkshire stated specifically that all were forbidden there that spring.[67] The reforms of 1547–8 left only one Palm Sunday ceremony still legal, the appearance of the 'prophet' and the reading or singing of the Passion. None the less, people seem to have been discouraged from providing that also, either actively or because the removal of so much else deprived it of a context. In Yorkshire in 1548 it was replaced by a sermon.[68] It vanishes from the surviving London accounts after 1547. Only at two parishes in the sample, one in Reading and one in Bristol, did it last longer. There it persisted until 1549, when it was abandoned as part of the complete reform of the liturgy.[69] In 1548 the government expressed its dislike of Whitsun processions as well as those at Corpus Christi. This prevented them in London, and the most elaborate recorded in the provinces, at Leicester, was also abandoned.[70]

The campaign launched by Cranmer against the principal remaining Easter rituals was equally effective. In 1548 the sepulchre was no longer watched in London or Westminster at any of the churches which have left accounts.[71] The same is true of most of the rest of the country, both in towns and villages. In many cases the sepulchre itself was sold (if it happened to take the form of a box) or hacked down (if it was a stone structure), during this year and the next. At the important administrative centre of Ludlow in Shropshire, at one Canterbury parish and one at Worcester, and at the southern Lancashire village of Prescot, the sepulchre was prepared and watched in 1548; clearly its pattern of survival by then owed more to the strength of local feeling than to a remote or rural situation. This impression is strengthened by the survival that year of the sepulchre in at least two cathedrals. One was Worcester, where the chapter compromised by dropping the hallowing of the Easter Eve fire but retaining the other Easter rites. The other was Winchester, and the appearance of the sepulchre there resulted in the summoning of the bishop, the once-powerful conservative Gardiner, before the Privy Council to apologize. He defended himself by insisting, quite correctly, that the ceremony was still lawful, and suffered no direct penalty.[72] The episode must, none the less, have helped to ensure what followed; that after Easter 1548 there is only one, very doubtful, mention of the existence of the custom anywhere in England as long as Edward lived.[73] Almost exactly the same rate of decline beset Cranmer's other targets, the paschal candle and the blessing of the fire upon Easter Eve. The former is recorded in 1548 only at Prescot, Ludlow, Halesowen in north Worcestershire, two Oxford parishes, the market town of Bungay in Suffolk, and Worcester cathedral, where it was set up but not blessed.[74] There is no trace of it in 1549. The fire was blessed at an Oxford parish in that latter year,[75] but it is recorded nowhere else, and by 1550 the rite seems to have vanished.

Given that the archbishop had already tried, in the previous reign, to abolish ringing for the dead on the feast of All Saints, it would have been most unlikely had he not attempted to accomplish this in the much more promising circumstances of 1547–8. After all, the custom was linked to the doctrine of Purgatory, which was officially condemned in those years. Yet the injunctions, proclamations, acts, and articles seem to have ignored it, and it might be easy to conclude that there was no official prohibition were it not for the chance survival of a letter from the royal visitors to the West Country, mentioned earlier. If the other teams enforcing the injunctions made the same addition, then this would help to explain why the ringing atrophied at the same rate as the other old ecclesiastical rituals. In

1548 it vanished from virtually all the parishes in which it is recorded till then. The exceptions are Halesowen (again), North Elmham in central Norfolk, and the market town of Thame in eastern Oxfordshire. At Thame the ringers were heard again in 1549, but then the payment to them ceased.[76] A similar fate met the Rogation processions around the parish bounds and fields. The panoply of crosses, banners, and holy water employed in these would have been offensive to Protestants, but the directives of the Crown and bishops seem to have passed over them. We are left to wonder what the visitors had to say, and to reflect upon the testimony of the Greyfriars Chronicle and of Robert Parkyn, the curate near Doncaster. The former states that the processions were stopped in London by governmental direction in 1548, and the latter that none took place in his area during that summer, because the crosses at which they had halted were being thrown down.[77] Such a campaign helps to explain the general collapse of the ritual during that year. It vanishes from those accounts in which it had been recorded up till then.[78] Only at Long Sutton in the Lincolnshire Fens is there any mention of the perambulations in 1548, and after then it ceased there as well.[79] In the next three years many parishes, in both town and country, sold off the banners which had been carried on them.

Thus, within eighteen months of its inception, the government of Protector Somerset had virtually demolished the seasonal rituals of the English Church and the ornaments and institutions which had underpinned them. In 1549 it proceeded to build upon the ruins by publishing its new liturgy, the Book of Common Prayer, prescribed by a parliamentary Act of Uniformity. It rendered the whole service into English, confirmed the abolition of the old feast days and ceremonies, and expunged prayers to individual saints and for intercession on behalf of the dead. With the force of statute behind it, the book was obtained by every parish from which accounts survive from that year, apparently by the specified date of Whit Sunday.[80] This provided the climax to a remarkable achievement of 'rapid reformation', and the obvious question to ask about it is how much it was driven on by the bombardment of official visitations and how much by Protestant enthusiasm at parish level. One test of the problem is to examine the evidence for positive inculcation of the Protestant message in the same accounts. In 1547 the government sponsored the publication of a *Book of Homilies*, sermons upon key topics and doctrines which could be read by clergy incapable of preaching. During the reign of Edward this was purchased by only twenty out of the 134 parishes in the sample from this period. The majority which did not obtain the volume were precisely those provincial communities where the priest would most need it. The government had more success with the English translation of the *Paraphrases* of Erasmus, probably because its purchase was enjoined by royal injunction. Of the parishes in the sample, forty-two had bought it before the end of 1548, and another twelve by the end of Edward's reign. How far this lively but scholarly work was understood by parishioners is, however, a different matter, and some of the entries recording the purchase do not encourage optimism. In the accounts of Yatton, Somerset, the book is called 'The Paraphrases and Erasmus', in those of St Dunstan, Canterbury, 'Parasimus', and in those of Sheriff Hutton, near York, 'Coloke of Herassimus'.[81]

The most complete success of the regime in ensuring the local acquisition of a Protestant work, the Prayer Book of 1549, directly and immediately provoked the bloodiest rebellion of the century. It covered all of Cornwall and Devon except the city of Exeter, where (as one citizen recorded) there were many who sympathized with the religious convictions of the rebels but put loyalty to Crown and city first.[82] Both the motivation of the rising and its demands included economic and social as well as pious elements, but there is no doubt that it intended to reverse the Reformation carried out over the previous two years.[83] Our only surviving Cornish churchwardens' account for the year, from Stratton at the far north end of the county, shows the parishioners restoring the rood and 'pageants' taken down a short while before, only to remove them again when the rebellion failed.[84] The absence of effective opposition to the rebels across the entire West Country, save at Exeter, is striking and significant. Instead the government needed its own armed forces to crush them, and these required three pitched battles to do the work, which were arguably won only because the westerners lacked cavalry and cannon. There was simultaneous unrest in the southern Midlands, expressing the same hostility towards the recent religious changes, and once again the Privy Council crushed it brutally.[85] The power and energy of the Council of the North kept that region fairly quiet, doubtless aided by the execution of so many religious conservatives after the Pilgrimage of Grace. But the appearance of the Prayer Book was still followed by a rising on the Yorkshire Wolds which lasted weeks and involved thousands before the Council routed it.[86] Only in East Anglia and the South-East is there no sign of widespread popular protest against the Edwardian Reformation that summer. The risings there, although very widespread, were almost wholly concerned with social and economic issues. That in Norfolk, indeed, complained of the inadequacy of the local clergy and asked for better preaching in a way with which Protestants would have sympathized. On the other hand it is perhaps notable that one of the assemblies which produced it was at Wymondham, where the people gathered to celebrate the feast of St Thomas Becket which had been abolished by Henry VIII.[87] None the less, the pattern of rebellion in that summer argues for a fairly wide measure of popular acceptance of the reforms since 1547 in the south-eastern quarter of the country. Elsewhere the energy of the visitations had clearly been the principal force behind the changes, so effective in enforcing the government's will that it left local people with no other choice than acquiescence or armed resistance.

From the point of view of the present book, it is particularly interesting that the regime of Protector Somerset had almost as shattering an effect upon the secular or semi-secular customs of the ritual year. Of the eighteen parishes which were regularly holding church ales in the early 1540s and which have also left good accounts for the reign of Edward, sixteen gave them up in the period 1547–9.[88] Whereas they are scattered across southern and midland England, the remaining two are both villages in one district of Oxfordshire,[89] where there is also evidence for ales at a third in the early 1550s.[90] In addition, one Somerset village was holding them at the same time,[91] but there is no trace of any other in the whole body of rural accounts preserved from the last four years of the reign. It may well have been as part of the same process that Wandsworth, then a Surrey village fairly near London, sold its maypoles in the year 1547–8.[92] Three villages at which the 'hogglers' or 'hognells' had collected have left accounts for the years 1547–51, and at each there is no more reference to them after 1547.[93] They appear nowhere in the later part of Edward's reign. The Hocktide captures and payments in the streets of provincial towns are documented at seven parishes which have left accounts for 1545–50; in every one they had ceased by 1549.[94] Again, there is no sign of them anywhere in the early 1550s.

Exactly the same is true of those Plough Monday gatherings which had continued to contribute to parochial finances in the 1540s. Three of them were in villages which have left good accounts for the period of Somerset's rule, and in every one they had ceased by 1548.[95] At Holbeach in the Lincolnshire Fens, the plough was cleared out of the church along with the images in 1547, and the stand upon which it had been mounted was sold off.[96] Accounts survive also from one of the midland villages where money had been collected around a dancing hobby-horse, Yoxall in Staffordshire's Needwood Forest. This also halted in 1547. At Holme Pierrepont in the Trent valley of Nottinghamshire a rate was settled on the parish in 1552 because its previous main source of income, 'gatherings with a hobby horse and lights', had been prohibited in the recent past.[97] In the period 1547–8 the London churches ceased to be decorated with birch at midsummer, roses at Corpus Christi, and garlands on Ascension Day. Holly and ivy continued to appear at Christmas in only one of those which has left records,[98] and vanish from the parish accounts of Bristol and Chester. The famous Coventry midsummer watches continued, but those upon St Peter's Eve were abolished in 1549.[99] As mentioned above, the government permitted the revival of the London Midsummer Eve parade in 1548, using soldiers destined for the war in Scotland. But it drew together 'a great rabble of the worst sort' (in the words of one anonymous observer) and was not repeated.[100] Records do not permit any knowledge of the fortunes of the other marching watches during the reign.

There is evidence that this atrophy of popular celebrations was the direct result of official hostility. The royal visitors to the West in 1547 forbade church ales because of the 'many inconveniences' arising, which they claimed had been reported to them.[101] A complete lack of data prevents us from determining whether those upon other circuits behaved differently and whether the survival of ales in central Oxfordshire was due to a more lenient local policy. In the same year the Corporation of London encouraged property-owners to punish their servants for attending May games. In 1549 it positively ordered them to do so, and directed them to apply the prohibition to 'youth' in general.[102] Since the riots of 1517 the maypole of record height which had stood in Cornhill had been hung on hooks in an alley. In 1549 a Protestant curate denounced it as an idol and some of his audience chopped it into pieces and burned them.[103] In May 1553 another pole was brought into Fenchurch parish which excited the admiration of many observers. It was painted white and green, and accompanied by a crowd of people in the same colours with a model giant and a morris troupe. They also erected a castle of gilded panels, with silk streamers. The response of the Lord Mayor was to take 'counsel' and to have pole and fortress broken up.[104] These examples can be multiplied by more from the provinces. The royal visitors forbade Plough Monday gatherings in southern Yorkshire, upon the grounds that they caused drunkenness and brawls. Henceforth both the owner of the plough and the households who gave money were to be fined.[105] If the teams in other parts of eastern England had made the same prohibition, it would explain the disappearance of the custom from the East Anglian accounts. The royal injunctions which they were enforcing directed that upon Sundays the populace should give themselves 'entirely to God', following church services with private prayer. By implication, they therefore struck at the summer games, which could most easily be held upon the day free from work. Bishop John Hooper went on specifically to condemn revels upon it.[106]

When all these official directions are joined with the collapse of ceremony and festivity recorded in the accounts, it becomes easy to understand why grumbles were heard that the Protestant Reformation had destroyed a happy society. In 1552 Dr John Caius either coined or appropriated what was to become an enduring expression, when he wrote of 'the old world, when this country was called merry England.'[107] Behind the reformers' attitudes seems to have lain a mixture of motives. A very powerful one was the fear of riot and rebellion during a period characterized not only by dramatic religious change but by inflation and harvest failure. This theme is clear enough in some of the pronouncements cited above, and there was a lot of historical justification for it. The Peasants' Revolt of 1381, Jack Cade's Rebellion in 1450, and the Prayer Book Rising of 1549 all broke out during the Whitsun holidays. So did local riots during the early Tudor period. The disturbances in London upon 'Evil May Day' 1517, directed against foreign merchants, have been mentioned, as has the assembly to celebrate the feast of St Thomas which helped to spark off the Norfolk revolt of 1549.[108] Any event which convened people in large numbers with leisure to discuss current affairs and alcohol to fuel their opinions was going to be treated warily by an insecure regime. But the injunction regarding Sunday reflected a different preoccupation, a restatement of the traditional Christian aspiration towards a greater godliness in society. And the animosity displayed by the preacher towards the Cornhill maypole embodied a Protestant rejection of material symbols and images which had not been present in the late medieval Church.

The reign of Edward did not bring all the traditional seasonal celebrations to an end. The dean and chapter of Chester cathedral still paid for a midsummer bonfire. In 1552 the corporation of Leicester noted that the citizens were still decorating their houses with boughs during summer holy days and ordered them to cut the foliage outside the town instead of from gardens.[109] The survival of a few church ales has been remarked upon. Furthermore, the government had no objection to festivities provided that they were officially sponsored and monitored, or at least supportive of its policies. The royal court itself held expensive revels at Shrovetide, with masks, costumes, and torches. Much of the theatrical activity in them consisted of parodying Catholic priests. There was also, under Somerset, a strong martial theme, as the Protector was bent upon eulogizing his campaigns in Scotland.[110] Secular civic pageantry developed in the metropolis to replace some of that swept away by religious reformation. Much of it had a comic and satiric theme which ran parallel to the abuse levelled by reformers against the old Church. At Easter 1553, for example, the sheriff of London rode through the streets followed by giants, morris dancers, and a piece of theatre to celebrate the death of Lent. The latter included Jake-of-Lent himself, his wife, a physician, and a cleric, all upon horseback and playing their parts with rough humour.[111]

It is not surprising, therefore, that Edward's reign was probably the golden age of the Lord of Misrule. This was one seasonal figure whom Henry VIII had not come to reject along with Robin Hood, the Boy Bishop, and the morris dance. Indeed, during the 1540s the old monarch tried consciously to propagate the fashion for him. In 1545 he wrote into the statutes of St John's College, Cambridge, which had been founded by his mother, a clause directing that its Christmas festivities should be supervised by such a 'lord'. The office was to be undertaken by each Fellow in turn, and he had to stage a fresh spectacle upon every one of the twelve nights. At neighbouring Trinity, founded in the following year, the same office was instituted at once.[112] Either its responsibilities or the excesses committed by its occupants soon became too much for the university, because at some time between 1548 and 1550 the heads of colleges agreed that nobody should be 'a lord of games at Christmas in whatever way he is titled'. This prohibition did not, however, extend to the summer season, and in May 1553 a 'Lord of St Andrew and his company' (parodying the hated Catholic primate of Scotland) was going around Cambridge collecting money.[113] At Oxford and in urban corporations the mock rulers continued to flourish in the face of royal approval. The Shrewsbury 'Abbot of Marham' embodied yet another opportunity to poke fun at the former religion, while at Gloucester the mayor, instead of appointing an 'abbot' of his own, invited the one attached to a gentleman's household to visit the city, band playing, at Christmas 1550.[114]

All these figures, naturally, paled beside that of George Ferrers, who brought the office of royal Lord of Misrule to its apogee in the last two years of the reign. He combined the traditional fun of inversion and parody with a dash of Renaissance metaphysics, both supported by considerable expense. At one Christmas he made his appearance out of a moon, at the next from 'a vast airy space'. He had his own coat of arms (a hydra) and his own crest (a holly bush). His retinue consisted of three pages, eight councillors, a clergyman, a philosopher, an astronomer, a poet, a physician, an apothecary, a Master of Requests, a civil lawyer, a fool, a Master of Horse, an ambassador (who spoke nonsense and was partnered with an interpreter), two gentlemen, jugglers, acrobats, comic friars, and guardsmen. His spectacles in the 1552–3 season included a triumphal entry, a naval battle on the Thames, a hunt, and a hobby-horse joust. His own robes were blue (for his entry), white (for his Christmas Day feast), red (upon New Year's Day), and purple (when he rode forth from court). He seems to have been chosen by the permanent Master of the Revels, but devised all his own entertainments and specified the money required for them. That his requirements were met seems largely due to the wish of the Privy Council to keep its boy monarch delighted. The first performances provided by Ferrers were said to have been commissioned by the new leader of the government, the Duke of Northumberland, in order to divert Edward's thoughts from the execution of its former leader, the fallen Lord Protector Somerset.[115]

Furthermore, George Ferrers could divert the Londoners as well. One of his annual escapades was to make a state entry into the capital, and to be welcomed by the sheriff's Lord of Misrule who had his own musicians and retainers in liveries of blue and white. The royal Lord was dressed at his grandest, in purple trimmed with ermine and braided with silver, and his followers included bagpipers, morris dancers, and gaolers bearing instruments of punishment. They would all ride through the City, the mock-sheriff bearing a sword of state before his royal equivalent, and deliver a comic proclamation. Ferrers then pretended to knight the sheriff's man and gave him a rich gown, while the 'royal cofferer' threw coins to the crowd. All then made procession again and were feasted by the Lord Mayor or the Lord Treasurer until dusk, when the royal retinue took boat again for Edward's winter residence of Greenwich. The spectacle impressed observers so much that all contemporary chroniclers or diarists recorded it.[116]

The regime of Protector Somerset was regarded by Protestants at the time, and has been characterized by historians since, as relatively moderate, cautious, and willing to compromise in the work of reform. Yet its impact upon the ritual year in England, and the ecclesiastical setting within which many of those rituals had been set, had been devastating. In this respect, all that the succeeding 'radical' administration of Northumberland had to do was mop up, by replacing the altars with communion tables, confiscating the now obsolete church goods, and revising the Prayer Book. In fourteen parishes in the sample, altars were removed under Somerset's rule. A third were in the capital but the others were scattered across nine counties from Devon to Sussex and Cheshire to Norfolk, in both town and country. The evidence does not allow us to determine in each case whether this was the result of local Protestant feeling or of a dislike taken by royal or ecclesiastical visitors to carvings upon the structure. In April 1550 Nicholas

Ridley, the new bishop of London, instituted a campaign to take down the rest. By the end of the year this had happened, not merely in every church in his diocese from which accounts survive but from all those in the sample from Bristol and some from a range of shires as distant from the capital as Devon, Worcestershire, and Yorkshire. Again, it is difficult to tell how much of this was due to the continuing barrage of visitations and how much to parochial protestantism. Whichever was true, the Privy Council could only have been exaggerating slightly, if at all, when it wrote to the bishops in November to claim that most of the altars in the nation had been taken down. It added a command to have the rest removed, to prevent disputes. This, driven home by more visitations, was complied with by virtually all the remaining parishes which have left accounts within one year: only Thame, already noted as a centre of conservatism, managed to postpone the work until December 1552.[117]

The government's campaign to lay its hands upon the church goods illustrates very neatly the extent of the power which it could bring to bear upon local communities. In 1547 the Privy Council ordered the bishops to ensure that inventories were made of the metal and textile ornaments kept by each church. Three years later county commissioners were appointed to repeat this process, and in January 1553 another set of commissions was issued, with instructions to seize all the surviving goods except linen, chalices, and bells. Plate, money, and jewels were to be sent to London, while robes, cloths, and base metals were to be sold locally and the proceeds sent up. All the surviving churchwardens' accounts register the activities of the commissioners, local worthies hand-picked for their obedience or enthusiasm. The wardens of Harwich had their initial inventory rejected, and the acceptance of the second postponed until the whole commission was present. The vicar of Morebath, on the Devon side of Exmoor, was interrogated four times over. After visiting the commissioners for the North Riding of Yorkshire five times and writing to them once, the wardens of Sheriff Hutton attended the Council of the North in a desperate attempt to save some of their church's goods. The only straightforward way for parishes to keep ornaments and vestments out of the government's hands was to sell them for their own profit before the commissioners arrived. Indeed, seventy-one sets of accounts in the sample record such sales between 1548 and 1552. Most occurred in London and the south-eastern counties, both more Protestant and (arguably) more conscious of the government's intentions.[118] The surviving inventories obtained by the commissioners[119] tell the same story. Thefts of goods, although nothing like as numerous as sales, had been very common. By 1552 most churches still had vestments and altar ornaments. But the Lenten veils, rood cloths, processional banners, and canopies for the sacrament were mostly gone.

The new Prayer Book was first read at St Paul's Cathedral upon All Saints' Day 1552, and did away with the name of 'mass', the sign of the cross, prayers for the dead, and priestly vestments, altering the communion service to a set of clearly Protestant formulae. The feast of All Saints was one of the few left to the Church by that date, following the further purge carried out by a parliamentary statute earlier in the year.[120] It abolished all days of individual saints except apostles, evangelists, Stephen the first martyr, and the archangel Michael. To these it added only Sundays, New Year's Day, Twelfth Day, Candlemas, the Annunciation, Ascension Day, Midsummer Day, All Saints, Holy Innocents, and the two days after Easter and Whitsun as permitted times of worship and recreation. Popular holy days such as those of St Nicholas and St George were consigned to oblivion.

In assessing how much the Edwardian reforms had altered the old ways, there are two main groups of evidence to add to that of the churchwardens' accounts. One consists of visitation returns and church court records, which bear out the impression left by the accounts of rapid and successful external enforcement. In Kent in 1548 people from just three parishes were accused of having failed to deface images removed from churches, and only one rector was summoned for having continued the ceremonies of paschal candle and Easter sepulchre. In late 1550, before altars were proscribed by the Privy Council, Archbishop Cranmer's officials were hounding members of fourteen Kentish parishes for not destroying them with sufficient speed, and excommunicating two priests until this was done. In Lancashire in 1552 a total of four parishes admitted to having failed to remove altars, and in Wiltshire in 1553 a single village confessed to having one. In the archdeaconry of Norwich in 1549, none of the parishes admitted to preserving images, tabernacles, or the old rituals. In the diocese of Ely during the whole of Edward's reign, visitations caused some concern about the quality of the clergy and their performance of the Protestant service, but none about the adaptation of the churches for Protestant worship. For Wales there exist no comparable records, but evidence of a sort is provided by the lament of a Glamorgan poet written near the end of the reign. He describes churches virtually empty of altars, roods, pyxes, and holy water stoops. The accounts suggest that the visitation returns were correct, and put together, all these sources bear witness both to a swift obedience to the reforms and to a ruthless enforcement of them upon the recalcitrant.[121]

But all this is an indication of external pressure. It is the other important category of evidence which provides our only insight into the process of alteration of belief: that of wills. A generation ago historians recognized that the formulae by which testators bequeathed their souls varied according to their theology. An adherent of the old Church and one of Protestantism would be strongly differentiated by the form of words employed, and thus wills could be used as a means to trace altering patterns of faith. It has subsequently been agreed that they may not, and in some cases certainly do not, reflect the views of the dying person so much as those of the clergy or scriveners who drew them up. But even when this is taken into account they can still act, like rebellions, as crude indicators of local belief, and they do show important changes over time. At present we have studies of their evidence for London, Kent, East Sussex, York, Yorkshire, Nottinghamshire, Devon, and Cornwall—three corners of the realm.[122] Unfortunately they do not share the same timescales and set of categories, but the following conclusions can be drawn from them. In London over the whole reign of Edward, 24 per cent of wills were traditional, 32 per cent Protestant, and 44 per cent avoided commitment to either. In Kent traditional wills fell from 39 per cent in 1547 to 6 per cent in 1553, and Protestant examples rose from 6 per cent to 8 per cent, 'neutral' formulae (which the writer concerned terms 'reformed') climbing from 52 per cent to 82 per cent. In East Sussex the drop in the traditional kind was from 70 per cent to 8 per cent, the increase in the Protestant sort from 1 per cent to 17 per cent, and that of the 'neutral' variety from 7 per cent to 66 per cent. At York most wills remained traditional in form, and the Protestant formulae comprised a total of 8.8 per cent. But in its county and in Nottinghamshire the old formulae sank to a minority in 1549 and by 1551 were only a third of the total; the scholar in question did not distinguish Protestant from neutral kinds. Finally, Protestant wills in Cornwall and Devon are said to have increased from 10 per cent in 1547–9 to 37 per cent in 1550–3. These figures, however, are so out of harmony with all the rest that we are left to wonder whether the South-West was evangelized to a remarkable degree or whether the historian concerned employed different definitions when consulting his material. Despite the problems of collating these studies, they do show an overall pattern. In all but one case traditional assertions of faith, used almost without exception in the 1520s, had fallen to a minority by the latter part of Edward's reign. But nowhere had Protestant formulae become a majority instead. It was, rather, the wills which avoided any explicit declaration of allegiance which had come to be the most common variety. This is powerful additional evidence for the argument that the Edwardian Reformation had been a tremendous destructive force but had achieved only a limited constructive impact.

And that achievement was now, of course, to be put to the most severe possible test, as Edward died and his sister Mary seized the throne in July 1553, determined to restore the old Church. At once she declared a temporary toleration of both creeds. In December a Parliament repealed the reforming statutes of Edward's reign and restored the service of 1546, whereupon the queen ordered every parish to build an altar and to hallow ashes upon Ash Wednesday, foliage upon Palm Sunday, and water on Easter Eve. In March she issued injunctions for the resumption of all former seasonal processions and all the old 'laudable and honest ceremonies'. Thus, within nine months the new regime had ordered the revival of the late medieval ecclesiastical year, with the exception of the minor feasts abolished in 1536.[123] The fact that most churchwardens did not date individual entries vitiates attempts to assess how much parishioners and priests anticipated the Crown's actions during the period of 'liberty' from July to December. But some certainly did. At Stratton, Cornwall, vestments were repurchased, a canopy for the sacrament made, and tapers bought, as soon as Mary took power. The wardens of Stanford, in Berkshire's White Horse Vale, sold the communion table with a reference to the past 'wicked time of schism'. Before October the high altar was made at Harwich and the mass restored at Halse in Somerset's Vale of Taunton Deane. In the London church of St Dunstan in the West, both altar and mass were back by the end of September. These hints bear out the picture presented by the literary sources, of a slight spontaneous revival of Catholicism in the capital and a more pronounced one in the provinces. It was a distinctly more impressive anticipation of policy than that accorded to Edward's Reformation in 1547, but the Protestants in those months, unlike the Catholics in 1553, had no legal freedom to act.[124]

Once the administrative machinery had been captured by the proponents of counter-reformation, it was worked with all the vigour which Protestants had given it. Metropolitan, episcopal, and archidiaconal visitations and royal commissioners passed through the provinces, and wardens were constantly returning inventories and statements to them. In December 1553 the Privy Council imprisoned a man from Maidstone, Kent, who had sponsored a petition for Protestantism in his parish, while in March it made four Essex gentry give bonds to erect altars in their respective parish churches. The wardens of St Pancras Soper Lane, in London, were ordered by Cardinal Pole's commissioners in 1555 not merely to rebuild a rood loft but to make it 5 feet long, with images, and to complete the work in 6 weeks. Those of another, the very Protestant community of St Botolph Aldgate, found themselves forced by Bishop Bonner to impose a rate to raise money for extensive rebuilding. In 1556 metropolitan visitors instructed those of St Neots, a Huntingdonshire market town, to rebuild every altar which had stood in their church in King Henry's time, within one month. Those of Bromfield, an Essex village, were excommunicated in 1558 because their church contained no images, while during two months in 1554 the wardens of Harwich, despite their previous enthusiasm, had to return three successive bills to the queen's commissioners.[125] All these places were in the more heavily Protestantized South-East.

Accounts from Mary's reign for 168 parishes have been employed for this book. They show a considerable homogeneity in the restoration of Catholic worship. By the end of 1554 all had rebuilt a high altar, and obtained vestments and copes, some or all of the utensils and ornaments of the mass, and some or all of the necessary books. During the remainder of the reign they added to this equipment, and most acquired a rood with flanking figures of Mary and John, some images or paintings of saints, a side altar, rood light, altar cloths, banners for processions, and a canopy. All the parishes which had removed their rood lofts under Edward, and for which records survive under Mary, rebuilt them. Where the purchase of items is not recorded, this may often mean that they were brought out of hiding or returned, and the frequent entries for mending old ornaments bear this out. In many parishes, a wooden crucifix was bought at first, to be replaced by a silver or gilded one, and the rood, Mary, and John were painted on a cloth until carved wooden figures could be paid for. The process slackened only slightly after the first year, and most of the parishes in the sample were carrying out further embellishments until the moment of Mary's death. The majority of these acquisitions were compulsory: the high altar and mass from December 1553, rood lofts and the rood, Mary, and John, from 1555, and images of patron saints of parishes by 1556. Yet many of the churches in the sample were decorated more lavishly than the law required.[126]

Within this setting, the restoration of ritual was fairly complete. Every church in the sample readopted the paschal candle. It is likely that the kindling of the holy fire and blessing of the font upon Easter Eve, so fundamental to Catholic practice, was also brought back universally. Certainly payments for coals for the fire are recorded for much the same proportion of parishes as under Henry VIII, twenty-five in the sample, virtually all of which were in towns, where this fuel was more economical.[127] The purchase of rood cloths, for the ceremonies of Lent and Palm Sunday, is specified at thirty-five places,[128] and is probably concealed by the general references to 'cloths' at many others. The veiling of the rood, together with the paschal candle, blessing of ashes and 'palms', Candlemas candles, and 'Creeping to the Cross', were rituals enforced by the visitations of Archbishop Pole of Canterbury and Bishop Bonner of London, and probably of other prelates.[129] The apparent lack of prosecutions consequent upon them would indicate that all were indeed widely readopted, although in the cases of the ashes, 'palms', and 'Creeping' the accounts cannot provide evidence as none needed parochial expenditure. None the less the adoration of the crucifix is recorded at Cambridge and at Tarring in western Sussex, and one of the London chronicles states that it was generally restored in the capital.[130] 'Palms' for Palm Sunday are mentioned at urban churches which had no easy access to woodland.[131] The purchase of 'trendles' to hold Candlemas tapers, and sometimes of the candles themselves, is entered in fifteen sets of accounts from all over southern England; much the same proportion and range as before the Edwardian Reformation.[132]

The Easter sepulchre was made compulsory in London in 1554[133] and features in eighty-four of the 168 sets of Marian accounts. As more villages are represented in them than in those from the early sixteenth century, this reflects about as wide a distribution as before, comprising all urban and many rural communities. The singing of the Passion upon Palm Sunday reappeared in a few urban parishes,[134] although its 'prophet' is apparently only recorded at Chester Cathedral, where he was rewarded with a jug of malmsey and a pair of gloves.[135] The ringing of bells for the dead after dark on All Saints' Day features in the accounts of twenty parishes from Devon to Lincolnshire, both urban and rural settlements.[136] This is as large a proportion as before the Reformation, and many parishes do not appear to have needed to pay for it as the Elizabethan evidence (to which we shall come) indicates that it was very common. The hanging of a brass or gilded star at Epiphany was always rare, and it is no surprise to find it under Mary only in two Chester churches.[137] The Boy Bishops seem only to have been reintroduced to London, although there they were clearly popular. On St Nicholas's Day 1554 a royal order specifically prohibited them, apparently because they would distract attention from the great ceremony of reconciliation with the papacy which was taking place on that date. But at least three City parishes defied the ban. By 1556 they were 'abroad the most part in London singing after the old fashion, and received with many good people into their houses, and had such good cheer as ever they had'. This was repeated in 1557.[138] The parish of St Mary at Hill recorded the purchase of a crucifix, mitre, and book for one. In St Katherine's, a woman who refused to admit the little bishop in 1556 was faced by an angry priest backed by a crowd, and had to make excuses for her behaviour.[139] The 'St Nicholas box' recorded at Prescot, in the Mersey valley of Lancashire, may indicate the presence of the custom, but otherwise the only provincial traces of it during Mary's reign are in cathedrals. The Boy Bishop from St Paul's sang before the queen. The sermon of one at Gloucester was published, although (or, rather, because) it was written by a prebendary.[140]

The most glamorous of the processions restored by the queen's proclamation were those at Corpus Christi. In that first year, of 1554, it was neglected by some London parishes, and a joiner tried to snatch the sacrament from one crossing Smithfield.[141] But from 1555 it is recorded in all the surviving sets of City churchwardens' accounts except one,[142] and in all those left to us from Bristol. Mary and her consort Philip led the progress of the host around their palace.[143] The ritual was also definitely revived at York, Chester, Lincoln, Norwich, Newcastle-upon-Tyne, Canterbury, Cambridge, and Coventry.[144] At Norwich the corporation set up a tree hung with 'flowers, grocery and fruit', and the grocers' guild paid for a carved and gilded griffon (its emblem) carried by three ladies, a pennant-bearer in a yellow wool coat, a 'crowned angel', and flowers bound in coloured thread. Other Corpus Christi processions wound their way around the towns of Dover, Bungay in Suffolk's Waveney valley, Ludlow, Sherborne in Dorset, Ashburton in Devon, and Louth on the Lincolnshire coast, and through several market towns and villages in Buckinghamshire, Kent, and Surrey. Just as before Edward's reign, they seem to have been mainly an urban phenomenon, although clearly now present in some rural communities of the South-East.[145] The Whitsun processions are likewise recorded in the same measure as before, being found at York, Leicester, Bristol, and London. It is noticeable, however, that the Leicester examples, formerly the most elaborate, were revived with much reduced expenses.[146] The royal couple personally encouraged the cult of St George, Philip leading the Knights of the Garter in procession upon his feast day in 1555. The column of dignitaries included priests in copes embroidered with gold, and three cross-bearers.[147] At York in 1554 the corporation ordered that on his day St George 'be brought forth and ride as hath been accustomed'. The next year he was accompanied by a dragon, St Christopher, a mock-king and mock-queen, and a 'May'. The riding at Leicester was also restored by that municipality, while at Norwich the city fathers resolved in 1555 to refound the saint's guild and his procession as of old. The saint also reappeared in the streets of Chester.[148] His images were set up again in parish churches in Devon, Essex, and Worcestershire, and may also have been carried in procession there.[149] Still, as before, the parades featuring George seem to have been few compared with those at Rogationtide. Once again, the sovereigns encouraged a revival both by admonition and example, Mary sending many of her own clergy to bless London carrying garlands and followed by banners, torches, musicians, choristers, and the sacrament carried under a canopy. The garrison of the Tower accompanied its priests around St Katherine's Fields.[150] Bishop Bonner insisted that all the City's churches have their banners ready for the Rogation perambulations in 1554,[151] and this is faithfully reflected in their surviving records. They also appear in the Marian accounts from Westminster, Chester, Leicester, Bristol, Salisbury, and eighteen villages and market towns scattered across southern and midland England.[152] As before the Reformation, the majority of rural communities do not seem to have needed to pay anything towards the ritual, but the Elizabethan evidence suggests that none the less they kept it up. The holders of certain pieces of property were expected to entertain the participants upon the way, obviating the need for parochial expense.

All this activity posed a serious financial problem: the meagre expenses of reformation had easily been covered by selling the obsolete church trappings, but restoration cost a great deal. Mary's Privy Council ordered ten of Edward's commissions to return to parishes those ornaments which they had received which were still intact. Apparently most were not, for the procedure was only of benefit to four churches in our sample. In nineteen the accounts record that parishioners presented goods (in some cases probably bought from the wardens under Edward) or money to obtain them. On the other hand, records of church courts from Mary's reign abound with suits against people who failed to disgorge such items when asked to do so. In many places objects were apparently brought out of hiding. But the accounts make it clear that the great bulk of the work of restoration had to be paid for. Rates, gatherings, and existing funds provided notable sources for this purpose. A multiplicity of local solutions was found, such as at South Littleton in Worcestershire's Vale of Evesham. There the priest agreed to pay for the necessary books on being given the right to cull and sell the pigeons which lived in the steeple.[153]

But another major means of paying for counter-reformation consisted of those forms of communal festivity which had mostly perished in the Edwardian Reformation and now sprang back to life. Church ales reappeared all over the half of England south and west of a line drawn between London and Chester, in county towns, market towns, ports, and (above all) villages. Over most of this huge region they feature in the majority of surviving rural accounts, although noticeably rarer in the three south-eastern shires.[154]

North and east of the line they were apparently seldom held, the only recorded cases being at Liverpool and the market towns of Melton Mowbray in Leicestershire and Long Melford in Suffolk. A 'Lord of Christmas' who gathered at the small western Norfolk town of Swaffham may not have been attached to an ale.[155] These events had always been less popular in the East Midlands than elsewhere, but the apparent failure to revive them on the old scale in East Anglia is noteworthy. A few of those recorded under Mary included summer kings, queens, lords, or ladies,[156] and some overlapped with a parallel revival of Robin Hood plays. The latter, also strikingly absent under Edward, appear in Mary's reign at six places, spanning the same wide variety of communities as the ales. They also cover a huge tract of country, from Cornwall and Devon up to the Midlands and as far north as Manchester. The plays seem not to have been revived in the Thames valley and South-East, where they were already declining before the Reformation, but they maintained their popularity in the South-West and perhaps increased their range in the middle and north-western parts of England. Glimpses of the performances occur. At Manchester one took place in the parish church, while at Chagford, just under Dartmoor in Devon, the players borrowed the town's armour. At Anthony in Cornwall, up a wooded creek from the Tamar, Robin was partnered with 'John Rowye', apparently providing us with a surname for Little John.[157] That other companion of parish revels, the morris dance, turns up in the reign at Reading (along with minstrels and a hobby-horse), at Crondall in the woods of eastern Hampshire,[158] and at London, as shall be described.

Some of the communities which did not hold ales or Robin Hood plays revived other old fund-raising customs instead. The ropes went out for Hocktide once again in ten parishes in the sample, found across almost the whole former extent of the practice and once again including villages as well as large towns. But the gatherings were none the less more thinly scattered than before.[159] The hogglers or hognels also re-emerged in nine places from which records survive. No longer were they found in the Lincolnshire Fenland and they were much rarer in the South-East, but they were once again well represented in their old stronghold of the West Country.[160] The Plough Monday gatherings likewise feature once more in the East Anglian accounts. Their range was much the same as in their heyday, from the Lincolnshire fens to Suffolk, but they can be located in only four communities. Furthermore, only the fenland one seems to have rekindled its 'plough light'.[161]

Other traditional secular or semi-secular calendar customs reappeared. Once again the churchwardens of large towns entered payments for holly and ivy at Christmas, and those of London often bought birch at midsummer and flowers at Corpus Christi as well.[162] At Holy Trinity, Chester, candles were wired to the holly, and at nearby St Mary on the Hill a star and moon were added. The surviving midsummer marching watches continued during the reign, but those abolished or curtailed at London and Coventry were not revived. At Canterbury there was discussion over whether or not to continue that at the feast of St Thomas Becket, but although a pageant of the martyrdom was added in 1554–5, the whole procession was apparently allowed to lapse thereafter. The continuing economic troubles of the city may have been responsible.[163] Christmas 'lords' and 'kings' continued to preside over the revels of Oxford colleges and reappeared at Cambridge.[164] But the 'Abbots' who had gambolled around certain towns in Edward's reign were tactfully retired upon the accession of a Catholic sovereign.[165] The same event removed the royal Lord of Misrule, perhaps because the pinnacle to which Ferrers had brought the office had caused it to be associated too closely with the regime which he had served. Mary's Master of the Revels was kept busy providing plays and masques at Christmas, Candlemas, Shrovetide, and All Saints' Day, but his ribald associate was never heard of again at court.[166] It may have been in part because of this example, in addition to the stated reason of economy, that in 1555 the corporation of London abolished the 'Lords' engaged by the mayor and sheriffs.[167]

Nevertheless, the reign of Mary Tudor was beyond any doubt a period in which the seasonal festivities of early Tudor England reappeared upon a grand scale. The obvious question provoked by this fact is how far the government itself encouraged the process. As has been indicated, the agents of Edward's administration did play a role in suppressing those customs. Did those of Mary either positively recommend a revival or, at the least, allow one to occur when people wanted one? Evidence for the first situation is apparently totally lacking, and there is actually some which is directly opposed. After Wyatt's rebellion in Kent, the Privy Council ordered the suppression of all May games in that county because 'lewd practises . . . are appointed to be begun at such assemblies'; the Marian regime shared with its predecessor a well-founded fear of the potential of popular gatherings.[168] When Edmund Bonner issued his episcopal injunctions for the diocese of London in 1554, he forbade the holding of plays or games on Sundays and holy days with a strictness which would have delighted his most severe medieval predecessors and Protestant enemies.[169] Yet it seems to be an inescapable conclusion that if the Council had made its prohibition national, or if the whole episcopacy had enforced Bonner's injunction, then the revival would have been much more muted than it was. The official attitude to such pastimes must in practice have been relatively relaxed. The fate of May games in London under Edward has been noted. But in June 1555 one was held at Westminster, near the royal palace and the refounded abbey, which included 'giants, morris pikes, guns and drums and devils, and three morris dances, and bagpipes and viols, and many disguised, and the lady of the May rode gorgeously with minstrels'. In May 1557 there was another one in the City, with a lord and lady, a morris dance with a sultan, young Moors, and an elephant 'with the castle' (we are not told whether it was real or a model).[170] Both passed off without interruption, and are good tests of the change in attitude which must have accompanied the religious counter-reformation.

Yet, as indicated, the revival of secular revelry was not entirely complete, some customs covering only a portion of their former range or being more thinly scattered across it. The ecclesiastical rituals had to be enacted without the accumulated trappings of centuries and in buildings denuded of the decorations of the medieval and early Tudor periods. In every case the new ornaments and utensils were less imposing and expensive than those destroyed under Edward. Three aspects of the old religion, pilgrimages, the cult of the saints, and the provision for souls in Purgatory, seem to have been seriously damaged by the Reformation. There was almost no investment in the first two under Mary, and the third was marked almost wholly by the ringing of bells without the additional support of guilds, chantries, and obits in the early Tudor manner. Even given the massive consumption of resources in restoring the fundamentals of Catholic worship, they all should have left more impression upon the records if the devotion to them had been as strong as before.[171] The crude evidence of preambles to wills, employed again, indicates how partial the process of reconversion remained by the end of the reign. In every county or city studied for the purpose, the proportion of wills with Catholic formulae rose considerably again, but never to the exclusion of any others. In Yorkshire and Nottinghamshire during the whole reign, Protestant and neutral forms represented a quarter, and in York itself a tiny minority. Further south they were more significant. In Kent in the last two years of Mary, Catholic forms never rose above 42 per cent and Protestant versions never sank below 5 per cent. In East Sussex, Catholic wills only stood at 50 per cent of the total in 1558 and Protestant examples, again, at 5 per cent. Protestant preambles also continued to make up 5 per cent of those surviving from Devon and Cornwall. In London less than 50 per cent of the sample are unequivocally Catholic and 20 per cent Protestant.[172]

As a total achievement, this was distinctly limited. But viewed as a starting-point for further Catholicization it was extremely healthy. There seem to have been very many more professed Catholics in England at the end of Mary's reign than there had been Protestants at the death of Edward. The same comparison is suggested by the incidence of rebellion. Whereas the religious changes of Henry and his son directly provoked revolts covering whole regions, those of Mary produced no equivalent. Instead she faced Wyatt's rising, which had no avowed religious aims and was directed instead towards halting the queen's wedding to Philip. It is certainly true that most of its leaders had either clear or probable Protestant sympathies, but they did not use these as a rallying-cry for their followers. In any case the latter rose only in one county, Kent, and their campaign collapsed without the need for any concessions from the government, as in 1536, or battle, as in 1549.[173]

Within this context can be set the picture presented by the visitation records. In Wiltshire in 1556, only two parishes admitted to having no altars and two others to lacking a rood, Mary, and John. In Lancashire in 1554, only one of thirty-one churches and chapels visited had no altar, one no images, and seven no ornaments; by 1557, three out of thirty-four had less than the full complement of books and ornaments and all had altars and images. Under Elizabeth, when exaggeration would have been politic, out of 153 Lincolnshire parishes, only four claimed to have had no rood under Mary, one no side-altars, ten no candlesticks, and five no mass books. Of 242 Somerset parishes visited in late 1557 and early 1558, twenty-one admitted to having no pyx (the container for the host), six to having no rood, twenty-two to having no Mary and John, two to having no rood loft, and one to having no crucifix. The slowest progress was recorded in Kent. There, thanks to a mixture (impossible to quantify) of more thorough physical reformation under Edward, more ingrained Protestantism, and more searching Catholic visitation, out of 243 parishes questioned in 1557, forty-five had no holy water stoops, fifty-three no rood light, twenty-two no rood, sixty no crucifix, forty-three no candlesticks, fifty-three no pyx, forty-seven no high altar, and ninety-three no side-altars, while sixty-one lacked some of the necessary books. All told, however, it was not a bad achievement for so few years. Putting the whole body of evidence together, it looks as if, had Mary reigned as long as Elizabeth did, the religion of her realm would have been emphatically Catholic but still rather different from that of the early sixteenth century: more uniform in its patterns of piety, more subject to direction from the centre, much less remarkable for local and personal cults. It would not have been the old Church revived, but neither was the Counter-Reformation Church upon the Continent, and the differences were more or less the same in the European case as those suggested here for England.[174] The Catholic ritual year would have been maintained and perhaps elaborated, in settings and with trappings gradually enhanced by communal expenditure and individual bequest. The fascinating, and unanswerable, question is what would have happened to the secular calendar customs as they encountered the economic and social strains of the late sixteenth century, without the element of Protestant reformation to compound those pressures.

Instead, of course, the death of Mary in November 1558 put religion into limbo yet again. Her successor Elizabeth issued a proclamation in December, ordering that the existing rites be continued pending a settlement, save that the Creed could be pronounced in English. When private persons attacked fittings, vestments, and books in a church in Sussex and one in London, the Privy Council directed that they be punished. Not until April 1559 did Parliament pass a statute prescribing use of a new Protestant liturgy, fundamentally that of 1552, with the ornaments and vestments which had been legal in 1548 unless the queen directed otherwise. It is thus hardly surprising to find that the Catholic rituals were maintained in virtually every church which has left accounts for the year, a total of 160, until after Easter. Only at Rye, a strong centre of Edwardian Protestantism, was any spontaneous move made towards reform, when the wardens removed the altars before Holy Week. By contrast, other parishes in early 1559 behaved as if Mary's religion was going to endure, such as St Andrew, Canterbury, where the crucifix was mended, Marston near Oxford, where a bequest was made to purchase one, and Ludlow, where a new canopy was made for the sacrament.[175]

The question of how exactly the Elizabethan church settlement was made, and what exactly the queen herself wished it to be, has been much debated in recent years, and the confusion of the evidence makes it probably unanswerable. It is certain that Elizabeth was an extremely conservative kind of Protestant, with a taste for ritual and decoration and a suspicion of evangelical preaching. What we may never know is how her Church would have looked if the bishops who had served under Mary had not refused almost unanimously to transfer their allegiance from the Pope to Elizabeth, thereby leaving the latter almost totally dependent upon committed Protestants. Furthermore, although it is clear that the actual settlement was some kind of compromise, it is debatable whether it was the one at which the sovereign would have aimed or whether it was forced upon her either by Catholic or by Protestant pressure.[176] Certainly, although the liturgy was in most respects the one achieved towards the end of Edward's reign, it was to be performed in a setting more similar to that which had obtained half-way through the boy king's rule. The same picture was emphasized in the injunctions which the queen issued in July. They instructed parishes to obtain the Bible and the *Paraphrases*. They forbade processions upon a practical ground (that they caused parishioners to compete for precedence), but exempted those of Rogationtide provided that they were a mere perambulation of parish boundaries without cross or banners and with the priest in secular dress. They left the decision of whether to remove altars and to substitute a communion table to the minister and churchwardens or to the royal visitors if there was local disagreement. And they ordered the destruction of monuments 'of feigned miracles, pilgrimages, idolatry and superstition', while not specifically forbidding the retention of images.[177] Taken at face value, these directions and the new Prayer Book should have put an end to the Catholic ritual year while permitting the Protestant services to take place, in some churches at least, within a setting of altars, statues, and pictures of saints, and rood lofts fully equipped with their figures.

But, as during the early years of Edward, the actions of the regime were considerably less moderate than its words. The injunctions were enforced by six teams of visitors, each with a region committed to its care. On paper they numbered a total of 125, including many peers and leading gentry, but in practice most of these notables failed to serve and the work was apparently done in each area by four or five individuals, usually lawyers and clerics. They were led by men who had been in exile in Mary's reign and represented some of the most determined Protestants in Elizabeth's realm. It is not surprising that in the bulk of the surviving churchwardens' accounts their arrival in a district was marked not only by the extinction of Catholic ritual but by the removal of altars and images. Several pairs of churchwardens had to re-submit accounts to them, and those of Steeple Ashton, in west Wiltshire, had to attend them six times and to hand in bills thrice. In London the visitors produced a trail of bonfires of roods and other statues and sometimes of vestments, banners, Easter sepulchres, cloths, and metal ornaments as well. At Exeter they forced the citizens who had most venerated the images to throw them into the flames. At Yatton near the north Somerset coast, the wardens begged in vain for a reprieve for their church's Mary and John. The temper of the queen's agents seems to have been summed up in a sermon delivered either then or later by one of those on the northern circuit, Edwin Sandys, glorifying his monarch for defacing 'the vessels that were made for Baal', breaking down 'the lofts that were builded for idolatry', and demolishing 'all polluted and defiled altars'.[178]

Indeed the impact of the Elizabethan Reformation upon ritual was very swift, apparently sweeping away that of the former Church even faster than Edward's measures had done. Almost none of it reappeared after that royal visitation of 1559. At Crediton, in the small hills of central Devon, the priest was still blessing Candlemas tapers in the following year even though his church's images, pictures, Easter sepulchre, tabernacle, cross, and censer had been smashed. The wardens of Ludlow bought a pound of candles for the same festival in 1562, but after that no more seems to be heard of the rite in England.[179] It was rather more difficult to persuade parishioners not to take banners on Rogationtide processions. In the first season of prohibition, 1560, they were displayed in Buckinghamshire and Cornwall, and in 1564 the wardens of Stanford in the Vale, Berkshire, were summoned to the archdeacon's court at Oxford for having taken a streamer.[180] After the middle of the decade such cases seem to disappear.

The ritual which the Elizabethan reformers found most tenacious was the ringing of bells for the dead on All Saints' Night. It got people into trouble all through the 1560s, in both villages and towns and in all regions.[181] The custom continued to be condemned in the visitation articles of bishops of Lincoln, Chester, and Hereford in the 1580s.[182] And indeed, individuals were still prosecuted for it during that decade in the courts of the dioceses of York and Oxford. In 1587 at Hickling in Nottinghamshire's Vale of Belvoir some men not only kept up the custom but 'used violence against the parson at that time to maintain their ringing'.[183] This is the latest such case uncovered in the writing of this present book, but the surviving records of other church courts may well contain others from the 1590s. When finally driven out of the churches the rite sometimes took to the fields. In the north of Lancashire, an area where popular Catholicism lingered longer than in any other, families assembled on hills at midnight on the eve of All Saints' Day. One held up a bunch of burning straw on a pitchfork and the rest knelt in a circle and prayed for the souls of friends and relatives until the bundle burned out. In the early nineteenth century such fires could still be seen all around the horizon of a few villages. The tradition died out at last before 1900, leaving the common local name of 'Purgatory Field' as the memory of their purpose.[184] It has been said earlier that faith in the efficacy of prayers for the dead was severely damaged by Protestant attacks from the reign of Henry VIII onwards.[185] But the persistence of the Hallowtide ringing indicates how strong a hold the belief maintained over some of the populace far into the reign of Elizabeth. It may be that it lasted so long because of particular devotion to it, or because out of all the Catholic seasonal rituals it was the one which could be carried on without the use of illegal ornaments or the participation of a priest, and after dark. Yet it was not to be the last survivor of those rites. This distinction was to go to the Christmas morning service prescribed by the Use of Sarum. The reading from the rood loft perished with the liturgy, and most of the lofts, in the Elizabethan Reformation. But the candlelit assembly before dawn, locally known as the Plygain, persisted in North Wales. It is recorded in some of the churchwardens' accounts of the region as the surviving examples begin in the seventeenth century, and was still general in the nineteenth.[186] It survives today in some villages of the Tanat valley in the Montgomery district of Powys. There the congregations preserve the final trace of the calendar customs of the medieval parish church.

But if the Elizabethan impact upon Catholic ritual seems to have been at least as swift as that of the Edwardian reformers, its clearance of the physical surroundings of the former worship appears to have been more tardy. In two churches at York, the altars were taken down only in 1561, and the images remained in one of them until 1562. The altars survived at Wing, Buckinghamshire, Stanford in the Vale, Berkshire, and Worfield, Shropshire, until 1561, at Stoke Charity, Hampshire, until 1561–2, at St Mary at Hill, Chester, until 1562, and at Thame, that very conservative Oxfordshire market town, until 1564. At Morebath, Devon, the high altar was simply covered with a board. In most of these cases the bishops or archdeacons had to exert considerable pressure to secure compliance, but secure it they did. The Elizabethan ecclesiastical visitation and court records bear out this picture. In Kent by 1569 the process of physical reformation had been very effective, leaving only a few holy water stoops and one crucifix undefaced. In the diocese of Norwich that year the changes were also more or less complete. In Essex in 1565–6 one church still had an altar and two still had images. In Lincolnshire, 153 parishes claimed in 1566 to have removed all trappings of Catholic worship, but the process had taken the full seven years and both altars and images were still in place at Belton in Axholme, overlooking the Humberside marshes, until just before the account was rendered. The metropolitan visitors of the diocese of Lichfield in 1560–1 had to order wardens from at least four Staffordshire villages to destroy altars. A church in Holderness, the remote eastern peninsula of Yorkshire, still had images and altars in 1567, and another still had images. Statues of saints survived in several Lancashire churches in 1563–4, and one altar remained in 1574. In 1567 the bishop of Bangor reported that he had recently found, in this most remote and mountainous of all dioceses, images with candles burned before them, altars, and relics which were carried in procession at feasts; a sample of all the structures and ceremonies condemned by Protestants since 1538.[187] But then this was an area in which the cult of St Beuno, whose holy day had been abolished over half a century before, was still kept up in 1589 at Clynnog Fawr on the Lleyn peninsula. The local people not only venerated Beuno, but sacrificed bullocks to him at Whitsuntide to make the rest of their herds prosper. It was a custom which must have predated over a thousand years of Welsh Christianity.[188]

All this evidence still suggests that the destructive aspects of the Elizabethan Reformation were relatively rapid and complete, and if comparable data had survived in the North and in Wales from Edward's reign they would probably show at most the same degree of conformity. But when evidence is available for comparison, the physical reforms of 1559 do appear to have been resisted and delayed to a slightly greater degree than those of 1547–50. There is no clear reason for this, although two can be offered here. One is that the ambiguous and moderate tone of the Elizabethan injunctions may, for all the fervour of the visitors, have offered more scope for the short-term survival of altars and images. The other, which is perhaps more likely, is that the future of English Protestantism in the 1560s depended upon the life of an unmarried woman who had no obvious heir of her own faith and who might be carried off by illness or murder at any moment. It seems logical that parishioners, having gone to such expense to rebuild the setting for Catholic worship under Mary, were in no hurry to dismantle it if it seemed possible that the mass would be reintroduced once more for a new reign. This situation also accounts for the fury and urgency of the devout Protestants, who were anxious to make such a reintroduction as difficult as possible. Evidence for such an interpretation is provided by the attitude of the two groups to rood lofts.

The Protestant objection to the lofts was that articulated by Sandys; that they had supported the churches' most important images, functioned as memorials to them, and would make their restoration easier. But they were also elaborate and beautiful structures upon which much money and pride had been lavished and which would be terribly expensive to rebuild. It is no wonder that they were the subject of the most determined struggles between reformers and parish officials. In 1560 the new bishop of London, Edmund Grindal, encouraged the Protestant parishioners of St Michael le Querne, in the City, to insist on the demolition of theirs. This course was taken by their fellow believers in nearby St Mary Woolnoth,

and in the same year by most of the other London churches which have
left accounts and by nine in the provinces, almost all of these being in
towns or in East Anglia. In October 1561, using the now traditional excuse
for a further step in reform, Elizabeth ordered that to prevent contention
in parishes all remaining lofts were to be cut down to the beam. This
direction was followed within the year in most of the remaining southern
and midland churches from which accounts survive and a few in the north,
but there are signs of considerable reluctance. In seven cases the accounts
record serious pressure exerted by diocesan officials to secure compliance,
and in three the wardens were excommunicated. In the province of York
most of the parishes in our sample ignored the order until in 1570–1, after
the military defeat of the northern Catholics and the appointment of
Grindal as archbishop, a comparable effort of enforcement was mounted.
During the next two decades most visitations resulted in the discovery and
destruction of one or two more lofts, and many parishes, either from choice
or coercion, further cut down the remnants of theirs. Even so, pre-
Reformation rood lofts, apparently unrestored, exist today at North Weald,
Essex, and in three churches in Somerset, five in Wiltshire, three in
Yorkshire, and ten in Wales, and more were removed during the last cen-
tury. They illustrate the extent to which a community could resist rela-
tively peripheral aspects of the Reformation if it was determined and lucky.
By contrast, only one pre-Reformation rood, Mary, and John survives in an
English or Welsh church (at Betws Gwerfyl Goch, near Corwen in the
Berwyn Mountains), and not a single medieval stone altar.[189]

As in the reign of Edward, the positive effects of the reforms are less
apparent in the accounts than the negative. Certainly, virtually all of them
record the new Prayer Book within a year of its issue. But only thirty-five
of the sample of 160 from the years 1559–62 enter the purchase of a new
Bible, although two payments for mending an old one suggest that an
unknown number were brought out of hiding. The *Paraphrases* were
definitely obtained by twenty-six parishes and, again, may have been
restored to others by private hands, while the revised *Book of Homilies* is
recorded in thirty-four. That this does in fact reflect most of the actual
numbers of Protestant works obtained by these churches is suggested by
the visitation returns for Kent in 1569. No parish then admitted to preserving an altar, image, or rood loft, but forty of the 169 returns recorded
the absence of either the Bible or the *Paraphrases*, and this was one of the
most perfectly reformed counties of the time.[190] Still, by 1570 the process
of transforming the churches of England and Wales from settings for ritual
into preaching-houses was virtually complete. It seems to be generally

accepted by historians that during the next two decades the decisive work of turning the overwhelming majority of the population against Catholicism was also accomplished. The old religious year had gone for ever. What remained was the complex of calendar customs which were partly or wholly secular in inspiration and which none the less had been woven into the communal life and finances of parishes in the course of the Middle Ages. Over the value of these Protestants were to become deeply divided, and it is this story which will be commenced in the next chapter.

4

Reformation of Manners

I N the course of the 1970s historians came to attach considerable importance to what they called the 'reformation of popular culture' or the
'reformation of manners' in early modern Europe. This was usually
defined in two complementary ways. One was the growth of a more obvious distinction between the tastes and pastimes of social élites and those of
the bulk of the population, and the increasing disparagement of the latter
by the former. The second was a greater readiness by the wealthy to police
the behaviour of their poorer neighbours and to prosecute practices which
had formerly been regarded with a greater tolerance. Considerable debate
was possible (and occurred) over the intensity and chronology of each
process and over exactly what was involved within the definition of each.
But certain things rapidly became clear. All over western and central
Europe during the sixteenth and seventeenth centuries reformers attacked
popular festivity and tried to enforce a stricter standard of sexual morality
and of personal decorum. A sharper separation was made between the
sacred and the profane and between the sophisticated and the vulgar, and
an attempt was made to create a more orderly and sober, as well as a more
pious, society. Vagrants, fornicators, and suspected witches were all perse-
cuted with a new intensity, and formal entertainments tended to replace
spontaneous and participatory celebrations.[1]

In seeking to explain these developments, those who studied them soon
attributed importance to three different contemporary processes. The first
was the major overhaul of western Christianity represented by the twin
movements of Reformation and Counter-Reformation, which both sought
to create a more godly society. The second was the continent-wide rise in
population between 1500 and 1640 and the associated inflation of prices.
This produced a marked increase in poverty and a society more sharply

polarized between the poorer social groups and those able to profit from the enhanced value of commodities and of land. The third was a marked increase in the wealth of Europe from trade, discovery, and conquest, and a concomitant growth in self-conscious refinement and education among the élites who obtained most of it. The problem for historians was to decide which of these possible causes was the most important and, as all were so pervasive and occurred simultaneously, the task was unlikely to be easy.

It was Keith Wrightson who emerged in the early 1980s as the best-known proponent of a solution for the particular case of England: that religious and economic factors had operated together.[2] In his view, Elizabethan Protestantism equipped parish élites with an ideology of social reformation even as the pressures of population and prices were defining them more clearly as a group and presenting them with new problems of poverty and potential disorder among their neighbours. It was a picture which could be substantiated fairly well for his main case-study, of Essex, and was swiftly endorsed for that county by William Hunt.[3] But during the remainder of the decade a series of criticisms were made of it. Martin Ingram presented a study of a Wiltshire village which suffered the same strains as those of Essex, and underwent a slow, small-scale increase in rigour of religious observance, but displayed no signs of evangelical Protestantism. He suggested that it seemed to be typical of its county, and perhaps more representative than Essex of England as a whole. There followed the work of Margaret Spufford and Marjorie McIntosh, cited earlier, revealing that periods of economic pressure during the Middle Ages had produced almost identical efforts to reform moral behaviour. The case against the religious factor, and in favour of socio-economic forces, appeared to have been clinched by Cynthia Herrup's work upon east Sussex. She showed that this area had undergone virtually no 'reformation of manners' during the Elizabethan and early Stuart ages, its magistrates showing little interest in prosecuting alehouses, sexual offences, and witchcraft in comparison with their colleagues in Essex. This was particularly striking in that it contained some of the most ardent evangelical Protestants in the nation. Its main port, Rye, had displayed marked enthusiasm for the reformed religion from the beginning, and some of its inland communities produced notable preachers and godly families with charismatic names, including the celebrated brothers Praise-God and Fear-God Barebone. Professor Herrup ascribed the difference to the relative economic prosperity and social stability of eastern Sussex.[4]

This present book is concerned with the fate of seasonal festivities and rites, rather than with other aspects of the social reformation. Nevertheless, its topic has usually been included with all the other varieties of regulation and manipulation grouped together in that process. And it may be said at once that, if that inclusion is correct, then something is obviously wrong with the emerging consensus described above. The impact of the reign of Edward, described in the last chapter, represented a very rapid and dramatic attack upon the traditional festive culture, propelled by religious and political forces. The rehabilitation of that culture under Mary, despite the continuation or intensification of the same long-term socio-economic developments, indicates the total irrelevance of the latter in the mid-Tudor period at least. In the succeeding hundred years Cynthia Herrup's east Sussex may not have displayed much interest in a legally imposed reform of 'manners', but it did lose its old calendar pastimes at the same rate as most of the nation. At Rye they collapsed in the 1560s, when the town was at the height of its prosperity.[5] It may be, therefore, that the issue of seasonal customs will have to be detached from the general model of explanation, and it is certain that much more information is needed to judge the matter. This chapter sets out to furnish such material. It is certainly more abundant for the reign of Elizabeth than for the preceding half-century. Churchwardens' accounts from a total of 332 parishes have been employed for this study, although only thirty-four sets cover the whole reign and almost all of these are urban, mostly metropolitan.[6] Every other variety of source is also considerably more abundant, with the exception of household accounts.

Something that emerges from this collection of evidence is that the accession of Elizabeth did not have the almost immediate impact upon secular festivities made by that of Edward. Indeed, the early and mid-1560s were a notable time for old-fashioned merry-making. Church ales are recorded in forty-seven parishes, as before most common in the West and the Midlands but extending into East Anglia and the South-East.[7] Some of the menus surviving make mouth-watering reading for a hungry researcher. At Northill, Bedfordshire, ten parishes gathered for a feast at Whitsun 1561 which consisted of bread, baked meats, fresh roast veal, fruit, spices, and beer. Five years later the parish of St Mary in the Suffolk town of Bungay held the first of three successive 'church ale games'. These also seem to have attracted participants from the whole district, and the fare included eggs, butter, currants, pepper, saffron, veal, lamb, honey, cream, bread, custards, pasties, and eight firkins of beer. The entertainments at these large celebrations were proportionately elaborate. Rural Northill paid for a minstrel, two fools, six morris dancers, and some fireworks. Urban St Mary's preferred plays, performed on a scaffold by its own inhabitants.

Masks were made for some, while the earl of Surrey, heir to the town's lord the duke of Norfolk, lent his own robes to dress the main characters. Surrey's patronage also permitted the parishioners to hold the events in the yard of Bungay Castle. Some lesser ales managed to afford a musician, some morris, a clown, or a maypole or two.[8] Seven parishes in the sample crowned summer kings or lords.[9] At Mere, on the Wiltshire chalk downs, the annual 'Cuckoo King' was assisted by a 'Cuckoo Prince' who was made king in the next year. Three villages in western Norfolk retained Christmas lords of the old East Anglian kind.[10] Robin Hood puts in an appearance in four of the recorded parish feasts. Three were at Devon villages, such as Braunton among the sandhills of the north coast where the outlaw was given a special coat and had a 'company' of attendants. The fourth was in the Thames valley town of Abingdon, at which the churchwardens set up his 'bower' in 1566.[11]

Other early Tudor customs which had been revived under Mary were still present in the next decade. Maypoles, morris, and hobby-horses seem to have been plentiful outside the context of church ales. One London merchant recorded a pole set up by the City's butchers and fishermen in May 1562, 'full of horns' to mock cuckolds, 'and they made great cheer'. In fifteen months during 1561 and 1562 the home of a Lincolnshire gentleman was visited by a hobby-horse player, a lone morris dancer, and a hobby-horse accompanied by four musicians.[12] Plough Monday gatherings helped out the parish funds of six communities which have left records for the 1560s, in Lincolnshire, Norfolk, and along the northern border of Suffolk. They include villages, market towns, and a parish in Norwich, the realm's third largest city.[13] Hocktide collections are noted in nine sets of churchwardens' accounts, from Southampton, Salisbury, Kingston upon Thames, Oxford, and two Hampshire villages.[14] The hogglers or hognells appear in four rural West Country parishes and one in Sussex.[15] Local drama flourished, plays being recorded during the 1560s in more than twenty parishes in Essex alone.[16] Lords of Misrule continued to appear each Christmas in some wealthy households, and in colleges, urban corporations, and Inns of Court.[17] The most renowned was the 'Prince Palaphilos' chosen at the Temple in 1561 and 1562. Shrewdly, the lawyers invited to the post none other than Lord Robert Dudley, the queen's favourite courtier. He went to the Inn on horseback in gilded armour and followed by eighty gentlemen 'riding gorgeously with chains of gold'. Twenty-four knights clad in white were his constant attendants. His 'rule' commenced after dark upon Christmas Eve and lasted until Twelfth Night, consisting almost wholly of presiding over feasting and dancing. The most elaborate and brutal fun came upon St Stephen's Night, when the 'Prince' was joined by the Lieutenant of the Tower of London, both in white armour. Supper was preceded by the hunting of a fox and a cat around the hall with about a score of hounds. The two animals were cornered and torn to pieces in front of the fire.[18]

Municipal archives bear out much the same story. The Coventry and Norwich religious drama was swiftly purged of passages offensive to the reformed religion. At Norwich the annual St George riding lost George himself and St Margaret, but the dragon continued to be paraded by popular demand.[19] Doubtless portions of other plays and pageants were discreetly excised in the same fashion, but on the whole the urban parades and dramatic cycles continued into the 1560s even as those of the Church vanished. Only those of Lincoln seem to have died with Mary. The earlier part of that decade saw an abundance of corporate celebration. At Rye the town treasury paid for a drummer and a breakfast 'for the May game'. The city fathers of Plymouth began modestly by rewarding morrismen and players, but went on in the course of the decade to supply a maypole, a hobby-horse, and fireworks. The mayor of Newcastle upon Tyne laid on a 'ship for dancing' at midsummer, minstrels and fools at Christmas, and troupes of actors and more musicians on other occasions.[20]

Records from the whole reign of Elizabeth enable us to have a much better look at customs which in the earlier period are only sketchily described. Philip Stubbes's picture of the fetching and decoration of a maypole has been quoted many times, especially since it was reprinted in Sir James Frazer's *Golden Bough*. But it is of such relevance to the matter of this book that a further appearance may be justified:

Against May Day, Whitsunday, or other time, all the young men and maids, old men and wives, run gadding overnight to the woods, groves, hills and mountains, where they spend all the night in pleasant pastimes; and in the morning, they return, bringing with them birch and branches of trees, to deck their assemblies withall. . . . But the chiefest jewel they bring from thence is their May-pole, which they bring home with great veneration, as thus. They have twenty or forty yoke of oxen, every ox having a sweet nose-gay of flowers placed on the tip of his horns, and these oxen draw home this May-pole (this stinking idol, rather), which is covered all over with flowers and herbs, bound round about with strings, from the top to the bottom, and sometime painted with variable colours, with two or three hundred men, women and children following it with great devotion. And thus being reared up, with handkerchieves and flags hovering on the top, they strew the ground round about, bind green boughs around it, set up summer halls, bowers and arbours hard by it. And then they fall to dance about it.[21]

The number of people and oxen involved suggests that Stubbes is picturing one of the huge urban or suburban poles, but most of the details can be substantiated from other sources. The specimens set up by the Plymouth corporation were painted and had flags and streamers hung from them and canvas set round them. That brought annually into Hinckley, Leicestershire, had a minstrel playing before it as it was fetched home and set up. There was an ample 'drinking' at the 'bringing home the summer rod' to the parish of Holy Trinity, Exeter. The prominent role of young people is confirmed at Eltham in south-eastern Kent, where the churchwardens bought a pole from 'boys', and at Nottingham where the city chamberlain paid 'to youth that brought in May'.[22] The custom whereby young adults went out overnight to pick flowers for May games is well attested, most lyrically by Edmund Spenser who portrayed them returning 'with hawthorn buds and sweet eglantine and garlands of roses and sops-in-wine'.[23] The bowers and arbours, other writers make plain, were there for the very practical purpose of affording shelter during a shower.[24] What is by no means obvious is whether any special dances were performed around the pole. The well-known modern variety, holding ribbons attached to the crest, was introduced from the Mediterranean region in the last century. The only illustration of an Elizabethan equivalent is a crude woodcut showing people of both sexes prancing in a circle facing the shaft.[25]

Stubbes included an almost equally famous description of a summer lord and his retinue:

First of all the wild heads of the parish conventing together, chose themselves a grand captain (of mischief) whom they enoble with the title of my Lord of Misrule, and him they crown with great solemnity, and adopt for their king. The king anointed, chooseth for the twenty, forty, three score or a hundred lusty guts like unto himself, to wait upon His Lordly Majesty, and to guard his noble person. Then every one of these his men he investeth with his liveries of green, yellow or some other light wanton colour. And as though that were not bawdy enough I should say, they bedeck themselves with gold rings, precious stones and other jewels: This done, they tie about either leg twenty or forty bells with rich handkerchieves in their hands, and sometimes laid across over their shoulders and necks, borrowed for the most part of their pretty Mopsies and loving Bessies, for bussying them in the dark. These things set in order, they have their hobby horses, dragons and other antiques, together with their bawdy pipes and thundering drummers, to strike up the Devil's Dance withall, then march these heathen company towards the church and churchyard, their pipers piping, drummers thundering, their stumps dancing, their bells jingling, their handkerchieves swinging about their heads like madmen, their hobby horses and other monsters skirmishing amongst the throng: and in this sort they go to the church (though the minister be at prayer or preaching) dancing and swinging their handkerchieves over their heads, in the church, like devils incarnate.[26]

The title 'Lord of Misrule' has often confused folklorists into identifying this picture with the mock-kings of Christmas, but the context makes it clearly a May game. The invasion of the church seems to have been a disorderly version of a custom whereby summer kings and queens formally attended a service before commencing their rule over the revels. Shortly after Stubbes, William Warner could write 'Lord and Lady gang till kirk with lads and lasses gay: Fra Mass and Evensong fa good cheer and glee on every green.'[27] But this tradition does seem to have been boisterous at times, and caused serious concern to senior churchmen as will be seen. Another good view of a summer lord comes from the end of the reign, in 1601 at South Kyme on the edge of the Lincolnshire Fens. There the games lasted much longer than the norm, right until the end of August. They included reciprocal visits of young men between villages, led by their own elected 'lords' and involving a tour of the pubs in each. The leader of the Kyme lads was the son of a prosperous yeoman and rode with an escort of about a dozen, including flag-bearers, drummers, and six guards carrying reeds with painted paper heads to simulate spears. The season ended on the last Sunday in August, with a maypole being erected and a play performed on the village green after evensong. Over a hundred people attended, from the whole district.[28] Sometimes summer queens were carried triumphally in chairs; the Protestant preacher Stephen Batman compared the Pope, transported in this manner, to 'whitepot queens in western May games' (whitepot being a cream custard). Another image of such a procession comes from Oxford in 1598, where a Queen of May was decked in garlands and brought into town by the militiamen, together with morris dancers, drummers and men attired in female dress.[29]

The 'Devil's Dance' described by Stubbes was, of course, the morris, and this is one of the best pictures of it under Elizabeth, when it completed its transformation from a court entertainment to a favourite one of the ordinary people. There is however no evidence that it had become standardized; the various images of it at this time have nothing in common except energetic movements and bells. It was almost wholly the preserve of men, either singly or in teams which normally numbered six. Handkerchieves of the sort portrayed by Stubbes were also common, as were colourful embroidered jackets and scarves attached to shoulders. The dancers were now often accompanied by a hobby-horse, a jester, and Maid Marian. The last two were survivals from the late medieval association of the dance with the mime of a fool who won a lady, the name of the latter being now taken from the companion of Robin Hood in the plays. But the Marians of the Elizabethan May games were there principally to provide rough humour, being men in female dress, often deliberately selected for their beards, brawny muscles, and general inability to make convincing transvestites. The courtship was now a parody, the fool usually clowning with the leather ball or bladder which was the symbol of his office, before collecting money from the observers in a wooden ladle.[30] The whole assemblage provided a potent mixture of music, costume, physical dexterity, and earthy fun.

Stubbes followed his jaundiced account of the summer lord with a classic description of a village 'king ale', substantiated in its component parts from many sets of churchwardens' accounts:

Then after this, about the church they go again and again, and so forth into the churchyard, where they have commonly their summer-halls, their bowers, arbours and banqueting houses set up, wherein they feast, banquet and dance all that day and (peradventure) all the night too. . . . They have also certain papers, wherein is printed some babblerie or other of imaginary work, and these they call 'my lord of misrule's badges': these they give to everyone that will give money for them. . . . And who will not be buxom to them, and give them money for these their devilish cognizances, they are mocked and flouted at not a little. . . . Another sort of fantastical fools bring to these hell-hounds . . . some bread, some good ale, some new cheese, some old, some custards, and fine cakes.[31]

Other old customs are well illustrated for the first time under Elizabeth. The vivid picture of the Lord of Misrule at the Temple was given above. The violence and excitement of Shrovetide football is pictured yet more vividly than before, with the added detail that bachelors would commonly play against married men.[32] There are also the very first references to rites which must have existed before the late Tudor period but are unrecorded till then because of the paucity of sources from the regions in which they flourished. One is apple-wassailing, mentioned in the first chapter. Another is 'rush-bearing', apparently confined to Westmorland, western Yorkshire, Cheshire, and Lancashire. All over the country fresh rushes were brought into buildings each summer and strewn upon the floors to afford comfort and warmth. But only in this region, apparently, were some of them woven with flowers and carried into the churches by women preceded by musicians, to be hung there.[33]

So what did happen to seasonal ceremonies and pastimes such as these during the reign of Elizabeth? The answer has long been known in outline: that they underwent a considerable decline. The quantity of information gathered here is sufficiently large to confirm this conclusion and to substantiate it in detail. It reveals that the attrition commenced in the middle of the 1560s and remained steady until the end of the reign and beyond it, although the 1570s seem to have been particularly significant in the process. It was then that church ales seem to have vanished from East Anglia, Kent, and Sussex and to have shrunk considerably in number over the rest of their former range. In many of the parishes in which they persisted, they became occasional contributions to parish funds instead of the mainstay. By the end of the reign they were confined to the West Country and to the valleys of the Thames and its tributaries.[34] Parish-sponsored May games disappeared at the same rate.[35] By 1600 Hocktide gatherings apparently contributed to parish funds only at Oxford and in the London area.[36] Over the same period hoggling became wholly confined to the western counties, and to fewer places within them.[37] Plough Monday collections ceased to have any connection with parochial finance,[38] leaving but a few relics of their importance to the official life of the eastern counties. At Leverton, in the Lincolnshire Fens, the churchwardens held a feast on that day until 1611. All through the seventeenth century the bells of Rolleston, upon the Trent in Nottinghamshire, were rung then. And into the eighteenth the parish funds of Waddington, in the uplands just south of Lincoln, were administered by 'ploughmasters' appointed then with much ringing and provision of music. Stuart ecclesiastical officials in these counties were occasionally annoyed to find the communal plough kept in the church, although the blessing of it had apparently ended with Elizabeth's Reformation.[39]

In each case the gap in fund-raising created by the separation of these customs from parish affairs was filled by rates or by rents charged for pews in the church. It is difficult to argue that the certainty or size of the yield was an important factor in the change, for the festivities had provided quite sufficient money over the previous hundred years. Only a significantly increased expenditure would substantiate such a contention, and the regular pecuniary needs of the Elizabethan parish church were less than those of the pre-Reformation equivalent, with its greater quantity of physical decoration and of ritual. Certainly the profits of the traditional revelry fell off in some places shortly before their disappearance, but this seems to reflect the same withdrawal of support which led to the abolition. What was happening was that a cultural pendulum which had swung to one extreme by the end of the fifteenth century was now moving back again, and communal festivity as a means of fund-raising was giving way to fixed exactions of the sort which seem to have been more the rule in the period before 1450. The alteration did not mean the automatic extinction of any of the pastimes concerned, except hoggling, which was wholly involved with the parish. The May games, Hocktide, and the Plough Monday collections remained in the orbit of private pleasure and profit, although the more vulnerable to attack there because of their uncoupling from parochial life. Nor had official sponsorship of them wholly retreated into remote rural districts. As indicated, it persisted in and around the Thames valley, the most densely populated and frequently travelled part of the realm. About half of the young men of the ruling classes went to study at Oxford, where every parish which has left records kept up Hocktide and two held annual Whitsun ales. The same tenacity was shown by villages near London and towns along the Thames between the capital and Oxford. Some of it may be accounted for in terms of the sheer quantity of people available in the region, representing potential customers; then as now, Merry England was a tourist attraction. But this factor alone is not a sufficient explanation, for the parishes of Cambridge, the other university town, almost ostentatiously failed to keep up any of these pastimes from the beginning of the reign. Likewise some of the villages near the metropolis abandoned them. The contrast between the two major seats of learning was a neat symbol of a division of taste and opinion growing within the nation.

A similar but not identical attrition occurred in ecclesiastical customs which, although not proscribed by the reformers, were bound up with the mentality of the old religion. One was the seasonal decoration of churches with greenery, especially with holly and ivy at Christmas. In the 1560s this was still quite common in towns (which, as before, preserve the only records of it as they alone had to purchase the vegetation concerned). It appears in all parish accounts existing for that decade in Bristol parishes and most of those in London. By 1570 it had vanished from all in Bristol and from several in the capital, and before the end of the century it was discontinued in almost every one where it is mentioned in the early part of the reign. The two exceptions were the churches flanking the royal palace of Whitehall.[40] The other tradition of this sort was the taking of communion upon the major feasts of the religious calendar, Easter above all. From the time of the Church Settlement most Elizabethan parishes either did not do this or did not think it worth special mention in the accounts. But some, scattered across the country, made a point of doing so in the 1560s. Most of them abandoned the practice in the next decade, and most of the remainder followed in the 1580s. Interestingly, the majority of those which persisted were in Kent and East Anglia, the regions which were most thoroughly affected by the evangelical Protestantism thought in general to be inimical to such an emphasis upon feast days and liturgy.[41] This survival pattern was almost the reverse of that of the traditional parish merry-making, and there was another important difference between the two. Whereas the decline of the festivities continued steadily beyond the end of the reign, in the last years of Elizabeth a revival of local interest in the liturgical year began, which was to become extremely important and which will be studied later.

Here it is necessary to document the fate of the old festivities from that other body of 'hard' evidence for the subject, the accounts and orders of municipal corporations. They reveal much the same pattern as the parish books. In the 1560s Rye gave up sponsoring May games and Coventry ended its famous midsummer marching watch and the play traditionally performed upon Hock Tuesday. Norwich stopped its Whitsun pageants and play cycle and York often suspended its own. Totnes in Devon abolished its midsummer watch. In the 1570s Coventry revived its Hocktide play, but ended the cycle on Corpus Christi Day, the most famous of all medieval English drama. Instead the craft guilds performed productions at midsummer, with Protestant texts. The almost equally celebrated cycles at York, Chester, and Wakefield also came to a permanent halt. The corporation of Newcastle upon Tyne allowed selections from that port's Corpus Christi plays to continue. Gloucester's midsummer watch disappeared. A mayor of Bristol, by contrast, instituted such marching watches in his city on Midsummer and St Peter's Eves, but only in compensation for the abolition of the traditional revels and shows upon those nights. The city fathers of Doncaster banned maypoles. Their action was reproduced in the 1580s by those of Lincoln, Banbury, Canterbury, and Shrewsbury. At Doncaster the municipality went on in the same decade to stop the Corpus Christi plays, which also ended at this time in Newcastle and Ipswich. The Newcastle council likewise withdrew support from midsummer bonfires, and that of Nottingham ceased to encourage May games. Plymouth abolished its midsummer watch. York developed one instead, in order to fill the void left by the drama. A schoolmaster was engaged to write some new plays for performance before the march, employing some of the old Corpus Christi pageant sets. But in the 1590s the corporation's interest faltered, watch and plays being moved to St Peter's Eve instead, with a much reduced expenditure. During that decade, also, the Hock Tuesday play finally vanished at Coventry and the drama still provided at times by craft guilds died out. The corporation also banned maypoles, a step now taken at Leicester. Norwich only intermittently paraded the model dragon which had been a regular entertainment on St George's Day, Gloucester abolished the play which had been the last survivor of its midsummer revels, and Sheffield ceased to pay for a piper, and his colourful coat, each Christmas.[42]

This sequence of events fits neatly alongside the developments detected in Elizabethan London by Ian Archer.[43] He found that communal celebrations such as those traditionally associated with midsummer and May Day atrophied still further during the reign, giving an enhanced importance to audience-based entertainments such as public theatre and bear-baitings. By the 1570s the only concern taken by the corporation for the old seasonal feasts was to double the watch during the most popular in order to avoid disturbances. The same pattern is found in village drama, which in the areas for which detailed studies exist, Essex, Norfolk, and Suffolk, collapsed around 1570 and was virtually gone by 1580.[44] Travelling theatre companies and troupes of musicians, who had been welcomed in increasing number by urban corporations during the late Middle Ages, suffered a reversal of fortune under Elizabeth. A large sample of municipal accounts reveals that towns became less and less ready to pay such entertainers. By 1600 some were starting to give them money *not* to perform, especially if they had aristocratic patrons who might be offended by a straightforward rebuff.[45] In that year only fragments of the old urban seasonal rituals remained, and some of these were about to be abolished in turn. A single cycle of Corpus Christi drama still existed at Kendal, in Westmorland, despite the grave reservations of the town council. Plymouth continued to hold its May games, and midsummer pageants and shows survived at Chester and Salisbury. The most widely tolerated of the traditional municipal ceremonies were the marching watches upon Midsummer Eve and St Peter's Eve. They could be held to testify to the martial spirit of a community, to exercise it in weaponry, and to help guarantee the public peace upon these nights, and as such they persisted at York, Nottingham, Bristol, Exeter, and Carlisle.[46] The most robustly conservative and festive town on record seems to have been Marlborough on the chalk hills of Wiltshire. True, it was in 1578 that it last provided wine and fireworks to welcome a visiting Lord of Misrule. But in 1590 its aldermen decided that on Midsummer Eve every one of them henceforth would invite the householders of his ward to his home to 'drink together as neighbours and friends'. The mayor would then host a party for them all. Unhappily we cannot tell how long this resolution remained in force before it was scored through in the order book and so abrogated.[47]

So what was the cause of all these changes in parish and town? Certainly not legislation, for the national law regulating these matters, in Church and state, did not alter after the first couple of years of the reign. The ecclesiastical settlement of 1559, as every student of the period knows, remained intact despite various efforts to reform it. That settlement, embodied in the royal injunctions and the Act of Uniformity, ordered all people to attend divine service upon Sundays and holy days and then to spend them in prayer, charity, and neighbourliness, working only as an absolute necessity. The list of holy days issued in 1560 was notably longer than that permitted by Edward's regime in 1552, including some of the most popular saints of the Middle Ages such as George, Lucy, Anne, Valentine, Mary Magdalen, Martin, Crispin, Cecilia, Catherine, and Clement, with some of special importance to the English such as Augustine of Canterbury, Alphege, Edward the Confessor, and Swithun. However, the guidelines issued the following year and the practice of church courts ensured that the restrictions on behaviour concerning holy days only applied to the feasts legal in 1552, essentially those of Christ and the Apostles. The 1563 Convocation revealed considerable dissatisfaction among many, though not most, clergy at the continued existence of saints' days. Elizabeth's first archbishop of Canterbury, Matthew Parker, responded to it with measures in both Convocation and Parliament to allow labour on those days. For unknown reasons the attempt failed in both bodies. Thus the secular and religious laws of the regime left a profound ambiguity concerning the number of seasonal feasts in the calendar and the pastimes which were to be encouraged or discouraged upon them and on Sundays.[48] To understand what happened it is necessary to look at the attitudes of the various members of the political and religious hierarchy, and of the society around them.

Elizabeth herself enthusiastically enjoyed some traditional forms of festivity, and had a taste for ornament and ritual greater than that of many Protestants. It is well known that she chose, from motives still in dispute, to retain a cross and candlesticks in her own chapel. Her gorgeous dresses, fans, and jewels are even more celebrated. It is of a piece with these traits that she carefully performed the rites which lent semi-sacred status to royalty. She devoutly washed the feet of poor women and men each Maundy Thursday, and then wiped them, made the sign of the cross over them, and kissed them. Each then received cloth, shoes, food, drink, a white bag holding as many pence as Elizabeth had years, and a red one containing twenty shillings. Each Twelfth Day, as her priests began to celebrate communion, she gave one of them a dish with papers containing the royal gold, frankincense, and myrrh. The courtly round of winter entertainments was kept with exuberance, plays, balls, and masques taking place at Christmastide and Shrovetide. The reciprocal New Year's gifts were measured out as before, the queen giving gold or silver plate in fixed quantity from the 136 ounces due to a favourite courtier such as Robert Dudley to the 2 ounces received by the court dwarf. In return she accepted rich clothing, money, or jewels, and presents in kind down to the marzipan sent by her cook. She drew up lists of nobles who were expected to attend her at each Twelfth Day dinner, when the Children of the Chapel Royal launched the musical accompaniment with a carol. The royal halls were decorated with holly, ivy, and bay leaves every Christmastide, and hobby-horses were hired. The only development in the course of the reign was that from the late 1570s festivities were no longer held at Candlemas, perhaps because of its Catholic associations with the Virgin Mary. Elizabeth's personal opinion upon the propriety of sports and revels upon Sundays was also clear. She enjoyed dancing and watching jousts upon that day in various years, and in 1569 she licensed a London poulterer with four small children to arrange Sunday games to supplement his income.[49]

The queen was also fond of the old summer festivals. In the last two years of her life she still went out to visit favoured gentry on May Day and to dance at their residences. In the very first year of her reign a May game had been held around London which included a giant, drummers, the Nine Worthies of Christendom, St George and the dragon, Robin Hood, Little John, Maid Marian, Friar Tuck, and morris dancers. The following day Elizabeth had it ordered up to Greenwich Palace to be played before her; it is hardly necessary to look further to understand why such revels persisted in the metropolis longer into her reign than into that of her brother.[50] In 1569 the queen pressed the corporation of London to revive its once-famous midsummer marching watch. The Lord Mayor pleaded his own ill-health and the presence of plague in the city, and engaged the most influential royal minister, Sir William Cecil, to persuade Elizabeth to accept those excuses; significantly, the corporation showed no greater interest in the parade when a less sickly mayor and summer came along.[51] Courtiers also introduced items from the popular revels into the entertainments which they provided for their monarch. Most famous are those laid on by Robert Dudley himself, by then earl of Leicester, at Kenilworth Castle in 1575. They included a harvest queen riding in a cart, a morris dance, and the Coventry Hock Tuesday play, directed by the muster master of that city. It made the claim that the custom of bindings had originated in a victory over the Danes, after which the women of Coventry led the defeated warriors in bonds. The theme was patriotic, and could have particular appeal to a female monarch, and royal appreciation enabled the performers to revive the play in the city itself, as described above.[52] But there were other such occasions, such as the moment when the queen, staying with the marquis of Hertford, was awoken by musicians 'in ancient country attire' who sang of a 'Lady of the May with garlands gay'.[53] There was no suggestion that either the monarch or these aristocrats were seriously concerned about the fate of the customs concerned; rather, they could provide occasional variety among the succession of deities, nymphs, satyrs, and allegorical figures usually produced to amuse Elizabeth and to proclaim her virtues. But it can at least be concluded that the decline of traditional seasonal customs took place despite the personal tastes of the monarch.

What, then, of the Privy Council, with which the queen was, as political and diplomatic historians well know, sometimes at variance? Its clearest statement upon such issues was made on 24 May 1589, in an order directed to the lord-lieutenant of Oxfordshire in response to a local attempt to ban summer festivities in the Banbury district. It declared that maypoles and 'like pastimes' were lawful and that people who tried to prevent them were to be arrested and sent before the Council. But it added that if the merrymakers themselves proved disorderly they were to be punished like any breakers of the peace. The councillors who signed this judgement included every member of the board except the archbishop of Canterbury, Whitgift, whose absence does not seem to have been significant.[54] Three years later virtually the same team qualified its ruling a little further when it was informed that Lancashire Catholics were trying to lure people away from the national Church by holding May games and other festivities in service time. It ordered the lord-lieutenant of that county to ensure that any who contrived this were apprehended.[55] In an earlier incarnation during the 1570s, the Council had been directly responsible for the demise of the Chester cycle of Whitsun plays. The local churchmen had convinced it that the content was too Catholic and it had bullied successive mayors until the performances lapsed. Near the end of the reign, in 1597, it halted an attempt by the Suffolk town of Hadleigh to hold a cyclical Whitsun play of its own, on the grounds that it was a time of famine when assemblies encouraged people to riot.[56] But by its ruling of 1589 it showed a readiness to protect the old pastimes if they were not politically dangerous or religiously offensive. What prevented this from becoming of major consequence was that it made no attempt to formulate a national policy upon the matter. Its rulings were always pragmatic responses to local difficulties, to which its attention had been drawn. Still, like the queen, it cannot be regarded as a factor in the widespread decline of parochial and urban festivity.

Directly beneath the monarch in the parallel hierarchy of the Church came the archbishops, bishops, and archdeacons. These had much more reason than the Privy Council to be interested in seasonal celebrations, and indeed took notice of them in four different ways: direct executive action, visitation articles, publications, and personal sponsorship. The clearest examples of the first came in the 1570s, as part of a policy of repression and reform following the rebellion of 1569. That rising put a halt to the elaborate church ales at Bungay, Suffolk, by bringing about the fall of the duke of Norfolk whose family had encouraged them. Its failure also removed the most determined of all the conservative magnates of northern England, and opened up that region to a more determined Protestant evangelism. A zealous reformer, Matthew Hutton, had already been made dean of York, and in 1570 he was joined by a new archbishop, Edmund Grindal. Both soon received support from the earl of Huntingdon, a notable patron of the new religion who was made president of the Council of the North. It was at this time that axes were put to many of the northern rood lofts, as described above. Between 1572 and 1576 the ecclesiastical commission which these men dominated destroyed most of the religious drama of the region. It forbade the Corpus Christi plays of Wakefield on the grounds that they degraded the life of Christ by representing it upon stage. It abolished what it termed the 'very rude and barbarous custom' on St Thomas's Day (21 December), when 'two disguised persons' called Yule and Yule's Wife rode through York 'very undecently and unseemly'. And it stopped the famous Corpus Christi cycle of that city. In 1568 Dean Hutton had threatened the corporation with the displeasure of 'the learned' and 'the state' if the drama continued, and Grindal subsequently impounded the texts. In 1579 the city council asked if the latter might be 'corrected' to the churchmen's satisfaction, but although whole sections were indeed ripped out no performances resulted. It was also Grindal and Huntingdon who propelled the Privy Council into suppressing the Chester plays.[57]

In southern England, however, examples of such direct episcopal interference are much harder to find, largely because of the absence of such bodies as the northern commission and of rebellions which would have invited a similar mopping-up operation. There seems to be only one clear case on record, when a new bishop of Winchester, Cooper, wrote to the ministers and chief gentry of his diocese in 1584 to stop morris dancers and similar 'heathenish and ungodly customs'. Although he certainly disliked such pastimes, he was specifically concerned with a report that they were taking place in service time and keeping people from church; it was this, rather than the activities themselves, which he wanted to prevent.[58] Even in the north, the reforming clerics were not concerned to wipe out any species of seasonal celebration except the religious drama. In 1595 the commission at

York prosecuted three Ripon men for 'keeping summergames on festival days', but this seems to have been an isolated incident.[59] Indeed, very occasionally leading churchmen employed their power to the opposite end; in 1586 the vice-chancellor and heads of colleges at Cambridge rebuked a minister who had preached in the university against Sunday sports and plays. They held that such recreations were lawful if they did not disturb religion.[60]

The second category of evidence consists of the visitation articles, those questionnaires sent out by senior churchmen to parish clergy and church-wardens to ensure conformity and decency in religious life. During the 1560s those of Elizabeth's bishops were concerned primarily with extirpating Catholic worship. But in 1569 Parkhurst of Norwich attacked the East Anglian custom of having Christmas Lords of Misrule enter churches at service time, 'playing their lewd parts with scoffing, jesting or ribaldry talk'. On arrival at York, Grindal extended the same ban to rushbearers and summer lords or other 'disguised persons', musicians or dancers. He also prohibited feasts and dances in the church or churchyard. Grindal repeated this (save only the reference to the northern custom of rushbearing) on his translation to Canterbury in 1576. He was copied in the 1570s by two bishops (of Winchester and of Worcester), in the 1580s by five (of Chester, Lichfield, Lincoln, Chichester, and Hereford), and in the 1590s by one more (of London). In 1577 Richard Barnes, bishop of Durham, wanted to know if ministers frequented May games.[61] All this represented quite a large number of prelates and, cumulatively, most of England. But it still left a lot of bishops who apparently did not trouble with such matters, and was in itself no more than a continuation of the sporadic medieval attempts to keep clerics and sacred places separate from potentially drunken or ribald festivity. Only one of Elizabeth's bishops, Coldwell of Salisbury in 1595, condemned Sunday merry-making, in this case church ales ('minstrelsie, dancing and drinking under colur thereby to procure some contribution towards the repairing of their church'). And only one other, Richard Cox of Ely in 1579, made a general denunciation of 'feasting', 'wanton dancing', and 'lewd maygames sometime continuing riotously with piping all whole nights in barns and such odd places, both young men and women out of their fathers' and masters' houses'. And he does not seem to have provoked any presentments under this clause.[62] In general the attention paid by episcopal articles to seasonal rites consisted of trying to ensure that the Church's own feasts were properly observed, including the Rogationtide perambulations, and that the correct liturgy was used for them.

The same pattern obtains in the publications of those who were, or subsequently became, Elizabethan bishops. Hardly any were concerned with the issue of popular revelry. Near the opening of the reign, in 1563, the episcopal bench issued the *Book of Homilies* as an aid to ministers who had difficulty in composing their own sermons. This suggested that merry-making should be avoided (but not prohibited) upon Sunday.[63] None of Elizabeth's prelates seem to have published tracts against the old forms of festivity, and at least one apparently enjoyed them. This was the most important of all, Archbishop Whitgift, who in 1592 or 1593 paid for a pageant to end a summer season spent at his rural residence of Croydon. It included scenes of 'Maying' and of reapers bringing 'harvest home to town' and country dances of 'maids and clowns'.[64] Ironically, the best-known example of an impassioned personal reaction against festive customs in a bishop's residence concerns a Catholic clergyman. He was a Jesuit imprisoned with a number of priests of his faith at Wisbech Castle in 1597. The castle was part of the estate of the bishop of Ely, but the see was vacant and the building used as a royal gaol. At Christmas some of the officials in charge of it brought a hobby-horse into the hall to entertain their captives and themselves, and the Jesuit took grave offence at its gambols, a sign of how in England, as on the Continent, the Counter-Reformation was producing an alteration in the attitudes of some towards the old festivities even as the Reformation had done.[65] No Elizabethan bishop is known to have kept a Lord of Misrule, but they still featured at the university colleges, which were staffed by clergy and led by men who were frequently promoted to sees. The only restriction placed on them during the reign was a royal injunction at Cambridge in 1569 or 1570 which laid down that each had to be approved by the heads of the colleges.[66]

What all this indicates is that the responsibility of the leaders of Church and state for the decline of traditional festivity was at most marginal. There is at least as much evidence that they encouraged or defended aspects of it. The principal force behind the alterations must have lain elsewhere in the nation and must now be sought there. One obvious place to begin is with those authors who attacked all or some of the old-style merry-making, producing what is frequently known to historians as 'complaint literature'. Elizabethan England seems to have produced thirty-five of these, and the first two stated between them the main concerns of most of the rest. One was Thomas Becon, an evangelical Protestant preacher well known since the reign of Henry VIII, who had returned from exile at the accession of Elizabeth and been presented to some lucrative London livings. In 1560 he produced a catechism which directed that Sunday be devoted wholly to religion and condemned upon that day labour, trade, dancing, and 'laughing'.[67] As mentioned in the previous chapter, the day upon which most people rested from work was a favourite one for summer games and ales. In 1563 a 23-year-old London lawyer called Barnaby Googe, a client of Cecil, published his first volume of poems. Part of their purpose was to turn the Greek and Roman tradition of pastoral verse, celebrating the innocence and joy of rural life, to glorify God and inculcate moral lessons. Thus, ingeniously, a literary form which might have been employed to commend country merry-making was employed to criticize it. 'Pleasant May' was associated with 'sport of fruitless price' and Whitsuntide with 'idle days'. In 1570 he went on to publish a translation of a poem by the European Protestant polemicist Thomas Naogeorgus, describing Catholic rituals and folk customs in Germany and the Netherlands. Most of these had been, or were, known in England as well, and Googe's point was that the latter were part of the same 'Popish kingdom' as the former.[68]

One year later the same link was made in a much briefer list of calendar rituals provided by a Dorset clergyman, William Kethe, preaching at Blandford Forum. He felt completely ill at ease in the county, having gained a benefice there after serving as chaplain to Robert Dudley's brother, the earl of Warwick, on campaigns to aid the French Protestants and to suppress the Catholic rising in northern England. Kethe was clearly as fervent in the reformed faith as his master, and on arrival in Dorset immediately denounced dancing upon Sunday and church ales. He told the story of a minister (perhaps himself) who had clashed with his parishioners when the latter obtained a licence for such an ale from a local justice. What resulted was a complete breakdown of communication. The licence had been granted on condition that there was no disorder. To the minister the dancing, drinking, and blood sports which took place represented disorder in themselves. To the villagers the event had been orderly, because sober and peaceful. By preaching against them and airing his other views at Blandford, Kethe provoked much hard feeling and had to publish to defend himself.[69] In the same year a group of radical Protestants who were campaigning for further reformation of the Church, and would shortly launch the presbyterian movement, demanded the abolition of 'lewd customs' in parishes, 'either in games or otherwise'. They suggested that this be obtained not by legislation but through a campaign of preaching by clergy.[70]

Their suggestion was followed at once by Humphrey Roberts, minister at King's Langley, Hertfordshire, who condemned sports in general and dancing upon Sunday in particular.[71] He was echoed in turn by John

Northbrooke, who had held a living at Bristol but resigned because he thought the Church still too Catholic. In 1577 he condemned dancing as an incitement to lust, and two years later he added an invective against all plays and games as devices of the heathen Romans (citing many prurient details of ancient amorality to colour this assertion).[72] In 1577 another Protestant divine, the Essex rector William Harrison, commented with satisfaction upon the dramatic decrease in church ales. He suggested that all remaining saints' days be concentrated in the weeks following Christmas, Easter, and Whitsun, resulting in the abolition of May Day and Midsummer Day as times of leisure.[73] Between 1577 and 1581 seven other clergymen published against recreations upon Sunday.[74] All directed their message specifically to 'the godly', which was no polite and general term but one denoting enthusiastic and strenuous Protestants anxious for a more perfectly reformed society and Church. Six of them were actual or aspiring clients of that group of powerful families, Dudley, Sidney, Carey, Hastings, and Bacon, who were the leading patrons of evangelical clergy. Five were preaching or writing in the capital, and two were associated with the presbyterian movement. All of them attacked drinking and dancing, and five would allow no activities on Sunday except worship and charity. One, employed by the London Skinners' Company, denounced Lords of Misrule as 'devilish inventions', while another denied the necessity for church ales as people had in any case a duty to contribute to parish funds.

In these same four years the rector of Medbourne, Leicestershire, published a protest against the holding of the parish dedication feasts, or wakes, upon Sunday. He pointed out that they easily led to drunkenness and disorder. His work was dedicated to the bishop of London and, added to further publications upon Christian living, brought him rapid promotion culminating in a post in the Chapel Royal.[75] But hostility to popular festivity was much more marked at the radical end of the English Protestant spectrum. Anthony Gilby, one of those demanding further reformation, called for the abolition of all holy days except the feasts of Christ.[76] A curate at Ipswich, who very clearly ranked himself with 'the godly', denounced 'light dancing', Lords of Misrule, and Hocktide bindings, as contrary to the spirit of order and sobriety radiated by the Scriptures.[77] The most memorable attack in this period was, however, delivered not by a cleric but by a young gentleman recently graduated from Cambridge and looking for a post in government service. His college had been Pembroke, a self-conscious nursery of evangelical Protestantism, and he looked for preferment to that knot of families mentioned above who represented the aristocratic sponsors of that faith. His name was Edmund Spenser, and he adopted Googe's device of using pastoral as a vehicle for piety and moraliz-ing. But whereas the feebleness of Googe's muse is obvious even in the few examples reproduced above, Spenser's *Shepherd's Calendar* remains one of the landmarks of English letters, remarkable not just for its technical virtuosity but for its assimilation of European and classical literary models.[78] Its May Eclogue portrayed the traditional festivities of that month in language of such beauty that it has provided a quarry for many later writers wishing to celebrate them (and has featured already in this chapter). But whereas Spenser's precise place in the range of Protestant belief remains controver-sial, his opinion of May games is unequivocal. All the gorgeous speeches in praise of them come from a Catholic character, while the hero reveals them to be occasions for self-indulgence and idleness.

During the early 1580s the flow of complaint literature slackened, to a total of three surviving pieces between 1582 and 1584. One was another contribution to the argument that Sunday should wholly be reserved to religion, by a chaplain to Lord Hunsdon, head of the Carey family and scourge of the northern Catholic rebels.[79] The other two were among the most ferocious, and famed in posterity, of all the direct attacks upon popu-lar merry-making. The lesser, in 1582, was by the obscure Christopher Fetherston. His *Dialogue against Light, Lewd and Lascivious Daunting* not only made a lengthy condemnation of that activity, as conducive to noth-ing but sin, but went on to denounce drinking and football on Sunday and May games at any time. His targets included 'men in woman's apparell, whom you do most commonly call maymarions, whereby you infringe Deut. 22. 5' (the Mosaic law against transvestism). It accused the fool in the morris troop of insulting the divine gift of reason, and repeated an accusation made by one of the London preachers in 1577, that morrismen also 'danced naked in nets'. He produced another, that he had 'heard of ten maidens which went to set May, and nine of them came home with child'.[80] This last piece of gossip, or fantasy, was reiterated the next year in Philip Stubbes's gigantic *Anatomie of Abuses*. It was still possible for Stubbes's Victorian editor, himself a Christian socialist,[81] to feel some spon-taneous sympathy for him, as a person who dedicated his life to religion and charity. During the present century this has evaporated, and to folk-lorists in particular he has become a symbol of all that was worst in Puritanism, by any definition of the word: morbid and obsessive piety, an utter lack of humour, a suspicion of most forms of human pleasure, a delight in salacious or disgusting details, and determination to secure a society given over to religion, labour, and martial exercises. Even among the Elizabethan 'godly' he was notable for the range of targets against which he pitted his indignation, and if his intemperance was not unusual among the complaint literature, his stamina was. Although he clearly wished for further reform of the Church (ideally to a presbyterian structure), his main interest was in social improvement, by a systematic purge of extravagant clothing (save for the nobility), of profitless or frivolous recreations, and of any activities which might tempt participants to intoxication, fornication, financial extravagance, or social or religious disrespect. He was one of those who wanted to reduce ecclesiastical feasts to those of Christ and to reserve Sunday for worship. His views upon May games have been quoted (one tremendous advantage of his style being that it furnishes detailed description). Also relevant to the concerns of this book is his utter opposition to public dancing, church ales, wakes, and football. The *Anatomie* was a sufficient success to go into three more editions, each one enlarged, in the following twelve years. In view of all this, and the fact that he also published ten devotional works, it is remarkable how little we know of Stubbes. He was a gentleman who lived in London, and nothing more is certain. That he was not well connected is suggested by the dedication of the *Anatomie* to the earl of Arundel, a prominent noble but not a patron of evangelists, with the admission that Stubbes did not really know whom to approach with it.

After the *Anatomie* anything in its genre would have seemed an anticlimax, but even without it some such sense ought to have been natural. From 1585 until the end of Elizabeth's life—almost twenty years and almost half the reign—only a dozen authors attacked seasonal revelry even obliquely. Furthermore, half of these published in the last four years, making the period between the mid-1580s and mid-1590s appear particularly sparse in such literature. In part this may have been due to the failure of the parliamentary campaign to reform the Church by legislation during the period 1584–6. One of its most successful measures was a bill to achieve the minimum demanded by sabbatarians, by prohibiting fairs, football, dicing, card-playing, blood sports, and wakes upon Sunday. It was pushed through Parliament by the enthusiasm of the Commons, apparently aided by the support of royal ministers as the Speaker (a government nominee) extolled it and Cecil (now Baron Burghley) sat on the committee which processed it in the Lords. But the queen vetoed it and, in default of any firm evidence, historians have surmised that she objected not so much to the contents as to the principle that Parliaments might intervene any further in religious matters.[82] After such a disaster it is not surprising that in the next ten years only three publications addressed such issues, and that two were by outright opponents of the existing Church of England. In

1589 one of the notorious Marprelate tracts, attacking the episcopacy, returned to the complaint that 'the summer lord with his May game or Robin Hood with his morris dance' distracted youths from attending services. It added the accusation that at Halstead in Essex's Colne valley the minister had shortened his sermon in order to join the fun himself.[83] The separatist Henry Barrow agreed and went further, to attack Lords of Misrule and wassail cups and to condemn the established liturgy for, among other things, still allowing Rogationtide processions.[84] Two more orthodox clergy did, however, return to the problem of Sunday activities. In 1588 Gervase Babington, a client of the earls of Pembroke, wrote against plays, summer games, and ales on that day. Pembroke was head of the Herberts, one of the noble families celebrated as patrons of evangelists, and it was through his influence that Babington was made bishop of Llandaff three years later. But the queen liked him well enough subsequently to promote him in the episcopacy.[85] In 1591 a London minister, Richard Turnbull, wrote against Sunday feasting, dancing, and plays.[86]

The revival of literary interest in such issues after 1595 derived from two inter-related factors. One was the attention paid to parish evangelism by clerics who wished for further reformation in the Church as a whole but temporarily despaired of any legislative alterations. They preached and wrote for godly Protestants at a local level, the most famous being based in East Anglia. The second factor was an intensified interest in the sabbatarian question sparked off by one of their number, Nicholas Bownde, a Suffolk rector. His 1595 publication, *The Doctrine of the Sabbath*, was primarily intended to instruct ministers in all aspects of the subject, including the assertion that legislation was needed to prohibit all Sunday recreations save charitable works and the reading of Scripture. As Kenneth Parker has pointed out, this was hardly new. But Archbishop Whitgift banned the book as part of his long campaign to enforce a greater conformity among the Church's personnel, feeling that it was presumptuous of Bownde to lay down doctrine in this manner.[87] During the next seven years the ruling upon recreations in *The Doctrine* was defended by a minister at Bury St Edmunds and the celebrated Cambridge divine William Perkins. Perkins also wrote that Christmas was nothing more than a human custom, not ordained by Scripture, that New Year's gifts were a pagan tradition rightly condemned by early Christians, and that dancing by mixed sexes was an invitation to sin.[88] This last point was echoed by the notable Cambridgeshire minister, Richard Greenham, while the rector of Welbourn, in Lincolnshire's wooded Kesteven region, called for an end to maypoles, wakes and dancing, as Catholic survivals.[89] Much further away, the minister of

Aberffraw, on the coast of Anglesey, was unique in devoting a tract exclusively to calling upon magistrates to take down maypoles. To him 'your mischevious pole', your 'maddening pole' was a focus of idolatry and an incitement to drink and lust.[90] All of these writers, with the possible exception of the last, belonged to that movement which desired further reform of the Church. Their views were shared to a much more limited extent by two members of the ecclesiastical hierarchy. One was the bishop of Salisbury quoted earlier, the other John King, archdeacon of Nottingham, who protested that too many people took dancing and drinking more seriously than religion upon Sunday.[91]

The complaint literature as a whole presents certain obvious patterns. Most was produced by clergymen, generally of the more enthusiastic variety of Elizabethan Protestant, most prominent in the early campaigns of evangelism and subsequently least happy with the Church's structure and ceremonies. The laity who contributed tended to be of the same sort. It must be noted, however, that very few of them were closely concerned with seasonal festivities, generally considering them in association with other preoccupations such as dancing, plays, and Sunday observance.[92] Indeed, even given that the total of publications examined here can only have been the visible tip of an enormous mass of sermons, a read through the works listed in the *Short Title Catalogue* of Elizabethan literature reveals that they represent only a small percentage of the outpourings even of 'the godly'.[93] Furthermore, they are clearly not distributed evenly across the reign. Although commencing early, they really began to amount to a campaign after 1569 and reached their peak in 1577–84. It was at that time also that two bishops took a direct and hostile interest in popular merrymaking. Still, the concentration of publications at various times would afford them an impact which in some measure compensated for a relatively small overall total. The pattern of publication does bear some relationship to the decline in municipal and parochial ritual celebration. And the total is not so small in absolute terms. It becomes still more significant when we realize that for most of the reign this literature went virtually unanswered.

This is the more remarkable in that one of the principal genres of Elizabethan poetry was pastoral. Its practitioners turned out thousands of lines in which English gentlemen appeared in fancy dress as classical shepherds, usually lovesick. The landscape in which they declaimed was often recognizably that of England (during an uncommonly good summer), its foliage and flowers lovingly portrayed. But virtually all Elizabethan pastoral verse almost ostentatiously avoids incorporating any of the traditional country festivities into its evocation of a timeless rural dreamland.[94] As said above, the two poets who did during the first half of the reign intended to condemn them. The message was clear enough: such merry-making by boors was of use as an occasional amusement for jaded and refined palettes at court or household entertainments, but no fit subject for serious literature and not worth celebrating in itself. Pagan deities might be honoured, but not summer lords or morris dancers. Likewise, for most of the reign nobody thought it worthwhile to write a defence of orderly Sunday recreations. The Privy Council could issue a mandate for them when pushed by events, but there was no literary campaign in their favour. The few references to seasonal customs in drama were usually to provide a simile or a metaphor, such as when Shakespeare compared Jack Cade to a prancing morris dancer or Helena to a painted maypole.[95] Or else, very occasionally, a hobby-horse or morris would be put on stage to add some rough fun to a plot.[96] The attitudes of the educated are illus-trated again in a survey of English social problems published in 1581 by William Stafford, the younger son of an Essex knight, who was hanging around the royal court hoping for preferment. His book was one means of trying to win this. In it he noted that May games and wakes had recently been much abandoned, but did so in a quite neutral tone, as if there were no issue to be debated in the fact.[97]

Yet there were exceptions to each part of this rule, and they began to appear more often as the reign drew to a close. David Norbrook has pointed out the significance of George Puttenham, another aspiring courtier, who in 1579, at the height of the literary agitation against popular revels, presented the queen with a set of verses tactfully supporting the project of her marriage with the French duke of Anjou. This union with a Catholic prince was opposed by many of the more fervent English Protestants, and Puttenham rounded upon the latter for encouraging disorder and barbarism while claiming to do the opposite. As part of this he held that it was wrong to 'forbid peasants their country sport'.[98] The condescension in the tone still marked the same attitude which caused most genteel writers to ignore, deride or condemn the 'sport', and Puttenham remained obscure and an isolated voice. The first beginnings of a real change only came in 1586, with the first edition of *Albions England* by the London lawyer and writer William Warner. He was a tremendous classicist, a translator and imitator of ancient texts. It was Ovid's *Metamorphoses* which gave him the idea for a parallel treatment of incidents in British history and myth, to produce a work at once patriotic, sententious, and ebulliently entertaining. And also extremely successful, going into four more, and bigger, editions in the rest of the reign. What was remarkable about the short passage on festivity was the manner in which it celebrated the whole traditional round of seasonal revelry: Christmas feasting, Plough Monday games, Shrovetide 'pan-puffs', morris, Maying, Robin Hood plays, summer lords and ladies, and midsummer bonfires. It made them seem not only delightful but part of the English heritage, belonging equally to the whole nation.[99] In 1591 the madrigal writer Thomas Morley, producing a form of song especially favoured by polite society, could evoke the excitement of running to see a passing morris troupe. He invited his listeners to see the dancers as doing honour to their whole community, with the skill of their performance.[100] Two years later Warner's friend Michael Drayton made the link between pastoral poetry and folk custom. In one of his first publications, *The Shepheards Garland*, he had his rustics paying a piper to play for a morris dance, feasting on a village green with a summer queen, and crowning their loves with flowers before revelling with them in summer bowers.[101] The *Garland* was written in imitation of Spenser's *Calendar*, which Drayton much admired and was not intending to parody. It was dedicated to Robert Dudley, of the family which had sponsored zealous preachers but also supplied a Lord of Misrule and included country celebrations in royal entertainments. As Drayton was wholly dependent upon upper-class patronage for his living, his attitude must have reflected a belief that tastes were changing, as well as personal preference.[102] It seems that sophisticated society was starting to take up the despised or disliked seasonal festivals in much the same way as it was later to treat Scottish Highlanders and native Americans.

During the last four years of Elizabeth's life this trend showed a marked reinforcement. In 1598 another friend of Drayton, the aged antiquary John Stow, published *A Survey of London*. Although a conforming Anglican, there seems little doubt that Stow had quiet regrets about the Reformation, and part of the task of his *Survey* was to record lovingly the calendar customs of May and midsummer which had vanished from the city during his long lifetime together with the old religion. Extracts have been quoted already in this work, as in many others. In 1602 Richard Carew produced a companion volume, *The Survey of Cornwall*. As a JP, MP, and squire of Anthony, in the wooded hills near the Tamar, Carew was in an excellent position to pronounce upon the practical advantages and disadvantages of popular revelry. While he ignored May games, he heartily commended most traditional Cornish entertainments and provided a famous defence of saints' days and church ales. Both, he insisted, promoted neighbourliness, and ales raised more money with better feelings than compulsory levies. He suggested that they be inserted between divine worship and 'manlike activities' such as sports, and be provided with only moderately strong beer, elders supervising the young.[103] Around 1600 two writers for the London stage, John Marston and Thomas Dekker, turned out plays which portrayed summer queens and the morris with a marked sympathy. Dekker's was performed before the queen.[104]

A couple of years later Nicholas Breton, a gentleman living in the capital, took the potential of verse a little further. During the 1590s he had written pastoral lyrics of the conventional kind, set in a classical never-never land.[105] Now in 1602 he brought out a moving evocation of an older England full of peace, honesty, and low prices, in which folk revels represented innocent gaiety, 'when all the churchyard might be full of laughter', 'when hearty welcome fills the wassail bowl', and 'pipe and tabor made as merry glee as at a may-pole one would wish to see'.[106] In the same period a few clergy began to extol calendar feasts and recreations. In 1600 the minister of Stockton, amid Wiltshire's chalk downs, dedicated a tract to his bishop (of Salisbury), praising the celebration of Christmas, Easter, and Whitsun as memorials to Christ.[107] In 1601 a bishop's brother, rector of a Worcester parish, published a defence of all the official holy days, as invitations to meditate upon religion.[108] And in 1602 the vice-chancellor of Oxford, John Howson, replied to the sabbatarian writers by holding that games and entertainments could take place on Sunday once church services were over.[109] All told, by the time of Elizabeth's death the critics of festivity were facing the very beginning of a powerful reaction.

So much for the literary sources. It is time to return, finally, to the local scene and to see whether other evidence survives to account for the pattern discerned in the parochial and municipal records analysed earlier. First, in the towns. At York it is clear that the repressive work of the ecclesiastical commission was made possible by the collaboration of a few enthusiastic Protestants in the corporation, whom the influence of Grindal and Huntingdon brought to power. It is also obvious that the changes were very unpopular with most of the citizens.[110] At Coventry the lapse in the Hock Tuesday play in the early 1570s was ascribed to the influence of Protestant ministers, and its revival in 1575 won 'great commendation' from the populace. The latter continued to agitate for drama of some kind after the Corpus Christi cycle was put down, and the corporation experimented with a number of new plays until 1602 when, supported by the clergy, it called such performances 'toys' and imprisoned one of the Drapers' Company who campaigned for them.[111] At Kendal the head burgesses, probably feeling the cold breath of the ecclesiastical commission on their necks, recorded that they permitted the Corpus Christi plays to continue because of vociferous public demand.[112] In the case of Chester local hostility to the Whitsun cycle may be indicated by the case of a man who borrowed and lost the register of performances in 1568 and a dyer who refused to pay the pageant expenses of his guild in 1575.[113] But it is hard to see why the archbishop of York had to call in the Privy Council to push a mayor into suppressing the plays in that latter year if he could have raised many local allies. Things had changed a generation later, in 1599–1600, to the extent that the mayor himself, Henry Hardacre, could be a religious zealot. He turned upon the Midsummer's Eve show which was left as the principal civic pageantry, had its model giants smashed, and forbade the inclusion of the customary dragon, 'naked boys', and 'feathered devil'. But his actions were unpopular enough for his successor to 'set out the giants and the midsummer show as of old'.[114]

Some evidence also exists for the fate of urban May games. At Lincoln in the mid-1580s the corporation was divided between a faction which banned the games and poles along with Sunday trading, and one represented by the next mayor, who restored all of these. The latter group was larger, but the former strengthened by the support of the bishop and the Secretary of State, Sir Francis Walsingham, who thought them the more committed Protestants and so more reliable defenders of the regime.[115] The interventions of individual mayors, with motives which are not recorded, were also important at Shrewsbury, Canterbury and Leicester. In all cases they clashed with townspeople. In the first, in 1588, the opposition came from members of the Shearmens' Guild, in response to a ban on maypoles. The mayor concerned threw them in prison when they fought the officials taking down a pole. At Canterbury the same prohibition in the same year earned the mayor of that city a morris dance made in protest outside his house, whereupon (of course) he arrested the dancer. The man who presided over Leicester in 1599 was much more moderate, for he allowed youths to erect a maypole in the town at Whitsun. When, however, they did so uproariously, with morris dancing and firing of guns, he had it broken. The snapped shaft was fixed back together by the revellers and a man denounced the mayor, who committed him to gaol. In 1603 the corporation issued a declaration that the poles had been banned from the town because of 'manifold inconveniences and disorders' caused by 'the multitude of rude and disorderly persons' who accompanied them.[116]

What all these cases show is pressure to remove the old customs exerted from above, through or from members of the urban élite and against the wishes of at least some of the populace. Where a reason for the pressure is given it is usually religious, although at Leicester a growing concern with order was apparently more important. The same pattern holds at county and at village level. The disappearance of church ales from several Devon parishes in 1595 is explained by an order made at the midsummer quarter sessions. It declared that ales had already been forbidden on Sundays. Now it abolished Sunday plays and May games too and added that ales could only take place in daylight, without music or dancing, and with drink provided by licensed alehouse-keepers. This was because they caused 'the dishonour of Almighty God, increase of bastardy and of dissolute life and very many other mischiefs'. In 1600 a second order forbade ales completely for reasons 'which with modesty cannot be explained'.[117] The context of these measures is missing, but we now have a little of that for the parallel decrees in Somerset in 1594 and 1596, flatly prohibiting ales.[118] The moving spirit behind them was the judge Sir John Popham, who wrote to probable sympathizers to drum up support for the abolition of what he termed 'licentious' events. One recipient of his letters was Sir Francis Hastings, a gentleman of pronounced religious zeal, who himself left sums in his will to five Somerset parishes to provide funds for their regular needs. These he bequeathed on condition that they never again held ales, which he held to profane the Sabbath, cause drunkenness and riot, and to train youth in 'wantonness'.[119] Popham's family were also notable patrons of godly preaching ministers. But a particular scandal may have precipitated the action of the justices. One of the signatories of their orders was Roger Sydenham, Ranger of Exmoor.[120] In 1592 he had accused his relative Humphrey Sydenham of Dulverton of poaching the royal deer. To pay for a countersuit, Humphrey decided to hold a series of ales. His tricks included stealing up to 400 gallons of beer stored for a parish feast, mustering his militia company to take part in the events, and inviting seventeen parishes to one of them alone. He had raised £60 by this means before the county bench banned ales in 1594 and halted him.[121]

Also well documented, and much better known among historians, is the clash in Oxfordshire in 1589 which provoked the Privy Council ruling upon May games quoted above. It was commenced by an alliance between the evangelical minister of Banbury; his uncle, who was high constable of the local hundred; and Sir Anthony Cope, who had been a campaigner for further reform in the Church. They sent out warrants to forbid wakes, maypoles, church ales, May games, and morris dancers, and provoked riots by attempts to enforce them in the nearby villages. They were opposed by the high sheriff of the county, Sir John Danvers, whom they described as a 'disorderly liver', on bad terms with his own local clergymen and said to have danced instead of attending church at Christmas. The Council's order gave victory to Danvers, and while Banbury itself became a notably godly and sober community, a village in its hundred like South Newington could continue to hold annual Whitsun ales.[122] In the same year there was another well-recorded row in Hertfordshire. Lady Bacon, one of the gentry sponsors of evangelists, had brought to St Albans one William Dyke, a preacher already suspended from his ministry in Essex for refusal to conform to the established Church. He immediately set about a condemnation of one of the few survivors of the county's church ales, held annually at nearby Redbourn. Dyke did not attempt to claim that it was badly behaved, but averred that it was 'abused' by piping, dancing, and the custom whereby a Maid Marian came into church to kiss parishioners and make them laugh. Redbourn people denounced him in turn to the bishop of London for preaching against the church hierarchy and liturgy, and he was promptly silenced again. His own congregation enlisted the support of Burghley, the local magnate and still the queen's principal minister of state, who agreed that Dyke was a fine preacher and probably innocent as charged. But the bishop was apparently unmoved.[123] At about this time the formidable John Bruen became active in Cheshire, in an episode as familiar to historians as that at Banbury. This is because of the biography of him by a local cleric, describing how Bruen, who died in 1625, had first enjoyed summer games and then, in the latter part of Elizabeth's reign, got religion and turned against them. Using his influence as a landowner, he conducted a campaign to abolish wakes and stop Sunday revelry of any kind in his district, the north-western part of the county. His biographer implies that he met with considerable success.[124]

A few miles from Bruen's neighbourhood, across the river Mersey, lay Lancashire and the setting for another fairly well-known sequence of events about which more can now be said. It began at Burnley in 1579, when a Robin Hood play (the most northerly recorded) provoked some kind of trouble, either actual misbehaviour or just dislike on the part of some local people. A group of JPs in the Manchester area, the most notable part of the county for enthusiastic Protestantism, decided that these customs only led to 'wantonness', by provoking lust and other bad impulses which harmed Christianity. They enlisted the support of the ecclesiastical commission and wrote to magistrates further north directing them to ban the revels and threatening them not only with the commission but with the Privy Council.[125] They themselves acted at once to ban fairs and music on Sunday in the hundred around Manchester. At the summer assizes in 1587 the preacher, Edward Fleetwood, persuaded the royal judges to extend this to the whole county with a prohibition on all Sunday ales, wakes, and other revelry. Fleetwood and his clerical and gentry allies now commenced a campaign to enlist the support of the bishop of Chester and turn that of the Privy Council into a reality. Both were persuaded by playing upon their fear of Catholicism, with the assertion that the very numerous Lancashire Catholics were sponsoring merry-making to keep people away from church. As mentioned earlier, the Council ordered a campaign against any such attempts. By 1590 the justices had started to act against traditional customs in the Pennine valleys, prosecuting the piper of Clitheroe and two spinsters of Goosenargh for playing and for rush-bearing on a Sunday, respectively.[126]

The patchy survival of Elizabethan legal archives may conceal other orders such as those issued for Devon, Somerset, and Lancashire. The same records and those of church courts furnish further evidence for attitudes to the old seasonal entertainments. Their most valuable service is to reveal the existence of people hostile to these activities as low down in society as the level of the wealthy farmers who made up churchwardens and jurymen. As early as the 1560s some in southern Essex presented individuals for going 'a-mumming' from house to house at Christmas, while at a nearby village a man was in trouble for morris dancing in service time. In the same decade villagers in south-east Kent denounced men for making bonfires on Midsummer Eve and St Peter's Eve. The minister of another village of Kent, in the Isle of Thanet, was cited for lighting a Peter's Eve fire, and the midsummer pyrotechnics were also a source of complaint in Hampshire. Their symbolic importance as a point of friction between local religious reformers and conservatives was well revealed in 1561 at Canterbury, where the latter controlled the council and found themselves confronting ardently Protestant preachers just installed in the cathedral. Aldermen encouraged both May games upon Sundays and an unusually large number of fires upon both Midsummer Night and St Peter's Night, which the Protestant clergy considered to be 'in contempt of the Christian religion, and for upholding the old frantic superstitions of papistry'. Each invective from the cathedral pulpits produced a further flaring of blazes in the streets, culminating in a huge one made at the Bull-stake on the evening of St Peter's Day with the help of the sheriff and a constable. A local wag nicknamed 'Railing Dick' led a procession of boys around it, carrying birch boughs and singing bawdy songs.[127] The fact that bonfires did not feature in the visitation articles and appeared very little in the complaint literature shows an interesting divergence between the priorities of national and local élites. By the 1580s they had converged a little, a man at Boughton in Nottinghamshire's Sherwood Forest being cited for setting up a maypole in the churchyard.[128] At Wootton, just west of Oxford, 'the youth were somewhat merry together in crowning of lords' one Midsummer Day at evening prayer, and were denounced to the archdeacon for irreverence (he dismissed the case).[129] In the 1590s the erection of a maypole upon a Cheshire green 'where a piper and divers youth were playing and dancing' could be reported to the archbishop of York, although the deponent could not remember if it had been on a Sunday or not.[130] In Essex an Elmstead man was cited for setting up a pole in service time, while the churchwardens of White Notley themselves neglected worship to instal one. Those of Wivenhoe were accused of allowing morris on a Sunday. By that decade, also, church ales were sufficiently unpopular with some Berkshire people for the wardens at Thatcham, in the Kennet valley, to be presented at the assizes for making one.[131]

Doubtless a comprehensive search of all surviving legal records would reveal more such cases, but they do seem extraordinarily rare and appear to reflect a genuine disinclination on the part of local people to report each other for such activities. Some examples, moreover, are of dubious value for the preoccupations of this book. At Warbleton in the Sussex Weald, a young carpenter was shot and killed as he and others were trying to remove a maypole from the village green. This episode has twice been linked with the recent arrival of a zealously Protestant minister, to suggest that the incident was provoked by hostility to the poles.[132] But the fact that the dead man came from another village might suggest that he and his companions were trying to steal this one as a trophy, a custom well recorded in the Stuart period.[133] Certainly the paucity of firm evidence relating to festivity in the legal records contrasts with the large quantity concerning Rogation perambulations. It is easy for a researcher to spend days without coming across any of the former, but only an hour or two in a diocesan court archive will suffice to turn up the latter. This of course reflects their proportional importance in visitation articles, but is not explained by episcopal interest alone: the cases would not exist without parishioners willing to bring them. The results show that the processions met with plenty of difficulties in the reign of Elizabeth, even excluding those created by the minister adhering to some of the Catholic rites. In Cheshire, Essex, Nottinghamshire, and Cambridgeshire parsons or laity objected to the custom on the grounds that it was popish in itself. Most colourful was a man at Westlebury in Essex during 1565, who pointed to a boundary marker and asked 'Is there an idol here to be worshipped that you have a drinking?' But these incidents, which between them span the reign, were very rare, numbering one or two in each county in this little sample. More common was neglect, because of squabbles between the minister and the parish élite, because the route had been blocked by a new wall, hedge, or ditch, or because of lack of interest on the part of cleric, parishioners, or both. The situation was most fraught in towns, where boundaries were often badly defined. Three Colchester parishes threw up accusations more often than any others in Essex. Likewise, in 1597 some twenty-five out of 542 involved in a visitation of Norfolk were slack in perambulating, but eight of these were in the city of Norwich. East Suffolk seems to have had exceptionally severe problems even in rural areas, for out of 260 parishes questioned in the same year, thirty-five had no such processions, while in sixteen more the minister did not take part.[134] Such a situation seems, even given the lack of comparable evidence for the earlier period, to have been a creation of the Reformation, undermining support for the old tradition. But the fact that so many people were prepared to report breaches, and that they apparently did not occur in the great majority of parishes, indicates that it was still widely respected.

So it is time to consider the whole body of evidence laid out above and to attempt to answer from it the question posed at the opening, of why municipal and parochial festivity declined so steadily in the reign of Elizabeth. What emerges is the paramount importance of evangelical Protestantism. This is, given the contrast between the fortunes of such festivity under Edward and under Mary, very much what we would already expect. The text of that religion, the Bible, provides an ample enough understanding of why hostility to seasonal customs should have abounded among those most conscious of Scripture and most determined to remould the world according to its decrees. The Books of Kings and those of the prophets are filled with fulminations against the veneration of stones and trees, and of deities represented in masonry or timber, which an impressionable mind might easily transfer to the reading of prayers before a parish boundary marker or the erection of a maypole. Most notorious of such examples, of course, was the dance of the Israelites around the golden calf, and it is worth reminding some modern readers that this offended Moses so much that he did not merely rebuke them but had 3,000 of them killed.[135] The prurience of some of the Elizabethan complaint literature is partly explained by the lubricity of diatribes against the heathen by the authors of the Books of Ezekiel and Hosea. The fear and hatred of 'wantonness' which these passages could inspire would be reinforced by Christ's own praise for those who made themselves 'eunuchs for God' and St Paul's recommendation of celibacy as the finest of human conditions for those who (like himself) were able to bear it. To him marriage was only a means of escaping the sin of fornication, against which he repeatedly thundered. Likewise St Peter warned people to avoid 'lewdness'.[136] Furthermore, the heroes and heroines of the Old Testament are never shown enjoying a bois-terous social life (the most spectacular example of which is Belshazzar's Feast). Christ's meals were likewise quiet and businesslike affairs, while both Peter and Paul told Christians to shun drunkenness, banquets, and revels.[137] The Bible was not written by people who would have appreci-ated a village ale or a morris dance.

Of course, it required certain types of personality to respond more intensely to these passages than to the many others in Scripture, and Christians versed in Holy Writ could argue that celebrations which did not involve intoxication, gluttony, or fornication were perfectly permissible. The enemies of popular merry-making did not merely quote Biblical texts but used four different arguments, all articulated in the publications and orders cited above. The first was that revels profaned the Lord's Day. In fact the theological status of the Christian Sunday was anything but clear, as it was not after all the Jewish Sabbath (which falls on Saturday) and as Christ had abrogated the strict rules of the latter, to some extent, for his followers. The opposition of many devout Protestants to Sunday recreations arose not so much from a clear scriptural warrant as from an instinct that just as secular activities should be kept out of sacred places so they should be kept away from the day of worship.[138] The second major charge was that the traditional festive customs were Catholic—a natural enough one in that they had flourished so obviously in the time of the old Church, had overlapped with its institutions, and had reflected a love of ceremony and display characteristic of late medieval religion. The recasting of the Catholic faith itself, which began before the reign of Elizabeth and which has been called the Counter-Reformation, was in fact to produce an official disapproval of customary merry-making among the adherents of Rome (such as the captive Jesuit at Wisbech) almost as strong as that among their enemies. As said earlier, the 'reformation of manners' was a phenome-non common to most of European Christendom. But the perception of many Tudor Protestants, that the 'manners' which they wished to reform descended from an older world with a different religion, was perfectly accu-rate.

The third charge was that the customs were heathen. In part this was simply a gloss of Old Testament rhetoric, but it was also the product of humanist learning. In 1502 the famous Italian scholar resident in England, Polydor Vergil, had published *De Rerum Inventoribus*, an attempt to discover the origins of religion, government, law, science, and social customs. As part of this he traced many religious and secular rites to pagan origins, including Candlemas candles, feasting, New Year's gifts, dancing, mumming, Maying, Christmas lords, Shrove Tuesday revelry, and midsummer bonfires. His purpose was not simply to instruct or entertain but to criticize and reform, pointing out that all these activities were capable of abuse, that dancing had become immoderate, and that the wearing of masks was inexcusable. The book went into thirteen more editions over the next hundred years, and supplied material for the direct and comprehensive attack upon Catholic ritual published by Thomas Becon (whose sabbatarian views have been quoted) in 1563.[139] All of it, he suggested, derived from the whims of individual Popes or from paganism. The heathendom to which these writers referred was not the Celtic twilight beloved of nineteenth- and twentieth-century folklorists but that of ancient Rome, revealed in classical texts, and some of the lines of descent which they inferred seem very questionable. But they supplied what seemed to be sound ammunition to many Protestants.

The fourth charge was, of course, that of disorder. As seen above, this could involve some severe difficulties of semantics, determined reformers attaching the label to activities which seemed perfectly dignified to those involved in them (and also to historians). There is, furthermore, something absurd about the notion that late Tudor villagers could hold their drink less well, and that Elizabethan girls were more prone to lose their maidenheads while going a-Maying, than those of the reign of Henry VII. As shown, popular festivals did indeed lead to riot and rebellion at times from the fourteenth to the early sixteenth century, without making local or central government inclined to forbid them. In addition, social and legal scholars seem agreed that violence or fornication rarely occurred at them in the late Tudor and Stuart periods, and that patterns of marital conception, let alone of bastard-bearing, have little relationship to seasonal revelry.[140] It is certainly true that the change from ales and other festive gatherings to rates, rents, and pew-rents as a means of financing the parish was part of a wider reform of English local government. In the course of the Elizabethan age the imposition of rates to provide poor relief, a militia, and lesser services became a feature of town and village life. It must be noted also that William Stafford, the courtier writing in 1581, said that ales were commonly laid aside as too expensive.[141] But, as said above, the regular expenditure upon religion of the Protestant parish was less than that before the Reformation, and church ales did continue to raise very large sums under Elizabeth, keeping up well with the rate of inflation.[142] Furthermore, the survival of early Elizabethan poor law records is too slight to permit any insight into whether parishes abandoned ales as part of the same process as the move to systematic poor relief. Indeed, their scarcity may be due to the fact that few ever existed. It was not until 1598 that overseers of the poor had to be appointed in every parish, and although an act of 1572 had directed the imposition of rates, it seems to have been very haphazardly obeyed.[143] The chronology seems wrong to account for the relatively early, and sustained, decline in fund-raising by festivity.

Given all this, it is quite possible to talk away all considerations of social and economic pressure and to allocate all responsibility to a reformed religion, employing a social rhetoric as one argument for its wishes. But that would be to ignore the evidence that the talk of disorder and misbehaviour in connection with revels became more pronounced in the course of the reign. Also, that the connection between the 'godly' and the enemies of popular festivals was rather less absolute in the early Stuart period, as will be discussed. It is already stretching the available information to assume that all the justices who signed the orders against ales in Somerset and Devon were religious enthusiasts; Sydenham for one had clear alternative motives. And a reduction to the religious factor would ignore another clearly established and important context for the alteration in attitudes to revelry. This is the undoubted growth in poverty and social polarization consequent upon population and monetary inflation in the sixteenth century, mentioned at the opening of the chapter. It certainly created a much more general and constant fear of famine and social unrest among the local élites of late Elizabethan England and a much greater propensity to regulate the behaviour of the populace and to reduce opportunities for unruly crowd activity and for sexual encounters which might result in bastard or pauper children for whom the parish would have to pay. Thus it may be suggested here that during the reign of Elizabeth religion was the most potent source of attitudes to traditional festivity, but that social anxieties also became important towards its end. This is to reverse the priorities of much of the recent historiography of the 'reformation of manners', although to draw this conclusion for popular revels is not necessarily to do so for other aspects of the social reformation.

Finally, something must be said about the positive aspects of the process. Protestantism did not, after all, simply eradicate aspects of an old culture, but substituted important replacements and alternatives of its own.[144] One of these was a new national calendar festival, to mark the anniversary of the accession of Elizabeth on 17 November. Its importance was first stressed at the four hundredth anniversary, in 1958, by Elizabeth's biographer Sir John Neale and (more particularly) by the art historian Sir Roy Strong.[145] Sir John noted that a few London parishes rang bells upon that day from the tenth anniversary, in 1568, but that the custom became national as a result of an upsurge of feeling towards the queen provoked by the rebellion of 1569 and the papal bull excommunicating her in 1570. He showed that it was added to the rota of holy days in 1576, and illustrated its celebration at Bridgnorth in Shropshire (where the corporation sometimes had a bonfire), at Ipswich in Suffolk (where the schoolmaster presented pageants in 1583), and at St Andrew Holborn in London (where the parish instituted a dole to poor women in 1584). He quoted a commentator upon the last official celebration, in 1602, who remarked that the day passed 'with the ordinary solemnity of preaching, singing, shooting, ringing and running'. Sir Roy endorsed this account of the feast's origins and added that at court it was celebrated by a ceremonial tournament in which the queen received the homage of nobles and gentry, who often rode there in ornate carriages accompanied by allegorical figures who addressed the sovereign.

He also provided a much more detailed study of its civic and parochial festivity, covering eleven towns and twenty-six parishes. In this he showed that bells had been rung at Worcester as well as at London in 1568, and that although the custom spread across most of southern and central England in the 1570s it reached Norfolk and Suffolk only in the next decade and some Durham parishes only in the 1590s. He illustrated the same range of municipal display for the occasion as Neale had done, across his wider sample, and also showed how it could evolve over time. Thus Oxford corporation paid for a sermon in 1571, and added organ music in 1572, fireworks in 1573, music and almsgiving in 1585, a drummer in 1587, and bonfires in 1590. Maidstone had bell-ringing, fireworks, a militia review, an open-air venison roast, and a pageant carried through the town by child players. In 1589 Northampton built a model castle on the town conduit, which was besieged, taken, and burned. Sir Roy suggested that the festival brought to reality the project proposed by Morison in the 1530s, of an anti-papal annual holiday, and allowed a revival of the civic display which had been dampened down by the Reformation. The official prayer book for the day was published in 1576 and enlarged in 1578, with Thomas Bentley publishing a set of private prayers and meditations for the date in 1582 and Edmund Bunny, subdeacon of York, adding some commentaries in 1585. These prayers stressed the sacred nature of godly monarchy and hailed Elizabeth as the restorer of peace, liberty, and the true religion. The service also gave an opportunity to clergymen from Whitgift downwards to preach and publish sermons on the same theme, usually treating the queen as spiritual heiress of the righteous sovereigns of the Old Testament. Sir Roy also showed that the observation of the day was attacked by the occasional radical Protestant, like Robert Wright, chaplain to Lord Rich, who thought the praise given to Elizabeth idolatrous. But it was, he added, far more the target of Catholic polemicists, who were angered by the unprecedented dedication of a holy day to a living human being. He also noted that three churches in the London area, one in Kent, and one in Salisbury added a tradition of ringing bells upon the queen's birthday, 7 September.

Strong's essay remains the basic study of the subject, but in 1975 Frances Yates added further details upon the royal jousts and in 1989 David Cressy incorporated a chapter upon the whole feast into his book upon Protestant festivity.[146] The former established that the tilts are first recorded in 1581 and were in large measure the responsibility of Sir Henry Lee, himself a formidable competitor. He last took part in 1590, wearing gilt armour with crowns upon the caparison to indicate that he was the queen's champion. Her favourite courtier at that time, the earl of Essex, was armoured in black, and the decorations of the tiltyard included a pavilion representing the Temple of the Vestal Virgins (a compliment, of course, to the Virgin Queen) and a crowned pillar written with verses extolling the sovereign. Earlier costumes for retainers had included those of native Americans and Gaelic Irish. The surviving speeches draw upon the imagery of medieval chivalry, full of knights, hermits, shepherds, and fairies, linking the world of Protestantism with that of the Middle Ages. Professor Cressy reworked and amplified Sir Roy's material, looking at more sermons and more parochial and municipal celebrations. He suggested that the most common name for the festival was 'Crownation Day', the day on which Elizabeth took the crown, distinguished carefully from Coronation Day, which took place in 1559 and was never commemorated thereafter. He also drew attention to official sponsorship in spreading the celebrations, by local leaders such as the bailiff of Ludlow, the mayors of Oxford and Liverpool, and the chancellor of the bishop of Gloucester. He stressed the much smaller scale of attention paid to Elizabeth's birthday, lesser sums always being expended on the ringers. He also noticed that in parts of the East Midlands parishioners called the day by its pre-Reformation name, the feast of St Hugh of Lincoln, the popular local patron. Lincoln College, Oxford, tactfully rang for both the queen and the saint. Professor Cressy traced observation of the day back to 1567, at Lambeth, and found it at a second London church in 1568. He established that it not only became general in southern England during the 1570s but spread into the north in the middle of that decade. He averred that it was never a true holy day like the feasts of Christ and the apostles, because no rest from work was enjoined, and so the bell-ringing and services took place in the evening.

Nothing can be added here upon the royal jousts, and little on the municipal celebrations, but a much larger sample of church records does allow of some further suggestions about the observation of the day at parish level. For one thing it seems to answer Professor Cressy's question concerning whether the propagation of it depended more upon local enthusiasm or pressure from the central government. It reveals a spontaneous expression of loyalty to the queen on the part of a few parishes in the metropolis and large southern provincial towns in the late 1560s,[147] greatly swelled by the rebellion and plots of the years 1569–71. Official recognition of this did not come until almost a decade had passed and bells were being rung for 17 November in virtually all southern counties, most of those in the Midlands, and in Chester and York.[148] Doubtless accidents in the survival of records conceal a still wider distribution. The pattern of appearance was for major urban centres to take it up first, followed by market towns and villages, and the effect of official recognition was to push observation into more rural communities and additional urban parishes in the south, and into the countryside and lesser towns of the north. But there was no neat movement from major to minor settlements, and parishes with the most illustrious patronage were not necessarily the first to get involved. St Margaret, Westminster, at the gate of one of the monarch's principal residences, did not ring bells until 1570, and St Martin in the Fields, near the other gate of the palace, began in 1572. The university church of Cambridge trailed four years behind a less distinguished parish, while no Oxford church seems to have done anything until the official prayers were issued. The process of adoption clearly depended greatly upon local whim. In the City of London, the church of St Botolph Bishopsgate was already ringing for 'the queen's day' when its records begin in 1568. Another London parish began that year, and another in 1569, after reading the royal homily issued against rebellion. Nineteen more started in the 1570s, one in the 1580s, and one more in the 1590s,[149] while St George Botolph Lane and Holy Trinity Minories never seem to have bothered. By the time that Elizabeth died her accession day was honoured in every county in her realm for which records survive, but in twenty-one parishes in the sample, from every region, the celebration of it was only commenced in the last ten years.[150] And there are another forty-nine, again from every region, which had still not taken notice of it.[151] Most were small villages or poorer urban parishes, but then so were many of those where the bells were rung. At Cranbrook in Kent, Cratfield in Suffolk, and Dursley in Gloucestershire, observation was commenced and then abandoned.

Thus to describe the festival of the queen's accession as a 'national' one is both accurate and misleading; the complex of communities which made up the nation adopted or ignored it at will. Likewise the custom of ringing again upon the queen's birthday was adopted by fifteen out of the forty-three London churches which have left late Elizabethan records, all of those in Salisbury, one out of four in Norwich, and three out of nine in Bristol. It also appeared at Hereford, the Wiltshire chalkland town of Devizes, and a Kent village on the main road to Dover, but not, apparently, in cities like York or Chester. Lambeth, by the archbishop's palace, was the only other village in the sample. This birthday salute in every case began later than the accession day one, appearing at Lambeth in 1574 and at the effusively loyal London church of St Botolph Bishopsgate and at one in Bristol[152] two years later. By 1590 it was present in the Kent village, a Salisbury parish, those around the palace of Whitehall, one in Norwich, and one more in London,[153] but all the rest which took it up, the majority in the sample, only did so in the 1590s. It was, pre-eminently, a tribute to an aged sovereign. The tendency to call the accession day 'St Hugh's' was also a matter of local caprice. As Professor Cressy remarked, it was chiefly found in the huge territory of the pre-Reformation diocese of Lincoln with which the saint's cult had especially been associated. But not only did it overspill it, to reach out as far as Hertfordshire, Warwickshire, Nottinghamshire, and Derbyshire, but within that great area only a minority of communities which have left records in each county opted for that piece of pious nostalgia.[154] Generally, the earlier entries for celebration of the event, between 1568 and 1576, went to some lengths to make clear exactly what it commemorated, the queen's accession. But later it was known simply by its date, or as 'the queen's day', 'the queen's night', 'the queen's holy day', or (especially common among those churches who took it up after 1585) 'Coronation day'. Professor Cressy's form, of 'crownation', is actually quite rare, while 'coronation' is so common and so plainly spelled in the 1590s that it seems obvious that many churchwardens had forgotten exactly what they were celebrating.

Nor is it clear that there was, indeed, much celebration. The principal form was to ring the bells, paying the ringers in cash or in bread and beer. They also usually required candles, as the job was done in the dark, and the appearance of the label 'queen's night' for the occasion in several parishes would confirm Professor Cressy's suggestion that the peals rang out in the evening once most people had finished work. But at Mildenhall in the west Suffolk heathlands the bells were busy at daybreak instead, and so it may have been elsewhere. Only a few places held a communion,[155] and some attention must be paid to the statement of the vice-chancellor of Oxford in 1602, while eulogizing the day, that services upon it were thinly attended.[156] Even given the fact that mid-November is not the best time in the English year for outdoor festivities, it is notable that the parish funds were not used to provide any entertainments except the reward to the ringers. And out of the whole sample only St Lawrence, Reading, managed to supply this reward by a collection among parishioners.[157] At Bishop's Stortford, Hertfordshire, this was attempted, and failed,[158] and elsewhere the bells were swung by individuals paid out of the general parish stock. As no release from work was allowed that day, the various activities described by the writer in 1602 quoted by Neale referred to clergy, courtiers, and garrisons such as that of the Tower. At St Oswald, Durham, the churchwardens supplied a tar barrel (for a bonfire), but this does not seem to have happened elsewhere.[159] Even the impressive catalogue of municipal celebration compiled by Sir Roy Strong and David Cressy must be viewed with two qualifications. One is that several corporations do not appear to have launched public entertainments for that day, examples including Newcastle upon Tyne, York, Marlborough, and Plymouth. The other is that those which did tended to provide them in some years but not in all.[160] Adoption of the day into the local calendar was not part of the same process as the abolition of traditional seasonal merry-making; parishes which ceased to sponsor ales or May games only sometimes observed the queen's day, and in most of these cases the former happened long before the latter. In some communities the old-style festive fund-raising and the ringing for Elizabeth took their place together in the ritual year.[161] After all, the new honour paid to the state did not fulfil, and therefore did not replace, the functions of the old annual celebrations. But when this is said, the commemoration of the royal anniversary was certainly a very widespread, very common, and very important event by the middle of the reign, and even more so by its end.

To sum up. Although the personal predilections of the queen slowed up the process, the drive against the secular and semi-secular customs of the old ritual year, an obvious feature of the Edwardian Reformation, was resumed as part of the Elizabethan. It succeeded in severing the link between those customs and parish or municipal affairs in most communities of the realm. Furthermore, reinforced by economic pressures it produced a new intolerance of those entertainments when carried on by persons acting outside of any official framework. And it created a new calendar festival, of worship and formal rejoicing directed towards the service of the state. But the old-fashioned sponsorship of the traditional celebrations remained in some of the most populous and important parts of the country, and the leaders of Church and state did not themselves subscribe to the campaign against them. Furthermore, by the end of the Elizabethan period there were signs of a sentimental reaction in favour of old-style popular merry-making among writers and their patrons. There were also traces of a tendency to eulogize ceremony, and the feasts of the Christian year, among churchmen. If these movements were to strengthen, and to combine, then the rites and recreations of the seasons would become controversial and divisive in a way in which they had never been under the Tudors. And this was, of course, exactly what was now to occur.

The Battle for Merry England

IN 1983 Sir Keith Thomas, invited to deliver the Creighton Trust Lecture at London university, chose as his theme 'The Perception of the Past in Early Modern England'.[1] Among many topics examined under this heading, he drew attention to the tendency of Elizabethans and Jacobeans to view the past as a golden age of prosperity and harmony.[2] In the process he carried out much pioneering work of importance to this present book, including the identification, noted above, of the earliest appearance of the term 'Merry England'. He also demonstrated the tendency of commentators to locate the vanished age of merriment in the relatively recent past: by Elizabethans, in the time before the Reformation; by early Stuart writers, in the reign of Elizabeth; and by late Stuart authors, in the early seventeenth century. This he attributed to the enchantment of backward vision which is the essence of nostalgia. But in an important sense all these sources were both objective and realistic. The early Tudor culture of seasonal celebration *was* in decline over the whole subsequent period of a century and a half. Thus it was quite correct at any one stage of the process to identify more of that traditional culture in the preceding age. But this nostalgia was at its peak in the years between the accession of James I and the collapse of Charles I's Personal Rule. It became during that time a serious political issue, of which historians of early Stuart England have always been conscious. The intent of this chapter is to co-ordinate for the first time all the various aspects of this issue, and to add to the evidence for them.

In their observation of the ritual year, local communities showed an awareness that the death of Elizabeth closed an era. The annual celebration of her accession day ended promptly with the reign.[3] With less obvious reason, those few communities which had instituted a yearly commemoration of the defeat of the Spanish Armada, the parishes of Salisbury and the corporation of Norwich, also wound that up at the passing of the queen.[4] Norwich churches had also rung bells ever since 1549 to mark the defeat of Kett's Rebellion; most ceased to do this at the death of Elizabeth.[5] The people of England were self-consciously drawing a line under the Tudor period. The attitude of the new monarch to festive pastimes, as suggested by his record as king of Scots, appeared to be balanced. On the one hand he had presided over ecclesiastical assemblies which had issued strict orders against work and sports upon Sunday.[6] His own book, *Basilikon Doron*, held that the Sabbath was to 'be kept holy' and 'no unlawful pastime used'. But the same work suggested that holy days, such as Christmas and May Day, ought to be marked by 'honest games', martial exercises, 'covening of neighbours', and merriment.[7]

Upon arrival in his new realm, James pursued the dual policy which his previous record had promised. Upon his way down to London he was entertained in Northamptonshire by a morris dance, provided by local people on their own initiative.[8] Soon after the completion of his journey he issued a proclamation intended to win favour with the English by addressing grievances left over from the time of the old queen. We cannot be certain upon whose advice the list was compiled, but it ended with the substance of the sabbatarian bill which Elizabeth had vetoed in 1584. James now obtained most of the ends of that measure by royal decree, forbidding 'common plays', baiting of animals, 'or other like disordered or unlawful exercises' on Sunday.[9] The vague nature of the last phrase allowed considerable latitude to reformers, although it soon became obvious that dramatic performances at court were not 'common', and so continued to take place on the Lord's Day.[10] When the king wanted one on Christmas night 1608, and was told by his 'lords' that it was not the fashion, he snapped that he would make it one.[11] From the opening of the reign a pattern was established of having plays at court on almost every evening of the Twelve Days, with a masque upon Twelfth Night. The principal Christian feasts of Christmas, Easter, and Whitsun were marked by sermons delivered by senior churchmen in the Chapel Royal, of whom Lancelot Andrewes had emerged by 1605 as James's favourite festival preacher. Shrovetide remained, as before, the other notable season for court revels.[12] All this made it most unlikely that the king would pay attention to that clause of the Millenary Petition, presented to him as he entered England by ministers wishing for the further reform of the Church, to reduce the status of holy days. But, as noted, he was prepared to act upon another part of that petition, for stricter observance of

Sunday. A year after the royal proclamation, the latter issue was raised again at the Hampton Court Conference, called by James so that the proponents of reform could confront the bishops. All present agreed upon the need for more action upon it, and the subsequent Canons, while unpalatable to the reformers in many respects, abolished permission for Sunday labour in harvest time.[13]

Thus James's attitude to the ritual year was very similar to that of Elizabeth but with a slightly tougher sabbatarian line. Much the same may be said about his bishops. They included men such as Gervase Babington and John King who had published against Sunday entertainments under Elizabeth. By 1615 King had been promoted to London and asked the churchwardens of the diocese if May games and ales 'profaned' the Lord's Day and 'led people away' to 'lewdness'.[14] In 1616 one of the royal chaplains, Lewis Bayly, was made bishop of Bangor. Four years earlier he had published *The Practice of Piety*, a book so popular that it went into thirty-six editions in the next two decades. It recommended that all recreations and sports be forbidden on Sunday, and asserted that only 'long custom' permitted the retention of saints' names for holy days.[15] In the 1614 Parliament a bill was sent up to the Lords which forbade, among other things, morris dancing and bear-baiting upon Sunday. The current archbishop of Canterbury, George Abbot, held that it was a godly measure which deserved full support, and his colleagues of Lincoln and Oxford agreed. But the only other bishop whose views upon it are recorded, James Montagu of Bath and Wells, held that dancing and merry-making were things approved by Scripture and that Sunday recreations were allowed even in Calvin's Geneva.[16] We are left to wonder what the rest of the episcopal bench thought, and further discussion of the bill was prevented by the dissolution of the Parliament. Certainly most of the Jacobean episcopacy, including Abbot, paid little attention in their published visitation articles to the prohibition of Sunday entertainments. They were more concerned with stopping labour and trade on that day and, as before, with making sure that revels did not disturb church services or draw people away from them. They also, as embodied in the northern ecclesiastical commission, seem to have put the finishing touches to the suppression of the old Corpus Christi drama. The only recorded example to survive Elizabeth, as described, was at Kendal in Westmorland. In 1605 the town council had to pay for journeys by representatives to attend the commissioners at York, and thereafter all references to the play cease.[17] But like the king, his bishops generally showed a firm commitment to the existing cycle of Church holy days.[18]

The sabbatarian bill which failed in 1614 was one of two such measures introduced in the earlier Parliaments of the reign. It had a predecessor in 1606 which tried to prohibit Sunday blood sports, plays, morris and other dances, rush-bearing, May games, and wakes. This passed the Commons within three weeks and without a division, but it died in its committee stage in the Lords, for reasons which remain unclear and which occasioned no controversy.[19] We cannot be sure whether the proposed measure of 1614 was identical and therefore whether changes in the proposals or in the mood of the peers account for its greater success. Certainly the Lord Chancellor supported it as well as both archbishops and most who debated it, whether clerics or noblemen, and it does seem that both Houses would have passed it if the dissolution had not intervened.[20] Unsurprisingly, the surge of sabbatarian literature which had commenced in the last decade of Elizabeth's reign continued into the first decade of the new one. Some existing works went into further editions. They included those of Perkins, and the controversial book by Nicholas Bownde, which was reprinted in 1606[21] and was said by later observers to have had a widespread impact, especially among town councillors.[22] Its appearance fitted into the middle of a run of five new publications of similar import by six different authors between 1603 and 1608. Three were, unsurprisingly, associated with the campaign for further reform of the Church, the most outspoken being Richard Rogers, minister at Wethersfield in northern Essex. He not only called for the reservation of the Lord's Day for religion but for a complete end to 'dissolute merry May kings' and to 'cursed fellowships' such as plays, May games, Lords of Misrule, and the morris.[23] But William Crashawe, preacher to the Temple and somebody who was contented with the government and liturgy of the Church, could still declare that plague would strike London again if (among other things) the Lord Mayor did not stop the 'abuse' of Sunday by trading, May games, morris, wakes, and feasts.[24] A minister at Portsmouth could plead for games, banquets, and dances to be kept to weekdays, compare maypoles and summer bowers to plague-infected houses, and accuse Lords of Misrule of insulting Christ.[25] A parson at Thornbury in Gloucestershire's Vale of Berkeley called feasting, dancing, games, maypoles, church ales, and plays 'heathenish vanities', to be kept away from Sunday.[26] And in 1612, as described, the future Bishop Bayly published very similar views. None the less, it is notable that in all the ten years between 1608 and 1618 Bayly's was the only further contribution to the 'complaint literature'. This comparative silence suggests that either the authors of such works felt that the point had been made effectively, or they felt cowed. The reward given to Bayly and the progress of the 1614 bill tell against the latter interpretation, and so do the local records. Their evidence may be considered now.

The open-ended nature of the 1603 proclamation certainly resulted in its use as a weapon by some local vigilantes. One high official in the East Midlands, whose identity is not preserved, immediately issued instructions to parish constables to stop all ales or wakes and prevent piping or dancing on Sunday. He cited the proclamation as authority for these measures.[27] The sabbatarian agitation also had a clear impact on some communities. At Buxted in the Sussex Weald the parishioners entered their decision in the register in 1613 to postpone the annual wake if it fell on a Sunday 'as we desire to keep this day in holiness after the example of Nehemiah and his people'.[28] Kenneth Parker has noted how in the dioceses of Chichester and Ely, sabbatarian offences tried before church courts multiplied from being an occasional event in the middle years of Elizabeth to the most important business under James.[29] Most of these cases, however, concerned labour, trade, or absence from church. Where recreations caused offence, it tended still to be in forms constant through the Middle Ages, of interfering with worship or consecrated ground. In these categories would fall, for example, the maypoles erected by crowds at Dagenham in southern Essex during service time, and those put up in the churchyards at Wylye, among the Wiltshire downs, and at Rudgwick, another Wealden village.[30] Likewise, when church ales and 'hogglers' featured in diocesan courts (which they rarely did), it was normally because of disputes over the fate of the profits.[31] A hunt through surviving quarter sessions records reveals even fewer cases concerning recreations, even in those counties where the justices had issued orders restricting them. That the latter had not in fact annihilated the activities concerned is indicated by their regular repetition. That made in Devon in 1595 was reissued in 1600 and extended in 1615 to cover baiting of bulls and bears, with the comment that two ales in the previous July had ended in manslaughter.[32] The Somerset ruling was reissued in 1600, 1607, 1612, and 1615, and once again the only court cases arising were of activities associated with the events rather than the ales themselves. The charges testify to the continued vitality of the custom in some communities at least, such as one against a professional bull-baiter who toured five church ales in the summer of 1607.[33] In 1616 the Lancashire bench renewed its ban upon piping, dancing, or 'profanation' on Sunday at any time or on holy days during services, yet not one presentment relating to those activities had been made since the reign began.[34] Such evidence can only support the inference often drawn from it before, that the orders were intended to regulate, not to annihilate, the pastimes concerned.

Having said that, it is equally plain from other sources that the decline of those pastimes, and the attacks upon them, continued steadily through the early Jacobean period. Churchwardens' accounts show that some of the relatively few parishes which maintained regular church ales, Hocktide collections, or 'hoggling' until the end of Elizabeth's reign now gave them up or reduced them to occasional events. The story is the same all over the region—consisting of the West Country, Wessex, and the Thames valley—into which they had shrunk. The parochial revels could collapse suddenly in places at which they were apparently popular. Wootton St Lawrence, in the woods of northern Hampshire, crowned a long tradition of 'king ales' with a 3-day one in 1603. But after 1605 it ceased to hold any.[35] The municipal records tell the same story. The corporation of Leicester took down all the town's maypoles in 1603.[36] In 1606 York last held its midsummer marching watch, and the following year Nottingham's council, noting that its own Midsummer Eve and St Peter's Eve watches were 'slenderly performed', abolished the latter and imposed fines on citizens who refused to serve in the former.[37] The Innkeepers' Company of Chester was vexed by the same concerns in 1611, rebuking many of its members for not attending the midsummer show. That year the corporation voted to reschedule the event if it fell upon a Sunday.[38]

The same span of years also furnishes more material than before for a picture of the local tensions which lay behind these changes. Once again, some of the best illustrations come from towns. The destruction of the Leicester maypoles was precipitated by a particularly unruly May Day for which some of the populace had stolen timber from the estates of the earl of Huntingdon. To make matters worse, the date fell upon a Sunday, the revels proceeded 'with a most tumultuous uproar and outcry', and the crowds failed to disperse when required to do so by the watch. The ringleaders were all of low social status, such as butchers, but were encouraged by some corporation members. Nevertheless most of the city government, and some of the citizens, had long harboured reservations about the May festivities, and the opportune arrival of James's proclamation concerning the Lord's Day made them feel the more confident in acting. The earl of Huntingdon, unsurprisingly, agreed.[39] Also very well documented, and much better known to historians, are the elaborate May games at Wells in 1607. They began on 3 May and ended with June, taking place almost every Sunday from near the end of divine service until the middle of the night. At times over 3,000 people spectated. The participants included 'morris dancers, loving dancers, men in women's apparel, new-devised lords and ladies', drummers, trumpeters, pipers, ensign-bearers, pikemen, musketeers, Robin Hood, St George, and other heroes of fiction. The most controversial part, culminating in a Star Chamber case, was the satirizing and mobbing of individuals who had expressed their dislike of such revels, especially a rich clothier and constable, John Hale, and a Mrs Yard. The games were sponsored by the churchwardens of St Cuthbert's, who needed funds for repairs, and by the bishop's bailiff, who hoped for a boom in tolls from traders attracted by the crowds. Most streets of the town competed to provide costumed characters, and they were supported by the dean and (in direct contrast to Leicester) the corporation leaders and the local magnate, the marquis of Hertford. The bishop and assize judges, however, disapproved, and the affair almost certainly inspired that year's renewal of the Somerset JPs' orders against church ales. Wells itself does not seem to have held any more.[40]

In other major towns change was propelled by a factor already important under Elizabeth: a reforming mayor. The one at Salisbury in 1611 was determined to stop the traditional merry-making on Midsummer Eve because that year it fell upon a Sunday. The Tailors' Company had commenced a morris dance during service time, and he ordered them to continue in the privacy of their homes. They stopped the dance and recommenced it after evening prayer instead, but the mayor first tried (and failed) to persuade youths to attack the dancers and then bound over the Tailors' wardens to answer a charge of profanation at the next quarter sessions. They cited neighbourliness, legality, custom, and the approval of the other city leaders. He cited God. They then appealed to the Crown, at which point the records run out.[41] Their tactic of recourse to central government was also adopted by some Guildford men whose maypole was pulled down by its mayor. They cunningly informed the lord-lieutenant of Surrey that this was an insult to the king, as they had placed the royal arms at the top. He agreed, and ordered an investigation, the results of which are not known.[42]

In smaller urban centres and rural communities, the arrival of a disapproving cleric could be as potent a force as before, and David Underdown and Jeremy Goring have between them collected many such cases for the Jacobean period. At Lyme Regis from 1606 John Geare mounted a campaign to stop both the traditional Whitsun processions to bring in leafy boughs to decorate the town, and the annual ale to raise funds to repair the breakwater. He won over some of the churchwardens and burgesses, but the majority of the latter resisted him.[43] The denunciation of the people who put up the maypole at Rudgwick, already mentioned, was the work of another recent arrival in the pulpit. His victims included some of the most prosperous of his parishioners. Alexander Cooke obtained the benefice of Leeds, Yorkshire, in 1615, and immediately found followers who smashed the instruments of musicians at a rush-bearing. This provoked the anger of some of the town's wealthiest traders.[44] The curate of Winsley, in north-west Wiltshire, described all women who danced or sang at midsummer revels as whores. The vicar of Iron Acton, at the south-west end of Gloucestershire, controlled the living of Rangeworthy chapel. In 1611 he told its congregation that they could only hold their usual Whitsun revel if they moved it to the Monday and attended a three-hour sermon first. They agreed, only to have their feast interrupted by the local high constable, who accused them of 'unlawful' games and 'beastly' drinking, and tried to arrest the musicians. He and his men were beaten up, and when he prosecuted their assailants in Star Chamber, the accused argued that the revel was decent and orderly and that the constable was motivated by an excessive religious zeal which also prompted him to criticize the established Church.[45]

At times figures of authority actively abetted village festivities. Christopher Windle, vicar of Bisley in the middle of the Cotswold hills, preached that maypoles and dances were wholly lawful, and had his son made the Whitsun lord in 1610. He was presented to the consistory court at the behest of the 'honest and religious' of his parish and the next. The south Devon gentleman Walter Wootton appeared before Star Chamber in 1606, where it was said that he had told the villagers of Harberton that he would get them a church ale and Whitsun lord and lady again, plus a 'fool and his horns'. In the same year Sir Edward Parham of Poyntington in southern Somerset turned up in the same court, alleged to have promoted an ale and danced in the morris himself. He proudly admitted both, declaring that such events promoted good neighbourliness. In neither case were the gentlemen being tried for these views or actions, but for breaches of the peace.[46] Below the level of the social or religious élite, rural opinion could be sharply divided. In 1612 a Wiltshire hundredal jury presented the churchwardens of Donhead St Mary in the southern downs, for holding an ale on a Sunday, even though it was after evening prayer.[47] In 1607 the church ale at the south Somerset market town of Yeovil was funded by collections made by a mock sheriff, with his retinue. Those who refused were accused of hostility to the national Church and threatened with being ridden on a rail.[48] At Longdon in Worcestershire's Vale of Severn, the youth held an annual May game on a Sunday afternoon. In 1614 and 1615 it was visited by louts from other villages who got drunk and brawled. In 1616 the constable decided to stop the dancing and so anticipate any further trouble, but was driven off with threats of violence. In 1617 the young people decided to dance every Sunday, whereupon he appealed to the county bench. The justices responded moderately, by ordering that the troublemakers from other communities be on good behaviour and that anybody dancing during divine service be arrested.[49]

What we have here is a complex pattern of individual and communal reactions to activities which changes in religious and social attitudes had called into question. It remains unclear how far the one common theme, of division, reflects a general situation, or how much the disputes themselves created records which a greater unanimity, which may have prevailed in other communities, would not. One method of coping with the evidence has been to suggest that certain kinds of local society were more inclined to retain the seasonal celebrations than others. It seems to have been Christopher Hill who first started this line of reasoning in 1964, by declaring that magistrates in cloth-working areas were particularly opposed to church ales. His perception was based upon a Marxist analysis, that the embryonic capitalism represented by master clothiers wished to replace an old cycle of feasts suitable for a feudal and agrarian society with a 7-day one better fitted to industrial production.[50] Joan Thirsk and Alan Everitt went on to interpret the same picture in anthropological terms, by suggesting that agrarian regions of nucleated villages with comparatively little industry or immigration and powerful resident gentry were less inclined to radicalism in politics or religion than those of wood, pasture, and cloth-working, which had larger, looser, less stable, and less well-supervised communities.[51] But it was left to David Underdown in 1985 to provide detailed research to substantiate this notion, in his celebrated case study of Somerset, Wiltshire, and Dorset.[52] His conclusions upon the matter have been the subject of considerable debate, and the consensus at present seems to be against accepting many of them.[53] It is a little unfair that the concentration of interest upon his topographical arguments has deflected attention from other aspects of an immensely rich study of regional history and popular culture and politics upon which this present work has leaned heavily at times. But the latter itself must deal directly with those same arguments. Of a piece with his other suggestions concerning regional differences, Professor Underdown asserts that festivities declined much faster in the pastoral and clothing areas of the West Country than in the chalk downlands and arable lowlands, with their more cohesive social order.[54]

A careful consideration of this argument has already been made for Wiltshire by Martin Ingram,[55] who concluded that it was incorrect for that county at least. He found that ales and revels were going out of fashion all over it in this period, which he ascribed to the growing bureaucratization of church finances, not to religion. He added that they survived best in small villages in each type of economic region, although sporadically in large communities in each, and that those which had an especially vigorous festive tradition were not all especially socially or physically cohesive. A number of points can be made here. The first is that there is a problem of evidence. The survival of early Jacobean churchwardens' accounts for the West Country is not sufficient to provide a large enough sample to answer questions of topography, and these represent the only sound source for the existence of parochial celebrations. In default of them Professor Underdown relies heavily upon the records of church and secular courts, in which the kind of merry-making which features most commonly is the 'revel', an annual village feast very similar to the church ale but not associated with parish funds. Even revels do not turn up very often in these legal archives, and, having emulated him, the present writer can only congratulate Professor Underdown upon the care with which he has detected them. But, as said earlier, in only a minority of cases were the revels, ales, or games themselves being prosecuted. In most cases the court was interested in incidents or claims associated with them. Thus a local entertainment which did not become linked with a controversy would not appear, and any chart based upon this material is at best very crudely one of the distribution of festivity. A second basic point is that upon a map of Somerset, Wiltshire, and Dorset the chalk downs and arable lowlands take up a much larger area than the clothing and dairying districts, offering more territory to produce evidence of merry-making. A third is that the national sample of churchwardens' accounts employed for this study, and every other category of source, supports Dr Ingram's findings for Wiltshire regarding the rate of survival of ales and revels.

But having said all this, in one respect the material gathered for this present book tends to corroborate David Underdown's view rather than that of Martin Ingram. It concerns the latter's assertion that the decline of parish feasts was due to a 'bureaucratization' of parochial finances rather than to religious factors. This surmise was not supported by evidence, but was reasonable enough considering that parish funds were becoming more systematized and regulated around 1600 and that there is no record of religious or social tension in most communities which were giving up ales at this time. The trouble is that there is no other reason apparent for the demise of the old festivities in these parishes, and that faced with the bare fact that they were obviously declining both Professor Underdown and Dr Ingram are selecting likely explanations in default of sufficient evidence. In this situation it is telling that where case studies do exist, like those cited above, religious beliefs and the fear of disorder are very prominent. It is also striking that many of these examples are drawn from areas of fervent popular Protestantism such as the Sussex Weald and that in which Gloucestershire, Somerset, and Wiltshire meet. If ales *did* cease to be a reliable means of raising money compared with rates, this may well have been due to a subtraction of local support because of ideological factors, as said before. Against the belief that a change in the structure of finance was the decisive factor may be set the Tudor material discussed in the last two chapters. Thus, although David Underdown's schematization of cultural regions does seem to be far too rigid, his stress upon the power of ideology may well be correct.

Certainly, some parishes still maintained the traditional revelry consistently throughout the first two-thirds of James's reign. The ale at Lyme Regis has been mentioned, and they were important also at such places as Williton, a large village on the edge of Exmoor, Bere Regis, another sizeable rural community on the road between Dorchester and Poole, and the Cornish fishing-port of St Ives.[56] Whitsun games were maintained at Bramley in the north Hampshire forest lands, and across the Kennet valley at Ashampstead the villagers bought a new maypole in 1613.[57] At Dursley in the Cotswolds and Cheddar beside the Mendip Hills the hogglers still made their rounds.[58] The legal records combed by Professor Underdown and Dr Ingram reveal many examples of West Country ales and revels flourishing during these years. The pattern is repeated elsewhere, though more sparsely and for entertainments not linked to parish finance. Examples from Essex and Sussex have been quoted, and the vagaries of fortune provide glimpses of merry-making elsewhere, such as that around the maypole at Fenton in Staffordshire's Trent valley. It is only known to history because a man was put in the stocks for fixing a libel to it in 1605.[59] Parishes which now only intermittently held church ales sometimes compensated for frequency with scale, such as Seal in southern Surrey which in 1611 hosted a 5-day extravaganza requiring musicians, a fool, silk points and laces as emblems for guests, ten barrels of beer, a quarter of wheat, three calves, eleven lambs, and a fat sheep.[60] Some urban communities maintained ritual and revelry with gusto. Carlisle, in national terms a remote border town, held an Ascension Day perambulation of the bounds by corporation and craft guilds with musicians, clowns, and jugglers, followed by feasting. Its council also paid for a 'Lord Abbot' to preside over the Christmas holidays, sponsored plays and games upon Shrove Tuesday, and feasted and provided music upon Midsummer Eve and St Peter's Eve.[61]

Upon those two nights also, the marching watches still paraded at Exeter and Nottingham, the latter's processions decked with ribbons and garlands.[62] But perhaps the most striking of all was the continuing vitality of old-fashioned celebration at Oxford and around London, where it was most highly visible to the political nation. Although the university church of St Mary abandoned Hocktide collections in 1603, the other parishes of the town kept up both those and Whitsun ales.[63] The celebrations in the London area are well recorded in the literature produced under James in defence of the traditional merry-making.

The latter makes a remarkable contrast to that published under Elizabeth, in that its volume actually exceeds that of works criticizing the same pastimes. Unlike the Elizabethan examples, also, it has received much attention from scholars of English letters, of whom Leah Marcus is the most significant in this regard.[64] Unfortunately, the contribution of these scholars to the present study is limited by their natural tendency to concentrate upon major figures such as Jonson and Herrick, ignoring the broader context of the genre. They have also attached a slightly misleading importance to the Cotswold Games sponsored by the lawyer Robert Dover from the 1610s. These have only attracted attention because of the famous set of verses, *Annalia Dubrensia*, addressed to Dover by his literary friends. The latter included a few of the defenders of the old-style revels, as we shall see, but the Cotswold event was not one of these. Rather, it was a new departure taking its model from ancient Rome and consisting of sports, with the emphasis on competition and prowess. Being held on the Thursday and Friday after Whitsun, it avoided both the Sabbath and traditional holy days.[65] The importance of Warner, Drayton, and Breton, suggested in the last chapter, seems to have gone unremarked. The last two were still active under James, and Breton returned to the theme of festivity in 1605, when he extolled feasting as well as fasting to produce a balanced annual cycle of existence.[66] Drayton was temporarily interested in other themes, but in 1612–15 he gathered round him in London a set of young poets, most of them law students, who shared his admiration for Spenser and his taste for pastoral verse.[67] In 1614 all of these—William Browne, George Wither, John Davies, and Christopher Brooke—collaborated upon a collection called *The Shepheards Pipe*. Its poetry celebrated Whitsun ales, village revel days, maypoles, Ladies of the May, harvest queens, summer bowers, garlands, and songs and dances on village greens. Around this time, also, Wither brought out *A Christmas Carol*, which lauded the merriment, charity, and social bonding of the Twelve Days and mentioned approvingly a string of their customs, including decking with holly and ivy, wassailing, mumming, carols, and party games such as Rowland Hoe and The Wild Mare.[68]

Before them other writers around the metropolis had been celebrating popular revelry. One of the wildest was Thomas Coryate, a courtier who earned his maintenance by his wit and his tales of his travels, to which he returned each time his audience in the royal entourage began to weary of him. In 1611 he went back to his native Odcombe, in the south Somerset arable lands, and got himself made its summer lord for a church ale. His retinue marched with him to nearby Yeovil to advertise the event. He subsequently boasted of its success in a pamphlet dedicated to King James and his family, comparing such ales not only to pagan Roman festivals but to early Christian love-feasts. Thus he attacked the complaint literature upon part of its own ground, making parochial festivity stand in the tradition of the Church's founders as well as that of ancient civilization (which, indeed, he loved and respected in its own right).[69] In about 1613 the more decorous Thomas Campion, a lawyer living in London like Drayton's friends, published a book of songs. One praised the simple delights of those who 'skip and trip it on the green, and help to choose the Summer Queen', and who take their places at the 'Country Feast'.[70]

Two publications of this kind stand out from the rest. One was in 1607, by Thomas Rogers, a Suffolk minister and a chaplain to the archbishop of Canterbury. It was a direct reply to all the sabbatarian literature and in particular to that of his near neighbour Bownde. Moved partly by personal animosity and partly by genuine feeling, he attempted to link the whole campaign for stricter observance of Sunday with that for the further reform of the Church, and to discredit both. Rogers held that only worship and abstinence from work were necessary upon the Lord's Day, opening the way for all manner of legal sports and merry-making.[71] The other piece of work was remarkable in being, at least apparently, a eulogy of rural pleasures which was not written by a Londoner. Its setting was a horse-race at Hereford in 1609, attended by many local gentry, led by Lord Herbert of Raglan. One of the amusements there was a morris danced by ten very old men, accompanied by an elderly female Maid Marian, four 'whiflers' or 'wifflers' to clear the way, a hobby-horse, a fiddler, and a taborer. The ages of the performers seem almost impossibly great, provoking suspicions of burlesque, but the pride expressed in Herefordshire morris rings true, and the descriptions of the costumes are the best we have for the period. Musicians and dancers were in 'long coats of the old fashion, high sleeves gathered at the elbows and hanging sleeves behind, the stuff red buskin striped with white, girdles with white, stockings white, and red roses to their shoes'. They wore red or white caps, with jewels and long feathers. The Marian 'was attired in colours: the wifflers had long staves, white and red'.[72]

In the same period, playwrights continued to incorporate folk pastimes in the way which had begun to be fashionable around 1600. The greatest of all did so in 1611, when Shakespeare added a rural revel to *The Winter's Tale*.[73] Two years later Drayton's friend Francis Beaumont produced *The Knight of the Burning Pestle*, which dwelt exuberantly upon the seasonal customs of young artisans from the London suburbs.[74] These included wrecking brothels on Shrove Tuesday, choosing a May Lord 'with scarves and rings and posy' and 'gilded staff', and providing a morris troupe. The play confirms what slightly later literature was to endorse: that the morris had become the English equivalent of the fiery dances for young men, involving leaping and kicking, found in peasant societies across Europe and beyond. The dexterity and stamina involved was considerable enough to make a good team a matter for local pride, as Marston and the Herefordshire tract had already suggested. But when the next year the same author composed a Shrovetide masque for the royal court, he chose to parody the dance by including a pair of fools and of baboons. They 'capered rudely', and the audience drowned the music with its laughter.[75] Likewise when in 1617 Barten Holyday had a morris to represent Music in an allegorical play about the arts, he included a clowning hobby-horse, which knocked over the other performers.[76] The dance had become an acceptable subject for the stage, but sophisticated patrons still liked to be reminded that it was the pastime of clods.

To this subject-matter Ben Jonson, who has been called its literary 'father',[77] actually came rather late and reluctantly. His combination of a love of the capital, lowly social origins, and a prodigious classical education, carefully acquired, made him something of a snob where country people were concerned. He had been at the Spencer seat of Althorp in Northamptonshire in 1603 when James and his queen passed through on their way to London. His plans to devise an entertainment for them, evoking the ancient world, were marred when, as he wrote bitterly, 'the clowns thereabout . . . most officiously presented themselves . . . to introduce a morris'. When the king granted their request, Ben penned a speech to preface it, terming it 'a kind of masque' and patronizing the dancers heavily, inviting them to 'stir their hobnailed stumps'. To make the mockery plainer, the speaker was dressed in breeches 'coming up to his neck, with his arms out at his pockets and a cap drowning his face'. But the dramatist's rage was completed when the noise of the crowd, come to watch the dance, drowned the words.[78] He could subsequently praise Sir Robert Wroth for his lordly hospitality to the common people around his rural seat, including a 'jolly wassail', but this did not indicate much sympathy with the commoners themselves.[79] It seems to have been his desire to pander to the king's animosities, rather than a feeling for country sport, which made him create the famous character of Zeal-of-the-land Busy in *Bartholomew Fair*, first performed before the court in 1614.[80] In Busy he gloriously personified the connection made by Thomas Rogers between sabbatarianism and those who wished to reform the liturgy and government of the Church. The king had made his distaste for the latter abundantly clear during the previous ten years. Since the 1560s their enemies had applied to them the term 'puritans'. Jonson himself doubtless had reason to dislike them, not least because of the hostility expressed by some of their number towards the theatre. But he still refrained from praising the popular pastimes attacked by Busy. In 1616 Ben responded to a speech made by the king in Star Chamber, calling for landowners to spend Christmas in the countryside dispensing hospitality and charity in the old fashion instead of remaining in London. On the next Twelfth Night he presented *Christmas his Masque* before the court, to glorify London and to defend the feast against charges (only made by the most radical of English Protestants) that it was a mere survival of Catholicism. In the process he personified many of the features of the season, including Lords of Misrule, carols, mince pies, gambling, mumming (in a pied suit and mask), wassailing (with a brown bowl decorated with ribbons and rosemary), and New Year's gifts (which in this case included oranges, more rosemary, brooches, gingerbread, marzipan, and wine). And yet, once again, a strong satirical theme prevented the tone from being purely one of celebration, the self-indulgence of the Twelve Days, and of the City, coming in for moments of censure.[81]

As must be obvious, the typical author of works in praise or defence of the old popular revels was somebody living in the capital or following the court, usually a lawyer or professional man of letters. Conspicuously missing were the sort of provincial gentry or (with the exception of Rogers) ministers who had to reckon with the practical problems of such merrymaking. Its proponents were essentially people who enjoyed it on trips out of town. One symbolic difference in their attitudes from those of genuine rustics was the way in which pretty May queens featured most prominently in their verse instead of the summer lords who are far more important in the recorded ales and games of the countryside. It is ironic that the preoccupations of provincials, from a region very remote from the capital, were to have more direct impact upon the formulation of royal policy than all the metropolitan writers put together, although the latter may have helped to predispose the king towards the course which he now took. The story has been well told already,[82] and can be repeated here very swiftly.

It commenced on 8 August 1616, when the Lancashire JPs, as described above, completely banned piping, dancing, or any other 'profanation' upon Sunday. The order was made too late in the year for it to have much impact upon that summer season, but as the warm weather returned in 1617 it clearly produced controversy in the shire. Fortune provided the measure's opponents with the highest of all courts of appeal, in the form of King James, who happened to pass through Lancashire in August on his way back from a visit to Scotland. His main business there had been to infuse more hierarchy and ceremony into the Scottish Kirk, making him even more conscious than usual of those who disliked such aspects of religion in both countries. At Myerscough Hall, on 13 August, he received objections to the justices' ruling and showed some sympathy with them. As a result, on the next Sunday, the 17th, he himself watched a rush-bearing, with music, after the morning service at Houghton in the Pennines, and enjoyed a masque and dancing after supper. But in the nearby parish of Over, dances took place in service time, provoking a new set of complaints supported by the local bishop (of Chester), Thomas Morton. James let the leader of the offending revel be fined and its musician be put in the stocks, but he also asked the bishop to draft a royal declaration for Lancashire, mitigating the severity of the quarter sessions order and clearing up the ambiguities in the royal proclamation of 1603. Morton was very willing to do this, having banned recreations only during time of worship in his own visitation articles. His proposals were of a piece, permitting piping, dancing, archery, athletics, and rush-bearing on Sunday once evening prayer was over, and banning plays, bowling, and baiting of animals. No Sunday festivity was to be permitted to Catholics, and nobody was to attend it in parishes other than their own. Within twenty-four hours the bishop was back with the draft, which James signed on the 27th at Gerrards Bromley, having added a preface of his own. Whereas Morton was conscious of the danger from Catholics, the king concentrated more upon 'puritans and precise people' and their misquotation of his earlier ruling (which, it must be said again, had lent itself to this very treatment). He declared that strict sabbatarianism would leave people idle, unhealthy, and disaffected, and ordered 'puritans' to accept his view or leave the country. At court that winter, the declaration clearly became the subject of debates which have left no trace in the records, for on 24 May 1618 it was reissued at Greenwich Palace. This time James complained that both puritans and

Catholics were misrepresenting what he had laid down in Lancashire. He accordingly repeated its provisions, added May games, Whitsun ales, morris, and maypoles to the permitted recreations, and made it binding upon the whole country. His only concession to sabbatarian feeling was that whereas the Lancashire document had to be read in all churches there, the national one did not enjoin this. Rumour attributed this to the cautious advice of the archbishop of Canterbury, George Abbot.

No literary debate of the declaration ensued, perhaps because of fear of royal anger, perhaps because clergy were not required to take notice of it, and perhaps because those interested in the theology of the Sabbath were diverted by a new controversy over whether Saturday was not the true Lord's Day.[83] But it made the subject of folk festivity even more fashionable among poets and playwrights. Breton and Drayton both rushed back to it. The former immediately produced a dialogue between a courtier and a rustic, in which the former's scoffing at country boorishness and *naïveté* was answered by the latter's eulogy of village celebrations. He wrote of 'true mirth at honest meetings . . . about the may-pole, where the young folks smiling kiss at every turning, and the old folks checking with laughing at their children, when dancing for the garland'.[84] In 1619 Drayton brought out a collection of poems including an exquisite description of a king ale in a summer bower woven with flowers, the participants feasting upon plums, cherries, cheese, curds, clotted cream, spiced syllabubs, and 'cider of the best' before piping and singing.[85] During the same year, Londoners were treated to the now famous *Pasquils Palinodia*, usually attributed to another of the literary men resident in the capital, William Fennor. A satire upon the manners of the City and suburbs, it used the huge permanent maypole in the Strand as a symbol of 'harmless mirth and honest neighbourhood'. It attacked 'capricious constables' and the 'peevish Puritan' and 'overwise churchwarden' who called such poles idols and Trojan horses. To the author, as to Breton, the days of ubiquitous May games and Whitsun ales had been times of innocence, love, charity, and probity. He rued the replacement of the wassail cup and the 'summer bower of peace and neighbourhood' with social and religious divisions.[86]

Other writers hastened to swell the flow of such publications following the declaration. The ebullient vicar of Bisley, now in Gloucester gaol for debt, appealed to the king to release him in a tract which justified merrymaking and Sunday recreations from Scripture. Doubtless remembering the time when his son was a summer lord, he insisted that such fun was better for youngsters, being supervised, than letting them slip into alehouses. He added that even the gaol had its maypole and 'May pyramid' (of greenery and flowers).[87] Ben Jonson himself cashed in, with a play called *The May Lord*. Although lost, it apparently displayed all the massive condescension with which both courtiers in general and Ben in particular viewed its subject; in his words, it showed the 'foolish sports' of 'clowns'.[88] Much less equivocal was the dramatist John Fletcher, who created for the London stage the character of Hope-on-high Bomby, reluctant hobby-horse player with a morris team. Having been convinced by his puritan wife that the model horse is the 'beast of Babylon', that dances are 'the Devil's measures', and that maypoles are 'tilt staves' aimed against the Church, he continues to play his part in order to earn the glory due to a martyr.[89] It must surely be to this period too that we can attribute the poetic exhortation to the minister of Bewdley, Worcestershire, by the ambitious young Oxford fellow, Richard Corbett. It satirized this individual for his known hostility to maypoles, and drew the king's connection between this attitude and disloyalty to Church and monarchy.[90]

The impact of the declaration on village life was limited by the slack provision for its distribution. Not only was it not necessary for ministers to read it, but no bishop mentioned it in visitation articles. Assize judges do not seem to have recommended it, and how well it was understood by some JPs may be indicated by the case of one in east Devon, who believed that it was intended for 'Lincolnshire' or 'Leicestershire' and had no relevance for his county.[91] Nevertheless, news of it did get around, and it had some effect. A young Lancashire gentleman, who had noted the decline in rush-bearing in 1617, and then joined the royal entourage to watch that at Houghton, enjoyed a summer game on a Sunday in 1618 with no sense of controversy.[92] In that year at Marlborough in Wiltshire, once such a centre of festivity, the minister informed midsummer merry-makers that they served the Devil and their morris dancer took the part of an idol. In reply to him they cited the king's declaration.[93] There was another show-down at Weymouth in June, when a group of youths, reproved by the mayor for beating drums, sounding a trumpet, and firing muskets on a Sunday, claimed that they had been going to fetch a summer pole. But they had none, and he bound them over for breach of the peace.[94] It is probably no coincidence that at this time the village of Thatcham, Berkshire, revived its Whitsun ale.[95] At Fuston in Yorkshire the parson preached against both rush-bearing and the royal declaration, and caused a fight amongst his audience. At a Leicestershire village the rector prolonged the service in order to keep his congregation in church until darkness prevented any games. In neighbouring Northamptonshire two JPs, Sir Edward Montagu and John Williams (who was also a minister) clashed over attempts by the former to regulate the wake in the parish of the latter. Both appealed to friends at court.[96] Thomas Wilson, the evangelical minister of Stratford upon Avon, quoted Perkins's writings against dancing and Sunday recreations and so persuaded the corporation to cut down the maypole in 1619.[97]

But such direct resistance to the royal will was always dangerous. The proper platform for criticism of the Crown's policies had always been Parliament, and the next one met in 1621. Within two days of its settling down to business, the Dorset MP Sir Walter Earle introduced a bill which banned, among other things, ales, May games, and dancing upon Sunday. At its second reading on 16 February, it was, as is well known, opposed vociferously by a young lawyer from the same county, Thomas Shepherd, who held that it was contrary to both Scripture and the king's declaration. All observers agreed that Shepherd's tone, more than his words, gave general offence, and he was expelled from the House. Even the solicitor-general and members who normally supported the court joined in censuring him. None the less, a privy councillor, Sir George Calvert, did say that the king thought the bill 'puritan' and wanted it amended. Three days later James himself confirmed this while accepting the punishment of Shepherd. A Devon gentleman, James Chudleigh, objected that the royal declaration encouraged vice, but he was not supported and a committee was appointed to bring bill and declaration into harmony. On 1 March it reported, having effectively reduced the prohibitions in the former to those made in the latter. As the declaration had not mentioned wakes, the bill banned these on Sunday in addition. The Lords took over two months to consider it, but when they did confer with the Commons upon it on 24 May, the only objection was a doubt over the propriety of its use of the word 'Sabbath', raised by Archbishop Abbot. Five days later it passed both Houses, only to be vetoed by the king, an action which, in view of all the trouble expended upon it, represented the most brutal possible snub and a warning to MPs that this area was out of bounds to them.[98] The strictest sabbatarian among his bishops, Lewis Bayly, remonstrated with him and incurred his lasting anger.[99]

The attitude of the Commons apparently gave some heart to local enemies of the declaration. Church ales vanished again at Thatcham. A constable tried to stop the midsummer celebrations of 1621 at Brinklow near Coventry, claiming that maypoles encouraged immorality and drunkenness and profaned the Sabbath. Fisticuffs resulted.[100] When three London playwrights presented *The Witch of Edmonton* in that same year, they cleverly mixed attitudes. The village pride in the morris team appeared, as in the work of Marston and Beaumont, with the additional information that some had bells which rang in different tones. But the fiddler who played for this one was a devil in disguise.[101] In the next year a reply to *Pasquils Palinodia* appeared, entitled *Vox Graculi*, likewise a satire on London life but one which termed maypoles 'long wooden idols' and sneered at the 'greasy churls' and 'dirty sluts' who enjoyed them and spent May morning embracing in ditches.[102] The Professor of Divinity at Oxford, John Prideaux, preached that recreation, cheerfulness, and liberality were all proper aspects of Sunday. But it is noteworthy that he did not dare to publish these views, even in Latin.[103] Most striking is the action of the Devon JPs. Four of these had been prominent in support of Earle's bill in Parliament, and now the whole bench flagrantly ignored the royal Declaration of Sports. At the 1622 midsummer sessions they cited various complaints made of the holding of church ales and declared that their earlier prohibitions were still in force.[104]

In view of all this, it is striking that these same years seem to have seen the flowering of the talent which for the modern world evokes more than any other the romantic eulogization of traditional seasonal customs; although it remained, like Prideaux's sermon, unpublished at this time. Robert Herrick graduated from Cambridge in 1617 and was a well-known literary figure by 1625. He fitted the general type of those who idealized rustic festivity, being a Londoner by residence and indeed in his case by birth. Unlike the others he actually went to live in the country, when appointed to be parson of a south Devon parish in 1630. His reaction was one of dislike and boredom, and acute homesickness for the capital. It is almost impossible to decide which of his poems were written before his departure from it. Some upon calendar celebrations, such as his masterpiece, 'Corinna's going a-Maying', and his portrait of apple-wassailing, can be dated from internal references of subject-matter to the Devon years. Even so, the interests and attitudes of Herrick's poetry are so consistent that they must have been developed during that earlier period in which it became familiar to the literary world. The tradition from which it stems is that of Drayton and Breton, of a timeless rural paradise which is at once the world of Greek pastoral verse and of the contemporary English villager. But Herrick lovingly portrayed not only the summer games but harvest celebrations and winter traditions which included the wassail bowl, mumming, Christmas pies, New Year's gifts, and decking with greenery. Next to Stubbes, he has been the folklorists' favourite quarry for quotations.[105]

Three scholars have discerned political implications in Herrick's treatment of festivity. Leah Marcus has pointed out that it embodies a very paternal and slightly patronizing notion of good lordship, set within an

ordered and hierarchical society.[106] Earl Miner makes it typify the
'Cavalier' mode of poetry in its love of ceremony within both the Church
and folk life, and the sense of cycle which it gives to the year and also to
the development of individuals.[107] To Peter Stallybrass it was part of that
general process of the regulation of popular celebration by the élite mentioned at the opening of the last chapter. He asserts that it was also an
emotional response to an England in the process of transformation by agrarian capitalism and nascent industrialization. In his scheme, Dover's Cotswold Games and Herrick's verses were engaged in the same work of trying
to create 'a mythical unity of prince, gentry and people', characterized by
ceremony, conformity, and royal authority.[108] Professor Marcus proves her
case, but some caution may be needed in accepting those of her colleagues.
Both enemies and defenders of old festive customs were probably in part
reacting to social change, although current Tudor and Stuart historians
would speak in terms of population pressure and inflation rather than the
dynamics portrayed by Peter Stallybrass. The main problem with Herrick
as a representative of the defenders is that none of the others managed to
combine *all* his qualities of royalism, classicism, élitism, social benevolence,
sensuality, intense love of ritual, Christian piety, and a deeply ambivalent
attitude towards the countryside. He is such an extreme of the genre that
he can hardly typify it. It cannot be a coincidence that, to a generation
which bought edition after edition of *Eikon Basilike* and hankered after the
restoration of monarchy and maypoles, the publication of Herrick's
Hesperides was a non-event.

Poetry was certainly not enough to soothe the feelings of the next House
of Commons, which convened in 1624. The bill vetoed at the end of the
previous Parliament was reintroduced on the third day and passed all its
stages in eleven more. The Lords saw it through without a division or a
conference and it was duly offered for the royal assent. At the end of the
session James vetoed it again. It has been customary among historians to
characterize the Parliament of 1624 as the most harmonious and productive
of the second half of the reign. While this is true, the judgement is only
relative. There is no mistaking the sourness of the king's tone at the dissolution, nor the bitterness felt by many MPs, and some of both was aroused
by the failed bill. James said that it still contradicted his declaration (which
was true only in respect of wakes, and there only implicitly), and that it
would 'give the Puritans their way, who think religion consists in two sermons a day'.[109] Certainly that year those who wanted 'their way' despite
the king's attitude seem to have been further encouraged by the Commons'
efforts. The Easter sessions of the Somerset JPs repeated the earlier orders

banning church ales.[110] At Keevil in the west Wiltshire dairying country, the minister had already persuaded the manorial court to demolish the 'king house' used for summer revels. Now he presented five of his younger parishioners, including a lad from a wealthy family, to the archdeacon for dancing in a bower on a Sunday. They pleaded, apparently with success, that they had done so after evening prayer according to 'the king's book'.[111] When Ben Jonson wrote a masque for presentation to the prince of Wales at Kenilworth Castle, he seems to have hedged his bets. He referred to the famous entertainment of 1575 and presented a character as Captain Cox, defender of the Coventry Hock Tuesday play. But Cox was made a figure both of sympathy and ridicule, and when Jonson called his city 'wise' for having subsequently banned May games, it is impossible to tell whether he was being sincere or ironic.[112]

Thus James I's attempt to protect some traditional pastimes did no more than slow down the war of attrition waged against them. Furthermore, his protection did not in itself stem from any affection or respect for them, but from his dislike of radical Protestantism which sharpened still further in the latter part of his reign. In two respects the king's attitude was mistaken. One was that the proponents of measures such as the sabbatarian bills in Parliaments and the local orders against ales included a large number of people who never displayed anything but contentment with the established hierarchy and liturgy of the Church. The second was that a religion 'consisting in two sermons a day' was becoming steadily less and not more the fashion in England during his reign. Parallel to the attack on secular revelry ran a profound growth in religious ceremony and adornment, plainly revealed in early Stuart churchwardens' accounts. It is partly manifested in a growing size of payments for wine and bread, suggesting a larger number of people taking communion. Charges for washing the surplice also increase, suggesting that the minister was wearing it more frequently. But for a book devoted to the ritual year there are three customs mentioned in the accounts which stand out: the decking of churches at Christmas, perambulations, and the provision of communion on feast days.

As said earlier, the old practice of decorating urban churches (where it can be traced) with seasonal greenery had declined for most of Elizabeth's reign. By the 1590s it was almost gone. Yet in that decade the first traces appear of a revival, which was to grow steadily until the end of the 1630s.[113] Initially it was slightly more pronounced in western towns such as Chester and Bristol, but it gained pace equally in both capital and provinces. By 1639 it obtained in twenty-three out of the fifty-one London parishes which have left good records for the period. Only at Norwich does it seem to have remained unpopular, the proportion there being one church out of four. The Christmas decking acquired a new sophistication, especially in London, as rosemary and bay leaves were used to add their astringent fragrance to the holly and ivy, or to replace them. Laurel was purchased at the single Norwich church recorded as reviving the custom. The pre-Reformation garnishings at midsummer and Ascension Day did not reappear, although upon the latter feast Temple church in Bristol took to putting garlands around its cross. The Bristol churches also began to fix up holly for All Saints' Day, while Easter was celebrated amid rosemary at St Petrock, Exeter, and box and yew at St Lawrence, Reading. Whitsun was marked with flowers and herbs at St Peter Westcheap in London.

It seems that the conclusions drawn by scholars upon the fortunes of the Rogation processions may have been misled by overdependence upon one category of source, the diocesan records. Under the early Stuarts, just as in the Elizabethan period, these contain many reports of controversy and neglect. Ministers, parishioners, or both, could be unwilling to make the processions, while those living along the route sometimes blocked it with enclosures or refused to provide customary hospitality to the walkers.[114] This material persuaded Sir Keith Thomas, in his monumental study of early modern English religion and magic, to conclude that the custom was one in prolonged decline. He suggested that the loss of its sacred and arcane associations at the Reformation left it enfeebled to face the agrarian changes of the subsequent period, of which enclosure was the most relevant and which cut the traditional paths around the boundaries. Thus economic self-interest joined hands with further attacks upon the religious associations of the custom by ministers such as William Brudenell, appointed to the northern Oxfordshire parish of Deddington in 1631. He first refused to wear his surplice on the walk and to read the gospel at the customary mark of a cross carved in the earth. Later he declined to go at all.[115] Sir Keith's view was later endorsed by David Underdown,[116] who used West Country examples to support the same picture of long-term decay. But clergy such as Brudenell were very rare. In the archdeaconry of Lewes (most of east Sussex) between 1581 and 1641 only a single parson is recorded as refusing to go on perambulation. In the diocese of Bath and Wells (most of Somerset) eight ministers failed to do so in the years 1625 to 1640, but of these one was ill, one lame, one under arrest, and one prevented by a boundary dispute. In every collection of diocesan records the cases of actual lack of perambulation seem to be outnumbered by those concerning damage to boundary markers or withdrawal of traditional refreshments. Even these are not very numerous. The archdeaconry of

Chichester (most of west Sussex) threw up fourteen complaints of any kind regarding the custom during the 1620s. Of fifty-five Cambridgeshire parishes which made visitation returns in 1638, every single one claimed to observe it.[117] No early Stuart archive yet studied reveals anything like the degree of neglect documented in Elizabethan Suffolk. In Essex, where good comparable records for the two periods exist,[118] they indicate better performance in the latter one.

This impression is borne out by the churchwardens' accounts. In 1590 none show regular payments for celebrations associated with the processions. In the course of the following decade a London church, St Bartholomew the Less, and one in Westminster, St Martin in the Fields, began to make them. By 1639 they feature in the records surviving from every single City parish except one, St Mary Aldermanbury. It had become a tradition for the boys in each to be taken around the boundaries every Ascension Day by the minister and leading inhabitants, and to be given some reward as part of the experience. In many cases this consisted of ribbons ('points') to pin or tie upon their clothing; a large parish like St Mary Woolnoth ordered ten dozen of these each year. Often the children received cakes, fruit, bread, nuts, or beer instead of, or in addition to, these trophies. The boundary markers were regularly touched up with paint as part of the tour, and the adults concerned frequently treated themselves to a dinner or supper on the parish funds. The major growth of the custom was in the reign of James, when it was adopted by thirty parishes, but ten more followed under Charles I. In the same span of years the processions began to be marked by parish feasts and bell-ringing at other Westminster churches and in Bristol, Canterbury, Cambridge, Hereford, Ipswich, Chester, Stafford, Norwich, Warwick, Winchester, York, Gloucester, and Reading.[119] The same thing happened in a scatter of villages and small towns across the South and Midlands,[120] though there the major development was after 1625. Most rural communities still obtained their food and drink from parishioners *en route*, according to the tradition documented in the diocesan court records. Northern towns such as Durham, and local capitals further south such as Oxford and Exeter, apparently did not invest parish funds in increasing the attraction and the importance of the processions. But there is copious evidence for the large number of communities which did so.

In the case of 'festival communion', like that of seasonal greenery, a story of decline and diminution for most of Elizabeth's reign turns into one of revival, commencing in her last years and massively reinforced under her successor. As before, the bare record of payments for bread and wine did not necessarily mean that they were not consecrated on the principal feasts of the Church. Nevertheless it must be significant that so many wardens ceased to record communions on Sundays of a month, or as seasonal totals, and began to enter them as occurring on holy days. The identity of the latter varied according to local taste; Easter was of course the favourite, followed by Christmas and Whitsun, but All Saints, Michaelmas, and Midsummer Day also featured quite often. As mentioned before, a few widely scattered places had never abandoned the custom, but their number was now very considerably augmented. In the 1590s it was increased by such varied parishes as Kirby Malzeard in the Yorkshire Dales, Lindfield in the Sussex Weald, St Aldate in Gloucester, South Cadbury and Charlton Musgrove in southern Somerset, Aston Abbots in Buckinghamshire's Vale of Aylesbury, Cratfield in eastern Suffolk, and St Martin in the Fields, Westminster.[121] By the end of the 1630s the custom was the rule virtually everywhere. The most glaring exception was the City of London itself, where, in contrast to the vogue for Ascension Day perambulations, only six of the surviving sets of parish accounts record festival communions.[122] In the whole of Cheshire (including Chester) only one set does so, and only a minority note it at Bristol.[123] Everywhere else the proportions were reversed and it was only a few churches which failed to go over to the revived stress upon providing the consecrated bread and wine upon sacred calendar dates. Under the early Stuarts, also, a few communities, most in Lincolnshire and Yorkshire's East Riding, took to greeting Christmas Day with a peal of bells.[124]

This religious development to some extent ran counter to a secular one which had occasioned James's proclamation in 1616, which had in turn prompted Jonson's masque and probably Withers's poem: a decline in the traditional Christmas entertainments and hospitality at gentry seats. The royal opinion was endorsed fifteen years later by the Londoner John Taylor, friend of Jonson and Breton. A waterman who eked out his income by writing, Taylor was well placed to understand the feelings of the poorer sort of people, and his *Complaint of Christmas* remains one of his best-known works. It accused landowners of preferring to stay in the capital during the Twelve Days and so save money, rather than providing charity, receiving guests, and permitting the 'honest mirth' of the Lord of Misrule. Taylor closed his tract with an idyllic picture of the feast as kept among ordinary rural folk, drinking spiced ale in which hot apples floated, playing cards and party games, dancing, and entertaining friends. He depicted the carrying of the wassail bowl as the means by which charity was given at that social level, a company of maids entering with it and receiving white bread, cheese, and mince pies.[125]

Felicity Heal, in her comprehensive survey of early modern English hospitality, was inclined to credit these beliefs with truth, partly because it was logical that they would have some basis in it and partly because the Thynne family accounts supported them perfectly. Probably because of the cost of their monstrous new house at Longleat, the Thynnes took to spending at least some Christmas seasons in the capital during the 1600s, living modestly.[126] To this example one might add that of the earl of Clare in the 1620s, who complained that his grandfather had 'flushed all his revenues down the privy' with festive entertainment of strangers, and clearly was not emulating him.[127] But Dr Heal also found rather more cases which may be taken as exceptions to this putative rule, including gentry such as the Petres, Stanleys, and Mildmays, parsons such as the rectors of Barley in Hertfordshire and of Penshurst in Sussex, and (top of the league of generosity) John Warine, bishop of Rochester, and Toby Matthews, archbishop of York. The last of these held six huge feasts between 26 December 1624 and 3 January 1625, just one of which fed a hundred people. Viewing things from the other end of the process, a woman accused of theft in the Isle of Ely in 1617 turned out to have spent the period between Christmas and New Year moving between five gentry households in the Stilton area and getting fed at each.[128]

It seems that there are two different issues at stake here, identified by Taylor when he wrote that many people still entertained their friends but seldom did the same for strangers and the poor. It is easy to suppose that the growing amount of poverty in the period, and the imposition of rates to deal with it, would have made landowners reluctant to feast the indigent when there were so many more of them and they were being supported in any case by a levy on property. Dr Heal proved that memories of heroic quantities of Christmas largesse were no mere nostalgia by recovering several examples from the Tudor age.[129] But it is not entirely clear that they are more numerous than those located by her in the early Stuart years. The household accounts of late medieval and early Tudor England, appraised in Chapter 2, do not suggest that many gentry kept open house in the Twelve Days, let alone from Christmas to Candlemas as Taylor held to have been the case. The rule seems to have been to entertain relatives, friends, neighbours, and sometimes tenants as well, and this certainly persisted into the seventeenth century.[130] Perhaps some of the complaints of declining charity were fuelled by the swelling of poverty itself, which made seasonal generosity seem more important than ever. It is true that zealous Protestantism could do some damage to observation of the feast of the Nativity. Lady Margaret Hoby was a gentlewoman imbued with that vari-

ety of faith, living in the East Riding around 1600. Her diary shows no celebration of the season except attendance at church each holy day.[131] Much
more radical was the widow of a separatist lay preacher at Bristol in the
1630s, who kept her grocer's shop open on Christmas Day to signify that
the festival was nothing except a Papist survival.[132] Her opinion was apparently shared by a number of country people in the same decade around
Beaconsfield in Buckinghamshire, who were accused by the local rector of
honouring only Sunday.[133] But such views seem to have been extraordinarily rare. Even Lord Brooke, whose beliefs were sufficiently extreme by 1640
to make him wish to abolish episcopacy and to permit some degree of
Protestant worship outside the national Church, still paid for musicians at
Christmas.[134] The Barringtons of Essex, allies of Brooke and his group,
enjoyed them as well in the 1630s and managed simultaneously to sponsor
'puritan' clergy, local wassailers, and a Lord of Misrule.[135]

These 'Lords' persisted in other gentry houses and in their Elizabethan
strongholds of the universities and Inns of Court; the presence of one was a
sign of a lavish Christmas celebration. The father of the diarist John Evelyn
gave his the right to break down the doors of anyone in the household
who tried to shut him out.[136] It was said that a fellow of Christ's College,
Cambridge, preached against them in 1610 and was forced to resign as a
result.[137] Their appearance in universities was occasional but spectacular, a
college deciding to have one after a gap of many years and then investing
a lot of effort in his rule. The best-documented in the early Stuart period
was at St John's, Oxford, in 1607, the first choice of a 'Christmas Prince'
there since the 1570s. He was elected by the students from amongst their
number, named a council of nine ministers with their own individual
insignia, and presided over plays, revels, and disputations on all holy days
during the long period from St Andrew's Day (30 November) until Shrove
Tuesday.[138] The Inns most associated with such figures were still the two
in the Temple. On Twelfth Eve 1628 the companions of one Temple 'Lord'
were arrested by the Lord Mayor for extorting money from householders in
the surrounding streets. As their Inn was to present the next Shrovetide
masque at the royal court, Charles I had them released upon provision of
an apology and compensation.[139] Seven years later the king himself asked
the Middle Temple to appoint a 'Lord', to provide diversion for his
nephew the Prince Palatine who was visiting England. A young
Cornishman, Richard Vyvyan, was duly elected 'Prince d'Amour', and contributed £6,000 of his own money towards the £20,000 which the Inn
spent in total upon feasts and dances from Christmas Day onward, culminating in another masque at Shrovetide.[140] No wonder such 'grand

Christmases' came rarely. But the students were quite capable of choosing such leaders without either public scandal or great expense resulting. A prim young man at the Middle Temple, Symonds D'Ewes, was irritated by the drunken antics of the 'Lord of Lincoln's Inn' who visited with his retinue at the close of the celebrations in January 1623. Over the same period the Middle Temple elaborated its own ritual calendar, reviving the old custom of entertaining notable men to dinner on All Saints' Day, with dancing after the meal.[141]

The period in which a larger investment in religious ceremonial has been identified was also that of the rise of a party within the Church associated with (among other things) a heavier emphasis upon ritual and order. Its enemies termed it Arminianism, a tag which has proved convenient to historians in lieu of any better one. An obvious question to pose is whether the two developments were connected. Certainly at first sight they appear to be in the case of one prominent individual, John Cosin. He was one of a group of young clergy patronized by Richard Neile, appointed bishop of Durham in 1617, who secured posts attached to that cathedral. The whole group believed in beautifying the fabric of the building and attaching greater importance to the ceremonies within it. When Neile was translated he left his protégés behind, and it was from Durham in 1627 that Cosin published *A Collection of Private Devotions*. This was a sequence of personal prayers matched to the successive Sundays and feasts of Christ and the Apostles in the cycle of the year. It was prefaced by the full calendar of holy days prescribed in 1560 which, it reminded readers, was still technically in force. The book won much praise at the royal court, being regarded, correctly, as an Anglican reply to the Catholic devotional handbooks matched to hours of prayer which were a feature of the time.[142] But it provoked an equivalent horror among those who felt that to pattern any worship after Papist examples was a step backwards from the Reformation. Their spokesman became Henry Burton, a former Clerk of the Closet to King Charles who had been dismissed for his furious hostility to the 'Arminians' and was now rector of a London parish. Burton's rebuttal accused Cosin of trying to lead England back towards Rome and called upon the Parliament of 1628 to disable him and clergy like him from promotion to high office.[143] The Commons' committee for religion did indeed question him and some other clerics.[144]

Soon after, John Cosin became the centre of more controversy, when the senior prebendary of Durham, Peter Smart, attacked him and some of their colleagues. Smart had been a favourite of Neile's predecessor as bishop. He believed most religious ceremonies to be unnecessary and any images or organ music in churches to be abominable. In a sermon in the cathedral on 7 July 1628 he accused his fellow prebendaries of multiplying all three, asserting that they had broken the law in the process. What especially caught the imagination of newsmongers was his charge that Cosin had revived the old Candlemas ceremonies by lighting over 200 candles upon that feast, sixty on the new stone communion table placed like a Catholic altar. Smart was summoned before the northern ecclesiastical commission for his words, and retaliated by charging his colleagues before the Durham summer assizes. The two judges and grand jury agreed that no law had been breached, although one of the former said that he approved of the sermon. Smart now published two tracts based upon it and prepared an appeal to the next session of Parliament. The leaders of the Church divided over the issue, old Archbishop Abbot defending Smart, and his rival and heir apparent, William Laud, supporting Cosin's group. To complicate matters, the existing bishop of Durham, John Howson, differed sharply from Smart in his attitude to religion but supported him because he felt that the others were too careless of his own authority. The result, in 1631, was a compromise imposed by Charles I. Howson agreed not to harass Cosin and his allies, while the latter agreed to employ only the rituals and ornaments customary at Durham before 1628. Smart was asked to consent to a reconciliation with his colleagues, and when he repeatedly refused he was degraded from the clerical profession.[145]

The whole affair may well have been misunderstood by historians hitherto because of a tendency to accept Smart's charges at face value; his account of the events at Durham on Candlemas Day 1628 are usually quoted without question. It is worth remembering that he repeated all his accusations to the Long Parliament in 1640, and once again it was the one about the candles which made the greatest impact and helped most to persuade the Commons to impeach Cosin. But the latter then entered detailed answers to each charge, asserting that in every case his enemy had misrepresented the truth. Thus the sixty candles on the communion table shrank to two, the total number was the same as that lit at Christmas and intended only to illuminate the huge church better, and none were employed in any ritual. The House of Lords, on receiving the impeachment and hearing all the evidence, could find little to act upon. Smart was restored to his prebend, but the impeachment of Cosin foundered.[146] The removal of the Durham Candlemas from the record of evidence for attitudes of churchmen to the ecclesiastical year corrects an anomaly in the whole. The import of the latter is that calendar feasts and rituals were not really an issue in the appearance of the division between so-called

Arminians and their enemies. Burton, attacking Cosin's book, said that the calendar of saints' feasts was tedious, not offensive; he concentrated his fire on the notion of hours of prayer. The elaboration of ceremony so obvious in the churchwardens' accounts cut across party lines. That same Burton presided over the development of the perambulation of his London parish into a lavish event, his churchwardens walking with him handing out figs, raisins, and almonds to the boys.[147] The reappearance of Christmas greenery at Chester also occurred in churches which were the livings of prominent 'puritan' ministers.[148] The practice of festival communion does appear to be a more reliable test of more general attitudes towards the rivalries of the day: it does not seem to have been adopted in parishes with incumbents who attacked the 'Arminians'. On the other hand, it appeared in many whose clergy were never denounced for sympathy with Laud, Cosin, and their kind. None of these three kinds of widespread ritual development were enjoined by the latter. They represent a movement in parish religion largely independent of national ecclesiastical politics.

Furthermore, the rival groups in the Church all promoted the development of the new Protestant festival calendar which had commenced with the celebration of Elizabeth's accession day. It was natural that, after 1603, this anniversary should be replaced by the date at which James acceded in turn, 24 March. Revised prayers were accordingly issued for this new annual celebration. But the king also had a second date to which he was personally attached, that of an escape from an attempt to kidnap him, and perhaps to murder him, led by the earl of Gowrie in Scotland a few years before. The day of his escape, 5 August, was kept by him ever after in thanksgiving, and when he arrived in England prayers were issued for that as well. In addition his coronation, which was held upon 25 July, the holy day of the apostle James the Great, could represent another anniversary for loyal celebration. So could his birthday upon 19 June. Thus, within a few months of his accession, the new monarch had provided his subjects with four possible new calendar festivals, and in 1606 a Parliament added another, by passing an act for a perpetual celebration of the second lucky escape of James's life, from the attempt by a few Catholics to blow him up in the Gunpowder Plot. As the whole Parliament had been intended to die with him, the new anniversary gave opportunities to celebrate representative government as well as monarchy, and to attack Catholics with particular fervour. The motion was formally proposed by the fervently Protestant Northamptonshire MP Sir Edward Montagu, who was to feature in the next decade as an enemy of village wakes, and it passed the Commons within two days. Based upon the ancient Hebrew tradition of days of deliverance, it ordered all people to attend church on the morning of each 5 November, and all parish clergy to read not only prescribed prayers but the act of Parliament itself, which justified the continuation of laws against Catholic worship.[149]

The first study of the reaction to this set of new choices has been made by David Cressy.[150] Clergy were supposed to remember four out of the five festivals (the exception being the birthday), although only one had statutory authority and required the attendance of the laity. Professor Cressy found that some parishes ignored all of them, many celebrated them irregularly, and most remembered 24 March, 5 August, and 5 November. The pattern was one of local choice and erratic behaviour; thus the Dorset market town of Sherborne let every royal anniversary pass unnoticed in 1620, rang bells for 24 March and 5 August in 1621, substituted 5 November for 5 August in 1622, and remembered all three in 1623. At Salisbury the wealthy parish of St Edmund rang peals on all three dates in the same years, and made an unusual addition by remembering James's birthday as well. David Cressy believed that the most popular date of them all was Gunpowder Treason Day. The king himself heard a sermon each year, according to statute, while rich citizens endowed them in several London parishes. Often in the metropolis more was spent on rewards to the ringers than on any other of the royal anniversaries. By the 1620s it merits the name of a national celebration, focused upon towns where— as in examples as scattered as Canterbury, Norwich, Carlisle, and Nottingham—corporations provided music and artillery salutes and attended church in scarlet robes of office. Professor Cressy also noted that, contrary to the assertions of some modern folklorists, the Gunpowder Treason celebrations derived directly from the misfortunes of Guy Fawkes and his partners and not from any pagan tradition of kindling bonfires and burning effigies at the onset of winter.

The research for the present book has supported all these points, and the following additions can be suggested. First, in denying that the 5 November bonfires had pre-Christian antecedents, David Cressy was attacking a belief well entrenched among folklorists until recently and expressed as late as 1982 and by such a fine scholar as Bob Bushaway. It derives largely from the undoubted existence in Wales and north-west England, until the last century, of Hallowe'en fires and rites connected with them which were fairly clearly descended from the pagan feast of Calan Gaea (Samhain in Ireland), the ancient Celtic New Year. Furthermore certain customs recorded at the Guy Fawkes celebrations, such as leaping the flames for luck, were also a feature of the clearly very old midsummer fire festival, and almost certainly transferred from it. None the less, Professor Cressy's point, that there is no sign of such a festival at this time of year across most of England until the statute of 1605, remains correct.[151]

Second, it is interesting to see, in a larger sample of material, how slowly the 5 November festivities spread despite the unequivocal text of the statute. At Pitstone Green in Buckinghamshire's Vale of Aylesbury, the prayers for the day only arrived in the financial year 1607–8. Chetton, in Shropshire, initially got the date wrong.[152] Most parishes which came to observe it did so in the 1610s, with some following in the next two decades. Overall, it was indeed the most popular state commemoration of the reign, with bells being rung for it in 139 parishes for which records survive. Eighty-eight rang for the accession day, and eighty for what they called 'Gowrie's Day', or 'the king's triumphing day'. Interestingly, the predominance of 5 November was not achieved because of popularity in London and its area, where 24 March was most commonly honoured. It was its adoption in market towns and villages, especially in Devon, Somerset, Staffordshire, and Shropshire, which swung the balance to it so heavily in the overall figure.[153] Whether this was because it had the force of law behind it, or whether because of hatred of Catholicism, we do not know. Certainly, as Professor Cressy believed, by 1625 it was found in all parts of England and its progress had been occasioned by the whims of parish élites.

Certainly, also, those whims could be enormously varied. Throughout the early Stuart period, most rural parishes failed to observe any of these days, and neither did some of those in towns, including eight in London.[154] In some of these urban cases the reason may have been poverty and a sense of marginality, but in those of comparatively important livings like the two Ipswich churches, the suspicion arises that a dislike of paying salutations to human sovereigns may have inspired the response. In several communities it was the king's escape from the Gowrie conspiracy which particularly caught the imagination. They ranged from the very wealthy Bristol suburb of Redcliffe, where the thirteen ringers received new gloves on that date, to villages such as Repton in Derbyshire's Vale of Trent and London parishes such as St Benet Fink and St Ethelburga the Virgin. Only eleven in the sample remembered the coronation day, though these were scattered across the country,[155] and only the more important of Salisbury's churches seem to have honoured James's birthday.[156] That of New Windsor rang bells occasionally in his reign on 5 August and 5 November, but under Charles it bothered only when royal children were born or the monarch arrived at the castle. Great Marlow, beside the Thames in Buckingham-shire, kept its peals for welcoming the royal train when it passed through.

It is unclear what happened in most places upon any of these dates, except the ringing of bells. At court James continued upon his accession day the custom of jousts which Elizabeth had instituted upon hers. We have the added detail that the king made gifts to the best competitors, but despite this the chief nobility had lost interest so much by 1618 that an angry James had to order them to take part. He also heard a sermon each year from a bishop, and the Tower garrison and royal guards fired their guns.[157] Beside this date 5 August and 5 November were modest points in the royal year, marked by sermons usually delivered by Lancelot Andrewes and by a few creations of knights.[158] His birthday was celebrated with only a better than usual feast and another honours list.[159] In parish churches it may be assumed that if the bells were rung then a service was held, but this is only certain in those few where communion was provided[160] or ser-mons endowed[161] on 5 November. Things are a little clearer in some large towns, where the corporations sponsored the quite elaborate Gunpowder Treason festivities noted by Professor Cressy. Canterbury was perhaps the most spectacular, with armed parades and volleys, although Bristol's annual twin bonfires and firework display were equally notable.[162] Yet there is no trace of comparable efforts in most urban centres. The statute did not spec-ify a day off from work, only attendance at a morning service. The fre-quency with which ringers were provided with candles may indicate that the bells were often swung before daybreak to fit the prayers in before the opening of business hours, rather than in the evening to encourage merry-making.

Another perception of David Cressy, which can be followed up further, is that the accession of Charles I soon brought about a totally novel situa-tion, of Protestant calendar festivals being used against the Crown instead of in its honour. On James's death his anniversary of 5 August was scrapped altogether, while the accession day ringing was transferred to 27 March, the date when Charles came to the throne. It remained a very important concern, being performed in eighty churches which have left accounts, once again spanning the nation and including some villages.[163] But the absence of it in most parishes in cities such as Oxford, York, and Chester is striking[164] and does seem to indicate a waning of enthusiasm among some of the communities most conscious of national events. This phenomenon is further emphasized by the continuing intensification of pop-ular interest in 5 November. What lent this a double edge was the new king's marriage to a Catholic French princess, which made gestures of hatred towards Catholicism potentially offensive to the Crown. The multiplication, rather than diminution, of Gunpowder Treason celebrations was in part a judgement on the marriage. It was in the period 1625–40 that the date becomes to some extent Bonfire Night, with fires and burning tar barrels being paid for by some parishes in London, Cambridge, and Durham.[165] Images of the Pope or Devil were burned in unofficial blazes in the capital. In 1628 an observer recorded 'trumpets and psalms' there as well.[166]

A much more calculated insult to the new queen lay in the revival of the cult of the old one, by the reappearance of celebrations upon Elizabeth's accession day. In the second half of James's reign, when his own wife converted to the faith of Rome and many of his more zealously Protestant subjects began to press for war with Spain, a few London churches began to ring bells once again on 17 November.[167] In 1620 a parishioner left money for an annual sermon that day at St Pancras Soper Lane. But on the arrival of Queen Henrietta Maria, that allowance was doubled by the man's son.[168] Professor Cressy found that in that year Queen Elizabeth's Day sprang into life again at five more churches in the City and two in Westminster.[169] To his total can now be added eleven more in London.[170] That still leaves thirty-seven London parishes from which accounts survive but which apparently did not ring bells then. Outside the capital, Professor Cressy only found it at Lambeth (opposite Westminster), at one Cambridge parish, and at 'puritan' Dorchester.[171] To this tiny number only two Bristol parishes can be added.[172] Still, the minority of metropolitan churches which paid for ringing on 17 November could set up quite a clangour, and the gesture was more effective in that a cruel providence had placed the real queen's birthday on the 16th and the king's on the 19th. In 1630 the contrast between the court's tilts in honour of Henrietta Maria and the City's pealing and lighting fires the next day for Elizabeth was obvious to all.[173] Ben Jonson presented Her Majesty with a poem, complimenting her and suggesting that public celebrations would have been appropriate.[174] Two days later the Privy Council was ready when nothing happened in London to mark King Charles's nativity, and summoned the Lord Mayor to demand that this be remedied. He at once ordered ringing in the City and suburbs, and the citizens obediently lit over a thousand fires in the streets.[175] Thereafter most London parishes, twenty-five out of the sample of the fifty-five which have left contemporary records, continued to ring for Charles's birthday. Nine managed to ring for Henrietta Maria as well.[176] Only one of those which had honoured Elizabeth now ceased to do so (St Michael Queenhithe), but only two of those which persisted failed to salute the king as well.[177] So a satisfactory compromise had clearly been reached. The whole squabble was a metropolitan one, provincial churches not troubling to take up the royal birthdays any more than to revive the tribute to Elizabeth. But it was not the less important for that.

The incident was essentially an exchange between the royal couple and the more intolerantly Protestant Londoners. It did not involve the differing sets of churchmen, and the latter were not in general divided over the new additions to the calendar any more than they were over the surviving ancient Christian feasts. It must already be obvious from the pattern of adoption sketched out above that there was no campaign by state or Church to enforce the celebration of these political anniversaries. It was left up to individual bishops whether or not they enquired after them upon visitation. The great majority did not. The two successive archbishops of Canterbury, Abbot and Laud, included 5 November in their metropolitan articles, and Abbot added 5 August. Under James the most enthusiastic proponent of the royal holy days seems to have been John Overall, bishop of Norwich, who enquired after 24 March, 5 August, and 5 November. The equivalents under Charles were the bishops of Carlisle in 1627 and Norwich in 1629, and Matthew Wren, appointed to Norwich and then Ely in the 1630s.[178] All asked about Gunpowder Treason Day and the accession day, but none were noted as launching a campaign against wardens who confessed that they did not remember them, even though in the returns to Wren's visitation of Ely this was the most common fault admitted.[179] In the summer of 1640 Convocation did pass a canon at Laud's behest, enjoining better observation of the accession day,[180] but this was the action of a desperate regime, sensing widespread disaffection and about to crumble. Until that point both the Arminians and their critics promoted 5 November as their favourite among the new anniversaries. The difference was that in 1635 Laud and his colleagues issued a new form of prayer for the day to emphasize the sin of rebellion in general as well as the danger from Catholicism.[181]

All parties looked benevolently upon the development of Protestant civic pageantry to replace that removed by the Reformation. The urban junketings on first 17 and then 5 November are some examples of this. Another is the steady elaboration of the London Lord Mayor's Show on 29 October. Having commenced in the mid-Tudor period, as described earlier, it remained based upon the custom that, having travelled by water to Westminster to take his oath of office, the new Lord Mayor would be rowed back and conducted from the wharf to the Guildhall with pageantry supplied by his craft company. From 1585 onward popular dramatists were hired to write the entertainments and published them. Until the 1590s they were largely religious in content, but after that referred overwhelmingly to classical mythology, British history, and moral allegory. Under James a pageant on the Thames was added to that upon land, while the latter expanded to include an even greater number of mechanical devices such as ships, chariots, and model animals. Under Charles acrobats appeared. The scripts, carefully penned by the professionals, managed to celebrate both City and Crown adroitly and thus gave offence to nobody.[182]

All in positions of national and metropolitan authority seem also to have shared the same ambivalence towards the development of Shrove Tuesday into a major time of misrule for London apprentices. Before 1598 there are no references to disturbances on that feast in the Middlesex quarter sessions records, although Lord Mayors did double the watch and warn the 'prentices' to stay indoors.[183] After that, it seems clear that they started to ignore that advice with spectacular results, for Shrove Tuesday riots occurred in twenty-four out of the twenty-nine years of early Stuart London, normally in the suburbs and especially in the northern suburbs, where traditional areas of recreation were situated. They could involve thousands of people, craftsmen reinforcing the youths, and their favourite targets were brothels and playhouses. In 1612–14 one Shoreditch bordello was attacked every year until it was demolished. On Shrove Tuesday 1617, a new playhouse in Drury Lane was wrecked, the inmates of Finsbury prison released, and several houses at Wapping destroyed.[184] Such actions were certainly criminal, and ringleaders sometimes received heavy fines and gaol sentences.[185] But they were directed against targets disliked by respectable people and could be regarded as a form of community policing. Three London satirists in the period, with very different attitudes to festivity, dealt with Shrove Tuesday. *Vox Graculi* deplored its gluttony but glossed over the commotions.[186] *Pasquils Palinodia* spoke complacently of apprentices 'indulging to the utmost' in sports of all kinds and of artisans 'coming close' to riot.[187] John Taylor wrote with more candour, admitting that 'youth armed with cudgels, stones, hammers, rules, trowels and hand-saws, put play-houses to the sack, and bawdy-houses to the spoil', smashing glass and ripping up tiles, chimneys, and feather beds. The zest with which he described the actions of these 'ragged regiments' was balanced by his recognition of the 'contempt of justice: for what avails it for a poor constable with an army of reverend rusty bill-men to command these beasts, for they with their pockets instead of pistols, well charged with stone-shot, discharge against the image of authority, whole volleys as thick as hail'.[188]

In view of all this it is ironic that what brought Charles I directly into collision with some of his subjects over calendar customs was not his treatment of either old Christian nor new royal holy days, but of semi-secular rural revelry. The irony lies principally in the fact that his character, austere, dignified, and humourless, was most unsuited to any personal appreciation of the merriment concerned. His reign began with an immediate concession to its enemies, when in his first Parliament he gave consent to the sabbatarian bill which his father had twice vetoed and which the Commons at once resurrected. It made statutory law of James's prohibition of plays and baitings on Sunday and of his injunction upon people to remain in their own parishes for such recreations as were 'lawful'. Unlike the royal declaration it did not name the latter, and so left their identity somewhat ambiguous. A single JP had authority to convict and punish offenders. Two years later the king assented to a second act, again passed through both houses without controversy, to forbid Sunday carting, driving, and slaughtering.[189]

As upon each occasion before, the demonstration of feeling within Parliament against 'profanation' of the Sabbath seems to have had an impact upon merry-making in general. It was in 1625–6 that church ales ended at Bere Regis in the Dorset chalklands, Hocktide collections at Alton in the central Hampshire forests, and 'hoggling' at Dursley in the Cotswolds.[190] All were important local centres where these activities were long established. At York the crafts finally gave up paying rents for the old pageant houses which had kept the sets for the Corpus Christi plays.[191] In July 1627 the judges riding the Western Circuit were persuaded by the Dorset JPs to add their authority, and thus that of the Crown, to an order prohibiting revels and church ales. When they moved on to Exeter they did the same for the Devon justices who had been enraged to find their previous rulings flouted by an exuberant Whitsun revel at Chivelstone.[192] The next year Chief Justice Denham, holding the Somerset spring assizes, was petitioned by six local ministers to give the same support to the orders issued by the bench for that county. He obliged.[193] In 1628, also, the chamberlain of Bristol was paid by the corporation to get rid of a maypole which had appeared in the city.[194] The next year a bishop, Barnabas Potter of Carlisle, issued articles forbidding rush-bearings, May-games, morris dances, and ales upon the 'Sabbath', in addition to those activities explicitly banned by statute.[195] Denham repeated his prohibition at the assizes in Dorset in 1631 and Somerset in 1632.[196] Hostility to the old festivities did not just operate among élites, even at parish level. On Midsummer Day 1633 a labourer of St Aldate's parish, Oxford, got into trouble for attacking a procession carrying a garland, according to tradition, into St Peter's church on the far side of the city. He turned out to be an individual of ardent Protestant religiosity.[197]

Voices raised upon the other side included the pair who had lauded the old rural revelry since the previous century. In 1626 Nicholas Breton brought out *Fantastickes*, which combined it with the feasts of the Church to suggest that a yearly cycle of religious ceremonial and ritualized social entertainments promoted both personal and communal well-being. The Lord of Misrule, maypole, and morris took their place alongside the Christmas and Easter eucharists as part of a single pattern of spiritual and physical refreshment. Four years later, Drayton, whose work had always been less obviously polemical, published another collection of pastoral verse, lauding the Lady of the May and the village king ale.[198] But three more, very different, writers contributed to the same end. One was Richard Rawlidge, denouncing the habit of tippling in 1628, who accused Elizabethan preachers of driving people into alehouses by closing down communal drinkings. In the same year a young fellow of an Oxford college, John Earle, included in a set of comic character-studies 'A She Precise Hypocrite' or female puritan, mean-minded, selfish, and a vicious gossip, who rages against a maypole and urges her husband to break the fiddler's head.[199] In 1628 also another Oxford scholar, Robert Burton, brought out the first edition of his subsequently famous work upon madness. It approved 'May-games, feasts, wakes and merry meetings' and 'Dancing, Singing, Masking, Mumming, Stage-plays' as preventions of mental disturbance. Burton went on to defend the Declaration of Sports against those whom he termed 'severe Catos', and commended all sports and recreations 'opportunely and soberly used'.[200]

Their views were, of course, soon to be endorsed by King Charles himself in the most powerful possible way. The story of this has always been well known, and the reasons for his action and its effects have been increasingly better understood, thanks to the work of Tom Barnes, Kenneth Parker, Julian Davies, and Kevin Sharpe.[201] The first two agreed that the principal impulse behind it was the conviction of Charles's favourite cleric, William Laud, that the Church needed to assert its independence of the laity (excepting the sovereign) in order to prosper. Professor Barnes suggested that he was accordingly annoyed when, in 1632, Chief Justice Denham's order against Somerset church ales contained a clause directing all clergy in the county to publish it. Although as yet only bishop of

London, Laud was already the king's chief ecclesiastical adviser, and it was probably he who persuaded Charles to command his Western Circuit judges to revoke the whole order in the spring of 1633. One of them, Chief Justice Richardson, obeyed in Dorset but not in Somerset, where feeling against ales was apparently stronger. His negligence was reported to the monarch, probably by the local gentleman Sir Robert Phelips, who disliked Richardson and was hoping to win royal favour. In May Charles requested a full report from Phelips and two friends, and swiftly got one, formally repeating the criticism of the judge and asserting the value of church ales. The king now commanded Richardson to revoke the order at the next Somerset assize, that summer. The Chief Justice complied, but with obvious bitterness and an invitation to JPs to petition Charles to change his mind. Twenty-five signed such an appeal, led by Phelips's principal local rival Lord Poulett. That left twenty-four who declined, among them of course Phelips, who complained of the incident to the king. Charles at once set up an inquiry, which culminated in November when Richardson was rebuked by the full Privy Council and disgraced by removal to the least prestigious circuit. On 4 October Laud, now archbishop of Canterbury, had written to the bishop responsible for Somerset to canvas the 'gravest' clergy upon the merits of ales. This individual, Piers of Bath and Wells, was one of Laud's principal allies, but he may well have been reporting accurately when, on 5 November, he replied that he had found seventy-two parish clergy who thought wakes and ales beneficial to both Church and people. But the archbishop had not, in any case, waited for this endorsement. On 18 October he had persuaded his sovereign to reissue James I's Declaration of Sports, this time including wakes in the permitted Sunday recreations and directing that it be read in all parish churches in the realm.

To this story Professor Parker has added the following details. Laud had not objected to the 1628 assize order against ales, even though he was then bishop of Wells himself. But he became concerned about Sunday observance after translation to London, when its Lord Mayor issued an order for strict enforcement of the recent statutes within the precincts of his own cathedral, encroaching upon episcopal authority. Thus, runs the argument, he exploited the controversy in Somerset to augment the power of the Church. At the same time the readiness of that county's JPs to oppose ales was increased by a riot at Coleford in the north-eastern clothing district, caused by heavy drinking at an Ascension Day church ale. Drs Davies and Sharpe differ from both their predecessors principally in crediting the king himself with the principal responsibility for the renewed declaration. They point out, convincingly, that this was believed by a number of commentators in the 1630s, that those who blamed Laud had good reason for making him the scapegoat in order to spare the monarch, and that Charles was not somebody who presided over initiatives which he did not himself endorse. Both of them also, however, appear to recognize that clear proof for the relative importance of sovereign and archbishop in propelling the sequence of events is missing.

None of the composite work of these historians seems to be at all faulty. In trying to build upon it, three themes should perhaps be disentangled: Judge Richardson, Somerset ales, and Sunday observance. The Chief Justice was examined in London by a committee of the Council, the decision of which was endorsed by the full body. It consisted of Laud (of course), plus the earls of Manchester and of Arundel, and Lord Coventry. At his trial twelve years later the archbishop insisted that the last two, as well as the king himself, had been infuriated by Richardson's reaction to a royal command,[202] and it is quite easy to believe that they would have been. Laud alone could not have pushed those aristocrats into a verdict, although he plainly urged them on. There is no reason to think that either he or the king were very enthusiastic about church ales themselves. Laud's behaviour in 1628 speaks for itself, but so does that at his trial, when he showed no inclination to defend them.[203] In his letter to Piers he sought further advice upon the subject, because Charles did not immediately trust the reassurances given by Phelips and his allies about the orderly nature of most. When the Somerset petition against ales had reached him, the king had listened with some sympathy.[204] If the ales were essentially a secondary issue, it is hardly surprising that the bishop's reply was not awaited before the Declaration was reissued.

On reading Laud's defence at this point of his trial, it is noteworthy that he never denied that he thoroughly believed in the revised declaration, only insisting that the king and the Lord Keeper, Coventry, did so as well. He based his attitude upon the issue of the extent of Sunday observance.[205] His loyal follower and biographer, Peter Heylyn, later held that the archbishop's determination to do something about the issue was first aroused by a book published in 1632 by Theophilus Brabourne, one of that small and eccentric group who believed that the true Lord's Day was Saturday, after the Jewish practice.[206] Thus Heylyn also makes it clear that sabbatarianism was the vital question for the government from the beginning, and there seem to have been two aspects to it. One was that to which Professors Barnes and Parker drew attention, largely because Heylyn himself did so,[207] of resisting lay encroachment on clerical preserves. The other, and perhaps more important, was that which had inspired James to

the original Declaration of Sports. It figured prominently in Laud's own letter to Piers, in which he said that what concerned the king most was his
belief that 'humourists' (puritans) abounded in Somerset and were responsible for the campaign against ales.[208] Both of them seem to have taken this,
and the pressure upon Sunday entertainments, as one thrust of a general
design to alter the Church from below. It was in the natures of the two
men to believe in the need to detect enemies within the realm and to deal
with them. It is possible that Brabourne's book, as Heylyn suggested,
impressed them as a warning that such foes were at work. But Brabourne
was a representative of such an atypical little set of thinkers that it is possible that Heylyn was being disingenuous in blaming him. It is difficult to
believe that the government's attitude to the Sunday question was not
inflamed far more seriously by a different publication of that same year
1632, resulting in legal action all through 1633: *Histrio-Mastix*, by William
Prynne, a lawyer based at Lincoln's Inn. It has long been celebrated as the
most intemperate and sustained attack upon stage plays and players. It was
also, however, a sabbatarian treatise of a radicalism unusual for an author
who conformed to the established Church. Prynne had expressed a belief
that, whereas St Ambrose and St Augustine had wished to abolish pagan
festivals altogether, a Pope, Gregory the Great, had made the error of com-
bining them with Christianity in order to facilitate conversion. In his view,
Christmas had become a feast in which the heathen elements predominated.
He therefore felt that it and all other holy days should be officially
demoted in status to enhance the position of Sunday which would (of
course) be reserved wholly for religious activities. He added a comprehensive condemnation of all dancing for purposes of pleasure, and averred that
the morris derived from the ritual cavorting of the Roman priests of Mars,
Bacchus and Cybele.[209] Prynne's savage punishment by the Crown was one
measure of the alarm felt by Charles and his advisers at what they saw as a
challenge to existing norms in government, religion, and society. The reissued declaration was another, as the church ales controversy followed
directly after the book.

Laud now set out to ensure that sabbatarianism would never function as
a Trojan horse for puritanism. He used his office as a censor to alter passages in works intended for publication, deleting the very word 'sabbath' in
one sermon (feeling, like Abbot before him, that it was not appropriate to
the English Lord's Day). He also amended a book asserting the divine
institution of episcopacy, by Joseph Hall, to make it more hostile to strict
Sunday observance.[210] His disciple Heylyn, who had presented the case
against *Histrio-Mastix* at Prynne's trial, now ensured the translation and

publication of John Prideaux's sermons in favour of Sunday recreations, delivered in 1622.[211] The king commissioned Heylyn himself to write a massive work upon the issue, which rearranged Elizabethan and Jacobean history to make sabbatarianism wholly an aspect of puritanism. It fiercely mocked the reverence for Sunday displayed by some English Protestants and stated (clearly on Charles's behalf) that the new declaration had been necessary because magistrates and ministers were extending the bounds of the 1625 act upon their own initiative.[212] The king also requested a book from Francis White, bishop of Ely, who obliged with one identifying sab-batarians with those who wished to make the Church less Christian and more Jewish.[213] In addition the opportunity was seized by young clergymen who supported the archbishop's policies and sought preferment; between 1635 and 1637 six of these published to defend Sunday recreations, although their theology sometimes differed.[214]

Poets and playwrights also made efforts to exploit the issue. The veteran Ben Jonson was first off the mark, producing in 1633, when the king's attention was being drawn to church ales, a pair of plays drawing upon rural pleasures. One, performed first before Charles, included a country wedding, with the bride 'dressed like an old May-Lady' in scarves and 'a great wrought handkerchief, with red and blue and other habiliments'. The other also involved bridal customs, and promised 'antique proverbs, drawn from Whitsun Lords and their authorities at wakes and ales'. It must surely be from this period too that dates Jonson's *The Sad Shepherd*, first published in 1640. A tale of Robin Hood, it poured disdain on 'the sourer sort of shepherds', who reviled traditional revels while being themselves guilty of the sins of covetousness and anger.[215] At Shrove Tuesday 1634 Nicholas Carew adroitly produced a court masque which praised the king for defending merriment in the higher causes of religion and wisdom.[216] Two years later, William Sampson's play *The Vow Breaker* included a sym-pathetic and very technical account of the work of a hobby-horse dancer. It described the bells, plumes, and frizzled mane of the model and the difficult business of imitating the movements of a real horse. The play also paid tribute to the morris in general, the team concerned including both a Maid Marian and a model dragon.[217] In 1636, also, Michael Drayton edited the famous collection of verses in homage to his friend Robert Dover, patron of the Cotswold Games. As suggested earlier, these games were a very differ-ent phenomenon from old-style rustic merry-making, but three of the thirty-four contributors did seize the opportunity to salute both. John Trussell thought the substitution of religious exercises for neighbourly con-viviality the sign of a sick society. He praised Lords of Misrule, wakes, rush-bearings, Whitsun ales, May games, and Hocktide. William Durham celebrated the exuberance of youthful pleasures on holy days. Thomas Randolph eulogized May revels, decried the 'melancholy swains' who opposed them, and suggested that country people were too innocent to indulge in vice (a comment which could only have come from a young Londoner). All three joyfully accepted the pagan roots of rural festivity.[218] Finally, another metropolitan literary man, Thomas Nabbes, produced a masque to amuse the young prince of Wales, representing the joys of May and involving a morris dance.[219]

Given the monarch's clearly expressed views, only the very brave and very foolish would raise voices on the other side, and even fewer would print their words. The one who printed most was the London rector Henry Burton, who had been Cosin's critic in the 1620s. In 1636 he delivered four separate attacks upon current ecclesiastical policy. In one he answered White's book upon Sunday, pointing out that views which the bishop had associated with Judaism had actually been propounded by such good Anglicans as King James's favourite festival preacher, Lancelot Andrewes.[220] Another cited fifty-five cases of personal disaster which had come to individuals who worked or played upon the Sabbath since the royal declaration had appeared.[221] The speed with which he collected them testifies to his place in a network of 'the godly' covering southern England. Part of it certainly centred upon the rich clothier John Ashe of Freshford near Bath, who was sent 200 copies of the book, which he distributed in turn to selected ministers who could inform their flocks of its contents.[222] Burton then chose Gunpowder Treason Day to preach two sermons attacking Laud for innovations in the Church, including the new prayers for the day and the declaration concerning Sunday sports. He asserted that the reference in the 1625 act to 'unlawful pastimes' signified dancing and revels, so that the declaration broke the law of the land.[223] Both sermons were printed as well, and the collective result of all this publishing was to land Burton in the dock, along with Prynne and John Bastwick, who had collaborated in writing and distributing further attacks on Laud and his allies. As is well known, all were mutilated and imprisoned. At the same time Laud made sure that the faithful Heylyn and another protégé put out replies to Burton's views on the Lord's Day. The only sort of negative comment which could be safely made upon popular revelry consisted of the sophisticated disdain which it had incurred before. Wye Saltonstall mocked 'poor villagers' whose 'zeal hangs so after the tabor and pipe'.[224] To James Shirley morris was a sordid business in which the dancers 'sweat through twenty scarves and napkins' and the Marian ends up 'dissolved to a jelly'.[225] The London stage now rarely treated such subjects as it had done so often under James; the royal protection of them had made them more, not less, risky subjects for portrayal. Nor did Charles himself care for them, so contrary were they to the tone of frigid dignity and refined aesthetic which he had set for his court.

All this while the distribution and enforcement was proceeding of what is described in the churchwardens' accounts of the time as 'the Book of Recreation', 'the King's Book', 'the Book of the Sabbath', 'the King's Instructions', 'the Book of Toleration', 'the Book of Liberty', and, occasionally, by the name which was to be more consistently attached to it in the 1640s and has been adopted by historians: 'the Book of Sports'. This process has been well studied by Julian Davies,[226] who found no sign that it was enforced in eleven of the nation's dioceses. Bishop Potter of Carlisle, who had earlier condemned all May games, reputedly declared that he would have nothing to do with it. Two of his colleagues, Bancroft of Oxford and Lambe of Peterborough, declared their support for the Book but suspended nobody for refusing to read it. Suspension did occur in the dioceses of Gloucester, Bristol, Ely, London, Llandaff, St David's, Lichfield, and Lincoln, yet the total number of clergy who suffered did not exceed five in any of these, and they were individuals already notorious for nonconformity. The same pattern, significantly, was followed by Laud himself at Canterbury. Bishop Curle of Winchester did suspend 'several', and then proceeded to restore all but two of them. The record of the overwhelming majority of the episcopacy therefore throws into even sharper relief the behaviour of Piers in Somerset and Matthew Wren in the diocese of Norwich, the former suspending at least twenty-five and the latter thirty.

Dr Davies has also pointed out that it is impossible for the historian to calculate the number of clergy who actually failed to read the Book, and the reason for this also helps to explain the low number of punishments resulting in most areas: that the declaration was full of loopholes. Clergy did not have to certify that they had read the book to an audience, or even in person if a neighbouring minister or a surrogate would oblige. They were also free to read it and then preach against its implications immediately afterwards.[227] All this is true, and yet it is important also to bear in mind the problem stressed by Kevin Sharpe, that the distress and anxiety aroused by the Book was out of all proportion to the number of prosecutions of its opponents. Not only did many more clergy refuse to read it initially and buckle under episcopal pressure or resort to subterfuges like those listed above, but even the obedient could harbour hard feelings. It offended not merely 'puritans' but many conformist, even conservative, laity, who were concerned about threats to order and morality. 'Perhaps more than any other of Charles I's injunctions', Dr Sharpe concludes, the Book 'raised opponents who were not natural enemies to the Church'.[228] It is interesting that among the churchmen who quietly declined to endorse it was John Cosin, who in every other way was closely associated with the ideals of Laud, Wren, and Piers but happened to believe in a strict keeping of Sunday.[229] How much resentment could simmer beneath the surface of acquiescence to the measure is revealed in the diocese of Ely, where Wren, translated thither from Norwich, found apparent complete obedience in the matter during a visitation in 1638. Only two years later, when the Long Parliament met, about a thousand of its inhabitants seized the opportunity to condemn him furiously for it.[230]

The king and the archbishop had defended traditional secular revelry in order to protect a Church which embodied hierarchy, ceremony, and dignity, and the ritual calendar of that body was central to their vision. Charles chose to be crowned at Candlemas, the old feast of the Virgin; which could be why no churches ever rang thereafter to commemorate the anniversary of the event. It was at Candlemas 1634 that the monarch prepared to watch a masque by the Inns of Court to celebrate the publication of the Book of Sports; the lawyers asked to stage it the next day as that year the festival fell on a Sunday, and Charles, somewhat surprised, agreed.[231] The Jacobean tradition of masques upon Twelfth Night and Shrove Tuesday continued, and from 1631 the royal couple instituted the custom of performing the Shrovetide extravaganzas for each other. Thus their love and marriage, as well as monarchy, piety, and hierarchy, could be formally celebrated.[232] As Laud came increasingly to identify sabbatarianism with opponents of his religious policy, so he tended to venerate calendar feasts more profoundly. In the Court of High Commission and those of his diocese he made a particular point of punishing those who ignored holy days. When bishop of Norwich, Matthew Wren not only enforced those of Christ and the Apostles but those of St Paul and St Barnabas as well.[233] When the rustic pleasures which he protected threatened order or touched holy places, the archbishop turned upon them as swiftly as any traditional prelate; he allowed the parishioners of Clungunford in the western Shropshire hills to revive their old Easter Day communal supper only provided that it was decently behaved and not held in the church.[234] As in the matter of the Book of Sports, his attitudes won some literary support. Successive editions of the cleric Daniel Featly's work on Christian living, *Ancilla Pietatis*, eulogized holy days ever more strongly.[235] In 1635 the poet George Wither wrote a celebration of the Rogationtide processions, and an attack upon those who neglected or obstructed them.[236] The young churchman Robert Sanderson, who had contributed to the defence of Sunday recreations, preached before the king in 1639 that early Christians had been happy to adopt pagan trappings. He reprimanded those who were now more 'rashly supercilious'.[237]

It is difficult to tell how far the Book of Sports reversed the decline in the old seasonal merry-making. There was still plenty of the latter about in the 1630s. Burton's victims of divine retribution included participants in maypole revels in 1634, 1635, and 1636 at Dartmouth, Gloucester, Thornton near Chester, Simbury in Dorset, Woolston in Worcestershire, Ivy Hinckley near Oxford, Glastonbury in Somerset, and Battersea, opposite Westminster on the Thames. His catalogue of tragedy involved church ales at Hempsted near Gloucester, Corsham and Sherston in Wiltshire, and Tolpuddle in Dorset, and summer sports at Brinkley in Essex. He indicated that the book had encouraged people to hold such events,[238] but we cannot tell whether they had been dormant in each place until it appeared. The legal records used by David Underdown refer to a scatter of ales and revels all over Somerset and Wiltshire in that decade. Only one, however, at Dundry overlooking Bristol, was definitely the first to be held in its place for a long time.[239] The same problem attends contemporary records of May games in central Shropshire[240] and southern Warwickshire.[241] It appears that the book could be overruled by urban by-laws, for maypoles and summer festivities do not seem to have reappeared in towns from which they had earlier been excluded. During the 1630s the corporation of York banned Sunday games without any sign of hesitation, or of suffering royal displeasure as a result.[242] It was also possible for parishioners (or at least the most powerful among them) to terminate traditional merry-making if they agreed to do so; the maypole at Cerne Abbas in the Dorset downs was chopped down and made into a ladder in 1635.[243] On the other hand, the West Country JPs made no further attempts to ban ales and revels, and confined themselves to dealing with those which became disorderly, such as the youths around a maypole at Dartmouth in 1634, who drank 'till they could not stand so steady as the pole did'.[244] Some parishes certainly revived ales at this time, such as South Newington in Oxfordshire's Cherwell valley and the Thames valley market town of Great Marlow, which held a 3-day church ale in 1639 instead of imposing a rate.[245] What seems incontrovertible is that old festive culture would have declined at a much greater rate had the Crown not declared in its favour.

For this was the principal development of the early Stuart period in the history of that culture: to turn it into a national political issue. Under

Elizabeth its condition had been for the most part determined by local initiatives. Before the reign of James had ended, it was apparently reacting to the views expressed in each Parliament, as well as to the interventions of the monarch. It had once again, as in the mid-Tudor period, become part of a conflict in national culture, represented in literature, religion, and statecraft. The concern of the next chapter will be to determine how that conflict related to the others of the time, and how far it was resolved by the bloody events to follow.

6

Puritan Revolution

THE difference between divisions of attitude to popular festivities in mid-Tudor and early Stuart England was, of course, that the division during the latter period separated the monarch from the majority of successive Houses of Commons. It shared this characteristic, equally obviously, with various other issues, and all were resolved with the meeting of the Long Parliament in November 1640. The Book of Sports was swept away with the other measures of the Personal Rule, and an end put to many of the activities which it was designed to preserve.

The new House of Commons immediately included the book among the grievances which it wanted to have redressed, upon the motion of Sir Benjamin Rudyard, who had criticized a number of royal policies in previous Parliaments.[1] Members soon began to raise the cases of ministers suspended for refusing to use it, and in early 1641 the Commons' committee for religion recommended the restoration of several of these and also questioned some who had been denounced for supporting the book with especial fervour.[2] The Lords seconded these actions by sentencing John Pocklington, whose defence of Sunday games had been particularly intemperate, to be deprived of his living while his work was burned at London and in the universities.[3] But although any enforcement of the Book of Sports ended with the convention of the Parliament, the king did not rescind it. Instead the Commons acted unilaterally in August, when the end of the first session of the Parliament was imminent. On the 31st they determined to order that communion tables be removed to the body of parish churches, rather than being placed in the east end where the pre-Reformation high altars had stood. Sir Symonds D'Ewes, who as a law student had been disgusted by the gambols of a Lord of Misrule, suggested that a condemnation of the Book of Sports be added. The next day the

Commons duly included a total prohibition of Sunday dancing and sports in a declaration condemning most of the ecclesiastical 'innovations' of the 1630s. The same clause encouraged sermons on Sunday afternoons and directed all ministers and churchwardens to certify compliance with the ban and all justices and mayors to report defaulters. This measure was agreed without a division and subsequently printed and published with the whole set.[4] The orders were, however, left with very doubtful legal stature because the Lords, let alone King Charles, refused to endorse them. Accordingly the MPs turned to the subject again in December, during a discussion of how to suppress whoring, swearing, drinking, and profanation of the Sabbath. On the 24th a committee reported with a draft measure to secure this. It was D'Ewes, again, who called for specific legislation against the liberty given in the Book of Sports, and two legal experts were asked to draw up a bill to this end.[5] It was never produced, for the work was overtaken in turn by the growing crisis between the king and his opponents in Parliament which led to the Civil War.

In theory, therefore, a state of tolerance existed from November 1640 in which people were equally free to denounce or to enjoy Sunday recreations, and revelry upon other days was left entirely able to flourish. The reality was very different. Every time that traditional seasonal festivity had been criticized by previous Houses of Commons it had shrunk a little more, in apparent direct response. The appearance of a House of such unprecedented power and determination to reform had a proportionately greater effect. After its convention no more books were published in praise of rural frivolity or in defence of Sunday sports. Instead eight appeared in early and mid-1641 to argue against any activities upon the Lord's Day except those related to religion and charity.[6] The Whitsun ales and Hocktide collections at Oxford, which had gone on stubbornly all through previous criticisms of such activities, came to an end in 1640.[7] Both vanished at the same time in Brentford, by the Thames in Middlesex, where they must have thrived on visitors from London and Westminster. Of all the surviving churchwardens' accounts, only two show takings from church ales by the summer of 1641, at little South Newington in Oxfordshire and remote St Ives in Cornwall. At each place they ended then. In the financial year 1640–1 the wardens of Wandsworth in Surrey dug up the village maypole.[8] From this time, also, there is no more trace of Lords of Misrule in colleges, inns, or private households. At Stafford, money had been raised for the parish ever since before the Reformation by a hobby-horse dancer accompanied by a fool; they disappear, too, in 1640.[9] The midwinter Horn Dance at nearby Abbots Bromley, of a hobby-horse and six men holding reindeer antlers, fell into abeyance around that time as well.[10] In 1641 a Lancashire gentleman, William Blundell, could look back ruefully to 'the harmless mirth of . . . peaceable times' in his district, when young people from six villages would gather to dance hornpipes and around the maypole.[11]

Urban ceremony also withered. The London Lord Mayor's Show was cancelled in 1640 because of the tense political situation, and did not reappear thereafter.[12] The Chester midsummer procession was stopped, and its model giants left rotting in a storehouse.[13] The Nottingham midsummer marching watch disappeared,[14] and indeed there is no record of such a watch held anywhere else after 1640. At Salisbury in that year the Tailors' Guild replaced its own traditional midsummer display, at which a giant had been paraded, with a quiet business meeting.[15] Only at Norwich do remnants of the Tudor civic pageantry seem to have continued for a while. Probably many village revels and private celebrations continued, invisible to history, although the tone of comments such as Blundell's suggests that in some areas at least these were much diminished. But it does appear that the political changes of 1640–1 destroyed the connection between the formal life of parish and town and the pre-Reformation festive culture, which had been weakening ever since the time of Elizabeth. Perhaps the uncertainties and divisions of those years themselves had a dampening effect upon public celebration, and the approach of civil war in 1642 contributed to the abandonment of ales and feasts. But the outbreak of hostilities did not occur until the main summer festive season was over, and the preparations did not affect daily life in much of southern England. It is hard to believe that a tradition which had flowered through the Wars of the Roses, the rebellions of early Tudor England, and the epidemics, harvest failures, and religious tensions of the reign of Mary would have succumbed so easily had the people who now apparently held the initiative in government not been hostile to it.

Sacred festivals fared much better, because even the Commons were deeply divided in their opinions of them. In December 1640 the 'Root and Branch' petition from London, which asked MPs for extensive reform of the Church, included a request that holy days be reduced in number and their status downgraded in comparison to that of Sunday. It held that the existing situation not only smacked too much of Catholicism but encouraged idleness and poverty in the national work-force.[16] This was the same alteration which had been suggested by Prynne and before him by very radical Elizabethan and Jacobean Protestants. It was duly incorporated into the campaign of county petitions to the Commons and by MPs within the House to secure wholesale reform, which is well known to historians and which came to grief against the determination of most Members to defend the existing liturgy. It may be observed, furthermore, that even the 'Root and Branch' campaigners did not call for the abolition of the Church's principal seasonal feasts. Conrad Russell has noted how, in 1640 and 1641, even the most prominent extremists among the reformers, such as the nobleman Lord Brooke and the London alderman Isaac Pennington, still held household celebrations at Christmas. The only distinction in their behaviour was to term the festival 'Christ-tide' to eliminate any association with the mass.[17] Conversely, the Commons agreed upon the primacy of the Lord's Day, committing to prison in March 1641 the rector of St Clement Abchurch, London, who had preached that Sunday to Christmas was as 'the chaff compared to the corn'.[18] It is of a piece with all this that churchwardens' accounts display no significant decline in festival communion and Rogationtide perambulations during the period 1640–2. There was the occasional zealot like the curate John Jones, at Tarporley in western Cheshire, who in 1641 abandoned the Prayer Book, the perambulation, and the celebration of Christmas and all saints' days.[19] But they do seem to have been very rare. Likewise all groups in the Commons combined to propose a new, if temporary, political calendar ritual, a fast to be kept all over the realm upon the last Wednesday of each month until the rebellion which broke out in Ireland in October 1641 was subdued. The Lords concurred at once and the king agreed, issuing a proclamation upon 8 January 1642. His subjects were ordered to abstain from food during the day and to attend a church service at which prayers were offered for the defeat of the rebels.[20] As before, also, all factions or parties united to observe the anniversary of the Gunpowder Plot, the only distinction being that, as before, those most anxious for reform preached sermons upon the horrors and dangers of Catholicism, while more conservative clerics dwelt upon the sin of rebellion.[21]

Thus it is clear enough that the Book of Sports and the Book of Common Prayer, with its accompanying festival calendar, fell into two categories. The first belonged to those 'innovations' of the 1630s which the majority of the House of Commons were determined to sweep away, the latter to that older England which many Members were inclined to admire and defend. Few if any historians would find such a distinction controversial. Yet it has been blurred by those scholars who have tended to see the differing opinions of popular festivity during the early Stuart period as representing one of the issues or instinctual cleavages which divided the parties of the English Civil War. Christopher Hill and David Underdown have both very obviously tended towards such a conclusion, in their work considered in the previous chapter. But its most succinct expression was made by Patrick Collinson, in an unjustly neglected series of lectures published in 1988.[22] He suggested that writers who see the Civil War as an 'undesired, unintended event' are suffering from a failure of imagination, because tensions and disagreements were plainly present in pre-war English society. One of these, he points out, was over the Book of Sports and ran through the antecedent disputes over the virtues and vices of traditional festivity. At this point Professor Collinson drew back from the firm conclusion towards which his argument had been tending. He did not trace 'any causal, explanatory sequence' between those arguments and the development of the wartime parties. But he suggested that there might be one.[23]

There is, of course, rather a large gap between suggesting that very few people wanted to go to war in 1642 and that there were no pre-existing tensions in England. The problem is that anybody who has studied the sources from that fatal year will know that only a tiny number of the partisans left any record of the reasons for their choice of sides.[24] We are therefore left to surmise those motives from the state of pre-war politics and society, and in such surmises there is room for a great deal of hazard. The debate over Professor Underdown's theory of regional cultures is one example of this, and so, it might be suggested here, is Patrick Collinson's proposal made above. At first sight there is plenty of evidence to support it. After all, it has been argued above (more strongly than by several colleagues) that religious factors were paramount in the Tudor campaigns to suppress old-fashioned revelry. Attention has been drawn to the prominence of godly Protestants of varying shades in the same sort of campaign under the early Stuarts. As the 'godly' were, quite clearly, in the vanguard of the wartime parliamentarian cause, a leap of imagination to connect one with the other is very easy to make. But it may be a false one.

As mentioned earlier, even towards the end of Elizabeth's reign individuals were engaging in the struggle to suppress maypoles and ales who were apparently more concerned with the threat of disorder than with considerations of religion. It was a concern which did not necessarily produce parliamentarians. One of the clearest pieces of evidence for the identity of protagonists in the struggle over 'Merry England' is the petition against church ales signed by Somerset justices in 1633.[25] Sure enough, a few of the names are those of gentry who were evangelical Protestants and later supporters of Parliament in the war. But otherwise it is a list of leading royalist families, Paulets, Hoptons, Stowells, Doddingtons, Wyndhams, and Portmans. Thomas Barnes faced up to this problem in his pioneering study of the controversy by suggesting that the clash was essentially one between political factions, with the ales merely employed as a pretext.[26] But whereas it is certainly possible to view Phelips and his friends as opportunists seizing upon the issue to win royal favour, a very large number of the opposing group must already have been set against ales if we are to account for the orders already issued by the Somerset bench to suppress them. More to the point seems to be Conrad Russell's observation about Sir John Stowell, who signed the petition, denounced Bishop Piers to the Commons in 1640, and then became one of the Civil War's most stubborn royalists: that all three actions were probably motivated by his ingrained fear of the common people and their potential to cause trouble.[27] The same might easily be supposed of his fellow justices who followed him into the same party. It was noted above that many disliked the Book of Sports who were in general religious conservatives. At the time observers pointed out that many clergy who were regarded as 'puritans' agreed to read it, while some who refused were not apparently opposed to the Church on other grounds.[28] Conversely, only thirty-four out of 2,425 ministers who were ejected from their livings by Parliament during the war had an enthusiasm for the Book, or for revels in general, included among the charges against them.[29] George Wither, the poet who had lauded rural merry-making, Christmas games, and Rogation processions, became a celebrated parliamentarian. Of the three writers who had explicitly defended traditional festivities in *Annalia Dubrensia*, one was dead by the time of the war, one took no obvious part, and one, William Durham, became another ardent supporter of Parliament.[30] Sir Thomas Barrington managed to patronize 'puritan' clergy, wassailers, Lords of Misrule, and morrismen before going on to be one of the mainstays of the parliamentarian cause in Essex.[31] All this suggests that attitudes to maypoles and ales in the preceding three decades were no good indicators of Civil War loyalties. Like Ship Money and the reforms presided over by Archbishop Laud, the Book of Sports was essentially an issue decided in 1640–1. It, and all it stood for, had little to do with the bloody quarrel which followed.

Nevertheless, the traditional revels and the Church calendar were eventually both to get mixed up in it. At first the points of contact seem to have been incidental. At Ludlow and nearby Croft in 1642 partisan hatreds were united to seasonal rejoicing by Marcher folk when crowds erected maypoles with 'a thing like a head' on top, 'and shot at it in derision of roundheads'. That year at Oxford a man did the same to a picture of a godly college official.[32] Soldiers burned down the hut in which the village revel at Newnton, in the north Wiltshire lowlands, had always been held; although their motives may not have been ideological.[33] The increasing pressure of war taxation led to a revival of 'hoggling' at Cheddar in 1643, as door-to-door collection seemed more reliable than the assessment of rates; the custom lasted until the end of the fighting and then vanished, this time for ever in England.[34] In February of that year Parliament hammered another nail into the coffin of the Book of Sports, by ordering ministers to instruct their congregations that the war was a divine punishment for the nation's sins, including Sunday games 'formerly encouraged even by authority'.[35] The regime at Westminster also devoted some effort to persuading people in the territory which it controlled to take the new monthly fast more seriously. In August 1642 it required clergymen to report to MPs the names of those who were not bothering to attend church then and of the others who turned up for the service but then spent the afternoon working, drinking, or playing sports.[36] Seven months later the Commons were grumbling over the lack of respect paid to this ordinance and wondering what to do about it.[37] For his own part, the king noted that fast-day sermons in parliamentarian quarters were often employed to attack his cause, so deprived them of legality in October 1643 by proclaiming that the fast would be moved to the second Friday in every month and that a form of prayer condemning all rebellion would henceforth be employed for it.[38] Meanwhile, one London cleric, Thomas Fuller, had already confronted a much larger issue which the fast day was going, sooner or later, to force into the open. He pointed out that on 28 December 1642 the day fell upon a traditional Church feast, that of Holy Innocents. He wondered which should take precedence, and went on to imply that the status of Christmas itself might be called into question when the fast collided with that much more important festival. His own answer was an uneasy compromise, whereby the young should be allowed to be 'addicted to their toys and Christmas sports' while elders should 'mourn while they are in mirth'. But no other speaker or writer seems to have drawn attention to the same problem in that first winter of the war.[39]

What changed everything was the Solemn League and Covenant, the alliance signed between Parliament and the Scottish government in September 1643. One of the clauses promised a further reformation of the Church of England, in terms which were left vague but made large-scale change of some sort now inevitable. Religious radicals were thereby encouraged to take the initiative, and the traditional ecclesiastical calendar was one of their targets. Hitherto even the 'Root and Branch' campaigners had spoken only of abolishing saints' days and ceasing to enforce the former strict cessation from work on seasonal feasts. Now the very existence of the latter came under attack. On Christmas Day 1643 some Londoners kept their shops in Cheapside open, and were duly attacked for their impiety by apprentices. Some ministers also kept their churches closed, having preached against the festival as 'superstitious'. More significant was the gesture of some MPs and peers, who turned up at the Houses of Parliament in sufficient numbers to make both quorate and (both Speakers being present) to transact business. The main royalist newspaper, *Mercurius Aulicus*, expressed both mockery and disapproval of those who ignored the Nativity. The parliamentarian journal which attempted especially to speak for Londoners, *Mercurius Civicus*, commented warily. It agreed that the feast was indeed 'superstitious', but recognized that to defy it on private initiative would 'give occasion of disturbance and uproar', and urged readers to refrain from doing so 'till such time as a course shall be taken by lawful authority with matters of that nature'. Another London newsbook, *The Scottish Dove*, took the same line. It set out the case for reform: that the Bible nowhere commanded the observation of Christ's birthday, so that the decision to do so was wholly the responsibility of the state, as in the case of the services on 5 November. It added that change was needed as Christmas not only commemorated 'the idol of the mass' but was 'frequently abused to carnal liberty'. Yet it also urged people not to act before the law had been changed.[40]

Parliament did not take the hint, perhaps because it was divided over the matter and perhaps because it was reluctant to act upon it until churchmen had pronounced. Instead, in March 1644, it turned its attention back to the legislation for Sunday observance which had been shelved upon the outbreak of war. Pressed forward with particular vigour by the notably godly MP Sir Robert Harley and the comparably devout Lord Wharton, an ordinance was passed after unspecified amendments on 8 April. It demanded enforcement of the legislation of the 1620s and extended it to ban all commerce, travel, and labour, all wakes, ales, and dances, and all 'sport or pastime whatsoever' upon the Lord's Day. Constables and churchwardens were directed to remove maypoles, as a 'heathenish vanity' which had 'greatly occasioned' profanation of the day. The Book of Sports was to be burned by JPs and urban magistrates. The insult to the king in this last action was arguably the only detail in the measure which would have differed greatly from one framed by the united House of Commons of 1641.[41]

By contrast the question of feast days hung fire through the year, save for a reply to the criticisms of Christmas, published at royalist Oxford in April by Edward Fisher.[42] The latter was not a cleric but a gentleman, who defended the festival as one established by the Church Fathers and not to be amended by an illegal regime such as that at Westminster. The latter nevertheless had its hand forced at the close of the year. For one thing, on 19 November the assembly of ministers convened by Parliament to reform the Church began discussing the liturgy intended to replace the Prayer Book. They resolved at once to condemn rush-bearings and all parish feasts, and to recognize Sunday as the 'only standing holy day under the New Testament'. Within one more week the divines had decided that this meant therefore that they would have no other such days at all.[43] Furthermore, in December 1644 the monthly fast at last clashed with Christmas Day, and on the 19th Parliament issued another ordinance, that the former should be kept 'with the more solemn humiliation' because the latter had turned into a 'liberty to carnal and sensual delights'.[44] Its own preachers, and its party's newspapers, drew attention to the need to secure some 'fires and plum pottage' for the young people who had lost their Christmas fun.[45]

Upon 4 January 1645 Parliament issued the new Directory for the Public Worship of God compiled by the assembly of divines. As expected, it decreed that Sunday was the only holy day and that neither work nor recreation were permitted upon it. In place of the old feasts, it recognized the existing monthly fast and any individual fast days which the Houses might appoint in response to national (and partisan) disasters and afflictions. Triumphs, in particular military victories, were to be celebrated with days of thanksgiving. These, however, were to be devoted to religion and 'holy duties' just like Sundays; indeed, they would only be distinguished from fast days by the fact that the prayers would be more cheerful and people would be allowed to have something to eat.[46] That March the Commons made further inroads into the pre-war calendar by ordering Londoners not to solemnize King Charles's accession day 'with the accustomed triumphs'; in this as in other respects the notion that the war was not being waged against his person was wearing a bit thin. The principal almanac published in the City, Booker's, deprived the date of the red letter which indicated special importance.[47]

That spring and summer further efforts were made to repress remnants of the old festive culture within parliamentarian territory. At Norwich the nation's main surviving example of civic pageantry was forbidden when, as St George's Day approached, it was ordered that there would be no 'beating of drums or sounds of trumpets; no snap dragon, or fellows dressed up in fools' coats and caps; no standard with the George thereon, nor hanging of tapestry cloth, nor pictures in any of the streets'.[48] Village ales had lingered in one hundred of east Sussex, where they were prohibited by an order of the midsummer sessions which constables were directed to announce in all churches.[49] Response to the Directory, however, was delayed by the fact that it was only enforceable in the two-thirds of England which Parliament now controlled, and that even there the distribution of copies had hardly commenced by August.[50] The Houses at Westminster made their own quiet adaptations of the new yearly cycle, starting to transact business on fast-day afternoons and to avoid it on 5 November to reinforce the importance of that date.[51]

By the end of the year the time had come for the first trial of strength over the enforcement of the new ecclesiastical calendar, at least in the capital and other major towns held by Parliament. There was never apparently much fuss over the loss of the saints' days, and religious observation of Easter and Whitsun could be concealed under the fact that they were combined with a Sunday. The real battle was joined over Christmas, traditionally the longest period of celebration at the season when joy was most badly needed. The pattern for succeeding years was set immediately at London: no churches were open, but neither were more than about forty shops, and apprentices carried out vigilante actions once more against these. It was easier to remove the religious commemoration of the day than the secular one. The parliamentarian newspapers commented bitterly upon this fact and one of them, *The True Informer*, was unable to appear that week because of 'the temper and disposition of the vulgar . . . being wholly taken up with recreation'. *The Scottish Dove*, as before, was the most imaginative, suggesting that personal New Year covenants with God be substituted for the traditional exchange of gifts. It is hard to tell how the situation varied in the rest of Parliament's territory, although churches were certainly closed in Gloucester, Yarmouth, Newbury, and Abingdon. In the dwindling royalist quarters, of course, the feast was celebrated as before, and the Oxford newsbooks spoke of their enemies' ban as sacrilegious and socially harmful. Old John Taylor, who had once defended the festival against misers, now pointed out the damage to grocers, who 'were wont to take more than £100,000 for fruit and spice to make plum pottage, mince pies and other cookery kickshaws'. The fact that Taylor had to pay for his tract to be printed, and to append a desperate appeal for patronage, indicated all too clearly that, however eloquent his words, they were those of a dying cause.[52]

By the next summer the victory of Parliament was clear, and it was able to begin the process of attempting to settle the country, which involved the acceptance of the new calendar arrangements and the new sabbatarian laws. It soon became clear that the victors had succeeded in linking the Book of Common Prayer, Christmas dinner, the maypole, and the royal accession day as a set of symbols around which opposition to the regime could be rallied. The attitude of so many royalists to Sunday entertainments had been so hostile that nobody wrote to defend them. The old summer games were only celebrated in print in the post-war years by the publication of the poems of Thomas Randolph, who was long dead, and of Robert Herrick, which, as said before, were the product of over twenty years and now passed almost unnoticed.[53] But maypoles formed gathering-points for popular uprisings in May 1648 at Bury St Edmunds in Suffolk and in Kent.[54] Accession Day celebrations provided an obvious means of displaying sympathy with the imprisoned king and impatience with the government. The two Houses themselves continued to ignore the date in the absence of any settlement with Charles. The City followed their practice until 1648, when the clear domination of Parliament by the supporters of the army led to an explosion of monarchist fervour. More bonfires were kindled than for twenty years. One observer noted that 'all coaches which passed by them were stopped and whosoever in the coaches were made to drink the king's health.' Suspected supporters of the regime were 'made most punctual to perform' this gesture. In Friday Street an image of Charles's gaoler, Colonel Hammond, was dragged along by the neck, hanged, and burned. The Lord Mayor locked himself in his house and the Commons ordered supporters to close the City gates in case the crowds sallied forth to attack Parliament.[55] At Norwich the mayor gave his permission for fires and feasts. Parliament summoned him to answer for it, thus precipitating a rising by his supporters which had to be suppressed by soldiers.[56] The issue divided Cambridge university, bonfires being lit at Jesus, St Catherine's, and Christ's Colleges, but not at Trinity and Caius.[57] At Oxford, students of that Trinity College and of New College kindled them upon the birthday of the prince of Wales, 29 May, as well.[58] London churchwardens were generally cautious enough not to pay for ringing on Accession Day, the brave exceptions being at St Dunstan in the East and St Michael Queenhithe.[59] Those of Salisbury, Oxford, and Gloucester, however, seem to have continued the custom until the execution of Charles left them no king for whom to ring.

The greatest rallying-point for disaffection in the calendar, however, was Christmas. In the first post-war December, of 1646, a group of apprentices ensured that all shops stayed closed on the day in Bury St Edmunds. When constables tried to disperse them, there was a fight.[60] A year later, when popular disgust with the regime had increased, there was a much more widespread disobedience. The lads of Bury were out again, armed with clubs stuck through with nails. The local JPs managed to provide a guard to keep one shop open, but succeeded only after a brawl.[61] Parliament ordered that the militia of London, Westminster, and Southwark be raised to prevent similar 'affronts, abuses and prejudices' there.[62] It faced an 'affront' upon its very doorstep, at St Margaret's, where the wardens decked the church with winter greens and a clergyman, one Bernard, prepared to preach on the Incarnation. The Commons had all three arrested and imprisoned.[63] Over in the City people had decorated the conduits with holly and ivy, and the Lord Mayor was running around 'very zealous' to pull it down and receiving 'divers affronts' in the process. A few ministers tried to preach, and most were stopped by 'some from the Parliament'. There were even fewer shops open than in the previous three years.[64]

In other parts of the country 'the church doors were kept with swords and other weapons defensive and offensive whilst the minister was in the pulpit'. At Norwich the day was preceded by a war of words between preachers petitioning the mayor for 'a more speedy and thorough reformation' and apprentices clamouring for festivities. He seems to have kept aloof from both. At Ipswich the defenders of Christmas held a 'great mutiny', and one of them was killed attempting to rescue their leaders from the watch.[65] But the most celebrated festive disturbances were at Canterbury, where a crowd 'threw up and down' the wares of twelve shopkeepers who obeyed the mayor's direction to open for business. It then swelled in number and took over the streets, some setting up holly bushes at their doors and giving free drinks. Others pelted a presbyterian minister and opened the city gaol. These successes led to a royalist revolt, and the seizure of the local magazine, that weekend.[66] All these episodes were manifestations of that upswelling of resentment which led to the rebellions forming part of the Second Civil War in the following summer. The crushing of them resulted in a much quieter Christmas in 1648, the main disturbance being at London where some actors were imprisoned as soon as they tried to perform.[67]

Parliament's reaction to these displays of feeling was generally to send in soldiers. In December 1646 it issued another ordinance complaining of neglect of the monthly fast, and directing local magistrates and constables to enforce it.[68] Not until the following February did the Houses pay any attention to the issue raised by *The Scottish Dove*, of providing any substitute for the fun which they had abolished with the old holy days. In that month a petition was presented by London apprentices, for 'lawful recreations for the needful refreshments of their spirits, without which life itself is unpleasant and an intolerable burden'. Nothing immediate was decided, but on 20 April a second appeal stirred the Commons into setting up a committee to frame an ordinance, granting the second Tuesday in each month as a time of pleasure. Its members were instructed to limit both the hours for liberty and the pastimes permitted in them, and to couple the measure with one for the formal abolition of the old feasts. At Easter, a week before, King Charles had issued a much-publicized statement that the festival of the Resurrection was as scriptural as Sunday. The government printed a denial of his view, holding that Easter had been instituted by the primitive Church and could now be abrogated by a reformed one. Its ordinance was a means of giving effect to this response.[69] The committee took until 7 June to make its report, but the result passed both Houses in just three days. This was despite the fact that the MPs who had framed it were unable to arrive at any decision upon the hours and games to be allowed. As a consequence, upon 10 June 1647 Christmas, Easter, Whitsun, and all other former Church feasts ceased to exist in England by both secular law and ecclesiastical ruling. Instead, a monthly day of recreation was added to the monthly fast and the weekly day of religion. Upon it, the populace was in theory free to engage in any diversions which were not (like maypoles) already illegal.[70] It was certainly ready to adopt new festivals if not fasts, and on the second Tuesday in July most of the shops in London were closed to inaugurate the new custom.[71] In the whole traditional calendar, the regime now formally recognized only one celebration, that of the foiling of the Papists and of the salvation of Parliament upon 5 November. In 1647 the Houses returned to business after a sermon, and then adjourned after nightfall to watch a firework display in Lincoln's Inn Fields. Fireballs and rockets burst, wheels spun, and figures materialized picked out in flames, to represent the prevention of the Gunpowder Plot. Royalists too were able to appreciate the fun, drinking the king's health instead of that of Parliament.[72] All told, the victors of the Civil War had created a completely new cycle of self-denial and self-indulgence, with a great deal more of the former than the latter but still giving regular scope for pleasure. It had two immediate shortcomings. The first was that it was associated with a government regarded by much of the population as detestable. The second was that, in its zeal to avoid any taint of paganism, it took no notice of the seasons. One of the most prominent parliamentarian newsbooks, *The Kingdomes Weekly Intelligencer*, made unconscious testimony to the sort of difficulty thus created in successive issues during mid-December 1647. Even while condemning those who kept Christmas and sneering at their 'superstitious' ways, it referred lugubriously to the 'depth of the winter' and later to 'the sloth of these winter nights'.[73]

The various regimes of the Interregnum contributed only a single subtraction and addition to the new framework. The former was made by the so-called Rump Parliament which established the Commonwealth, when, about a month after the abolition of the monarchy, it cancelled the monthly fast. The reason given in the ordinance was that the fast was by then so generally ignored that continuation was pointless, and *ad hoc* days of national 'humiliation' should be substituted.[74] Our only independent source for the keeping of this ill-starred day consists of the famous diary of the Essex minister Ralph Josselin. It lends support to the Parliament's assertion, in five complaints, spread over as many years, that the fast was commonly neglected. On the other hand, there were occasions upon which he had 'the greatest audience' upon it, and on most he made no comment. It was only with the regicide that he noted that the custom was now 'so exceedingly' neglected that it would have to be 'laid down'.[75] After this no further legislative attention was paid to the calendar until 1657, when the second Parliament of the Protectorate made two elaborations. One was to declare that no 'common profaner of the Lord's Day' could be an MP. The other was a statute designed to stop the continued occurrence of such profanation. It carefully defined the offence, including dancing, secular songs, music, wakes, revels, feasts, church ales, maypoles, 'or any other sports and pastimes'. The act was to be read in every parish church by the minister on the first Sunday of each March. Anybody who published arguments against it was to be fined £5 or sent to the local House of Correction.[76]

So what was the impact of these measures? In a very influential essay published in 1982, John Morrill argued that it was limited. He was the first Stuart historian to make extensive use of churchwardens' accounts, assembling a sample from 150 parishes in East Anglia and western England. He noted what has been confirmed in this book, that before 1643 the general pattern was for communions to be held upon great feasts such as Easter, Christmas, and Whitsun. What surprised and impressed fellow historians most was that 85 per cent of his parishes still did so in 1646, and 43 per cent still held an Easter communion in 1650. After this, the proportion rose, and did so still faster after 1657, until by Easter 1660 just over half were doing so.[77] The sample gathered for this book provides a total of 367 parishes for the 1650s, covering the whole country. While it bears out the basic trend of Dr Morrill's findings, it also departs from them in lesser respects. It confirms beyond doubt that most of those churches which observed 'festival communion' ceased to do so in the period 1645–9, at a fairly steady rate. This reflects the impact of the reforms made by the Directory and confirmed by ordinance. However, that process continued into the next decade, as parishes were still abandoning the custom.[78] By contrast, the number of those which revived it, all during the late 1650s, is much smaller. More than half of them did so in 1659, when the future of the republic was already in doubt.[79] Only thirty-four parishes out of the 367 (9 per cent) consistently recorded festival communions throughout the Interregnum,[80] and a further sixteen held them regularly on Easter Day though not upon the other old feasts.[81] To these may be added a church in Gloucester, one in Bristol, and three in London, which did not record communions at Christmas but were still regularly decorated with greenery at that season. A fourth London church still strewed herbs at Whitsuntide.[82] Several other parishes ignored the traditional festivals for religious purposes but regularly paid wages, gave doles, or held dinners upon them.[83] With the sole brave exception of one London example, St Mary Woolchurch Haw, the churches which continued to hold festival communions were all in small villages. The pattern does suggest that the old religious calendar was in serious decline by the mid-1650s and that had the republic survived longer, it might have been reduced to private observation. In this respect the Puritan Revolution bid fair to emulate the achievements of the Reformation, something the more remarkable in that it had itself dismantled the traditional process of visitation and inquiry. Clerical discipline was enforced by local communities of parliamentarian worthies, but they were apparently much more concerned with personal adequacy and political conformity than liturgical uniformity.[84] None of this, however, vitiates the main thrust of Dr Morrill's argument, which was to question earlier assumptions about the popularity of the religious reforms and to prove a widespread nostalgia for the pre-war Church. The signs of revival of the old feasts in 1659, when the future of the republic appeared to be in doubt, have already been mentioned. At Easter 1660, when a royal restoration had become extremely likely, the trickle of examples becomes a deluge, and here a larger sample once again bears out that used by John Morrill. Just under half of the parishes which have left accounts recorded the taking of the sacraments upon that day.[85]

The accounts add a relatively objective corroboration to the impression given by literary sources. John Evelyn's diary has long provided evidence of how a devout conservative Anglican could often manage to find a communion in London on the old feasts. But it was a difficult business. From 1652 to 1655 he sought in vain for a church open on Christmas Day. In 1656 he heard a sermon and took the sacrament, but from a clergyman operating in private lodgings, crowded out by his informal congregation. The next year, as is well known, he attended a service in the earl of Rutland's chapel and the whole company there was arrested and interrogated by Major-Generals

Whalley and Goffe. They released Evelyn 'with much pity of my igno-rance'. In 1658 he understandably stayed out of the capital and attended a private service at his cousin's home. The next year, however, central gov-ernment had collapsed altogether in December, and the cleric apprehended two years before (Dr Gunning) was holding semi-public worship without molestation in the City. At Easter 1654 Evelyn took communion from a visiting minister, in his own library, and a year later listened to sermons in two London churches, 'the ruling powers conniving' at the use of the old Prayer Book at one of them, St Gregory by St Paul's. He went back to St Gregory's and found communion in 1656, and had the same at a private service in 1657 and at St Gregory's again at Whitsun that year. In 1658 he went to St Mary Woolchurch Haw for Easter and received the sacrament from Gunning in private at Whitsun.[86] The army's crackdown on Christmas services in London in 1657 also turned up one held by 'some old choristers and new taught singing boys' at Garlickhithe.[87] Otherwise there is little evidence either that the former holy days were widely observed for religious purposes or that the authorities were greatly concerned when they were. Clergymen and pious laymen continued to dispute the theological basis of Christmas until 1656, but their exchanges were obviously sterile. As both sides generally agreed that there was no scriptural foundation for the feast and that it was based upon tradition and episcopal and royal com-mand, their attitudes turned upon their differing opinions of that tradition and those powers.[88]

It certainly signified a great deal, however, that the attempt to vilify the festival to a popular audience was virtually stillborn. A rather feeble satire appeared in January 1646,[89] but after that the field was left clear for tracts extolling the charity, fellowship, and jollity associated with the feast, which overlapped with the religious defence of it and continued until 1652.[90] It remains true, none the less, that there were not very many of these, and that half those surviving owed their existence to the ebullience and indi-gence of Christmas's old friend, the royalist poet John Taylor. In large part their relative scarcity may be accounted for by the fact that their audience was so thoroughly converted that it needed little persuasion. As before, London supplied most of the evidence. In 1650, 1652, 1656, 1657, and 1659 Parliaments and Councils of State commenced (and usually completed) fresh measures to put down the revelry in the City. In 1650 the Council noted 'the general keeping of shops shut'. In 1652 a newsbook testified to wide-spread feasting and singing of carols. In 1654 the Venetian ambassador reported that the celebrations lasted almost a week. In 1656 MPs com-plained that scarcely a shop was open between the Tower and

Westminster. In 1657 the Venetian observed that the hunt for Christmas services had not persuaded any more shopkeepers to do business. All these sources also testify to the general closure of churches, supporting the impression that the religious aspect of the day had been eradicated far more effectively than the merriment to which its critics often objected most. A few Londoners did strongly support the abolition of both, but they all seemed to have belonged to the radical minority who worshipped in gathered congregations. Among them were Samuel Chidley, who urged Parliament to stronger measures in 1652, and ministers such as Christopher Feake and Henry Jessey, who held a day of fasting and prayer that year to atone for the sins of the feasting City.[91]

Once again, the evidence from the provinces is much sparser but suggests a similar situation. A group of ministers given livings in place of ejected clergy complained in 1654 that they were 'much abused' by parishioners for refusing 'customary and promiscuous communions at Easter and Christmas' and being 'zealous against the superstitious and profane observances . . . in their unChristian Christmas revellings'.[92] An exemplar of them was the rector of Everleigh in the Wiltshire chalklands, who held out against demands for 'the riotous custom of Christmas ales' by 'the ruder sort of the parish' all through the Interregnum.[93] A royalist newsbook in December 1654 boasted of how churches were 'excellently adorned with rosemary and bays' and told a cautionary tale of how a 'Canaanite' had just tried to cut down the famous thorn tree at Glastonbury. This always flowered around Christmas and was popularly cited as testimony to the sanctity of the feast. The fanatic swung an axe at it (so the story went) but only cut himself.[94] The seasonal mumming was put down around Woodplumpton, in the low-lying Fylde district of Lancashire, in 1648,[95] but was still in progress around Calne, another community in the Wiltshire chalk country, in 1655. The latter group is only known to history because they denounced a baker for selling ale without a licence, an example of the sort of accident necessary to provide evidence of these popular customs under the Protectorate.[96] The hostility of the London apprentices to shops opened at Christmas was shared by those of Bristol, where in 1654 the corporation ordered them to work on the day of the feast and not to terrorize shopkeepers who obeyed the law and attempted to do business.[97] When John Taylor wrote in 1652 he suggested that if the jollity of the Twelve Days was under attack in the capital it was still the rule in Devon and Cornwall, where country people played cards, sang carols, 'went nimbly dancing', consumed roasted apples in ale, and enjoyed 'Hotcockles, Shoeing The Wild Mare and the like harmless sports'.[98]

Something of this can be borne out for the gentry by diaries and account books. Evelyn, at his mansion in north-west Kent, gave dinner to some of his neighbours on Holy Innocents Day 1657 and spent the whole Twelve Days the following year as the guest of a cousin.[99] The London lawyer John Greene offered hospitality at Christmas in 1649, 1652, and 1656.[100] On his prospering farm near Reading, Anthony Blagrave gave dinner to sixty-nine poor folk at the same season in 1653 and exchanged entertainments with friends of his own class as well.[101] Young Anthony Throckmorton, from a prominent Catholic family, paid for music at Christmas and for New Year's gifts when a student at Cambridge in 1654. In 1655 and 1658 he enjoyed the celebrations at the family home in Buckinghamshire, and he made gifts to musicians and mummers when a guest at an Oxfordshire manor house in 1657. The same sorts of performer were rewarded again at his own seat at Christmas 1659, when he also made a dole of money to the poor.[102] All three were passive royalists, and enthusiasm in commitment to the Nativity may have increased in proportion to that to the king's cause; the gentlemen who rose for Charles II in Wiltshire and Dorset in early 1655 were noted for having just kept 'great Christmases after the usual time with sets of fiddlers'.[103] But Giles Moore, a clergyman whose loyalty to the Protectorate was sufficiently apparent for him to be given a Sussex rectory, still presented money 'to several persons, towards the feast of Christmas', even if he did not keep it himself.[104] The godly Captain Adam Eyre, of Penistone in the Yorkshire Pennines, did not celebrate it either, but he rested at home then instead of working.[105] Sir Miles Stapleton, of Carlton in the same county, seems to be a rare case of a landowner who failed to make any payments at all connected with the festival, during the whole time of the Protectorate. His motives for keeping quiet must, however, have been precisely the opposite to those of the enemies of the feast, for he was a Roman Catholic living under the suspicion of the republican government.[106]

The abolition of the traditional religious calendar and liturgy ought in theory to have removed the Rogationtide perambulations as well. Yet in view of the obvious utility of teaching youngsters where the parish boundaries lay, and the former enthusiasm for the custom shown even by such opponents of royal policy as Henry Burton, one might expect it to continue in many places and not to be disturbed by the authorities. Evidence bears out inference. Of the sixty-two London parishes which have left accounts from the Interregnum, forty-two (68 per cent) kept on perambulating. So did some in Oxford, Cambridge, Bristol, York, Winchester, Westminster, Ipswich, Norwich, and Chester.[107] The fact that it could be preserved at St Margaret's, next to the twin seats of the central executive and legislature at Westminster, indicates how little animosity the successive republican regimes must have felt towards it. As ever, rural parishes generally do not record payments, as traditional hospitality probably provided the costs. But the widespread distribution of those which did feature them indicates a comparable survival of the perambulations in villages.[108]

Unsurprisingly, the continued survival of summer revels is much harder to document. During the Interregnum they played no part whatsoever in parochial fund-raising in any community from which records survive. The diocesan courts, the second principal source of information for them hitherto, had ceased to exist. In default of these, two categories of evidence might, in theory, be expected to be fruitful. One is the complaints and boasts of local notables, such as ministers, mayors, and justices, some of whom had been such notable opponents of the merry-making before the wars. The other consists of quarter-sessions orders and indictments, enforcing the new legislation against sabbath-breach and maypoles. Incidental comment and literary reference ought to add a little more to this body of material. Yet a sampling of each kind of source yields very little information. This may indicate that there was in fact not much of the old-style communal feasting and dancing going on, the reforms of 1644 having effectively put an end to it. Or it could be that its enemies now had much more serious worries, in the form of the poverty, physical destruction, and religious radicalism exacerbated or created by the wars. To both the godly and those more immediately concerned with order, plotting royalists, maimed soldiers, and Quakers could seem considerably more problematic than maypoles and morris. To some extent the evidence supports both views.

David Underdown certainly identified a number of village revels in their traditional stronghold of the West Country. At Woodborough, one of those Wiltshire chalk country communities which feature so prominently in the history of Merry England, a 'lewd company' from the whole district gathered in 1652. It marched noisily behind a drummer and fiddler to Pewsey, where it drank heavily and 'very disorderly danced the morris dance'. The next summer a tithingman and churchwarden of Holwell, at the Dorset end of the Blackmore Vale, impudently organized a revel on a national fast day, 'with great rejoicing and feasting'.

In 1649 the JPs for Somerset reissued the old orders against such festivities. In 1650 they were defied at Langford Budville in the Vale of Taunton Deane, where there was 'fiddling and dancing and a great rout of people'. A tithingman bringing the justices' ruling was chased away by a group of

Wellington men shouting 'We will keep revel in despite of all such tithing calves as thou art.' In 1653 there was a fight at the 'wonted revel or wake day' at Kingweston in central Somerset. In 1655 a woman confessed to the bench that she had got pregnant after the village feast at Staple Fitzpaine on the far side of Taunton. The next year men hauled a load of beer southwards from Bristol to Timsbury, for a revel attended by 'a great concourse' and producing 'many disorders and abuses'. In 1659 a reveller at Whitestaunton in the Blackdown Hills assaulted a watchman, declaring himself to be Robin Hood.[109] Professor Underdown understandably interpreted this impressive collection of incidents to mean that the traditional summer gatherings had not only survived easily enough, but were actually reviving in districts from which they had formerly disappeared, as rallying-points for disaffection under a hated regime. He may well be correct, but it is difficult to dispose absolutely of the objection that they are recorded so often because of an even more intense hostile interest in them on the part of their opponents.

The same pattern, and problem, occurs in other counties. As soon as the Devon Quarter Sessions was revived after the Great Civil War, the bench restated all former prohibitions of revels and ales, noting that several were being planned. Ten years later it glumly declared that revel days were 'yet observed in divers parishes', giving rise to 'all manner of disorder, as drunkenness, swearing, fighting'.[110] In 1655 the Warwickshire magistrates forbade the traditional erection of maypoles and may-bushes for morris dancing and other recreations at Henley in Arden.[111] The Sussex bench acted to stop an ale planned at Herstmonceux in 1652.[112] That year eleven tailors were in court in Staffordshire for having performed a morris dance in Wolverhampton despite the wishes of a gathering of ministers, and then got drunk. That they were not an impromptu collection of performers is suggested by the fact that they included a tabor-player, sword-bearer, flag-carrier, and fool. In 1655 ringleaders of wakes at Lapley and Stretton in the woods to the north were hauled in. They were husbandmen and alehouse-keepers, several of them Catholic.[113] There is one comparable case from Shropshire, where a Lord of Misrule and 'the Vice called the Lord's son' sallied out of Broseley parish with their youthful retinue on Whit Monday. They went to the nearby town, Much Wenlock, and got into trouble when they refused to pay for their drinks.[114] The next year hundreds of people processed by beat of drum to Wellington, near Shrewsbury, to watch some morris. On this occasion the justices did not need to intervene, for soldiers of the Shrewsbury garrison mistook the gathering for a potential uprising and dispersed it by force.[115]

The relevant records for other former centres of the summer games, such as Oxfordshire, Gloucestershire, and Cornwall, are missing. Where they exist in other regions they show few or none of these cases. In Middlesex a spinster of St Katherine's parish, by the Tower, was apprehended in June 1659 for 'dancing at a garland at twelve o'clock at night and carrying of the garland home on her head in company'. She was already considered 'idle, lewd and disorderly'.[116] There is nothing of interest for this present purpose in the published quarter sessions books and rolls of Hertford-shire,[117] Surrey,[118] Nottinghamshire,[119] and Essex,[120] although none of these are complete. Nevertheless, it needs to be emphasized that even in the West the attention paid to revels represented just a tiny amount of that devoted to other social problems and misdemeanours. While there were many, and widespread, prosecutions for working and drinking on the Sabbath, there seem to have been none in this sample of evidence for com-munal festivity upon it. Nor, despite the firm legal prohibition after 1644, does anybody seem to have been indicted for putting up a maypole, the more generalized order against the dances at Henley-in-Arden being the sole appearance of the poles in the court papers.

Certainly, also, a variety of other sources testify to the continued exist-ence of the summer recreations. There is mention of a maypole being raised at Wolverhampton, the year after the morris-men had performed there, to celebrate the expulsion of the so-called Rump Parliament.[121] At Throckmorton Manor, Worcestershire, the Catholic owners rewarded visit-ing musicians and mummers on May Day 1654.[122] George Fox, the most famous of the early Quaker leaders, later recalled how he had gone around the East Midlands in 1649, 'testifying against their wakes and feasts, their May-games, sports, plays and shows . . . and the days they had set forth for holy days'. His words suggest that some of each, at least, survived then.[123] Further north, at Spofforth in central Yorkshire, the rector, churchwardens, and principal villagers recorded a pact in the register in May 1654, to stop working, sports, and tippling on Sunday. This was ten years after the Parliamentary ordinance should have done so.[124] Two Danish travellers crossing Oxfordshire in June 1652 came across the last recorded of the old-style Robin Hood plays at Enstone in the fringe of the Cotswolds.[125] The London area does not seem to have preserved any of these recreations, but the citizens still went a-Maying. Indeed, although May Day itself was no longer holy, the wealthier Londoners now developed a formal practice of promenading in Hyde Park that afternoon. Pious women were scandalized to learn of ladies who rode 'round and round, wheeling of their coaches about and about, laying of the naked breast, neck and shoulders over the boot, with lemon and fan-shaking' to greet 'vain roisterers' on horseback.[126]

No more than in the 1640s did royalist propaganda seize upon the summer games as rallying-points for opposition to the enemy. Instead casual references to them crop up occasionally in literature during the Interregnum, with the same disregard for the ethics of those in power as the fashionable society in Hyde Park. In 1653 one Robert Cox wrote and staged (presumably in private) a pastoral masque including a revel about a maypole, a morris, and other country dances.[127] A collection of festive verses published in 1657 celebrated the erection of a maypole with the words 'I'll drink to the garlands around it, / But first unto those/ Whose hands did compose / The glory of flowers that crown'd it.' In 1658 Sir Aston Cokain mocked the 'zealots' who hated the poles 'with all their souls'.[128] Another set of joyous poems in that year included 'leaping o'er a Midsummer bonfire' among various games which it lauded.[129] All this would suggest, in terms of the traditional folk culture, business as usual. Against it, however, must be put the numerous instances, cited below, of observers who commented upon the revival, in 1660, of maypoles and morris after a long period of disuse. The antiquarian John Aubrey asserted that midsummer fires were put 'quite out of fashion' by the Civil War and never regained their previous popularity.[130] The most likely surmise to make from all this conflicting evidence is that the reforms of the 1640s did indeed deal further serious blows to the old festival culture, but that some of it did continue despite rather desultory persecution, the latter being more likely if its participants were disorderly or of known bad character. What they seem to have achieved almost wholly is to break its remaining links with municipal and parochial life and to drive it out of Sunday.

John Morrill has censured the victorious enemies of Charles I for another aspect of their attitude to the cycle of the year: their failure to establish a new public holiday to celebrate the Revolution.[131] This undoubted truth may be ascribed to the fear that any regular attempt to commemorate either of the key actions of that event, the regicide and the abolition of the monarchy, would have revealed how deeply unpopular both had been. Instead, the governments of the Interregnum held to the monthly Tuesday of recreation (which was such a success that historians have barely noticed it) and to Gunpowder Treason Day. Both Dr Morrill and Professor Cressy have noted that the latter was left as virtually the only date upon which churches regularly rang their bells.[132] David Cressy discovered that four in his sample, in London, Salisbury, Cambridge, and Devon, nevertheless ceased to do so during the mid-1650s. The much larger collection of accounts employed here reveals just one additional case to these, in London.[133] By contrast, it contains seven, widely scattered, cases of parishes which took up the custom during the Interregnum.[134] In all, 169 of the 367 sets of accounts used for this book (46 per cent) contain payments for it, a larger absolute and relative number than before the wars and an illustration of how communities were taking to the anniversary or hanging on to it in default of any other now nationally recognized. Its penetration of the countryside was also greater than ever before, even though a few places took a little while to work out what was required; the extreme case being Whalley, in the Lancashire Pennines, which rang for six years on 1 November, as its people had done for the dead a century before, until in 1658 they corrected the date.[135]

Some communities made their own attempts to celebrate political anniversaries. In 1651 Trinity College, Cambridge, paid for a bonfire to commemorate the regicide, and down the street Corpus Christi College held a 'thanksgiving'.[136] The people of Gloucester and Taunton rejoiced each year upon the dates of the relief of their towns from sieges by royalist armies during the Great Civil War.[137] One Bristol church in the sample and seven in London continued to ring upon Queen Elizabeth's Day.[138] Another one in Bristol and two in the metropolis abolished the custom when the republic was proclaimed, apparently because honours paid to any monarch might now be questionable.[139] Yet another in the City took it up at that time, presumably because the English Deborah had been a leader whose memory was honoured by Protestants of all shades, an example of how quite opposite use could be made of the same gesture.[140] Ludlow, the major regional centre in the midst of the Welsh Marches, made an apparently unique experiment by ringing upon Oliver Cromwell's birthday. It also took to ringing in the New Year, as did Winkleigh in central Devon, to create another calender celebration which would pass the scrutiny of the government.[141] The same dispensation was apparently not accorded to the Shrove Tuesday romps of urban youth. A literary work published in 1646 made a metaphor out of the traditional throwing at an effigy of Lent on that day, while another in 1648 did the same for the associated sport of pelting cocks.[142] But there is a significant lack of records of Shrovetide disturbances in Interregnum London, while the magistrates of Bristol annually forbade the usual pastimes of the time, itemizing cock-throwing, dog-tossing, and football. On Shrove Tuesday 1660, when demonstrations against the government were breaking out all over southern England, the Bristol apprentices kept within the letter of the prohibition while insulting the spirit. Outside the Mayor's house they threw at geese and hens and tossed up bitches and cats, and knocked down the sheriff who came to fulminate.[143]

Their actions helped to usher in a year in which, as is well known, monarchy, episcopacy, and holy days were restored together. The spontaneous return of so many parishes to Easter communion has been noted. A few weeks later came May Day and the reappearance of the maypole as a widespread popular symbol of triumph over the republic. Again, the most striking cases are celebrated. Many have read before of how Samuel Pepys saw the people of Deal setting up two or three poles with flags on them and drinking the royal health while the garrison of the castle glowered at them.[144] Those at Oxford are almost as famous, thanks to Anthony Wood who drew particular attention to the one by the Bear Inn, intended 'to vex the Presbyterians and Independents'. The vice-chancellor and beadles of the university were beaten off when they tried to saw it down. On Ascension Day the citizens were 'so violent for may-poles in opposition to the Puritans that there was numbered twelve . . . besides three or four morrises etc.'.[145] Another well-thumbed account is that of the minister Henry Newcome who, crossing Rutland in June, was horrified to find 'May-poles in abundance as we came, and at Oakham I saw a morris-dance, which I had not seen of twenty years before'.[146] These sources are, of course, confirmed by those less widely known. One Hertfordshire parish paid for 'the Maypole painting again',[147] an entry not found in any known churchwardens' accounts since the 1610s. At Gravesend on the Kent shore of the Thames, two festive symbols were combined when a pole was stuck on a tar barrel. A Wiltshire gentleman who had supported the republic, Sir Walter St John, put one up at Wootton Bassett in an unsuccessful attempt to prove to its people that he had changed his allegiance and to secure his election as MP.[148] David Underdown has collected several other references. One of the godly at Newcastle upon Tyne complained that 'May-poles and players . . . now pass current.' The Lord Mayor of London removed a pole erected by 'the rabble' in Cheapside. The parish clerk at Myddle in the western Shropshire hills told revellers that 'it was as great a sin to set up a may-pole as it was to cut off the King's head.' He was dismissed and fined for his words. Some of the parishioners of Steeple Ashton, in the west Wiltshire lowlands, complained of disorders 'at the setting-up of summer houses'. At Ramsbury, eastward in the chalklands, a constable who removed a pole received many 'ill words'.[149] As the restored monarch neared London for his state entry, royalty and revelry briefly came together on Blackheath. He was met by 'a kind of rural triumph, expressed by the country swains, in a morris-dance with the old music of the tabor and pipe'. Like his grandfather in 1603, Charles passed the sight with amusement.[150]

Most of these cases portray conflict, an immediate renewal of the local battles of the early Stuart period, inviting in turn a royal or parliamentary intervention. This is the context of the famous tract *Funebriae Florae* by Thomas Hall, minister of King's Norton in the western Warwickshire hills, published in July. It extended Prynne's arguments about the classical pagan origins of Christmas and summer festivities, and fused them with a country parson's practical concerns about the stealing of poles from rival communities and the disorders and bad company that could be found at the games. In verse he contrasted the beauty of the setting:

> Bowers of May-sprigs gaily built
> With flowers and garlands all bedecked
> In tufts of trees, in shady groves . . .

with the revellers:

> The scum of all the rascal crew,
> Of fiddlers, peddlers, jailscaped slaves,
> Of tinkers, turncoats, tosspot knaves
> Of thieves and scape-thrifts many a one,
> With bouncing Bess and jolly Joan,
> With idle boys and journeymen
> And vagrants, that their country run.[151]

Hall's intention was to help sway the sentiments of the new regime against such activities. The Convention Parliament which restored the monarchy made some effort to salvage the sabbatarian legislation of the 1640s. In that same July its House of Commons resolved to ask the King to issue a proclamation to 'quicken the execution' of previous laws against the profanation of the Lord's Day, drunkenness, and swearing. It also set up a committee, mixing Prynne with men who supported the restoration of episcopacy, to frame a bill to extend them. This got two readings in August, and on running out of session in September the House repeated its request for a royal proclamation. When it reconvened in November the bill was sent up to the Lords. At this point it certainly encountered some opposition among MPs, Sir John Masham speaking against a strict observation of the Sabbath, but Prynne and some other former parliamentarians supported it effectively enough to get it through without a division. Strict it certainly was, for it banned, along with most kinds of work, wakes, revels, church ales, parish feasts under any other name, maypoles, 'or any other sports and pastimes'. In the Lords it made two readings, again apparently lacking in serious controversy, before dissolution intervened and it was lost.[152] With much more urgent business on their hands, the Commons as a whole clearly did not attach much importance to the measure, and failed to comment in the winter upon the fact that Charles had ignored both their addresses for a proclamation; either he and his councillors considered the issue to be still less pressing, or they were intent upon keeping it open. The latter approach was certainly adopted towards the parallel question of holy days. During 1660 these were neither banned nor enforced, but left up to the taste of individual parishes. Festival communion remained the preserve of the parishes practising it at Easter, while Christmas services were once again legal and performed most prominently by the deans and other cathedral or collegiate clergy restored with the King and bishops.[153] Likewise the Sunday recreations were regulated by the occasional urban magistrate, such as the mayor of Norwich who banned them during May.[154]

During the first half of 1661 such matters still seemed debatable. The former presbyterian ministers who discussed a Church settlement with episcopalians at the Savoy during May required the abolition of saints' days while accepting the revival of the feasts of Christ.[155] Up in Cheshire one of their party, Adam Martindale, was engaged in a confrontation of the sort which had taken place many times over the past hundred years. A 'rabble of profane youths, and some doting fools' put up a maypole on his route to his church of Rostherne. Taking his cue from Hall, he preached that it 'was a relic of the shameful worship of the strumpet Flora in Rome', and a little later his wife and three friends sawed it down at night. Shortly after this, however, a hostile neighbour set up another, for 'drinking to debauchery in the evening'.[156] This exchange was one of the very last of its kind, for that same month the meeting of the Cavalier Parliament and the Convocation of the Church led to the re-establishment of the traditional liturgy in a manner quite unacceptable to those who had requested its reform at the Savoy. By the end of the next year the traditional calendar was back with the force of law behind it, and Hall, Martindale, Newcome, and the sabbatarian mayor of Norwich were all ejected from their livings and offices. With them went many other enemies of popular revelry in Church and town. The attitude of the royal government was symbolized neatly on 14 April 1661, when the King's brother and heir, acting in his capacity as Lord High Admiral, sent sailors to help erect a giant maypole in the Strand to replace the one removed in 1644. It measured 134 feet, bound at two points with iron and bearing the royal arms at its crest, richly gilded. Once it was up, a morris dance took place around it. A week later Charles rode past on his way to be crowned, and it formed a focal point for the celebrations of the people of London and Westminster that summer and for fifty years after.[157]

The image is so fine, the story brought to this point so neat, that it would be tempting to end the book here, with the Anglican ritual year and the traditional popular festivities having apparently been triumphantly reasserted after a century of controversy which had almost culminated in their extirpation. But to do so would be to ignore too many questions. What, in fact, had been restored, and how long did it last? In what respects did the ritual year under the later Stuarts differ from that in the early seventeeth century, and how far did the history of both represent part of a pattern which can be traced back through the Tudor period and forward into the eighteenth century? These problems will form the matter of the final chapter.

7

Merry Equilibrium

I<small>T</small> was remarked at the opening of the fourth chapter that historians of England in the period 1500 to 1700 have portrayed a process of 'Reformation of Manners', whereby a flourishing tradition of communal festivity was increasingly challenged by the social élite, motivated partly by evangelical religious renewal and partly by economic alterations. In this fashion, not only was much of the festival culture destroyed but a novel gulf was opened between the educated and the populace. What is particularly striking is that historians of the period from 1700 to 1850 have told precisely the same story, in all those respects, without either group of scholars perceiving any paradox in the situation.[1] If both are correct, then there would seem to be two different explanations immediately apparent. One is that both are perceiving successive phases of the same phenomenon, carrying on slowly over 400 years. The other is that the traditional festive culture was somehow revived in the late seventeenth century, to be attacked and diminished all over again in a new social polarity. Alternatively, each group of historians may in reality be discussing a different phenomenon.

Three authors have taken some notice of the problem. Thirty years ago Christopher Hill characterized the whole period between 1500 and 1800 as one of emergent capitalist systems of production, dragging religious and social change in their wake. Thus the 'Puritan Sunday' had to survive the defeat of other aspects of the Puritan Revolution, because the new economic structures demanded a regular working week instead of seasonal holy days.[2] In the 1980s David Underdown, in his study much referred to above, noted that rural recreations 'appear to have been more freely practised than ever in the century after the Restoration, as the gentry's desire, and the church's power, to enforce strict Sabbath observance declined'. Yet he also suggested that the cultural divide between the socially respectable and the poor, created in the Tudor and early Stuart periods, was deepened and consolidated in the succeeding hundred years by the appearance of a more self-assured and larger middle class. Thanks to a 'new economic universe', 'the Restoration compromise could no more arrest the gradual erosion of the old ideas of paternalism and community than the earlier short-lived Laudian reaction had done'.[3] If behind Professor Hill ultimately stood the figure of Karl Marx, behind Professor Underdown were not only Hill himself but the social historians of the 1970s, summed up and to some extent led by Keith Wrightson. It was he who, more than any other, had drawn attention to the polarization of society around 1600, created by inflation and associated economic pressures, as 'the most central theme in the social drama of the age'. He included communal rituals and recreations among the casualties of this cleavage and suggested that because of it by the Restoration period the educated could regard the world of the common people as something alien: 'the poor had become not simply poor, but to a significant degree culturally different'.[4]

Economic explanations of cultural changes are very attractive to historians, including many who do not instinctively regard religion as a cloak for material needs or creativity as essentially a product of prosperity. Economic developments can be measured, quantified, and assessed in a way that alterations in fashion, changes of communal mood, and shifts in the 'spirit of an age' may not be. In this sense they appear to *explain* more, whereas references to the latter phenomena can easily appear to be a dereliction of duty, an appeal to processes which are themselves intangible. As seen above, economic developments can be useful and convincing at times as factors conditioning or propelling the changes which are the subject of this book. Nevertheless, for three successive periods they have already been found wanting as complete or even as primary explanations of change. The structure so neatly proposed by Professor Underdown and inspired in part by Dr Wrightson was included in a textbook published by the third of our recent commentators, J. A. Sharpe.[5] Although he endorsed it in general and lacked the means to criticize it from his own research, he still felt compelled to sound an unfashionable note of caution:

it is worth pondering that the 'decline of popular culture', like 'the rise of the middle classes', is probably one of those phenomena which can be found in any period where historians seek it determinedly enough. Popular culture is something which changes, adapts and assimilates, and it would perhaps make more sense to approach its history in those terms rather than by using any simple model of decline.

With that laudable caveat in mind, it is time to see what can be learned about seasonal revelry in late seventeenth-century England.

One very striking conclusion is that the contribution of social jollity to parish funds remained almost as dead as the Long Parliament had left it. Of the 705 parishes which have contributed late Stuart churchwardens' accounts to the sample used for this book, only one seems to have held church ales. This was Williton in Somerset, nestling between the Brendon Hills and the Bristol Channel, which revived an annual ale in 1662, and continued even though the new excise on beer was levied upon that brewed by the wardens and reduced the profits. During the 1680s the latter fell off seriously, presumably because of declining support, and the custom was killed by the Window Tax imposed on the nation after the Glorious Revolution, causing the parish to lease out the church house, where the ale was held and upon which payments were now due.[6] Of all the Oxford parishes which had stubbornly held Whitsun ales and Hocktide collections until the end of the 1630s, none restored the former and only two, St Peter in the East and St Cross, returned to the latter at the Restoration. The St Cross accounts run out too soon for anybody to track the subsequent fate of the tradition, but at St Peter it was abandoned finally in 1677, for reasons which are not recorded.[7] With that, Hocktide makes its exit from formal parochial life, to remain a source of private amusement and profit in many communities until the last century. Apart from these cases, only Pinner, in Middlesex, made any attempt to raise funds for the church from festivity. It did so by reviving its eccentric habit, documented under the early Stuarts, of buying cocks at Shrovetide so that people could pay to engage in the seasonal sport of throwing at them. But it does not seem to have survived the 1660s.[8]

All this does not mean that parishes did not engage in festivity under the later Stuarts, only that recreations no longer contributed to their finances. The custom of rush-bearing in the North, invisible or in abeyance during the Interregnum, resurfaces after the Restoration. Churches in Cheshire and Westmorland paid ringers to salute the arrival of the garlands;[9] as mentioned above, in the latter county the practice still obtains. It is also recorded in the West Riding of Yorkshire in 1682, as will appear below. Churchwardens also made occasional payments to encourage local fun and games from which they had ceased to profit. At Wolverhampton, the scene of sport under republican rule, they sponsored maypoles, a peal of bells, and a 'gathering of May' on May Day 1665, and contributed towards similar activities on the same feast in 1671–2 and 1702.[10] All Saints', in the town of Stamford, rang on May Day 1707,[11] and the church of Soham, in the Cambridgeshire Fens, did the same in most years of the 1680s.[12] In 1686 the wardens of St Mary le Strand paid to have the huge maypole in that street, erected under princely patronage, repaired with copper, iron, and lead.[13] Those of Yarnton, near Oxford, invested in a village pole in 1663, and those of St Ives, Cornwall, did the same in 1686.[14] The inhabitants of Eling, on Southampton Water, still held a 'dinner at the church house' on most Whitsuns in the 1660s and 1670s, the difference being that now the parish funds made a donation to it instead of receiving from it.[15] Likewise, churchwardens in East Anglia and the East Midlands sometimes paid to ring bells on Plough Monday. What had changed was that they no longer profited from the gathering behind the plough.[16]

A parallel shift had occurred in municipal ceremony. At Chester in 1660 the corporation 'made anew the dragon' and paid 'six naked boys to beat at it' on St George's Day. It also restored the Midsummer Show. But in 1678 the show was abolished again, this time for ever, and after that there was no sign of the St George festivities either.[17] The 12-foot giant and black hobby-horse paraded by the Tailors' Company of Salisbury at the town's own midsummer feast had a longer and happier history; both survived to the present and are in the town museum. But the feast did not last with them. It was revived only in 1668, 1695, and 1709, by the latter date moved to the Monday after St Peter's Day. Then it was heard of no more, and the models were used in municipal parades held on special occasions.[18] Similarly, 'Old Snap', the Norwich St George's Day dragon, made it as far as the nineteenth century because the corporation, on seizing the endowments of the guild in 1548, had turned the parade on that feast into the year's principal civic occasion. It became the time at which the new mayor took office, and 'Old Snap' was brought out as part of a procession to honour him, and the city, rather than the saint.[19] It is of a piece with this that the London equivalent, the Lord Mayor's Show, was also successfully and permanently relaunched at the Restoration. Its late seventeenth-century pageantry was as lavish as that under James I and Charles I, with official civic poets being hired to prepare the speeches.[20] By contrast, not a single midsummer marching watch ever reappeared. Eighteenth-century England was rich in civic ceremony and display, but it tended to be associated with political and administrative occasions such as the inaugurations of officials, local and parliamentary elections, fairs, royal accessions, coronations and visits, and national victories and treaties.[21] It had become at once less obviously bound up with the cycle of the seasons and with religion, and more particularized, different towns tending to hold annual celebrations at different dates.

When Christopher Hill suggested that the 'Puritan Sunday' had triumphed, one of his arguments was that none of the late Stuarts attempted to issue a defence of Sunday sports as both James I and Charles I had done. Those latter monarchs, however, had been motivated primarily by a desire to flush out 'puritans' from the Church and to a much lesser extent from local government; this work was performed far more crudely and savagely by the Second Restoration Settlement of 1661–2. In this important sense a Book of Sports would have been unnecessary in Restoration England. It is striking, when collecting statements against popular revelry and Sunday games during the latter period, to find how many were articulated by individuals who would before 1662 have enjoyed authority at parish level but now had none. The cases of Prynne, Hall, Newcome, and Martindale have been mentioned. In the 1670s, Richard Baxter published classic restatements of hard-line Sabbatarian thinking, arguing that all Sunday games and recreations were ungodly and condemning 'voluptuous youths that run after wakes, and May games, and dancings and revellings, and are carried by the love of sports and pleasure . . . into idleness, riotousness and disobedience to their superiors'.[22] But Baxter had been ejected from his living in 1662. Another clergyman, Oliver Heywood, could contemplate the May Day pleasures of Halifax in 1680 and mutter to his diary that 'Hell is broke loose.' He had similar negative feelings about a rush-bearing at Haworth, but, like Baxter, he now wielded power only over a dissenting congregation.[23] The early Quakers spoke and wrote against dancing, May games, and ales; but these commoners, who might otherwise have been an important element in campaigns against such activities at parish level, were now generally mocked and reviled for their religious views.[24]

Having said all this, however, it is important to remember, once again, that many Civil War royalists had been no friends to popular revelry, and this sentiment was carried over by some into the next period. When John Evelyn published a book upon trees in 1670, he included a fulmination against

those riotous assemblies of idle people who under pretence of going a maying (as they term it) do oftentimes cut down, and carry away fine straight trees, to set up before some alehouse, or revelling place, where they keep their drunken Bacchanalias . . . I think it were better to be quite abolished amongst us, for many reasons, besides that of occasioning so much waste and spoil . . . to adorn their wooden idols.[25]

It is language hardly short of that of Stubbes. Evelyn was undoubtedly a prig, but even a gentleman like John Aubrey, who had an unusual enthusiasm for country customs and a lively sense of humour, still believed that the drunkenness and rudeness of village revels required reformation.[26] Nor did all beneficed clergy feel very differently upon such matters from Baxter, Heywood, and their like. The parson of a Yorkshire Dale parish tried to stop rush-bearings there in 1682 because of the 'barbarous heathenish manner' in which his flock feasted afterwards. All that he achieved was to have his doors broken and his person abused.[27] What is striking about such incidents is the new ineffectuality of those who condemned the merry-making, even when members of the current élite.

A second component in Dr Hill's description of the victory of the 'Puritan Sunday' was the insight, taken from W. B. Whitaker's pioneering work into Stuart Sabbatarianism, that the Lord's Day observance legislation of the 1620s was extended under Charles II.[28] An important distinction must none the less be made: the comprehensive legislation of 1644 and 1657 was never repeated. This was not, however, for want of trying upon the part of some in the legislature, a story which has never been told and will probably always be mysterious in some respects. After the loss of the bill of 1660, MPs in the next, 'Cavalier', Parliament repeatedly introduced fresh sabbatarian legislation. Bills to this effect appeared in 1662, 1663, 1664, 1667, 1670, and 1673, and in the second of those years one got as far as the Lords. None has survived, and nor have any notes of debates upon them, but it seems to have been the pressure of other business, rather than animosity or controversy, that prevented the passage of any before the end of sessions. They appear to have been supported by individuals from quite a wide range of groups and with differing attitudes to the Church, including Prynne, Sir William Morrice, Francis Goodrich, and Sir Robert Holt. In 1662 the Commons formally asked the king to issue a proclamation upon the subject pending legislation, as the Convention Parliament had done. Once again he declined to get involved, for motives which are not on record.[29] The bill which did pass, in 1677, was remarkable in that it started in the House of Lords. It began as a measure to improve the provision of baptism and catechism as well, and this heavily ecclesiastical character, its origin in the Lords, and the fact that the bishop of Rochester chaired the committee which discussed it, strongly suggest that it was an episcopal initiative. It would fit into a set of measures introduced into the same house simultaneously, concerning clandestine marriages, the growth of Popery, and the education of future royal children and representing a reform package produced by the bishops with the agreement of Charles II and his first minister Danby.[30]

This being so, it is interesting that the bill proposed to resurrect the draconian sabbatarian legislation of the Civil War and Interregnum in its entirety, by forbidding not only all work and trade, but 'all sports and pastimes' on the Lord's Day. This comprehensive measure was drastically amended at the first proper discussion of it on 4 April, after opinions had been taken from the judges. First it was agreed to be too unwieldy, and catechism and baptism were removed to be considered in a separate bill. Then games and recreations were removed from its provisions, leaving only the ban on work, which passed into law at record speed. The amended bill was out of committee on 12 April and down to the Commons the next day. On the 16th they decided by twenty-one votes to consent to it without further discussion, and so it was duly offered to Charles and given his approval.[31] Irritatingly, nobody seems to have made any record of these debates, contemporaries (and therefore historians) being distracted by the dramatic political and diplomatic aspects of the session. We can only wonder if the peers, in their decisive rejection of a ban on Sunday festivities, were guided by sentiments similar to those expressed in a famous paper of advice offered to Charles II by the marquis of Newcastle back at the Restoration.[32] One of its heads was to urge the king to revive

May-games, morris dancers, the Lords of the May and Lady of the May, the fool—and the hobby-horse must not be forgotten. Also the Whitsun Lord and Lady, thrashing of hens at Shrovetide, carols and wassails at Christmas, with good plum porridge and pies which are now forbidden as profane ungodly things . . . and after evening prayer every Sunday and holy day—the country people with their fresher lasses to trip on the town green about the May-pole to the louder bagpipe there to be refreshed with their ale and cakes.

His point was that commoners distracted and contented by such fun would be unlikely to discuss politics and to rebel; it was the old argument for the Roman circus. Newcastle was, however, dead by 1677, and there appears to be no good evidence to suggest whether his views in this respect were typical of a late Stuart aristocrat, or eccentric.

Nor is there much more for the views of bishops. On the full restoration of the old disciplinary machinery in 1662, episcopal visitation articles were issued for every see.[33] When dealing with the calendar and with festivity, as in almost every other respect, they were wholly traditional and conservative. As before the wars, they prohibited work and tippling on both Sundays and holy days, and enjoined the custom of Rogationtide perambulations. Those for Lincoln, Durham, Peterborough, St David's, Oxford, and Chichester repeated the warning, instituted under Elizabeth, to keep morris-dancers, musicians, and other merry-makers out of churches. It was of a piece with this that the Canons issued by Convocation in 1683 re-enacted the medieval ban on plays, feasts, or ales in church or churchyard.[34] Nothing in any of it provides a parallel for the total proscription of recreations first included in the sabbatarian bill of 1677. The same lack of interest seems to characterize the efforts of the late Stuart incarnation of local moral reformers, the Societies for the Reformation of Manners. These were, after all, the very bodies which furnished the term which historians have come to apply to the process of cultural transformation, including attacks upon traditional merry-making, which characterized the sixteenth and early seventeenth centuries. The first appeared in London in 1690, and they spread across the nation towards the end of that decade, attracting considerable support from leading churchmen and within Parliaments. Essentially, they were vigilante groups of devout laymen, mostly tradesmen and artisans, who campaigned against vice and profanity. One of their principal targets was Sunday trading and labouring, and they occasionally published against sports on the Lord's Day as well. Yet they devoted very little energy to campaigning against Sunday recreations and none to dancing and revelry in general, in sharp contrast to their equivalents a hundred years before. This was no doubt partly a consequence of the fact that they were wholly an urban phenomenon, but that in itself is something remarkable.[35] County benches seem to have paid equally little attention to such matters; there does not appear to be an order issued by JPs against village feasts between the Restoration and 1710, when those of Gloucestershire banned wakes. They renewed the direction at the next sessions, stating that it had been granted on the petition of the 'ministers and principal inhabitants' of the Cotswold Edge villages of Coley, Frocester, and Nympsfield against 'unlawful wakes and revels and other disorderly meetings upon several Lord's Days . . . where rioting and drunkenness, lewdness, and debauchery and other immoralities are committed'. With that the local struggles were renewed, and were to continue through the eighteenth century.[36]

Literature seems to tell the same story. The strictures of Baxter and Evelyn have been mentioned, as isolated voices bereft of a wider debate of the sort which had existed before the wars. One Nicholas Smith did oppose Baxter with regard to Sunday recreations, observing that 'without doubt sports and pastimes at seasonable times may be used' on both the Lord's Day and seasonal holy days.[37] In point of law he was, of course, wholly correct. Yet in 1708 an anonymous pamphleteer could bewail the fact that England was 'loaded with the pretended statutes of reformation', by which he meant the sabbatarian legislation. He added sourly that 'were we but once rid of some of our pretended zealots for good manners, whose pretences have still made too much impression, even in our days; we might still have some hopes that those days of liberty might be restored.' The 'days' concerned were the early Stuart period, and his favoured instrument for the restoration was a new positive royal declaration in favour of Sunday sports and dances, like those of the former kings.[38] The tract is of particular interest in that it suggests that Lord's Day recreations, though legal, had been curtailed in practice, although it does not make clear whether this situation had obtained ever since the Interregnum or was a feature of the 1700s. Once again, no exchange seems to have resulted. Sabbatarianism was not an issue in which late seventeenth-century English clerics took much interest, just as there was no disposition among poets and dramatists to treat the subject of popular merry-making. It had no place in the spectacular and exotic dramas or the comedies of sophisticated society which were the favourite genres of the stage. Pastoral verse had mostly returned to a formal and timeless classicism.

The writer who took most interest in popular pastimes was Shadwell, whose rococo play *The Royal Shepherdesse* was produced before the king in 1669. It included country folk who danced and sang of a list of genuine English rural games, such as 'trap, keels, barley-break, golf [and] stool-ball' and made light of exactly those aspects of the summer revelry which most disturbed moralists:

> About the May-pole we dance all around,
> And with Garlands of pinks, and of roses are crown'd
> Our little Kind tributes we cheerfully pay
> To the gay Lord and the bright Lady of the May.
> And when we have done we laugh and lie down
> And to each pretty lass we give a green gown.

Lords of the May are also mentioned in a romantic pastoral play by Aphra Behn, while Dryden's patriotic drama *King Arthur* features a realistic harvest-home song and 'round country dance' by 'peasants', who boast of cheating the parson out of his tithe. Dryden also produced a Jacobite poem, known under various titles, which used a May Queen as its central image. This, however, seems to be all, and it is no accident that the one play of the age actually to portray a morris and a parish revel remained unfinished, let alone staged, being the only foray into creative writing of the thoroughly eccentric John Aubrey.[39]

Instead, the characteristic variety of Restoration writing to deal with such matters belonged to those relatively novel figures, the natural scientists and antiquaries. It was the Elizabethan William Camden who developed the medieval and early Tudor tradition of the travel itinerary to include occasional information upon local customs and historical traditions. The first edition of his masterpiece, *Britannia*, appeared in 1586. He never, however, treated of 'vulgar' sports and rites of the sort which have been the focus of this book. This work was left to the local studies of Stow and Carew, mentioned earlier, and they had no successors for two generations, until the Oxford scholar Robert Plot brought out his *Natural History of Oxfordshire* in 1677. As well as surveying the county's flora and fauna, it contained notices of human phenomena, including a few examples of sport and ritual which struck the author as curious: the rights of wood-gathering at Eynsham on Whit Monday, the reading of a gospel in a cellar during the Rogation perambulation at Standlake, practical jokes at Shrovetide and gatherings on the officially defunct feast of St Blaise, Hocktide bindings, and the former carrying of a model giant around Burford on Midsummer Eve.[40] The work was a tremendous success, earning its author the posts of secretary to the newly formed Royal Society in 1682 and Professor of Chemistry and keeper of that other novel institution, the Ashmolean Museum, in 1683.[41] Three years after that he published a companion volume, *The Natural History of Staffordshire*, which contained accounts of beliefs about the mating of birds upon Valentine's Day, the collection of money by poorer villagers on the feast of Clement, the setting-up of May boughs, and the Abbots Bromley Horn Dance.[42] Something of Plot's approach was adopted for a rather different end by the Catholic gentleman Thomas Blount, who turned to scholarship because his religion debarred him from proceeding far in the legal profession. In 1679 he brought out a collection of examples of ancient tenures and manorial customs, intended to illustrate problems in land law but including some entertaining accounts of local traditions, of which the most notable was the description of the Lamb Feast at Kidlington near Oxford.[43] The same period saw the burgeoning of the tradition of the county history, made especially popular by the achievements of Sir William Dugdale. This genre concentrated upon the social élite, wholly ignoring popular activities, but the example which it set of detailed local history and topography acted with that of Plot to inspire a parson to produce a meticulous account of his parish and its district in 1695. The man, White Kennett, was a scholar of considerable talent destined to become a bishop, and his description of the border country of Oxfordshire and Buckinghamshire includes a valuable account of village wakes.[44]

To historians, however, the figure who towers over these others is John Aubrey. As the author of the first work of archaeology in the modern sense, the first substantial collection of English folklore, and the first

English book entirely devoted to the elucidation of place-names, it is easy to see why he has won such acclaim. Yet it is equally obvious to his admirers that his appetite for knowledge and the breadth of his interests were not matched by any ability to analyse and present information; he was a compulsive jotter-down of notes. As a result, he commenced and abandoned one literary project after another, and his immense labours yielded only one publication before his death, a collection of occult lore in 1695. His fame has therefore been in the main a posthumous creation, as his notebooks were edited and brought out by others, a process which continues to the present.[45] Those relevant to the history of the ritual year comprise his collections for a topographical account of his native region, north Wiltshire[46] and for a work upon popular rites, traditions, and superstitions which he termed *Remaines of Gentilisme and Judaisme*.[47] The first included a small amount of information upon revels, the latter a large quantity of data upon seasonal customs of many different kinds, witnessed by Aubrey himself or described to him by correspondents. To this he added apparent parallels or origins for the activities concerned from the Bible and from a range of Roman and medieval authors. There was no doubt in Aubrey's mind that much folk ceremonial and belief derived from pagan roots, but like his predecessors in this opinion, stretching back to Polydor Vergil, he was so book-bound that he could only conceive of the ancient British as a blank sheet upon which the Romans inscribed their own traditions. What seems to have driven Aubrey, apart from sheer intellectual curiosity and a mind to which anecdote and information adhered like flies to sticky paper, was a vague nostalgia for the world before the Reformation. He was remarkably free from the hostility to Catholicism which characterized most of his generation, being able to consider that religious processions were 'fine pleasing diversions' and that monastery bells made 'very pretty music'. As a boy he was 'always enquiring of my grandfather of the old time, the rood loft, etc., ceremonies, of the priory, etc.'. In this sense he stood in that tradition of romantic conservatism which had produced John Stow and William Warner.[48]

What is striking about the attitude of all this set of writers to seasonal pastimes is their utter objectivity. Certainly the subject was incidental to the concerns of most of them, and even formed only a small part of Aubrey's interests. Yet it is worthy of note that none seem to have provided any indication that it was at all controversial, Kennett alone remarking that wakes had fallen into disuse in much of southern England because of 'popular prejudice' and then making no personal comment upon the latter. It is also notable that this approach did not last. Later folklorists who placed Aubrey at the head of their discipline's list of founders usually considered a Newcastle clergyman, Henry Bourne, second in succession to him;[49] Bourne's book on 'vulgar antiquities', published in 1725, was indeed the first systematic collection of popular customs and beliefs after the *Remaines*.[50] Its tone, however, puts it with the 'complaint literature' of an earlier age. Bourne also recognized that the traditions derived from a mixture of ancient and medieval practices, but termed the one 'the produce of heathenism' and the other 'the inventions of indolent monks'. His aim was to suggest which of the customs were harmless and which 'sinful and wicked' and deserving of repression; the list of the latter included mumming, gathering greenery on May Day, maypole dancing, and wakes. The tone and purpose of the work fits in very well with others published in the early and mid-eighteenth century, condemning the superstition and disorder of popular festivities. A few were composed to answer them and defend the pastimes concerned.[51] It was not until the latter part of that century that scholars once again began to record festivities with the detachment displayed by those of Restoration England.

The relative lack of interest shown in them by the social élite makes it difficult to assess how prosperous those festivities were in the late seventeenth century. The glimpses of them are usually incidental. We have, as noted already, Kennett's assertion that wakes were still found widely across the Midlands and northern England and Plot's that people still went a-Maying in Staffordshire. Blount's description of the Kidlington Lamb ale reveals that it always included a morris dance and was presided over by a Lady. It is also clear from the sources considered earlier that rush-bearing was flourishing and that in some parishes wardens were contributing funds to dances and feasts, although it must be pointed out that this occurred in seven cases in a sample of over 700. Aubrey and Bourne agreed that it was still common to go a-Maying, and that midsummer bonfires were still kindled, although apparently much more in the North than the South of England. Aubrey testified to the continued vitality of wassailing, and Bourne to that of mumming.[52]

A scatter of other references bear out these statements. A May Day procession carrying a garland in northern Kent came to public notice in 1672 because it was ambushed by a press-gang seeking recruits for a war with the Dutch.[53] On the same day in 1679 dancers on the village green at Waresley in Huntingdonshire got into trouble by firing off guns.[54] At Oxford Anthony Wood thought that after 1660 'the rabble flagged in their zeal' for May-games, but one or two poles still appeared every year.[55] Samuel Pepys came across morris in Leadenhall Street, London, on the evening of May Day 1663, and commented that he had not seen the dance 'in a great while'. Exactly four years later he ran into some milkmaids near Drury Lane 'with their garlands upon their pails, dancing with a fiddler before them'.[56] By the end of the century it had grown into a custom for the maids to tie up silver plate with the garlands and to carry it on their heads instead of pails, dancing from door to door of their regular customers to the music of a bagpipe or fiddle.[57] As for village feasts, the diary of a Lancashire apprentice refers casually to attendance at a wake at Ashton in Makerfield, in the southern part of the county, in August 1664.[58] A young Northamptonshire gentleman noted another at Maidwell in September 1672, where 'from singing they came to fighting'.[59] Among the scores of north Wiltshire villages investigated by John Aubrey for his topographical survey, three still held annual revels.[60] As for apple-wassailing, payments appear in the account books of a Sussex gentleman and a rector in the same county, to boys who came to 'howl' away bad fortune from their trees in the 1670s and 1680s.[61] All this suggests that the old festive culture, if not perhaps as ubiquitous as a hundred years before, was still flourishing even though it had been uncoupled from local finance. Furthermore, most observers seemed to take it in their stride. The furious parsons had become very rare, the altercations between revellers and constables, churchwardens and tithingmen almost disappeared, the justices lost interest. Why?

It must be obvious from the survey above that a historian interested in this question suffers from a loss of important evidence such as the parliamentary debates of 1677, though this lack of records is itself significant. In default of them, a socio-economic reply might perhaps be proposed: that late Stuart England did not suffer from the pressure of a rising population and prices which had been so apparent around 1600. Therefore, the argument could run, the threat of disorder was less apparent and the local élites less likely to worry about the activities of their inferiors. The symmetry of this model is attractive, and it may have some foundation in reality. But its flaws are also obvious. Economic historians seem to be agreed that conditions were improving from the 1630s onwards, yet what followed was not a gradual softening of élite attitudes towards revelry, but the Puritan Revolution. There also seems to be general acceptance of the idea that economic circumstances during the early eighteenth century were very similar to those in the late seventeenth. Yet from 1700 onwards the traditional merry-making seems to have become controversial once again. The relatively easy economic climate of the late Stuart age still coincided with the Societies for the Reformation of Manners, which according to those who have studied them were the product of religious developments coupling with a fear of the social consequences of the strains produced by war.[62] Instead of an economic model of explanation, a religious and political one is proposed here, with four parts. First, that after 1660 the former enemies of Merry England were bitterly divided, into Anglican and Dissenters, royalist and republican, Tory and Whig. Second, that for the dominant, Anglican and royalist, groups, the proscription of ales, maypoles, and revels had become too uncomfortably associated with the Interregnum to be a cause easily espoused by them. Third, that those who feared disorder and sin most were now presented with much more obvious incarnations of both, in the shape of nonconformist conventicles, republican plotters, and (for some, and later) Catholics or Deists. The hunt for these must have engrossed most of their energy. It was perhaps only when the new terrors, resentments, and animosities began to ameliorate a little, after 1700, that concern with festive disorder could reappear. Fourth, and most speculative, the snapping of the links between the traditional festivity and the established religion, by chasing the former out of churches, churchyards, parish fund-raising, and Sunday, may have been achieved to an extent which represented a victory for the most important aim of the Protestant opponents of revelry.

All this, however, is to ignore the main thrust of the views of Keith Wrightson and David Underdown, outlined above; that although the old celebrations continued, their significance had altered because the unified communities which they served had been polarized by economic change. Dr Wrightson indeed suggested that the new interest in popular customs shown by antiquarians such as John Aubrey was itself a consequence of this change, making the world of the populace essentially alien to the educated élite.[63] This last, and specific, point does not easily stand up to examination. Blount's references to such customs are wholly incidental, while Plot was not concerned with popular culture in general but only in aspects, usually oddities, which helped to make points about human behaviour. Aubrey's investigations into the subject were certainly much broader, but not only was he a thoroughly unusual figure but he was steeped in rural society. As a child he had loved its stories, and his easy familiarity with it shows in all his work. His purpose in collecting information upon it was partly one dimension of a magpie-like mind and partly for a scientific purpose, to amass arcane lore of all kinds which might prove to be of practical utility. Indeed, he was mocked for this aspiration by more sceptical contemporaries, and in this respect was far less 'modern' or 'detached' than a writer like Reginald Scot a hundred years before who had collected similar folk beliefs only to ridicule them as superstition. There certainly was a common spirit which animated the late Stuart antiquarians, and it was relatively novel, but 'it was not the product of social polarization; it was that intense curiosity about the workings of the world and desire to amass information upon them which has been given the nickname of 'The Scientific Revolution'.[64] The phenomenon described by Dr Wrightson, of a study of popular culture by scholars to whom it had effectively become a foreign country, was indeed to occur. It belongs, however, to the late eighteenth and nineteenth centuries.

None the less, the basic assumption of the historians cited above seems incontrovertible: there was a polarization of wealth and power within English society, and especially rural society, between about 1550 and 1650. The difficulty is to demonstrate whether this in fact undermined communal rites and revels as Professor Underdown seems to suggest.[65] It is possible that some social historians of the Tudor and Stuart periods tend to overestimate the cohesion of medieval communities. Recent studies of the workings of pre-Reformation parishes and towns, and of the value of ceremony to them, have stressed that they were imbued with a profound ethic of hierarchy as well as of communality.[66] There seems no reason in principle why that function should not be made to serve a still less equal, more divided, social order. But appeals to principle are rarely admissible; to test this point it is necessary to look at the changing fortunes of certain calendar traditions which have featured in this study.

One of the most important was midwinter feasting and entertainment. The earliest literary portraits of this in Britain seem to be in early medieval Welsh poems, which concentrate wholly upon royal courts and show the season to be an opportunity for rulers to relax with their most important subjects and to reward and entertain them.[67] This aspect of it remained constant through the rest of the Middle Ages, most splendidly revealed in the poem *Sir Gawaine and the Green Knight*. The information upon royal Christmastide revels collected in this book indicates that nothing altered throughout the Tudor and early Stuart period except the inevitable presence of a greater civility and formality. Charles II revived the tradition of balls and parties during the Twelve Days, and especially upon Twelfth Night, the only distinctions from his father's time being that masques were out of fashion and gambling was encouraged.[68]

The first evidence for Christmas entertainments lower down in society consists of manorial records, abundant enough by the thirteenth century to permit some generalization. Most specified that villeins were to do no work on the lord's land during the Twelve Days and that the lord would provide a feast for them; but they were also expected to bring him gifts, which being normally in farm produce would actually provide most of the meal. Some custumals made one explicitly conditional on the other.[69] The household accounts for the late medieval and Tudor period, analysed earlier in this book, indicate that the manorial feast had ceased to be an expected custom; instead landowners entertained relations, friends, and also tenants if they decided that this was fitting. Some certainly fed the local poor, or even kept open house, but it was also suggested above that such flamboyant generosity was always exceptional. The late seventeenth-century evidence presents much the same picture. At one extreme was Sir George Downing, the newly risen financial expert and state servant, who gloated over the money which he saved by giving only broth to the neighbours whom he entertained at his country seat.[70] At the other was the Northamptonshire squire Sir Justinian Isham, who fed the paupers, labourers, and 'better class inhabitants' of two villages on successive evenings.[71] Sir John Reresby, in Yorkshire, feasted his tenants, local gentry, local clergy, and local tradesmen on different days, while commenting that this degree of munificence was unusual. Over in Lancashire Nicholas Blundell sometimes kept open house.[72] There is no suggestion that any were trying to obtain a greater social control over their guests, only that they were trying to promote local harmony and to fulfil an onerous traditional ideal of social responsibility. It was more common for gentry to provide for their tenants and neighbours,[73] while members of corporations entertained each other,[74] as did state officials of the second rank like the young Samuel Pepys.[75] Occasionally there is mention of a parson giving dinner to his parishioners, like the rector of Clayworth in Nottinghamshire's Vale of Trent.[76] The Quakers did not believe in any holy days, but one from the landed class, like Sarah Fell of Swarthmoor Hall, Furness, still exchanged gifts of venison and game birds with neighbouring gentry families at Christmas.[77] A ballad published at some time between 1672 and 1696 claimed that the feast had been revived with such liberality that 'All travellers as they do pass on the way / At gentlemen's halls are invited to stay.'[78] It is more likely, though still very hard to prove, that the generosity of provision had declined still further since the early Stuart period as the historian of hospitality, Felicity Heal, has suggested.[79] Any such change, if it existed, would have been one of degree rather than of form, and the patterns of entertainment at late Stuart Christmases seem remarkably timeless. So do the entertainers, musicians, and players being rewarded by the great houses as they had been since the Middle Ages. The one notable alteration wrought by the seventeenth century had been the disappearance of the Lord of Misrule; after a taste of genuine misrule during the

Interregnum, nobody in the ruling élite seems to have had any stomach for simulating it.

Nothing very much seems to have altered during the next century either, the observations upon late Stuart Christmases being reproduced throughout the whole Hanoverian period.[80] In Devon in 1816 the tradition of liberality was still sufficiently alive for labourers to claim, and be given, food and drink on demand from any farmer whose corn they had reaped in the autumn. The debate over the due extent of hospitality was sufficiently energetic in 1820 for Washington Irving to produce a literary portrait of an Essex squire who attempted to keep open house in the Twelve Days after the 'old style', only to have 'the manor overrun by all the vagrants of the county'. He subsequently 'contented himself with inviting the decent part of the neighbouring peasantry to call at the hall on Christmas Day',[81] which was, one might add, still somewhat more generous than many of his Stuart predecessors had been, and considerably more so than a high medieval lord.

The thirteenth-century custumals reveal a second communal meal of considerable symbolic importance, that provided by landowners at the end of harvesting.[82] It served such an obvious function that it passes almost unnoticed through the Tudor and Stuart periods, arousing no controversy and therefore little comment. Yet Tusser in the sixteenth century, Aubrey in the seventeenth, and Bourne in the early eighteenth all refer to it as ubiquitous,[83] and this is confirmed in the late eighteenth and nineteenth centuries when systematic observation of rural customs begins. There was general agreement by then (and presumably long before) that any farmer who failed to provide a substantial harvest supper to reward his fieldworkers was failing seriously as an employer; indeed sometimes this meal, and refreshments during the reaping, stood in lieu of money wages.[84]

But what of the classic expression of village communal solidarity, the parish feast, whether incarnated as an ale, a rush-bearing, a wake, or a revel? Here there certainly was dramatic change, in that church ales died out altogether in the seventeenth century, and wakes became scarce in the South. In the western counties and southern chalklands, the function of the latter was, however, preserved by revels. In the eighteenth century parochial feasting, under one name or another, is recorded widely across all of England except East Anglia, the South-East, and the London area; in these latter regions it was noted that their function was fulfilled by fairs.[85] As indicated earlier, there were clear religious reasons for the extinction of church ales and the decline of wakes, and there are no good grounds for supposing that the communities of the south-eastern quarter of England were very different in social and economic composition from those else-where. Throughout the whole period from the fifteenth to the nineteenth century the purpose of these events, to promote friendship and neighbour-liness, remained the same. So did the attendant risks, drunkenness, brawl-ing, and sexual misconduct amongst the young. Aubrey's picture of a late seventeenth-century revel at Bishopston, Wiltshire, the old men sitting on a 'hock bench' to keep order while the young danced, does not suggest a community in which social polarization had affected the traditional festivi-ties.[86] The description of an early nineteenth-century summer lord at King's Sutton, Northamptonshire, presiding over the feasting and morris with a mace plaited with silk ribbons,[87] is hardly different from the be-ribboned May lord with his gilded staff in *The Knight of the Burning Pestle*. The eighteenth-century Whitsun ale at Woodstock near Oxford could take its place indistinguishably beside a Tudor equivalent, with its lord and lady, its morris-dancers, its maypole, and its bower. It had only ceased to raise funds for the church.[88]

Shrovetide likewise remained a time for misbehaviour, within or beyond generally acceptable limits, from the twelfth to the nineteenth century. This was despite the decay of the tradition of the Lenten fast which had provoked it, established first as part of the cycle of the medieval Christian year and maintained by Tudor and Stuart Protestant regimes to nurture the fishing fleet upon which not only economic prosperity but recruitment for the navy partly depended. The history of the Shrovetide revelry has been traced above up till 1660. Under the Restoration monarchy there was no renewal of the violence by London apprentices, an absence rather curi-ous as they made intermittent serious trouble on other dates.[89] Those of York certainly celebrated Shrove Tuesday in the old disreputable way in 1673, forcing their way into the Minster to hold their traditional games there and smashing the windows of the Dean's house because he tried to keep them out. In 1670 and 1685 the magistrates at Bristol had to punish lads for causing affrays on the same feast.[90] Less lawless games and feasting remained the rule upon the day, occasionally sponsored by parishes; the cocks at Pinner have been mentioned, while St Benet Gracechurch, London, invested in a 'pancake bell' in the 1690s, to announce the beginning of the general eating and drinking.[91] Although during the eighteenth century the fast of Lent disintegrated into a matter for private choice, Shrove Tuesday remained characterized by pancakes, fritters, football, cock-throwing, and brawling, representing a constant problem for law-enforcement officers.[92]

If all these seasonal customs seem to show a remarkable continuity of form and function, what then does one make of the powerful argument advanced by Peter Burke, in his famous pioneering study of early modern popular culture? Using a set of vivid examples, he suggested that from 1600 onwards the literate classes of Europe tended to withdraw from a popular culture which formerly they had shared, and to despise it.[93] This he ascribed to the social and economic changes of the age. In the single and limited field of seasonal festivals there is much in Dr Burke's work which this one has endorsed, notably his insight that hopes and fears formerly expressed in religion and in ritual came increasingly to be transmuted into secular politics. But, as must be abundantly clear, it questions his suggestion of the primacy of social and economic forces in producing change, and it must now consider how calendar ceremonies fit into his model of increasing divergence in cultures. He himself certainly included English examples in his picture. Do they actually belong there?

The answer is that they certainly do, for the simple reason that to Peter Burke 'early modern' signified the whole span of time between 1500 and 1800, and the process which he was describing was not by any means complete even by the latter date. By contrast Keith Wrightson concentrated upon the years 1580 to 1680, and David Underdown on those between 1603 and 1660. Dr Burke also took a look at late medieval culture and made no easy and generalized assumptions about its communal and homogeneous nature. Instead he recognized that there were already major distinctions between the life-styles and interests of social élites and those of ordinary people; his point was rather that they overlapped, and that customs moved between them, more than by the beginning of the modern age. He also recognized a range of sub-cultures at each level of the social order. It may be suggested here that the Midsummer Eve bonfires noted much earlier, kindled by the pages in the hall of Henry VIII, by the wealthy villager outside his house at Long Melford, and by principal householders in the streets of London, were a pre-Christian religious symbol used simultaneously, to reinforce a sense of communality and inequality, of deference and responsibility, within complementary communities. As was also suggested earlier, an alteration in Christianity, rather than a failure of the custom to serve its social purpose, left it as an entertainment of the populace alone, in increasingly marginal areas. The royal court got bored with Robin Hood plays and morris, and the common people eventually tired of the plays also, but the dance continued among them because it had successfully fused so many perennial aspects of entertainment. In place of the fires, the plays, and the dancers, the whole political and social hierarchy of the land could share new celebrations more acceptable to a Protestant nation and private customs which were not affected by changes in religion. The former included the political anniversaries of royal accessions, birthdays, coronations, and the Gunpowder Plot, the latter New Year's gifts and Valentines.[94] As shown above, late seventeenth-century gentry continued to give money to local or itinerant players, musicians, and dancers as their early sixteenth-century predecessors had done. On May Day 1515 Henry VIII rode up Shooter's Hill to meet Robin Hood and feast in a summer bower. In 1661 Charles II joined the customary May Day exodus of Londoners to Hyde Park, with 'an innumerable appearance of the gallantry on rich coaches'.[95]

It is certainly true that descriptions of local festivity in the Tudor period are never sufficiently detailed to determine whether some elements of society had withdrawn from it by the end of the seventeenth century. There is, however, no evidence that any had. By contrast, there is no mistaking the alteration of mood in the years between 1740 and 1850. Then the literate really did come to regard traditional popular pastimes as belonging to a different world to their own, and to record, transform, or suppress them according to personal tastes and circumstances. This is the tremendous shift noticed by social historians of the eighteenth and nineteenth centuries, and by Peter Burke. It would seem to be an error, however, to project it backward into Tudor and Stuart England.

What, then, of those other beneficiaries of the Restoration, the seasonal ceremonies of the established Church? Following the spontaneous return to the sacrament at Easter in so many parishes in 1660, it is hardly surprising that churchwardens' accounts show a widespread adoption of festival communion. In all, some 411 of the 703 parishes in the sample used here for the years 1660 to 1700 (58 per cent) employed the practice. Yet that does leave a very large number which did not, and the distribution of both sorts is very revealing. The overwhelming majority of churches where the sacraments were offered at feasts were rural, either in villages or market towns. By contrast only one London parish, St Alphage London Wall, made a point of recording it, and none did in Bristol. Although one or two did so in other large towns, York is the only important urban centre where a majority of parishes which have left accounts mention the custom. Otherwise, it is well scattered, being found in every English county and in all in Wales from which records survive. It seems to have flourished particularly in the countryside of the whole midland region, of Norfolk, and of Kent, but not to a much greater degree than the national norm. The readoption of it was a steady and slow business, after the rush of 1660. Parishes continued to take it up at an even rate throughout the four decades until the end of the century, and the process was still in full flow under William

III. The feasts selected were almost wholly those of Christ, the communions at All Saints' Day, Michaelmas, and Midsummer, which had featured fairly regularly in rural churches before the Civil War, now being rare.[96]

As perambulations at Rogationtide had continued in so many parishes throughout the Interregnum, when it was no longer an official ceremony, there is no surprise in discovering that the custom was very widely revived when it became legal again at the Restoration. The rector of Clayworth, Nottinghamshire, noted how the custom was reintroduced in his district with much rejoicing and lavish provision of hospitality along the route; he added sourly that 'when this hot fit was over the charity began to wax cold'.[97] None the less, the processions were sustained, and are recorded more frequently in late Stuart churchwardens' accounts than in early seventeenth-century equivalents. Only ten out of seventy-five London parishes in the sample did not mention the custom,[98] and in some of these inadequate book-keeping is apparent. Parishes in every corporate town observed it, and once again it is mentioned in a scatter of villages across the country from one end to another. As before, the suspicion is that it was in these parishes that charity had most 'waxed cold', rather than that the processions were kept there with especial affection; it may be significant in this regard that they were most common in the countryside of East Anglia and Kent,[99] but the case cannot be proven.

The ample evidence from the Restoration period furnishes insights into the further development of the custom. London parishes began to pay for wands or rods (usually specifically white in colour), with which the children could beat the boundary markers and so increase their chances of committing them to memory.[100] At the fishing port of St Ives in West Cornwall, it was the boys who were beaten at the marks instead, to the same end;[101] both practices survived commonly in Rogation processions into the present century. At Gateshead on the Tyne the file of parishioners was accompanied by Northumbrian pipers.[102] Those of North Petherton, in Somerset's Parrett valley, had to hire a boat to follow the boundary accurately.[103] Entertainments had a tendency to become more elaborate: thus by the 1670s the wardens of one London parish were ensuring that the children in the Ascension Day procession were getting almonds, raisins, ribbons, and silk points, while the adults had bottles of wine. At Whiston in South-West Yorkshire, they provided bread, beer, tobacco, pipes, and a bonfire at the end of the walk.[104] At Cuckfield, a large parish in the Sussex Weald, the perambulation took three days and so was held very irregularly. When it was decided to do so, the curate, parish clerk, and boys stayed the whole course, but adult parishioners tended to come along for only one of the days, along the section closest to their homes. They all chanted psalms as they walked.[105]

Some communities demonstrated an enhanced interest in the traditional ritual year by paying to have special peals of bells rung at certain of its feasts, in a way which had not hitherto been noticeable. The favourite time for this was on Christmas Day, either just after midnight or at dawn. Although parishes which instituted this can be found thinly all over the country,[106] they were noticeably concentrated in the north-east Midlands[107] and in and around Chester.[108] The distribution can only be ascribed to local whim and example. One London church was included, one of the most important in Norwich, and the principal one of Great Yarmouth. Otherwise only Chester and Salisbury have recorded the practice among all the large towns, while the rural examples include small boroughs, market towns, and all sizes of village. Fourteen of them, in the Midlands and East Anglia, took up the habit of ringing in the New Year as well,[109] while the Norwich church added St Stephen's Day, Easter, and Easter Monday and the Yarmouth one, uniquely, rang out at the feasts of St Stephen, St Michael, and St John the Baptist as well. As in the case of festival communion, so festival campanology developed slowly, increasing over the whole forty years after the Restoration. It also provides a context for the adoption of the well-loved North Welsh tradition of the plygain, the Christmas dawn singing, which has been described above. As was pointed out there, it seems to derive from the pre-Reformation Christmas morning service. Nevertheless, the churchwardens' accounts reveal that it spread notably in the 1680s, having been rare until that time.[110]

These developments all suggest that the Church of England possessed a capacity for local choice and innovation in ritual practices, over and above the common liturgy, which was still considerable despite the narrowing of its membership in the legislation and expulsions of the Restoration settlements: it is a conclusion which parallels that which John Spurr has already drawn for its theology and political attitudes.[111] Still, the overall trend was towards a greater emphasis upon ceremony, and upon the celebration of the ritual year. It was paradoxically coupled with an apparent slackening willingness to enforce the sanctity of the calendar of holy days. In his groundbreaking work in the 1960s, Christopher Hill suggested that after 1660 nobody attempted to enjoin the observation of saints' days.[112] He seems to have been half-correct. The Restoration episcopacy certainly commanded the observation of all holy days, as said above, and a case study suggests that churchwardens seem to have been every bit as ready as before to present fellow parishioners for working on them, including the feasts of saints.[113] On the other hand, in that same case the wardens rarely named individuals and no prosecutions seem to have resulted from these reports.[114] The imposition of the ritual calendar upon the laity was starting to break down, although they were formally required to pay the same respect to it.

The same impression of local variety and choice within developing national fashions is suggested by a study of political anniversaries. As is well known, the Convention Parliament added two more to the list, directing that the Restoration be henceforth celebrated by a thanksgiving service every 29 May and the execution of Charles I mourned by a fast and another service every 30 January.[115] The first date was not that of the formal proclamation of the restored monarchy, which had taken place three weeks before, but of the 'completion' of the process by Charles's formal entry into London. More to the point, it was also his birthday, just as the date of the regicide was of course his accession day. Thus, for as long as he lived, two dates which would have invited commemoration in any case were neatly taken up with rites of passage out of the traumas of the Interregnum. The royal birthday had already been celebrated privately by loyal royalists, some of whom had also mourned the martyred king with a private fast.[116] The proposals to make both into formal acts of piety were so swiftly and enthusiastically supported in the Commons that it does not seem possible to tell from whom they derived.[117]

It is only a little easier to discover how far they were adopted. Like the statute imposing the 5 November service, the new pair did not prescribe any penalties for those who ignored them. The only bishops who enquired after observation of them in that first visitation of 1662 were old Piers of Bath and Wells, Henchman of Salisbury, Ironside of Bristol, and Hacket of Lichfield. All these also asked after the Gunpowder Treason services; and that other veteran, Matthew Wren, restored to Ely, wanted to know about this latter commemoration alone, as did his colleague at St Asaph.[118] Returns have survived for Henchman's and Wren's dioceses and reveal a total of one parish, Alton Barnes in the Wiltshire chalklands, which confessed that it did not keep the required days; some of those in Cambridgeshire went to the trouble of stating that they honoured all three.[119] Some towns, such as Sherborne, Exeter, Bury St Edmunds, Holesworth in Suffolk, Stamford, Reading, and Oundle, instituted the celebration of 29 May with particular fervour, involving the burning of republican leaders in effigy and of the Solemn League and Covenant.[120] The problem, of course, is to determine how much this spontaneous enthusiasm was sustained in the following years.

For this, we depend upon incidental comment and churchwardens' accounts. The latter are in fact a very rough guide to the keeping of the services, because the activity paid for is the ringing of bells upon the dates concerned, the absence of which does not necessarily indicate a lack of religious observation. The entries testify, instead, to a relative enthusiasm. The difficulties are increased a little by the fact that in the course of the reign of Charles II most London parishes began to pay a regular sum to teams of ringers, ending the rewards upon specific dates which provided a guide to seasonal observations. Yet enough evidence survives outside the metropolis for a comparative study to be made. Of the 616 parishes in the sample used here which have left itemized payments to ringers from the reign of Charles, 233 (39 per cent) rang bells on 29 May.[121] They include, unsurprisingly, all large churches in provincial towns, but also a great many in villages, spread across the whole country. Some of these rural communities were very small, giving the lie to the notion that poverty was an important determinant of the distribution. Some went to further efforts on the day: St Ives in Cornwall provided a tar barrel and a drummer, two Oxford parishes lit bonfires, the wardens of Ashby Folville in Leicestershire treated 'the neighbours', Mildenhall in Suffolk held firework displays, and Dallinghoo in the same county and St Oswald in Durham town held communions.[122] These financial records are paralleled by the occasional notice of urban celebration. At Cambridge in 1669, for example, the city fathers filed out of church in their scarlet gowns and went off to the town hall for a dinner of salt fish, mutton, veal, bacon, beef, lamb, salads, capons, rabbits, and claret, at the public expense.[123] Cathedral clergy also added to the merriment, those of Worcester kindling a huge fire in the Close each year.[124]

Although some of the smaller parishes failed to ring every year, observation of the new festival was remarkably consistent, and hardly responded to the political tensions of the reign. All Saints' parish in Dorchester, did, it is true, stop the ringing when feeling began to run against the government during the Exclusion Crisis. But neighbouring Holy Trinity never faltered,[125] and at the town of Ludlow and the villages of Munslow, Alderbury, and Milton Regis, in Shropshire and Kent respectively, the parish actually took up the custom during that crisis, as if rallying to the Crown.[126] None the less, there are signs that elsewhere enthusiasm for the festival ebbed even though it was not wholly neglected. Pepys noted a 'very solemn observation' of it in London in 1662, with bonfires in the evening, but by the next year feeling was already running against the regime so strongly that although no shops were open 'hardly ten people' attended some churches, and the general atmosphere was 'ill'. By 1666 the date was still kept as a holiday, and bells rang all over the City at dawn, but there were few fires there later, although Westminster was full of them.[127] Out in Kent Evelyn noted nothing amiss until the Exclusion Crisis, in 1679, when suddenly his local church had so 'thin a congregation' that the minister did not bother to preach.[128] The attendance, however, recovered. In the next year of that crisis, 1680, Anthony Wood recorded that the shops were still closed at Oxford, but business was being done as usual in London, as a blatant insult to the king.[129] This was, however, partly the Crown's own doing, for the Privy Council had prohibited all fires and fireworks for fear of an uprising or riot. Certainly the holiday atmosphere was restored by 1682, Whigs and Tories holding rival demonstrations with burning of effigies, and the defeat of the former that year left the way clear for loyal commemoration.[130]

There is no indication that the fast of 30 January was not solemnly observed throughout the reign, people in general abstaining from work although many may, like Pepys, have only abstained from food when they forgot to lay in a stock.[131] Most contemporaries remembered the day for its sermons, which have been well studied.[132] The Prayer Book had already prescribed St Matthew's account of the trial and crucifixion of Christ as a lesson for that day, and the form of prayer prescribed in 1661 built on the obvious parallel to stress the sacred nature of kingship. Preachers accordingly made the sacrilege of resistance to the monarchy their favourite theme, the only development being that whereas before the Popish Plot their favourite targets were Protestant dissenters, some thereafter included Catholics as well. A cleric in 1685 estimated that 3,000 sermons were preached on this day every year. In addition, the new reign provided two more opportunities for celebration, although neither was statutory. One was the coronation date, which was fixed, with wonderful imagination on the part of Charles and his advisers, for the feast of the national saint, George. This meant that each year, as the monarch processed at Windsor in the restored ceremony of the Order of the Garter, his subjects could join if they wished in a tribute to both Crown and country. As it happened, not many did so, to judge from the payments for bell-ringing which occur in just eighty-one parishes out of the 616 (13 per cent) in the sample. Most were smaller than those for Restoration Day. Even the dean and chapter of Worcester, while ensuring a peal from the cathedral belfry, did not stretch to a bonfire.[133] Still, the sheer variety of English parochial practice meant that for most of the reign this was the only political anniversary upon which bells rang at the Trent valley village of Rolleston, North

Somercotes on the Lincolnshire coast, the Norwich parish of St Lawrence, and the important Thames Valley town of Great Marlow.[134] The other date attracted very little attention, being the birthday of Charles's queen, Catherine of Braganza, who was both a Catholic and a self-effacing personality. Only eight churches in the sample, all in London, chose to ring on 15 November and so extend to her the tribute given by more to the even less popular Henrietta Maria.[135] Although their records give out, it seems hard to believe that they would have continued to do so once she fell under suspicion among many people of complicity in the Popish Plot. Yet this is when court commemoration of the day came into its own. As part of his gallant determination to stand by his wife, Charles ensured that when she was first rumoured to be implicated in the plot her customary birthday ball was 'never so brave'. To mark their final triumph over the Whigs, in 1684, he commanded 'fireworks upon the Thames before Whitehall, with pageants of castles, forts and other devices of gyrandolas, serpents, the King and Queen's arms and Mottos, all represented in fire. . . . It is said this sole triumph cost £1500: which was concluded with, a great ball, where all the young ladies and gallants danced.[136]

Yet, as David Cressy has pointed out, the most widely celebrated political anniversary during the reign was Gunpowder Treason Day, which now built upon the growing attachment to it during the early Stuart years and the Interregnum. He noted that churchwardens regularly spent as much upon the ringing then as upon Restoration Day, and that some provided more entertainments, such as bonfires at Cambridge and tar barrels at Darlington on the Tees in County Durham. He also repeated Samuel Pepys's observations of boys flinging 'crackers' in London streets in 1661, the day having been kept 'very strictly' there, and of bonfires in the City in 1664, so thick that coaches could not pass. He cited John Evelyn's regular attendance at sermons on 5 November, and went on to point out that once again the success of the day derived largely from the flexibility of its message: to some it was an opportunity to berate Catholics, to others one to eulogize monarchy and condemn all rebellion.[137]

These conclusions are well borne out by the further evidence employed here. Of the sample of 616 parishes, some 337 (55 per cent) recorded payments during the reign for ringing upon 5 November. Almost all of those which rang upon St George's Day and Restoration Day did so then as well, often with extra expenditure, while in many it was the only anniversary thus honoured. Those which remembered it included a large number of villages, in every part of the realm. Among them were Grasmere in the centre of the Cumbrian Mountains, where most payments were for the killing of ravens which menaced the flocks, and St Buryan near Land's End, one of the last strongholds of the ancient Cornish language.[138] At Worcester the cathedral chapter kindled more bonfires.[139] It must be stressed that this predominance was present from the beginning of the reign, and that of those 337 communities only seventeen[140] took up the ringing at the presumed exposure of the Popish Plot or during the ensuing Exclusion Crisis when fear of Catholicism was generally accentuated. Indeed, three, in Westmorland, Cheshire and Kent, actually dropped the habit during the crisis as if it had become too much associated with Whiggery.[141] None the less, there is no mistaking the manner in which Londoners developed the holiday during the 1670s into a tremendous display of hatred for Popery. It has been the subject of a number of studies.[142] The acceleration of activity began upon the heels of the heir presumptive's declaration of his conversion to the faith of Rome, in 1673. That 5 November, apprentices commenced a tradition of parading effigies of the Pope and burning them at Temple Bar which was enacted almost every year for the rest of the decade and into the early 1680s. Between 1679 and 1681 the Whigs sponsored far more elaborate and expensive processions, with many more models and a much bigger fire. To avoid competition with local demonstrations, they held these spectacular shows upon that other favourite festival of radical Protestants, 17 November. Destiny had delivered it, once again, an exquisite capacity to insult a reigning Monarch, for just as Charles I's Catholic wife had been born on the 16th, so Catherine of Braganza's birthday was on the 15th. During the 1660s Queen Elizabeth's Day was only rung for by a few parishes, all in London.[143] The fact that of the six which recorded it only one (St Giles Cripplegate) rang for Catherine as well still made some kind of point, and during the Exclusion Crisis the clamour of bells was said to be general in the City as each 17 November dawned. The ringing and processions were imitated at Salisbury and Taunton. They ebbed, as is well known, with the crisis. In 1682 a Tory corporation had the pageants at London destroyed when still under construction, and the militia tried to put out all bonfires. By 1684 both Gunpowder Treason Day and Queen Elizabeth's Day were quiet in the City, and observation of the latter had ceased altogether outside it.

Much less scholarly attention has been paid to the development of the festive calendar under James II. His reign automatically multiplied it, for although he carefully held his coronation on St George's Day like his brother, his birth and accession had almost inevitably to occur on different dates, 14 October and 6 February respectively. Forms of prayer were duly issued for these, and the forms already in existence for Restoration Day revised accordingly. The increased complexity of the political ritual year ought in theory to have decreased observation of some, at least, of its component parts. Yet this does not seem to have occurred, perhaps because the party of Crown and High Church was fully in control, and perhaps because the new state calendar got swept up in that enthusiasm for seasonal ceremony manifest in the Church of the time. The preaching on 30 January does not seem to have diminished in volume nor altered in its nature.[144] Of 565 parishes which have left itemized expenditure upon ringing from the reign, 261 (46 per cent) swung the bells upon 29 May, a larger proportion than in the first decade after the Restoration itself. Once again, they included most of those in towns but many in the countryside, representing every county. Anthony Wood noted 'bonfires, bells, gaudies' at Oxford on Restoration Day 1687,[145] and comparable celebrations should have occurred in other communities. Coronation Day, the feast of George, fared similarly well, being rung for in 115 out of the sample of 565 churches (20 per cent). The concentration in urban centres is more pronounced, but this still leaves many rural communities in the number. Two of the city parishes, St George Colegate in Norwich, and St Ethelburga Bishopsgate in London, began paying for bonfires in addition to the peals which they had provided under Charles,[146] and Wood recorded fires and bells all over Oxford on St George's Day 1688.[147]

James himself certainly made much of his birthday. Not only did the court hold balls of particular splendour and the Tower guns fire salutes, but the royal guards paraded in Hyde Park.[148] Upon the first occasion, in 1685, the Lord Mayor ordered bonfires as well as bells in London, and at least four parishes paid for them formally, two (St Katherine Coleman and St Peter Cornhill) adding rather stiffly that this was done under direction.[149] The next year the government forbade any fires in the City, apparently for fear of disturbances. Westminster, however, was lit up with them, and the shops of the twin cities and the suburbs were closed as if for a holy day.[150] At Oxford the initial celebration in 1685 was a lively business, with bells by day and fires in colleges and streets by night, around which merry-makers drank the royal health. Thereafter the number of bonfires dwindled, and they ceased altogether in 1688, although some colleges held parties.[151] Altogether, some eighty-two of the 565 parishes in the sample (15 per cent) paid to ring bells on this date. They mostly represented the more important churches of towns, although the urban centres involved ranged from cities to small local centres such as Braintree in Essex, Wem in Shropshire, and Louth in Lincolnshire. There were also nineteen villages included, stretched across the south and east of the realm from Dorset to

Durham.[152] All these rang consistently through the reign, though by its last year one Norwich parish and one in London felt obliged to record that they did so by order of their mayors.[153] Cambridge formed an interesting exception among important towns in not paying the salute, and the overall total is obviously much lower than for ringing on 29 May and 23 April. Nevertheless, more churches were saluting the birthday of James II than had acclaimed those of any of his predecessors, saving only the case of Charles II's, which had been subsumed in a statutory political commemoration. As the fourth Stuart was very clearly not a personality whom his subjects held in higher esteem than previous monarchs, the new attention paid to his nativity indicates a general growth in the cult of kingship, reflected in the development of the calendar.

That this is so is suggested by the fortunes of other significant dates. One was 25 September, the birthday of James's queen, Mary of Modena, yet another Catholic and therefore no more dear to the hearts of her subjects than her two predecessors. No London church recorded ringing for this even by precept, and those which did do so consisted only of St Margaret, Westminster and New Windsor, both at the gates of royal residences, and Kingston upon Thames and St Laurence, Norwich, which were presumably carried away by loyalty or courtesy.[154] By contrast three out of the six metropolitan parishes which have left accounts for ringing in the reign continued to salute the last queen to die a Protestant, Elizabeth.[155] The king's accession day was quite a different matter, incurring the respect due to the royal office. It was, however, celebrated much less than in earlier reigns; of the sample of 565 parishes only seventy (12 per cent) recorded ringing then. The distribution of these reveals the cause for the decline, for most were in villages and in those western and northern counties such as Somerset, Warwickshire, Shropshire, and Lancashire where the royal birthday was not observed. The natal feast was effectively replacing that of the accession, the two rarely being rung for in the same place. Although James's regime had issued prayers for the latter, as said, it is possible that he himself was responsible for the change of emphasis. Certainly it appears that his birthday was commemorated much more lavishly at court than his accession, perhaps because the latter reminded him too forcefully of his brother's agonizing death.[156]

Amid this shifting pattern, the symbolic flexibility of Gunpowder Treason Day enabled it to do more than hold its own, 333 of the 565 (59 per cent) parishes recording ringing upon it. That churches under the king's nose could keep it up, in Westminster and Windsor, reinforces the point made by the lack of any attempt to issue a new Form of Prayer for the day: as it stood it was a splendid opportunity for preaching against resistance to the royal will. Yet the enhanced popularity of it under James arouses an almost overwhelming suspicion that its associations with hatred of Catholicism made it all the more apposite under a Catholic king. The handful of villages which tactfully stopped ringing on the date[157] is more than outweighed by this higher proportion of an overall total which did. The inhabitants of Prestbury, on the Cotswold Edge, must have been making a calculated gesture when their wardens paid for a hundred pieces of wood to build a gigantic bonfire on the first 5 November of the Popish monarch's reign.[158] This is borne out by David Cressy's look at the Gunpowder Treason sermons of the reign, which included several against Catholicism;[159] indeed at Westminster it was a matter for comment when one fell into this category, but at Oxford it was just as much an event when one did not.[160] Some attempt was made by the government to regulate popular celebration of the day, including a retention of the ban on bonfires in the City of London upon that night (for fear of Pope-burnings). In 1686 youths there paraded candles upon sticks instead, to the annoyance of the king, and the next year the Lord Mayor obediently set a watch to stop 'disorders' of this sort.[161] The order against fires or fireworks on 5 November seems to have been extended to cover the whole nation in 1686, for the Yorkshire diarist Adam de la Pryme recorded that in large provincial towns it was circumvented by the placing of candles in windows as a witness against Catholicism.[162] If it was ever made general, it was spectacularly flouted at Oxford in 1688, when a passionately anti-Catholic sermon at the university church was followed by a record number of fires in streets and colleges, 'in spite to the papists'.[163]

The overall view suggests that had James II not undergone a personal, and deeply felt, conversion to the faith of Rome, then his reign would have seen the acceptance of a more elaborate political ritual year, in harmony with a national church more given to ceremony, than in the time of Charles II. Yet as all know, this was not to be. Even as the bonfires were lit at Oxford the army of William of Orange was landing in Tor Bay, and within three months James was gone and the vacant throne offered to William and Mary. Political festivals had to be altered once again, and more drastically than in 1685. The principal element of continuity, as it had been through the Interregnum, was Gunpowder Treason Day, and it now reached its greatest importance as it commemorated the deliverance of 1688 as well as that of 1605. The new prayers for the day drove the point home, as did the bell-ringers at St Mildred, Canterbury, who refused to accept any payment for their work on 5 November 1689, while their fellow parishioners paraded with tubs of fire 'in contempt of the sacrifice of the mass'.[164] The joint monarchs were occupied at that same moment with 'a splendid ball, and other festival rejoicings'.[165] Of the 537 parishes in the sample which have itemized expenditure on ringing for the 1690s, 306 (57 per cent) paid for Gunpowder Treason Day. Of these, two in London, that of Horsell in the Surrey woods and that of Madeley in the Staffordshire heathlands, all began to pay for bonfires as well as bells in 1689.[166] Yet the figure gives some pause; it is much the same proportion as under James. Furthermore, official encouragement of the festivities rapidly made respectable citizens at last start worrying about the practical dangers of pyrotechnics. At Oxford by 1692 bonfires were mostly confined to colleges, and townspeople preferred to light up their windows.[167] The same development had been anticipated at London in 1691, where the night 'was celebrated with illuminations, that is, by setting up innumerable lights and candles in the windows towards the street, instead of squibs and bonfires, much mischief having been done by squibs'.[168] Burns and scorch-marks were inducing the same results as the precepts of the deposed king. None the less, the importance of the date remains unmistakable, for the simple reason that it was thrown further into prominence by the relative decline in importance of most of the others.

It is true that the fast upon 30 January seems to have held up well, although the evidence for this is somewhat impressionistic. Evelyn regularly attended its services in London during the 1690s, without comment.[169] The day was 'solemnly kept' at Oxford in 1690, and this appears to have been the case thereafter.[170] Sermons preached upon it during the decade survive in much the same numbers as before; they called, as before, for submission to the established government, the principal change being that they were no longer used to attack Protestant nonconformity.[171] It is noticeable that in comparison Evelyn went to only two Restoration Day services in the whole decade, and upon one of those commented that the traditional office for the day was not used, and indeed no attention was paid to its historic significance.[172] At Oxford sermons were a more regular and notable occurrence on 29 May, but bonfires were few, and not heard of after 1693.[173] In his survey of Jacobitism, Paul Monod discovered that even prominent Tories did not pay much attention to the day in the reigns of William, Mary, and Anne, although it had a resurgence of popularity after 1714.[174] The churchwardens' accounts underpin this circumstantial evidence. Only sixty out of the 537 sets in the sample for the 1690s (11 per cent) record ringing on the day. Most of these were major urban parishes which were probably dutifully obeying the statute which prescribed celebration, although the number included a clutch in rural Staffordshire.[175] It was a very eccentric community which insisted, like St Nicholas, Durham, or Ludlow, on ringing more on Restoration Day than any other; the festival was clearly too closely associated in the public mind with the exiled royal family. Unsurprisingly, the St George's Day celebrations died out altogether at the change of dynasty, as the new monarchs chose, deliberately, to be crowned upon a different date.

On the other hand, despite their impeccable Protestantism and parliamentary title, those sovereigns did not succeed in establishing their own political anniversaries to anything like the extent that James had done. Their accession day seems to have been rung for only in Oxford, and there Anthony Wood noticed a lack of popular enthusiasm; in 1690 it was celebrated only by a bear-baiting in one suburb and in 1693 by some illuminations in the High Street. He added that the reign had become associated with high taxes, and thus people felt that there was little to commemorate.[176] Perhaps because the date was also linked to the deposition (or 'abdication') of the previous monarch, more communities preferred to remember the new coronation day, 11 April. Yet they only numbered forty-four in the sample (8 per cent), some major urban parishes and some a scatter of villages across southern England. It was almost half the total which had rung for St George's Day. Evelyn only once attended a service upon this date, while Wood charted the decline in enthusiasm for it at Oxford. In 1690 there were indeed bonfires, but the next year only one, lit by boys, and by 1692 none were visible and only some colleges rang bells, so that the observation was already far less than it had been in King James's time. There was no revival of interest thereafter.[177] William's birthday should have fared better, if only because the same providence which had provided the Protestant Wind of 1688 and parked two nativities of Catholic queens next to Queen Elizabeth's Day had placed it on 4 November. This ought to have lent itself to a euphoric double bill of loyal and Protestant celebration on that and the following day. Instead, it was rung for in only forty-six of the parishes in the sample (9 per cent), often the same which remembered his coronation and again often in towns, although there was also a notable concentration in rural Kent and Buckinghamshire.[178] Evelyn never mentions the day as special, and when the wardens of St Benet Gracechurch, London, made a bonfire on it in 1692, they entered the familiar chilly comment that it was in response to the Lord Mayor's orders.[179] Wood is more eloquent upon the matter: in 1692 the date was already 'little observed' at Oxford with just a few bonfires in colleges, and by 1693 there were only 'some crackers and squibs made at St Mary's church door'. Interest resumed fitfully in 1695, some bonfires reappearing, but that was upon news that the king himself was near Oxford.[180] Mary's birthday ought to have been honoured considerably more than that of most royal wives, for she was not only a queen regnant and joint sovereign but has commonly been supposed by historians to have enjoyed a popularity denied to her husband and father. Yet it was remembered only a little better than that of her Catholic namesake and stepmother, an almost random total of eleven towns and village churches recording ringing for her.[181]

All this would suggest that the Glorious Revolution of 1688, far from triumphantly developing the 'royal ritual year', did much to wither it. Doubtless, as Wood suggested, this had something to do with the popularity of the new government, but a different point also needs to be made about the process. From time immemorial the English, like all human beings, had celebrated communal successes with festivity, and the Protestant monarchy of Elizabeth took over this tradition by appointing special days for this purpose, sometimes with forms of prayer issued for them; the most notable of all being after the defeat of the Spanish Armada. The Civil War had the effect of making these far more frequent, as the opposed parties won battles against each other, and the republican governments did the same to celebrate successes over insular and foreign foes. Charles II took over the practice, to mark naval victories and treaties, and James ordered thanksgivings for his defeat of Monmouth's rebellion and the birth of his heir. All these were marked by the clamour of bells and sometimes the flaring of bonfires as well. The regime of William and Mary made such events annual, and sometimes more frequent than that, as the public were invited to celebrate gains in Ireland and the Netherlands, the escape of the king from a Jacobite conspiracy, or merely his return to the country from foreign expeditions. The parishes which rang bells for any of the calendar dates, and a few which did not, obediently held services and sent in the ringers for these *ad hoc* festivities. Thus the new regime turned the political year into more of a progress report upon its good government and less a commemoration of monarchy itself; in this respect, as in his austere Calvinist faith and his disdain for the old idea that sovereigns could heal by touch, William helped to create a less 'sacerdotal' kingship than that of James II.

Looking at the same issues from the opposite direction, it seems clear that during the seventeenth century parish élites, especially outside London, had a remarkable freedom of choice concerning their political calendar. They selected anniversaries for commemoration, and altered their selection according to changing circumstances in ways which did not always reflect the wishes and priorities of the central government. There is also the matter of the 'silent minority', 118 out of the 705 (17 per cent) in the sample for the years 1660–1700, which never recorded ringing for a single political occasion but got on with their own local business. It is not a surprise to find that virtually all were rural, with one from a poor quarter of a provincial town.[182] Nor is it unexpected to find that many are in Wales and Herefordshire. But they are present in virtually every county in the sample, rare in the North, Midlands, and West Country, and quite common in Kent and East Anglia. At Hounslow, on one of the main roads to and from London, the bells were only put to work when a king passed by.[183] They tended to be parishes without resident gentry (to judge from pew rents and rating lists), but then so were many which did ring. The presence of the seat of the Duke of Beaufort within earshot of Great Badminton church did not cause its ringers to ply their art for any other political date or event than the birth of a prince of Wales in 1688.[184] Such records do provide some of the many materials for the study of a rich and complex local political culture in late Stuart England, a process which has at present hardly begun. Likewise, when the records of secular and ecclesiastical courts from the late seventeenth century have been inspected with the same thoroughness, and the same questions in mind, as some of those for the late Tudor and early Stuart periods, then the context for attitudes to popular festivity, and morality, will be much better understood.

When I first planned the research project from which this book has derived, around 1980, I expected it to document, rather better than before, the way in which an immemorial folk festival culture, derived ultimately from pagan roots, encountered first an attack upon religious grounds, consequent upon the English Reformation, and then one upon secular grounds, resulting from the social changes of the eighteenth and nineteenth centuries. This expectation rested upon the views prevalent in the 1970s among folklorists and social historians. By 1985 initial explorations had made clear to me that some of it, at least, did not fit the data. I was increasingly less certain that many customs could be traced to pagan origins, or indeed whether we really knew very much about ancient British paganism at all. Instead, I seemed to be discovering that many of the activities removed or criticized during the Reformation period had been adopted locally, if not actually conceived, during the late Middle Ages. I therefore formed a model to explain what I was now calling the rise and fall of Merry England, a story of how the high value of real wages and the collapse of the manorial system in the fourteenth and fifteenth centuries fostered the growth of a lively popular festival culture based upon parish, guild, and town. This culture, in my scheme, was to be undermined and destroyed by the inflation and fall of wage values in the subsequent 200 years, polarizing and collapsing the local communities upon which it depended. Such a scheme was heavily influenced by social historians such as Keith Wrightson, and effectively filled out research that they had already carried out for the later period, while adding a neat late medieval dimension to it. My problem was that further work failed to support my expectations: the economic explanation for the growth of ritual seemed, if not itself refutable, at least increasingly hard to prove, while religious factors appeared to be increasingly important to the subsequent process. When I came to study the late seventeenth century, I could not find that my model applied at all.

The story that the records seemed to suggest was as follows: during the late Middle Ages a religion which embodied the concept of salvation by works encouraged a tremendous elaboration of sacred buildings, ornaments, and rites. In turn, and perhaps assisted by propitious economic factors in some areas, the fashion grew of utilizing communal merry-making and semi-secular calendar customs to raise money for the parish. It was a society in which ritual and festival was utilized for many different purposes at many different levels. Then came a direct ideological challenge from early Protestantism, which stood not merely to reform the physical and ideological context of worship but to destroy much of the festive culture with which the old Church had been bound up. This challenge was to a considerable extent successful, reinforced in its later stages by a growing fear of popular disorder among local élites, created by novel economic pressures. It did, however, provoke a double reaction in turn, consisting of a renaissance of ceremony in many churches and a nostalgia for the old communal merry-making among poets and dramatists. Both parts of this reaction were reinforced, and made more contentious, by the policies of the early Stuart kings. The events of 1640–6 represented a complete victory for the intentions which the early Protestant reformers had cherished towards religious ritual and communal festivity, producing a Church and society in this respect very close to that aimed at by the governments of Edward VI. The Restoration provided a compromise, a considerable quantity of ceremony restored to the Church and the attack on secular merry-making called off for half a century, but the link between that merry-making and religious buildings and funds finally broken. Civic ritual was likewise detached from that of ecclesiastics. All these developments took place within a society which, despite the economic strains of the years around 1600, remained remarkably unchanging in its basic structure. As said, the story outlined above seems to be that dictated by the sources themselves, as the previous seven chapters ought to have shown. What is noteworthy, and perhaps disturbing, is that, like the earlier shifts in the author's expectations, it fits into a wider historiographical pattern, the current tendency to suspicion of economic and social determinism and a revival of belief in the importance of religious and political factors as forces for change in their own right. It will be fascinating to see if further research reveals this view to be any more objective than those before.

Appendix

L ISTED below are the churchwardens' accounts used for this book, being all those which were available to a researcher when I was working upon it. I attempted in the end to read all those surviving from before 1690, a date chosen because the very large number of extant accounts which begin in the following decade would have required a proportionate amount of additional work, while those which began earlier and continued through William's reign gave me a sufficient sample for those years. My ambition was inevitably a failure. For one thing it is almost certain that more accounts remain hidden in the vestries of their native parishes. For another, and more important, over a hundred of the sets lodged in county record offices have been declared unfit for production, according to the wildly varying tastes of individual archivists. The extreme case is Dorset, where about a third of the total stock is now out of bounds, including some used earlier by David Underdown and David Cressy. It can only be hoped that I was unlucky enough to work in an interval between the imposition of more rigorous standards of conservation and the microfilming of delicate documents, although the financial constraints upon local archives make this sadly unlikely.

Nevertheless, the list below may still be useful to future researchers. In the designation of repositories, 'L' signifies 'Library', 'RO' 'Record Office', and 'CRO' 'County Record Office.' In the description of documents, 'impf.' (imperfect) indicates that occasional years are missing in the run, while 'v. impf.' (very imperfect) means that only occasional years are present. Always excluded are those spans of time for which only summary totals of income and expenditure are entered. Hundreds of sets of accounts held by record offices consist wholly of this kind, and they also are eliminated, so that the catalogue consists of detailed records of income and expenditure except in very occasional cases in which, as indicated, only one or the other survives. In citing publication of items, I have omitted those which (as in the Malone Society and Records of Early English Drama series) only concern themselves with very limited categories of entry.

BEDFORDSHIRE

CLIFTON 1543, 1589, 1604, 1608. In CRO, P7/1/1. Ed. J. Farmiloe and R. Nixseaman, Bedfordshire Historical Record Society, 33 (1953).

NORTHILL 1561–1612, 1665–1709. In CRO, P10/5/1–2. Ed. Farmiloe and Nixseaman, to 1600.

SHILLINGTON *c*.1571–1666. In CRO, P44/5/1–2. Ed. Farmiloe and Nixseaman, to 1600.

KEMPSTON ALL SAINTS 1617–18, 1671. In CRO, P60/5/1–3.

FLITTON 1632, 1658–9. In CRO, P12/5/1.

PULLOXHILL 1638–40, 1679–84. In CRO, P13/5/1.

HUSBORNE CRAWLEY 1672–1702. In CRO, P49/5/1.

FLITWICK 1674, 1685–1740 impf. In CRO, P59/5/1.

BOLNHURST 1676–1766 impf. In CRO, P46/5/1.

HARLINGTON 1677–1918. In CRO, P75/5/1.

MILTON BRYAN 1678–1729. In CRO, P15/5/1.

CARDINGTON 1680–1715. In CRO, W1301.

BERKSHIRE

ST LAWRENCE, READING 1432–51 impf., 1498–1651 impf. In CRO, D/P 97/5/1–3. Extracts ed. Charles Kerry, *History of the Municipal Church of St Lawrence, Reading* (Reading, 1881).

BRIGHTWALTON 1481–1620 v. impf. In CRO, D/P 24/5/1.

ST GILES, READING 1518–1808 impf. In CRO, D/P 96/5/1. Ed. W. L. Nash, *The Churchwardens' Account Book for the Parish of St Giles's, Reading* (Reading, 1883).

NEW WINDSOR 1531–63 impf. In CRO, D/Ex 554.

1616–87 impf. In CRO, D/P 149/5/1.

STANFORD IN THE VALE 1551–1705. In CRO, D/P 118/5/1. Ed. to 1602 by W. Haines, *The Antiquary*, 17 (1888), 71–213.

ST HELEN, ABINGDON 1555–74. Extracts ed. Prof. Ward, *Archaeologia*, 1 (1770), 140–2.

ST MARY, READING 1555–1602. Ed. F. and A. Garry, *The Churchwardens' Accounts of the Parish of St Mary's Reading* (Reading, 1893).

THATCHAM 1561–1629. In CRO, D/P 130/5/1A. Extracts ed. Samuel Barfield, *Thatcham, Berks* (1901).

CHILDREY 1568–1604, 1612–30, 1654–87. In CRO, D/P 35/5/1.

KINTBURY 1583–8. In CRO, D/P 78/5/1.

WARFIELD 1586–1758 impf. In CRO, D/P 44/5/2.

NEWBURY 1602–1724. In CRO, microfiche 97/12A–B.

ASHAMPSTEAD 1611–41, 1665–87. In CRO, D/P 8/5/1.

HAMPSTEAD NORREYS 1636–40, 1655–1779. In CRO, D/P 62/5/1.

BRIMPTON 1640–78 impf. In CRO, D/P 26/5/1.

WANTAGE 1657–1758. In CRO, D/P 143/5/1.

BRIGHTWELL 1666–98 impf. In CRO, D/P 25/5/1.

CAVERSHAM 1672–1707. In CRO, 162/5/1.

STRATFIELD MORTIMER 1681–1768. In CRO, D/P 120/5/1.

CHADDLEWORTH 1687–1836. In CRO, D/P 32/5/1.

CUMNOR 1687–1719. In CRO, D/P 45/5/1.

BRISTOL

ALL SAINTS *c*.1446–93 impf., 1536–42, 1549–52, 1553–1662. In City RO, P/AS/ChW/3.

ST EWEN 1454–1632. In City RO, P/St E/ChW/1–2. Ed. to 1560 by B. Masters and E. Ralph, Bristol and Gloucester Archaeological Society (1967).

ST NICHOLAS 1520–1727. Destroyed. Extracts printed by E. G. C. Atchley, *Transactions of the St Paul's Ecclesiological Society*, 6 (1906), 36–67.

CHRIST CHURCH 1531–44 impf., 1545–7, 1551–1655 impf., 1656–1708. In City RO, P/xch/la–c.

ST JOHN THE BAPTIST 1532–56, 1557–81 impf., 1635–1728. In City RO, P/St JB/ChW/2.

ST THOMAS 1544, 1552, 1564–1670 impf., 1697. In City RO, P/St T/ChW/1–102.

ST WERBURGH 1548–1710. In City RO, P/St W/ChW/3a–b.

ST MARY REDCLIFFE 1548–9, 1551–1734. Six volumes kept in church vestry.

ST PHILIP AND ST JACOB 1564–1782. In City RO, P/St P and J/ChW/3a.

TEMPLE 1582–1687 impf. In City RO, P/Tem/ChW/1 Ca 1–24.

BUCKINGHAMSHIRE

WING 1527–1723. In CRO, PR 234/5/1.

AMERSHAM 1529–30, 1539–41, 1597–1607, 1646, 1680–95. In CRO, PR 4/5/1–2. Extracts in *Records of Buckinghamshire*, 7 (1891), 43–51.

ASTON ABBOTS 1562–1630. In CRO, PR 7/5/1. Extracts ed. W. Bradbrook, *Records of Buckinghamshire*, 10 (1910–16).

LUDGERSHALL 1565–1607, 1661–1800. In CRO, PR 138/5/1.

WINGRAVE 1575–1610. In CRO, PR 235/5/1.

GREAT MARLOW 1593–1675. In CRO, PR 140/5/1.

PITSTONE GREEN 1604–24. In CRO, PR 166/5/2.

MIDDLE CLAYDON 1635–45. In CRO, PR 52/5/1.

BLEDLOW 1640–75 impf. In CRO, PR 17/5/1.

DINTON 1650–73. In CRO, PR 62/5/1.

WEST WYCOMBE 1663–1774. In CRO, PR 227/4/2.

CLIFTON REYNES 1665–1774. In CRO, PR 54/5/1.

QUAINTON 1668–1735. In CRO, PR 169/5/1.

STEWKLEY 1671–1750. In CRO, PR 193/5/1.

RADCLIVE 1672–1732. In CRO, PR 171/5/1.

WOTTON UNDERWOOD 1673–1943. In CRO, PR 246/5/1.

BOARSTALL 1673–1703. In CRO, PR 20/5/1.

BEACONSFIELD 1678–1821. In CRO, PR 14/5/1.

HUGHENDEN 1681–1756. In CRO, PR 110/5/1.

PRINCES RISBOROUGH 1682–1707. In CRO, PR 175/12/2.

EDLESBOROUGH 1685–1743. In CRO, PR 69/5/1.

NEWTON LONGVILLE 1689–1723. In CRO, PR 155/5/1.

CAMBRIDGESHIRE

LEVERINGTON 1494, 1497–8, 1520–80. Extracts in *Fenland Notes and Queries*, 7 (1907–9), 184–90.

BASSINGBOURN 1497–1538. In CRO, P11/5/1–2.

GREAT ST MARY, CAMBRIDGE 1504–1699 impf. In CRO, P30/4/1–2. Ed. 1504–55 by J. Foster, Cambridge Antiquarian Society (1905).

HOLY TRINITY, CAMBRIDGE 1504–69. In CRO, P22/5/1–2.

ALL SAINTS, CAMBRIDGE 1569–1690. In CRO, P23/5/2–3.

ST MARY, ELY 1572–1630 impf. In CRO, P68/5/1. Ed. R. Holmes, *St Mary's Parish Church, Ely* (Ely, 1965).

COTON 1576–1607. In CRO, P49/5/1.

ST BOTOLPH, CAMBRIDGE 1599–1715. In CRO, P26/5/1–2.

ORWELL 1653–1756 impf. In CRO, P127/5/1.

SOHAM 1663–1762 impf. In CRO, P142/5/1.

CHESHIRE

HOLY TRINITY, CHESTER 1532–1684 impf., 1687–1718. In CRO, P1/11–12. Transcript 1532–1640 in British L, Harl. MS 2177.

ST MARY ON THE HILL, CHESTER 1536–1689. In CRO, P20/13/1.

ST MICHAEL, CHESTER 1560–1717. In CRO, P65/8/1–2.

ST OSWALD, CHESTER 1575–1629, 1676–1704. In CRO, P29/7/1–3.

FRODSHAM 1609–32, 1634–46, 1651–1717. In CRO, P8/13/1–6.

MARBURY 1618–58 impf. In CRO, P39/8/1.

MIDDLEWICH 1635–40, 1648–67, 1684–1721. In CRO, P13/22/1–2.

ST JOHN, CHESTER 1636–1744. In CRO, P51/12/1–2.

BUNBURY 1655–1709. In CRO, P40/13/1.

TARPORLEY 1662–1703 impf. In CRO, P22/11/1.

CHURCH MINSHULL 1668–1746. In CRO, P12/12/1.

ROSTHERNE 1672–1758 impf. In CRO, P47/8/1.

OVER PEOVER 1674–1938 impf. In CRO, P77/8/1.

STOKE 1677–90. In CRO, P31/3/1.

ST MARTIN, CHESTER 1682–1816. In CRO, P16/6/1.

ALDERLEY 1682–1722. In CRO, P143/9/1.

DARESBURY 1683–1706. In CRO, P66/12/1.

MACCLESFIELD 1686–1751. In CRO, P85/10/1.

DAVENHAM 1687–1751. In P6/10/1.

WYBURNBURY 1687–1716. In CRO, P37/15/1.

CORNWALL

LAUNCESTON 1405–1547 v. impf., 1558–1654 v. impf. Those 1529–58 survive in CRO, DDP 221/5/2. The rest printed in Richard and Otho Peter, *The Histories of Launceston and Dunheved* (Plymouth, 1885), 124, 356–75.

STRATTON 1512–77. In British L, Add. MS 32243.

POUCHILL 1525–59 impf., 1578–97. In CRO, DDP 192/5/1.

ST BREOCK 1529, 1541, 1566–98. In CRO, DDP 19/5/1.

NORTH PETHERWIN 1530–1612 v. impf. In CRO, DDP 167/5/1.

CAMBORNE 1538–77 impf., 1677–1780 impf. In CRO, DDP 322/1 and DDX 510.

ANTHONY 1550–84. In CRO, DDP 7/5/1.

MENHENIOT 1555–75. In CRO, DDP 144/5/2.

KILCHAMPTON 1563–1605. In CRO, DDP 102/5/1.

ST IVES 1570–1689. Ed. in John Hobson Matthews, *A History of St Ives* (1892), 144–288.

ST COLUMB MAJOR Receipts 1585–1660, Whole 1660–1700. In CRO, DDP 36/8/1.

LISKEARD 1598–1660. In CRO, DDP 126/4/1.

ST NEOT 1602–1709 impf. In CRO, DDP 162/5/1.

PADSTOW 1638–1707 impf. In CRO, DDP 170/5/1.

BRADOC 1666–1947. In CRO, DDP 17/5/1.

MORWENSTOW 1666–1752. In CRO, DDP158/5/1.

BOYTON 1670–93. In CRO, DDP 16/5/1.

ST AUSTELL 1671–1743 v. impf. In CRO, DDP 8/8/1.

ST STEPHEN BY SALTASH 1673–4. In CRO, DDP 214/5/1.

LANDOWEDNACK 1674–1760. In CRO, DDP 105/5/1.

ST BURYAN 1674, 1692–1742. In CRO, DDP 23/5/1.

ST DOMINIC 1693–1844. In CRO, 50/5/1.

CUMBERLAND

GREAT SALKELD 1547–9. Ed. C. Bouch, *Transactions of the Cumberland and Westmorland Antiquarian and Archaeological Society*, NS 49 (1950), 135–7.

ST ANDREW, PENRITH 1655–1801. In Cumbria (Carlisle) RO, PR 110/1/75.

STANWIX 1688–1790. In Cumbria (Carlisle) RO, 117/26.

DENBIGHSHIRE

LLANELIDAN 1650–1755. In Clwyd (Ruthin) RO, PD 54/1/10.

LLANYRNOG 1655–81 impf., 1683–1728. In Clwyd (Ruthin) RO, PD 47/1/30–1.

CHIRK 1661–1743. In National Library of Wales, Chirk Collection.

WREXHAM 1661–6, 1668–74. In Clwyd (Ruthin) RO, PD 101/1/133–4.

GRESFORD 1661–7. In Clwyd (Ruthin) RO, PD 34/1/158.

MARCHWIEL 1663–1777. In Clwyd (Ruthin) RO, PD 78/1/39.

LLANGYNHAFAL 1663–1727. In Clwyd (Ruthin) RO, PD 67/1/20.

LLANWRST 1664–82 impf. In Clwyd (Ruthin) RO PD 69/1/75.

BRYNEGLWYS 1664–82, 1687–1740. In Clwyd (Ruthin) RO, PD 111/1/12–13.

LLANFAIR TALHEARN 1665–1718 impf. In Clwyd (Ruthin) RO, PD 56/1/21.

LLANFERRES 1673–1718. In Clwyd (Ruthin) RO, PD 57/1/30.

DENBIGH 1679. In Clwyd (Ruthin) RO, PD 24/1/58.

CLOCAENOG 1684–1703. In Clwyd (Ruthin) RO, PD 20/1/1.

RUTHIN 1692. In Clwyd (Ruthin) RO, PD 78/1/39.

DERBYSHIRE

ALL SAINTS, DERBY 1465–1527 v. impf., 1620–1881. Ed. J. Charles Cox and W. H. St John Hope, *The Chronicles of the Collegiate Church or Free Chapel of All Saints, Derby* (1881).

REPTON 1583–1635. Ed. J. Charles Cox, *Journal of the Derbyshire Archaeological and Natural History Society*, 1 (1879), 27–41.

MARSTON ON DOVE 1602–1827 impf. In CRO, D812A/PW1.

ST WERBURGH, DERBY 1668–1707. In CRO, D1145A/PW1.

DEVON

TAVISTOCK 1392–1575 impf. In CRO, Tavistock PW1–26. Ed. R. N. Worth, *Calendar of the Tavistock Parish Records* (Plymouth, 1887).

ST JOHN'S BOW, EXETER 1412–1626 v. impf. In CRO, DD36765–75.

HOLY TRINITY, EXETER 1415–1556 v. impf. In CRO 1718A add./PW1–41B.

ST MARY STEPS, EXETER 1421–1856 v. impf. In CRO, DD70920.

ST PETROCK, EXETER 1425–1650 impf. In CRO, Exeter St Petrock PW1–5.

DARTMOUTH 1430–1539 v. impf. Years 1495–1553 survive in CRO, DD61218–DD61391A. All printed in Hugh R. Watkin, *Dartmouth* (1935), i. 300–52.

ASHBURTON 1479–1580. Ed. A. Hanham, Devon and Cornwall Record Society, 1970.

CHAGFORD 1480–1547, 1551–60. Ed. Francis Marden Osborne, *The Churchwardens' Accounts of St Michael's Church, Chagford* (Chagford, 1979).

ST ANDREW, PLYMOUTH 1483–5. In West Devon RO, W129/46.

DARTINGTON 1484–5, 1554–1638. In CRO, Dartington PW1–2.

WINKLEIGH 1513–1648. In North Devon RO, 2989A/PW1.

BROADHEMPTON 1517–1676. In CRO, Broadhempton PW1/V.

MOREBATH 1520–84, 1684–1766. In CRO, PW1–2. Ed. to 1573 by J. E. Binney, *The Accounts of the Wardens of the Parish of Morebath* (Exeter, 1904).

WOODLAND 1527–9. In CRO, Woodland PW1.

WOODBURY 1538–1637, 1651–71. In CRO, Woodbury PW3–4V.

OKEHAMPTON 1543, 1548. In CRO, Okehampton PW1, PW3.

CREDITON 1551–99. In CRO, Crediton PW1/V.

COLDRIDGE 1552–1620. In CRO, Coldridge PW1/V.

SOUTH TAWTON 1554–1613. In CRO, South Tawton PW1/V.

BRAUNTON 1554–1670. In North Devon RO, 1677A/PW1–1A.

KILMINGTON 1556–1608. Ed. R. Cornish, *Kilmington Churchwardens' Accounts* (1901).

MOLLAND 1557–77. Ed. Sir John Phear, *Transactions of the Devonshire Association*, 35 (1902), 211–37.

CHUDLEIGH 1561–1651. In CRO, Chudleigh PW1/V.

SHOBROOKE 1562–1620. In CRO, Shobrooke PW1.

EXBOURNE 1565, 1568. In CRO, Exbourne PW1, PW4.

FARWAY 1565–91, impf. receipts only. In CRO, Farway PW1.

HONITON 1570–1651. In CRO, Honiton PW1/V.

NORTHAM Receipts only 1581–98. In North Devon RO, 1843/PW1.

BRIXHAM 1588. In CRO, Brixham PW1.

DAWLISH 1588–1630, 1686–1718. In CRO, Dawlish PW1a–b.

HARTLAND 1597–1706. In North Devon RO, 1201A/PW1.

WOLBOROUGH 1600. In CRO, Wolborough PW1.

AWLISCOMBE 1600–37, 1649–94. In CRO, Awliscombe PW2–8.

BERE FERRERS 1602–50. In CRO, D1815/Z/P21.

CULLOMPTON 1609–18, 1669–1758. In CRO, Cullompton PW1–2.

NORTH TAWTON 1611–99. In CRO, North Tawton PW1.

STOKE GABRIEL 1611–22. In CRO, Stoke Gabriel PW1.

MODBURY 1622–1842. In CRO, Modbury PW8.

HABERTON 1626–31, 1680–1704. In CRO, Heberton PW1–2.

UPLYME 1633–99 impf. In CRO, Uplyme PW1.

BOW 1633–60 impf., 1661–1700. In CRO, Bow PW1–3.

TEDBURN ST MARY 1642–72. In CRO, Tedburn St Mary PW1.

GITTISHAM 1649–1762. In CRO, Gittisham PW1.

HOLCOMBE BURNELL 1657–82, 1684–1731. In CRO, Holcombe Burnell PW1–2.

HIGH BRAY 1658–83, 1687–1715. In North Devon RO, 815A/PW2–3.

AXMINSTER 1660–85. In CRO, R7/2/25.

DREWSTEIGNTON 1661–98. In CRO, Drewsteignton PW1.

INSTOW 1661–90. In North Devon RO, 3064A/PW1.

BROADHEMBURY 1662–1700. In CRO, Broadhembury PW1.

BUCKLAND IN THE MOOR 1662–1700. In CRO, Buckland in the Moor PW1.

ST MARY ARCHES, EXETER 1662–1716. In CRO, Exeter St Mary Arches PW1.

ASHWATER 1663–1700. In CRO, Ashwater PW1.

ABBOTSKERWELL 1663–1700. In CRO, PW1.

ASHPRINGTON 1671–1700. In CRO. Ashprington PW1.

WOOLFORD ISWORTHY 1672–88. In CRO, Woolford Isworthy (East) PW1.

WEMBURY 1674–1757. In West Devon RO, 125/8.

ALL HALLOWS GOLDSMITH STREET, EXETER 1676–1763. In CRO, Exeter All Hallows Goldsmith Street PW1.

SOWTON 1681–2. In CRO, Sawton PW1–2.

WARKLEIGH 1691–1718. In North Devon RO, 1701A/PW1.

COMBE MARTIN 1692–1717. In North Devon RO, 4025A/PW1.

BROADWOOD KELLY 1692–1861. In North Devon RO, 1772A/PW2.

DORSET

WIMBORNE MINSTER 1403–1696 impf. In CRO, PE/WM CW1–42.

SHERBORNE 1514–1700. In CRO, PE/SH/CW1/4–169. Published to 1554 in *Somerset and Dorset Notes and Queries*, 23 (1939–42).

BRIDPORT 1556. Published in *Somerset and Dorset Notes and Queries*, 8 (1902–3), 120–2.

CORFE CASTLE 1570–7 impf., 1689–1703. In CRO, PE/COC/CW1/1, 5.

CHARLTON MARSHALL 1583–1642, 1657–1707. In CRO, PE/CHM/CW1/1–2.

MOTCOMBE 1604–1713 impf. PE/MOT/CW1/1.

BERE REGIS 1607–33 impf., 1655–7, 1682–1740. In CRO, PE/BER/CW1–10.

CERNE ABBAS 1628–85. In CRO, PE/CEA/CW1.

LONGBURTON 1634–74 impf., 1686–1770. In CRO, PE/LOB/CW1–2.

LANGTON LONG BLANDFORD 1636–97 impf. In CRO, PE/LAL/CW1.

BEAMINSTER 1646–1719. In CRO, PE/BE/CW1.

ALL SAINTS, DORCHESTER 1649–1738. In CRO, PE/DO (AS) CW1.

MILTON ABBAS 1653–89 impf. In CRO, PE/MIL/CW1.

SEABOROUGH 1656–1839. In CRO, PE/SEA/CW1/1.

SYMONDSBURY 1656–8, 1681–2. In CRO, PE/SYM/CW1/1.

PUDDLETOWN 1657–72, 1689–1722. In CRO PE/PUD/CW1/1.

TARRANT HINTON 1658–1740. In CRO, PE/TTH/CW1/1.

STOUR PROVOST 1660–1743. In CRO, PE/SPV/CW1.

MELBURY OSMOND 1661–1749. In CRO, PE/MBO/CW1.

COMPTON VALENCE 1669–1781 impf. In CRO, PE/COV/CW1.

LONGBREDY 1669–1781 impf. In PE/LBY/CW1.

KINGSTON MAGNA 1673–1790. In CRO, PE/KIM/CW1/1.

SWANAGE 1673–1700 impf. In CRO, PE/SW/CW1/1.

FONTHILL MAGNA 1675–1717. In CRO, PE/FOM/CW1.

FROME VAUCHURCH 1679–1788. In CRO, PE/FRV/CW1.

ABBOTSBURY 1683–1772. In CRO, PE/ABB/CW1.

PIDDLEHINTON 1686–1766. In CRO, PE/PDH/CW1/1.

COUNTY DURHAM

ST OSWALD, DURHAM 1580, 1595–1644, 1652–1700. Ed. Surtees Society (1888).

PITTINGTON 1584–1641. Ed. Surtees Society (1888).

HOUGHTON LE SPRING 1592–1669. Ed. Surtees Society (1888).

RYTON 1597–1790. In CRO, EP/Ryt 4/1–3.

MERRINGTON 1621–1700 impf. In CRO, EP/Mer 34.

ST MARY, GATESHEAD 1626–78. In CRO, EP/Ga SM 4/1.

LONG NEWTON 1629–53 impf. In CRO, EP/LN 11.

ST CUTHBERT, DARLINGTON 1630–97. In CRO, EP/Da SC 35.

BISHOPWEARMOUTH 1661–89. In CRO, EP/Bi W 129.

HEIGHINGTON 1666–77. In CRO, EP/He 12.

ST NICHOLAS, DURHAM 1666–1703 impf. In CRO, EP/Du SN 4/1. Ed. Surtees Society, 1888.

ST MARY LE BOW, DURHAM 1678–92. In CRO, EP/Du MB 10.

BILLINGHAM 1682–1782. In CRO, EP/Bi 4/1.

ESSEX

SAFFRON WALDEN 1439–85. In CRO, D/P 192/5/1. Extracts printed by W. Mepham, *Essex Review*, 54 (1945), 57.

GREAT HALLINGBURY 1526–79 impf. In CRO, D/P 27/5/1.

GREAT DUNMOW 1526–1619 v. impf. In CRO, D/P 11/5/1. Extracts printed by L. A. Majendie, *Transactions of the Essex Archaeological Society*, 2 (1863), 227–37.

BROOMFIELD 1540–1, 1553–1610 impf. In CRO, D/P 248/5/1.

WALTHAM ABBEY 1542, 1554. Extracts printed by Prof. Ward, *Archaeologia*, 1 (1770), e–h.

HARWICH 1550–60. In Colchester RO, T/A 122/1.

HEYBRIDGE 1554–60. Ed. John Pridden, *The Churchwardens' Accounts Belonging to the Parish of Heybridge* (n.d.).

CHELMSFORD 1558–1641 impf., 1659–68. In CRO, D/P 94/5/1.

WIVENHOE 1560–75, 1676–1797. In Colchester RO, D/P 277/5/1–2. Extracts printed by G. M. Benton, *Essex Review*, 37 (1928), 156–7.

GREAT EASTON 1577–1616, 1630–1. In CRO, D/P 232/8/1.

THAXTED 1583, 1597–1636, 1661–84, 1686–97 impf. In CRO, D/P 16/5/2–7.

SOUTH WEALD 1584–1638, 1643–86, 1698–1718. In CRO, D/P 128/5/1.

WRITTLE 1588–1643 impf. In CRO, 50/5/1.

HORNCHURCH 1590–1678 impf. In CRO, D/P 115/5/1.

HEYDON 1599–1620. In CRO, D/P 135/1/1.

AVELEY 1600–1. In CRO, D/P 157/5/6.

WALTHAM HOLY CROSS 1624–70. In CRO, D/P 75/5/1.

BROMLEY 1626–1806. In Colchester RO, D/P 103/5/4.

WEST HAM 1643–1710. In CRO, D/P 256/5.

BOCKING 1670–1734. In CRO, TA 433/1.

NAZEING 1674–1711. In CRO, D/P 321/12/1.

THEYDON GARNON 1677–1714. In CRO, D/P 152/5/1.

DOWNHAM 1683–5. In CRO, D/P 257/5/4.

BRAINTREE 1684–1793. In CRO, D/P 264/5/1.

FLINTSHIRE

MOLD 1654–63. In Clwyd (Hawarden) RO, D/KK/111.

CILCAIN 1657–1705. In Clwyd (Hawarden) RO, P/14/1/21.

HAWARDEN 1660–5, 1668–1840 impf. In Clwyd (Hawarden) RO, P/28/1/42 and D/BJ/315.

CAERWYS 1674–1711. In Clwyd (Hawarden) RO, P/13/1/20.

HANMER 1683–1726. In Clwyd (Hawarden) RO, P/27/1/26.

NORTHOP 1683–1717 impf. In Clwyd (Hawarden) RO, P/45/1/74.

YSCEIFOG 1687–1785. In Clwyd (Hawarden) RO, P/72/1/30.

GLAMORGAN

ST MARY, SWANSEA 1558–69, 1579–1627. In Swansea University L, Corporation Records D2.

LLANTWIT FADRE 1679–80. In CRO (Cardiff), CL MS 4. 1108.

LLANGYNWYD 1685–6. In CRO (Cardiff), CL MS 5. 52.

GLOUCESTERSHIRE

St Michael, Gloucester 1545–91, 1603–39, 1643–1746. In CRO, P154/14/1–3.

Minchinhampton 1555–1687 impf. In CRO, P217/CW/2/1.

Tewkesbury Abbey 1563–1700 impf. In CRO, P329/CW/2/1.

St Aldate, Gloucester 1563–1617 impf. 1620–41. In CRO, P154/6/CW1–2.

Dursley 1566–1738 impf. In CRO, P124/CW/2/4.

Lechlade 1567–70. In CRO, P197/CW/2/1.

Winchcombe 1602–3, 1661–2. In CRO, P368/CW/2/1.

Barnsley 1609–37 impf. In CRO P34/CW/2/1–2.

Kemble 1612–30 impf., 1640–70 impf. In CRO, P186/CW/2/1.

St Lawrence, Stroud 1623–1715. In CRO, P320/CW/2/1.

St Mary, Tetbury 1626–1703 impf. In CRO, P328/1/CW/2/14.

Bromsberrow 1631–40, 1661–2. In CRO, P63/CW/2/1.

Twyning 1638–1703. In CRO, P243/VE/2/1.

Mickelton 1639–59 impf. In CRO, P216/CW/2/1.

Withington 1539–79 impf. In CRO, P374/CH/1.

Standish 1642–85 impf. In CRO, P305/CW/2/2.

Chedworth 1645–1923. In CRO, P77/CW/2/1.

Deerhurst 1646, 1690. In CRO, P112/CW/2/1.

Mitcheldean 1655–7, 1674–1889. In CRO, P220/VE/2/1.

Bibury 1655–91. In CRO, P44/CW/2/4.

Rockhampton 1662–1725. In CRO, P271/CW/2/1.

Westbury on Severn 1664–84 impf. In CRO, P354/CW/2/1.

Prestbury 1675–1866. In CRO, P254/CW/2/1.

Great Badminton 1676–1839. In CRO, P32/CW/2/1.

Old Sodbury 1678–1710. In CRO, P302/CW/2/1.

Kingswood 1681–1949. In CRO, P193/CW/2/2.

Painswick 1681–1906. In CRO, P244/CW/2/1.

Upton St Leonards 1682–1922. In CRO, P347/CW/2/1.

Stinchcombe 1683–4. In CRO, P312/CW/2/1.

Bourton on the Hill 1685–1921. In CRO, P54/CW/2/1.

Newnham 1686–1814. In CRO, P228/CW/2/1.

HAMPSHIRE

Bramley 1523–1613. In CRO, 63M70/PW1.

Stoke Charity 1541–4, 1548–1600, 1657–79. In CRO, 77M84/PW1. Tudor parts ed. John Foster Williams, *The Early Churchwardens' Accounts of Hampshire* (Winchester, 1913).

Crondall 1543–57, 1561–1600. Ed. Williams.

Ellingham 1543–4, 1555–63, 1584. In CRO, 113M8/PW1. Ed. Williams.

St John, Winchester 1549–1824. In CRO 88M81/PW1–2. Tudor part ed. Williams.

WOOTON ST LAWRENCE 1559–1640 impf., 1662–75. In CRO, 75M72/PW1. Tudor part ed. Williams.

PORTSMOUTH 1564–7. Ed. Williams.

NORTH WALTHAM 1593–1688. In CRO, 41M64/PW1.

HAMBLEDON 1600–19 impf. In CRO, 46M84/PW1.

FORDINGBRIDGE 1602–49 impf. In CRO, 24M84/PW2.

HOLDENHURST 1609, 1621. In CRO, 9M75A/PW1.

SOUTH WARBERTON 1611–49, 1663–81. In CRO, 70M76/PW1.

CHAWTON 1621–1813. In CRO, 1M70/PW1.

OVERTON 1623–8, 1679–1724. In CRO, 81M72/PW1–2.

ALTON 1625–1826. In CRO, 29M84/PW1.

UPHAM 1640–64 impf. In CRO, 74M78A/PW1.

MINSTEAD 1641–79 impf. In CRO, 90M71/PW1.

HEADBOURNE WORTHY 1645–52. In CRO, 21M62/PW1–2.

ODIHAM 1654–95. In CRO, 47M81A/PW1.

EASTON 1655–1820. In CRO, 72M70/PW1.

SOBERTON 1658–73. In CRO, 50M73A/PW1.

FAWLEY 1661–85, 1692–1718. In CRO, 25M60/PW1–2.

BINSTEAD 1663–88, 1690–9. In CRO, 1M67/PW1.

STRATFIELD SAYE 1664–1720. In CRO, 15M83/PW1.

ST MARY BOURNE 1664–1759. In CRO, 96M82/PW1.

ELING 1667–91. In CRO, 4M69/PW1.

NORTH BADDESLEY 1674–1734. In CRO, 51M67/PW1.

ST SWITHUN UPON KINGSGATE, WINCHESTER 1676–1720. In CRO, 74M81W/PW1.

ANDOVER 1677–1721. In CRO, 60M67/PW1.

BRAMSHOTT 1677–1704. In CRO, 57M75A/PW1.

ROCKBOURNE 1677–87. In CRO, 39M68/13.

BURGHCLERE 1679–1788. In CRO, 148M82/PW1.

HURSTBOURNE TARRANT 1686–8. In CRO, 68M79A/PW1.

SELBOURNE 1687–1833. In CRO, 32M66/PW1.

HEREFORDSHIRE

STOKE EDITH 1532–40, 1542–6, 1566–70. In Hereford CRO, J72/8.

ST NICHOLAS, HEREFORD 1601–70. In Hereford CRO, AG 81/22–3.

HENTLAND 1628–1705 impf. In Hereford CRO, N13/1.

BODENHAM 1652–67 impf. In Hereford CRO, M61/14.

BRAMPTON ABBOTS 1673–1766. In Hereford CRO, AA 15/18.

GARANEW 1678–84. In Hereford CRO, AC 75/16.

HERTFORDSHIRE

BISHOPS STORTFORD 1431–40, 1482–1661 impf., 1680–8. In CRO, D/P 21/5/1–2. Ed. J. Glasscock, *The Records of St Michael's Parish Church, Bishop's Stortford* (1882).

BALDOCK 1540–53, 1634, 1641–50, 1677–8. In CRO, D/P 12/5/1. Tudor part ed. Anthony Palmer, Hertfordshire Record Society (1985).

BARKWAY 1558. In CRO, D/P 13/5/1. Ed. Palmer.

ASHWELL 1562–1664, 1680–3, 1698–1736. In CRO, D/P 7/5/1. Ed. Palmer till 1600.

ST PETER, ST ALBANS 1573–1717. In CRO, D/P 93/5/1–2. Ed. Palmer.

STEVENAGE 1575–7. In CRO, D/P 105/8/1. Ed. Palmer.

BERKHAMSTEAD 1589–1639, 1657–67, 1687. In British L, Add. MS 18773.

KNEBWORTH 1598–1609. In CRO, D/P 62/1/1. Ed. Palmer.

TOTTERIDGE 1613–24. In CRO, D/P 463/5/1.

WATTON AT STONE 1631–3. In D/P 118/5/1.

BENGEO 1632–3. In CRO, D/P 17/12/1.

BARNET 1656–1760 impf. In CRO, 15/5/1.

LITTLE HADHAM 1663–4. In CRO, D/P 43/5/1.

WELLINGTON 1667–1710 impf. In CRO, D/P 115/5/1.

LILLEY 1674, 1687–1796. In CRO, D/P 67/5/1.

HITCHIN 1686–1717. In CRO, D/P 53/5/1.

HUNTINGDONSHIRE

RAMSEY 1511–52 impf. In CRO, 2449/25.

HOLYWELL 1547–99 impf. In CRO, 2280/28.

GREAT PAXTON 1615–42. In CRO, 2119/3.

FENSTANTON 1627–73. In CRO, 2688/5.

GREAT STAUGHTON 1637–1744. In CRO, 2735/5/1.

ST NEOTS 1674–1785 impf. In CRO, 2519/116.

STANGROUND 1676–8. In CRO, 2776/12/1.

KENT

HYTHE 1412–13. Ed. in *Archaeologia Cantiana*, 10 (1876), 245–8.

ST DUNSTAN, CANTERBURY 1484–1508, 1514–33, 1538–50, 1558–80 impf. In Canterbury Cathedral L, U3/141/4/1–4. Ed. to 1563 by J. Cowper, *Archaeologia Cantiana*, 16–17 (1886–7).

ST ANDREW, CANTERBURY 1485–1528, 1538–9, 1545–8, 1549–1625. In Canterbury Cathedral L, U3/5/4/1. Ed. C. Cotton, *Archaeologia Cantiana*, 32–6 (1917–22).

BETHERSDEN 1515–73 impf. Ed. F. Mercer, Kent Record Society (1928).

ST MARY, DOVER 1536–58. In British L, Egerton MS 1912.

BRENZETT 1546–68. In Centre for Kentish Studies (Maidstone) (hereafter CKS), P46/5/1.

SMARDEN 1546–68. Extracts ed. F. Haselwood, *Archaeologia Cantiana*, 9 (1874), 225–35.

HAWKHURST 1547–60. Extracts ed. W. Lightfoot, *Archaeologia Cantiana*, 5 (1862–3), 56–72.

ELTHAM 1554–69. Ed. A. Vallance, *Archaeologia Cantiana*, 47–8 (1935–6).

STROOD 1555–1763. In British L, Add. MS 36937.

Hoo All Hallows 1555–1613. In Medway Area Archives Office (hereafter MAAO), P188/5/1.

Cranbrook 1560–1647, 1664–94. In CKS, P100/5/1.

Harrietsham 1565–99 impf. In CKS, P173/5/1.

Charing 1590–1658 impf., 1661–1724. In CKS, P78/5/1–2.

Loose 1613–53 impf., 1656–94. In CKS, P233/5/1–2.

Tenterden 1614–1715. In CKS, P364/5/1–14.

St Mary Bredman, Canterbury 1628–1706 impf. In Canterbury Cathedral L, U3/2/4/1.

Sutton Valence 1629–33. In CKS, MF 1056.

St Alphege, East Greenwich 1630–40. Ed. J. W. Kirby, *Transactions of the Greenwich and Lewisham Antiquarian Society*, 4 (1953), 270–84.

Shorne 1630–81. In MAAO, P336/5/1.

Burham 1632–1756. In MAAO, P52/5/1.

Chatham 1634–57, 1673–96. In MAAO, P85/5/1.

Hartlip 1635–6, 1667–91 impf. In CKS, P175/5/1–1A.

East Farleigh 1636–1708 impf. In CKS, P142/5/1.

Headcorn 1638–57 impf., 1662–7 impf., 1672–1726. In CKS, P81/4/1–2.

Brookland 1643–90. In CKS, P49/4/1.

St Mildred, Canterbury 1650–1737. In Canterbury Cathedral L, U3/89/4/1.

Milton Regis 1652–94 impf. In CKS, P253/5/1.

Sandhurst 1652–93 impf. In CKS, P321/5/1.

Sellindge 1654–1706. In CKS, P329/5/1.

Bredgar 1660–96. In CKS, P43/5/1.

St Mary Northgate, Canterbury 1662–1716. In Canterbury Cathedral L, U3/103/4/1.

Benenden 1663–1744. In CKS, P20/5/1.

New Romney 1663–1711. In CKS, P309/4/1.

Swanscombe 1663–1736. In MAAO, P362/5/1.

Cobham 1663–1731. In MAAO, P85/5/1.

Birling 1663–1729. In MAAO, P29/5/1.

Kenardington 1664–1705. In CKS, P206/5/1.

Otham 1664–87. In CKS, P280/5/1.

Staplehurst 1665–1715. In CKS, P347/5/1.

St Clement, Sandwich 1667–1724. In Canterbury Cathedral L, U3/172/4/1.

Knockholt 1671–1825. In CKS, P214/5/1.

Dartford 1672–1714. In MAAO, P110/5/1.

Edenbridge 1679–1837. Ed. Granville Leveson-Gower, *Archaeologia Cantiana*, 21 (1895), 118–25.

LANCASHIRE

Prescot 1523–1607, 1663–98. Ed. to 1607 by F. Bailey, Lancashire and Cheshire Record Society (1953). Later portion in CRO, PR 2880/1.

CARTMEL 1597–1659, 1674–1812. In Cumbria (Kendal) RO, WPR/89/W1–2.

PADIHAM 1623–87. In CRO, PR 2863/2/1.

WHALLEY 1636–1709. In CRO, PR8.

CLITHEROE 1656–1802 impf. In CRO, PR 1962.

STANDISH 1679–1839. In CRO, MF 8/30.

CROSTON 1681–1709. In CRO, P249.

ASHTON UNDER LYME 1689–96 impf. In CRO, PR 2566.

LEICESTERSHIRE

ST MARY DE CASTRO, LEICESTER 1490–1, 1652–1729 impf. In CRO, 8D59/1/1–5, and 8D59/2.

ST MARTIN, LEICESTER 1544–1744. In CRO, DE 1564/1384, 1386. Ed. to 1562 by James Thompson, *History of Leicester* (1849), i. 237–9 and appendix J, and to 1571 by Thomas North, *A Chronicle of the Church of St Martin in Leicester* (1866).

MELTON MOWBRAY 1547–1612 impf. In CRO, DG 36/140/1–40.

HINCKLEY 1574–1620. In CRO, DE 1225/65.

LOUGHBOROUGH 1584–1684. In CRO, DE 667/62.

BELTON 1602–15. In CRO, DE 1965/41.

MARKET HARBOROUGH 1603–13. Ed. J. E. Stocks, *Market Harborough Parish Records* (Oxford, 1926), 36–48.

SHAWELL 1609–49 impf. In CRO, DE 734/6.

WALTHAM ON THE WOLDS 1609–1708 impf. In CRO, DE 625/18.

WIGSTON MAGNA 1615–60 impf., 1661–1704. In CRO, DE 384/36.

LYDDINGTON 1626–1824 impf. In CRO, DE 1881/41.

STATHERN 1631–77. In CRO, DE 1605/34–5.

GADDESBY 1652–1704. In CRO, DE 751/10–11.

MUSTON 1664–1728. In CRO, DE 830/32–3.

ASHBY FOLVILLE 1674–1729. In CRO, DE 960/23.

PECKLETON 1675–1704. In CRO, 19D 33/4.

ENDERBY 1675–1739. In CRO, DE 766/1.

ROTHERBY 1676–1743. In CRO, DE 4/1.

BREEDON ON THE HILL 1676–83 impf. In CRO, DE 2478/18.

BRANSTON 1677–1731. In CRO, DE 720/6.

EDMONDTHORPE 1677–1732. In CRO, DE 690/9.

THUREASTON 1680–91. In CRO, DE 625/18.

LINCOLNSHIRE

ST MARY, GRIMSBY 1411–12. Ed. E. E. Gillett, *Lincolnshire Architectural and Archaeological Society Reports and Papers*, 6 (1955–6), 27–36.

WIGTOFT 1484–7, 1499–1543. Extracts printed by John Nichols, *Illustrations of the Manners and Expenses of Antient Times* (1797), 196–229.

SUTTERTON 1490–1530 impf. In Bodleian L, Rawlinson MS D786. Ed. Edward Peacock, *Archaeological Journal*, 39 (1882), 53–63.

LEVERTON 1492–1619 impf. In CRO, 'Leverton 7/1'. Ed. Edward Peacock, *Archaeologia*, 41 (1867), 236–65.

ST JAMES, LOUTH 1500–24, 1528–54, 1560–1756. In CRO, 'Louth St James 7/1–5'. Ed. to 1524 by Reginald C. Dudding, *The First Churchwardens' Book of Louth* (Oxford, 1941).

INGOLDMELLS 1542–89. In CRO, 'Addlethorpe 10'.

LONG SUTTON 1543–73. In CRO, 'Long Sutton R7'.

WITHAM ON THE HILL 1550. In CRO, 'Witham on the Hill 7/1'.

KIRTON IN LINDSEY 1564–5, 1573–1677 impf. In CRO, 'Kirton in Lindsey 7/1'. Extracts ed. Edward Peacock, *Antiquary*, 14 (1889), 20.

SAXILBY 1565. In CRO, 'Saxilby 7/1'.

HECKINGTON 1568–1602. In CRO, 'Heckington 7/1'.

ADDLETHORPE 1571, 1655–1709 impf. In CRO 'Addlethorpe 7'.

ALVINGHAM 1574–83. In CRO, 'Alvingham 7/1'.

BROUGHTON BY BRIGG 1576–96 impf. In CRO, 'Broughton by Brigg 7/1'.

WADDINGTON 1600–2. In CRO, 'Waddington 10'.

ST BENEDICT, LINCOLN 1652–1712 impf. In CRO, 'Lincoln St Benedict 7/1'.

NORTH SOMERCOTES 1668–1820 impf. In CRO, 'North Somercotes 7'.

CARLBY 1677. In CRO, 'Carlby 7/1'.

SOUTH CARLTON 1685–1773. In CRO, 'South Carlton 7/1'.

LONDON

ST MARY AT HILL 1420–1559. Ed. Henry Littlehales, Early English Text Society (1905).

ST PETER WESTCHEAP 1441–1601 impf. 1601–1702. In Guildhall L, 645/1–2.

ST NICHOLAS IN SHAMBLES 1452–1546 v. impf. In St Bartholomew Hospital Archives, SNC 1, HA1/1.

ST ANDREW HUBBARD 1454–1550, 1552–1658. In Guildhall L, 1297/1–3. Ed. in *British Magazine*, 31–5 (1847–9).

ALL HALLOWS LONDON WALL 1455–1536, 1566–1745. In Guildhall L, 5090/1–3.

ST MICHAEL CORNHILL 1456–75, 1548–1608 impf., 1608–1702. In Guildhall L, 4071–2. Ed. to 1608 by William Henry Overall, *The Accounts of the Churchwardens of the Parish of St Michael, Cornhill* (1871).

ST BOTOLPH ALDERSGATE 1464–7, 1637–79. In Guildhall L, 1454, 1455/1.

ST MARTIN ORGAR 1471–2, 1574–1707 impf. In Guildhall L, 959/1.
1517–22. In Lambeth Palace L, CM ix/14.

ST STEPHEN WALBROOK 1474–1538, 1549–50, 1551–1738. In Guildhall L, 593/1–2, 4.

ST STEPHEN COLEMAN STREET 1486–1507, 1586–1640, 1656–85. In Guildhall L, 4457/1–3.

ALL HALLOWS STAINING 1491–1628, 1645–1706. In Guildhall L, 4956/1–3. Extracts in James Peller Malcolm, *Londinium Redivivum* (1802), ii. 21–2.

ST DUNSTAN IN THE EAST 1494–1509, 1635–1705. In Guildhall L, 4887, 7882/1–3.

ST MARGARET PATTENS 1506–25, 1548–53, 1555–1760. In Guildhall L, 4570/1–3.

St Martin Outwich 1509–45 impf., 1632–1743. In Guildhall L, 6842, 11394/1. Extracts 1509–45 in C. Goss, *Transactions of the London and Middlesex Archaeological Society* NS vi (1933).

St Michael le Querne 1514–48, 1549–1718. In Guildhall L, 2895/1–2.

St Dunstan in the West 1516–57, 1558–1700. In Guildhall L, 2968/1–6.

St Mary Magdalen Milk Street 1518–1606 impf., 1606–67. In Guildhall L, 2596/1–2.

St Alphage London Wall 1527–1722. In Guildhall L, 1432/1–5.

St Lawrence Pountney 1530–50, 1579–1681. In Guildhall L, 3907/1.

St Mary Woolnoth 1539–1641. In Guildhall L, 1002/1A–B.

Christ Church Newgate Street 1546–8. In St Bartholomew Hospital Archives, SNC/1.

St Andrew Holborn 1547–60. Extracts in Malcolm, *Londinium*, ii. 186–7. 1667–91. In Guildhall L, 19592 and 4250A.

St Botolph Aldgate 1547–85. In Guildhall L, 9235/1.

St Margaret Moses 1547–97, 1689–1761. In Guildhall L, 3476/1–2.

St Matthew Friday Street 1547–1643, 1650–1744. In Guildhall L, 1016/1–2. Ed. to 1603 by W. S. Simpson, *Journal of the Archaeological Association*, 25 (1869), 362–73.

St Benet Gracechurch 1548–1724. Guildhall L, 1568. Extracts in Malcolm, *Londinium*, i. 314–16.

St Pancras Soper Lane 1555. Extracts in Malcolm, *Londinium*, ii. 169.

St James Garlickhithe 1555–1699. In Guildhall L, 4810/1–2.

St Mary Woolchurch Haw 1560–1824. In Guildhall L, 1013/1–2.

Holy Trinity Minories 1566–97 impf. In Lambeth Palace L, MS 3390.

St Botolph Bishopsgate 1567–1662. In Guildhall L, 4524/1–2.

St Ethelburga Bishopsgate 1569–1729. In Guildhall L, 4241/1–2. Ed. C. B. Cobb, *The Church of St Ethelburga the Virgin within Bishopsgate* (1905).

St Mary Aldermanbury 1569–92, 1631–1737. In Guildhall L, 3556/1–3.

St Giles Cripplegate 1570–80, 1596–1607. In British L, Add. MS 12222. 1648–69. In Guildhall L, 6047/1.

St Andrew by the Wardrobe 1570–1704. In Guildhall L, 2088/1–2.

St Christopher le Stocks 1572–1685. Ed. Edwin Freshfield, *Accomptes of the Churchwardens of the Paryshe of St Christopher's in London 1572 to 1662* (1885), and *The Account Book of the Parish of St Christopher Le Stocks in the City of London 1662–1685* (1895).

St Antholin Budge Row 1574–1708. In Guildhall L, 1046/1.

St Bartholomew the Less 1575–1665. In St Bartholomew Hospital Archives, SBL 21/1–2.

St Margaret New Fish Street 1576–1754. In Guildhall L, 1176/1–2.

St Lawrence Jewry 1579–1698. In Guildhall L, 2593/1–2.

Holy Trinity the Less 1582–1725. In Guildhall L, 4835/1–2.

St Alban Wood Street 1584–1675. In Guildhall L, 7673/1–2.

St Mary Staining 1586–8, 1657–1718. In Guildhall L, 1542/1–2.

Sᴛ Oʟᴀᴠᴇ Jᴇᴡʀʏ 1586–1705. In Guildhall L, 4409/1–2.

Sᴛ Jᴏʜɴ Zᴀᴄʜᴀʀʏ 1591–1785 impf. Ed. W. Mc. Murray, *The Records of Two City Parishes* (1925).

Sᴛ Jᴏʜɴ Wᴀʟʙʀᴏᴏᴋ 1595–1728. In Guildhall L, 577/1–2.

Sᴛ Gᴇᴏʀɢᴇ Bᴏᴛᴏʟᴘʜ Lᴀɴᴇ 1596–1676 impf., 1676–1769. In Guildhall L, 951/1–2.

Sᴛ Bᴀʀᴛʜᴏʟᴏᴍᴇᴡ Exᴄʜᴀɴɢᴇ 1596–1698. Ed. Edwin Freshfield, *The Account Books of the Parish of St Bartholomew Exchange* (1895).

Sᴛ Sᴡɪᴛʜᴜɴ Lᴏɴᴅᴏɴ Sᴛᴏɴᴇ 1602–1725. In Guildhall L, 559/1.

Sᴛ Bᴏᴛᴏʟᴘʜ Bɪʟʟɪɴɢsɢᴀᴛᴇ 1603–1854. In Guildhall L, 942/1–2.

Sᴛ Bᴇɴᴇᴛ Pᴀᴜʟ's Wʜᴀʀꜰ 1605–57. In Guildhall L, 878/1.

Sᴛ Kᴀᴛʜᴇʀɪɴᴇ Cᴏʟᴇᴍᴀɴ 1609–36, 1641–2, 1646–1724. In Guildhall L, 1124/1–2.

Sᴛ Bᴇɴᴇᴛ Fɪɴᴋ 1610–99. In Guildhall L, 1303/1.

Sᴛ Tʜᴏᴍᴀs Aᴘᴏsᴛʟᴇ 1612–1779. In Guildhall L, 662/1.

Aʟʟ Hᴀʟʟᴏᴡs Hᴏɴᴇʏ Lᴀɴᴇ 1614–84. In Guildhall L, 5026/1.

Aʟʟ Hᴀʟʟᴏᴡs ᴛʜᴇ Gʀᴇᴀᴛ 1616–1708. In Guildhall L, 818/1.

Sᴛ Pᴀɴᴄʀᴀs Sᴏᴘᴇʀ Lᴀɴᴇ 1616–1740. In Guildhall L, 5018/1.

Sᴛ Mɪᴄʜᴀᴇʟ Cʀᴏᴏᴋᴇᴅ Lᴀɴᴇ 1617–93. In Guildhall L, 1188/1.

Sᴛ Mɪᴄʜᴀᴇʟ Bᴀssɪɴsʜᴀᴡ 1618–1716. In Guildhall L, 2601/1.

Sᴛ Mɪᴄʜᴀᴇʟ Wᴏᴏᴅ Sᴛʀᴇᴇᴛ 1619–1718. In Guildhall L, 524/1.

Sᴛ Dɪᴏɴɪs Bᴀᴄᴋᴄʜᴜʀᴄʜ 1625–1729. In Guildhall L, 4215/1.

Sᴛ Mɪᴄʜᴀᴇʟ Qᴜᴇᴇɴʜɪᴛʜᴇ 1625–1706. In Guildhall L, 4825/1.

Sᴛ Bᴀʀᴛʜᴏʟᴏᴍᴇᴡ ᴛʜᴇ Gʀᴇᴀᴛ 1629–93 impf. In Guildhall L, 3989/1.

Sᴛ Mᴀʀʏ Aʙᴄʜᴜʀᴄʜ 1629–92. In Guildhall L, 3891/1.

Sᴛ Oʟᴀᴠᴇ Sɪʟᴠᴇʀ Sᴛʀᴇᴇᴛ 1630–1719. In Guildhall L, 1257/1–2.

Sᴛ Aɴɴ ᴀɴᴅ Sᴛ Aɢɴᴇs 1636–87. In Guildhall L, 587/1–1A. Ed. McMurray, *Two City Parishes*.

Sᴛ Cʟᴇᴍᴇɴᴛ Eᴀsᴛᴄʜᴇᴀᴘ 1636–56, 1665–1740. In Guildhall L, 977/1.

Sᴛ Mᴀɢɴᴜs ᴛʜᴇ Mᴀʀᴛʏʀ 1638–1734. In Guildhall L, 1179/1.

Sᴛ Bʀɪᴅᴇ Fʟᴇᴇᴛ Sᴛʀᴇᴇᴛ 1641–1701. In Guildhall L, 6552/1–2.

Sᴛ Sᴇᴘᴜʟᴄʜʀᴇ Hᴏʟʙᴏʀɴ 1648–83. In Guildhall L, 3146/1–2.

Sᴛ Mᴀʀʏ Mᴀɢᴅᴀʟᴇɴ Fɪsʜ Sᴛʀᴇᴇᴛ 1648–1721. In Guildhall L, 1341/1.

Sᴛ Mɪʟᴅʀᴇᴅ Bʀᴇᴀᴅ Sᴛʀᴇᴇᴛ 1648–93. In Guildhall L, 3470/1A.

Sᴛ Mᴀʀᴛɪɴ Lᴜᴅɢᴀᴛᴇ 1649–90. In Guildhall L, 1313/1.

Sᴛ Kᴀᴛʜᴇʀɪɴᴇ Cʀᴇᴇ 1650–91. In Guildhall L, 1198/1.

Sᴛ Hᴇʟᴇɴ Bɪsʜᴏᴘsɢᴀᴛᴇ 1655–1715. In Guildhall L, 6844/1.

Sᴛ Pᴇᴛᴇʀ Cᴏʀɴʜɪʟʟ 1664–90. In Bodleian L, Rawlinson MS D897.

Sᴛ Nɪᴄʜᴏʟᴀs Aᴄᴏɴs 1675–1794. In Guildhall L, 4291/1.

Sᴛ Bᴇɴᴇᴛ Sʜᴇʀᴇʜᴏɢ 1675–1735. In Guildhall L, 838/1.

Sᴛ Aɴɴ Bʟᴀᴄᴋꜰʀɪᴀʀs 1676–94 impf. In Guildhall L, 1061/1–13.

Aʟʟ Hᴀʟʟᴏᴡs Bʀᴇᴀᴅ Sᴛʀᴇᴇᴛ 1678–99. In Guildhall L, 5038/1.

MERIONETHSHIRE

Lʟᴀɴꜰɪʜᴀɴɢᴇʟ ʏ Tʀᴀᴇᴛʜᴀᴜ 1686–1766. National Library of Wales, MS 9046C.

MIDDLESEX

EAST BEDFONT 1593–1629. In Greater London RO, DRO 84/35.

CHELSEA 1594–1670. Extracts in Daniel Lysons, *The Environs of London* (1792), ii. 145.

LALEHAM 1610–22, 1665–83. In Greater London RO, DRO 21/29/1.

BRENTFORD 1621–40. Extracts in Lysons, ii. 54–5.

PINNER 1622–1757 impf. In Greater London RO, X56/5.

FULHAM 1637–51, 1665–70. In Shepherd's Bush Public L.

ISLEWORTH 1649–90. In Hounslow Local History Centre.

HAMPTON 1654–1704. In Greater London RO, Acc. 333/1/1.

STAINES 1658–81 impf. In Greater London RO, DRO2/B2/1.

HAMPSTEAD 1671–1710 impf. In Greater London RO, P81/JN1/1A.

NORFOLK

EAST DEREHAM 1413–71 v. impf., 1478–98 impf., 1597–1692 impf. In CRO, Phi/461, 607–10.

TILNEY ALL SAINTS 1443–1589 impf. In CRO, Bradfer-Lawrence II (e).

ST NICHOLAS, GREAT YARMOUTH 1465. Extracts in Henry Swinden, *The History of . . . Great Yarmouth* (Norwich, 1777), 810–11. 1576–1728. In CRO, Y/C39/1–3.

SNETTISHAM 1468–1546 whole but impf., 1550–79 receipts only, 1579–81 whole. In CRO, PD 24/1 (S).

SWAFFHAM 1505–94, 1627–53. In CRO, PD 52/71–2.

DENTON 1507–38, 1608–39. In CRO, PD 136/56–7.

SHIPDAM 1511–79, 1581–1634, 1636–63 v. impf., 1676–1710. In CRO, PD 337/85–8.

GREAT WITCHINGHAM 1528–56 receipts only, 1556–62, 1569–71, 1596–1627, 1656–1837 impf. In CRO, PD91/21 (S).

NORTH ELMHAM 1538–69 impf., 1586–1627. In CRO, PD 209/153–4. Ed. A. G. Legge (Norwich, 1891).

WYMONDHAM 1544–6. Kept in church vestry.

LODDON 1554–7, 1565, 1595–1739. In CRO, PD 595/19.

ST MARGARET, NORWICH 1563–98. In CRO, PD 153/42.

PULHAM MARKET 1563–90, 1595–1620. In CRO, D/N/PRG/14.

NORTH WALSINGHAM 1580–1643. In CRO, MF/RO 461/4.

ST PETER MANCROFT, NORWICH 1580–1704. In CRO, PD 26/71–2.

BRESSINGHAM 1581–94, 1600–1905. In CRO, PD 111/69–70.

DITCHINGHAM 1581–1600, 1681–1759. In CRO, PD 301/45–6.

HARDWICK 1584, 1635, 1644, 1686–98 impf. In CRO, PD 437/14.

ST MARY COSLANY, NORWICH 1586–1657. In CRO, COL 3/4 T130A.

ST LAURENCE, NORWICH 1590–6, 1603–1736 impf. In CRO, PD 58/38 (S).

FERSFIELD 1606–76 impf. In CRO, PD 144/43.

EAST HARLING 1610–29 impf., 1629–51 impf., 1663–1736 impf. In CRO, PD 219/27.

ST BENEDICT, NORWICH 1613–1891. In CRO, PD 191/23.

CAWSTON 1615–16, 1679–81. In CRO, MC 254/2/7 and PD 193/79.

GREAT RYBURGH 1619–36 impf. In CRO, PD 621/51.

HILGAY 1619–39 impf. In CRO, PD 382/29.

BANHAM 1621–1726. In CRO, PD 155/15.

ST SAVIOUR, NORWICH 1623. In CRO, Accn. 11. 9. 70. (R.154 D).

CARLETON RODE 1625–7, 1667, 1672, 1678–1836. In CRO, PD 254/63–4.

BALE 1632–1763. In CRO, Accn. Store 9. 2. 70. (R. 155 D).

BESTHORPE 1635–49 impf., 1672–1724 impf. In CRO, PD 309/34.

SAHAM TONEY 1636–7. In CRO, PD 566/56.

AYLSHAM 1637–1848 impf. In CRO, PD 602/70.

GISSING 1640–88. In CRO, PD 50/37.

HEYDON 1654–85 impf. In CRO, PD 435/19.

BERGH APTON 1660–81. In CRO, PD 497/25 (S).

GARBOLDISHAM 1660–1788. In CRO, PD 197/64.

BACONSTHORPE 1663–1713. In CRO, NRS 21142/45/A1.

HOUGHTON NEXT HARPLEY 1663–1727 impf. In CRO, PD 413/12.

ST JOHN DE SEPULCHRE, NORWICH 1664, 1673, 1685–1712. In CRO, PD 90/09 (S).

BLICKLING 1667–1786 impf. In CRO, PD 434/10.

HOCKWOLD 1669–1895 impf. In CRO, PD 311/16.

TUNSTEAD 1672–1725. In CRO, PD 285/38.

FORNCETT ST PETER 1672–84, 1691–2. In CRO, PD 421/58 (S).

WILTON 1674–1861 impf. In CRO, PD 311/26.

ST GEORGE COLEGATE, NORWICH 1678–1716. In CRO, PD 7/37.

FELMINGHAM 1679–1788. In CRO, PD 399/11.

EAST RUSTON 1682–1844. In CRO, PD 38/20.

TOPCROFT 1683–1824. In CRO, PD 389/41.

DISS 1686–1713. In CRO, PD 100/62.

WITTON 1688–1720. In CRO, PD 70/32.

SPARHAM 1689–1770. In CRO, MC 217/1.

NORTHAMPTONSHIRE

ST JOHN, PETERBOROUGH 1467–1546, 1554–73. Ed. in W. T. Mallows, *Peterborough Local Administration* (Northamptonshire Record Office, 1939), 1–169.

CULWORTH 1531–1607 impf., 1653–1742. In CRO, 94P/21–3.

NORTON BY DAVENTRY 1549–80 impf. In CRO, 243P/209.

BURTON LATIMER 1559–70, 1608–45. In CRO, 55P/55–9.

BRINGTON 1600–79. In CRO, 49P/GB1d.

MARSTON TRUSSELL 1607–1704 impf. In CRO, 206P/64.

ASTON LE WALLS 1629–1709. In CRO, 19P/1.

IRCHESTER 1629–33. In CRO, 177P/Ir/1.

BYFIELD 1635–7. In CRO, 56P/42.

BRAWNSTON 1656–1787. In CRO, 46P/35.

WAPPENHAM 1657–75 impf. In CRO, 339P/19.

EYDON 1663–79. In CRO, 120P/46.

UFFORD 1663–88. In CRO, 331P/12.

RADSTONE 1676–85, 1689–1771. In CRO, 277P/7.

NORTHUMBERLAND

HEDDON ON THE WALL 1671–85. In CRO, EP 37/23.

CORBRIDGE 1676–81. In CRO, EP 57/125.

BYWELL ST PETER 1683–1711, impf. In CRO, EP 45/16.

NOTTINGHAMSHIRE

WORKSOP 1546, 1552–1750 impf. In CRO, PR 22765–6.

HOLME PIERREPOINT receipts only 1552, 1560, 1566–1667 impf., whole 1667–1722. In CRO, PR 547.

UPTON 1600–44. In CRO, PR 1709.

CODDINGTON 1631–1754 impf. In CRO PR 1517.

OLLERTON 1638. In CRO, PR 240.

ELKESLEY 1674–1804 impf. In CRO, PR 190.

ROLLESTON 1681. In CRO, PR 778.

STAUNTON 1681–5. In CRO, PR 1091.

NORWELL 1685–1881 impf. In CRO, PR 965.

OXFORDSHIRE

ST MARY MAGDALEN, OXFORD 1404, 1562. In CRO, Par Oxford St Mary Magdalen c. 64, d. 8.

ST MICHAEL, OXFORD 1404–1600 impf., 1601–99. In CRO, Par Oxford St Michael a. 1–4. Ed. to 1600 by E. W. Weaver, Oxfordshire Archaeological Society (1933).

ST ALDATE, OXFORD 1440, 1520–1732 impf. In CRO, Par Oxford St Aldate b. 17–19, c. 15.

ST PETER IN THE EAST 1440, 1482–1639 impf., 1640–1733. In CRO, Par Oxford St Peter in the East a. 1–2, c. 1, d. 1.

THAME 1442–1665. Ed. to 1524 by J. P. Ellis, *Berks, Bucks and Oxon Archaeological Journal*, 7–20 (1901–15). Survive from 1455 in CRO, Par Thame b. 2.

ST MARY THE VIRGIN, OXFORD 1509–1833 impf. In CRO, Par Oxford St Mary the Virgin c. 33.

HENLEY 1521–30. Ed. P. Briers, Oxfordshire Record Society (1960).

SPELSBURY 1526–33. In CRO, MS DD Spelsbury d. 5. Ed. F. Weaver and G. Clark, Oxfordshire Record Society (1925).

MARSTON 1529–53, 1557–1632, 1669–1732. In CRO, MS DD Marston b. 7, c. 2. Ed. to 1570 by Weaver and Clark.

ST MARTIN, OXFORD 1544–1680, 1682–98. In CRO, Par Oxford St Martin a. 1–2.

PYRTON 1548–1880. In CRO, MS DD Pyrton b. 1, c. 1. Ed. to 1613 by Weaver and Clark.

SOUTH NEWINGTON 1553–1684. Ed. E. Brinkworth, Banbury Historical Society (1964).

ALL SAINTS, OXFORD 1606, 1692–1713. In CRO, Par Oxford All Saints a. 1.

ODDINGTON 1609, 1626–50. In CRO, MS DD Par Oddington e. 3.

YARNTON 1610–1740. In CRO, MS DD Par Yarnton b. 7.

LANGFORD 1626–1750 impf. In CRO, MS DD Par Langford c. 2.

EYNSHAM 1640–65. In CRO, MS DD Par Eynsham b. 12.

ST CROSS, OXFORD 1652–67. In CRO, Par Oxford St Cross e. 6.

GREAT HASELEY 1668–1773. In CRO, MS DD Par Great Haseley b. 7.

SHIPLAKE 1677–1714. In CRO, MS DD Par Shiplake c. 6.

EWELME 1681–1768. In CRO, MS DD Par Ewelme b. 7.

AMBROSDEN 1686–1759. In CRO, MS DD Par Ambrosden b. 7.

PEMBROKESHIRE

CAREW 1622–9, 1667–1776. In Dyfed (Haverfordwest) RO, HPR/68/33.

RADNORSHIRE

CEFNLLYS 1684–1764. In National Library of Wales, MS 3555F.

RUTLAND

UPPINGHAM 1633–88 impf. In Leicestershire CRO, DE 1784/17.

MORCOTT 1686–1773. In Leicestershire CRO, DE 2876/16/1–11.

SHROPSHIRE

LUDLOW 1469–71. Ed. L. Jones, *Transactions of the Shropshire Archaeological and Natural History Society*, 2nd ser. 1 (1889), 236–50.

1540–1600. Ed. T. Wright, Camden Society (1869).

1608–1702. In CRO, 2881/2/1.

WORFIELD 1500–36. Ed. H. Walters, *Transactions of the Shropshire Archaeological and Natural History Society*, 3rd ser. 3–9 (1903–9).

1541–56, 1558–60, 1561–1645. Ed. Walters. Survive in CRO, 1374/48.

1649–1722. In Glamorgan CRO (Cardiff), MS 4/888.

CHESWARDINE 1544–8, 1564–1628. In CRO, 4728/ChW/1.

ST MARY, SHREWSBURY 1550–1626 impf., 1627–55 v. impf. In CRO, 1041/Ch/1–2.

CONDOVER 1577–97, 1604–89. In CRO, 1977/4/1–5.

ST OSWALD, SHREWSBURY 1579–1616 impf. In CRO, 3965/Ch/1–2.

CHETTON 1599–1743. In Shrewsbury Local Studies L, MS 4387.

KENLEY 1600–80 impf. In CRO, 2310/1.

ALBRIGHTON 1608–37 impf. In CRO, 1379/CW/1.

WHITCHURCH 1619–70, 1688–1712. In CRO, 3091/3/1–4.

COUND 1625–47, 1683–1811. In CRO, 790/1, and 1250/1.

DONNINGTON 1629–40, 1650–83, 1697. In CRO, 3793/1.

TONG 1630–80. In CRO, 3848/CW/1.

ST JULIAN, SHREWSBURY 1632–93 impf. In 2711/Ch/1.

SHAWBURY 1633–1711. In CRO 2959/4/1–2.

MADELEY 1641–51, 1662–1712. In CRO, 2280/6/1a.

MORE 1651–64 impf., 1665–1713. In CRO, 1053/Ch/1–2.
CHURCH PULVERBATCH 1653–1707. In CRO, 3416/3/1/1–2.
ALDERBURY 1656–77 impf., 1679–1702. In CRO, 4369/ChA/1–2.
ST LEONARD, BRIDGNORTH 1656–99 impf. In CRO, 3662/Ch/1.
WROXETER 1658–1716. In CRO, 2656/18–19.
MUNSLOW 1661–1709. In CRO, 1705/43.
CHETWYND 1662–1722. In CRO, 2151/24.
HUGHLEY 1665–1784. In CRO, 3903/Ch/1.
EDGMOUND 1672–1754. In CRO, 4227/Ch/2.
WEM 1683–1739. In CRO, 4351/ChA/1.
ELLESMERE 1685–1726. In CRO, 3372/Ch/1.
LYDHAM 1686–8. In CRO, 2958/8.

SOMERSET

BRIDGWATER 1318–1549 v. impf. In CRO, D/B/bw.
ST MICHAEL, BATH 1349, 1420–1546 v. impf., 1547–63 impf. Ed. C. B. Pearson, *Somersetshire Archaeological and Natural History Society Proceedings*, 23–4 (1877–8).
ST JOHN, GLASTONBURY 1366–1650 v. impf. In CRO, D/P/gla. j. 4/1.
TINTINHULL 1434–1543 impf., 1582–1678. In CRO, D/P/tin/4/1/1–2. Ed. to 1543 by Bishop Hobhouse, Somerset Record Society (1890).
YATTON 1445–1559, 1583–1604. In CRO, D/P/yat/1/1/1–4. Ed. to 1559 by Hobhouse.
CROSCOMBE 1474–1539, 1545–8. Ed. Hobhouse; originals lost.
PILTON 1498–1530, 1626–41. In CRO, D/P/pilt/4/1/1, 3. Ed. Hobhouse.
STOGURSEY 1502–46. In CRO, D/P/stogs/4/1/1. Extracts in Historical Manuscripts Commission 6th Report, appendix pp. 348–9.
NETTLECOMBE 1507–46. In CRO, DD/WO/BOX 49/1.
BANWELL 1515–1602, 1607–51, 1688–1779. In CRO, D/P/ban/4/1/1–3.
HALSE 1540–55, 1627–36. In CRO, D/P/hal/4/1/1, 4.
ILMINSTER 1543–9, 1567–1608, 1632–72. In CRO, D/P/ilm/4/1/1.
GOATHURST 1545, 1553–4. In CRO, D/P/gst/4/4/1.
LANGFORD BUDVILLE 1550–1610 impf., 1612–35, 1637–1714. In CRO, D/P/lanf/4/1/1–3, 6.
LYDEARD ST LAWRENCE 1550–9. In CRO, D/P/1. st. 1./4/1/1.
WINSFORD 1552–74 v. impf. In CRO, D/P/wins/4/1/1.
FROME 1567–8. In CRO, DD/LW/35.
AXBRIDGE 1570–1670. In CRO, D/P/ax/4/1/1.
LANGPORT 1577–1618 impf. In CRO, D/P/langp/4/1/1.
SOMERTON 1581–1729. In CRO, D/P/som/4/1/1–2.
CHARLTON MUSGRAVE 1584–1649 impf. In CRO, D/P/ch. mu./4/1/1.
STAPLEGROVE 1585–1623. In British L, Add. MS 30278.
BISHOPS' HULL 1590–1615 impf. In CRO, D/P/b.hl./4/1/1.
WILLITON 1590–1713. In CRO, DD/WY/37/1.
SOUTH CADBURY 1593–1810 impf. In CRO, D/P/cad.j./4/1/1.
EAST QUANTOXHEAD 1602–98. In CRO, D/P/qua.e./4/1/1–3.

BURRINGTON 1605–84, impf., 1686–1735 impf. In CRO, D/P/bur/4/1/1.

MONKSILVER 1610–51, 1660–88, 1691–1767. In CRO, D/P/mon/4/1/1–3.

WELLINGTON 1611–37, 1652–82. In CRO, D/P/wel/4/1/3–4.

CHEDDAR 1612–74. In CRO, DD/SAS SE14.

GOATHURST 1615–38 impf. In CRO, D/P/gst/4/4/1.

SHEPTON MALLET 1617–1704. In CRO, D/P/she/4/1/1.

THORNE COFFIN 1622–53 impf. In CRO, D/P/th.co./4/1/1–2.

CREWKERNE 1625–1700 impf. In CRO, D/P/crew/4/1/1.

NORTH PETHERTON 1626–33, 1664–1734. In CRO, T/PH/Dev 5, and D/P/pet.n./4/1/1–2.

RODE 1627–35, 1664. In CRO, D/P/rode/4/1/1.

SWAINSWICK 1631–1712. In CRO, D/P/swk/4/1/1.

LOCKING 1633–83 impf. In CRO, D/P/lock/4/1/1.

DURSTON 1633–1719. In CRO, D/P/durn/4/1/1.

HINTON ST GEORGE 1633–73. In CRO, D/P/hin.g./4/1/1–2.

KILTON 1634–6, 1675–1736. In CRO, D/P/kln/4/1/1–2.

MINEHEAD 1637–94. In CRO, D/P/m.s.m./4/1/1.

CHURCHILL 1639–76. In CRO, D/P/chl/4/1/1.

NORTH WOTTON 1645–87. In CRO, D/P/n.wo./4/1/1.

ST CUTHBERT, WELLS 1649–1729. In CRO, D/P/w.st.c./4/1/1–2.

CHARLINCH 1650–3. In CRO, DD/SAS/HV/34.

STOCKLAND BRISTOL 1652–1732. In CRO, D/P/stoc.b./4/1/1–2.

MISTERTON 1657–1782. In CRO, D/P/mis/4/1/1–2.

SEAVINGTON ST MICHAEL 1659–1706. In CRO, D/P/sea.ml./4/1/1.

LUCCOMBE 1659–1701. In CRO, D/P/luc/4/1/1.

WEST PENNARD 1660–1776. In CRO, D/P/w.pen./4/1/1.

WESTON ZOYLAND 1662–99. In CRO, D/P/w.zoy./4/1/1.

CREECH ST MICHAEL 1663–93. In CRO, D/P/crch/4/1/1.

PUXTON 1665–1754 impf. In CRO, D/P/pux/4/1/1.

PITMINSTER 1668–1731. In CRO, D/P/pit/4/1/1.

BATCOMBE 1669–1702. In CRO, D/P/bat/4/1/1.

CHILTHORNE DORMER 1671–1712 impf. In CRO, D/P/chi.dom./13/2/2.

WEST BUCKLAND 1672–1748. In CRO, D/P/w.bu./4/1/1.

BATHEALTON 1672–3, 1698–1754. In CRO, D/P/bal/4/1/1.

MIDDLEZOY 1672–1728. In CRO, D/P/m.zoy./4/1/1.

CURRY RIVEL 1673–1726. In CRO, D/P/curr/4/1/1.

BUTLEIGH 1673–1766. In CRO, D/P/butl/4/1/1.

FIDDINGTON 1674–7. In CRO, D/P/fid/4/1/1.

FARRINGTON GURNEY 1676–1799. In CRO, D/P/far.g./4/1/1.

EAST BRENT 1677–92 impf. In CRO, D/P/brnt.e./4/1/1.

LYNG 1679–1747. In CRO, D/P/lyn/4/1/1.

TIMBERSCOMBE 1680–1807. In CRO, D/P/timb/4/1/1.

WIVELSCOMBE 1681–1741. In CRO, D/P/wiv/4/1/1.

BADGWORTH 1681–1779 impf. In CRO, D/P/badg/4/1/2.

LOVINGTON 1681–1757. In CRO, D/P/lov/4/1/1.

MORLINCH 1682–1703. In CRO, D/P/mor/4/1/1.

STREET 1684–1770. In CRO, D/P/str/4/1/1.

WAYFORD 1684–1894. In CRO, D/P/wa/4/1/1.

BACKWELL 1685, 1698–1701. In CRO, D/P/back/4/1/1.

THORNFALCON 1686–1774 impf. In CRO, D/P/th.f./4/1/1.

NORTON ST PHILIP 1686–1752. In CRO, D/P/n.ph./4/1/1.

STAFFORDSHIRE

WALSALL 1462–1531. Ed. G. P. Mander, *Collections for a History of Staffordshire*, 52 (1928), 175–267.

ST MARY, STAFFORD 1528–9. In William Salt L, Stafford, Salt MS 366(1). 1612–44. In CRO, D1323/E/1.

YOXALL 1541–9. In CRO, D1851/1/13/20.

PATTINGHAM 1583–1646, 1652–92. In CRO, D345/2/2–3.

ST PETER, STOKE ON TRENT 1589–1703 impf. In William Salt L, Stafford, 13–14/46.

BIDDULPH 1609–1703. In CRO, D3539/3/1.

CHECKLEY 1628–69 impf., 1671–93. In CRO, D113/A/PC/1–2.

HANBURY 1634–1714. In CRO, D1528/4/1.

ST MICHAEL, STONE 1634–81. In CRO, D4605/2/1.

BETLEY 1635–1706 impf. In CRO, 689/PC/1/1.

MAVESYN RIDWARE 1643–97. In CRO, D3712/4/1.

KINGSLEY 1648–56, 1662–74. In CRO, D124/A/PC/1–2.

BLITHFIELD 1663. In CRO, D1386/2/1/4.

GNOSALL 1669–1724. In CRO, D951/3/1.

ALREWAS 1673–1748 impf. In CRO, D783/2/1/1.

NORBURY 1681–1755. In CRO, D1718/4.

MADELEY 1683–1731 impf. In CRO, D3412/3/1.

ASHLEY 1685–1753. In CRO, D44/A/PC/1.

SUFFOLK

MILDENHALL 1446–54, 1504–53 impf., 1578–1661, 1661–70 impf. In West Suffolk RO, EL 110/5/1, 3, 5, 7.

WALBERSWICK 1450–99, 1583–1700 impf. In East Suffolk RO, FC 185/E1/1–2.

BRUNDISH 1475–1542. In East Suffolk RO, FC 89/A2/1.

METFIELD 1486–1702 impf. In East Suffolk RO, FC 91/E5.

CRATFIELD 1490–1560. Ed. John James Raven, *Cratfield* (1895). Section 1533–60 survives in East Suffolk RO, FC 62/E1/3.

ST MARY, BUNGAY 1523–1800. In Lowestoft RO, 116/E1/1.

BARDWELL 1524–31. Ed. F. E. Warren, *Proceedings of the Suffolk Institute of Archaeology*, 11 (1903), 112.

BOXFORD 1530–96 impf., 1608–96. Tudor section ed. Peter Norteast, Suffolk Records

Society 23 (1982). All in West Suffolk RO, FB 77/E2/2–3.

HORHAM 1531, 1601–35 impf. In East Suffolk RO, FC 85/E1/2–3.

MICKFIELD 1538–48. In East Suffolk RO, FB 19/E4/2.

DENNINGTON 1539–40, 1568–1697 impf. In East Suffolk RO, FC 112/E1/1.

LONG MELFORD 1547–57, 1561–3, 1575–81. In West Suffolk RO, FL 509/1/15.

MENDLESHAM 1552, 1572–1693 impf. In East Suffolk RO, FB 159/E7/1–108.

FRAMLINGHAM 1557–1671 v. impf. In East Suffolk RO, FC 101/E2/1–39.

HOLY TRINITY, BUNGAY 1558–1613. In Lowestoft RO, 115/E1/1.

MONK SOHAM 1565. In East Suffolk RO, FC 98/A1/1.

EARL SOHAM 1570–1643 impf. In East Suffolk RO, FC 119/E1/1.

WATTISFIELD 1573–1607. In West Suffolk RO, FL 668/519.

ST MATTHEW, IPSWICH 1573–1636. In East Suffolk RO, FB 95/A2/1.

ST MARGARET, SOUTH ELMHAM 1586–1685 v. impf. In Lowestoft RO, 150/E1/1–21.

STRADBROKE 1588–98, 1631–6, 1649–95. In East Suffolk RO, FC 83/E1/1.

EXNING 1590–1620. In West Suffolk RO, FL 567/5/1.

ST MARY, WOODBRIDGE 1593–1693. In East Suffolk RO, FC 25/E1/1.

ST CLEMENT, IPSWICH 1594–1642. In East Suffolk RO, FB 98/E3/1.

GISLINGHAM 1595–1699 v. impf. In East Suffolk RO, FB 130/E3/1–43.

STONHAM ASPEL 1598–1686. In East Suffolk RO, FB 22/E1/1.

WEYBREAD 1599–1738. In East Suffolk RO, FC 99/E1/1.

CRETINGHAM 1602–56 impf., 1657–89. In East Suffolk RO, FB 51/E2/1–2.

MELLIS 1611–28. In East Suffolk RO, FB 123/E1/1.

CLARE 1613. In West Suffolk RO, FL 501/5/1.

LAXFIELD 1613–27 impf. In East Suffolk RO, FC 80/E4/1–3.

ST MARY TOWER, IPSWICH 1614–55, 1663–1744 impf. In East Suffolk RO, FB 91/E1/1, and 91/A1/2.

EARL STONEHAM 1621–1708. In East Suffolk RO, FB 23/E1/1A–B.

GREAT BARTON 1622. In West Suffolk RO, E9/4/1.

RUMBURGH 1623–83 impf. In Lowestoft RO, 141/E2/3–27.

THWAITE 1627–32. In East Suffolk RO, FB 153/E1/1.

SUDBOURNE 1631. In East Suffolk RO, FC 169/A1/1.

PEASENHALL 1634–1717. In East Suffolk RO, FC 67/E1/1.

BREDFIELD 1640–67, 1697–1757. In East Suffolk RO, FC 27/E1/1.

WESTLETON 1644–1724 impf. In East Suffolk RO, FC 63/E1/1.

WILBY 1646–7, 1657–8, 1685–6. In East Suffolk RO, FC 88/E2/1–3.

WALSHAM LE WILLOWS 1646–1709. In West Suffolk RO, FL 646/5/1.

WICKHAM MARKET 1652–63. In East Suffolk RO, FC 103/A1/1.

CHEDISTON 1653. In East Suffolk RO, FC 191/E1/1.

COTTON 1653–74 impf. In East Suffolk RO, FB 161/E1/3.

IXWORTH 1656–9, 1661–84, 1686–7. In West Suffolk RO, FL 505/5/1.

MONKS ELEIGH 1657–8, 1662–1742 impf. In West Suffolk RO, EL 111/1/1.

MELTON 1657–1758. In East Suffolk RO, FC 30/E1/1.

KETTLEBURGH 1659–79. In East Suffolk RO, FC 109/E1/1.

GREAT FINBOROUGH 1659. In East Suffolk RO, FB 212/A1/1.

HUNTINGFIELD 1660–90. In East Suffolk RO, FC 57/E1/1.

THEBERTON 1662–74. In East Suffolk RO, FC 70/A2/1.

DALLINGHOO 1662–80, 1690–1826. In East Suffolk RO, FC 115/E1/1.

BURGATE 1663–87. In East Suffolk RO, FB 136/E4/1.

WORLINGHAM 1663–4, 1672, 1696–7. In Lowestoft RO, 167/A2/1.

PAKENHAM 1668. In West Suffolk RO, FL 614/5/1.

GLEMSFORD 1670–1711 impf. In West Suffolk RO, FL 575/1/1.

COOKLEY 1672–1723. In East Suffolk RO, FC 58/E1/1.

HEVENINGHAM 1674–9, 1694–1775. In East Suffolk RO, FC 68/E1/1.

LANGHAM 1674–1760. In West Suffolk RO, FL 599/5/2.

STANSFIELD 1680–1785. In West Suffolk RO, FL 627/1/2.

ERWASTON 1680–1730. In East Suffolk RO, FB 185/A1/1.

ST JAMES, SOUTH ELMHAM 1688–1704. In Lowestoft RO, 149/E1/1.

SURREY

ST MARGARET, SOUTHWARK 1444–55. Ed. J. Collier, *British Magazine*, 32 (1847), 481–7.

KINGSTON UPON THAMES 1497–1538, 1567–1681, 1684–1708 impf. In Kingston upon Thames RO, KG/2/1–4. Extracts printed in Historical Manuscripts Commission 3rd Report, appendix pp. 331–2.

LAMBETH 1504–22, 1554–7, 1565–1642. Ed. C. Drew, Surrey Record Society (1940–3).

HORLEY 1507–9, 1542. In British L, Add. MS 6173.

WANDSWORTH 1545–1640, 1646–1742. In Greater London RO, P95/NIC/94–5. Ed. C. Davis, *Surrey Archaeological Collections*, 15–17 (1900–2).

BLETCHINGLEY 1546–52. In Folger Shakespeare L, Washington DC, MS b. 84–5. Ed. T. Craib, *Surrey Archaeological Collections*, 29 (1916).

ST SAVIOUR, SOUTHWARK 1552–3. In Greater London RO, P92/SAV/591.

BATTERSEA 1559–1603, 1604–45, 1646–67. Ed. John George Taylor, *Our Lady of Batersey* (1925).

COBHAM 1588–1601, 1629–31. In Guildford RO, PSH/COB/5/1.

SEALE 1588–1641 impf., 1651–1723. In Guildford RO, PSH/SEA/2/1. Extracts ed. William Henry Hart, *Surrey Archaeological Collections*, 2 (1864), 27–43.

ELSTEAD 1591–3, 1600–4. In Guildford RO, PSH/EL/6/1. 1652. Ed. W. H. Hart, *Surrey Archaeological Collections*, 2 (1864), 27–43.

HORSELL 1600–1748. In Guildford RO, PSH/HORS/7/1.

WEYBRIDGE 1622–3, 1653–75, 1697–1701. In Kingston upon Thames RO, 2384/3/1. Ed. Eleanor Lloyd, *Surrey Archaeological Collections*, xxi (1908), 130–64.

MORTLAKE 1652–1709. In Kingston upon Thames RO, 2397/3/1.

BERMONDSEY 1671–1752. In Greater London RO, P71/TMS/1.

CAMBERWELL 1671–1720 impf. In Greater London RO, X15/19.

SUSSEX

ARLINGTON 1455–79. In British L, Add. MS 33192.

COWFOLD 1460–85, 1636–1718 impf. In West Sussex RO, Par 59/9/1–2.

ROTHERFIELD 1509–1675 impf. In East Sussex RO, Par 465/10/3/1. Ed. Canon Goodwyn, *Sussex Archaeological Collections*, 41 (1898), 29–48.

WEST TARRING 1515–96 impf. Ed. W. J. Pressy, *The Churchwardens' Accounts of West Tarring* (1934).

STEYNING 1519–22. Ed. T. Medland, *Sussex Archaeological Collections*, 8 (1855), 133–4.

BILLINGHURST 1520–45 impf., 1550–1639 impf. In West Sussex RO, Par 21/9/1.

ASHURST 1522–47 impf., 1553. In West Sussex RO, Par 11/9/1.

WORTH 1528–46, 1550–4, 1560–3. In West Sussex RO, Par 516/9/1.

BOLNEY 1536–40. Ed. J. Dale, *Sussex Archaeological Collections*, 6 (1853), 244–50.

ST ANDREW, LEWES 1542–6. Ed. H. M. Whitley, *Sussex Archaeological Collections*, 14 (1902), 41–50.

ST ANDREW AND ST MICHAEL, LEWES 1546–9, 1552–4, 1559, 1601–66 impf. In East Sussex RO, Par 414/a/1a–c. Ed. Whitley, 50–7.

RYE 1546–60. In East Sussex RO, Rye Corporation Records 147/1.

BREDE 1546–56. In East Sussex RO, Par 253/9/1.

SOUTHOVER 1560–1. Ed. W. Hudson, *Sussex Archaeological Collections*, 48 (1905), 22.

ALL SAINTS, HASTINGS 1572–89. Ed. Thomas Ross, *Sussex Archaeological Collections*, 23 (1871), 99–117.

LINDFIELD 1580–1610, 1666–1723 impf. In West Sussex RO, Par 416/9/1.

SLINFOLD 1585–1616. In West Sussex RO, Par 176/12/1.

HELLINGLY 1592–1600 impf. In East Sussex RO, Par 375/12/1.

TILLINGTON 1602–78 impf. In West Sussex RO, Par 516/9/1.

ASHBURNHAM 1607. In East Sussex RO, Par 233/9/1.

HORSHAM 1610–1770 impf. In West Sussex RO, Par 106/9/1.

WEST CHILTINGTON 1613–1705 impf. In West Sussex RO, Par 48/9/1.

ST THOMAS AT CLIFFE, LEWES 1622–1704. In East Sussex RO, Par 415/9/1a.

CUCKFIELD 1633–42, 1670–1, 1693–1701. In West Sussex RO, Par 301/9/1.

HENFIELD 1645–1755 impf. In West Sussex RO, Par 100/9/1.

CHIDDINGLEY 1662. In East Sussex RO, Par 292/9/1.

BURWASH 1674–1740. In East Sussex RO, par 284/9/1.

BERWICK 1679–1743 impf. In East Sussex RO, Par 239/9/1.

ST PETER THE LESS, CHICHESTER 1684–1757. In West Sussex RO, Par 45/8/1. Extracts ed. F. H. Arnold, *Sussex Archaeological Collections*, 44 (1901), 161–77.

HURSTPIERPOINT 1685–1755 impf. In West Sussex RO, Par 400/9/1–28.

WARWICKSHIRE

SOLIHULL 1534–43, 1662–76. In CRO, DRB 64/63–4.

ST NICHOLAS, WARWICK 1547–1768. In CRO, DRB 87/1–2.

ROWINGTON 1554–89. Ed. J. W. Ryland, *Records of Rowington* (Oxford, 1922), ii.

GREAT PACKINGTON 1557–1631. In CRO, DR 158/19.

HOLY TRINITY, COVENTRY 1559–1619. In CRO, DR 581/45, 801/13.

KINGSBURY 1572–87, 1662. In CRO, DR (B) 3/38.

BIDEFORD 1582–97. In CRO, DR 602/40.

SOUTHAM 1582–1647 impf. In CRO, DR 50/9.

SHIPSTON 1593–1617. In CRO, DR 446/21.

BERKSWELL 1603–18. In CRO, DR 613/74.

RYTON ON DUNSMORE 1615–43 impf. In CRO, DR 11/20.

WELFORD ON AVON 1617–18. In CRO, DR 911/6/1.

OFFCHURCH 1619–53 impf. In CRO, N4/18.

BARCHESTON 1626–1725. In CRO, DR 5/6.

NETHER WHITACRE 1632–1702 impf. In CRO, DRB 27/5.

KINETON 1639–40. In CRO, DR 212/30.

CASTLE BROMWICH 1641–1805. In CRO, DRB 105/10.

ALCESTER 1651–85 impf. In CRO, DR 360/63.

COLESHILL 1657–9. In CRO, DRB 100/20.

SHERBORNE 1671–1783 impf. In CRO, DR 82/6.

KNOWLE 1672–1760. In CRO, DRB 56/54.

MONKS KIRBY 1673–1757. In CRO, DR 155/122.

TREDINGTON 1674–84, 1690–1758. In CRO, DR 79/35.

OLDBERROW 1676–1768 impf. In CRO, HR 61/1.

POLESWORTH 1677–1777. In CRO, 369/70.

WYKEN 1684–1730. In CRO, DR 39/8.

WESTMINSTER

ST MARGARET 1460–1692. In Westminster Central L, St Margaret E1–73. Extracts 1550–62 printed in Malcolm, *Londinium*, iv. 136–7.

ST MARTIN IN THE FIELDS 1525–1692 impf. In Westminster Central L, St Martin in the Fields F1–48. Ed. to 1603 by John V. Kitto, *St Martin in the Fields: The Accounts of the Churchwardens* (1901).

ST MARY LE STRAND 1601–50, 1677–98. In Westminster Public L, St Mary Le Strand M/f 22.

WESTMORLAND

ASKHAM 1580, 1640, 1674–1780. In Cumbria (Kendal) RO, WPR/11.

MORLAND 1588–1751 impf. In Cumbria (Kendal) RO, WPR/76/W1.

HEVERSHAM 1601–1828. In Cumbria (Kendal) RO, WPR/8.

HAWKSHEAD 1612–1797 impf. In Cumbria (Kendal) RO, WPR/83.

BEETHAM 1618–1886. In Cumbria (Kendal) RO, WPR/43.

HOLY TRINITY, KENDAL 1658–87, 1688–1732. In Cumbria (Kendal) RO, WPR/38.

GRASMERE 1661–1735. In Cumbria (Kendal) RO, WPR/91/W1.

KIRKBY LONSDALE 1669–1734. In Cumbria (Kendal) RO, WPR/19.

WILTSHIRE

St Edmund, Salisbury 1461–1694. In CRO, 1901/1–86. Ed. Henry Swayne, Wiltshire Record Society (1896).

St Mary, Devizes 1499–1633 v. impf., 1634–1734. In CRO, 189/1–2.

Calne 1527–1678 impf. Ed. A. E. W. Marsh, *A History of the Borough and Town of Calne* (Calne, 1903), 367–72.

Winterslow 1542–1661. Ed. W. Symonds, *Wiltshire Archaeological and Natural History Magazine*, 36 (1909–10), 29–43.

Steeple Ashton receipts only 1542–58, whole 1558–60. In CRO, 730/97/1.

St Thomas, Salisbury 1545–1724. Ed. Swayne, Wiltshire Record Society (1896).

Marlborough 1555–7, 1569–1700. In CRO, 1197/21.

Mere 1556–1853. Ed. to 1582 by T. Baker, *Wiltshire Archaeological and Natural History Magazine*, 35 (1908), 24–72.

Longbridge Deverill 1557–8, 1562–71. In CRO, 1020/25.

St Martin, Salisbury 1567–1653 impf., 1654–1700. In CRO, 1899/65–6.

Stratford sub Castle 1574–1666 impf. In CRO, 1076/19.

North Newnton 1576, 1646. In CRO, 1271/18.

Chilton Foliat 1577. In CRO, 735/19.

Sutton Mandeville 1602–36. In CRO, 2119/1.

Broad Blunsdon 1616–54, 1664–76. In CRO, 1565/35–6.

Highworth 1620–1705. In CRO, 1184/19.

Hannington 1635–1822. In CRO, 1819/13.

Stockton 1660–1763. In CRO, 203/7.

Seend 1664–70. In CRO, 1048/23.

Christian Malford 1666–1761. In CRO, 1710/32.

Cricklade 1670–1730. In CRO, 1632/18.

Grittleton 1672–1799. In CRO, 1620/17.

Seagry 1683–1704. In CRO, 2096/7.

Durrington 1689–1769. In CRO, 1885/10.

Farley 1689–1720. In CRO, 1891/14.

Hullavington 1690–1850. In CRO, 1819/13.

Baverstock 1695–1805. In CRO, 1085/8.

Luckington 1697–1822. In CRO, 1108/8.

WORCESTERSHIRE

Halesowen 1487–1582. Ed. F. Somers, Worcestershire Historical Society (1957).

St Helen, Worcester 1519–20. Ed. J. Amphlett, Worcestershire Historical Society (1896).

Badsey 1525–71, 1624–1837. In CRO (St Helen's), 850/Badsey/BA, 5013/2 and 1895. Ed. to 1571 by E. A. B. Barnard, *Churchwardens' Accounts of the Parish of Badsey* (Hampstead, 1913).

ST MICHAEL IN BEDWARDINE, WORCESTER 1543–1603. Ed. Amphlett, Worcestershire Historical Society (1896).

SOUTH LITTLETON 1548–1727. In CRO (St Helen's), 850/1284/1.

ELMLEY CASTLE 1632–72. In CRO (St Helen's), BA 8883/5.

YORKSHIRE

ST JAMES, HEDON 1350–1477 v. impf. In East Yorkshire RO, DDHE/29/B. Extracts in J. R. Boyle, *The Early History of the Town and Port of Hedon* (1895), appendix BB.

RIPON 1354–1440 impf. Ed. J. Fowler, Surtees Society 81 (1886), 207–34.

ST AUGUSTINE, HEDON 1371–1547 v. impf. In East Yorkshire RO, DDHE/29/A. Extracts in Boyle, *Hedon*, appendix W.

ST NICHOLAS, HEDON 1379–1476 v. impf. In East Yorkshire RO, DDHE/29/C. Extracts in Boyle, *Hedon*, appendix CC.

ECCLESFIELD 1524–45 impf., 1568–1626, 1638–40, 1680. In Sheffield Reference L, M/A80 and PR 54/87.

ST MICHAEL SPURRIERGATE, YORK 1537–48, 1594–1710. In Borthwick Institute, York, PR Y/MS 2, 3, 5. Extracts 1518–46 in John Nichols, *Illustrations of the Manners and Expenses of Antient Times*.

SHERIFF HUTTON 1537–59 impf. Ed. J. Purvis, *Yorkshire Archaeological Journal*, 36 (1944–7), 181–9.

MASHAM 1542–1675 impf., 1677–1793. In North Yorkshire RO, MIC 995–6. Extracts in John Fisher, *The History and Antiquities of Masham* (1865), 581–2.

ST MARTIN CONEY STREET, YORK 1553–1637. In Borthwick Institute, York, MS Y/MCS 16–17.

SHEFFIELD 1557–70. In Joseph Hunter, *Hallamshire*, ed. Alfred Gatty (1869), 246–8.

HOLY TRINITY GOODRAMGATE, YORK 1558–1712. In Borthwick Institute, York, R. X11 Y/HTG/12.

ST MARTIN MICKLEGATE, YORK 1560–1670. In Borthwick Institute, York, Y/MG/1a.

THORNTON WATLASS 1574–1641 impf., 1663–1954. In North Yorkshire RO, MIC 2032.

KIRBY MALZEARD 1576–1641, 1649–51. In North Yorkshire RO, MIC 1204.

BEDALE 1584–1607 impf., 1668–1721. In North Yorkshire RO, MIC 995, 1161.

ST JOHN OUSEGATE, YORK 1585–1648, 1690–1703. In Borthwick Institute, York, Y/J/17.

ST MARY, BEVERLEY 1592–1963. In East Yorkshire RO, PE1/51–90.

HOWDEN 1593–1666 impf. In East Yorkshire RO, PE 121/37.

WRAGBY 1603–12, 1618–20, 1622–6. In West Yorkshire RO, D99/1.

DONCASTER 1619–20. In Doncaster Archives Department.

SCARBOROUGH 1622–88 impf. In East Yorkshire RO, PE 165/241.

MILLINGTON 1622–63 impf. In Borthwick Institute, York, MIL/10.

COXWOLD 1632–42, 1649–90. In Borthwick Institute, York, COX/19.

ALL SAINTS NORTH STREET, YORK 1645–1734. In Borthwick Institute, York, Y/ASN/10.

EAST ARDLEY 1652–5, 1690–5. In West Yorkshire RO, D16/5/1.

ROYSTON 1656–1726. In West Yorkshire RO, D36/5/2.

NORTH FERRIBY 1658–1723 impf. In East Yorkshire RO, PE 36/30.

COTTINGHAM 1660–1890 impf. In East Yorkshire RO, PE 2/43.

ROOS 1666–1755 impf. In East Yorkshire RO, PE 44/23.

SIGGLESTHORPE 1669–76 impf. In East Yorkshire RO, 144/23.

HELMSLEY 1671–1785. In North Yorkshire RO, MC 995.

ST LAWRENCE, YORK 1574–85. In Borthwick Institute, York, Y/L/33.

THORNHILL 1674–1743. In West Yorkshire RO, D14/5/1.

BOLTON PERCY 1679–1787. In Borthwick Institute, York, BP/6.

WHISTON 1682–1705. In Sheffield Reference L, PR 37/38.

HOLY TRINITY MICKLEGATE, YORK 1683–1773 impf. In Borthwick Institute, York, Y/HTM/17.

NOTES

The following abbreviations have been used:

BL	British Library
Bod. L	Bodleian Library
CW	Churchwardens' Accounts (listed in Appendix)
DNB	*Dictionary of National Biography*
EETS	Early English Text Society
EHR	*English Historical Review*
HMC	Historical Manuscripts Commission
JEFDSS	*Journal of the English Folk Dance and Song Society*
L	Library
PRO	Public Record Office
RO	Record Office
TRHS	*Transactions of the Royal Historical Society*

All titles published in London unless otherwise stated.

CHAPTER 1

1. As will become evident from the endnotes below.
2. In *Local History and Folklore* (1975), 21–5.
3. Those listed in the Appendix for London, Rye, Coventry, Chester, Worcester, Oxford, Salisbury, Ludlow, Thame, and Bristol.
4. Chester City RO, St Mary on the Hill, vol. i; East Sussex RO, Rye Corporation Records, 147/1.
5. John Stow, *A Survey of London*, ed. Charles Lethbridge Kingsford (Oxford, 1908), i. 97.
6. Quoted in A. R. Wright, *British Calendar Customs*, ed. T. E. Lones (Folklore Society, 1936), iii. 243.
7. *The Use of Sarum*, ed. Walter Howard Frere (Cambridge, 1898), i. 111–33; James Pellar Malcolm, *Londinium Redivivum* (1802), ii. 71; Thame (Oxon.) CW, years 1442–1524; St Michael, Oxford CW, years 1425–1544; St Edmund, Salisbury (Wilts.) CW, pp. 1–83; Halesowen (Worcs.) CW, pp. 1–90; All Saints, Bristol CW, years 1464–1545; St Werburgh, Bristol CW, years 1547–8.
8. Alexander Murray, 'Medieval Christmas', *History Today* (Dec. 1986), 35.
9. T. Tusser, *Five Hundred Pointes of Good Husbandrie*, ed. W. Payne and S. J. Herrtage (English Dialect Society, 1878), 68.
10. Ian Lancashire, 'Orders for Twelfth Day and Night . . . in the Second Northumberland Household Book', *English Literary Renaissance*, 10 (1980), 14–15;

Records of Early Drama: Cumberland, Westmorland and Gloucestershire, ed. Audrey Douglas and Peter Greenfield (Toronto, 1986), 360–1; HMC Middleton MSS, pp. 331–7 (Willoughby accounts); BL Harleian MS 6388, fo. 28ᵛ (notes upon Coventry).

11. Lancashire, 'Orders for Twelfth Day and Night', 15–16; *Cumberland, Westmorland and Gloucestershire*, ed. Douglas and Greenfield, 356–9; HMC Rutland MSS (Rutland accounts), p. 312; *Letters and Papers, Foreign and Domestic, of the Reign of Henry VIII*, ed. J. S. Brewer (1864), II. ii. 1444; St John's College L (Cambridge), D91/19, fo. 121 (Lady Margaret Beaufort's accounts); *Household Books of John Duke of Norfolk and Thomas Earl of Surrey*, ed. John Payne Collier (Roxburgh Club, 1844), 144–5.

12. Graham Mayhew, *Tudor Rye* (Falmer, 1987), 58; *Records of Early English Drama: Devon*, ed. John M. Wasson (Toronto, 1986), 343; HMC 14th Report, appendix viii. 124 (Bury St Edmunds Abbey accounts); *Journal of Prior William More*, ed. Ethel S. Fegan (Worcestershire Historical Society 30, 1914), 76–7; *Records of Plays and Players in Kent 1450–1642*, ed. Giles Dawson (Malone Society, 1965), 23–5.

13. J. Charles Cox, *Churchwardens' Accounts* (1913), 269 (for Ashburton, Great Yarmouth, and Tintinhull); Great Dunmow (Essex) CW, years 1530–42; Swaffham (Norfolk) CW, 1536–67; Halesowen (Worcestershire) CW, p. 60; William Kelly, *Notices Illustrative of the Drama . . . of Leicester* (1865), 14.

14. e.g. Murray, 'Medieval Christmas', 35; HMC Middleton MSS, pp. 331–2 (Willoughby accounts).

15. Lancashire, 'Orders for Twelfth Day and Night', 12.

16. A. E. Green, 'Popular Drama and the Mummers' Play', in David Bradby, Louis James, and Bernard Sharratt (eds.), *Performance and Politics in Popular Drama* (Cambridge, 1980), 139–66; E. G. Cawte, Alex Helm, and N. Peacock, *English Ritual Drama: A Geographical Index* (1967); Craig Fees, 'Mummers and Momoeri: A Response', *Folklore*, 100 (1989), 240–7; Frederick B. Jonassen, 'Elements of the Traditional Drama of England in *Sir Gawain and the Green Knight*', *Viator*, 17 (1986), 221–54; Thomas Pettit, 'Early English Traditional Drama: Approaches and Perspectives', *Research Opportunities in Renaissance Drama*, 25 (1982), 1–30; Alex Helm, *The English Mummers' Play* (Folklore Society, 1981); Gareth Morgan, 'The Mummers of Pontus', *Folklore*, 101 (1990), 143–51. For the latest discussion of 'Beelzebub', see Ronald Hutton, *The Pagan Religions of the Ancient British Isles* (Oxford, 1991), 150–1, 162, 318–19, 328. For the pre-Reformation quack doctor, see *Non-Cycle Plays and Fragments*, ed. Norman Davis (EETS, 1970), 74–8.

17. Robert Ricart, *The Maire of Bristow Is Kalendar*, ed. Lucy Toulin Smith (Camden Society, 1872), 85–6; *Records of Early English Drama: Chester*, ed. Lawrence M. Clopper (Manchester, 1979), 56; *Memorials of London and London Life*, ed. Henry Thomas Riley (1868), 658, 669.

18. E. K. Chambers, *The Medieval Stage* (1963 edn.), i. 403–19, and sources listed there; Stow, *Survey of London*, ed. Kingsford, i. 97; St John's College L, Cambridge, D91/24 (Lady Margaret Beaufort's accounts); *Records of Plays and Players in Norfolk and Suffolk 1330–1642*, ed. D. Galloway and J. Wasson (Malone Society, 1980), 8, 81, 93, 100–2, 192; Polydor Vergil, *Works*, trans. John Langley (1663), 194–5; Great Dunmow (Essex) CW, years 1530–42; Dennington (Essex) CW, years 1539–40; PRO, SP 1/99, fos. 203–4 (deposition against Harwich priest); *The Black Books of Lincoln's Inn*, ed. J. W. Walker (1897), i. 181–90.

19. Chambers, *Medieval Stage* (1963 edn.), i. 342–59; Neil Mackenzie, 'Boy into Bishop',

History Today (Dec., 1987), 11–15; *Extracts from the Accounts Rolls of the Abbey of Durham*, ed. Canon Fowler (3 vols.; Surtees Society, 1898–1900), *passim*; Wells Cathedral L, Communard Books for years 1327–1538 (using catalogue compiled by L. S. Colchester).

20. Chambers, *Medieval Stage* (1963 edn.), i. 358–9, ii. 248–9; *Records of Early English Drama: Cambridge*, ed. Alan H. Nelson (Toronto, 1989), 78–80, 1064, 1106; *Letters and Papers*, ed. Brewer, II. ii. 1453, 1458, 1463–4, 1469, 1480, III. ii. 1533–47, and IV. i. 869 (King's Books of Payments 1509–21); PRO, E. 101/420/11, *passim* (King's Book of Payments 1528–31); John Brand, *Observations on the Popular Antiquities of Great Britain*, ed. Sir Henry Ellis (1908), i. 423–4.

21. Chambers, *Medieval Stage* (1963 edn.), i. 358–9; St Nicholas (Bristol) CW, pp. 36–55; Ricart, *The Maire of Bristowe Is Kalendar*, 80–1; Cox, *Churchwardens' Accounts*, 276; Revd G. Huelin, 'Christmas in the City', *Guildhall Miscellany*, NS 111 (1977–9), 165; All Hallows, Staining (London) CW, fo. 143; BL Stowe MS 871, fos. 32–3 (inventory of St Peter Mancroft, Norwich); Nelson (ed.), *Cambridge*, 1053; Boxford (Suffolk) CW, p. iv; Lambeth (Surrey) CW, pp. 55–6; St Andrew, Lewes (Sussex) CW, pp. 42–5; Halesowen (Worcs.) CW, pp. 39, 45; Walsall (Staffs.) CW, pp. 186–7, 255, 263; Horley (Surrey) CW, fo. 4; Sherborne (Dorset) CW, no. 24; George Hall, *The Triumph of Rome* (1655), pp. 25–6; *Players in Kent*, ed. Dawson, 91–9; Imogen Luxton, 'The Reformation and Popular Culture', in Felicity Heal and Rosemary O'Day (eds.), *Church and Society in England: Henry VIII to James I* (1977), 61; St Martin, Leicester, CW, year 1552.

22. U. Lambert, 'Hognel Money and the Hogglers', *Surrey Archaeological Collections*, 30 (1917), 54–60; Molland (Devon) CW, pp. 211–37; Sutterton (Lincs.) CW, year 1525; Croscombe (Somerset) CW, pp. 4–40; Pilton (Somerset) CW, pp. 54–74; Wigtoft (Lincs.) CW, pp. 220–9; Tintinhull (Somerset) CW, pp. 178–205; Wandsworth (Surrey) CW, p. 82; Bletchingley (Surrey) CW, p. 26; Bolney (Sussex) CW, pp. 247–8; Rotherfield (Sussex) CW, pp. 37–48; Arlington (Sussex) CW, years 1455–79; Ashburton (Devon) CW, pp. 49–140; Launceston (Cornwall) CW, pp. 371–5; Banwell (Somerset) CW, pp. 118–26; Chagford (Devon) CW, nos. 1–4; Coldridge (Devon) CW, pp. 9–27; Winkleigh (Devon) CW, no. 15; Minchinhampton (Gloucs.) CW, 6–68; Dursley (Gloucs.) CW, years 1579–1626; Nettlecombe (Somerset) CW, years 1507–46. The Elizabethan description is in Somerset RO, D/D/Cd 28, Badgworth churchwardens *v*. Hyde, 25 Jan. 1600.

23. Brand, *Observations*, ed. Ellis, i. 2–7; *Festive Songs and Carols*, ed. W. Sandys (Percy Society, 23; 1847), 19–20; BL Add. MS 38,174, fo. 36 (Henry VII's Household Ordinances).

24. The Fordwich reference was uncovered by Dr James Gibson, and will be published by him in the volume which he is editing in the Records of Early English Drama series; I only feel able to cite it here, with his permission, because I identified for him the nature of the custom which was being paid for. The other citations are from *The Poems of Robert Herrick*, ed. L. C. Martin (Oxford, 1965), 264; F. Sawyer, 'Sussex Folklore', *Sussex Archaeological Collections*, 33 (1883), 256.

25. Tusser, *Five Hundred Pointes*, 68; *Festive Songs*, ed. Sandys; *Specimens of Old Christmas Carols*, ed. T. Wright (Percy Society, 4; 1841), and *Festive Songs and Carols*, ed. Wright; Murray, 'Medieval Christmas', 37.

26. *The Earl of Northumberland's Household Book*, ed. Bishop Thomas Percy (1905), 328–32;

Lancashire, 'Orders for Twelfth Day and Night', 14–15; HMC Middleton MSS, pp. 337–94 (Willoughby accounts); HMC Rutland MSS, i. 266–9 (Rutland accounts); *Letters and Papers*, ed. Brewer II. ii. 1444, 1497 (King's Book of Payments); *Journal of Prior More* (Worcestershire Historical Society, 1914), 76–7; *Household Books of John Duke of Norfolk and Thomas Earl of Surrey*, ed. John Payne Collier (Roxburgh Club, 1844), 146; Vergil, *Works*, ed. Langley, 193; Tusser, *Five Hundred Pointes*, 68; BL Add. MS 38,174, fo. 36ᵛ (Henry VII's Household Ordinances).

27. BL Add. MS 38,174, fo. 35ᵛ (Henry VII's Household Ordinances); Lancashire, 'Orders for Twelfth Day and Night', 14–15; Kelly, *Drama . . . of Leicester*, 14; Sydney Anglo, 'The Court Festivals of Henry VII', *Bulletin of the John Rylands Library*, 43 (1960–1), 21.

28. Chambers, *Medieval Stage* (1963 edn.), ii. 45–9, for St Nicholas, Great Yarmouth (Suffolk), St Lawrence, Reading (Berks.), St Martin (Leicester), St Andrew, Canterbury (Kent), and Holbeach (Lincs.); St Ewen, Bristol CW, pp. 6, 83, 87; Great St Mary, Cambridge CW, pp. 1–77; Ripon (Yorks.) CW, ii. 207; St Mary on the Hill, Chester CW, year 1544.

29. BL Add. MS 38,174, fos. 35–6 (Henry VII's Household Ordinances); *Cumberland, Westmorland and Gloucestershire*, ed. Douglas and Greenfield, 356–9 (Buckingham's household accounts); Lancashire, 'Orders for Twelfth Day and Night', 19–20; Anglo, 'Court Festivals', 21; HMC Rutland MSS, pp. 266–81; *Letters and Papers*, ed. Brewer, II. ii. 1444, 1497 (King's Books of Payments).

30. *Records of Plays and Players in Lincolnshire 1300–1585*, ed. S. J. Kahrl (Malone Society, 1969), p. xxvii (for Grimsby); *Players in Norfolk and Suffolk*, ed. Galloway and Wasson, 16, 87 (for Great Yarmouth and Snettisham); M. W. Barley, 'Plough Plays in the East Midlands', *JEFDSS* 7 (1953), 72 (for Donington, Lincs.); Revd R. M. Serjeantson and Revd H. Isham Longden, 'The Parish Churches and Religious Houses of Northamptonshire', *Archaeological Journal*, 2nd ser. 20 (1913), 382, 416, 425; Leverington (Cambs.) CW, pp. 186–7; *County Folklore*, v. *Lincolnshire*, ed. Mrs Gutch and Mabel Peacock (1908), 171–4 (for Leverton, Sutterton, Kirton-in-Lindsey, and Wigtoft); W. Marratt, *The History of Lincolnshire* (Boston, 1814), 104–7 (for Holbeach); St John, Peterborough (Northants.) CW, p. 92.

31. *Select Works of John Bale*, ed. Revd H. Christmas (Parker Society, 1849), 528; *Dives and Pauper*, ed. P. H. Barnum (EETS 1976), 157.

32. Tusser, *Five Hundred Pointes*, 108, 307.

33. *Players in Norfolk and Suffolk*, ed. Galloway and Wasson, 79–82, 92, 100–1, 138 (for Shipdam, Snettisham, Swaffham, Tilney All Saints, Boxford); Leverington (Cambs.) CW, pp. 186–7; Saxilby (Lincs.) CW, year 1565; *County Folklore*, v. *Lincolnshire*, ed. Gutch and Peacock, 171, 174 (for Addlethorpe, Leverton, and Wigtoft); St John, Peterborough (Northants.) CW, pp. 1–92; Great Dunmow (Essex) CW, years 1526–40; Cratfield (Suffolk) CW, pp. 19–32; Great St Mary, Cambridge CW, pp. 20–1; Holy Trinity, Bungay (Suffolk) CW, p. 2; Brundish (Suffolk) CW, years 1475–1542; Denton (Norfolk) CW, years 1507–36.

34. J. E. Tiddy, *The Mummers' Play* (Folcroft, 1923), 240–57; E. K. Chambers, *The English Folk Play* (New York, 1964), 89–122; Thomas Davidson, 'Plough Rituals in England and Scotland', *Agricultural History Review*, 7 (1959), 27–37; Barley, 'Plough Plays', 68–95; Alan Brody, *The English Mummers and their Plays* (Philadelphia, 1969), *passim*; Cawte, Helm and Peacock, *English Ritual Drama, passim*.

35. H. M. Shire and K. Elliott, 'Pleugh Song and Plough Play', *Saltire Review*, 2: 6 (1955), 39–44, identify a Scottish 'Pleugh Song' dating from *c*.1500 as a parallel to the Plough Monday play and indicative of the latter's antiquity. But as it describes the slaughter of a dying ox and the harnessing of a new one, it has nothing in common save the theme of death and renewal (in this case by replacement not resurrection). Nor is there any proof that the actions of the song were mimed out as the authors suggest. Barley, 'Plough Plays', 70–1, cites a Tudor parish play recorded at Donington, Lincs., as Plough Monday drama. But there is no evidence of its calendar date of performance, and the cast list (which is all that we have) bears little resemblance to those of the later plays.

36. *Mirk's Festial*, ed. T. Erbe (EETS 1905), 56–7; Joshua Stopford, *Pagano-Papismus* (1675), 237–43; *Manuale ad Usum Percelebris Ecclesiae Sarisburiensis*, ed. A. Jeffries Collins (Henry Bradshaw Society, 1960), 7–9; BL Add. MS 38,174, fo. 5 (Henry VII's Household Ordinances); *Northumberland's Household Book*, 321; HMC Middleton MSS, p. 331 (Willoughby accounts).

37. Yatton (Somerset) CW, p. 100; Bethersden (Kent) CW, pp. 5–24; Bolney (Sussex) CW, p. 244; Arlington (Sussex) CW, years 1475–9; Tavistock (Devon) CW, p. 4; Dartmouth (Devon) CW, pp. 300–52; Winterslow (Wilts.) CW, p. 36; Ripon (Yorks.) CW, p. 207; All Hallows Staining (London) CW, fo. 30; Nettlecombe (Somerset) CW, years 1507–46.

38. HMC 14th Report, appendix 8, pp. 267–8 (List of Grimsby feasts); Charles Phythian-Adams, 'Ceremony and the Citizen', in Peter Clark (ed.), *The Early Modern Town* (1976), 109–10; *Cambridge*, ed. Nelson, 1058–1129; Eamon Duffy, *The Stripping of the Altars* (New Haven, Conn., 1992), 20.

39. Wright, *British Calendar Customs*, ed. Lones, i. 138–9; HMC Middleton MSS, pp. 353, 365 (Willoughby accounts).

40. First recorded in the accounts of the corporation of Hull, who feasted on that day in the early sixteenth century: George Hadley, *History of . . . Kingston-upon-Hull* (Hull, 1788), 823–6.

41. William Kethe, *A Sermon Preached at Blandford Forum* (1570), quoted in Brand, *Observations*, ed. Ellis, i. 308.

42. *Memorials of London*, ed. Riley, 571 and n. 2.

43. Joseph Strutt, *The Sports and Pastimes of the People of England*, ed. J. Charles Cox (1903), 96, 224; *Chester*, ed. Clopper, pp. li–liii; Morris Marples, *A History of Football* (1954), 22–39; Brand, *Observations*, ed. Ellis, i. 79.

44. *Festyvall* (1511), quoted in Brand, *Observations*, ed. Ellis, i. 95–6.

45. *Dives and Pauper*, ed. Barnum, 99–101; Henry John Feasey, *Ancient English Holy Week Ceremonial* (1897), 1–49.

46. Brand, *Observations*, ed. Ellis, i. 111.

47. Bassingbourne (Cambs.) CW, years 1497–1538.

48. Feasey, *Holy Week Ceremonial*, 1–12.

49. Ibid. 53–83; Cox, *Churchwardens' Accounts*, 253–4; *Dives and Pauper*, ed. Barnum, 26, 89; *Mirk's Festial*, ed. Erbe, 114; *Sarum Manual*, ed. Collins, 12–14; Nicholas Doncaster, *The Doctrine of the Mass Book* (1554), quoted in Brand, *Observations*, ed. Ellis, i. 125–6; Anthony Sparrow, ed., *A Collection of Articles* (1671), 9; Duffy, *Stripping of the Altars*, 23.

50. Feasey, *Holy Week Ceremonial*, 53–4.

51. Cox, *Churchwardens' Accounts*, 253–8 (for St Peter Cheap (London), St Andrew Hubbard (London); St Margaret, Westminster; St Lawrence, Reading (Berks.); St Stephen Walbrook (London); St Margaret Pattens (London); St Mary Woolnoth (London); St Alphege London Wall (London); Ludlow (Shropshire); and St Ewen, and St John Baptist (Bristol); *Chester*, ed. Clopper, 45; St Andrew, Canterbury (Kent) CW, p. 39; St Andrew, Lewes (Sussex) CW, pp. 43–5; Dartmouth (Devon) CW, pp. 300–52; St Martin in the Fields, Westminster CW, p. 28; St Nicholas, Bristol CW, pp. 53–4; Thame (Oxon.) CW, pp. 35–40; Denton (Norfolk) CW, fos. 3ʳ–4ᵛ; Christ Church, Bristol CW, years 1545–7; All Saints, Bristol CW, years 1481–1536; St Mary Magdalen Milk Street (London) CW, years 1518–47; Sir W. Parker, *The History of Long Melford* (1873), 72.

52. Cox, *Churchwardens' Accounts*, 249–52, 258–9; *Use of Sarum*, ed. Frere, i. 142–3; Feasey, *Holy Week Ceremonial*, 84–92. Cox and Feasey cite London, Salisbury, and Exeter cases. I can add East Sussex RO, Rye Corporation Records 147/1, fos. 1–111. The only rural one which I can find is Badsey (Worcs.) CW, p. 23, where the 'Judas candles' may have been for the Tenebrae.

53. Brand, *Observations*, ed. Ellis, i. 143–7; *Rites of Durham*, ed. Canon Fowler (Surtees Society, 107; 1907), 77.

54. Feasey, *Holy Week Ceremonial*, 95–113; H. Owen and J. B. Blakeway, *A History of Shrewsbury* (1825), i. 336.

55. Cox, *Churchwardens' Accounts*, 259.

56. Brand, *Observations*, ed. Ellis, i. 150–1.

57. Feasey, *Holy Week Ceremonial*, 114–28; Cox, *Churchwardens' Accounts*, 259; *Dives and Pauper*, ed. Barnum, 2, 26, 87–9; Chambers, *Medieval Stage* (1963 edn.), ii. 17–19, 310–11; F. M. Salter, *Medieval Drama in Chester* (Toronto, 1955), 19; *Northumberland's Household Book*, ed. Percy, 322–3.

58. Chambers, *Medieval Stage* (1963 edn.), ii. 20–1, 312–15; A. Heales, 'Easter Sepulchres', *Archaeologia*, 41 (1867), 263–303; Feasey, *Holy Week Ceremonial*, 129–78; *Rites of Durham*, ed. Fowler, 12–13; Karl Young, *The Drama of the Medieval Church* (Oxford, 1933), ii. 511–38; Stratton (Cornwall) CW, fo. 18; Yatton (Somerset) CW, p. 153; St Mary at Hill (London) CW, p. 63; Stogursey (Somerset) CW, years 1502–46; St Lawrence, Reading (Berks.) CW, p. 43; Great St Mary, Cambridge CW, p. 29; Leverton (Lincs.) CW, pp. 338–59; Cox, *Churchwardens' Accounts*, 259–61; *Household Books of Norfolk*, ed. Collier, 185; Serjeantson and Longden, 'Parish Churches . . . of Northamptonshire', 267–430; Duffy, *Stripping of the Altars*, 29–33.

59. Bramley, Stoke Charity, Crondall, and Ellingham (Hants.); Croscombe, Halse, Banwell, and Nettlecombe (Somerset); Dennington, Metfield, Brundish, Mickfield, and Bardwell (Suffolk); Bolney and Steyning (Sussex); Launceston (Cornwall); Winterslow (Wilts.); Sheriff Hutton (Yorks.); Horley (Surrey); North Elmham (Norfolk); Addlethorpe Ingoldmells (Lincs.); Bassingbourn (Cambs.); Stoke Edith (Herefordshire). The larger totals for Hampshire, Somerset, and Suffolk are probably only due to the greater survival of rural accounts in those counties.

60. Those appear in the extant accounts for London, Bristol, Dover, Worcester, Leicester, Reading, Oxford, Lambeth, Peterborough, Westminster, Ludlow, Henley, and Stafford.

61. Feasey, *Holy Week Ceremonial*, 179–234; Cox, *Churchwardens' Accounts*, 54–60; *Sarum Manual*, ed. Collins, 19–25; *Rites of Durham*, ed. Fowler, 10–11.

62. *Rites of Durham*, ed. Fowler, 12–13; Heales, '*Easter Sepulchres*', 176; St Nicholas, Great Yarmouth (Suffolk) CW, year 1525.

63. *Northumberland Household Book*, ed. Percy, 333; Henley (Oxon.) CW, years 1521–30; Dartmouth (Devon) CW, pp. 300–52; Kingston (Surrey) CW, years 1503–16; St Lawrence, Reading (Berks.) CW, p. 237.

64. *Sarum Manual*, ed. Collins, 64–81.

65. *Mirk's Festial*, ed. Erbe, 129.

66. Brand, *Observations*, ed. Ellis, i. 154–7, 172–5.

67. *Chester*, ed. Clopper, 23; Melton Mowbray (Leics.) CW, no. 1.

68. Revd Samuel Denne, 'Memoir on Hokeday', *Archaeologia*, 7 (1785), 244–68; Phythian-Adams, 'Ceremony and the Citizen', 113 (for Coventry); Boxford (Suffolk) CW, years 1540–7; St Lawrence, Southampton (Hants.) CW, years 1540–2; Kingston upon Thames (Surrey) CW, years 1508–39; *Cambridge*, ed. Nelson, 1081–1112; Henley (Oxon.) CW, years 1499–1532; Dursley (Gloucs.) CW, years 1556–70; St Andrew, Canterbury (Kent) CW, xxxii. 212–43, xxxiv. 24–36; St Mary at Hill (London) CW, pp. 228–309; St Dunstan, Canterbury (Kent) CW, years 1490–1538; St Giles, Reading (Berks.) CW, pp. 1–36; St Lawrence, Reading (Berks.) CW, p. 239; Thame (Oxon.) CW, years 1488–1524; St Michael (Oxford) CW, 1471–1530; Lambeth (Surrey) CW, pp. 2–14; Badsey (Worcs.) CW, pp. 9–10; St Martin in the Fields (London) CW, pp. 1–21; St Edmund, Salisbury (Wilts.) CW, pp. 47–104; St Thomas, Salisbury (Wilts.) CW, p. 273; Holy Trinity, Bungay (Suffolk) CW, p. 3; Bassingbourn (Cambs.) CW, years 1497–1538. The custom was certainly present at Worcester in 1450, but not after, and there are probable references to it at Shrewsbury and at Walsall (Staffs.): Chambers, *Medieval Stage*, i. 155–6, and Walsall CW, pp. 186–7.

69. *Records of Early English Drama: Norwich*, ed. David Galloway (Toronto, 1984), 23–30; *Records of Early English Drama: Newcastle-upon-Tyne*, ed. J. J. Anderson (Toronto, 1982), 13–15; *Northumberland Household Book*, ed. Percy, 333; St Ewen, Bristol CW, p. 46; All Saints, Bristol CW, years 1446–1536; Croscombe (Somerset) CW, pp. 32–6; Thomas Sharp, *A Dissertation on the Pageants or Dramatic Mysteries . . . at Coventry* (Coventry, 1825), 161; Kelly, *Drama . . . of Leicester*, 37–9; *Players in Norfolk and Suffolk*, ed. Galloway and Wasson, 76–7; R. Whiting, 'For the Health of my Soul', *Southern History*, 5 (1983), 80; Alan H. Nelson, *The Medieval English Stage* (Chicago, 1974), 51.

70. Stow, *Survey of London*, ed. Kingsford, i. 98–9; Vergil, *Works*, ed. Langley, 194.

71. HMC Middleton MSS, p. 382 (Willoughby accounts); Wing (Bucks.) CW, fo. 21; Cratfield (Suffolk) CW, p. 18; Yatton (Somerset) CW, pp. 81–143; Tintinhull (Somerset) CW, pp. 178–88; *The Chronicles of the Collegiate Church or Free Chapel of All Saints, Derby*, ed. Revd J. Charles Cox and W. H. St John Hope (1881), 51–2; Charles Pendrill, *Old Parish Life in London* (Oxford, 1937), 62–3; Guildhall L (London), MS 4,249, fo. 222ᵛ (observations of Thomas Bentley); and see Appendix for the other CW referred to in the text.

72. Roscoe E. Parker, 'Some Records of the Somyr Play', in Richard Beale Davis and John Leon Lievsay (eds.), *Studies in Honor of John C. Hodges and Alwin Thaler* (Knoxville, 1961), 19–26.

73. *Players in Norfolk and Suffolk*, ed. Galloway and Wasson, 87–93; Bramley (Hants.) CW, years 1529–30; Cratfield (Suffolk) CW, p. 17.

74. Cox, *Churchwardens' Accounts*, 205; *Players in Norfolk and Suffolk*, ed. Galloway and Wasson, 191–2.

75. *Records of the Borough of Nottingham* (Nottingham, 1885), iii. 382; William Chappell, *Old English Popular Music*, ed. H. Ellis Woodbridge (New York, 1961), i. 33; HMC New Romney, pp. 540–1; Launceston (Cornwall) CW, p. 124; St Mary, Devizes (Wilts.) CW, year 1499.

76. *Players in Norfolk and Suffolk*, ed. Galloway and Wasson, 87–93.

77. Stow, *Survey of London*, ed. Kingsford, i. 99, 143.

78. Parker, 'Records of the Somyr Play', 20–1 (for Wistow, Yorks.); St John's College L (Cambridge), D91/20 (for Colyweston, Leics.); Henley (Oxon.) CW, pp. 198–229; Andover (Hants.) CW, year 1472; Calne (Wilts.) CW, pp. 369–70; St Nicholas, Bristol CW, p. 67; Bramley (Hants) CW, years 1529–30; Croscombe (Somerset) CW, pp. 5–7; St Lawrence, Reading (Berks.) CW, pp. 235–6; Steyning (Sussex) CW, pp. 133–4; St Edmund, Salisbury (Wilts.) CW, pp. 13–85; Halesowen (Worcs.) CW, p. 26; Sherborne (Dorset) CW, xxiii. 311–13, xxiv. 6–140; Winterslow (Wilts.) CW, pp. 29–37 (also mentions the Deane lord); Melton Mowbray (Leics.) CW, nos. 1–2; Great Dunmow (Essex) CW, years 1530–9; W. St L. Finny, 'Medieval Games and Gaderyngs at Kingston-upon-Thames', *Surrey Archaeological Collections*, xliv (1936), 127–9. Sandra Billington, *Mock Kings in Medieval Society and Renaissance Drama* (Oxford, 1991), 65–85, argues for a tradition of midsummer 'king games' held upon hills, using apparent references to them in Tudor literature. I find no trace of these in the local records, and the literary allusions seem unconvincing to me. Likewise, her assertion (p. 56) that English villagers held lord and lady games before midsummer and all-male games thereafter appears to be a neat distinction which is not substantiated by the local evidence: 'ladies' were always rare in these events, and in the form of Maid Marian they sometimes appeared in July. The sources are listed above and below.

79. By far the best overall study is David Wiles, *The Early Plays of Robin Hood* (Cambridge, 1981). I have added material from J. C. Holt, *Robin Hood* (1981 edn.), 33, 148–95; *The Journal of Prior More* (Worcestershire Historical Society, 1914), 87, 293, 309, 332, 405; Croscombe (Somerset) CW, pp. 4–38; St Nicholas, Bristol CW, p. 67; Tintinhull (Somerset) CW, p. 200; St John, Glastonbury (Somerset) CW, no. 11; St Andrew Hubbard (London) CW, years 1538–40; Henley (Oxon.) CW, pp. 125–89; Graham Mayhew, *Tudor Rye* (Falmer, 1987), 58; Edward Hall, *Hall's Chronicle* (New York, 1965), 582; *Letters and Papers*, ed. Brewer, I. ii. 1504 (royal revels account); Kelly, *Leicester*, 60–1.

80. Holt, *Robin Hood*, 33.

81. Wiles, *Early Plays of Robin Hood*, 16–17, 45–53.

82. *Staffordshire Suits in the Court of Star Chamber*, ed. W. K. Boyd (William Salt Archaeological Society, Collections for a History of Staffordshire, NS 1; 1907), 80–1; Wiles, *Early Plays of Robin Hood*, 27; *Devon*, ed. Wasson, 119; Peter Clark, 'Reformation and Radicalism in Kentish Towns c.1500–1553', in *The Urban Classes, the Nobility and the Reformation* (Publications of the German Historical Institute, 5; 1979), 112.

83. Owen and Blakeway, *History of Shrewsbury*, i. 331–3; *Staffordshire Suits*, ed. Boyd, 80–1.

84. Barbara Lowe, 'Early Records of the Morris in England', *JEFDSS*, 8: 2 (1957), 61–3;

Lancashire, 'Orders for Twelfth Day and Night', 15; *Records of Nottingham*, iii. 362; St Lawrence, Reading (Berks.) CW, pp. 235–6; Chappell, *Old English Popular Music*, i. 34; *Players in Kent*, ed. Dawson, 100; John Forrest, *Morris and Matachin* (1984), chs. 1–2.

85. By saying this, I take a stand on the question of the famous window which was formerly set into the manor house at Betley, Staffs. It is certainly more recent than the 1460s, for most of the figures were clearly copied from a copper engraving made by Israhel von Mecheln or Meckenem in that decade. The absence of beards upon the men, and the fact that the sequence includes the arms of the Audley family, who gave up Betley in 1536, make an early Tudor date seem more likely. One expert upon stained glass, Charles Bridgeman, has indeed claimed it for that period. But the lettering across the maypole is no earlier than the Elizabethan age, and most authorities upon such glass assign it to then or to the early seventeenth century when the building in which it is first recorded was erected. I therefore follow this latter view: C. Bridgeman, 'Note on the Betley Morris Dance Window', *Collections for a History of Staffordshire*, NS 16 (1923), 1–5; Herbert Read, *English Stained Glass* (1926), 240–9; E. J. Nichol, 'Some Notes on the History of the Betley Window', *JEFDSS*, 7: 2 (1953), 59–67.

86. Lowe, 'Early Records', 61–3; Kingston-upon-Thames (Surrey) CW, p. 331; Wiles, *Early Plays of Robin Hood*, 13.

87. E. C. Cawte, *Ritual Animal Disguise* (Folklore Society, 1978), 3–23; St Mary (Stafford) CW, year 1528–9; Barley, 'Plough Plays', 70.

88. *Use of Sarum*, ed. Frere, i. 173–4; *Rites of Durham*, ed. Fowler, 104–5; St Edmund, Salisbury (Wilts.) CW, pp. 1–85.

89. Found in all early Tudor CW listed in Appendix under London, Bristol, Chester, Salisbury, Oxford, and Reading, plus Tavistock (Devon) CW, p. 18; Halesowen (Worcs.) CW, p. 41; Long Sutton (Lincs.) CW, fos. 16–18; Leverington (Cambs.) CW, p. 188; Denton (Norfolk) CW, years 1515 and 1520; Cox, *Churchwardens' Accounts*, 263–5 (for Bassingbourn, Dover, and Saffron Walden).

90. *Mirk's Festial*, ed. Erbe, 149; *Visitations in the Diocese of Lincoln 1517–1531*, ed. A. H. Thompson (Lincoln Record Society, 33; 1940), 67, 76, 81; *Norwich Consistory Court Depositions*, ed. Revd E. Stone and B. Cozens-Hardy (Norfolk Record Society, 10; 1938), no. 412.

91. Serjeantson and Longden, 'Parish Churches . . . of Northamptonshire', 277, 292, 311, 336, 383.

92. *Mirk's Festial*, ed. Erbe, 150–2.

93. Recorded in all the surviving early sixteenth-century accounts for the City and Westminster.

94. *Rites of Durham*, ed. Fowler, 104–5.

95. St Michael, Oxford CW, a. 1–2; St Edmund, Salisbury (Wilts.) CW, pp. 1–85; St Mary, Bungay (Suffolk), pp. 3–11.

96. Cox, *Churchwardens' Accounts*, p. 265.

97. Kelly, *Drama . . . of Leicester*, 7–10; *Devon*, ed. Wasson, 355–75; *Chester*, ed. Clopper, p. liv.

98. Stow, *Survey of London*, ed. Kingsford, 101–4.

99. BL Harleian MS 2345, fo. 49ᵛ (Sermons 'monachi Winchelcumbensis'); Stow, *Survey of London*, ed. Kingsford, 101; William Kethe, *A Sermon Preached at Blandford Forum*

(1570), and Richard Nicholls, *London's Artillery* (1616), rep. in Brand, *Observations*, ed. Ellis, i. 308, 326–7; *Mirk's Festial*, ed. Erbe, 182; Corporation of London RO, Journal 12, fo. 329; Parker, *Long Melford*, 73.

100. Anglo, 'Court Festivals of Henry VIII', 28–43; *Letters and Papers*, ed. Brewer, II. ii. 1446 and III. ii. 1536, 1541 (King's Books of Payments); BL Arundel MS 97, fos. 20ᵛ, 76 (King's Book of Payments 1539–41); HMC Middleton MSS, p. 333 (Willoughby accounts); Sharp, *Dissertation on . . . Coventry*, 175; R. Burne, 'Chester Cathedral in the Reigns of Mary and Elizabeth', *Journal of the Architectural, Archaeological and Historic Society of Chester and North Wales*, 38 (1951), 56–7; Peter Clark, 'Reformation and Radicalism in Kentish Towns c.1500–1553', in *The Urban Classes, the Nobility and the Reformation* (Publications of the German Historical Institute, 5; 1979), 111.

101. Sharp, *Dissertation on . . . Coventry*, 175. The London CW concerned are St Martin Outwich, pp. 272–3; St Martin in the Fields, pp. 13–21; St Peter Cheap, year 1534; St Mary at Hill, pp. 81–309; and St Andrew Hubbard, xxxii. 278–393 and xxxiv. 18–187.

102. Tavistock (Devon) CW, pp. 2–20; Pilton (Somerset) CW, pp. 62–75; Saffron Walden (Essex) CW, p. 57.

103. George Unwin, *The Guilds and Companies of London* (1925), 269–70; S. Williams, 'The Lord Mayor's Show in Tudor and Stuart times', *Guildhall Miscellany*, 10 (Sept. 1959), 4–6; Cawte, *Ritual Animal Disguise*, 24–6; *A Calendar of Dramatic Records in the Books of the Livery Companies of London*, ed. Jean Robertson and D. J. Gordon (Malone Society, 3; 1954), 1–36; Nicolls, quoted in Brand, *Observations*, ed. Ellis, i. 326–7.

104. Sharp, *Dissertation on . . . Coventry*, 181–200; *Chester*, ed. Clopper, pp. li–lii; Charles Hoskins, *The Ancient Trade Guilds and Companies of Salisbury* (1912), 171; *Calendar of the Plymouth Municipal Records*, ed. R. N. Worth (Plymouth, 1893), 105; *Records of Nottingham* (1885), iii. 361; *The Great Red Book of Bristol*, pt. 1, ed. E. Veale (Bristol Record Society, 1933), 26–7; J. A. Picton, *Memorials of Liverpool* (1875), 45; *Cumberland, Westmorland and Gloucestershire*, ed. Douglas and Greenfield, 301; *Devon*, ed. Wasson, 132–9, 279–80, 342.

105. *Newcastle-upon-Tyne*, ed. Anderson, 15; *Records of Early English Drama: York*, ed. Alexandra F. Johnston and Margaret Rogerson (Manchester, 1979), *passim*; David Palliser, *Tudor York* (Oxford, 1979), 80, 152.

106. Sharp, *Dissertation on . . . Coventry*, 181–200; *Chester*, ed. Clopper, pp. li–lii.

107. James Thompson, *History of Leicester* (1849), i. 149–50; *York*, ed. Johnson and Rogerson, 1–289, 689–839; *Rites of Durham*, ed. Fowler, 89–90; St Mary at Hill (London) CW, pp. 81–305; St Martin Outwich (London) CW, pp. 84–90; St Andrew Hubbard (London) CW, xxxi. 248–536, xxxii. 273–395, xxxiii. 564–78, xxxiv. 18–675; St Martin in the Fields (London) CW, pp. 1–105; St Peter Cheap (London) CW, years 1477–1534; All Hallows Staining (London) CW, fos. 3–167; St Lawrence Pountney (London) CW, years 1530–47; St Mary Woolnoth (London) CW, fos. 1–24; St Mary Magdalen Milk Street (London) CW, fos. 1–91; St Michael le Querne (London) CW, fos. 3–120; St Peter Westcheap (London) CW, years 1537–8; St Stephen Walbrook (London) CW, years 1474–1538; St Dunstan in the East (London) CW, years 1494–5; St John, Bristol CW, fos. 1–34; St Ewen, Bristol CW, pp. 31–158; All Saints, Bristol CW, years 1469–1542; Christ Church, Bristol CW, years 1545–7; Stow, *Survey*, ed. Kingsford, i. 230–1; Sharp, *Dissertation on . . .*

Coventry, 160–72; *The Records of the City of Norwich*, ed. Revd William Hudson and John Cottingham Tingey (Norwich, 1910), ii. 230; Chambers, *Medieval Stage* (1963 edn.), ii. 338–99 (for Beverley, Bury St Edmunds, Hereford, Ipswich, Bungay, King's Lynn, Shrewsbury, Worcester, Great Yarmouth); A. F. Johnston, 'The Guild of Corpus Christi and the Procession of Corpus Christi in York', *Medieval Studies*, 38 (1976), 372–84; *Records of Maidstone* (Maidstone, 1926), 2; *Henley Borough Records*, ed. P. Briers (Oxfordshire Record Society, 1960), 199–225; *The Account Books of the Guilds of . . . Nottingham*, ed. R. Hodgkinson (Thoroton Society Record Series, 1939), *passim*; *Plymouth Municipal Records*, ed. Worth, 29–35; *Devon*, ed. Wasson, 101–39, 348–85 (for Exeter); Devon RO, Dartmouth Corporation Records, Mayors' Accounts, years 1526–33; Richard Welford, *History of Newcastle and Gateshead* (1885), ii. 97–508; St Dunstan, Canterbury (Kent) CW, xvi. 304–19, xvii. 93–110; St Andrew, Canterbury (Kent) CW, xxxii. 208–43, xxxiii. 3–59; St John, Peterborough (Northants.) CW, pp. 82–161; Louth (Lincs.) CW, pp. 186–98; St Lawrence, Reading (Berks.) CW, pp. 234–5; St Michael, Oxford CW, a. 1–2; Ludlow (Salop) CW, pp. 22–5; Sherborne (Dorset) CW, xxiii. 209–333; St Mary, Devizes (Wilts.) CW, years 1499–1500.

108. *Players in Norfolk and Suffolk*, ed. Galloway and Wasson, 2, 100, 159; Great Dunmow (Essex) CW, years 1526–46; Ashburton (Devon) CW, pp. 1–114; Saffron Walden (Essex) CW, years 1441–76.

109. Miri Rubin, 'Corpus Christi Fraternities and Late Medieval Piety', in W. J. Sheils and Diana Wood (eds.), *Voluntary Religion* (Studies in Church History, 23; 1986), 97–109.

110. Cox, *Churchwardens' Accounts*, 268–70; Sherborne (Dorset) CW, years 1512–48; *Players in Norfolk and Suffolk*, ed. Galloway and Wasson, p. xi; Great Dunmow (Essex) CW, years 1526–39; *Players in Lincolnshire*, ed. Kahrl, pp. xxiii–xxxvi.

111. *Players in Norfolk and Suffolk*, ed. Galloway and Wasson, 2, 100.

112. Chambers, *Medieval Stage* (1963 edn.), ii. 338–98; *Players in Lincolnshire*, ed. Kahrl, 76–84; Harold C. Gardiner, *Mysteries' End* (New Haven, Conn., 1967), ch. 3; V. A. Kolve, *The Play Called Corpus Christi* (1966); A. Leach, 'Some English Plays and Players 1220–1548', in *An English Miscellany Presented to Dr Furnivall* (Oxford, 1901), 206–34; Alan H. Nelson, *The Medieval English Stage* (Chicago, 1974); William Tydeman, *The Theatre in the Middle Ages* (Cambridge, 1978), 114–20.

113. Sharp, *Dissertation on . . . Coventry*, 4–75; *Records of Early English Drama: Coventry*, ed. R. W. Ingram (Manchester, 1981), 1–174; Nelson, *Medieval English Stage*, chs. 3, 8; *York*, ed. Johnston and Rogerson, 1–289, 689–839; Clifford Davidson, *From Creation to Doom* (New York, 1984); Kolve, *Corpus Christi*.

114. Nelson, *Medieval English Stage*, ch. 2; Tydeman, *Theatre in the Middle Ages*, 114–20.

115. In 'Ritual, Drama and Social Body in the Medieval English Town', repr. in his collected essays *Society, Politics and Culture* (Cambridge, 1986), 17–41.

116. Sharp, *Dissertation on . . . Coventry*, 175–201; *The Little Red Book of Bristol*, ed. Francis B. Bickley (Bristol, 1900), ii. 122–89; *Great Red Book of Bristol*, ed. Veale, 26–7; Picton, *Liverpool*, 45; *Cumberland, Westmorland and Gloucestershire*, ed. Douglas and Greenfield, 27, 301; *Devon*, ed. Wasson, 139; *Newcastle-upon-Tyne*, ed. Anderson, 15, 24; Stow, *Survey*, ed. Kingsford, i. 101, ii. 284; Kethe, *A Sermon*, reprinted in Brand, *Observations*, ed. Ellis, i. 308; HMC Middleton MSS, p. 336 (Willoughby accounts).

117. Canterbury Cathedral L, Literary MS C13, fo. 10 (description of Canterbury watch); *Players in Lincolnshire*, ed. Kahrl, 24–69; Nelson, *Medieval English Stage*, ch. 6.

118. Tusser, *Five Hundred Pointes* (English Dialect Society, 1878), 129–32.

119. Milton, quoted in Sir James Frazer, *The Golden Bough* (abridged edn. 1922), 405; William Benchley Rye (ed.), *England as Seen by Foreigners in the Days of Elizabeth and James the First* (1865), 111 (Paul Hentzner's journal).

120. BL Additional MS 38174, fo. 34^v (Henry VII's Household Ordinances).

121. Kethe, *A Sermon*, and *Festyvall* (1511), repr. in Brand, *Observations*, ed. Ellis, i. 308, 392; *Northumberland Household Book*, ed. Percy, 320, 324; Rye (Sussex) CW, years 1540–7; *Mirk's Festial*, ed. Erbe, 269; HMC Middleton MSS, pp. 330, 349, 369 (Willoughby accounts); Leverington (Cambs.) CW, pp. 188–9; Bramley (Hants.) CW, years 1522–3; Leverton (Lincs.) CW, p. 356; Great Dunmow (Essex) CW, years 1529–34; Wigtoft (Lincs.) CW, p. 220; Heybridge (Essex) CW, pp. 153–82; Bethersden (Kent) CW, p. 43; St Michael, Oxford CW, a. 1; Bletchingley (Surrey) CW, p. 27; Ashburton (Devon) CW, pp. 4–102; St Petrock, Exeter (Devon) CW, years 1427–8; St Mary at Hill (London) CW, p. 149; St Edmund, Salisbury (Wilts.) CW, p. 14; St Thomas, Salisbury (Wilts.) CW, p. 274; Worfield (Staffs.) CW, p. 235; Shipdam (Norfolk) CW, fo. 4; Long Sutton (Lincs.) CW, fos. 16–18; Bramfield (Essex) CW, p. 3; St Mary, Bungay (Suffolk) CW, pp. 3–4; Bassingbourn (Cambs.) CW, years 1497–1538; Denton (Norfolk) CW, fos. 3–40; Swaffham (Norfolk) CW, fos. 1–140; Woodbury (Devon) CW, years 1538–41; St Michael, Bath (Somerset) CW, pp. 25–117; Christ Church, Bristol CW, years 1545–7; St Lawrence Pountney (London) CW, years 1530–47; St Mary Woolnoth (London) CW, fos. 1–19; Amersham (Bucks.) CW, pp. 44–5; Bridgewater (Somerset) CW, pp. 56–96.

122. St Mary (Stafford) CW, years 1528–9.

123. HMC 14th Report, appendix viii, pp. 267–8 (list of Grimsby feasts); *Players in Lincolnshire*, ed. Kahrl, pp. xxvii, 11–12; Hadley, *Kingston-upon-Hull*, 823–6.

124. Duffy, *Stripping of the Altars*, 47.

125. Cawte, *Ritual Animal Disguise*, *passim*; and see also S. Addy, 'Guising and Mumming in Derbyshire', *Derbyshire Archaeological and Natural History Society Journal*, 29 (1907), 30–42, and Chambers, *Medieval Stage* (1963 edn.), ii. 302.

126. Robert Plot, *The Natural History of Staffordshire* (Oxford, 1686), 434.

127. Thomas Blount, *Fragmenta Antiquitatis* (1845), 529–32.

CHAPTER 2

1. Listed in the Appendix.

2. *Medieval Framlingham: Select Documents*, ed. John Ridgard (Suffolk Records Society, 27; 1985) (Framlingham manor and castle 1286–7, 1324–5, 1386–8); Nottingham University L, M:A/1 (Lord Grey of Condor, 1304–5); 'Household Accounts at Hunstanton 1328', ed. G. H. Holley, *Norfolk Archaeology*, 2 (1920–2), 77–96; BL Add. Roll 63207 (Dame Katherine de Norwich, 1336–7); Magdalen College (Oxford) L, Moulton Hall 160 (Moulton of Moulton, 1343–4); Berkeley Castle Muniment Room, Select Roll 64 (Lord Berkeley, 1345–6); Norfolk RO, N. H. 8 (Le Strange, 1348–50); Shakespeare's Birthplace Trust, DR 37, box 3 (Montfort, n.d. but clearly late 14th cent.); B. Ross, 'The Accounts of the Talbot Household at Blakemere in

the County of Shropshire 1394–1425' (Australian National University Ph.D. thesis; Canberra, 1970); PRO, E. 101/511/15 (John Catesby, 1392–3) and E. 101/512/17 (William Moleyn, 1400–1); Northamptonshire RO, Westmorland (Apethorpe), box 9, parcel 20/4 (Duke of York, 1409–10); *The Household Book of Dame Alice de Bryene*, ed. Vincent B. Redstone (Suffolk Institute of Archaeology and Natural History, 1931) (for 1412–13); Longleat House, Miscellaneous MS IX (Earl of Warwick, 1420–1); Somerset RO, DD/L/P37/10 (Luttrell, 1425–6); Essex RO, D/DPr 137 (Earl of Oxford, 1431–2); *Compota Domestica Familiarum de Bukingham et d'Angouleme*, ed. W. B. Turnbull (Abbotsford Club, 1836) (Duke of Buckingham, 1443–4, and Duchess of Buckingham, 1463–4); 'The Account of the Great Household of Humphrey, First Duke of Buckingham, for the Year 1452–3', ed. Mary Harris, *Camden Miscellany*, 28 (Camden Society, 4th ser. 29; 1984), 1–57; Bod. L. MS DD Per Weld C19/4 (Eyre of Hassop, 1466–91); Lincolnshire RO, M.M. 1/3/26 (Skipwith of South Ormsby, 1467–8); PRO, C47/37/7 (Elizabeth Stonor, 1478). I owe many of these references to the work of Christopher Dyer.

3. *A Roll of the Household Expenses of Richard de Swinfield, Bishop of Hereford*, ed. Revd John Webb (Camden Society, 59; 1853, and 62; 1854); 'Household Roll of Bishop Ralph of Shrewsbury' (1337–8), ed. A. H. Thompson, *Somerset Record Society Collectanea*, 1 (1924), 72–174; Cambridge University L, EDR/D5/3, 5 (Bishop of Ely, 1381–8); BL Harleian MS 3,755 (Bishop of Salisbury, 1406–7); Staffordshire RO, D1734/3/3/264 (Bishop of Lichfield, 1461).

4. *The Account Book of Beaulieu Abbey*, ed. S. F. Hockley (Camden Society, 4th ser. 16; 1975); *Documents Illustrating the Rule of Walter de Wenlok, Abbot of Westminster, 1283–1307*, ed. Barbara F. Harvey (Camden Society, 4th ser. 2; 1965); *The Early Rolls of Merton College, Oxford*, ed. J. R. Highfield (Oxford Historical Society, NS 18; 1964); *Extracts from the Account Rolls of the Abbey of Durham*, ed. Canon Fowler (Surtees Society, 99, 100, 103; 1898–1900); K. L. Wood-Legh (ed.), *A Small Household of the XVth Century* (Manchester, 1965); *Records of Early English Drama: Cambridge*, ed. Alan H. Nelson (Toronto, 1986), *passim* (for King's College); Warwickshire RO, M1 272 (Maxstoke Priory, 1432–95); Bod. L, MS All Souls C276 (All Souls' College, 1448–9).

5. *Rotuli de Libertate ac de Misis et Praetestis Regnante Johanne*, ed. T. Duffus Hardy (Record Commission, 1844); *Records of the Wardrobe and Household 1285–1286*, ed. Benjamin F. Byerly and Catherine Ridder Byerly (HMSO, 1977), and *Records of the Wardrobe and Household 1286–1289*, ed. Benjamin F. Byerly and Catherine Ridder Byerly (HMSO, 1986).

6. John Brand, *Observations on the Popular Antiquities of Great Britain*, ed. Sir Henry Ellis (1908), i. 10–17; Alexander Murray, 'Medieval Christmas', *History Today* (Dec. 1986), 33; *Medii Aevi Kalendarium*, ed. R. T. Hampson (1841), 132.

7. Bede, *Ecclesiastical History*, ch. 30.

8. Nathaniel J. Hone, *The Manor and Manorial Records* (1906), 98; *Patrologiae Cursus Completus . . . Series Latinae*, ed. J. P. Migne, 202 (Paris, 1855), 141.

9. H. H. Scullard, *Festivals and Ceremonies of the Roman Republic* (1981), 104–5; *Cormac's Glossary*, ed. John O'Donovan and Whitley Stokes (Dublin, 1868), 15; Pliny, *Natural History*, XVIII. lxx.

10. Miranda Green, *The Gods of the Celts* (1986), 164–5, and 'Jupiter, Taranis and the Solar Wheel', in Martin Henig and Anthony King (eds.), *Pagan Gods and Shrines of the*

Roman Empire (Oxford, 1986), 65–75; T. Brown, '72nd Report on Folklore', *Transactions of the Devonshire Association*, 107 (1975), 188; Ronald Hutton, *The Pagan Religions of the Ancient British Isles* (Oxford, 1991), 103–7, 156, 164–5.

11. John T. McNeill, *The Celtic Churches* (1974), 109–18, 196–7; Mary Clayton, *The Cult of the Virgin Mary in Anglo-Saxon England* (Cambridge, 1990), ch. 2; Brand, *Observations*, ed. Ellis, i. 44; John Dowden, *The Church Year and Calendar* (Cambridge, 1910), 27–35, 40–4, 80, 105–7; *Councils and Synods . . . 871–1066*, ed. D. Whitelock, M. Brett, C. N. L. Brooke (Oxford, 1981), 220; Henry John Feasey, *Ancient English Holy Week Ceremonial* (1897), 114–28; A. R. Wright, *British Calendar Customs*, ed. T. E. Lones (Folklore Society, 1936), i. 149; *Documents Illustrative of English Church History*, ed. Henry Gee (1896), 22–3; *Medii Aevi Kalendarium*, ed. Hampson, 221.

12. See sources at Ch. 1 n. 51.

13. Feasey, *Holy Week Ceremonial*, 179–240; *Councils and Synods . . . 1205–1313*, ed. F. M. Powicke and C. R. Cheney (Oxford, 1964), 56, 178, 318, 513, 715–16, 1006, 1123.

14. E. K. Chambers, *The Medieval Stage* (Oxford, 1963), ii. 8–16; A. Heales, 'Easter Sepulchres', *Archaeologia*, 42 (1867), 263–70.

15. *Inventory of Church Goods temp. Edward III*, ed. Dom. A. Watkin (Norfolk Record Society, 19; 1948), *passim*.

16. See Appendix. It appeared (e.g.) at Pilton (Somerset) in 1507; at Yatton (Somerset) in 1455; at St Nicholas, Great Yarmouth (Suffolk) in 1465; at Walberswick (Suffolk) in 1464; at St Dunstan, Canterbury (Kent) in 1491; at St Michael, Oxford in 1500; at Arlington (Sussex) in 1465; at Tavistock (Devon) in 1543; at Dartmouth (Devon) in 1494; at Halesowen (Worcs.) in 1527; at Worfield (Staffs.) in 1502; at Stratton (Cornwall) in 1530; at Saffron Walden (Essex) in 1443; and at St Dunstan in the West (London) in 1525. All these accounts go back for years before. It is also present in some sets as they commence in the fifteenth century.

17. *Inventory of Church Goods*, ed. Watkin, *passim*.

18. John Chandos (ed.), *In God's Name* (1971), 41; Chambers, *Medieval Stage* (1963 edn.), chs. 13–15; Neil Mackenzie, 'Boy into Bishop', *History Today* (Dec. 1987), 10–11.

19. *Records of Early English Drama: York*, ed. Alexandra F. Johnston and Margaret Rogerson (Manchester, 1979), 687–8; Chambers, *Medieval Stage* (1963 edn.), i. 340–58.

20. Chambers, *Medieval Stage* (1963 edn.), i. 321–5, 340–52; Mackenzie, 'Boy into Bishop', 15.

21. See sources at n. 4, plus *Medii Aevi Kalendarium*, ed. Hampson, 80.

22. 'A Brief Summary of the Wardrobe Accounts of the Tenth, Eleventh and Fourteenth Years of King Edward the Second', *Archaeologia*, 26 (1835), 342; *Cambridge*, ed. Nelson, 1053.

23. e.g. they appeared at Louth in 1502 (apparently as part of a greater importance of the church after major rebuilding); at Lambeth in 1522; and at Halesowen in 1515. What is significant about this tiny number of cases is that it actually represents the majority of parishes in which the Boy Bishops are known which have accounts good enough to show when the custom began. For the extent of the 'bishops', see Ch. 1 n. 21.

24. Miri Rubin, 'Corpus Christi Fraternities and Late Medieval Piety', in W. J. Shiels and Diana Wood (eds.), *Voluntary Religion* (Studies in Church History, 23; 1986), 97–104, and 'Corpus Christi: Inventing a Feast', *History Today* (July 1990), 15–17;

John Wodderspoon, *Memorials of the Ancient Town of Ipswich* (1850), 156–62; *Inventory of Church Goods*, ed. Watkin, p. xxxix; Thomas North, *A Chronicle of the Church of St Martin in Leicester* (1866), 184–8; *Cambridge*, ed. Nelson, 5; Alan H. Nelson, *The Medieval English Stage* (Chicago, 1974), chs. 8, 10.

25. e.g. at Bridgewater torches appeared in 1428–9, and at Nottingham torches in 1473 and banners in the 1490s: *Bridgewater Borough Archives*, ed. T. Dilks (Somerset Record Society, 58; 1943), 62–101; and *The Account Books of the Guilds of St George and St Mary in the Church of St Peter, Nottingham*, ed. R. Hodgkinson (Thoroton Society Record Series, 1939), 16–23. At St Michael (Oxford), the banners for the parish procession were added in 1434: CW in Appendix.

26. David Scott Fox, *St George* (1983), 17–18; H. F. Westlake, *The Parish Guilds of Medieval England* (1919), *passim*.

27. *Records of the Guild of St George in Norwich*, ed. M. Grace (Norfolk Record Society, 9; 1937), 17–112.

28. See sources at Ch. 1 n. 69.

29. St Margaret, Westminster (London) CW, p. 3 (year 1491); St John, Glastonbury (Somerset) CW, no. 11 (year 1498); Stoke Courcy (Somerset) CW, year 1507–8; Croscombe (Somerset) CW, p. 32 (year 1511); St Edmund, Salisbury (Wilts.) CW, p. 64 (year 1518–19); St Augustine, Hedon (Yorks.) CW (year 1531–2); and St Lawrence, Reading (Berks.) CW, year 1534.

30. *Household Expenses of Richard de Swinfield*, ed. Webb, 22–31.

31. *Household Book of Dame Alice de Bryene*, ed. Redstone, 25–9; Longleat House, Misc. MS IX, n.p. (Warwick accounts).

32. Fits I–III.

33. *Councils and Synods*, ed. Powicke and Cheney, 313, 480. Two unequivocal references to the custom of summer kings appear in a monastic chronicle and a poem or song, both referring to events in 1306 and apparently contemporary or only slightly later than them: *Flores Historiarum*, ed. H. R. Luard (Rolls Series, 1890), iii. 130, and *Historical Poems of the XIVth and XVth Centuries*, ed. Russell Hope Robbins (New York, 1959), 16.

34. Repr. in *Medii Aevi Kalendarium*, ed. Hampson, 231–3.

35. Roscoe E. Parker, 'Some Records of the Somyr Play', in Richard Beale Davis and John Leon Lievsay (eds.), *Studies in Honor of John C. Hodges and Alwin Thaler* (Knoxville, 1961), 19–20.

36. Joseph Strutt, *The Sports and Pastimes of the People of England*, ed. J. Charles Cox (1903), 276; Kenneth Hurlstone Jackson (ed.), *A Celtic Miscellany* (1951), 87–9.

37. H. C. March, 'The Giant and Maypole of Cerne', *Proceedings of the Dorset Natural History and Antiquarian Field Club*, 22 (1901), 104.

38. Hutton, *Pagan Religions*, 178–83.

39. Kevin Danaher, *The Year in Ireland* (Cork, 1972), 95–100.

40. *Materials for the History of Thomas Becket*, ed. Revd James Craigie Robertson (1877), iii. 9.

41. *Two Lives of Saint Cuthbert*, trans. Bertram Colgrave (Cambridge, 1940), 219; Feasey, *Holy Week Ceremonial*, 95–103; Wright, *British Calendar Customs*, ed. Lones, i. 62–3; Arnold Kellett, 'King John's Maundy', *History Today* (Apr. 1990), 34–9.

42. Alexander Murray, 'Medieval Christmas', *History Today* (Dec. 1986), 37; Brand, *Observations*, ed. Ellis, i. 481–5.

43. Brand, *Observations*, ed. Ellis, i. 2; *Medii Aevi Kalendarium*, ed. Hampson, 100–2.

44. Brand, *Observations*, ed. Ellis, i. 53–4; Wright, *British Calendar Customs*, ed. Lones, i. 138–9. And see sources at Ch. 1 n. 39.

45. *York*, ed. Johnston and Rogerson, 689; A. Leach, 'Some English Plays and Players 1220–1548', in *An English Miscellany Presented to Dr Furnivall* (Oxford, 1901), 208–9; *Records of Plays and Players in Norfolk and Suffolk 1330–1642*, ed. D. Galloway and J. Wasson (Malone Society, 1980), 38–55.

46. *Records of Early English Drama: Coventry*, ed. R. W. Ingram (Manchester, 1981), 1–12; *Records of Early English Drama: Devon*, ed. John M. Wasson (Toronto, 1986), 357–8; *Records of Early English Drama: Chester*, ed. Lawrence M. Clopper (Manchester, 1979), 6–7; *Records of Early English Drama: Newcastle-upon-Tyne*, ed. J. J. Anderson (Toronto, 1982), 3.

47. *Records of Plays and Players in Lincolnshire 1300–1585*, ed. S. J. Karhl (Malone Society, 1969), 76–84.

48. *Coventry*, ed. Ingram, 1–174; *York*, ed. Johnston and Rogerson, 1–83; *Chester*, ed. Clopper, 1–43.

49. *Memorials of London and London Life*, ed. Henry Thomas Riley (1868), 419–20, 488; *Devon*, ed. Wasson, 359; *Coventry*, ed. Ingram, 7–8, 16; *Chester*, ed. Clopper, p. lii.

50. Listed in Richard Valpey French, *Nineteen Centuries of Drink in England* (1884), 81–4.

51. See e.g. Yatton (Somerset) CW, pp. 81–6 (house built 1448); Tintinhull (Somerset) CW, pp. 178–97 (house built 1497); Walberswick (Suffolk) CW, pp. 1–6 (ales begin 1451); St Michael (Oxford) CW, a.1, year 1457–8; Launceston (Cornwall) CW, year 1485–6; St Edmund, Salisbury (Wilts.) CW, pp. 1–13 (ales begin 1469–70); St John, Glastonbury (Somerset) CW, nos. 1–7 (ales begin 1428).

52. Chambers, *Medieval Stage* (1963 edn.), i. 156.

53. ll. 1210–11.

54. Chambers, *Medieval Stage* (1963 edn.), i. 155 n. 3; *Memorials of London*, ed. Riley, 561–2, 571.

55. *Cambridge*, ed. Nelson, 1091–1103.

56. St Michael (Oxford) CW, a.1, year 1471; Thame (Oxon.) CW, year 1488; St Dunstan, Canterbury (Kent) CW, xvii. 297 (year 1490); Bassingbourn (Cambs.) CW, year 1497; St Edmund, Salisbury (Wilts.) CW, p. 47 (year 1497–8); Henley (Oxon.) CW, year 1499.

57. Sources at Ch. 1 n. 68.

58. David Wiles, *The Early Plays of Robin Hood* (Cambridge, 1981), 43–6 and appendix 1.

59. The sources for the period 1450–1540 are collected at Ch. 1 n. 18, above, to which I have added a little here from Chambers, *Medieval Stage* (1963 edn.), ii. 403–4. Those for the years 1300–1450 are well set forth in Sandra Billington, *Mock Kings in Medieval Society and Renaissance Drama* (Oxford, 1991), 30–3. I differ from her only in failing to find any firm evidence of midwinter mock rulers between the royal bean king in 1335 and 'Prester John' in 1414. The reference which she finds in William Langland, *The Vision of Piers Plowman . . . together with Richard the Redeless*, ed. Revd Walter W. Skeat (Oxford, 1886), passus IV, i. 1, seems to me to be to a 'Christian king' not a 'Christmas king' as she believes.

60. Barbara Lowe, 'Early Records of the Morris in England', *JEFDSS*, 7/2 (1957), 61–6; and sources at Ch. 1 n. 84 above.

61. Sandra Billington, 'Routs and Reyes', *Folklore*, 89 (1978), 184–203.

62. E. C. Cawte, *Ritual Animal Disguise* (Folklore Society, 1978), 11–23.

63. Chambers, *Medieval Stage* (1963 edn.), i. 235–59.

64. See (e.g.) Westlake, *Parish Guilds*; Alan Kreider, *English Chantries: The Road to Dissolution* (Cambridge, Mass., 1979); J. J. Scarisbrick, *The Reformation and the English People* (Oxford, 1984), chs. 1–2; B. A. Hanawalt, 'Keepers of the Lights: Late Medieval Parish Guilds', *Journal of Medieval and Renaissance Studies*, 14 (1984), 21–37; Ronald Hutton, 'The Local Impact of the Tudor Reformations', in Christopher Haigh (ed.), *The English Reformation Revised* (Cambridge, 1987), pp. 115–16; Robert Whiting, *The Blind Devotion of the People* (Cambridge, 1989), chs. 1–3.

65. *Players in Lincolnshire*, ed. Karhl; *Players in Norfolk and Suffolk*, ed. Galloway and Wasson; *Players in Kent*, ed. Dawson; *Devon*, ed. Wasson.

66. Christopher Dyer, *Standards of Living in the Later Middle Ages* (Cambridge, 1989), 1–9; F. W. Maitland, *Township and Borough* (Cambridge, 1898), 85; Joel T. Rosenthal, *The Purchase of Paradise* (Toronto, 1972), 1.

67. Eleanor Searle, *Lordship and Community* (Toronto, 1972), 365–6; A. R. Bridbury, *Economic Growth: England in the Later Middle Ages* (2nd edn., Brighton, 1975); John Hatcher, *Rural Economy and Society in the Duchy of Cornwall 1300–1500* (1977), chs. 7–8, and *Plague, Population and the English Economy 1348–1500* (1977); R. B. Dobson, 'Urban Decline in Late Medieval England', *Transactions of the Royal Historical Society*, 5th ser. 27 (1977), 1–22; Charles Phythian-Adams, 'Urban Decay in Late Medieval England', in D. Abrams and E. A. Wrigley (ed.), *Towns in Societies* (Cambridge, 1978), 159–85; Alan Dyer, 'Growth and Decay in English Towns 1500–1700', *Urban History Yearbook* (1979), 60–72; Charles Phythian-Adams, 'Dr Dyer's Urban Undulations', *Urban History Yearbook* (1979), 73–6, and *Desolation of a City* (Cambridge, 1979); Christopher Dyer, *Lords and Peasants in a Changing Society* (Cambridge, 1980), 189–305; Douglas Moss, 'The Economic Development of a Middlesex Village', *Agricultural History Review*, 28 (1980), 104–14; Ann Kussmaul, *Servants in Husbandry in Early Modern England* (Cambridge, 1981); A. R. Bridbury, 'English Provincial Towns in the Later Middle Ages', *Economic History Review*, 2nd ser. 34 (1981), 1–24; Christopher Dyer, 'Deserted Villages in the West Midlands', *Economic History Review*, 2nd ser. 35 (1982), 19–34; Cicely Howell, *Land, Family and Inheritance in Transition* (Cambridge, 1983), 50–70; Andrew Jones, 'Bedfordshire: Fifteenth Century', in P. D. A. Harvey (ed.), *The Peasant Land Market in Medieval England* (Oxford, 1984), 179–251; M. K. McIntosh, *Autonomy and Community* (Cambridge, 1986), ch. 6; R. H. Britnell, *Growth and Decline in Colchester 1300–1525* (Cambridge, 1986); Christopher Dyer, *Standards of Living in the Later Middle Ages* (Cambridge, 1989); A. F. Pollard, *North-Eastern England during the Wars of the Roses* (Oxford, 1990), chs. 1–8; Maurice Keen, *English Society in the Later Middle Ages 1348–1500* (1990), chs. 3–4.

68. Canterbury Cathedral L, Literary MS C13, fo. 10.

69. 'Puritanism and Social Control?', in Anthony Fletcher and John Stevenson (eds.), *Order and Disorder in Early Modern England* (Cambridge, 1985), ch. 1.

70. 'Local Change and Community Control in England 1465–1500', *Huntington Library Quarterly*, 49 (1986), 219–42.

71. Wiles, *Early Plays of Robin Hood*, 45.

72. Lowe, 'Early Records of the Morris', 61–6.

73. Wiles, *Early Plays of Robin Hood*, appendix 1.

74. Phythian-Adams, 'Urban Decay', 173–8.

75. Harold C. Gardiner, *Mysteries' End* (New Haven, Conn., 1967), ch. 3; *Coventry*, ed. Ingram, 40, 79–80, 136, 148–9; *York*, ed. Johnston and Rogerson, 62, 697.

CHAPTER 3

1. The principal examples being C. A. Haigh, *Reformation and Resistance in Tudor Lancashire* (Cambridge, 1976); F. Heal, 'The Parish Clergy and the Reformation in the Diocese of Ely', *Proceedings of the Cambridge Antiquarian Society*, 166 (1976–7), 141–63; Peter Clark, *English Provincial Society from the Reformation to the Revolution* (1977), and 'Reformation and Radicalism in Kentish Towns', in *The Urban Classes, the Nobility and the Reformation* (German Historical Institute 5; 1979); D. Palliser, *Tudor York* (Oxford, 1979); A. M. Johnson, 'The Reformation Clergy of Derbyshire', *Journal of the Derbyshire Archaeological and Natural History Society*, 100 (1980), 49–63; G. Williams, 'Wales and the Reign of Mary I', *Welsh History Review*, 10 (1980–1), 334–58; E. Sheppard, 'The Reformation and the Citizens of Norwich', *Norfolk Archaeology*, 38 (1981–3), 44–55; M. A. Cook, 'Eye (Suffolk) in the Years of Uncertainty 1520–1590' (Keele University Ph.D. thesis; 1982); G. Mayhew, 'The Progress of the Reformation in East Sussex', *Southern History* (1983), 38–67; Diarmaid MacCulloch, *Suffolk and the Tudors* (Oxford, 1986), pt. 2; and Robert Whiting, *The Blind Devotion of the People* (Cambridge, 1989).
2. Ronald Hutton, 'The Local Impact of the Tudor Reformations', in Christopher Haigh (ed.), *The English Reformation Revised* (Cambridge, 1987), 114–38.
3. See Appendix.
4. St Lawrence, Reading (Berks.); Stratton (Cornwall); St Mary on the Hill, Chester (Cheshire); St Michael, Oxford; Thame (Oxon.); St Margaret, Westminster; St Martin in the Fields, Westminster; Ashburton (Devon); Morebath (Devon); St Petrock, Exeter (Devon); Badsey (Worcs.); Boxford (Suffolk); St Mary, Bungay (Suffolk); Wing (Bucks.); All Hallows Staining (London); St Alphege London Wall (London); St Dunstan in the West (London); St Mary Magdalen Milk Street (London).
5. *Councils and Synods, with Other Documents Relating to the English Church*, ed. D. Whitelock, M. Brett, and C. N. L. Brooke (Oxford, 1981), i. 218; *A Collection of the Laws and Canons of the Church of England*, ed. John Johnson (Oxford, 1850), i. 219.
6. Kenneth L. Parker, *The English Sabbath* (Cambridge, 1988), 8–23.
7. Ibid.; *Councils and Synods*, ed. F. M. Powicke and C. R. Cheney (Oxford, 1964), 197, 202, 265, 303, 622, 722, 1044; *Records of Early English Drama: Devon*, ed. John M. Wasson (Toronto, 1986), 318, 328; Robert of Brunne, *Handlying Synne*, ed. F. J. Furnivall (EETS; 1901), 283–90.
8. *Councils and Synods*, ed. Powicke and Cheney, 313, 480; Richard Valpey French, *Nineteen Centuries of Drink in England* (1884), 81–4.
9. *Devon*, ed. Wasson, 328; Bishops Stortford (Essex) CW, year 1490; Elham (Kent) CW, pp. 66–7; PRO, SP 1/99, pp. 203–4 (deposition regarding Harwich).
10. Robert of Brunne, *Handlying Synne*, 36, 156, 283.
11. *The Eclogues*, ed. Beatrice White (EETS; 1928), 5th Eclogue, ll. 807–24.
12. *Popular Culture in Early Modern Europe* (1978), ch. 8.
13. *Bonfires and Bells* (1989), 3.
14. See Chs. 1–2, above, but also Ronald Hutton, *The Pagan Religions of the Ancient British Isles* (Oxford, 1991), 133–4, 179–83, 290–2, 324–30.

15. e.g. *Manuale ad Usum Percelebris Ecclesia Sarisburiensis*, ed. A. Jeffrey Collins (Henry Bradshaw Society; 1960); and *Councils and Synods*, ed. Powicke and Cheney, 321–5.

16. Hutton, *Pagan Religions*, 291–2, 297–8; *Dives and Pauper*, ed. P. H. Barnum (EETS; 1976), 5, 29, 157; *Mirk's Festial*, ed. T. Erbe (EETS; 1905), 44–5.

17. Out of a large literature, examples of different approaches are provided by Burke, *Popular Culture*; William A. Christian, *Local Religion in Sixteenth-Century Spain* (1981); Robert Scribner, 'Interpreting Religion in Early Modern Europe', *European Studies Review*, 13 (1983), 89–105, and *Popular Culture and Popular Movements in Reformation Germany* (1987); A. E. Green, 'Popular Drama and the Mummers' Play', in David Bradby, Louis Jones, and Bernard Sharatt (eds.), *Performance and Politics in Popular Drama* (Cambridge, 1980), 139–66; Natalie Zemon Davis, 'Some Tasks and Themes in the Study of Popular Religion', in Charles Trinkhaus and Heika A. Oberman (eds.), *The Pursuit of Holiness in Late Medieval and Renaissance Religion* (Leiden, 1974), 307–38, and 'From "Popular Religion" to Religious Cultures', in Steven Ozment (ed.), *Reformation Europe: A Guide to Research* (St Louis, 1982), 321–42.

18. 'The Recent Historiography of the English Reformation', *Historical Journal*, 25 (1982), 995–1007.

19. Yatton (Somerset) CW, years 1547–50; Stoke Charity (Hants) CW, year 1550–1; Great Packington (War.) CW, year 1561–2.

20. *Documents Illustrative of English Church History*, ed. Henry Gee and William John Hardy (1896), 150, 172–3.

21. [Anthony Sparrow (ed.)], *A Collection of Articles* (1671), 167–8.

22. J. B. Sheppard, 'The Canterbury Marching Watch and the Pageant of St. Thomas', *Archaeologia Cantiana*, 2 (1878), 37–9; Eamon Duffy, *The Stripping of the Altars* (New Haven, Conn., 1992), 394–8.

23. *Records of Plays and Players in Norfolk and Suffolk 1330–1642*, ed. D. Galloway and J. Wasson (Malone Society, 1980), 170–83.

24. Halesowen (Worcs.) CW, p. 78. See also Sherborne (Dorset) CW, no. 19.

25. *Documents*, ed. Gee and Hardy, 276–9.

26. Halesowen (Worcs.) CW, p. 78; All Saints, Bristol CW, year 1538–9.

27. Whiting, *Blind Devotion of the People*, 58.

28. Patrick Collinson, *The Birthpangs of Protestant England* (1989), 50.

29. Swaffham and Tilney All Saints (Norfolk); Boxford, Brundish, and Cratfield (Suffolk).

30. Bramley (Hants); Yatton (Somerset); St Margaret, Westminster; St Michael Spurriergate, York; St Andrew, Lewes (Sussex); Ashburton (Devon); Badsey (Worcs.); St Martin Outwich (London); Stogursey (Somerset); St Nicholas, Bristol; Long Sutton (Lincs.); St Martin, Oxford; St Mary, Bungay (Suffolk); All Hallows Staining (London); St Dunstan in the West (London); and St Mary Magdalen Milk Street (London).

31. Hutton, 'Local Impact', 117–18.

32. *Letters and Papers*, xiv. *1539*, no. 1144; Charles Wriothesley, *A Chronicle of England*, ed. W. D. Hamilton (Camden Society; 1875), i. 100; S. Williams, 'The Lord Mayor's Show in Tudor and Stuart Times', *Guildhall Miscellany*, 10 (Sept. 1959), 4–6; *Harleian Miscellany*, ix. 389–408 (account of midsummer watch). The anxieties of the Council are first reported in the *Calendar of State Papers Spanish*, iv. ii, no. 1091 (28 June 1533); I owe this reference to Diarmaid MacCulloch.

33. BL Arundel MS 97, fos. 20^v, 76 (King's Book of Payments 1539–41). Compare the

rest of this book and the next, BL Add. MS 59900 (for years 1542–3), when a gift is still made to the grooms of the hall but no fire is mentioned.

34. *Records of Early English Drama: Coventry*, ed. R. W. Ingram (Manchester, 1981), 148–9.

35. *Records of Plays and Players in Lincolnshire 1300–1585*, ed. S. J. Kahrl (Malone Society, 1969), 60–9.

36. *Records of Early English Drama: Chester*, ed. Lawrence M. Clopper (Manchester, 1979), 40–2.

37. Sydney Anglo, 'An Early Tudor Programme for Plays and Other Demonstrations against the Pope', *Journal of the Warburg and Courtauld Institutes*, 20 (1957), 176–9; Duffy, *Stripping of the Altars*, 425–6.

38. *Tudor Royal Proclamations*, ed. Paul L. Hughes and James F. Larkin (New Haven, Conn., 1964), i, no. 188; Duffy, *Stripping of the Altars*, 426.

39. Hutton, 'The Local Impact', 118.

40. *Proclamations*, ed. Hughes and Larkin, i, no. 202.

41. BL Arundel MS 97, fo. 158, and Add. MS 59900, fo. 54 (King's Books of Payments 1539–44).

42. Boxford (Suffolk); Sherborne (Dorset); St Andrew, Lewes (Sussex).

43. A St Clement was erected at St Nicholas, Bristol, in 1541 (CW, p. 62).

44. Hutton, 'The Local Impact', 117–19.

45. Ibid. 118.

46. W. B. Whitaker, *Sunday in Tudor and Stuart Times* (1933), 14–15.

47. Thomas Cranmer, *Miscellaneous Writings*, ed. J. E. Cox (Parker Society, 1844), 415; John Foxe, *Acts and Monuments*, ed. Revd Stephen Reed Cattley (1938), v. 561–2.

48. Great Witchingham (Norfolk) CW, year 1543; R. M. Fisher, 'Reform, Repression and Unrest at the Inns of Court, 1518–1558', *Historical Journal*, 20 (1977), 783.

49. *Acts of the Privy Council of England*, ii. 25–6; St Botolph Aldgate (London), CW, 17 July 1547; *The Letters of Stephen Gardiner*, ed. J. A. Muller (Cambridge, 1933), 273–6.

50. e.g. Halesowen (Worcs.) CW; Ludlow (Salop) CW; Winterslow (Wilts.) CW; Stratton (Cornwall) CW; Thame (Oxon.) CW; Great Hallingbury (Essex) CW; Christ Church, Bristol, CW; Wandsworth (Surrey) CW; Marston (Oxon.) CW; St Mary on the Hill, Chester (Ches.) CW; Bletchingley (Surrey) CW; Ashburton (Devon) CW.

51. Hutton, 'The Local Impact', 120; HMC Dean and Chapter of Wells MSS, ii. 264–5 (Visitors to Chapter).

52. Corporation of London RO, Journal 15, fo. 322, and Letter Book Q, fos. 210^v and 214.

53. E. Cardwell, *Documentary Annals of the Reformed Church of England* (Oxford, 1884), i. 42.

54. J. Strype, *Ecclesiastical Memorials* (Oxford, 1822), ii. 2. 125.

55. Hutton, 'The Local Impact', 121–2.

56. [Sparrow (ed.)], *A Collection of Articles*, 20–30; Duffy, *Stripping of the Altars*, 460–1.

57. Hutton, 'The Local Impact', 121–2.

58. Susan Bridgen, *London and the Reformation* (Oxford, 1989), 429.

59. St Ewen, Bristol, CW, years 1547–8; Morebath (Devon) CW, p. 160; St Martin, Leicester, CW, year 1547–8; Hawkhurst (Kent) CW, year 1547–8; Great St Mary, Cambridge, years 1547–51; Wandsworth (Surrey) CW, year 1548–9; Halesowen

(Worcs.) CW, p. 92; Great Hallingbury (Essex) CW, year 1549–50; All Hallows Staining (London) CW, fo. 176.

60. As in Morebath (Devon) CW, p. 164; St Martin, Leicester CW, year 1547–8; Great St Mary, Cambridge CW, years 1547–51; Ashburton (Devon), p. 121; St Andrew Hubbard (London) CW, year 1547; St Thomas, Salisbury (Wilts.) CW, year 1547–8; Ludlow (Salop) CW, year 1548; Stratton (Cornwall) CW, fo. 46; Holy Trinity, Exeter (Devon) CW, year 1548.

61. 'An Account of the Company of St. George in Norwich', *Norfolk Archaeology*, 3 (1852), 341–2; *Records of Early English Drama: Norwich*, ed. David Galloway (Toronto, 1984), 26–30; *York Civic Records*, ed. Angelo Raine (Yorkshire Archaeological Society Record Society; 1946), v. 3–4; William Kelly, *Notices Illustrative of the Drama of Leicester* (1865), 50–1.

62. *Acts of the Privy Council*, ed. J. R. Dasent, 186; Foxe, *Acts and Monuments*, ed. Cattley (1838), vi. 351–2.

63. See e.g. *John Bon and Master Parson* (printed by Luke Shepherd; 1548).

64. *Monumenta Franciscana*, ed. Richard Howlett (Rolls Series; 1882), ii. 216–20. The surviving London CW confirm this chronicle.

65. Holy Trinity, Chester, CW, years 1547–9; St Dunstan, Canterbury (Kent) CW, years 1547–50; Ashburton (Devon) CW, 119–22; St Edmund Salisbury (Wilts.) CW, years 1547–9; St Nicolas, Bristol, CW, p. 63; Ludlow (Salop) CW, years 1547–9.

66. *Records of Early English Drama: York*, ed. Alexandra F. Johnston and Margaret Rogerson (Manchester, 1979), 291–3; *Coventry*, ed. Ingram, 174–93; *Chester*, ed. Clopper, p. liv; *Players in Lincolnshire*, ed. Kahrl, 64; *Norwich*, ed. Galloway, 10–36.

67. 'Robert Parkyn's Narrative of the Reformation', ed. A. G. Dickens, *English Historical Review*, 62 (1947), 66–7. South Littleton, Worcs., bought tapers for Candlemas 1550, but as it also did for other major feasts, they were probably only to illuminate the church: CW, year 1549–50.

68. 'Robert Parkyn's Narrative', ed. Dickens, 67.

69. St Lawrence, Reading (Berks.) CW, p. 238; St Nicholas, Bristol, CW, year 1549.

70. *Monumenta Franciscana*, ii. 217; Kelly, *Leicester*, 7–10.

71. St Matthew Friday Street; St Andrew Hubbard; St Botolph Aldgate; St Margaret Moses; St Martin in the Fields; St Michael Cornhill; St Mary at Hill; St Benet Gracechurch; All Hallows Staining; St Margaret Pattens; St Alphege London Wall; St Dunstan in the West; St Mary Woolnoth; St Mary Magdalen Milk Street; St Michael le Querne; St Margaret, Westminster.

72. Ludlow CW, year 1548; St Dunstan, Canterbury (Kent) CW, year 1547–8; St Michael, Worcester CW, pp. 19–22; Prescot CW, pp. 25–6; Duffy, *Stripping of the Altars*, 460–1; Transcript of Worcester (St Helen's) RO, 009/1/BA 2636, parcel 11, fos. 155–9, lent to me very kindly by Diarmaid MacCulloch who is publishing a report on it.

73. This is in A. Heales, 'Easter Sepulchres', *Archaeologia*, 43 (1867), 304, where it is stated that the sepulchre was still watched at Minchinhampton (Gloucs.) in 1551. The subsequent loss of these accounts makes it impossible to tell if this was a misreading (e.g. of the sale of the object rather than its use). It is so out of conformity with all the other evidence that a suspicion must exist.

74. Prescot CW, p. 26; Halesowen CW, p. 90; Ludlow CW, year 1548; St Martin, Oxford, CW, a.1, year 1547–8; St Michael, Oxford CW, a.2, year 1547–8; St Mary, Bungay

CW, year 1547–8; Worcester (St Helens) RO, 009/1/BA 2636, parcel 11, fos. 155–9. This is to assume that the 'St Mary light' mentioned at Prescot is actually the paschal, which seems to be the case, rather than an (illegal) candle burned before a statue.

75. St Michael, Oxford, CW, a.2, year 1549–50.

76. Halesowen (Worcs.) CW, p. 93; North Elmham (Norfolk), fo. 51; Thame (Oxon.) CW, years 1547–9.

77. *Monumenta Franciscana*, ii. 217; 'Robert Parkyn's Narrative', ed. Dickens, 67.

78. In London, Westminster, Bristol, and Salisbury.

79. Long Sutton CW, fos. 33–4.

80. Hutton, 'The Local Impact', 125.

81. Ibid. 124–5.

82. John Hooker, *The Description of the Citie of Ercester* (Devon and Cornwall Record Society; 1919), 67–8.

83. Julian Cornwall, *Revolt of the Peasantry, 1549* (1977); Joyce Youings, 'The South-Western Rebellion of 1549', *Southern History*, 1 (1979), 99–122; Barrett L. Beer, *Rebellion and Riot* (1982), ch. 3.

84. Stratton CW, fos. 48^v–9.

85. A. Vere Woodman, 'The Buckinghamshire and Oxfordshire Rising of 1549', *Oxoniensa*, 22 (1957), 78–84.

86. A. G. Dickens, 'Some Popular Reactions to the Edwardian Reformation in Yorkshire', *Yorkshire Archaeological Journal*, 34 (1938–9), 158–68.

87. Cornwall, *Revolt of the Peasantry*; Diarmaid MacCulloch, 'Kett's Rebellion in Perspective', *Past and Present*, 84 (1979), 36–59, and *Suffolk and the Tudors* (1986), 300–9; Beer, *Rebellion and Riot*, ch. 4; J. D. Alsop, 'Latimer, the Commonwealth of Kent and the 1549 Rebellions', *Historical Journal*, 28 (1985), 379–83; Peter Clark, *English Provincial Society from the Reformation to the Revolution* (1977), 78–81; Lawrence Stone, 'Patriarchy and Paternalism in Tudor England', *Journal of British Studies*, 13 (1974), 19–23.

88. Boxford (Suffolk); Bramley (Hants); Crondall (Hants); Morebath (Devon); Yatton (Somerset); St Michael, Oxford; St Martin, Oxford; Ashburton (Devon); Winterslow (Wilts.); Worfield (Salop); Melton Mowbray (Leics.); Sherborne (Dorset); Halse (Somerset); Ilminster (Somerset); West Tarring and Ashurst (Sussex); Mildenhall (Suffolk).

89. Marston, Thame.

90. Pyrton.

91. Winsford.

92. CW, p. 90.

93. Banwell (Somerset) CW, pp. 125–8; Ashurst (Sussex) CW, years 1541–6, 1550–3; Worth (Sussex) CW, years 1540–5, 1550–3.

94. St Andrew, Canterbury (Kent); Wing (Bucks.); St Lawrence, Reading (Berks.); St Michael, Oxford; St Martin, Oxford; St Edmund, Salisbury (Wilts.); St Thomas, Salisbury (Wilts.).

95. Boxford (Suffolk); Cratfield (Suffolk); Swaffham (Norfolk).

96. W. Marrat, *The History of Lincolnshire* (Boston, 1814), 104–7.

97. CW, p. 2.

98. All Hallows Staining.

 99. *Coventry*, ed. Ingram, 181.

100. *Harleian Miscellany*, ix. 389–408.

101. HMC Dean and Chapter of Wells MSS, ii. 264–5 (Visitors to Dean and Chapter).

102. Corporation of London RO, Repertory 11, fo. 350 and 12, fo. 90ᵛ.

103. John Stow, *A Survey of London*, ed. C. L. Kingford (1908), 144.

104. *The Diary of Henry Machyn*, ed. John Nichols (Camden Society; 1848), 20.

105. *Visitation Articles and Injunctions of the Period of the Reformation*, ed. Walter Howard Frere (Alcuin Club Collections; 1910), ii. 175.

106. Parker, *English Sabbath*, 38–9.

107. Keith Thomas, *The Perception of the Past in Early Modern England* (Creighton Trust Lecture, University of London; 1983), 20.

108. Joyce Youings, *Sixteenth-Century England* (1984), 213–14; S. J. Goring, 'The Riot at Baynham Abbey, June 1525', *Sussex Archaeological Collections*, 116 (1978), 8.

109. R. Burne, 'Chester Cathedral in the Reigns of Mary and Elizabeth', *Journal of the Architectural, Archaeological and Historic Society of Chester and North Wales*, 38 (1951), 56–7; Kelly, *Leicester*, 72.

110. *Documents Relating to the Revels at Court in the Time of King Edward VI and Queen Mary*, ed. Albert Feuillerat (1914), 29–145; *Acts of the Privy Council*, NS ii. *1547–50*, 163.

111. Machyn, *Diary*, ed. Nichols, 33.

112. Sandra Billington, *Mock Kings in Renaissance Society and Drama* (Oxford, 1991), 37.

113. *Records of Early English Drama: Cambridge*, ed. Alan H. Nelson (Toronto, 1989), 178, 1123.

114. Sir E. Chambers, *The Medieval Stage* (1963 edn.), i. 408; H. Owen and J. B. Blakeway, *A History of Shrewsbury* (1825), i. 333; *Records of Early English Drama: Cumberland, Westmorland and Gloucestershire*, ed. Audrey Douglas and Peter Greenfield (Toronto, 1986), 296.

115. Billington, *Mock Kings*, 38–42; Feuillerat, *Revels at Court*, 29–145.

116. Machyn, *Diary*, 28; *Monumenta Franciscana*, ii. 235, 238–9; R. Holinshed, *Chronicles of England, Scotland and Ireland*, ed. J. Hooker *et al.* (1807–8), iii. 1033.

117. Hutton, 'The Local Impact', 125–6.

118. Ibid. 126–7.

119. PRO, E. 117.

120. *Statutes of the Realm* (1819), IV. i. 132–3.

121. Hutton, 'The Local Impact', 127.

122. Brigden, *London and the Reformation*, 483–5; Clark, *English Provincial Society*, 76; G. Mayhew, 'The Progress of the Reformation in East Sussex', *Southern History*, 5 (1983), 38–67; Palliser, *Tudor York*, 249–54; A. G. Dickens, *Lollards and Protestants in the Diocese of York 1509–1558* (Oxford, 1959), ch. 4; Whiting, *The Blind Devotion of the People*, graph 1. For a summary of the views concerning the utility of wills as sources for this purpose, and an excellent example of such use, see Duffy, *Stripping of the Altars*, ch. 15.

123. Hutton, 'The Local Impact', 127–8.

124. Ibid. 128.

125. Ibid. 128.

126. Ibid. 129.

127. At Chester, Warwick, Worcester, Oxford, Lewes, Salisbury, Ludlow, Thame,

Gloucester, Bristol, Westminster and, of course, London above all, but also at Crondall (Hants); Eltham and Bethersden (Kent); and Lambeth and Wandsworth (Surrey).

128. At London, Canterbury, Oxford, Exeter, Salisbury, Ludlow, Bungay, Sherborne, and villages in Cornwall, Devon, Somerset, Essex, Suffolk, Norfolk, Oxfordshire, Kent, Berkshire, and Surrey.

129. Henry John Feasey, *Ancient English Holy Week Ceremonial* (1897), 114–28; *Visitation Articles and Injunctions*, ed. Frere, ii. 346, 362.

130. Tarring (Sussex), CW, year 1556; Great St Mary, Cambridge, CW, years 1553–5; Charles Wriothesley, *A Chronicle of England*, ed. W. D. Hamilton (Camden Society; 1875), ii. 105.

131. All from London, Westminster, and Bristol, plus St Thomas, Salisbury (Wilts.); Ludlow (Salop); St Mary-on-the-Hill, Chester; St Martin, Oxford; Holy Trinity, Chester.

132. Strood and Bethersden (Kent); St Andrew, Lewes (Sussex); Mere (Wilts.); Thame (Oxon.); Holy Trinity, Cambridge; Swaffham (Norfolk); Crediton and Woodbury (Devon); All Saints, Bristol; Bridport (Dorset); St Michael, Worcester; St Michael, Oxford; St Mary Woolnoth (London); Anthony (Cornwall).

133. *Narratives of the Days of the Reformation*, ed. J. G. Nichols (Camden Society; 1859), 287; Wriothesley, *Chronicle*, ii. 113.

134. St Michael Cornhill (London); St Thomas, Salisbury (Wilts.); Thame (Oxon.); Christ Church, Bristol; St John, Bristol; St Botolph Aldgate (London).

135. *Chester*, ed. Clopper, 45–62.

136. Great Dunmow (Essex); Strood and Bethersden (Kent); Stanford in the Vale (Berks.); Ashburton (Devon); St Edmund, Salisbury (Wilts.); Addlethorpe, Ingoldmells and Long Sutton (Lincs.); Melton Mowbray (Leics.); Thame (Oxon.); St Mary, Bungay (Suffolk); Swaffham and Tilney (Norfolk); Dartington and Woodbury (Devon); St Alphage London Wall, St Mary Woolnoth, and St Michael le Querne (London); Christ Church and All Saints, Bristol.

137. Holy Trinity, and St Mary on the Hill.

138. Machyn, *Diary*, ed. Nichols, 77–8, 121, 160; Stow, *Annals*, 121, 160.

139. Foxe, *Acts and Monuments*, ed. Cattley, viii. 579.

140. R. T. Hampson, *Medii Aevi Kalendarium* (1841), i. 81; John Chandos (ed.), *In God's Name* (1971), 45–52.

141. *Monumenta Franciscana*, ii. 251; Machyn, *Diary*, ed. Nichols, 62–3.

142. St Botolph Aldgate.

143. Machyn, *Diary*, ed. Nichols, 139.

144. *York Civic Records*, ed. Raine, v. 105; *Coventry*, ed. Ingram, 205; *Chester*, ed. Clopper, 54–60; Chambers, *Medieval Stage* (1963 edn.), ii. 379, 388; *Records of Early English Drama: Newcastle-upon-Tyne*, ed. J. J. Anderson (Toronto, 1982), 26–7; *Norwich*, ed. Galloway, 37, 43–4; St Andrew, Canterbury (Kent) CW; Sherborne (Dorset) CW; Ashburton (Devon) CW.

145. St Mary, Dover (Kent) CW; St Mary, Bungay (Suffolk) CW; Ludlow (Salop) CW; Strood (Kent) CW; Lambeth (Surrey) CW; Wandsworth (Surrey) CW.

146. *York Civic Records*, ed. Raine, v. 105; St Martin, Leicester CW; St Ewen, Bristol, CW; St Michael Cornhill (London) CW; St Michael le Querne (London) CW; Kelly, *Leicester*, 7–10.

147. Machyn, *Diary*, ed. Nichols, 60, 85.

148. *York Civic Records*, ed. Raine, v. 105; Kelly, *Leicester*, 50–1; 'An Account of the Company of Saint George', *Norfolk Archaeology*, 3 (1852), 343; Alan Nelson, *The Medieval English Stage* (Chicago, 1974), 51; *Chester*, ed. Clopper, 55, 57.

149. Morebath (Devon) CW, p. 185; Chelmsford (Essex) CW, year 1558–9; Braunton (Devon) CW, year 1557–8; South Littleton (Worcs.) CW, p. 12.

150. Machyn, *Diary*, ed. Nichols, 61–3.

151. *Articles*, ed. Frere, ii. 345.

152. Snettisham (Norfolk); Stratton (Cornwall); Yatton (Somerset); Strood (Kent); Stanford in the Vale (Berks.); Lambeth (Surrey); Wandsworth (Surrey); Ashburton (Devon); Banwell (Somerset); Mere (Wilts.); Winterslow (Wilts.); Sheriff Hutton (Yorks.); Long Sutton (Lincs.); Melton Mowbray (Leics.); Heybridge (Essex); Crediton (Devon); South Littleton (Worcs.); St Michael, Bath (Somerset).

153. Hutton, 'The Local Impact', 129–30.

154. In all, thirty-three parishes: in Cornwall (Anthony, Poughill, Stratton); Devon (Morebath, Ashburton, Woodbury, Crediton, Braunton, Dartington, South Tawton); Somerset (Yatton, Halse, Winkleigh); Dorset (Sherborne); Wiltshire (Steeple Aston, Mere, St Edmund, Salisbury); Berkshire (Reading (2 parishes), Standford); Hampshire (Crondall and St John, Winchester); Surrey (Wandsworth); Sussex (Rye); Kent (St Mary, Dover); Oxfordshire (Marston, Pyrton, Thame, St Michael, Oxford); Warwickshire (St Nicholas, Warwick); Northamptonshire (Norton by Daventry); Worcestershire (Badsey).

155. *Liverpool Town Books*, ed. J. A. Twemlow (1918), i. 51; Melton Mowbray CW, nos. 6–7; Swaffham CW, year 1557; Long Melford, years 1555–7.

156. Winchester, Salisbury, Melton Mowbray, Crediton.

157. Owen and Blakeway, *Shrewsbury*, i. 333; Holy Trinity, Exeter (Devon) CW, years 1555–8; Anthony (Cornwall) CW, years 1555–8; David Wiles, *The Early Plays of Robin Hood* (Cambridge, 1981), appendix 1, for Chagford (Devon) and Melton Mowbray (Leics.); Hampson, *Medii Aevi Kalendarium*, 263–4, for Manchester (Lancs.).

158. Crondall CW, year 1555–6; St Mary, Reading (Berks.), CW, year 1556–7.

159. St Andrew, Canterbury (Kent); Bramley, Stoke Charity, and St John, Winchester (Hants); St Lawrence, Reading (Berks.); St Michael, Oxford; Lambeth (Surrey); St Edmund, and St Thomas, Salisbury (Wilts.); Holy Trinity, Bungay (Suffolk).

160. St Thomas, Launceston (Cornwall); Molland, Ashburton, Coldridge, and Winkleigh (Devon); Banwell and Halse (Somerset); Minchinhampton (Gloucs.); Worth (Sussex).

161. Leverton (Lincs.); St Mary, and Holy Trinity, Bungay (Suffolk); Swaffham (Norfolk); Long Melford (Suffolk).

162. In all the CW of the reign from Chester, Coventry, Worcester, Oxford, Ludlow, Bristol, and London.

163. Sheppard, 'Canterbury Marching Watch', 39.

164. Chambers, *Medieval Stage* (1963 edn.), i. 408; *Cambridge*, ed. Nelson, 186–206.

165. The most famous and long established being at Shrewsbury; Owen and Blakeway, *Shrewsbury*, i. 333.

166. *Revels at Court*, ed. Feuillerat, 149–242.

167. Corporation of London RO, Journal 1b, fo. 334.

168. *Acts of the Privy Council*, v (1554–6), 151.

169. *Visitation Articles and Injunctions*, ed. Frere, ii. 348.

170. Machyn, *Diary*, ed. Nichols, 89, 137.

171. Hutton, 'The Local Impact', 131–2.

172. Dickens, *Lollards and Protestants*, pt. VI, ch. 1; Palliser, *Tudor York*, 252–4; Clark, *English Local Society*, 76; Mayhew, 'The Progress of the Reformation', 46; Whiting, 'For the Health of my Soul', 90; Brigden, *London and the Reformation*, 628–9.

173. D. M. Loades, *Two Tudor Conspiracies* (Cambridge, 1965), 15–127; William B. Robison, 'The National and Local Significance of Wyatt's Rebellion in Surrey', *Historical Journal*, 30 (1987), 769–90.

174. Hutton, 'The Local Impact', 132–3.

175. Ibid. 133.

176. W. S. Hudson, *The Cambridge Connection and the Elizabethan Settlement of 1559* (Durham, NC, 1980); N. L. Jones, *Faith by Statute: Parliament and the Settlement of Religion, 1559* (1982), and 'Elizabeth's First Year', in Christopher Haigh (ed.), *The Reign of Elizabeth I* (1984), 32–48; G. Alexander, 'Bishop Bonner and the Parliament of 1559', *Bulletin of the Institute of Historical Research*, 56 (1983), 164–79; N. M. Sutherland, 'The Marian Exiles and the Establishment of the Elizabethan Regime', *Archiv für Reformation Geschichte*, 78 (1987), 253–86; John Guy, *Tudor England* (Oxford, 1988), 258–64; Christopher Haigh, *Elizabeth I* (1988), 27–40; Diarmaid MacCulloch, *The Later Reformation in England 1547–1603* (1990), 27–33; Hirofumi Horie, 'The Lutheran Influence on the Elizabethan Settlement', *Historical Journal*, 34 (1991), 519–38.

177. *Proclamations*, ed. Hughes and Larkin, i, no. 460.

178. Hutton, 'The Local Impact', 133–4.

179. Crediton CW, years 1559–61; Ludlow CW, p. 108.

180. Machyn, *Diary*, ed. Nichols, 236; Stanford in the Vale CW, p. 169.

181. Ralph Houlbrooke, *Church Courts and the People during the English Reformation* (Oxford, 1979), 249; Stanford in the Vale (Berks.) CW, p. 169; Bethersden (Kent) CW, year 1559–60; Borthwick Institute, York, HC/CP/1567–8; A. R. Wright, *British Calendar Customs*, ed. T. E. Lones (Folklore Society; 1936), iii. 133.

182. W. P. M. Kennedy, *Elizabethan Episcopal Administration* (Alcuin Club; Cambridge, 1924), 110, 191, 228.

183. *Tudor Parish Documents of the Diocese of York*, ed. J. S. Purvis (Cambridge 1948), 174–5; *The Archdeacon's Court*, ed. E. Brinkworth (Oxfordshire Record Society; 1942), 155; R. Hodgkinson, 'Extracts from the Act Books of the Archdeacons of Nottingham', *Transactions of the Thoroton Society*, 30 (1926–7), 29.

184. J. Weld, *A History of Leagram* (Chetham Society; 1913), 132–3.

185. See esp. Whiting, *The Blind Devotion of the People*, the conclusions of which are apparently confirmed by the absence of such entries in the churchwardens' accounts.

186. Revd J. Fisher, 'The Religious and Social Life of Former Days in the Vale of Clwyd', *Archaeologia Cambrensis*, 6th ser. 6 (1906), 155–7; Edmund Hyde Hall, *A Description of Caernarvonshire* (Caernarvonshire Historical Society; 1952), 319; Revd J. Fisher, 'Two Welsh–Manx Christmas Customs', *Archaeologia Cambrensis*, 6th ser. 84 (1929), 308–14; Roy Saer, 'The Christmas Carol Singing Tradition in the Tanad Valley', *Folk Life*, 7 (1969), 15–42, and 'A Midnight Plygain at Llyanymawddwy Church', *Folk Life*, 22 (1983–4), 99–107.

187. Hutton, 'The Local Impact', 134–5.
188. PRO, SP 12/224/74 (Mr Price's information).
189. Hutton, 'The Local Impact', 135–6; Houlbrooke, *Church Courts*, 168.
190. Hutton, 'The Local Impact', 137.

CHAPTER 4

1. Out of a very large literature, the following are especially relevant to the development of the subject in the English-speaking world: Mikhail Bakhtin, *Rabelais and his World* (Cambridge, Mass., 1968); John Christopher Coldeway, 'Early Essex Drama' (University of Colorado Ph.D. thesis, 1972); K. E. Wrightson, 'The Puritan Reformation of Manners with special reference to the Counties of Lancashire and Essex 1640–1660' (Cambridge Ph.D. thesis; 1973); Natalie Zemon Davis, *Society and Culture in Early Modern France* (1975), ch. 4; C. Phythian-Adams, 'Ceremony and the Citizen', in Peter Clark (ed.), *The Early Modern Town* (1976), 106–28; Jean Delumeau, *Catholicism between Luther and Voltaire* (1977), 174–8; Peter Burke, *Popular Culture in Early Modern Europe* (1978), chs. 8–9; Gerald Strauss, *Luther's House of Learning* (1978); Keith Wrightson and David Levine, *Poverty and Piety in an English Village: Terling 1525–1700* (1979); Steven Ozment (ed.), *Reformation Europe: A Guide to Research* (Center for Information Research; St Louis, 1982), 321–42; Keith Wrightson, *English Society 1580–1680* (1982); Peter Clark, *The English Alehouse* (1983); Kaspar von Greyerz (ed.), *Religion and Society in Early Modern Europe* (1984), chs. 4, 5, 9, 12, 14; R. W. Scribner (ed.), *Popular Culture and Popular Movements in Reformation Germany* (1987), ch. 2; Robert von Friedburg, 'Reformation of Manners and the Social Composition of Offenders', *Journal of British Studies*, 29 (1990), 347–85.

2. Developed in his thesis and his village study with Levine, cited in n. 1, and expressed most fully in *English Society*.

3. In *The Puritan Moment* (Cambridge, Mass., 1983).

4. Martin Ingram, 'Religion, Communities and Moral Discipline in Late Sixteenth- and Early Seventeenth-Century England: Case studies', in von Greyerz (ed.), *Religion and Society*, ch. 12; Margaret Spufford, 'Puritanism and Social Control?', in Anthony Fletcher and John Stevenson (eds.), *Order and Disorder in Early Modern England* (Cambridge, 1985), ch. 1; Marjorie McIntosh, 'Local Change and Community Control in England 1465–1500', *Huntington Library Quarterly*, 49 (1986), 219–42; Cynthia B. Herrup, *The Common Peace* (Cambridge, 1987).

5. Annabel Gregory, 'Witchcraft, Politics and "Good Neighbourhood" in Early Seventeenth-Century Rye', *Past and Present*, 133 (1991), 59–60.

6. See the Appendix, as before.

7. Two in Cornwall (Kilchampton and Stratton); nine in Devon (Morebath, Ashburton, Kilmington, Farway, Shobrooke, Crediton, Chudleigh, South Taunton, and Braunton); one in Somerset (Banwell); one in Gloucestershire (Minchinhampton); one in Dorset (Wimborne Minster); five in Wiltshire (St Edmund, and St Thomas, Salisbury, Mere, Winterslow, and Steeple Aston); three in Hampshire (Stoke Charity, Crondall, and Bramley); one in Sussex (West Tarring); one in Kent (Eltham); two in Warwickshire (Rowington and St Nicholas, Warwick); one in Shropshire (Worfield); one in Worcestershire (Badsey); one in Northamptonshire (Culworth); two in Leicestershire (Melton Mowbray and St Martin, Leicester); one

in Bedfordshire (Northill); three in Buckinghamshire (Aston Abbots, Ludgershall, and Wing); six in Oxfordshire (Marston, Thame, South Newington, Pyrton, Spelsbury, and St Michael, Oxford); three in Berkshire (St Mary, Reading, Thatcham, and Childrey); one in Hertfordshire (Ashwell); one in Essex (Monk Soham); and one in Suffolk (St Mary, Bungay).

8. Such as West Tarring, Aston Abbots, St Nicholas, Warwick, Winterslow, Eltham, and St Martin, Leicester, all above.

9. West Tarring, Melton Mowbray, Stoke Charity, Mere, Winterslow, Thatcham, and Northill.

10. Snettisham, years 1560–6, Swaffham, years 1560–5; Great Witchingham, year 1569.

11. St Helen, Abingdon (Berks.) CW, year 1566; *Records of Early English Drama: Devon*, ed. John M. Wasson (Toronto, 1986), 57 (Chudleigh); Farway (Devon) CW, year 1567; Braunton (Devon) CW, years 1560–2.

12. *The Diary of Henry Machyn*, ed. J. Nichols (Camden Society, 1848), 283; Lincolnshire RO, Ancaster MSS, HC xxiii. 40.

13. M. W. Barley, 'Plough Plays in the East Midlands', *JEFDSS* 7 (1953), 72 (for Saxilby and Donington, Lincs.); St Mary, Bungay (Suffolk) CW, years 1562–78; Holy Trinity, Bungay (Suffolk) CW, years 1560–93, Swaffham (Norfolk), years 1560–3; St Margaret, Norwich (Norfolk) CW, years 1563–9.

14. J. Silvester Davies, *A History of Southampton* (Southampton, 1883), 372 n. 3; Kingston-upon-Thames (Surrey) CW, years 1561–78; Stoke Charity (Hants) CW, years 1560–3; Bramley (Hants) CW, year 1563; St Thomas, Salisbury (Wilts.) CW, years 1560–81; St Edmund, Salisbury (Wilts.) CW, years 1560–84; St Mary the Virgin, Oxford, CW, year 1560; St Martin, Oxford, CW, years 1560–1641; St Michael, Oxford, CW, years 1561–1640.

15. Coldridge (Devon) CW, year 1560; Winkleigh (Devon) CW, year 1560; Minchinhampton (Gloucs.) CW, years 1560–72; Kilchampton (Cornwall) CW, years 1563–73; Worth (Sussex) CW, 1560–3.

16. Coldeway, 'Early Essex Drama', 68–76.

17. E. K. Chambers, *The Medieval Stage* (1963 edn.), i. 408–18.

18. Machyn, *Diary*, ed. Nichols, 273–4; John Nichols, *The Progresses . . . of Queen Elizabeth* (1788), i. 15–24.

19. Harold C. Gardiner, *Mysteries' End* (New Haven, Conn., 1967), 65–85; *Records of Early English Drama: Norwich*, ed. David Galloway (Toronto, 1984), 47.

20. Graham Mayhew, *Tudor Rye* (Falmer, 1987), 58; *Devon*, ed. Wasson, 238–64; *Records of Early English Drama: Newcastle-upon-Tyne*, ed. J. J. Anderson (Toronto, 1982), 29–58.

21. *Anatomie of Abuses* (1583), ed. Frederick J. Furnivall (New Shakespeare Society; 1879), 148–9.

22. *Devon*, ed. Wasson, 238–64; Hinckley CW, years 1586–93; Holy Trinity, Exeter (Devon) CW, year 1588; Eltham CW, year 1562; *Records of the Borough of Nottingham* (Nottingham, 1885), iv. 175.

23. *Poetical Works*, ed. J. C. Smith and E. de Selincourt (1926), 436.

24. Expressed most clearly in William Brown, *The Shepherds Pipe* (1614).

25. Stubbes, *Anatomie*, ed. Furnivall, 33.

26. Ibid. 146–7.

27. William Warner, *Albions England* (1602 edn.), bk. 5, p. 121.

28. Norreys Jephson O'Conor, *Godes Peace and the Queenes* (Oxford, 1934), 108–25.

29. Francis Douce, *Illustrations of Shakespeare and of Ancient Manners* (1807), 457; HMC Cecil MSS, viii. 201 (report on Oxford disturbances).

30. John Forrest, *Morris and Matachin* (EFDSS; 1984), 1–23; *Kemps Nine Daies Wonder* (1600); Barbara Lowe, 'Early Records of the Morris in England', *JEFDSS* 8: 2 (1957), 69–75; E. C. Cawte, *Ritual Animal Disguise* (Woodbridge, 1978), 54–5; David Wiles, *The Early Plays of Robin Hood* (Cambridge, 1981), 20–6; John Brand, *Observations on the Popular Antiquities of Great Britain*, ed. Sir Henry Ellis (1908), i. 254–6.

31. *Anatomie of Abuses*, 147–8.

32. Joseph Strutt, *The Sports and Pastimes of the People of England*, ed. J. Charles Cox (1903), 96; Morris Marples, *A History of Football* (1954), 13.

33. The Elizabethan references will follow. For the nature of the custom at later periods, see *The Journal of Nicholas Assheton*, ed. F. R. Raines (Chetham Society, 1848), 41–2, and T. F. Thistleton Dyer, *Church Lore Gleanings* (1892), 328–30. It is still carried on at Ambleside and Grasmere in the centre of the Lake District.

34. The following CW in the Appendix contain most of the evidence. Devon: Chudleigh (regular till 1581, end 1594); Honiton (regular till 1578, end 1581); Shobrooke (regular till 1584, end 1595); Woodbury (regular till 1577, end 1583); Morebath (end 1585); Kilmington (end 1578); Crediton (end 1565); Coldridge (end 1592); Braunton (regular till 1582, end 1595); South Tawton (regular till 1570, end 1588); Northam (end 1581). Cornwall: St Ives (continue); Kilchampton (end 1575); Poughill (end 1578). Somerset: Tintinhull (end 1601); Banwell (end 1575); Somerton (continue); Williton (continue). Gloucestershire: Minchinhampton (regular till 1583, end 1589); Dursley (end 1572). Wiltshire: St Edmund, Salisbury (end 1582); Mere (end 1582); Winterslow (regular till 1598, continue occasionally); Steeple Ashton (continue); Calne (regular till 1572, continue occasionally). Dorset: Wimborne Minster (regular till 1574, end 1590); Sherborne (end 1570); Corfe Castle (end 1572). Hampshire: Stoke Charity (regular till 1564, end 1579); Crondall (regular till 1572, end 1597); Bramley (regular till 1570, continue occasionally). Sussex: West Tarring (end 1568). Surrey: Seal (continue). Berkshire: Thatcham (regular till 1579, end 1598); Kintbury (end 1588); Childrey (end 1593). Buckinghamshire: Aston Abbots (regular till 1575, end 1579); Ludgershall (regular till 1575, end 1594); Wing (regular till 1584, end 1598); Great Marlow (continue); Bedfordshire: Northill (end 1565); Shillington (end 1575). Oxfordshire: Marston (end 1586); Pyrton (regular till 1572, continue occasionally); Thame (regular till end); South Newington (regular till 1596, continue occasionally); St Martin, Oxford (regular till end); St Michael, Oxford (regular till end). Warwickshire: Shipston (end 1593). Northamptonshire: Culworth (end 1570). Suffolk: St Mary, Bungay (end 1568). To this can be added data from David Underdown, *Revel, Riot and Rebellion* (Oxford, 1985), 83–4, on Glastonbury (end 1589), South Brent (over before 1600), and Blagdon (over before 1590), all in Somerset.

35. Cawte, *Ritual Animal Disguise*, 17–18 (Sleighford, Staffs., end 1584); Lowe, 'Early Records of the Morris', 67 (Potten, Beds., end 1592); Hinckley (Leics.) CW (end 1593); Berkhampstead (Herts.) CW (end 1589).

36. See Appendix for Hampshire: Bramley (regular till 1563, ends 1596). Wiltshire: St Edmund, Salisbury (ends 1581); St Thomas, Salisbury (ends 1580). Surrey: Kingston upon Thames (ends 1578), Battersea (ends 1565). Middlesex: Chelsea (continues). Oxford: St Mary the Virgin, St Martin, St Michael, and St Peter in the East (continues at all).

37. See CW in Appendix for Cornwall: Launceston (end 1596); Kilchampton (continue); Poughill (end 1595). Gloucestershire: Minchinhampton (regular to 1573, end 1596); Dursley (continue). And Somerset RO, D/D/Cd 28, for Badgworth where ending in 1590s.

38. See CW in Appendix for Suffolk: St Mary, Bungay (ends 1597); Holy Trinity, Bungay (ends 1593). Norfolk: Swaffham (ends 1563); St Margaret, Norwich (ends 1568). Lincolnshire: Leverton (ends 1577), Ingoldmells (ends 1575).

39. Leverton CW; Stradbroke (Suffolk) CW, years 1631–6, 1649–95; Leverington (Cambs.) CW, year 1575. Waddington CW, years 1642–1706; Barley, 'Plough Plays in the East Midlands', 72.

40. See Appendix for Ludlow (Salop) (ends 1573). Bristol: St Ewen (ends 1584); Christ Church (ends 1565); All Saints (ends 1566); St John (ends 1565); St Philip and St Jacob (ends 1570). St Edmund, Salisbury (Wilts.) (ends 1569). Lambeth (Surrey) (ends 1578). Cheshire: St Oswald, Chester (ends 1585). London: St Alphege London Wall (ends 1567); St Dunstan in the West (ends 1585); St Mary Woolnoth (ends 1578); St Peter Westcheap (ends 1584); St Michael le Querne (ends 1571); St Botolph Bishopsgate (ends 1575); St Benet Gracechurch (ends 1573); St Martin Orgar (ends 1583); St Mary Aldermanbury (ends 1574); St Matthew Friday Street (ends 1572); Westminster: St Martin in the Fields; St Margaret.

41. See the following CW in the Appendix. Hampshire: Bramley (ends 1570). Devon: Braunton (ends 1579); Dawlish (ends in 1590s). Wiltshire: Stratford sub Castle (ends 1583); St Mary, Devizes (ends 1562). Shropshire: Worfield (ends 1570); Cheswardine (continues). Cheshire: St Michael, Chester (continues). Berkshire: St Lawrence, Reading (ends in 1570s). Oxfordshire: South Newington (continues). Warwickshire: Great Packington (ends in 1580s); St Nicholas, Warwick (ends in 1568). Leicestershire: Loughborough (ends in 1580s); St Martin, Leicester (ends in 1560s). Bristol: St Ewen (ends by 1580); St Thomas (ends 1571); Christ Church (ends in 1560s). London: St Alphege London Wall (ends 1577); St Margaret Pattens (ends in 1560s); St Peter Westcheap (ends 1580). Lincolnshire: Heckington (continues). Norfolk: Swaffham (ends 1574); North Elmham (continues); St Margaret, Norwich (ends 1578); Putham St Margaret (continues); St Nicholas, Great Yarmouth (ends 1584); North Walsingham (ends 1588). Suffolk: Cratfield (ends 1578); Walberswick (ends in 1580s); Mildenhall (ends 1580); Mendlesham (ends in 1570s); St Mary, Bungay (continues). Essex: Thaxted (continues); Chelmsford (continues). Kent: Hoo All Hallows (continues). Yorkshire: Masham (continues).

42. Mayhew, *Tudor Rye*, 58–9; Gardiner, *Mysteries' End*, 79–87; Underdown, *Revel, Riot and Rebellion*, 46; Phythian-Adams, 'Ceremony and the Citizen', 123; *Norwich*, ed. Galloway, 47–102; Thomas Sharp, *A Dissertation on the Pageants or Dramatic Mysteries . . . at Coventry* (Coventry, 1825), 11–12, 133, 221–5; *Records of Nottingham*, iv. 133–200; PRO, SP 12/224/54 (order of constable of Banbury Hundred); David Harris Sacks, *The Widening Gate* (Berkeley, Calif., 1991), 191; *Devon*, ed. Wasson, 154–76, 238–69, 279–80; *Records of Early English Drama: Chester*, ed. Lawrence M. Clopper (Manchester, 1979), 63–197; *Records of Early English Drama: York*, ed. Alexandra F. Johnston and Margaret Rogerson (Manchester, 1979), 365–468; *Newcastle-upon-Tyne*, ed. Anderson (Toronto, 1982), 29–132; *Records of Early English Drama: Cumberland, Westmorland and Gloucestershire*, ed. Audrey Douglas and Peter Greenfield (Toronto, 1986), 1–27, 301–13; *Records of Plays and Players in Norfolk and Suffolk 1330–1642*, ed.

D. Galloway and J. Wasson (Malone Society, 1980), pp. xiii–xiv; *A Calendar to the Records of the Borough of Doncaster* (Doncaster, 1899–1903), iv. 24–86; PRO, SP 12/192/67 (deposition by Lincoln councillors); Peter Clark, *English Provincial Society from the Reformation to the Revolution* (1977), 157; John Wodderspoon, *Memorials of the Ancient Town of Ipswich* (1850), 174–5; William Kelly, *Notices Illustrative of the Drama . . . of Leicester* (1865), 100–2; *The Records of the Burgery of Sheffield*, ed. John Daniel Leader (1897), 48–74.

43. *The Pursuit of Stability: Social Relations in Elizabethan London* (Cambridge, 1991), 1, 3, 94.

44. Coldeway, thesis, 68–76; *Plays and Players in Norfolk and Suffolk*, ed. Galloway and Wasson, *passim*.

45. John Tucker Murray, *English Dramatic Companies 1558–1642* (1910), ii, appendices.

46. See sources at n. 42.

47. Underdown, *Revel, Riot and Rebellion*, 46; *The Orders, Decrees and Ordinances of . . . Marlborough*, ed. B. Howard Cunnington (Devizes, 1929), 17.

48. [Anthony Sparrow (ed.)], *A Collection of Articles* (1671), 73, 112–13; John Cosin, *A Collection of Private Devotions* (1627); David Cressy, *Bonfires and Bells* (1989), 7; Kenneth L. Parker, *The English Sabbath* (Cambridge, 1988), 50–1, 122–3.

49. W. Lambarde, 'The Order of the Maundy Made at Greenwich, March 19, 1572', *Archaeologia*, 1 (1770), 7–8; Leslie Hotson, *The First Night of Twelfth Night* (1954), 176–7; Bishop Lyttleton (ed.), 'Account of New Year's Gifts, Presented to Queen Elizabeth 1584–5', ed. Bishop Lyttleton, *Archaeologia*, 1 (1770), 9–12; W. Stevenson, 'Extracts from Lord North's Household Book', *Archaeologia*, 19 (1821), 292–301; Albert Feuillerat, *Documents Relating to the Office of the Revels in the Time of Queen Elizabeth* (Materialer zur Kunde des Älteren Englischer Dramas; 1908), *passim*; Richard L. Greaves, *Society and Religion in Elizabethan England* (Minneapolis, 1981), 417; W. B. Whitaker, *Sunday in Tudor and Stuart Times* (1933), 30–3; R. Chris Hassel, jun., *Renaissance Drama and the English Church Year* (Lincoln, Neb., 1979), 1–3.

50. Greaves, *Society and Religion*, 429, 457; Machyn, *Diary*, ed. Nichols, 201.

51. 'A Book Conteyning the Manner and Order of a Watche', *Harleian Miscellany*, 9 (1812), 389–408.

52. John Nichols, *The Progresses, Processions, etc. of Queen Elizabeth* (1823), iii. 135.

53. *The Complete Works of John Lyly*, ed. R. Warwick Bond (Oxford, 1902), i. 447–8.

54. PRO, SP 12/224/61 (the order); *Acts of the Privy Council of England, 1588–9*, 202.

55. Ibid. (1591–2), 549.

56. Gardiner, *Mysteries' End*, 79–83; *Plays and Players in Norfolk and Suffolk*, ed. Galloway and Wasson, 164.

57. *Tudor Parish Documents of the Diocese of York*, ed. J. S. Purvis (Cambridge, 1948), 173; *York Civic Records*, ed. Angelo Raine (1947), vii. 55; *York*, ed. Johnston and Rogerson, 689–839; J. S. Purvis, 'The York Religious Plays', in Alberic Stacpoole *et al.* (eds.), *The Noble City of York* (York, 1972), 854.

58. Folger Shakespeare Library, Washington DC, MS L. 6 183.

59. Roscoe E. Parker, 'Some Records of the "Somyr Play"', in Richard Beale Davis and John Leon Lievsay (eds.), *Studies in Honor of John C. Hodges and Alwin Thaler* (Knoxville, 1961), 24.

60. Parker, *English Sabbath*, 110–11.

61. *Visitation Articles and Injunctions of the Period of the Reformation*, ed. Walter Howard

Frere (Alcuin Club, 1910), iii. 209, 256–7, 271, 291, 383; W. P. M. Kennedy, *Elizabethan Episcopal Administration* (Alcuin Club, 1924), 59, 73, 110, 166, 194, 220, 228, 350.

62. Parker, *English Sabbath*, 62–4, 118–19.

63. The *Short Title Catalogue* lists the known publications of Elizabeth's bishops. Their sabbatarian writings are well discussed in Parker, *English Sabbath*, 43–4, 60, 89, 111, although the misleading impression is given there that John King and Richard Turnbull were Elizabethan bishops.

64. Thomas Nashe, *Works*, ed. R. B. McKerrow (1910), iii. 230–45.

65. Christopher Bagshaw, *A True Relation* (1601), 18.

66. Chambers, *Medieval Stage* (1963 edn.), i. 407–13 (for three Oxford colleges); *Records of Early English Drama: Cambridge*, ed. Alan H. Nelson (Toronto, 1989), 1145.

67. *DNB*; Parker, *English Sabbath*, 42, 55–6.

68. *Eglogs, Epytaphes and Sonettes* (1563); *The Popish Kingdom* (1570).

69. *A Sermon Made at Blandford Forum* (1571).

70. *A Second Admonition to Parliament* (1571), in *Puritan Manifestoes*, ed. Revd W. H. Frere and Revd C. E. Douglas (Church Historical Society, 72; 1907), 120.

71. *An Earnest Complaint of Divers Vain, Wicked and Abused Exercices* (1572).

72. *A Treatise Against Dicing* (1577), 145–83; *Spiritus est Vicarius Christi in Terra* (1579).

73. *The Description of England*, ed. Georges Edelen (Ithaca, NY, 1968), 36. The standard analysis of Harrison's thought is G. J. R. Parry, *A Protestant Vision* (Cambridge, 1987).

74. John Stockwood, *A Sermon Preached at Paules Crosse on Barthelemew Day* (1578), 50–1, 132–6, and *A Very Fruitful Sermon Preched at Paules Crosse* (1579), 25–8; John Walsall, *A Sermon Preached at Pauls Crosse* (1578), sigs. C1–C5; Thomas White, *A Sermon Preached at Pawles Crosse on Sunday the Thirde of November* (1578), 43–5; Abraham Fleming, *The Diamond of Devotion* (1581), 15–16; John Field, *A Caveat for Parsons Howlett* (1581), sig. D111, and *A Godly Exhortation* (1583), *passim*; John Knewstub, *Lectures of John Knewstub upon the Twentieth Chapter of Exodus* (1577), 72–5; Thomas Lovell, *A Dialogue between Custom and Veritie* (1581), *passim*.

75. Anthony Anderson, *The Shield of our Safetie* (1581), sig. T4; *DNB*.

76. *A Pleasant Dialogue Between a Souldior of Barwicke, and an English Chaplaine* (1581), sig. M4.

77. Samuel Byrd, *A Friendlie Communication* (1580), fos. 15–16; *DNB*.

78. The edition used here is by J. C. Smith and E. de Selincourt, 1926. Scholarly criticism of direct relevance to the concerns of this book includes Elizabeth A. F. Watson, *Spenser* (1967); Helena Shire, *A Preface to Spenser* (1978); John N. King, *Spenser's Poetry and the Reformed Tradition* (Princeton, NJ, 1990); David Norbrook, *Poetry and Politics in the English Renaissance* (1984), ch. 3.

79. Stephen Bateman, *The New Arrival of the Three Gracis into Anglia* (?1584), n.p.

80. pp. 1–5.

81. Frederick J. Furnivall (New Shakespeare Society; 1879).

82. J. E. Neale, *Elizabeth I and her Parliaments* (1957), ii. 58–60; Parker, *English Sabbath*, 121–3.

83. *Hay any work for a Cooper* (1589), 3–4.

84. *The Writings of Henry Barrow 1587–90*, ed. L. H. Carlson (Sir Halley Stewart Trust, 1962), 390–2.

85. *A Profitable Exposition of the Lord's Prayer* (1588), 189–91; *DNB*.

86. *An Exposition upon the Canonical Epistle of St James* (1591), fo. 249.

87. W. B. Whitaker, *Sunday in Tudor and Stuart Times* (1933), 59–65; Parker, *English Sabbath*, 92–6.

88. George Estey, *A Most Sweete and Comfortable Exposition upon the Tenne Commaundements* (1602), sigs. M4–N; *The Work of William Perkins*, ed. Ian Breward (Abingdon, 1970), 471; William Perkins, *Works* (1631 edn.), ii. 676.

89. Jeremy Goring, *Godly Exercises or the Devil's Dance* (Friends of Dr William's Library 37th Lecture; 1983), 11; Francis Trigge, *A Touchstone* (1599), 244.

90. Hugh Roberts, *The Day of Hearing* (Oxford, 1600).

91. *Lectures upon Jonas* (1597), 96.

92. For the bulk of which see Goring, *Godly Exercises*; Parker, *English Sabbath*, 42–108; Elbert N. S. Thompson, *The Controversy between the Puritans and the Stage* (Yale Studies in English, 20; 1903); Richard L. Greaves, *Society and Religion in Elizabethan England* (Minneapolis, 1981), 395–409, 455–8.

93. No exact figure is provided as the category is itself somewhat imprecise.

94. See the relevant work of Sir Philip Sidney, Richard Barnfield, Fulke Greville, Sir John Davies, Sir Edward Dyer, Thomas Lodge, John Lyly (except when staging his entertainment for Elizabeth), Sir Walter Raleigh, and Robert Sidney.

95. *2 Henry VI*, III. i. 364–6; *Midsummer Night's Dream*, III. ii. 296. Other Shakespearian references are in *Henry V*, II. iv. 25; *All's Well that Ends Well*, II. ii. 26. Also see Nashe, *Works*, ed. McKerrow, i. 83.

96. The references are collected by Cawte, *Ritual Animal Disguise*, 54–5, and Jane Garry, 'The Literary History of the English Morris Dance', *Folklore*, 94 (1983), 219–20.

97. *Compendious or Briefe Examination of Certayne Ordinary Complaints*, ed. Frederick J. Furnivall (New Shakespeare Society; 1876), 16.

98. *Ballads from Manuscripts*, ed. F. Furnivall and W. R. Morfill (Ballad Society, 1873), 72–91; and see Norbrook, *Poetry and Politics*, 70–1.

99. See bk. 5, p. 121, and, for Warner, *DNB*.

100. E. H. Fellowes, *English Madrigal Verse 1588–1632* (3rd edn.; Oxford, 1967), 143.

101. pp. 14, 65, 68.

102. See *DNB*; Bernard H. Newdigate, *Michael Drayton and his Circle* (Oxford, 1941), chs. 1–7; Joan Grundy, *The Spenserian Poets* (1969), 8–10.

103. The standard editions (used here) are by Charles Lethbridge Kingsford and F. E. Halliday (1958), respectively.

104. John Marston *et al.*, *Jacke Drums Entertainment* (1601); *The Dramatic Works of Thomas Dekker*, ed. Fredson Bowers (Cambridge, 1962), *Shoemakers' Holiday*, introduction and III. iii. 49–71.

105. *Brittons Bowre of Delights* (1591); *The Arbor of Amorous Devises* (1597).

106. *Olde Mad-Cappes New Galley-Mawfrey* (1602), sigs. C–D4.

107. John Terry, *The Trial of Truth* (Oxford, 1600), 125–6.

108. Robert Abbot, *The Exaltation of the Kingdome and Priesthood of Christ* (1601), 72.

109. John Howson, *A Sermon Preached at St. Maries in Oxford* (Oxford, 1602), sig. CIV.

110. David Palliser, *Tudor York* (Oxford, 1979), 243–8; *York*, ed. Johnston and Rogerson, 359–62.

111. Sharp, *Dissertation*, 11–12, 36–7, 50–77.

112. *Cumberland, Westmorland and Gloucestershire*, ed. Douglas and Greenfield, 17–18.

113. F. M. Salter, *Medieval Drama in Chester* (Toronto, 1955), 50.

114. *Chester*, ed. Clopper, pp. liv–lv, 197–206.

115. PRO, SP 12/192/67 (paper by Rishworth group); J. W. F. Hill, *Tudor and Stuart Lincoln* (Cambridge, 1956), 101–7, 227–32.

116. Greaves, *Society and Religion*, 426; Clark, *English Provincial Society*, 157; Kelly, *Leicester*, 100–12.

117. *Devon*, ed. Wasson, pp. 293–5.

118. T. Barnes, 'County Politics and a Puritan Cause Célèbre: Somerset Churchales, 1633', *TRHS*, 5th ser. 5 (1959), 109. This pioneering work missed the significance of the documents below.

119. Huntington L, HA 10,347 (Popham to Hastings); *The Letters of Sir Francis Hastings*, ed. Claire Cross (Somerset Record Society, 69; 1969), 117–18.

120. PRO, SP 16/96/7; William Prynne, *Canterburies Doome* (1646), 152.

121. Frederick Brown, 'Star Chamber Proceedings, 34th Elizabeth 1592', *Proceedings of the Somerset Archaeological and Natural History Society*, 29 (1883), 53–60.

122. PRO, SP 12/224/47–87 (papers on the case); South Newington (Oxon.) CW in the Appendix. See Patrick Collinson, *The Birthpangs of Protestant England* (1988), 8, 137–9.

123. William Urwick, *Nonconformity in Herts* (1884), 107–15, 291–2.

124. William Hinde, *A Faithfull Remonstrance of the Holy Life . . . of John Bruen* (1641), 11–12, 89–131.

125. Susan Maria Farington, *The Farington Papers* (Chetham Society; 1856), 128–30.

126. James Tait, 'The Declaration of Sports for Lancashire', *EHR* 32 (1917), 466–8; Christopher Haigh, 'Puritan Evangelism in the Reign of Elizabeth I', *EHR* 92 (1977), 53–5; *The Lancashire Lieutenancy under the Tudors and Stuarts*, ed. John Harland (Chetham Society, 1859), ii. 217–23; *Lancashire Quarter Sessions Records*, ed. James Tait (Chetham Society, 1917), 11, 51; Edward Baines, *History of the County Palatine and Duchy of Lancaster* (1836), i. 549–50; 'A Description . . . of the County of Lancaster', ed. F. R. Raines, *Chetham Miscellany*, 5 (1875); PRO, SP12/235/68 (Paper by secretary to bishop); *Acts of the Privy Council of England, 1591–2*, ed. J. R. Dasent, 549.

127. F. G. Emmison, *Elizabethan Life: Disorder* (Chelmsford, 1970), 27; 'Archbishop Parker's Visitation', ed. A. Hussey, *Home Counties Magazine*, 5 (1903), 208; Canterbury Cathedral L MS X/8/6, fo. 37ᵛ; Ralph Houlbrooke, *Church Courts and the People during the English Reformation* (Oxford, 1979), 249; E. J. Baskerville, 'A Religious Disturbance in Canterbury, June 1561', *Bulletin of the Institute of Historical Research*, 158 (1992), 340–8.

128. R. Hodgkinson, 'Extracts from the Act Books of the Archdeacons of Nottingham', *Transactions of the Thoroton Society*, 30 (1926), 42.

129. E. Brinkworth (ed.), *The Archdeacon's Court* (Oxfordshire Record Society; 1942), 43–4.

130. *Tudor Parish Documents of the Diocese of York*, ed. J. S. Purvis (Cambridge, 1948), 39.

131. F. Emmison, 'Tithes, Perambulation and Sabbath-Breach in Elizabethan Essex', in Frederick Emmison and Roy Stephens (eds.), *Tribute to an Antiquary* (1976), 202; Underdown, *Revel, Riot and Rebellion*, 60.

132. Goring, 'Godly Exercises', 3; Collinson, *Birthpangs of Protestant England*, 141.

133. e.g. Thomas Hall, *Funebria Florae* (1661), 10; *Warwick County Records*, ed. S. C.

Ratcliff and H. C. Johnson (Warwick, 1941), vi. 53; *Hertford County Records: Sessions Rolls 1581–1698*, ed. W. J. Hardy (Hertford, 1905), 34.

134. Emmison, 'Tithes, Perambulation and Sabbath-Breach', 184–92; Purvis, *Tudor Parish Documents*, 37–63; Essex RO, D/AEA 1–21 and D/ACA 3–25, *passim*; Hodgkinson, 'Act Books of the Archdeacons of Nottingham', 40–2; Cambridge University L, EDR B 2/15, fo. 4ᵛ; John Strype, *The Life and Acts of Matthew Parker* (Oxford, 1821), i. 303–5; Arthur Hussey, 'Visitations of the Archdeacon of Canterbury', *Archaeologia Cantiana*, 25 (1902), 22, 32; Greaves, *Society and Religion*, 428; *Bishop Redman's Visitation*, ed. Revd J. Williams (Norfolk Record Society, 18; 1946), *passim*.

135. Exod. 32.

136. Matt. 19: 11–12; Rom. 1: 29; 1 Cor. 6: 9; Gal. 5: 19; Eph. 5: 3; Col. 3: 5; 1 Pet. 4: 3. The quotations are from the King James version, but the Tudor translations have the same import.

137. 1 Cor. 5: 11; Gal. 5: 21; 1 Pet. 4: 3.

138. On which, see Patrick Collison, 'The Beginnings of English Sabbatarianism', in *Studies in Church History*, 1, ed. C. W. Dugmore and Charles Duggan (1964), 207–21; Greaves, *Society and Religion*, 395–409; Parker, *English Sabbath*, 1–117.

139. *The Reliques of Rome*, fos. 158–78.

140. Barnes, 'Somerset Church Ales', 107; Wrightson, 'The Puritan Reformation of Manners', 31; Peter Laslett and Karla Oosterveen, 'Long-Term trends in Bastardy in England', *Population Studies*, 27 (1973), 259; G. R. Quaife, *Wanton Wenches and Wayward Wives* (1979), 84–7.

141. *Compendious or Briefe Examination*, 16.

142. On this see Sedley Lynch Ware, *The Elizabethan Parish in its Ecclesiastical and Financial Aspects* (Johns Hopkins University Studies in Historical and Political Science; Baltimore, 1908), 73–4.

143. For an overview, see Paul Slack, *Poverty and Policy in Tudor and Stuart England* (1988), 123–7.

144. The finest current work on this is Collinson, *The Birthpangs of Protestant England*, and Cressy, *Bonfires and Bells*.

145. J. E. Neale, *Essays in Elizabethan History* (1958), 10–12; Roy C. Strong, 'The Popular Celebration of the Accession Day of Queen Elizabeth I', *Journal of the Warburg and Courtauld Institutes*, 21 (1958), 86–103.

146. Frances A. Yates, *Astraea* (1975), 88–108; Cressy, *Bonfires and Bells*, 50–7.

147. Already known are St Peter Cheap (London: 1568); St Edmund, Salisbury (Wilts.: 1569); St Michael Worcester (1568); Lambeth (Surrey: 1567); St Botolph Bishopsgate (London: 1568). Now may be added All Saints, Cambridge (1569); All Hallows London Wall (London: 1569).

148. Comprising sixty-two of the parishes in the Appendix, in London, Surrey, Sussex, Kent, Hampshire, Hertfordshire, Wiltshire, Bristol, Somerset, Devon, Worcestershire, Warwickshire, Bedfordshire, Cambridgeshire, Suffolk, Norfolk, Shropshire, Chester, and York.

149. The first three as in n. 147. Then St Michael Cornhill 1571; St Ethelburga Bishopsgate 1574; St Andrew Hubbard 1572–4; St Giles Cripplegate 1571; All Hallows Staining 1571; St Alphage London Wall 1576; St Andrew by the Wardrobe 1573; St Benet Gracechurch 1574; St Dunstan in the West 1572; St James Garlickhithe 1594; St Margaret Moses 1581; St Margaret Pattens 1573; St Martin

Orgar 1575; St Mary Aldermanbury 1570; St Mary Magdalen Milk Street 1575–80; St Mary Woolchurch Haw 1572; St Mary Woolnoth 1571; St Matthew Friday Street 1577; St Michael le Querne 1572; St Peter Westcheap 1574; St Stephen Walbrook 1575.

150. Stanford in the Vale (Berks.) 1599; Seal (Surrey) 1596; Leverton (Lincs.) 1596; St Andrew, Canterbury (Kent) 1594; Ashwell (Herts.) 1602; Honiton (Devon) 1595; Chudleigh (Devon) 1596; St Peter, Stoke-on-Trent (Staffs.) 1596; Hartland (Devon) 1597; Somerton (Somerset) 1594; Wimborne Minster (Dorset) 1594; Wootton St Lawrence (Hants) 1600; Berkhamstead (Herts.) 1594; Broomfield (Essex) 1594; St Nicholas, Great Yarmouth (Norfolk) 1595; North Walsingham (Norfolk) 1594; Thornton Watlass (Yorks.) 1594; Masham (Yorks.) 1595; Lindfield (Sussex) 1600; St Mary, Swansea (Glam.) 1598; and St James Garlickhithe, as above.

151. Knebworth (Herts.); St Breock (Cornwall); Coldridge (Devon); South Littleton (Worcs.); Pattingham (Staffs.); Marston (Oxon.); Tintinhull (Somerset); South Cadbury (Somerset); Culworth (Northants.); St Botolph, Cambridge; Clifton (Beds.); Cartmel (Lancs.); Heversham (Westmorland); Williton (Somerset); Charlton Musgrave (Somerset); Charlton Marshall (Dorset); Fordingbridge (Hants); Hambledon (Hants); Childrey (Berks.); Ludgershall (Bucks.); Aston Abbots (Bucks.); Wingrave (Bucks.); St Michael Spurriergate, York; Southam (War.); St Martin, Leicester; East Bedfont (Middx.); St George Botolph Lane (London); Holy Trinity Minories (London); Poughill (Cornwall); St Neot (Cornwall); Great Dunmow (Essex); Heydon (Essex); Stonham Aspel (Suffolk); Stradbroke (Suffolk); Gislingham (Suffolk); Loddon (Norfolk); East Dereham (Norfolk); Elstead (Surrey); Cobham (Surrey); Weybread (Suffolk); Exning (Suffolk); Boxford (Suffolk); Billinghurst (Sussex); Slinfold (Sussex); Cheswardine (Salop); Harrietsham (Kent); Hoo All Hallows (Kent); St Mary, Bungay (Suffolk); Great Witchingham (Norfolk).

152. St Philip and St James.

153. Respectively, Strood; St Thomas, Salisbury; St Martin in the Fields; St Margaret, Westminster; St Mary Coslany, Norwich; and St Christopher le Stocks, London.

154. In Hertfordshire, Bishop's Stortford and St Peter, St Albans. In Derbyshire, Repton. In Oxfordshire, South Newington. In Lincolnshire, Leverton, Louth, and Broughton by Brigg. In Bedfordshire, Shillington. In Buckinghamshire, Wing and Great Marlow. In Warwickshire, Rowington and Shipston. In Leicestershire, Loughborough. In Nottinghamshire, Worksop.

155. Bressingham (Norfolk); St Bartholomew the Less (London).

156. Howson, *Sermon*, 15.

157. St Lawrence, Reading (Berks.) CW, year 1583.

158. Bishop's Stortford CW, year 1579.

159. St Oswald CW, years 1580–1602.

160. Such as at Norwich, in 1589, 1591, and 1594, and Gloucester, in 1596 and 1602: *Norwich*, ed. Galloway, 95–106 and *Cumberland, Westmorland and Gloucestershire*, ed. Douglas and Greenfield 176–9.

161. e.g. St Ives (Cornwall), years 1579–1602; Kilchampton (Cornwall), years 1582–1602; Langport (Somerset), year 1589; Somerton (Somerset), year 1594; and all the Oxford parishes.

CHAPTER 5

1. Published as a pamphlet under that title by the university, that year.
2. pp. 13–21.
3. At Berkswell, in Warwickshire's Forest of Arden, it carried on one more year; Berkswell CW, in Appendix.
4. David Cressy, *Bonfires and Bells* (1989), 120.
5. CW for St Laurence, and St Mary Coslany, listed in Appendix. St Peter Mancroft was the recorded exception.
6. Kenneth Parker, *The English Sabbath* (1988), 117.
7. Leah Marcus, *The Politics of Mirth* (Chicago, 1986), 3.
8. *The Works of Ben Jonson*, ed. Francis Cunningham (1904), ii. 572–8.
9. *Stuart Royal Proclamations*, ed. James F. Larkin and Paul L. Hughes (Oxford, 1983), 14; Parker, *English Sabbath*, 116–17.
10. W. B. Whitaker, *Sunday in Tudor and Stuart Times* (1933), 70; Thomas Birch (ed.), *The Court and Times of James I* (1848), i. 71.
11. Birch (ed.), *Court of James I*, i. 69.
12. Ibid. i. 69, 71, 87, 96, 290, 356–8, 387, 452–4, and ii. 66; John Nichols, *The Progresses . . . of King James the First* (1828), i. 301–14, 479–90, 589–607, ii. 1–32, 43, 102–21, 161–74, 213–45, 266–82, 373–96, 408–11, 513–15, 591–600, 706–45, iii. 26–38, 123–31, 232–42, 452–64, 527; Lancelot Andrewes, *XCVI Sermons* (1629); R. Chris Hassel, *Renaissance Drama and the English Church Year* (Lincoln, Nebr., 1979), 5, 60.
13. Whitaker, *Sunday*, 67–8; Parker, *English Sabbath*, 116–17.
14. Parker, *English Sabbath*, 119–20.
15. pp. 377–455.
16. *Commons Debates 1621*, ed. Wallace Notestein, Frances H. Relf, and Hartley Simpson (New Haven, Conn., 1935), vii. 643–4; HMC Hastings MSS, iv. 265–7, 278–80 (record of debate). I can find no evidence to support the suggestion of Parker, *English Sabbath*, 130–1, that Mountagu was inspired by James himself; the bishop does seem to have been putting forward his own views.
17. *Records of Early English Drama: Cumberland, Westmorland and Gloucestershire*, ed. Audrey Douglas and Peter Greenfield (Toronto, 1986), 17–18.
18. Cressy, *Bonfires and Bells*, 35–7, supported by the various visitation articles.
19. Parker, *English Sabbath*, 128; *Journals of the House of Commons* (1803), i. 261–9; *Journals of the House of Lords*, ii. 375–400.
20. Sources at n. 16, plus *Commons' Journals*, i. 467–505 and *Lords' Journals*, ii. 706–10. Parker, *English Sabbath*, 129–30, is convinced that the 1606 and 1614 bills were the same.
21. *Sabbathum, Veteris et Novi Testamati* (1606).
22. Whitaker, *Sunday*, 59–65.
23. Richard Rogers, *Seven Treatises* (1603), 578. The other two authors in this category were John Dod and Robert Cleaver, *A Treatise or Exposition upon the Ten Commandments* (1603).
24. *The Sermon Preached at the Crosse, Feb. xiiii 1607* (1608), 169–74.
25. George Widley, *The Doctrine of the Sabbath* (1604), 98–113.
26. John Sprint, *Propositions, Tending to Proove the Necessarie Use of the Christian Sabbaoth* (1607), 36–7.

27. HMC Rutland MSS, i. 390–1. Parker, *English Sabbath*, 117, mistakes this for a royal command. The original document is in Belvoir Castle and not available to scholars.

28. T. F. Thistleton Dyer, *Old English Social Life* (1898), 206–7.

29. *English Sabbath*, 134–6.

30. *A Series of Precedents and Proceedings in Criminal Cases*, ed. William Hale (1847), 235; Jeremy Goring, *Godly Exercises or the Devil's Dance* (Friends of Dr Williams's Library, 37th lecture; 1983), 7; Martin Ingram, *Church Courts, Sex and Marriage in England* (Cambridge, 1987), 104–7.

31. Ingram, *Church Courts*, 105; David Underdown, *Revel, Riot and Rebellion* (Oxford, 1985), 58–63; Somerset RO, D/D/Cd 28 (*Badgworth churchwardens* v. *Hyde*, 25 Jan. 1600) and 71 (*Derrick* v. *Allen*, 5 Mar. 1632).

32. *Records of Early English Drama: Devon*, ed. John M. Wasson (Toronto, 1986), 294–6.

33. T. Barnes, 'County Politics and a Puritan Cause Célèbre: Somerset Church Ales, 1633', *TRHS*, 5th ser. 5 (1959), 107–9; Underdown, *Revel, Riot and Rebellion*, 98–9.

34. James Tait, 'The Declaration of Sports for Lancashire', *English Historical Review*, 32 (1917), 567–8.

35. See Appendix for CW of Stoke Newington (Oxon.) (regular ales end 1606); Winterslow (Wilts.) (ales end 1610); Chelsea (Middx.) (Hocktide ends 1611); Calne (Wilts.) (ales end 1603); Cullompton (Devon) (ales end 1616); Blagdon (Somerset) (hoggling ends c.1615); St Mary the Virgin, Oxford (Hocktide ends 1602); Stanford in the Vale (Berks.) (sold maypole 1610); Wooton St Lawrence (Hants).

36. William Kelly, *Notices Illustrative of the Drama . . . of Leicester* (1865), 102–12.

37. *Records of Early English Drama: York*, ed. Alexandra F. R. Johnston and Margaret Rogerson (Manchester, 1979), 520; *Records of the Borough of Nottingham* (Nottingham, 1885), iv. 286.

38. *Records of Early English Drama: Chester*, ed. Lawrence M. Clopper (Manchester, 1979), 268, 297.

39. Kelly, *Leicester*, 102–12.

40. Most of the information is in PRO STAC 8/161/1, to which C. J. Sisson, *Lost Plays of Shakespeare's Age* (Cambridge, 1936), 162–75, adds a little material from the Ellesmere MSS. Among modern scholars who have referred to these events are Martin Ingram, David Underdown, Roger Manning, and David Wiles.

41. PRO, SP 14/64/66 (deposition).

42. HMC 7th Report, appendix, p. 675 (Nottingham to More).

43. Underdown, *Revel, Riot and Rebellion*, 56–7.

44. Goring, *Godly Exercises*, 7.

45. Underdown, *Revel, Riot and Rebellion*, 59, 61–2.

46. Ibid. 59, 63.

47. *Records of the County of Wilts*, ed. B. Howard Cunnington (Devizes, 1932), 35.

48. M. Ingram, 'Ridings, Rough Music and the "Reform of Popular Culture" in Early Modern England', *Past and Present*, 105 (1984), 90.

49. HMC MSS in Various Collections, i. 294–5 (petition and order).

50. *Society and Puritanism in Pre-Revolutionary England*, 427.

51. Joan Thirsk, 'Industries in the Countryside', in F. J. Fisher (ed.), *Essays in the Economic and Social History of Tudor and Stuart England* (Cambridge, 1961), 70–88; Alan Everitt, 'Farm Labourers', in H. P. R. Finberg (ed.), *The Agrarian History of England and Wales* (1967), 462–5; Joan Thirsk, 'Seventeenth-Century Agriculture and Social

Change' and Alan Everitt, 'Nonconformity in Country Parishes', in Joan Thirsk (ed.), *Land, Church and People* (Reading, 1970), 148–77 and 178–99.

52. *Revel, Riot and Rebellion.*
53. See esp. his debate with John Morrill in the *Journal of British Studies*, 26 (1987), 451–79; Ann Hughes, *The Causes of the English Civil War* (1991), 138–45; Buchanan Sharp, 'Rural Discontents and the English Revolution', in R. C. Richardson (ed.), *Town and Countryside in the English Revolution* (Manchester, 1992), 251–72; and Martin Ingram, cited below, n. 55.
54. *Revel, Riot and Rebellion*, 74–98.
55. *Church Courts, Sex and Marriage*, 101–2.
56. See CW in Appendix for Williton (Somerset), Bere Regis (Dorset), and St Ives (Cornwall).
57. See CW in Appendix for Bramley (Hants) and Ashampstead (Berks.).
58. See CW in Appendix for Dursley (Gloucs.) and Cheddar (Somerset).
59. Staffordshire RO, Q/S Rolls, Easter 1605.
60. See Appendix for Seal (Surrey) CW.
61. *Cumberland, Westmorland and Gloucestershire*, ed. Douglas and Greenfield, 25–71.
62. *Devon*, ed. Wasson, 176–89; Charles Deering, *Nottinghamia Vetus et Nova* (Nottingham, 1751), 123–4.
63. See Appendix for CW of St Mary the Virgin, St Martin, St Michael, and St Peter in the East.
64. Esp. *The Politics of Mirth* (Chicago, 1986). The publications of others will be referred to below.
65. Christopher Whitfield, *Robert Dover and the Cotswold Games* (1962), ch. 1.
66. *An Olde Mans Lesson and a Young Mans Love* (1605).
67. Joan Grundy, *The Spenserian Poets* (1969).
68. *The Poetry of George Wither*, ed. Frank Sidgwick (1902), 178–81.
69. *Coryats Crambe* (1611).
70. *Campion's Works*, ed. Percival Vivian (Oxford, 1909), 127.
71. *The Catholic Doctrine of the Church of England* (1607). For discussions, see W. B. Whitaker, *Sunday in Tudor and Stuart Times* (1933), 71, and Parker, *English Sabbath*, 92–6, 113–14.
72. 'Meg Goodwin', *Old Meg of Herefordshire* (1609).
73. IV. iii. 164.
74. *The Knight of the Burning Pestle*, i. 135–6, iv. 8–60, v. 295–300, and v. 320–1.
75. *Masque of the Inner Temple and Gray's Inn*, in *The Dramatic Works in the Beaumont and Fletcher Canon*, ed. Fredson Bowers (Cambridge, 1966).
76. *Technogamia*, ed. Sister M. J. C. Cavanaugh (Washington, DC, 1942).
77. Marcus, *Politics of Mirth*, 9.
78. *The Works of Ben Jonson*, ed. Francis Cunningham (1904), ii. 572–8.
79. Ben Jonson, *Works*, ed. C. H. Herford Percy and Evelyn Simpson (Oxford, 1941), viii. 98.
80. Who is well discussed by Marcus, *Politics of Mirth*, 50–1.
81. Jonson, *Works*, ed. Percy and Simpson, vii. 437–45; Marcus, *Politics of Mirth*, 77–83.
82. James Tait, 'The Declaration of Sports for Lancashire', *English Historical Review*, 32 (1917), 561–8; Hill, *Society and Puritanism*, 195–6; Christopher Haigh, 'Puritan Evangelism in the Reign of Elizabeth I', *English Historical Review*, 92 (1977), 30–58;

Parker, *English Sabbath*, ch. 5. I have added a few extra details from John Barwick, *A Summarie Account of the Holy Life and Happy Death of . . . Thomas Late Lord Bishop of Duresme* (1660), 80–1.

83. Parker, *English Sabbath*, 161–8.

84. Nicholas Breton, *The Court and Country* (1618), 7.

85. Michael Drayton, *Pastorals* (1619), esp. *Ninth Eglogue*, ll. 40–50.

86. Sig. B3.

87. *A Book, for a Buck with a Parke* (1618).

88. Marcus, *Politics of Mirth*, 106.

89. *Women Pleased*, vi. 85–214, in *The Beaumont and Fletcher Canon*, ed. Bowers, i.

90. *The Poems of Richard Corbett*, ed. J. A. W. Bennett and H. R. Trevor-Roper (Oxford, 1955), 52–6.

91. *The Diary of Walter Yonge, Esq.*, ed. George Roberts (Camden Society, 1848), 64.

92. *The Journal of Nicholas Assheton*, ed. F. R. Raines (Chetham Society; 1848), 29–30, 41–2, 105–8.

93. Ingram, *Church Courts, Sex and Marriage*, 103.

94. H. J. Moule, *Descriptive Catalogue of the Charters, Minute Books and Other Documents of . . . Weymouth* (Weymouth, 1883), 59.

95. Thatcham CW (see Appendix), years 1617–20.

96. Underdown, *Revel, Riot and Rebellion*, 65–7; Parker, *English Sabbath*, 154–9.

97. Goring, *Godly Exercises*, 6, 17–18.

98. Parker, *English Sabbath*, 169–73; Robert Zaller, *The Parliament of 1621* (Berkeley, Calif. 1971), 42–5; *Commons Debates 1621*, ed. Notestein, Relf, and Simpson, ii. 95–150, iv. 52–64, v. 12, 467–8, 500–3, vi. 362; *Commons' Journals*, i. 524–5.

99. Parker, *English Sabbath*, 173–4; *DNB* 'Bayley'. The king's growing irritation with Bayly was greatly increased by the fact that the bishop's general sympathy with evangelical Protestants was coupled with a remarkable ineptitude in the running of his diocese: Kenneth Fincham, *Prelate as Pastor* (Oxford, 1990), chs. 1.3 and 3.4.

100. Ann Hughes, *Politics, Society and Civil War in Warwickshire, 1620–1660* (Cambridge, 1987), 83.

101. Thomas Dekker, John Ford, William Rowley, *The Witch of Edmonton* (1621), II. i. 36–85, III. i. 1–24, III. iv.

102. pp. 62–3.

103. John Prideaux, *The Doctrine of the Sabbath* (1634).

104. *Devon*, ed. Wasson, 297–8.

105. *The Poems of Robert Herrick*, ed. L. C. Martin (Oxford, 1965), 68, 149, 178–9, 230–1, 239, 255, 263–4, 285, 355; George Walton Scott, *Robert Herrick* (1974); S. Musgrove, *The Universe of Robert Herrick* (Auckland University College Bulletin, 38; 1950); Robert H. Deming, *Ceremony and Art: Robert Herrick's Poetry* (The Hague, 1974); A. Leigh Deneef, *This Poetic Liturgie* (Durham, NC, 1974).

106. *Politics of Mirth*, 140–50.

107. *The Cavalier Mode from Jonson to Cotton* (Princeton, NJ, 1971), 191–3.

108. '"We Feaste in our Defence": Patrician Carnival in Early Modern England and Robert Herrick's "Hesperides"', *English Literary Renaissance*, 16 (1986), 234–52.

109. Parker, *English Sabbath*, 174; *Commons' Journals*, ii. 671–2; PRO, SP 14/165/61 (Edward to John Nicholas).

110. Barnes, 'County Politics', 109.

111. Ingram, *Church Courts, Sex, and Marriage*, 117.

112. Jonson, *Works*, ed. Percy and Simpson, vii. 781–6.

113. Appears from 1590s: St Werburgh, Bristol; All Hallows London Wall (London); St Mary at Hill, Chester. Appears from 1600s: St Michael, Chester; St Oswald, Chester; St Michael, Gloucester; Temple, Bristol; Holy Trinity the Less (London); St Michael le Querne (London); Lambeth (Surrey). Appears from 1610s: St Andrew by the Wardrobe (London); St Peter Westcheap (London). Appears from 1620s: St Christopher le Stocks (London); St Michael, Oxford; All Hallows Staining (London); St Alphege London Wall (London); St Antholin Budge Row (London); St Martin Orgar (London); St Olave Jewry (London). Appears from 1630s: St Peter Mancroft, Norwich (Norfolk); St Mary Redcliffe, Bristol; St Lawrence, Reading (Berkshire); St Petrock, Exeter (Devon); St Peter in the East, Oxford; St Thomas, Bristol; All Saints, Bristol; St Philip and St James, Bristol; St Mary le Strand, Westminster; St Margaret, Westminster; St Stephen Coleman Street, St Stephen Walbrook, St Benet Paul's Wharf, All Hallows Honey Lane, St Michael Queenhithe, and St Clement Eastcheap (all London). See Appendix as usual, for all these CW.

114. Oxfordshire RO, MS Diocesan Papers C. 26–8, 118, 175 *passim*; *A Series of Precedents and Proceedings in Criminal Cases*, ed. Hale (1847), 243; Essex RO, D/ACA/21–51, *passim*. *Episcopal Visitation Returns for Cambridgeshire*, ed. W. Palmer (Cambridge, 1930), 15–73 *passim*; R. Hodgkinson, 'Extracts from the Act Books of the Archdeacons of Nottingham', *Transactions of the Thoroton Society*, 30–1 (1926–7), 30. 40–2, 31. 142; *Churchwardens' Presentments (17th Century)*, ed. H. Johnstone (Sussex Record Society; 1947–87), *passim*; W. Rensham, 'Notes from the Act Book of the Archdeaconry Court of Lewes', *Sussex Archaeological Collections*, xix (1906), 62; Borthwick Institute, York, V1633/CBI, *passim*; *The Churchwardens' Presentments for the Oxfordshire Peculiars of Dorchester, Thame and Banbury*, ed. Sidney A. Peyton (Oxfordshire Record Society, 1928), 144–5, 214, 245, 251, 299, 308, 312, 315; Margaret Stieg, *Laud's Laboratory* (Lewisburg, Pa., 1982), 194–5; Underdown, *Revel, Riot and Rebellion*, 77–81, 90–1, 96–7.

115. Keith Thomas, *Religion and the Decline of Magic* (1971), 62–5.

116. *Revel, Riot and Rebellion*, 77–81, 90–1, 96–7.

117. Sources all at n. 114.

118. Being the archdeaconry act and minute books in Essex RO, D/ACA and D/AEA. I sampled three years in every ten.

119. See the CW in Appendix.

120. See Appendix. Expenditure appears under James at Repton (Derbs.); Strood and Loose (Kent); Worfield (Salop); Axbridge (Somerset); Seale (Surrey); Upton (Notts.); and Banham (Norfolk). And under Charles at St Alphege, East Greenwich (Kent); Crewkerne (Somerset); Newbury (Berks.); Ryton on Dunsmore and Offchurch (War.); Stroud (Gloucs.); Kingston upon Thames (Surrey); Great Staughton and Fenstanton (Hunts.); St. Ives (Cornwall); and Lewes (Sussex).

121. See CW in Appendix.

122. St Alphege London Wall, St Dunstan in the West, St Ethelburga Bishopsgate, St Stephen Walbrook, St Ann and St Agnes, and St Clement Eastcheap.

123. Those which recorded it being, in each case, St Mary at Hill, Chester, and St Werburgh, and St Ewen in Bristol.

124. Such as Howden (E. Riding), Louth (Lincs.) and Kirton in Lindsey (Lincs.).

Temple (Bristol) also began to ring on Christmas morn, and Wimborne Minster (Dorset) upon New Year's Day.

125. *The Complaint of Christmas and the Tears of Twelfthtyde* (1631).

126. *Hospitality in Early Modern England* (Oxford, 1990), 148–9.

127. Gervase Holles, *Memorials of the Holles Family*, ed. A. C. Wood (Camden Society, 3rd ser. 4; 1937), 41–2.

128. Heal, *Hospitality*, 149, 173, 175, 219, 280–1, 293–4.

129. Ibid. 71–7.

130. In addition to those above, examples from different areas include *Early Stuart Household Accounts*, ed. Lionel M. Munby (Hertfordshire Record Society, 2; 1986), 89–159; Assheton, *Journal*, ed. Raines, 69–75, 122; *Cumberland, Westmorland and Gloucestershire*, ed. Douglas and Greenfield, 128–9, 142–4; Rachel Weigall, 'The Journal of Lady Mildmay', *The Quarterly Review*, 215 (1911), 134. *A Royalist's Notebook*, ed. Francis Bamford (1936), 232; Hugh Owen, 'The Diary of Bulkeley of Dronwy, Anglesey', *Anglesey Antiquarian Society and Field Club Transactions* (1937), 110–11, 136, 159–60.

131. *Diary of Lady Margaret Hoby 1599–1605*, ed. Dorothy M. Meads (1903).

132. *The Records of a Church of Christ in Bristol*, ed. Roger Hayden (Bristol Record Society; 1974), 85.

133. W. H. Summers, 'Some Documents in the State Papers Relating to Beaconsfield', *Records of Bucks*, 7 (1897), 98–9, 108.

134. Conrad Russell, *The Fall of the British Monarchies 1637–1642* (Oxford, 1991), 183–4.

135. W. Mepham, 'Essex Drama under Puritanism and the Commonwealth', *Essex Review*, 58 (1949), 181.

136. Sandra Billington, *Mock Kings in Medieval Society and Renaissance Drama* (Oxford, 1991), 35.

137. E. K. Chambers, *The Medieval Stage* (Oxford, 1963), i. 412.

138. Griffin Higgs, *The Christmas Prince*, ed. Frederick S. Boas (Malone Society, 1922).

139. Martin Butler, 'Entertaining the Palatine Prince', *English Literary Renaissance*, 13 (1983), 329–30; Thomas Birch, *The Court and Times of Charles I* (1848), i. 311, 313–14 (Mead to Stuteville). *The Earl of Strafford's Letters and Dispatches*, ed. W. Knowler (1739), i. 506–7; *The Diary of Thomas Crosfield*, ed. F. S. Boas (1935), 83.

140. Holles, *Memorials*, 236.

141. *The Diary of Sir Simonds D'Ewes (1622–1624)*, ed. Elisabeth Bourcier (Paris, 1974), 104, 113.

142. Keith A. Newman, 'Holiness in Beauty', in Diana Wood (ed.), *The Church and the Arts* (Studies in Church History, 28; 1992), 69–83.

143. *A Tryall of Private Devotions* (1628).

144. *The Acts of the High Commission Court within the Diocese of Durham*, ed. W. H. D. Longstaffe (Surtees Society, 1858), 197–8.

145. Ibid. 197–206; *The Correspondence of John Cosin*, ed. George Ornsby (Surtees Society, 1860), i. 141–210; Peter Smart, *A Sermon Preached in the Cathedral Church of Durham, 7 July 1628* (1628), and *The Vanitie and Downe-Fall of Superstitious Popish Ceremonies* (Edinburgh, 1628).

146. *To the Honourable . . . the Commons House of Parliament, The Humble Petition of Peter Smart* (3 Nov. 1640); *Acts of the High Commission Court*, 211–43.

147. St Matthew Friday Street (London) CW, years 1620–35.

148. M. J. Crossley-Evans, 'The Clergy of the City of Chester, 1630–1672', *Journal of the Chester Archaeological Society*, 68 (1986), 115.

149. Thomas Birch, *The Court and Times of James I* (1848), i. 46–51 (Hoby to Edmondes); *Journals of the House of Commons*, i. 258–60; *Journals of the House of Lords*, ii. 363, 365; *Statutes of the Realm* (1819), v. ii. 1067–8.

150. *Bonfires and Bells*, 57–8 and ch. 9.

151. Bob Bushaway, *By Rite* (1982), 66; John Brand, *Observations on the Popular Antiquities of Great Britain*, ed. Sir Henry Ellis (1908), i. 391 (for Dugdale on Lancashire); T. Gwynn Jones, *Welsh Folklore and Folk-Custom* (Cambridge, 1979), 147–9; J. Weld, *A History of Leagram* (Chetham Society; 1913), 132–3; R. V. Sayce, 'A Survey of Montgomeryshire Folk-lore', *Montgomeryshire Collections*, 17 (1942), 21.

152. CW in Appendix under Buckinghamshire and Shropshire.

153. Examples of adoption by villages and small towns under James are as follows. Devon: Bere Ferrers, Braunton, Buckland in the Moor, Hartland, North Tawton, Modbury, Uplyme, Woodbury, Cullompton, Stoke Gabriel. Somerset: Axbridge, Crewkerne, Churchill, Locking, Monksilver. Staffordshire: Pattingham, Checkley, Stone, Stokron Trent, Hanbury, and Betley. Shropshire: Worfield, Albrighton, Donnington, Cound, and Shawbury. But there are others from most counties.

154. St George Botolph Lane, St Margaret Pattens, St Mary Magdalen Milk Street, St Michael Le Querne, St Peter Westcheap, St Benet Paul's Wharf, St Botolph Aldersgate, and St Dunstan in the East. Provincial examples include St Werburgh, Bristol, St Michael, Lewes, St Mary Bredman, Canterbury, and St Clement and St Mary Tower, both in Ipswich.

155. Ecclesfield (Yorks.); St. Oswald, Oswestry (Salop); Prescot (Lancs.); Louth (Lincs.); Padiham (Lancs.); Bishop's Hull (Somerset); St Bartholomew Exchange (London); St Stephen Walbrook (London); St Mary at Hill, Chester (Ches.); Worfield (Salop); Newbury (Berks.).

156. St Edmund and St Thomas.

157. Birch, *Court and Times of James the First*, i. 358; Nichols, *Progresses*, ii. 43, 123, 408–11, 609–10, 759, iii. 134, 267, 471–2, 532–3, 592, iv. 659–60, 755, 968.

158. Ibid. ii. 145, 203, iii. 97, 119, 186, 215, iv. 755.

159. Ibid. iii. 533.

160. Like St Andrew, Canterbury (Kent), St Michael Crooked Lane (London), and Scarborough (Yorks.).

161. See Cressy, *Bonfires and Bells*, ch. 9, *passim*.

162. Ibid. 148; John Latimer, *The Annals of Bristol in the Seventeenth Century* (Bristol, 1900), 34.

163. Like Condover and Cound (Salop), Shorne (Kent), Bedale and Millington (Yorks.), Bromley (Essex), North Walsingham (Norfolk), Ryton (Durham), and Thatcham (Berks.).

164. In Oxford, absent at St Michael, St Peter in the East. In York, at Holy Trinity Goodramgate, St Martin Micklegate, St John Ousegate, St Martin Coney Street. In Chester, at St Mary at Hill, St Michael, St Oswald, Holy Trinity.

165. In London, St Ethelburga Bishopsgate, St Michael Wood Street, St Mary Abchurch. In Durham, St Oswald. In Cambridge, Holy Trinity and Great St Mary.

166. Cressy, *Bonfires and Bells*, 145–8.

167. Those on record being St John Walbrook and St Botolph Billingsgate. See Appendix.
168. Cressy, *Bonfires and Bells*, 134–5.
169. Ibid. 60–1, 134–7: St Bartholomew Exchange, St Katherine Coleman Street, St Stephen Coleman Street, St Botolph Bishopsgate, St Christopher le Stocks, St Martin in the Fields, and St Margaret Westminster.
170. Holy Trinity the Less, St Antholin Budge Row, St Dunstan in the West, St Lawrence Jewry, St Lawrence Pountney, St Swithun London Stone, St Thomas Apostle, St Michael Queenhithe, St Martin Outwich, St Olave Silver Street, and St Mary Abchurch.
171. Cressy, *Bonfires and Bells*, 61, 138.
172. Temple and St Mary Redcliffe.
173. Birch, *Court and Times of Charles the First*, ii. 80 (Mead to Stuteville).
174. Jonson, *Works*, ed. Percy and Simpson, viii. 239.
175. Birch, *Court and Times of Charles the First*, ii. 82 (Mead to Stuteville).
176. St Christopher le Stocks, St Thomas Apostle, St Benet Fink, St Michael Wood Street, St Martin Outwich, St Katherine Coleman, St Ann and St Agnes, St Swithun London Stone, St Michael Bassishaw.
177. St Bartholomew Exchange, St Antholin Budge Row.
178. As before, this is based upon the printed visitation articles catalogued by diocese in the British, Bodleian, and Cambridge University Libraries.
179. *Episcopal Visitation Returns*, ed. Palmer, 15–71, *passim*.
180. Cressy, *Bonfires and Bells*, 62.
181. The purchase of which is recorded in the accounts of most churches which kept the day.
182. *A Calendar of Dramatic Records in the Books of the Livery Companies of London*, ed. Jean Robertson and D. J. Gordon (Malone Society, 3; 1954), 37–118; Sheila Williams, 'The Lord Mayor's Show in Tudor and Stuart Times', *Guildhall Miscellany*, 10 (1959), 7–15; David M. Bergeron, *English Civic Pageantry 1558–1642* (1971), 123–240; F. W. Fairholt, *Lord Mayors' Pageants* (1843), i.
183. Ian W. Archer, *The Pursuit of Stability: Social Relations in Elizabethan London* (Cambridge, 1991), 1, 3.
184. K. Lindley, 'Riot Prevention and Control in Early Stuart London', *TRHS*, 5th ser. 33 (1983), 109–10.
185. e.g. Birch, *Court and Times of James the First*, ii. 3 (Chamberlain to Carleton).
186. Quoted in Brand, *Observations*, i. 65.
187. p. 20.
188. *Jack a Lent his Beginning and Entertainment* (1621), sig. B2.
189. Parker, *English Sabbath*, 175–7; *Statutes of the Realm*, v. 1, 25.
190. See CW in Appendix.
191. *York*, ed. Johnston and Rogerson, 572.
192. *Western Circuit Assize Orders 1629–1648*, ed. J. S. Cockburn (Camden Society, 4th ser. 17; 1976), 3–4, 33.
193. PRO, SP 16/96/7; Barnes, 'County Politics', 109.
194. Latimer, *Annals of Bristol*, 101.
195. *Articles to be Enquired of within the Diocese of Carlisle* (1629), 23.
196. Barnes, 'County Politics', 110.
197. Oxfordshire RO, MS Diocesan Papers c. 27, fo. 46.

198. *The Muses Elizium*, in which see esp. 'The Second Nimphall', ll. 219–22.

199. Earle, *Micro-cosmographie* (1628), sig. 43A; Keith Wrightson, 'Alehouses, Order and Reformation', in Eileen and Stephen Yeo, *Popular Culture and Class Conflict in England 1590–1914* (Brighton, 1981), 10.

200. *The Anatomy of Melancholy*, ed. Thomas C. Faulkner, Nicholas K. Kiessling, and Rhonda L. Blair (Oxford, 1989), ii. 76, 82.

201. Barnes, 'County Politics', 110–20; Parker, *English Sabbath*, 179–90; Julian Davies, *The Caroline Captivity of the Church* (Oxford, 1992), 174–80; Kevin Sharpe, *The Personal Rule of Charles I* (New Haven, Conn., 1992), 353.

202. *The Works of Archbishop Laud*, ed. James Bliss (Oxford, 1854), iv. 133–4, 255–7.

203. Ibid. iv. 256.

204. PRO, SP 16/247/24; *William Whiteway of Dorchester: His Diary 1618 to 1635*, foreword by David Underdown (Dorset Record Society, 12; 1991), 132.

205. Laud, *Works*, ed. Bliss, iv. 255–7.

206. Whitaker, *Sunday*, 132; Davies, *Caroline Captivity*, 174–5.

207. Parker, *English Sabbath*, 181.

208. PRO, SP 16/247/24.

209. pp. 233–63, 758–61.

210. Hill, *Society and Puritanism*, 198–202.

211. As *The Doctrine of the Sabbath* (1634). See *DNB*, 'Prideaux', and 'Heylyn'.

212. *The History of the Sabbath* (1636). See Parker, *English Sabbath*, 197–8.

213. *A Treatise of the Sabbath Day* (1635).

214. *The Works of Robert Sanderson*, ed. William Jacobsen (Oxford, 1854), v. 15–16; Christopher Dow, *A Discourse of the Sabbath and the Lord's Day* (1636), 45–75; and *Innovations Unjustly Charged upon the Present Church and State* (1637), fos. 73–107; John Pocklington, *Sunday No Sabbath* (1636); Gilbert Ironside, *Seven Questions of the Sabbath Briefly Disputed* (1637), 271–5; Edmund Reeve, *The Communion Book Catechism Expounded* (1635), 90–108; David Primrose, *A Treatise of the Sabbath and the Lords Day* (1636), 138.

215. *The King's Entertainment at Welbeck*; *A Tale of a Tub*; *A Sad Shepherd*, in *Works*, ed. Percy and Simpson, vii. 5–49.

216. *Coelum Britannicum* (1634). I am not quite persuaded by Marcus, *Politics of Mirth*, 15–16, who suggests that the anti-masque is an oblique criticism of the Book of Sports; rather, it condemns those who would abuse entertainments for their own ends, in contrast to the selfless sovereign.

217. The relevant passages are reprinted in Brand, *Observations*, i. 267–8; and *Shakespeare's England* (Oxford, 1916), ii. 438.

218. All in *Annalia Dubrensia* (1636).

219. *The Springs Glorie* (1638), sigs. F–G3.

220. *A Brief Answer to a Late Treatise* (1636).

221. *A Divine Tragedy Lately Acted* (1636).

222. HMC 3rd Report, p. 191 (Examination of clergy before Bishop Piers).

223. *For God and the King* (1636).

224. *Picturae Loquentes* (1635; republished by Luttrell Society, 1946), 67.

225. *The Dramatic Works and Poems of James Shirley*, ed. John Murray (1833), iv. 6–7.

226. *Caroline Captivity*, 180–95.

227. Ibid. 195–204.

228. *Personal Rule*, 353–9.

229. Davies, *Caroline Captivity*, 202–3.

230. Palmer, *Episcopal Visitation Returns*, 1–73.

231. Birch, *Court and Times of Charles I*, i. 72 (Chamberlain to Carleton); Whiteway, *Diary*, 138–9.

232. Kevin Sharpe, *Criticism and Compliment* (Cambridge, 1987), 182–3, 224, 227, 243, 247; Hassel, *Renaissance Drama*, 5, 60, 114.

233. Hill, *Society and Puritanism*, 158; Cressy, *Bonfires and Bells*, 39–40; H. R. Trevor-Roper, *Archbishop Laud* (1940), 159.

234. Ibid. 158–9.

235. Cressy, *Bonfires and Bells*, 41.

236. *Emblems*, quoted in A. R. Wright, *British Calendar Customs*, ed. T. E. Lones (1936), i. 130.

237. Sanderson, *Works*, i. 228–9.

238. Burton, *Divine Tragedie*, 7–21. David Underdown is confident that these are cases of revival: *Revel, Riot and Rebellion*, 68.

239. *Revel, Riot and Rebellion*, 67–8, 74, 86–8, 95, 98.

240. Richard Baxter, *Reliquiae Baxterianae*, ed. Matthew Sylvester (1696), i. 1–2.

241. *Warwick County Records*, ed. S. C. Ratcliff and H. C. Johnson (Warwick, 1941), vi. 53.

242. York City Archives Department, House Book 35, fos. 158, 273, 339.

243. Cerne Abbas (Dorset) CW, year 1635 (see Appendix).

244. Burton, *Divine Tragedie*, 9–10.

245. See Appendix for South Newington (Oxon.) CW, years 1636–41, and Great Marlow (Bucks.) CW, year 1639.

CHAPTER 6

1. *The Journal of Sir Simonds D'Ewes*, ed. Wallace Notestein (New Haven, Conn., 1923), 6, 38.

2. D'Ewes, *Journal*, ed. Notestein, 83, 298, 337, 343, 531. The only clergy named were Wray, Raymond, Wilson, and Burwel, who had been suspended.

3. *DNB*, Pocklington.

4. *Journals of the House of Commons* (1803), ii. 278–9, 283; Conrad Russell, *The Fall of the British Monarchies 1637–1642* (Oxford, 1991), 368.

5. *The Journal of Sir Simonds D'Ewes*, ed. W. H. Coates (New Haven, Conn., 1942), 308; *Commons' Journals*, ii. 348.

6. Kenneth L. Parker, *The English Sabbath* (Cambridge, 1988), 217.

7. See CW in Appendix for the parishes of St Martin, St Michael, and St Peter in the East.

8. See CW in Appendix.

9. See CW in Appendix.

10. Robert Plot, *The Natural History of Staffordshire* (Oxford, 1686), 434.

11. *Crosby Records: A Cavalier's Note Book*, ed. T. E. Gibson (1880), 233–6.

12. Sheila Williams, 'The Lord Mayor's Show in Tudor and Stuart Times', *Guildhall Miscellany*, 10 (1959), 12; David M. Bergeron, *English Civic Pageantry 1558–1642* (1971), 240.

13. Thomas Sharp, *A Dissertation on the Pageants or Dramatic Mysteries . . . at Coventry* (Coventry, 1825), 203–4.

14. Charles Deering, *Nottinghamia Vetus et Nova* (Nottingham, 1751), 123–4.
15. Charles Hoskins, *The Ancient Trade Guilds and Companies of Salisbury* (1912), 184–5.
16. *Documents Illustrative of English Church History*, ed. Henry Gee (1896), 542.
17. Russell, *Fall of the British Monarchies*, 183–4, 502.
18. *Commons' Journals*, ii. 96; D'Ewes, *Journal*, ed. Notestein, 485.
19. Anthony Fletcher, 'Factionalism in Town and Countryside', in Derek Baker (ed.), *The Church in Town and Countryside* (Studies in Church History, 16; 1979), 291.
20. *Commons' Journals*, ii. 356, 449; *Tudor and Stuart Proclamations*, ed. Robert Steele (Oxford, 1910), i, no. 1925.
21. *Commons' Journals*, ii. 306; David Cressy, *Bonfires and Bells* (1989), 156–8, 161.
22. *The Birthpangs of Protestant England*.
23. Ibid. 132–54.
24. Which is all I was saying in *The Royalist War Effort* (1981), 201–3, which I was flattered to find that Professor Collinson had selected for his chief opponent in this respect.
25. John Rushworth, *Historical Collections* (1721), ii. 193.
26. 'County Politics and a Puritan Cause célèbre: Somerset Churchales, 1633', *TRHS* 5th ser. 5 (1959), 116.
27. Russell, *Fall of the British Monarchies*, 223.
28. Parker, *English Sabbath*, 194.
29. A. G. Matthews, *Walker Revised* (Oxford, 1948), 80–2, 85, 147, 149–51, 153, 157, 161, 164, 170, 201, 207–8, 215, 218, 220, 247, 250, 329, 333, 340, 345–6, 375–6.
30. See the biographies of Trussell, Durham, and Randolph in Christopher Whitfield, *Robert Dover and the Cotswold Games* (1962).
31. W. Mepham, 'Essex Drama under Puritanism and the Commonwealth', *Essex Review*, 58 (1949), 181; Barbara Lowe, 'Early Records of the Morris in England', *JEFDSS* 7: 2 (1957), 73.
32. *Letters of the Lady Brilliana Harley*, ed. Thomas T. Lewis (Camden Society, 1854), 167; *True New News* (1642), 2–3.
33. John Aubrey, *Remaines of Gentilisme and Judaisme*, ed. James Britten (1881), 137–8.
34. Cheddar CW, in Appendix.
35. *Acts and Ordinances of the Interregnum*, ed. C. H. Firth and R. S. Rait (1911), i. 81; *Commons' Journals*, ii. 962, 964–5; *Journals of the House of Lords*, v. 593–607.
36. *Acts and Ordinances*, ed. Firth and Rait, i. 22–4; *Commons' Journals*, ii. 694, 702, 732, 735.
37. *Commons' Journals*, iii. 23.
38. Steele, *Proclamations*, i, no. 2492.
39. Christopher Durston, 'Lords of Misrule', *History Today* (Dec. 1985), 8. This essay, unfortunately given to a journal which allows no footnotes, is the pioneering work on the fate of Christmas during the Civil War and Interregnum.
40. *Mercurius Civicus* (21–8 Dec. 1643), 346; *The Scottish Dove* (22–9 Dec. 1643), 81–5; *Mercurius Aulicus* (24–30 Dec. 1643), 742; *Commons' Journals*, iii. 351; 'The Diary of John Greene', ed. E. M. Symonds, *English Historical Review*, 43 (1928), 393.
41. *Acts and Ordinances*, ed. Firth and Rait, i. 420–1; *Commons' Journals*, iii. 440–1, 447, 504; *Lords' Journals*, vi. 501, 503.
42. *The Feast of Feasts*.
43. *Minutes of the Westminster Assembly of Divines*, ed. A. F. Mitchell and John Struthers (Edinburgh, 1874), 3–11.

44. *Acts and Ordinances*, ed. Firth and Rait, i. 580.

45. Durston, 'Lords of Misrule', 19; *Kingdomes Weekly Intelligencer* (17–24 Dec. 1644), 693; *The Parliament Scout* (19–26 Dec. 1644), 436; Greene, *Diary*, 601–2; *The Diary of the Rev. Ralph Josselin*, ed. E. Hockliffe (Camden Society, 3rd ser. 15; 1908), 23.

46. *Acts and Ordinances*, ed. Firth and Rait, i. 598–606.

47. *Mercurius Aulicus* (23–30 March 1645), 1542.

48. David Underdown, *Revel, Riot and Rebellion* (Oxford, 1985), 259.

49. *Quarter Sessions Order Book 1642–1649*, ed. B. C. Redwood (Sussex Record Society, liv; 1954), 76.

50. John Morrill, 'The Church in England, 1642–9', in Morrill (ed.), *Reactions to the English Civil War* (1982), 93.

51. e.g. *Commons' Journals*, iv. 334.

52. Durston, 'Lords of Misrule', 13; Underdown, *Revel, Riot and Rebellion*, 261; *Kingdomes Weekly Intelligencer* (16–23 Dec. 1645), 1054; *The Arraignment, Conviction and Imprisoning of Christmas* (1646); *The Scottish Dove* (24 Dec. 1645–1 Jan. 1646), 905–8; *The Moderate Intelligencer* (24 Dec. 1645–1 Jan. 1646), 139; *Mercurius Academicus* (22–7 Dec. 1645); John Taylor, *The Complaint of Christmas* (Oxford, 1646).

53. Randolph's *Poems* were issued in 1646, Herrick's *Hesperides* in 1648.

54. *The Moderate Intelligencer* (11–18 May 1648), 1319; Rushworth, *Historical Collections*, vii. 1119; Alan Everitt, *The Community of Kent and the Great Rebellion* (Leicester, 1966), 243.

55. Bod. L, Clarendon MS 31, fo. 42 (newsletter 30 Mar. 1648).

56. David Underdown, *Pride's Purge* (Oxford, 1971), 91.

57. John Twigg, *The University of Cambridge and the English Revolution* (Cambridge, 1990), 150.

58. Charles Edward Mallet, *A History of the University of Oxford* (1924), 384.

59. See CW in Appendix.

60. Durston, 'Lords of Misrule', 14.

61. *A Perfect Relation of the Horrible Plot, and Bloody Conspiracie* (4 Jan. 1648).

62. *Commons' Journals*, v. 403.

63. St Margaret, Westminster, CW (in Appendix), year 1647; N. B[ernard], *The Still-Borne Nativitie* (1648).

64. 'Diary of John Greene', ed. Symonds, 108–9; *The Kingdomes Weekly Intelligencer* (21–8 Dec. 1647), 783.

65. Durston, 'Lords of Misrule', 14.

66. Everitt, *Kent*, 231–4.

67. Underdown, *Revel, Riot and Rebellion*, 260.

68. *Acts and Ordinances*, ed. Firth and Rait, i. 905–7; *Commons' Journals*, iv. 556, 678, 735, v. 7.

69. *Lords' Journals*, viii. 715; *A Perfect Diurnall* (19–26 Apr. 1647), 1559–60; *The Moderate Intelligencer* (15–22 Apr. 1647), 1032; *Certain Queries Proposed by the King* (27 Apr. 1647).

70. *Commons' Journals*, v. 202, 206; *Lords' Journals*, ix. 246; *Acts and Ordinances*, ed. Firth and Rait, i. 854.

71. *A Perfect Diurnall* (12–19 July 1647), 1663–4.

72. Cressy, *Bonfires and Bells*, 161–3.

73. Issues for 14–21 and 21–8 Dec. 1647.

74. *Acts and Ordinances*, ed. Firth and Rait, ii. 79–81.

75. *The Diary of Ralph Josselin*, ed. Alan Macfarlane (1976), 22, 50, 74, 76, 108, 129, 155.

76. *Acts and Ordinances*, ed. Firth and Rait, ii. 1050, 1162–9.

77. Morrill, 'The Church', 105–6, 114.

78. Such as Biddulph (Staffs.) in 1655; Oddington (Oxon.) in 1650; St Martin, Oxford, in 1650; Aston le Walls (Northants.) in 1652; Clifton (Beds.) in 1652; North Wotton (Somerset) in 1651; Warfield (Berks.) in 1652; Milton Abbas (Dorset) in 1654; Wimborne Minster (Dorset) in 1652; North Waltham (Hants) in 1653; Gaddersby (Leics.) in 1656; Hentland (Hereford.) in 1653; Charing (Kent) in 1650; Gissing (Norfolk) in 1655; Wandsworth (Surrey) in 1657. See Appendix.

79. Churchill (Somerset), Christmas 1659; Kemble (Gloucs.) in 1656; St Thomas, Bristol, Christmas 1659; St Neot (Cornwall) in 1657; Bale (Norfolk), Easter 1659.

80. In Staffordshire, Pattisham and Checkley. In Devon, Winkleigh and Holcombe Burnell. In Wiltshire, Hannington. In Oxfordshire, Pyrton, Eynsham, Langford, and Yarnton. In Northamptonshire, Brington and Culworth. In Somerset, Swainswick, Thorne Coffin, Tintinhull, and Stockland Bristol. In Dorset, Seaborough. In Hampshire, Chawton. In Berkshire, Stanford in the Vale and Childrey. In Yorkshire, Millington and Royston. In Warwickshire, Barcheston. In Gloucestershire, Withington and Chedworth. In London, St Mary Woolchurch Haw. In Shropshire, Condover. In Huntingdonshire, Fenstanton. In Nottinghamshire, Coddington. In Flintshire, Mold. In Kent, Headcorn, Sellindge, Brockland, and Burham. In Suffolk, Rumburgh.

81. In Devon, Bow. In Oxfordshire, Langford and Chinnor. In Somerset, Langford Budville, Churchill, and Locking. In Hampshire, Easton and Soberton. In Yorkshire, Coxwold and Masham. In Buckinghamshire, Bledlow. In Huntingdonshire, Great Staughton. In Suffolk, Cotton. In Kent, Milton Regis. In Norfolk, Banham. In Lincolnshire, Addlethorpe.

82. St Michael, Gloucester; St John Baptist, Bristol; St Lawrence Pountney, St Katherine Coleman, St Mildred Bread Street, and St John Walbrook.

83. Minehead (Somerset); St Giles, Reading (Berks.); Symondsbury and Milton Abbas (Dorset); St Michael Spurriergate, Holy Trinity Goodramgate, and All Saints North Street, York; Dinton (Bucks.); Nether Whitacre (War.); Twying (Gloucs.); St Cuthbert, Darlington (Durham); St Thomas, Bristol; St Dunstan in the East, London; Stradbroke and Walsham le Willows (Suffolk); St Peter, St Albans (Herts.); Tong (Salop); Holy Trinity, Chester; St Peter Mancroft, Norwich (Norfolk).

84. Morrill, 'The Church', 93, 102.

85. To be precise, 152 out of 340 (44.7 per cent). In a review of my book on the Restoration, printed in *Parliamentary History*, 6 (1987), 179, Ian Green criticized me for citing a sample of 306 churchwardens' accounts but not listing them. It seemed to me an understandable but not entirely reasonable objection. I remember thinking that although Dr Green had published work of the very highest quality and importance, he had never attempted a large book and had reason to appreciate the likely reaction of a publisher to having 306 references printed to underpin a single footnote. Now, however, I am delighted to draw his attention to the 705 sets of accounts covering the late Stuart period, listed in the Appendix to this book. I look forward to seeing the use that he makes of them.

86. *The Diary of John Evelyn*, ed. E. S. De Beer (Oxford, 1955), iii. 79, 92, 94, 145, 150, 164, 169, 185, 190, 193, 203–4, 211–12, 214, 225, 228, 230, 238–9.

87. Durston, 'Lords of Misrule', 13.

88. George Palmer, *The Lawfulness of the Celebration of Christ's Birth-Day Debated* (17 Oct. 1648); Robert Skinner, *Christ's Birth Misse-timed* (Dec. 1648); Joseph Heming, *Certain Quaeries Touching the Rise and Observation of Christmas* (Dec. 1648); *Christ's Birth not Mis-Timed* (Jan. 1649); [Edward Fisher], *A Christian Caveat to the Old and New Sabbatarians* (Jan. 1650); Thomas Mocket, *Christmas, the Christians Grand Feast* (26 Nov. 1650); [Alan Blayney], *Festorum Metropolis* (Aug. 1652); Henry Hammond, *A Letter of Resolution to Six Quaeries of Present Use in the Church of England* (Nov. 1652), 411–75; Edward Sparke, *Scintilla Altaris* (Nov. 1652); John Collinges, *Responsoria ad Erratica Piscatoris* (Feb. 1653); [Hezekiah Woodward], *Christmas Day, the Old Heathens Feasting Day* (Feb. 1656); Giles Collier, *Vindiciae Thesium de Sabbato* (Apr. 1656).

89. *The Arraignment, Conviction, and Imprisoning of Christmas* (Jan. 1646).

90. T. H., *A Ha! Christmas* (Dec. 1647); *Women Will Have their Will* (Dec. 1648); John Taylor, *Christmas in and out* (Dec. 1652), and *The Vindication of Christmas* (Dec. 1652).

91. *Calendar of State Papers Domestic*, ed. Mary Everett Green (1876), 1650, p. 484; 1657–8, p. 226; and 1658–9, p. 225; *Commons' Journals*, vii. 235–6, 475; *Diary of Thomas Burton, Esq.*, ed. J. T. Rutt (1828), i. 229–30; *The Weekly Intelligencer* (21–8 Dec. 1652), 733; *A Perfect Account* (22–9 Dec. 1652), 828; *Mercurius Democritus* (22–9 Dec. 1652); *The Flying Eagle* (25 Dec. 1652–1 Jan. 1653), 34–8; *Calendar of State Papers Venetian*, ed. A. B. Hinds (1931), 1655–6, p. 5; and 1657–9, pp. 150, 152.

92. *A Petition Humbly Presented to his Highnesse the Lord Protector* (1654), sig. A3 and p. 23.

93. Underdown, *Revel, Riot and Rebellion*, 263.

94. *The Weekly Post* (26 Dec. 1654–2 Jan. 1655), 4045–6.

95. K. E. Wrighton, 'The Puritan Reformation of Manners with Special Reference to the Counties of Lancashire and Essex 1640–1660' (Cambridge Ph.D. thesis; 1973), 210.

96. HMC MSS in Various Collections, i. 130 (Wiltshire Quarter Sessions deposition).

97. John Latimer, *The Annals of Bristol in the Seventeenth Century* (Bristol, 1900), 256.

98. Taylor, *Christmas in and out*, 6.

99. Evelyn, *Diary*, ed. De Beer, iii. 205, 225.

100. 'Diary of John Greene', ed. Symonds, 112–13, 115.

101. John Spurr, *The Restoration Church of England, 1646–1689* (New Haven, Conn., 1991), 1–2; Bod. L, MS Eng. Misc. E118 (Blagrave's diary).

102. E. A. B. Barnard, *A Seventeenth-Century Country Gentleman* (Cambridge, 1944), 18, 25, 41, 53–4, 72.

103. Underdown, *Revel, Riot and Rebellion*, 261.

104. R. W. Blencowe, 'Extracts from the Journal and Account Book of the Rev. Giles Moore', *Sussex Archaeological Collections*, i (1850), 72.

105. 'Adam Eyre, a Diurnal', ed. H. J. Morehouse, in *Yorkshire Diaries and Autobiographies* (Surtees Society, 65; 1877).

106. 'The Household Book of Sir Miles Stapleton, Bt.', ed. J. C. Cox, *The Ancestor*, 3 (Oct. 1902), 148–9.

107. St Mary the Virgin, Oxford; St Botolph, Cambridge; St John, Winchester; Holy Trinity Goodramgate, York; St Thomas, Bristol; St John Baptist, Bristol; St Mary Redcliffe, Bristol; St Margaret, Westminster; St Mary Tower, Ipswich; St John, Chester; Holy Trinity, Chester; St Peter Mancroft, Norwich. See Appendix, as usual.

108. Yarnton (Oxon.); Orwell (Cambs.); Cheddar (Somerset); Clitheroe (Lancs.); Fulham (Middx.); Condover (Salop); Gislingham and Woodbridge (Suffolk); Fenstanton (Hunts.); Chatham (Kent); Gateshead (Durham).

109. Underdown, *Revel, Riot and Rebellion*, 263–7.

110. A. H. A. Hamilton, *Quarter Sessions from Queen Elizabeth to Queen Anne* (1878), 139, 161.

111. *Warwick County Records*, ed. S. C. Ratcliff and H. C. Johnson (Warwick, 1941), iii. 271–2.

112. *Quarter Sessions Order Book 1642–1649*, ed. B. Redwood (Sussex Record Society; 1954), p. xxiii.

113. Lowe, 'Early Records of the Morris', *JEFDSS* 8: 2 (1957), 76.

114. Ibid. 76–7.

115. Henry Reece, 'The Military Presence in England 1649–1660' (Oxford D.Phil. thesis; 1981), 184.

116. *Middlesex County Records*, ed. J. C. Jeaffreson (Middlesex County Records Society; 1888), iii. 280–1.

117. *Hertford County Records: Sessions Rolls 1581–1698*, ed. W. le Hardy (Hertford, 1905) and *Hertford County Records: Calendar to the Sessions Books 1619–1657*, ed. W. le Hardy (Hertford, 1920).

118. *Surrey Quarter Sessions Records*, ed. Dorothy L. Powell and Hilary Jenkinson (Surrey Record Society, 1934).

119. *Nottinghamshire County Records*, ed. H. Hampton Capnall (Nottingham, 1915).

120. *Essex Quarter Sessions Order Book 1652–1661*, ed. D. H. Allen (Essex Edited Texts, 1; 1974).

121. Maurice Ashley, *The Greatness of Oliver Cromwell* (1957), 270.

122. Barnard, *Country Gentleman*, 7.

123. *The Journal of George Fox*, ed. John L. Nickalls (Cambridge, 1952), 37.

124. T. F. Thistleton-Dyer, *Old English Social Life* (1898), 207–9.

125. David Wiles, *The Early Plays of Robin Hood* (Cambridge, 1981), 28; A. Rhodes, 'Howde Men', *Notes and Queries*, 11th ser. 1 (1910), 494.

126. Daniel Lysons, *The Environs of London* (1792), 183; *The Mysteries of Love and Eloquence* (1658), 7–9; W. B., *The Yellow Book* (1 May 1656).

127. Robert Cox, *Actaeon and Diana* (Sept. 1653).

128. *A Pleasant Grove of New Fancies* (1657), 74; Sir Aston Cokain, *Small Poems of Divers Sorts* (1658), 209.

129. *The Garden of Delight* (1658), 76.

130. Aubrey, *Remaines*, 26.

131. Morrill, 'The Church', 113–14.

132. Ibid. 114; Cressy, *Bonfires and Bells*, 164–5.

133. St Mildred Bread Street, and the last appearance there was earlier in 1640.

134. Biddulph (Staffs.); Durston, and Stockland Bristol (Somerset); Padiham, and Whalley (Lancs.); St Werburgh, Bristol; Aylsham (Norfolk).

135. See Whalley CW, in Appendix.

136. Twigg, *Cambridge and the English Revolution*, 163.

137. St Michael, Gloucester, CW (in Appendix); Underdown, *Revel, Riot and Rebellion*, 289–90.

138. All Saints', Bristol; St Michael Cornhill; St Thomas Apostle; All Hallows the Great;

St Pancras Soper Lane; St Olave Silver Street; St Katherine Cree; St Mary Woolchurch Haw. See Appendix for CW as usual.

139. Temple, Bristol; St Andrew by the Wardrobe; St Mildred Bread Street.

140. St Alban Wood Street.

141. See Appendix, as usual.

142. *The Cyprian Academy* and *The Shepherd's Oracles*, quoted in John Brand, *Observations on the Popular Antiquities of Great Britain*, ed. Sir Henry Ellis (1908 reprint), i. 80, 101.

143. John Latimer, *The Annals of Bristol in the Seventeenth Century* (Bristol, 1900), 260, 292.

144. *The Diary of Samuel Pepys*, ed. Robert Latham and William Matthews (1970), i. 121.

145. *The Life and Times of Anthony Wood*, ed. Andrew Clark (Oxford Historical Society; 1891), i. 314, 317.

146. *The Autobiography of Henry Newcome*, ed. Richard Parkinson (Chetham Society; 1852), 121.

147. Alfred Kingston, *Hertfordshire during the Great Civil War* (1894), 101.

148. Henry Jessey, *The Lord's Loud Call to England* (Aug. 1660), 13; Wiltshire RO, Q/S Great Rolls A1/100, M 1660, fo. 139.

149. Underdown, *Revel, Riot and Rebellion*, 274–5.

150. *Englands Joy* (1660), 6.

151. Sig. G2.

152. *Commons' Journals*, viii. 95, 116, 139, 168, 180, 194; *Lords' Journals*, xi. 195, 211; *The Parliamentary or Constitutional History of England* (London, 1760), xxiii. 26–31; House of Lords RO, Parchment Collection Box 12, Act for the Lord's Day, 29 Nov. 1660.

153. Cf. Evelyn, *Diary*, ed. De Beer, iii. 265; Pepys, *Diary*, ed. Latham and Matthews, i. 323.

154. Norfolk RO, MCB 23, fo. 120.

155. *Reliquiae Baxterianae*, ed. Matthew Sylvester (1696), I. ii. 316–33.

156. *The Life of Adam Martindale*, ed. Richard Parkinson (Chetham Society; 1854), 156–8.

157. A. R. Wright, *British Calendar Customs*, ed. T. E. Lones (Folklore Society; 1936), i. 220.

CHAPTER 7

1. Among the most notable works for the later period are Robert W. Malcolmson, *Popular Recreations in English Society 1700–1850* (Cambridge, 1973), esp. 67–109, 151, 159; E. P. Thompson, 'Patrician Society, Plebeian Culture', *Journal of Social History*, 7 (1974), esp. 392–7; Bob Bushaway, *By Rite* (1982), esp. 13, 21–2; and Peter Borsay, '"All the Town's a Stage": Urban Ritual and Ceremony 1660–1800', in Peter Clark (ed.), *The Transformation of English Provincial Towns 1600–1800* (1984), 247–852.

2. *Society and Puritanism in Pre-Revolutionary England* (1964), 215–17.

3. *Revel, Riot and Rebellion* (Oxford, 1985), 281–5.

4. Keith Wrightson, *English Society 1580–1680* (1982), 140–8, 183–227.

5. *Early Modern England* (1987), 285–300.

6. See Williton (Somerset) CW in Appendix.

7. See CW in Appendix under Oxford.

8. Pinner CW in Appendix under Middlesex, years 1622, 1628, and 1662–8.

9. Hawkshead and Grasmere (Westmorland) CW; Daresbury (Ches.) CW; in Appendix.

10. A. R. Wright, *British Calendar Customs*, ed. T. E. Lones (Folklore Society; 1936), 209.

11. Ibid.

12. Soham (Cambs.) CW, in Appendix.

13. St Mary le Strand (Westminster) CW, in Appendix.

14. Yarnton (Oxon.) CW, and St Ives (Cornwall) CW, in Appendix.

15. Eling (Hants) CW, years 1661–77.

16. Stradbroke (Suffolk) CW, years 1662–88; Fenstanton (Hunts.) CW, year 1662; Rolleston (Notts.) CW, year 1681.

17. Underdown, *Revel, Riot and Rebellion*, 280; F. M. Salter, *Medieval Drama in Chester* (Toronto, 1955), 28.

18. Charles Hoskins, *The Ancient Trade Guilds and Companies of Salisbury* (Tisbury, n.d.), 38; Hugh Shortt, *The Giant and Hob-Nob* (Salisbury, 1982).

19. 'An Account of the Company of St George in Norwich', *Norfolk Archaeology*, 3 (1852), 354–74; William Kelly, *Notices Illustrative of the Drama . . . of Leicester* (1865), 48–50.

20. Peter Burke, 'Popular Culture in Seventeenth-Century London', *London Journal*, 3 (1977), 151–2; Sheila Williams, 'The Lord Mayor's Show in Tudor and Stuart Times', *Guildhall Miscellany*, 10 (1959), 12–15.

21. Borsay, '"All the Town's a Stage"', 230–2.

22. Richard Baxter, *A Christian Directory* (2nd edn., 1678), i. 390; W. B. Whitaker, *Sunday in Tudor and Stuart Times* (1933), 181–3.

23. *The Rev Oliver Heywood B.A. 1630–1702: His Autobiography, Diaries, Anecdote and Event Books*, ed. J. Horsfall Turner (Brighouse, 1882–5), ii. 272.

24. This is a theme of the Quaker tracts usefully gathered in Bod. L, 110; 63–4, 119–20, 125, 128–32, 239, 241.

25. John Evelyn, *Sylva* (1670), 206–7.

26. Michael Hunter, *John Aubrey and the Realm of Learning* (1975), 217.

27. Thompson, 'Patrician Society', 394.

28. Hill, *Society and Puritanism*, 215–17; Whitaker, *Sunday*, 192–3.

29. *Journals of the House of Commons* (1803), viii. 417, 424–5, 435, 437, 457, 467, 470, 492, 496, 515, 535, 539, 580–1, 636, ix. 4, 198, 209–10, 225, 234, 268, 270, 360.

30. On other aspects of which, see Mark Goldie, 'Danby, the Bishops and the Whigs', in Tim Harris, Paul Seaward, and Mark Goldie (eds.), *The Politics of Religion in Restoration England* (Oxford, 1990), 75–106.

31. *Commons' Journals*, ix. 421–2; *Journals of the House of Lords* (n.d.), xiii. 56–7, 91, 113, 120; *Statutes of the Realm* (1819), v. 848; House of Lords RO, Main Papers, Draft Bill 1 Mar. 1677, and Manuscript Minutes 16 Feb. 1673–7 May 1678 (29 Mar., 4 Apr., 9 Apr. 1677).

32. Sandford Strong (ed.), *A Catalogue of Letters and other Historical Documents Exhibited in the Library at Welbeck* (1903), 188–201.

33. Collected conveniently in Bod. L, Pamph. C118 and B. 7. 9 Line.

34. T. F. Thistleton-Dyer, *Church Lore Gleanings* (1892), 324.

35. T. C. Curtis and W. A. Speck, 'The Societies for the Reformation of Manners', *Literature and History*, 3 (1976), 45–64; E. J. Bristow, *Vice and Vigilance* (Dublin, 1977), ch. 1; Tina Isaacs, 'Moral Crime, Moral Reform and the State in Early Eighteenth-Century England' (Rochester University Ph.D. thesis; 1980); A. G. Craig, 'The Movement for the Reformation of Manners, 1688–1715' (Edinburgh University Ph.D. thesis; 1980); Tina Isaacs, 'The Anglican Hierarchy and the Reformation of

Manners, 1688–1738', *Journal of Ecclesiastical History*, 33 (1982), 391–411; David Hayton, 'Moral Reform and Country Politics in the Late Seventeenth-Century House of Commons', *Past and Present*, 128 (1990), 48–91; Robert B. Shoemaker, 'Reforming the City: The Reformation of Manners Campaign in London, 1690–1738', in Lee Davison, Tim Hitchcock, Tim Keirn, and Robert B. Shoemaker (eds.), *Stilling the Grumbling Hive* (Stroud, 1992), ch. 5.

36. Malcolmson, *Popular Recreations*, 146–7.

37. *A Sabbath of Rest to be Kept by the Saints* (1675), 12.

38. *A Brief Defence of the Several Declarations of King James the First, and King Charles the First, concerning Lawful Recreations on Sundays* (1708), 24.

39. For *The Royal Shepherdesse*, see *The Complete Works of Thomas Shadwell*, ed. Montague Summers (1927), i. 132–6. For Behn's *The Young King*, see *The Plays, Histories and Novels of the Ingenious Mrs Aphra Behn* (1871), ii. 94. For Dryden's *King Arthur* and 'The Flower and the Leaf', see *The Works of John Dryden*, ed. Sir Walter Scott and George Saintsbury (Edinburgh, 1884), viii. 195 and xi. 394. David Hopkins very kindly supplied me with all the versions of Dryden's Jacobite poem: *Poetical Miscellanies: The Fifth Part* (1704) (for 'The Lady's Song'); *Miscellaneous Works, Written by . . . George, Late Duke of Buckingham* (1704) (for 'The Beautiful Lady of the May'); Bod. L, MS Don. c 55, fos. 180–90^r (for 'A Song By Mr Dryden: May Day'); BL Add. MS 28253, fo. 65 (unnamed); and Leeds University L, Brotherton Collection, MS Lt 54, p. 448 (for 'The Queen of May'). For Aubrey's *The Country Revell*, see Bod. L, Aubrey MS A21.

40. *The Natural History of Oxfordshire* (Oxford, 1677), 116, 201–3.

41. *DNB* 'Plot'.

42. *The Natural History of Staffordshire* (Oxford, 1686), 430, 434.

43. *DNB* 'Blount'; Thomas Blount, *Fragmenta Antiquitatis* (1679), 149.

44. White Kennett, *Parochial Antiquities Attempted in the History of Ambrosden, Burcester . . . in the Counties of Oxford and Bucks* (Oxford, 1695), 609–14.

45. Anthony Powell, *John Aubrey and his Friends* (1948); Richard M. Dorson, *The British Folklorists: A History* (Chicago, 1968), 4–10; Michael Hunter, *John Aubrey and the Realm of Learning* (1975); David Tylden-Wright, *John Aubrey* (1991).

46. Edited from Bod. L, Aubrey MS A3 by J. E. Jackson, as John Aubrey, *Wiltshire: The Topographical Collections* (Devizes, 1862).

47. Edited with scholarly rigour by John Buchanan-Brown, in John Aubrey, *Three Prose Works* (Fontwell, Sussex, 1972), and with interesting additions by James Britten, as John Aubrey, *Remaines of Gentilism and Judaisme* (1881).

48. Hunter, *Aubrey and the Realm of Learning*, 40, 176.

49. Dorson, *British Folklorists*, sums up the orthodoxy of a century.

50. *Antiquitates Vulgares* (Newcastle Upon Tyne, 1725).

51. Malcolmson, *Popular Recreations*, 67–71, 146–7, 151–9; Bushaway, *By Rite*, 7.

52. Aubrey, *Remaines*, ed. Britten, 9, 18, 26, 40; Bourne, *Antiquitates*, 147–50, 200–2, 210–11.

53. Eveline Legh, Lady Newton, *The House of Lyme* (1917), 256.

54. C. F. Tebbutt, 'Huntingdonshire Folk and their Folklore', *Transactions of the Cambridgeshire and Huntingdonshire Archaeological Society*, 6 (1938–47), 142.

55. *The Life and Times of Anthony Wood*, ed. Andrew Clark (Oxford Historical Society, 1891), i. 317.

56. *The Diary of Samuel Pepys*, ed. Robert Latham and William Matthews (1970), iv. 120, viii. 193.

57. Roy Judge, *The Jack-in-the-Green* (Woodbridge, 1979), 4–5.

58. *The Diary of Roger Lowe*, ed. William L. Sachse (1938), 68.

59. *The Journal of Thomas Isham of Lamport*, ed. Robert Isham (Norwich, 1875), 65.

60. Aubrey, *Wiltshire*, ed. Jackson, 311–12; Bod. L, Aubrey MS A3, fos. 80, 140.

61. R. W. Blencowe, 'Extracts from the Journal and Account-Book of the Rev. Giles Moore', *Sussex Archaeological Collections*, 1 (1850), 110, and 'Extracts from the Journal and Account-Book of Timothy Burrell', ibid. 3 (1850), 122, 124.

62. See sources at n. 35 above.

63. *English Society*, 221.

64. On which see esp. Hunter, *Aubrey*, ch. 1.

65. *Revel, Riot and Rebellion*, 275–80.

66. See e.g. Mervyn James, 'Ritual, Drama and the Social Body in the late Medieval Town', *Past and Present*, 88 (1983), 3–29; Miri Rubin, *Corpus Christi* (Cambridge, 1991); Eamon Duffy, *The Stripping of the Altars* (New Haven, Conn., 1992), chs. 3–4.

67. Most colourfully in *Culhwch ac Olwen*, translated accessibly in *The Mabinogion*, ed. Jeffrey Gantz (1976), 137–40, and *Etmich Dinbych*, in Sir Ifor Williams, *The Beginnings of Welsh Poetry*, trans. Rachel Bromwich (1972), 163–70.

68. *The Diary of John Evelyn*, ed. E. S. De Beer (Oxford, 1955), iii. 308, 350, iv. 30; Pepys, *Diary*, iii. 300–1.

69. George Caspar Homans, *English Villagers of the Thirteenth Century* (Cambridge, Mass., 1942), 357–8.

70. Pepys, *Diary*, viii. 85.

71. Isham, *Journal*, 22–3, 78–9.

72. Felicity Heal, *Hospitality in Early Modern England* (Oxford, 1990), 168, 173, 186–7.

73. Ibid. 173; Blencowe, 'Journal of Timothy Burrell', 126; Evelyn, *Diary*, iii. 348, 367, 393, 503, iv. 82, 298, 495.

74. *The Diary of Samuel Newton*, ed. J. R. Foster (Cambridge Antiquarian Society 23; 1890), 7–8, 38.

75. Pepys, *Diary*, i. 322–3, ii. 2–7, 238–41, iii. 1–4, 292–4, iv. 433–8, v. 1, 356–7, vi. 1–5, 338–9, vii. 1–6, 420–2, viii. 589–90, ix. 12–13, 400–9.

76. Heal, *Hospitality*, 297.

77. *The Household Account Book of Sarah Fell*, ed. Norman Penney (Cambridge, 1920), 25–6, 167–8, 239.

78. *The Pepys Ballads*, ed. Hyder Edward Rollins (Cambridge, Mass., 1929–32), iii. 51–5.

79. Heal, *Hospitality*, 151, 168, 297.

80. Ibid. 355; Malcolmson, *Popular Recreations*, 26–7, 57–8.

81. Bushaway, *By Rite*, 128–30, 240–1.

82. Homans, *English Villagers*, 371.

83. Thomas Tusser, *Five Hundred Pointes of Good Husbandrie*, ed. W. Payne and S. J. Herrtage (English Dialect Society; 1878), 132–8; Aubrey, *Remaines*, 34; Bourne, *Antiquitates*, 229.

84. John Brand, *Observations on the Popular Antiquities of Great Britain*, ed. Sir Henry Ellis (1908), ii. 26–9; Malcolmson, *Popular Recreations*, 25–6, 55–69; Bushaway, *By Rite*, 128–36.

85. Heal, *Hospitality*, 358–65; Malcolmson, *Popular Recreations*, 16 23, 31–3, 54–5; Bushaway, *By Rite*, 250.

86. Aubrey, *Wiltshire*, 311–12.

87. T. F. Thistleton Dyer, *Church Lore Gleanings* (1892), 325.

88. A. R. Wright, *British Calendar Customs*, ed. T. E. Lones (1936), i. 154–5.

89. Shoemaker, 'The London "Mob"', 290.

90. John Latimer, *The Annals of Bristol in the Seventeenth Century* (Bristol, 1900), 353, 434.

91. St Benet Gracechurch (London) CW, years 1691–7, in Appendix. For the use of the bell, see John Taylor, *Jack a Lent his Beginning and Entertainment* (1621), sig. B2.

92. Brand, *Antiquities*, ed. Ellis, i. 68–91; Wright, *British Calendar Customs*, i. 9–23; T. F. Thistleton Dyer, *Old English Social Life* (1898), 205–6; Malcolmson, *Popular Recreations*, 36–7, 79, 119–22, 138–4; Bushaway, *By Rite*, 6, 36, 51, 171–2.

93. *Popular Culture in Early Modern Europe* (1978), esp. ch. 9.

94. For late Stuart Valentines see Wright, *British Calendar Customs*, i. 139 (for the royal court); HMC Rutland MSS, ii. 22 (for the aristocracy); Pepys, *Diary*, ii. 36, iii. 28–9, iv. 42, vi. 35, vii. 42, viii. 62 (for the upper middling sort); Plot, *Staffordshire*, 430 (for popular attitudes).

95. Evelyn, *Diary*, iii. 285.

96. The sample of parishes is listed in the Appendix.

97. *The Rector's Book: Clayworth, Nottinghamshire*, ed. H. Gill and E. C. Guildord (Nottingham, 1910), 143.

98. St Alphage London Wall; St Bartholomew the Great; St Lawrence Pountney; St Margaret Moses; St Martin Outwich; St Martin Ludgate; St Sepulchre Holborn; St Mildred Bread Street; St Helen Bishopsgate; St Ann Blackfriars.

99. e.g. Milton Regis, Swanscombe, Otham, Birling, and Chatham in Kent; and Gissing, Loddon, East Dereham, Hardwick, Garboldisham, Blickling, Hockwold, Forncett St Peter, Wilton, Sparham, and Starston in Norfolk.

100. St Andrew by the Wardrobe; St Benet Gracechurch; St John Walbrook; St Martin Orgar; St Mary Aldermanbury; St Botolph Billingsgate; St Nicholas Acons.

101. St Ives (Cornwall) CW, years 1679–91, in Appendix.

102. Gateshead (Durham) CW, years 1663–78, in Appendix.

103. North Petherton (Somerset) CW, years 1664–1700, in Appendix.

104. St Benet Sherehog (London) CW, years 1675–1700, and Whiston (Yorks.) CW, years 1682–1705, in Appendix.

105. Miss M. Cooper, 'A Perambulation of Cuckfield', *Sussex Archaeological Collections*, 61 (1920), 40–52.

106. In London, St Christopher le Stocks. In Staffordshire, Betley and Madeley. In Devon, Instow. In Westmorland, Kirkby Lonsdale. In Cumberland, Penrith. In Dorset, Bere Regis, Beaminster, and Abbotsbury. In Wiltshire, the Salisbury parishes of St Edmund and St Thomas. In Hampshire, Andover and Fawley. In Yorkshire, Bolton Percy, Beverley, Howden, and Whiston. In Warwickshire, St Nicholas, Warwick, and Nether Whitacre. In Gloucestershire, Mitchedean. In Shropshire, Ludlow and Whitchurch. In Suffolk, Westleton. In Sussex, Burwash. In Norfolk, St Peter Mancroft, Norwich, and St Nicholas, Great Yarmouth.

107. In Leicestershire, Ashby Folville. In Lincolnshire, South Carlton, North Somercotes, Addlethorpe, and Kirton in Lindsey. In Nottinghamshire, Rolleston, Holme Pierrepoint, Worksop, Coddington, and Elkesley. In Derbyshire, St Werburgh, Derby.

108. In Chester itself, St Mary at Hill, Holy Trinity, and St John. In Cheshire, Middlewich, Wyburnbury, and Frodsham. In Flintshire, Hawarden.

109. Rolleston; Kirton in Lindsey; Betley; Madeley; Whitchurch; Worksop; Coddington; St Mary at Hill, Chester; Middlewich; Frodsham; St Peter Mancroft, Norwich; St Nicholas, Great Yarmouth; South Carlton; and North Somercotes.

110. This seems to be the import of the following CW. Merionethshire: Llanfihangel Y Traethau (begins with accounts, 1686). Denbighshire: Chirk (begins with accounts, 1661); Bryneglwys (begins with accounts, 1664); Llandyrnog (begins 1683); Llanferres (begins 1685); Llanfair Talhearn (begins 1684); Llanwrst (begins with accounts, 1664); Wrexham (begins 1663). Flintshire: Hawarden (begins 1685); Cilcain (begins 1686); Caerwys (begins 1683); Ysceifog (begins with accounts, 1687). It is not recorded in the eleven other seventeenth-century North Welsh CW listed in the Appendix.

111. In *The Restoration Church of England, 1646–1689* (New Haven, Conn., 1991).

112. *Society and Puritanism*, 215–17.

113. This consists of the good contemporary records for the diocese of Salisbury, specifically Wiltshire RO, D/1/54/3/1, fo. 4; 3/2, fo. 3; 4/1, n.f., Rodbourne Cheney 1671; 6/3. fos. 2, 11, 18, 40, 41, 54, 71; 6/5. n.f., Boyston, Corton, Upton Scudmore, Codford St Mary, 1674; 10/2, fos. 31, 46; 11/1. n.f., Brinkworth 1686; 11/2, n.f., Wanborough, Rodbourne Cheney; 11/3. n.f., Lavington 1686; 12/3, n.f., St Thomas, Salisbury, 1689. I am very grateful to my graduate pupil, Henry Lancaster, for checking through the documents for me in case of oversights.

114. Again, I offer heartfelt thanks to Henry Lancaster for providing an independent opinion upon the same records, the Salisbury diocesan court books.

115. *Statutes of the Realm* (1819), v. 237, 288.

116. Helen W. Randall, 'The Rise and Fall of a Martyrology', *Huntington Library Quarterly*, 10 (1946–7), 136.

117. *Commons' Journals*, viii. 49–51, 175, 177, 179, 185, 197, 201–2, 207–8.

118. Bod. L, Pamph. C118 and B. 7. 9. Linc., *passim*.

119. Wiltshire RO, D1/54/1/2, fo. 9; *Episcopal Visitation Returns for Cambridgeshire*, ed. W. M. Palmer (Cambridge, 1930), 87, 95, 98, 99, 112–13.

120. *Mercurius Publicus* (30 May–6 June, 6–13 June 1661), *passim*.

121. See Appendix.

122. St Ives (Cornwall) CW; All Saints, Oxford CW; St Mary the Virgin, Oxford, CW; Ashby Folville (Leics.) CW; Mildenhall (Suffolk) CW; Dallinghoo (Suffolk) CW; St Oswald, Durham, CW.

123. Newton, *Diary*, 46–7.

124. Worcester Cathedral L, A. 26, *passim*.

125. David Underdown, *Fire From Heaven* (1992), 249.

126. CW in Appendix.

127. Pepys, *Diary*, iii. 94–5, iv. 163, vii. 135.

128. Evelyn, *Diary*, iv. 204.

129. Wood, *Life and Times*, ii. 487.

130. Tim Harris, *London Crowds in the Reign of Charles II* (Cambridge, 1987), 121, 166–8, 179.

131. Pepys, *Diary*, ii. 26, iii. 20, iv. 29, v. 31, vi. 25, vii. 30, viii. 36; Evelyn, *Diary*, iii. 314, 429, 474, 568, iv. 2, 52, 105, 128, 163, 237, 300, 364.

132. Randall, 'Martyrology', 144–55; Byron S. Stewart, 'The Cult of the Royal Martyr', *Church History*, 38 (1969), 175–81; Spurr, *Restoration Church*, 241–2.
133. Worcester Cathedral L, A. 26, *passim*.
134. Rolleston (Notts.) CW; North Somercotes (Lincs.) CW; Great Marlow (Bucks.) CW.
135. All Hallows Staining; St Andrew by the Wardrobe; St Dunstan in the West; St Olave Jewry; All Hallows the Great; St Giles Cripplegate; St Katherine Cree; St John Zachary.
136. Evelyn, *Diary*, iv. 101, 123, 157, 395.
137. David Cressy, *Bonfires and Bells* (1989), 171–4.
138. Grasmere (Westmorland) CW; St Buryan (Cornwall) CW, in Appendix.
139. Worcester Cathedral L, A. 26, *passim*.
140. South Newington (Oxon.); Tintinhull, and Puxton (Somerset); Northill, and Harlington (Beds.); Kendal (Westmorland); Stour Provost (Dorset); Alton, and Eling (Hants); Clifton Reynes (Bucks.); Muston (Leics.); Morwenstow (Cornwall); St Mary Tower, Ipswich (Suffolk); Carleton Rode, and East Harling (Norfolk); North Somercotes, and Addlethorpe (Lincs.).
141. Hawkshead (Westmorland), Tarporley (Ches.) and Birling (Kent).
142. Sheila Williams, 'The Pope-Burning Processions of 1679, 1680 and 1681', *Journals of the Warburg and Courtauld Institutes*, 21 (1958), 104–18; O. W. Furley, 'The Pope-Burning Processions of the Late Seventeenth Century', *History*, 44 (1959), 16–23; Harris, *London Crowds*, 26, 31, 93, 104–6, 120–1, 123–4, 157, 169, 180, 219; Cressy, *Bonfires and Bells*, 173–84.
143. St Ethelburga Bishopsgate; St Alban Wood Street; All Hallows London Wall; St Michael Cornhill; St Olave Silver Street; St Giles Cripplegate.
144. Stewart, 'Royal Martyr', 180–1; Randall, 'Martyrology', 144–55; Evelyn, *Diary*, iv. 499, 537, 568; Wood, *Life*, i. 208.
145. Wood, *Life*, iii. 267.
146. St George Colegate, Norwich (Norfolk) CW, in Appendix.
147. Wood, *Life*, iii. 265.
148. Evelyn, *Diary*, iv. 480, 526, 601.
149. St James Garlickhithe; St Peter Cornhill; St Katherine Coleman; St Magnus the Martyr.
150. Evelyn, *Diary*, iv. 526.
151. Wood, *Life*, iii. 166, 198, 240, 276.
152. Monksilver and Hinton St George (Somerset); Cerne Abbas, and Bere Regis (Dorset); Odiham, and Overton (Hants); Caversham, and Stratfield Mortimer (Berks.); Quainton, and Beaconsfield (Bucks.); Bolton Percy (Yorks.); Upton St Leonards (Gloucs.); Hartlip, and Swanscombe (Kent); Boxford (Suffolk); Thornhill (Norfolk); Murston (Leics.); Billingham, and Bishopswearmouth (Durham).
153. St Peter Mancroft, Norwich, and St Lawrence Jewry, London.
154. St Margaret, Westminster, CW; New Windsor (Berks.) CW; Kingston upon Thames (Surrey) CW; St Laurence, Norwich (Norfolk) CW.
155. All Hallows Staining; St Dunstan in the West; St Katherine Coleman.
156. Neither Evelyn nor Wood record any junketings on 6 Feb.
157. Princes Risborough (Bucks.); Misterton, and Weston Zoyland (Somerset); Horsell (Surrey); and Theydon Garnon (Essex).

158. Prestbury (Gloucs.) CW, year 1685.
159. Cressy, *Bonfires and Bells*, 185–6.
160. Evelyn, *Diary*, iv. 529; Wood, *Life*, iii. 199.
161. Cressy, *Bonfires and Bells*, 186.
162. *The Diary of Adam de la Pryme*, ed. Charles Jackson (Surtees Society 54; 1870), 10.
163. Wood, *Life and Times*, iii. 281.
164. St Mildred, Canterbury (Kent) CW, in Appendix.
165. Evelyn, *Diary*, iv. 650.
166. St Alphage London Wall; St Dunstan in the West; Horsell (Surrey); Madeley (Staffs.). CW all listed in Appendix.
167. Wood, *Life*, iii. 406.
168. Evelyn, *Diary*, v. 72.
169. Ibid. v. 4, 42, 86, 283.
170. Wood, *Life*, iii. 324, 415, 442, 478.
171. Stewart, 'Royal Martyr', 181–3.
172. Evelyn, *Diary*, v. 102, 288.
173. Wood, *Life*, iii. 303–4, 331, 391, 424, 454, 485.
174. Paul Kléber Monod, *Jacobitism and the English People 1688–1788* (Cambridge, 1989), 181–2.
175. Partingham, Checkley, Hanbury, and Madeley.
176. St Mary the Virgin, Oxford, CW (in Appendix); Wood, *Life*, iii. 325, 415.
177. Evelyn, *Diary*, v. 19; Wood, *Life*, iii. 329, 359, 386, 449, 483.
178. Hartlip, Milton Regis, Swanscombe, Sandwich, and St Mary Northgate, Canterbury (Kent); Wing, Great Marlow, Amersham, Beaconsfield, and West Wycombe (Bucks.).
179. See CW in Appendix.
180. Wood, *Life*, iii. 406, 434, 493.
181. Wantage (Berks.); Amersham (Bucks.); St Michael Spurriergate, and St John Ousegate, York; Bermondsey (Surrey); St Margaret, Westminster; St Alphage London Wall, and St Lawrence Jewry, London; Barnet (Herts.); Swanscombe (Kent); St Peter Mancroft, Norwich (Norfolk).
182. St Julian, Shrewsbury (Salop) CW, in Appendix.
183. Hounslow (Middx.) CW, in Appendix.
184. Great Badminton (Gloucs.) CW, years 1676–1700, in Appendix.

Index